Annotated Guide to Social Welfare Law

with annotations by

Professor Robert Clark

Associate Professor of Law,
University College
Dublin

LONDON
SWEET & MAXWELL
1995

Published in 1995 by
Sweet & Maxwell Limited of
South Quay Plaza,
183 Marsh Wall, London
Typeset by LBJ Enterprises Ltd.
of Aldermaston and Chilcompton
Printed and bound in Great Britain by
Butler & Tanner Ltd, Frome and London

A CIP catalogue record for this book is available
from the British Library

ISBN 0–421–52600–9

PREFACE

There has been a long felt need for a work that examines the legal aspects of social welfare legislation, for, despite the expansion of Irish legal publishing in the last decade, there exists no work that sets Irish social welfare law into ˙a proper legal context. Some excellent policy studies and essays have emerged (*e.g.* Gerry Whyte's works on the Equality Directive, Peter Ward's study on family breakdown, and Mel Cousins' book on social welfare policy come to mind immediately) and I hope that this book will provide a lawyerly addition to the literature. While the practice of law does not provide the general practitioner with many opportunities to go into the finer points of social welfare law and State income support issues, there are a substantial number of areas of general practice which interface with the social welfare code: accident compensation, family breakdown and employment law, for example, are generally very important areas of practice, and any practitioner should find this work of utility when social welfare issues arise.

The basis of this book is the 1993 Consolidation Act, although I have been teaching and researching in this field for almost two decades. In this time I have been able to view the ebb and flow of certain trends and fashions, from the heady days of pay-related benefits to the harsher realism of greater stress on means-tested payments. Irish social legislation has led to several innovations, such as social welfare benefits for strikers, a topical issue given the recent *Irish Press* controversy, but the overwhelming impression that emerges is that our policy makers and judges have tended to tinker with the existing framework rather than re-assess the basic objectives that the landmark legislation of 1838, 1897, 1911, 1933, 1952, 1970 and 1975 sought to advance. I hope that the contents of this work will prove relevant to any future reappraisal of the law.

I am grateful to my colleague Tony Kerr for providing a steady stream of unreported judgments over the years, to Anne Murphy for her word processing skills, and to Mary O'Malley for help in proofing the work. My greatest debt however is to Sweet and Maxwell and the typesetters for their efficiency and enthusiasm. The 1993 (No. 2) Act, the 1994 Act and the two Acts passed in 1995 are gathered up into the text, and it is my intention to provide a work that is up-to-date as of July 31, 1995.

I am sure that there are errors and inaccuracies in this book. I apologise in advance for any that exist. Some will be my own fault but others can be traced back to the complexity of the legislation, which in part can be attributed to the draftman's almost perverse desire to make this area of Irish Statute law completely impervious to the scrutiny of even the best informed legal professional, much less the hapless social welfare claimant!

Robert Clark
August 24, 1995.

v

CONTENTS

References are to page numbers

Social Welfare (Consolidation) Act, 1993 (as amended)

Contents

TABLE OF CASES

References are to the General Note to the specified section and to the Introduction

Table of Cases

Table of Cases

TABLE OF STATUTES

References are to the General Note to the specified section

TABLE OF STATUTORY INSTRUMENTS

References are to the General Note to the specified section

SOCIAL WELFARE (CONSOLIDATION) ACT, 1993 (AS AMENDED)*

(1993 No. 27)

ARRANGEMENT OF SECTIONS

PART I

PRELIMINARY

PART II

SOCIAL INSURANCE

CHAPTER 1

THE SOCIAL INSURANCE FUND

CHAPTER 2

EMPLOYED CONTRIBUTORS AND EMPLOYMENT CONTRIBUTIONS

CHAPTER 3

SELF-EMPLOYED CONTRIBUTORS AND SELF-EMPLOYMENT CONTRIBUTIONS

*Annotations by Professor Robert Clark, UCD.

CHAPTER 16

SURVIVOR'S PENSION

CHAPTER 17

ORPHAN'S (CONTRIBUTORY) ALLOWANCE

CHAPTER 18

DESERTED WIFE'S BENEFIT

CHAPTER 19

DEATH GRANT

CHAPTER 20

TREATMENT BENEFIT

PART III

SOCIAL ASSISTANCE

CHAPTER 1

DESCRIPTION OF SOCIAL ASSISTANCE

PART IV

CHILD BENEFIT

PART V

FAMILY INCOME SUPPLEMENT

PART VI

GENERAL PROVISIONS RELATING TO SOCIAL INSURANCE, SOCIAL ASSISTANCE AND INSURABILITY

Preliminary

CHAPTER 1

CLAIMS AND PAYMENTS

CHAPTER 2

PROVISIONS RELATING TO ENTITLEMENT

PART VII

DECISIONS APPEALS AND SOCIAL WELFARE TRIBUNAL

CHAPTER 1

DECIDING OFFICERS AND DECISIONS BY DECIDING OFFICERS

Appointment and Functions of Deciding Officers

Revised Decisions by Deciding Officers

CHAPTER 2

APPEALS OFFICERS, CHIEF APPEALS OFFICER AND DECISIONS BY APPEALS OFFICERS

Chief Appeals Officer

Procedures for Appeals

Revised Decisions by Chief Appeals Officers and by Appeals Officers

CHAPTER 3

SUPPLEMENTARY WELFARE ALLOWANCE— DETERMINATIONS AND APPEALS

FIRST SCHEDULE

EMPLOYMENTS, EXCEPTED EMPLOYMENTS AND EXCEPTED SELF-EMPLOYED CONTRIBUTORS

PART I

EMPLOYMENTS

PART II

EXCEPTED EMPLOYMENTS

PART III

EXCEPTED SELF-EMPLOYED CONTRIBUTORS

SECOND SCHEDULE

RATES OF BENEFITS

PART I

RATES OF PERIODICAL BENEFITS AND INCREASES THEREOF

PART II

OCCUPATIONAL INJURIES BENEFITS— GRATUITIES AND GRANT

PART III

DISABLEMENT PENSION

PART IV

INCREASES OF DISABLEMENT PENSION

THIRD SCHEDULE

RULES AS TO CALCULATION OF MEANS

PART I

UNEMPLOYMENT ASSISTANCE AND PRE-RETIREMENT ALLOWANCE

PART II

OLD AGE (NON-CONTRIBUTORY), BLIND, WIDOW'S AND ORPHAN'S (NON-CONTRIBUTORY) PENSIONS, DESERTED WIFE'S, PRISONER'S WIFE'S LONE PARENT'S AND CARER'S ALLOWANCES

PART III

SUPPLEMENTARY WELFARE ALLOWANCE

FOURTH SCHEDULE

RATES OF ASSISTANCE

PART I

RATES OF PERIODICAL SOCIAL ASSISTANCE AND INCREASES THEREOF

PART II

INCREASE OF OLD AGE (NON-CONTRIBUTORY) PENSION AND BLIND PENSION FOR ONE OF A COUPLE

PART III

AMOUNTS OF CHILD BENEFIT

FIFTH SCHEDULE

ENACTMENTS REPEALED

SIXTH SCHEDULE

COMMENCEMENT OF CERTAIN PROVISIONS

An Act to consolidate the Social Welfare Acts. [*9th November*, 1993]

INTRODUCTION AND GENERAL NOTE

The Social Welfare (Consolidation) Act, 1993 represents the most recent legislative measure bringing together the Irish law relating to social welfare provision into one body of legislation. As such, its predecessors are the Social Welfare Act, 1952 and the Social Welfare (Consolidation) Act, 1981. Since the 1981 Consolidation Act, legislative measures to further develop social welfare provision were yearly with twice yearly legislative features, inevitably resulting in a complex and fragmented body of legislation, made all the more opaque by the considerable amount of detail which reposed in statutory instruments.

The period between 1981 and 1993 was marked by a substantial amount of legislative innovation, sparked in part by the Report of the Commission on Social Welfare (pl. 3851) which reported in 1986. Important structural adjustments such as the introduction of social insurance for the self-employed in 1988 and substantial improvements in social assistance schemes were accompanied by the introduction of new programmes, such as Family Income Supplement, Carers' Allowance, Lone Parents' Allowance, as well as the streamlining of child dependant additions. One area where no real legislative activity has taken place, however, is in the area of social assistance provision for the disabled.

In this text the amendments to the Principal Act of 1993, which have been made by primary legislation, that is, the Social Welfare (No. 2) Act, 1993, the Social Welfare Act, 1994, the Social Welfare Act, 1995, and the Social Welfare (No. 2) Act, 1995, have been incorporated into both the text of the legislation as well as the text of the annotation. Recent statutory instruments which also modify the text of the Act, S.I. No. 312 of 1994 and S.I. No. 25 of 1995, are also included. The sources of such amendments appear in square brackets immediately following the amendment.

Social Welfare (Consolidation) Act 1993

Abbreviations

The following abbreviations are used:

Social Welfare (Consolidation) Act, 1993: the Principal Act.
Social Welfare (No. 2) Act, 1993: 1993 (No. 2) Act.
Social Welfare Act, 1994: 1994 Act.
Social Welfare Act, 1995: 1995 Act.

Citation

This Act may be cited as the Social Welfare (Consolidation) Act, 1993.
This Act and the 1993 (No. 2) Act the 1994 Act, and the 1995 Act may be collectively cited as the Social Welfare Acts, 1993 to 1995, although since 1993 this formula for collective citation has not been used in of any of the three amending Acts.

Statutory Instruments

Where relevant, the Statutory Instruments in force are cited in the annotations to each section.

Commencement

The 1993 Consolidation Act came into operation on November 16, 1993: S.I. No. 335 of 1993.

Parliamentary Debates

The Principal Act of 1993
433 *Dáil Debates* Col. 1728 (Second Stage).
434 *Dáil Debates* Cols. 1645–62 (Report and Final Stages).
137 *Seanad Debates* Cols. 779, 885, 1658–1674 (All Stages).

The 1993 (No. 2) Act.
436 *Dáil Debates* Cols. 321–345, 465–518, 577–586 (Second Stage and Referral to Select Committee)
436 *Dáil Debates* Cols. 1007, 1705–1732 (Committee and Subsequent Stages)
138 *Seanad Debates* Cols. 1484–1556 (All Stages)

The 1994 Act
439 *Dáil Debates* Cols. 1101–1143 (Second Stage)
439 *Dáil Debates* Cols. 1205–1258, 1360–1411 (Second Stage resumed and Committee referral)
440 *Dáil Debates* Cols. 975–1013 (Committee Stage and Report and Final Stages)
139 *Seanad* Debates Cols. 1467–1548 (All Stages)

The 1995 Act
450 *Dáil Debates* Cols. 1921–1982 (Second Stage)
451 *Dáil Debates* Cols. 11–77, 147–162 (Second Stage resumed)
451 *Dáil Debates* Cols. 425–476 and 569 (Report and Final Stage)
142 *Seanad Debates* Cols. 1485–1577 (Second Stage)
142 *Seanad Debates* Cols. 1602–1725 (Committee and Final Stages)

The 1995 (No. 2) Act
454 *Dáil Debates* Cols. 1122–1191, 1274–1286, 1499, 1501 (Second Stage)
454 *Dáil Debates* Cols. 1563–1601 (Committee Stage)
455 *Dáil Debates* Cols. 587–624, 665–694 (Committee and Final Stages)
144 *Seanad Debates* Cols. 705–760 (Second Stage)
144 *Seanad Debates* Cols. 1188–1228 (All later Stages)

Statutes referred to

Agriculture Act, 1931	1931 No. 8
Blind Persons Act, 1920	10 & 11 Geo. 5, c. 49
Central Bank Act, 1971	1971 No.24
Civil Liability Act, 1961	1961 No. 41

Civil Liability (Amendment) Act, 1964	1964 No. 17
Companies Act, 1963	1963 No. 33
Courts (No. 2) Act, 1986	1986 No. 26
Debtors Act (Ireland), 1872	35 & 36 Vic. c. 57
Dublin Institute of Technology Act, 1992	1992 No. 15
Enforcement of Court Orders Act, 1926	1926 No. 18
Enforcement of Courts Orders Act, 1940	1940 No. 23
Family Law (Maintenance of Spouses and Children Act), 1976	1976 No. 11
Fatal Injuries Act, 1956	1956 No. 3
Finance Act, 1969	1969 No. 21
Finance Act, 1970	1970 No. 14
Finance Act, 1975	1975 No. 6
Finance Act, 1980	1980 No. 14
Finance Act, 1986	1986 No. 13
Finance Act, 1992	1992 No. 9
Harbours Act, 1946	1946 No. 9
Health Act, 1947	1947 No. 28
Health Act, 1953	1953 No. 26
Health Act, 1970	1970 No. 1
Health Authorities Act, 1960	1960 No. 9
Health Contributions Act, 1979	1979 No. 4
Higher Education Authority Act, 1971	1971 No. 21
Housing (Private Rented Dwellings) Act, 1982	1982 No. 6
Income Tax Act, 1967	1967 No. 6
Labour Services Act, 1987	1987 No. 15
Local Government Act, 1941	1941 No. 23
Local Government (Superannuation) Act, 1956	1956 No. 10
Maternity Protection of Employees Act, 1981	1981 No. 2
Mental Treatment Act, 1945	1945 No. 19
Minimum Notice and Terms of Employment Act, 1973	1973 No. 4
National Council for Educational Awards Act, 1979	1979 No. 30
National Archives Act, 1986	1986 No. 11
National Health Insurance Act, 1933	1933 No. 13
National Insurance Act, 1911	1 & 2 Geo. 5 c. 55
Pilotage Act, 1913	2 & 3 Geo. 5 c. 31
Preferential Payment in Bankruptcy (Ireland) Act, 1889	52 & 53 Vic. c. 60
Probation of Offenders Act, 1907	7 Edw. 7
Public Assistance Act, 1939	1939 No. 27
Regional Technical Colleges Act, 1992	1992 No. 16
Road Traffic Act, 1961	1961 No. 24
Social Welfare Act, 1950	1950 No. 14
Social Welfare Act, 1952	1952 No. 11
Social Welfare Act (Occupational Injuries) Act, 1966	1966 No. 16
Social Welfare Act, 1973	1973 No. 10
Social Welfare Act, 1975	1975 No. 1
Social Welfare (Supplementary Welfare Allowance) Act, 1975	1975 No. 28
Social Welfare (Consolidation) Act, 1981	1981 No. 1
Social Welfare Act, 1988	1988 No. 7
Social Welfare (No. 2) Act, 1989	1989 No. 12
Social Welfare Act, 1991	1991 No. 7
Social Welfare Act, 1992	1992 No. 5
Status of Children Act, 1987	1987 No. 26
Superannuation Act, 1936	1936 No. 39
Statutory Declarations Act, 1938	1938 No. 37
Unemployment Insurance Act, 1920	10 & 11 Geo. 5 c. 55
Vocational Education Act, 1930	1930 No. 29
Widows' and Orphans' Pensions Act, 1935	1935 No. 29
Workmen's Compensation Act, 1906	6 Edw. 7. c. 58
Workmen's Compensation Act, 1934	1934 No. 9
Youth Employment Agency Act, 1981	1981 No. 32

Acts Cited Collectively

Adoption Acts, 1952 to 1991

Army Pensions Acts, 1923 to 1980
Companies Acts, 1963 to 1990
Connaught Rangers (Pensions) Acts, 1936 to 1964
Garda Síochána (Compensation) Acts, 1941 and 1945
Health Acts, 1947 to 1991
Housing Acts, 1966 to 1988
Income Tax Acts
Labourers Acts, 1883 to 1965
Local Authorities (Higher Education Grants) Acts, 1968 to 1992
Mental Treatment Acts, 1945 to 1966
Military Service (Pensions) Acts, 1924 to 1964
National Health Insurance Acts, 1911 to 1952
Protection of Employees (Employer's Insolvency) Acts, 1984 and 1991
Redundancy Payments Acts, 1967 to 1991
Superannuation Acts, 1834 to 1963
Workmen's Compensation Acts, 1934 to 1955

Be it enacted by the Oireachtas as follows:

PART I

PRELIMINARY

Short title
1.—This Act may be cited as the Social Welfare (Consolidation) Act, 1993.

Definitions
2.—(1) In this Act, save where the context otherwise requires—
"appeals officer" means a person holding office as an appeals officer under section 251;
"assistance" means assistance under Part III;
"beneficiary" means a person entitled to any benefit, assistance, child benefit or family income supplement, as the case may be;
"benefit" means, subject to section 210 and Part VI, benefit under Part II;
"benefit year" means the period commencing on the first Monday in a particular year and ending on the Sunday immediately preceding the first Monday in the following year;
"claimant" means a person who has made a claim for any benefit, assistance, child benefit or family income supplement, as the case may be;
"Collector-General" means the Collector-General appointed under section 162 of the Income Tax Act, 1967;
"contribution week" means one of the successive periods of seven consecutive days in a contribution year beginning on the 1st day of that contribution year, or on any 7th day after that day, the last day of a contribution year (or the last two days of a contribution year ending in a leap year) being taken as included in the last contribution week of that contribution year;
"contribution year" means a year of assessment within the meaning of the Income Tax Acts;
"credited contribution" means, in relation to any insured person, a contribution credited to that person by virtue of section 27;

"day of incapacity for work" has the meaning assigned in section 31(1);

"day of unemployment", in relation to Part II, has the meaning assigned in section 42, and in relation to Chapter 2 of Part III, has the meaning assigned in section 120(6);

"deciding officer" means a person holding office as a deciding officer under section 246;

"developing country" means any country which the Minister, having regard to the countries so designated by the United Nations, the World Bank or the International Labour Organisation as developing countries and after consultation with the Minister for Foreign Affairs, may determine, for the purposes of this Act, to be a developing country [1993 (No. 2) Act, section 11];

"disabled person's maintenance allowance" means a maintenance allowance under section 69 of the Health Act, 1970;

"employed contributor" has the meaning assigned in section 9(1);

"employer's contribution" has the meaning assigned in section 6(1)(a);

"employment contribution" has the meaning assigned in section 6(1)(a);

"entry into insurance" means, subject to sections 29(3), 102(7) and Chapters 12 and 13 of Part II, in relation to any person, the date on which he became an insured person [1994] Act, section 13];

"health board" means a health board within the meaning of the Health Act, 1970;

"incapable of work" means incapable of work by reason of some specific disease or bodily or mental disablement or deemed, in accordance with regulations, to be so incapable;

"infectious diseases maintenance allowance" means a payment under section 44 of the Health Act, 1947, to a person suffering from an infectious disease;

"insurable employment" means employment such that a person, over the age of 16 years and under pensionable age, employed therein would be an employed contributor;

"insurable (occupational injuries) employment" has the meaning assigned in section 50;

"insurable self-employment" means self-employment of such a nature that a person engaged therein would be a self-employed contributor;

"insured person" means a person insured under Part II;

"Member State" means a Member State of the European Communities;

"the Minister" means the Minister for Social Welfare;

"non-governmental agency" means any organisation which has as one of its functions the promotion of relief and development in developing countries through the sponsoring or aiding of projects involving the employment of volunteer development workers in those countries [1993 (No. 2) Act, section 11];

"occupational injuries insurance" has the meaning assigned in section 49(2);

"optional contribution" means a contribution paid under Chapter 4A of Part II;

"optional contributor" means a person engaged in share fishing paying optional contributions [1993 (No. 2) Act, section 3];

"orphan" means a qualified child—

(a) both of whose parents are dead, or

(b) one of whose parents is dead, unknown, has abandoned or has refused or failed to provide for the child and whose other parent—

(i) is unknown, or

(ii) has abandoned or has refused or failed to provide for the child, where that child is not normally residing with a step-parent or with a person who is married to and living with that step-parent [1995 Act, section 20];

"outworker" means a person to whom articles or materials are given out to be made up, cleaned, washed, altered, ornamented, finished or repaired or adapted for sale in his own home or on other premises not under the control or management of the person who gave out the articles or materials for the purposes of the trade or business of the last-mentioned person;

"pensionable age" means the age of 66 years;

"person engaged in share fishing" means a self-employed contributor who is a member of the crew of a fishing vessel and whose principal means of livelihood is derived from a share in the profits or the gross earnings of the working of the vessel [1993 (No. 2) Act, section 2];

"prescribed" means prescribed by regulations;

"qualifying contribution" means the appropriate employment contribution or self-employment contribution which was paid or would have been paid but for section 10(1)(c) or (e) or section 18(1)(d) in respect of any insured person or the appropriate optional contribution which was paid or would have been paid but for section 24B(1)(b) [1993 (No. 2) Act, section 2 and 1994 Act, Schedule C];

"reckonable earnings" means, subject to regulations and to section 78, earnings derived from insurable employment or insurance (occupational injuries) employment;

"reckonable emoluments", in relation to a self-employed contributor, means emoluments (other than reckonable earnings, non-pecuniary emoluments and such other emoluments as may be prescribed) to which Chapter IV of Part V of the Income Tax Act, 1967, applies, reduced by so much of the allowable contribution referred to in Regulations 59 and 60 (inserted by the Income Tax (Employments) Regulations, 1972 (S.I. No. 260 of 1972)) of the Income Tax (Employments) Regulations 1960 (S.I. No. 28 of 1960) as is deducted on payment of those emoluments;

"reckonable income" in relation to a self-employed contributor or an optional contributor [1993 (No. 2) Act], means the aggregate income (excluding reckonable earnings, reckonable emoluments, non-pecuniary income and such other income as may be prescribed), from all sources for the contribution year as estimated in accordance with the provisions of the Income Tax Acts, but without regard to section 2 or section 18 of the Finance Act, 1969, or (save in the case of a person to whom paragraph 1 of Part III of the First Schedule applies) to Chapter 1 (inserted by the Finance Act, 1980) of Part IX of the Income Tax Act, 1967, after deducting from the income so much of any deduction allowed by virtue of the provisions referred to in section 33 of the Finance Act, 1975, as is to be deducted from or set off against that income in charging it to income tax;

"regulations" means regulations made by the Minister under this Act;

"self-employed contributor" has the meaning assigned in section 17;

"self-employment contribution" has the meaning assigned in section 6;

"short-time employment" means employment in which, for the time being, a number of days is systematically worked in a working week which is less than the number of days which is normal in a working week in the employment concerned;

"the Social Insurance Fund" means the Fund to which section 7 relates;

"social welfare inspector" means a person appointed by the Minister under section 212 to be a social welfare inspector for the purposes of Parts II, III (other than Chapter 11), IV, V, VI and IX;

"statutory declaration" means a statutory declaration within the meaning of the Statutory Declarations Act, 1938;

"trade dispute" means any dispute between employers and employees, or between employees and employees, which is connected with the employment or non-employment or the terms of employment or the conditions of employment of any persons, whether employees in the employment of the employer with whom the dispute arises or not;

"voluntary contribution" has the meaning assigned in section 22;
"voluntary contributor" has the meaning assigned in section 21;
"volunteer development worker" means a person who is employed temporarily outside the State in a developing country and has secured such employment either—

(a) by or through the organisation known as the Agency for Personal Services Overseas or by or through a non-governmental agency in the State, or

(b) by or through a governmental or non-governmental agency in any Member State other than the State, or

(c) directly with the government of a developing country,

and who is employed by any of the aforesaid agencies or by the government of the developing country or by both under conditions of remuneration similar to local conditions applying in the said country and who was resident in the State immediately prior to taking up such employment [1993 (No. 2) Act, section 11];

"the Workmen's Compensation Acts" means the Workmen's Compensation Acts, 1934 to 1955, and the enactments repealed by the Workmen's Compensation Act, 1934.

(2) In this Act "adult dependent", subject to sections 170 and 245A, means in relation to any person—

(a) a spouse who is wholly or mainly maintained by that person but does not include—

　(i) a spouse in employment (other than employment specified in paragraph 4 or 5 of Part II of the First Schedule), or

　(ii) a spouse who is self-employed, or

　(iii) a spouse who is entitled to, or is in receipt of, any benefit, pension, assistance or allowance (other than supplementary welfare allowance) under Parts II or III of this Act, or disabled person's maintenance allowance, or

　(iv) a spouse who, by virtue of the provisions of section 47(1) or 125(3), is or would be disqualified for receiving unemployment benefit payable under Chapter 9 of Part II or unemployment assistance payable under Chapter 2 of Part III in his own right with the exception of a spouse who qualifies as an adult dependant by virtue of regulations made under paragraph (c), or

　(v) a spouse who is entitled to or is in receipt of an allowance the rate of which is related to the rates of unemployment assistance payable under section 121 or unemployment benefit payable under section 44 or 45 in respect of a non-craft full-time course approved by An Foras Áiseanna Saothair under the Industrial Training Act, 1967,

　or

(b) a person over the age of 16 years being wholly or mainly maintained by that person and having the care of one or more than one qualified child who normally resides with that person where that person is—

　(i) a single person,

　(ii) a widow,

　(iii) a widower, or

　(iv) a married person who is not living with and is neither wholly or mainly maintaining, nor being wholly or mainly maintained by, such married person's spouse, or

(c) such person as the Minister may by regulations specify to be an adult dependant for the purposes of this Act.

(3) Subject to section 114(3), in this Act "qualified child" means a person who is ordinarily resident in the State, is not detained in a reformatory or an industrial school, and—

(a) for the purposes of—
    (i) sections 34(2) and 45(2),
    (ii) section 121(1)(b)(ii) in the case of an applicant for unemployment assistance other than as referred to in paragraph (b),
    is under the age of 18 years or is of or over the age of 18 years and is regarded as attending a course of study within the meaning of section 126(3)(a),

(b) for the purposes of—
    (i) disability benefit payable by virtue of section 56 [1995 Act, Schedule E],
    (ii) sections 60(9), 62(1), 87(2), 91(2), 99(2), 102(7), 106, 113(1), 128(1)(b), 136(1), 148(1), 159(1), 165(1) and 198, and
    (iii) section 121(1)(b)(ii) in the case of an applicant who, in any continuous period of unemployment as construed in accordance with section 120(3), has been in receipt of unemployment benefit or unemployment assistance for not less than 390 days—
        (I) is under the age of 18 years, or
        (II) is of or over the age of 18 years and under the age of 22 years, and is receiving full-time education, the circumstances of which shall be specified in regulations [1995 Act, section 14].

GENERAL NOTE

This is the definition section. The 1993 (No. 2) Act inserted definitions of the phrases "optional contribution", "optional contributor", "person engaged in share fishing" and "qualifying contribution", as well as amending the definition of "reckonable income". The definition of "orphan" was amended by section 20 of the 1995 Act.

The definition of "adult dependant" in section 2(2) is not self-contained: S.I. No. 417 of 1994, article 6 defines adult dependants, for the purposes of section 2(2)(c), so as to include spouses with a weekly income below £60, as calculated in accordance with article 6.

The definition of "qualified child" in section 2(3)(b) was amended by section 14 of the 1995 Act so as to include persons in full-time education (as specified in S.I. No. 417 of 1994) who are under 22 years of age. This came into force between April 27, 1995 and May 3, 1995: S.I. No. 112 of 1995.

The definitions of "developing country", "non-governmental agency" and "volunteer development worker" were inserted by section 11 of the 1993 (No. 2) Act.

Interpretation generally

3.—(1) For the purposes of this Act—
(a) a person shall be deemed to be over any age therein mentioned if he has attained that age and shall be deemed to be under any age therein mentioned if he has not attained that age;
(b) a person shall be deemed to be between two ages therein mentioned if he has attained the first-mentioned age but has not attained the second-mentioned age;
(c) a person shall be deemed not to have attained the age of 16 years until the commencement of the 16th anniversary of the day of his birth, and similarly with respect to any other age;
(d) regulations may provide that, for the purpose of determining whether a contribution is payable in respect of any person, or at what rate a contribution is payable, that person shall be treated as having attained at the beginning of a contribution week, or as not having attained until the end of a contribution week, any age which he attains during the course of that week;
(e) the circumstances in which a person is to be regarded as living alone shall be specified in regulations.
(f) regulations may provide for determining the circumstances in which a person is or is not to be regarded to be wholly or mainly maintaining another person. [1995 No. 2 Act, section 10]

(2) Any reference in this Act to contributions shall, where the reference is without qualification, be construed, save whether the context otherwise requires, as including a reference to employment contributions, self-employment contributions and voluntary contributions.

(3) Regulations may, as respects any class or description of insurable employment or insurable (occupational injuries) employment, specify the persons to be treated for the purposes of this Act as the employers of employed contributors employed in that employment.

(4) References in this Act to an employed contributor's employer shall not be construed as including his employer in any employment other than insurable employment or insurable (occupational injuries) employment.

(5) Any question relating to the normal residence of a qualified child shall, subject to section 193(2), be decided in accordance with regulations made under this subsection.

(6) Where a child has been or becomes adopted pursuant to the Adoption Acts, 1952 to 1991, then for the purposes of this Act—
  (a) the child shall thereafter be treated as if he were the child of the adopter or adopters born to him, her or them and were not the child of any other person and, if he was an orphan immediately before the adoption, as having ceased to be an orphan, and
  (b) if there is one adopter only, in any application after the adoption with respect to the child of the definition of "orphan" contained in section 2(1), "the parent of whom is dead" shall be substituted in paragraph (a) of that definition for "both of whose parents are dead".

(7) References in this Act to any enactment shall be construed as references to that enactment as amended or extended by any subsequent enactment.

(8) References in any other enactment to the "Social Welfare Acts" means this Act and every enactment which is to be construed together with it as one.

(9) In this Act, a reference to a Part or Chapter, section or Schedule is to a Part or Chapter or section of or Schedule to this Act, unless it is indicated that reference to some other enactment is intended.

(10) In this Act, a reference to a subsection, paragraph, subparagraph or clause is to the subsection, paragraph, subparagraph or clause of the provision (including a Schedule) in which the reference occurs, unless it is indicated that reference to some other provision is intended.

(11) In this Act, any reference to this Act shall be construed as including a reference to regulations made under or applying the provisions of this Act.

(12) For the purposes of section 34(3), 45(3), 55(3), 87(3), 91(3), 99(3), 124(1), 128(3), 138, 165(4), 192(2), [1995 Act section 5(3)(a)], 245A [1995 Act, section 15(3)] and Chapter 11 of Part III, "spouse" means—
  (a) each person of a married couple who are living together, or
  (b) a man and woman who are not married to each other but are cohabiting as husband and wife.

(13) For the purposes of determining the entitlement of a person to an increase in respect of an adult dependant, references to a spouse in the definition of "adult dependant" contained in section 2(2) and regulations made thereunder shall be construed as including:
  (a) a party to a marriage that has been dissolved, being a dissolution that is recognised as valid in the State, or
  (b) a man and woman who are not married to each other but are cohabiting as husband and wife. [1995 (No. 2) Act section 10]

GENERAL NOTE
Subsection (5)
   Issues relating to normal residence are considered in article 7 of S.I. No. 417 of 1994.

General provisions as to regulations

4.—(1) The Minister may make regulations—
   (a) for any purpose in relation to which regulations are provided for by any of the provisions of this Act, and
   (b) for prescribing any matter or thing referred to in this Act as prescribed or to be prescribed.

   (2) Except in so far as this Act otherwise provides, any power conferred thereby to make regulations may be exercised—
   (a) either in relation to all cases to which the power extends, or in relation to all those cases subject to specified exceptions, or in relation to any specified cases or classes of case, and
   (b) so as to make, as respects the cases in relation to which it is exercised—
      (i) the full provision to which the power extends or any less provision (whether by way of exception or otherwise),
      (ii) the same provision for all cases in relation to which the power is exercised or different provision for different cases or classes of case, or different provision as respects the same case or class of case for different purposes of this Act,
      (iii) any such provision either unconditionally or subject to any specified condition.

   (3) Without prejudice to any specific provision in this Act, any regulations may contain such incidental or supplementary provisions as may appear to the Minister to be expedient for the purposes of the regulations.

   (4) The following shall be subject to the sanction of the Minister for Finance—
   (a) regulations for the purposes of section 2(2), 10, 11, 12, 13, 14, 17(2)(d), 19, 20, 22(1)(d), 32(3), 32(6), 39, 41I, 42(2), 42(4), 43(5), 49(3), 50(7), 50(8), 50(9), 80(1), 82(1)(a), 82(2), 83(5), 83(6), 84(7), 84(9), 84(12), 84(14), 88(6), 88(7), 89(3), 89(4), 89(6), 96(1), 96(2), 97, 102(3), 102(5), 110(1)(c), 111(3), 111(8), 115(3), 115(5), 120(1), 121(5), 129, 163(1), 169(2)(b), 179, 202(2), 202(3), 203(1), 239, 241, 245A, 282, 303, Rules 1(2)(m) and 1(6) of the Third Schedule, Rule 3(3) of Part II of the Third Schedule and Rule 2 of Part III of the Third Schedule, [1995 (No. 2) Act, section 11]
   (b) a draft of regulations under any of the provisions mentioned in subsection (5).

   (5) Where regulations are proposed to be made for the purposes of section 9(2), 9(3), 10(2)(a), 17(2)(a), 17(2)(b), 17(2)(c), 18(1)(f), 26, 32(5), 38(2), 41H(3), 43(4), 82(1)(c), 82(1)(d), 84(6), 89(2), 96(6), 102(2), 107(2), 111(2) or 115(2), a draft thereof shall be laid before each House of the Oireachtas and the regulations shall not be made until a resolution approving of the draft has been passed by each such House. [1994 Act, section 13(4)(b)]

   (6) Regulations or rules (not being regulations or rules of which a draft is required by this Act to be approved of by resolution of each House of the Oireachtas) shall be laid before each House of the Oireachtas as soon as may be after they are made and, if a resolution annulling the regulations or rules is passed by either House within the next 21 days on which that House has sat after the regulations or rules have been laid before it, the regulations or rules shall be annulled accordingly, but without prejudice to the validity of anything previously done thereunder.

(7) Where the Minister revokes regulations made under any of the provisions mentioned in subsection (5) and makes regulations which he certifies to be substantially to the like effect as the regulations so revoked, a requirement that a draft of the proposed regulations be laid before each House of the Oireachtas shall not apply.

GENERAL NOTE

It is important to note that several of the reforms implemented into Irish law in the arena of social welfare law have in fact been inspired by E.C. and E.U. law and that implementation has often taken place through delegated legislation. Examples include the compensation payments to Irish women due to late implementation of the Third Equality Directive in the 1985 (No. 2) Act, as highlighted by the litigation commenced by *Cotter* and *McDermott*. On this, see the European Communities (Social Welfare) Regulations, 1992 (S.I. No. 152 of 1992) made under the European Communities Act, 1972 and the decision of Miss Justice Carroll in *McClean and Tate v. Minister for Social Welfare* H.C. Unreported, February 3, 1995.

Similarly, the health and safety benefit regulations (S.I.s No. 312 and 313 of 1994 and S.I. No. 25 of 1995) were made under the European Communities Act, 1972.

Expenses

5.—(1) Any expenses incurred by the Minister or any other Minister in carrying this Act into effect shall, to such extent as may be sanctioned by the Minister for Finance, be paid out of moneys provided by the Oireachtas.

(2) There shall be paid to the Minister for Finance out of the Social Insurance Fund, at such times and in such manner as the Minister for Finance may direct, such sums as the Minister may estimate, on such basis as may be agreed upon between him and the Minister for Finance, to be the part of the said expenses of the Minister or any other Minister which relates to the scheme of social insurance provided for in Part II and any sums so paid shall be appropriated in aid of moneys provided by the Oireachtas for carrying this Act into effect.

(3) In estimating expenses for the purposes of subsection (2), there shall be included such amount as, in the opinion of the Minister for Finance, represents the amount of the accruing liability in respect of any superannuation or other retiring allowances, lump sums or gratuities accruing in respect of the employment of any officer or other person for the purposes of this Act.

(4) Any expenses incurred by An Post under the provisions of Part II, (determined on such basis as may be agreed upon between the Minister, the Minister for Finance and An Post) shall be paid by the Minister out of the Social Insurance Fund to An Post at such times and in such manner as the Minister for Finance may direct.

GENERAL NOTE

Monies provided by the Oireachtas are voted annually in the form of the Appropriation Acts.

PART II

SOCIAL INSURANCE

CHAPTER 1

THE SOCIAL INSURANCE FUND

Sources of moneys for benefits

6.—(1) For the purposes of providing moneys for meeting the expenditure on benefit and making any other payments which, under this Act, the

Redundancy Payments Acts, 1967 to 1991, and the Protection of Employees (Employer's Insolvency) Acts, 1984 and 1990, are to be made out of the Social Insurance Fund, there shall be—

(a) contributions (referred to in this Act as "employment contributions") in respect of employed contributors, each of which shall comprise a contribution by the employed contributor and a contribution (referred to in this Act as "the employer's contribution") by the employer of the employed contributor,

(b) contributions (referred to in this Act as "self-employment contributions") in respect of self-employed contributors,

(bb) contributions in respect of optional contributors, [1993 (No. 2) Act, section 5],

(c) contributions in respect of voluntary contributors, and

(d) payments out of moneys provided by the Oireachtas.

(2) Employment contributions, self-employment contributions, optional contributions and voluntary contributions shall be paid into the Social Insurance Fund.

DEFINITIONS

"employed contributor": section 9(1).
"optional contribution": section 2(1) added by section 3 of 1993 (No. 2) Act of 1993.
"optional contributors": section 2(1) added by section 3 of 1993 (No. 2) Act of 1993.
"self-employed contributor": section 17.
"voluntary contribution": section 22.
"voluntary contributor": section 21.

GENERAL NOTE

The original basis upon which social insurance was built was, in actuarial terms, a financial disaster. The National Insurance Act, 1911 sought to provide a limited range of benefits from a fund which was made up of employer and employee contributions, but following the mass unemployment of the 1920s, Irish and U.K. social insurance could not provide adequate levels of benefit without a large Exchequer subvention. Social insurance, therefore, is a tripartite system which relies upon payments from employers, employees and the State to finance benefit and pension payments.

The proportion of these contributions has fluctuated over the years: in 1978 the employer's share was 53.1 per cent, the employee's share was 26.6 per cent and the State subvention was 20 per cent, the balance of 0.3 per cent coming from investment income. In 1985 the employer's contribution had fallen to 48 per cent, the employee's share had fallen to 23 per cent while the State and investment income percentages were 28.8 per cent and 0.2 per cent respectively. In 1991 the employer's contribution had risen to 60.1 per cent, the employee's share stood at 26.2 per cent, the State contribution being 9.6 per cent, with investment income and self employment contribution standing at 0.2 per cent and 3.9 per cent respectively. The Social Insurance Fund, established by the 1952 Act, does not necessarily require a State contribution but the authors of the 1949 White Paper supported the principle that the community as a whole (*i.e.* the State) should bear its share of the burden of social insurance, as a matter of social equity, so as to keep the employee contribution down to a reasonable level. The Commission on Social Welfare (1986) agreed, on the basis that the cost of certain contingencies was spread across the community and that social insurance was broadly redistributive and a force for greater social cohesion. There have been some significant structural changes in recent years, these being in part due to the recommendations of the Commission on Social Welfare and in part due to a desire to effect administrative streamlining. Section 23 of the 1990 Act abolished the Occupational Injuries Fund, a separate Fund established in 1966 to finance occupational injuries payments. This Fund, financed exclusively from contributions levied on employers and from investment income, was in surplus to the tune of £52 million and this was transferred into the Social Insurance Fund. A similar reform was effected by section 24(4) of the 1990 Act in relation to the Redundancy and Employer's Insolvency Fund, a composite fund established under the Redundancy Payments Act, 1967 and the Protection of Employees (Employers Insolvency) Act, 1984.

Social Insurance Fund

7.—(1) The Social Insurance Fund (in this section and in section 8 referred to as "the Fund") established under the Social Welfare Act, 1952, and continued in being under section 122 of the Social Welfare (Consolidation) Act, 1981, shall continue in being and to comprise a current account and an investment account.

(2) The Minister shall manage and control the current account of the Fund.

(3) The Minister for Finance shall manage and control the investment account of the Fund.

(4) Save where otherwise specifically provided—

(a) sums payable into the Fund shall be paid into the current account of the Fund, and

(b) sums payable out of the Fund shall be paid out of that account.

(5) Moneys standing to the credit of the current account of the Fund and not required to meet current expenditure shall be transferred to the investment account of the Fund.

(6) Whenever the moneys in the current account of the Fund are insufficient to meet the liabilities of that account, there shall be transferred to that account from the investment account of the Fund such sums as may be necessary for the purpose of discharging those liabilities.

(7) Subject to subsection (6), moneys standing to the credit of the investment account of the Fund shall be invested by the Minister for Finance and income arising from any such investment shall be paid into that account.

(8) An investment under subsection (7) may be in any securities in which trustees are for the time being by law empowered to invest trust funds or in any of the stocks, funds and securities which are for the time being authorised by law as investments for Post Office Savings Bank Funds.

(9) (a) The amount by which the income of the Fund for any financial year is less than its expenditure shall be paid into the Fund out of moneys provided by the Oireachtas.

(b) The income and expenditure of the Fund for a financial year shall be determined for the purposes of this subsection by the Minister on such basis as may be agreed upon between him and the Minister for Finance.

(10) Any sum payable into the Fund under subsection (9)(a) shall be paid in such manner and at such times as the Minister for Finance may determine.

(11) Accounts of the Fund shall be prepared in such form, in such manner and at such times as the Minister for Finance may direct and the Comptroller and Auditor General shall examine and certify every such account and a copy thereof, together with the report thereon of the Comptroller and Auditor General, shall be laid before each House of the Oireachtas.

DEFINITIONS

"Minister": Minister for Social Welfare (section 2(1)).

GENERAL NOTE

This section sets out the structural features of the Social Insurance Fund. Subsection (1) is a saver provision which preserves the existence of the fund. The remaining provisions in the section direct that the Social Insurance Fund is to consist of a current account and an investment account and these provisions regulate the transfer of monies, the investment powers of the Minister and the auditing functions of the Comptroller and Auditor General. Subsection (9)(a) is the legislative basis upon which the State subvention is paid into the Social Insurance Fund, this being done under the provisions of the annual Appropriation Acts.

Payments from Fund for acquisition of land, etc.

8.—(1) Payments may be made out of the Fund in respect of expenditure by the Minister on the acquisition of lands, premises, furniture or equipment or the construction or reconstruction of premises, and any such lands, premises, furniture or equipment shall be held by the Minister on behalf of the Fund.

(2) A payment shall not be made under subsection (1) save with the consent of the Minister for Finance.

(3) The Minister may dispose of any lands, premises, furniture or equipment which he has acquired, constructed or reconstructed under this section and any moneys which he receives in respect of any such disposal shall be paid into the Fund.

(4) A disposal shall not be effected under subsection (3) save the consent of the Minister for Finance.

DEFINITIONS

"Minister": Minister for Social Welfare (section 2(1)).

GENERAL NOTE

This section empowers the Minister to expend monies from the Social Insurance Fund on certain capital items, those items being held by the Minister on behalf of the Social Insurance Fund. The Minister may also dispose of those items, the proceeds being payable to the Social Insurance Fund. These powers are subject to the overall control of the Minister for Finance.

CHAPTER 2

EMPLOYED CONTRIBUTORS AND EMPLOYMENT CONTRIBUTIONS

Employed contributions and insured persons

9.—(1) Subject to this Act—

(a) every person who, being over the age of 16 years and under pensionable age, is employed in any of the employments specified in Part I of the First Schedule, not being an employment specified in Part II of that Schedule, shall, subject to paragraph (b), be an employed contributor for the purposes of this Act, and

(b) every person, irrespective of age, who is employed in insurable (occupational injuries) employment shall be an employed contributor and references in this Act to an employed contributor shall be construed accordingly, and

(c) every person becoming for the first time an employed contributor shall thereby become insured under this Act and shall thereafter continue throughout his life to be so insured.

(2) Regulations may provide for including among employed contributors persons employed in any of the employments specified in Part II of the First Schedule.

(3) Regulations may provide for—

(a) excluding particular employments or any classes of employment from the employments specified in Part I of the First Schedule, or

(b) adding to the employments so specified particular employments or any classes of employment,

and, where the Minister considers that any modifications of this Act are appropriate having regard to the purpose for which the regulations are made, the regulations may make those modifications.

DEFINITIONS

"pensionable age": section 2(1).
"employed contributor": section 9(1).

GENERAL NOTE

Social insurance has developed and expanded considerably from its origins under the National Insurance Act, 1911. The 1911 Act confined national insurance, on an experimental basis, to certain trades and the insurance system, both in Britain and in Ireland, has gradually come to embrace both those employed under a contract of employment and those who are self-employed. The method adopted by the Oireachtas to designate those within social insurance has been simple enough: those workers liable to contribute to social insurance are set out in the list of employments which are referred to in section 9 of the 1993 Act and which are contained in Part 1 of the First Schedule to the Act. While this list has broadened and expanded considerably, this method of designating insurable employments was used under the Social Welfare Act, 1952 and the Unemployment Insurance Act, 1920.

The existing list of Part 1 Employments is as follows:

1. Employment in the State under any contract of service or apprenticeship, written or oral, whether expressed or implied, and whether the employed person is paid by the employer or some other person, and whether under one or more employers, and whether paid by time or by the piece or partly by time and partly by the piece, or otherwise, or without any money payments.

As we shall see, the central issue here is whether the employment consists of a contract of service or apprenticeship. We now turn to consider some of the key elements in this formula.

The Contract of Service

The contract of service is the basis upon which most worker-protection legislation is founded, whether the right in question relates to redundancy or employer insolvency, unfair dismissal or holiday pay entitlement. In establishing the status of servant or employee, as distinct from independent contractor (*e.g. The Minister for Social Welfare v. Griffiths* [1992] I.L.R.M. 667) or office-holder (*e.g. Carr v. Limerick VEC* H.C. Unreported, May 22, 1987), the employed person also establishes insurability against a number of contingencies that are typically outside the worker's control, such as involuntary unemployment. The employer may seek to minimise overheads, such as social welfare payroll taxes, by engaging persons on an independent contractor basis, and this is a perfectly legitimate business decision for the employer to make. However, the danger of allowing widespread non-observance of social welfare insurability obligations must be counteracted and several important industries have a history of producing employment arrangements which straddle this difficult line. Anti-fraud measures are directed particularly towards forestry and construction, the security industry, meat processing and the milk and fuel supply sectors.

Drawing the line between contracts of service and contracts for services is a notoriously difficult activity. Professor Wedderburn, in *The Worker and the Law* (3rd ed. Penguin) p. 111 observes that a contract of employment is rooted in the notion of service and that the concept goes back to feudal times: "The judges carried over the earlier concept of service, built from the fourteenth century upon the status and legal imagery of a pre-industrial society with agricultural and domestic labourers featuring prominently, and they used it to fill 'the empty boxes of the contract clauses . . . giving to the master powers to demand obedience that derive from the earlier relationships' ".

The Control Test

The essential feature of the concept of service, identified by two centuries of litigation, is the notion of control. Obviously, in the context of the rural or pre-industrial kind of society referred to above, the master was able to control and direct the work of the agricultural servant or labourer and, indeed, the master often asserted such a right. The right to control the manner in which the work was carried out was also a feature of this concept. As Wedderburn points out, the control test did not require that the master actually exercise this right, but rather, that the employer had the right to do so. The control test features prominently in many workmens' compensation cases in which the inquiry is directed at distinguishing between an independent contractor and a workman employed under a contract of service, and some early Irish social insurance cases direct attention to the control factor as if it was the sole factor (*e.g. Limerick C.C. v. I.I.C. and London* [1934] I.R. 364). Many of the early English cases stress that control was the only relevant issue, the best known example of this being the *dictum* of Bramwell B. in *Yewens v. Noakes* (1880) 6 Q.B.D. 530, where a servant was defined as "a person *subject to* the command of his master as to the manner in which he shall do his work". However, the control test was not always seen as reliable, particularly when the worker involved was a skilled or professional person such as an expert well-sinker (*Hughes v. Quinn* [1917] 2 I.R. 442), a harbour pilot (*Westport Harbour Comm. v. I.I.C.*) [1915] 2 I.R. 283) or a qualified medical practitioner (*Cassidy v. Ministry of Health* [1951] C.L.Y. 6870). One Irish judge expressed the view that questions under Part I of the First Schedule had to be decided by reference to the Statute: "there is an almost invincible tendency on the part of everybody concerned to generalise, . . . it represents a tendency which, when a particular case comes up for judicial determination, must be resisted. Each case must be decided on its own facts in the light of the legislation": *per* Johnston J. in *McArthur v. Minister for Industry and Commerce* [1928] I.R. 555 at 556, an approach recently reindorsed in *McAuliffe v. Minister for Social Welfare* [1995] 1 I.R.L.M. 189. However the Irish case that signals the search for new approaches to the issue of determining the employment status in borderline cases is *Graham v. Minister for Industry and Commerce* [1933] I.R. 156, and in particular the dissent of Kennedy C.J. The case concerned a dispute about whether a construction worker engaged by the appellant was an independent contractor or a servant. In testing this issue, admittedly by reference to unclear or disputed facts, Kennedy C.J. said, at pp. 159–60:

"The question whether a particular individual is an "employed person" (that is to say, a person engaged in employment under a contract of service whether paid by time or piece), or is an independent contractor, is a question of fact often difficult of solution depending in each case on the particular facts of that case. No exhaustive definition of either category has yet been settled and established either by statute or by judicial decision and there is a zone of uncertainty. A commonly accepted test is that of control. Is the alleged "employed person" (to whom I will refer by the neutral expression "engaged person") subject to be controlled by the employer in executing the work, *e.g.*, as to the order and manner in which he carries out the work in detail? As to the disposal of his time while engaged upon it? This, the most usual test is, it appears to me, far from sufficient as a single test. In my opinion there are other and equally important tests, *e.g.*, is the "engaged person" engaged to execute the whole of a given piece of work? Can the engagement be terminated before completion of the piece of work without cause assigned, or for misconduct, or only for malperformance of the work? Is the agreed remuneration on a wage basis or on a percentage or other commercial profit basis? Are the necessary materials to be procured by the engaged person on his own account and, if necessary, his own credit? Are such other workmen (if any) as have been taken into employment upon the work by the engaged person so employed by him as agent for the principal, or are they his own employees paid by and subject to him? Is the engaged person required to give all the time of his working day to the work until completed, or is he free to arrange his own time as he pleases? Is he a member of a trade union and are trade union rules and conditions applicable to the work?"

Many of the "tests" advanced above are clearly relevant to the enquiry in hand, but it would be inappropriate to describe them as tests *strictu sensu*. Rather, this judgment anticipates the evolution of multi-factor tests in which the question of control is probably the single most important element in resolving the status of the individual concerned. In this regard the decision of McKenna J. in *Ready Mixed Concrete (South East) v. Minister for Pensions and National Insurance* [1968] C.L.Y. 2560 has been influential. In this case McKenna J. indicated that there are three primary tests. Firstly, a servant will be obliged to perform the task as a matter of personal obligation. The freedom to do the job by one's own hand or by selecting another is inconsistent with a contract of service even though a limited power of delegation may not be. McKenna J. secondly, adopted the control test and it is evident from later cases that control remains an important factor. Thirdly, McKenna J. argued that the courts should seek to identify provisions in the contract that are inconsistent with the contract of service. Critics of the McKenna J. approach point out that the learned judge did not complete the process by identifying a method of weighing or "balancing" the factors or provisions in question. Nevertheless the courts have been able to produce coherent, if not uniform, guidelines on how the employment/self-employment divide is to be drawn. Particular attention has been given to the practice favoured by some tribunals and judges of drawing up separate lists of contractual terms, rights and obligations that are either positive, negative or neutral in respect of the classification contended for. Thus, the U.K. decisions on the multi-factor test reveal that questions such as the degree of supervision of the work that was undertaken or possible, the power of the employed person to engage a substitute to undertake the work, the method of remuneration or payment, particularly the question whether the employed person runs the risk of incurring a financial loss as well as a profit, are relevant to the inquiry. While some skilled workers, who are generally accepted to be servants, will customarily be required to provide their own tools, if a person is required to provide premises, plant and equipment, this will point towards self-employment. Other minor factors such as the deduction of social security contributions, the payment of holiday pay and the designation given by the parties themselves are of relevance. On balance, however, "no magic formula can be propounded for determining which factors should, in any given case, be treated as the determining ones. The plain fact is that it is a balancing operation, weighing up the factors which point in one direction and balancing them against those pointing in the opposite direction. In the nature of things it is not to be expected that this operation can be performed with scientific accuracy": *per* Atiyah, *Vicarious Liability and the Law of Torts* (3rd ed. Wiedenfeld & Nicholson) p. 38.

Even a professional person, such as a doctor engaged by a company, can be an employee, although it is evident that the employer will not exercise any real degree of control over the professional: see *McCurdy v. Bayer Diagnostics Manufacturing Ltd* [1993] E.L.R. 83.

The Organisation Test

Before leaving the issue of distinguishing the employed from the self-employed by reference to the dominant multi-factor test, it is worth mentioning the so-called organisational test most frequently associated with Denning L.J. and his judgment in *Stevenson, Jordan & Harrison v. MacDonald and Evans* [1952] C.L.Y. 666: "One feature which seems to run through the instances is that, under a contract of service, a man is employed as part of a business, and his work done as an integral part of the business; whereas, under a contract for services, his work, although done for the business, is not integrated into it but is only accessory to it".

The organisation or integration test was first articulated by Professor Kahn-Freund in (1951) 14 M.L.R. 504, but it is implicit in some earlier case law. One Irish example of this is the judgment of Johnston J. in *McArthur v. Minister for Industry and Commerce* [1928] I.R. 55. Here the issue was whether a boy employed to assist a bread roundsman was an employee of the roundsman or the bakery that supplied the bread to the roundsman. After looking at the relationship between the roundsman and the bakery, in particular the fact that the roundsman paid the bakery for the bread before he went out to sell it to his own customers, the absence of control by the bakery and the fact that the roundsman's income was largely determined by how hard he worked, Johnston J. concluded that "when he set out each morning with the van, of which he had the loan, and with his assistant, whom he had employed, he was in reality a retailer of bread".

As Wedderburn has pointed out (*op cit.,* p. 113) this test has the advantage of directing attention to the economists' distinction between one who sells his labour power to the enterprise of another and one who operates his own enterprise, but it is still somewhat imprecise and has been criticised for this reason. It has however proved influential in some cases in Ireland. In the case of *In Re Sunday Tribune* [1984] I.R. 505, the point to be decided was whether certain journalists who contributed copy to a newspaper were employed under a contract of service. Carroll J., following *Beloff v. Pressdram* [1973] C.L.Y. 420, held that two journalists, even though to some extent they were freelance, were nevertheless obliged to contribute copy and were under editorial control: their work was clearly an integral part of the business. However, not all newspaper contributors or columnists will be employees (*O'Riain v. Independent Newspapers* UD134/1978; (E.A.T.) *Kelly v. Irish Press* (1986) 5 J.I.S.L.L. 170).

In contrast stands *O'Coindealbhain (Inspector of Taxes) v. Mooney* H.C. Unreported April 21, 1988, in which the organisation test was given a vital rôle. Here, the branch manager of an employment exchange was held to be an independent contractor. Blayney J. said, applying *Market Investigations Ltd. v. Minister for Social Security* [1968] 3 All E.R. 732, approved in *Roche v. Kelly Ltd.* [1969] I.R. 100, that where the cumulative affect of the various approaches is applied these approaches are not contrasting but rather constitute examining these issues from different angles. See also *Ryan v. Shamrock Marine (Shannon)* [1991] E.L.R. 19 and *Lane v. Shire Roofing Co. (Oxford), The Times,* February 22, 1995.

Declarations by the Parties themselves

It has been stated in several U.K. decisions that the parties themselves cannot alter the essential nature of the employment relationship by expressly declaring that a particular relationship is to exist. This of course is self evident: if for tax or P.R.S.I. purposes, for example, an employment relationship is labelled as self-employment when all the circumstances point towards the conclusion that the self-employed person is clearly an employee, then the "label" will be ignored. In *Lamb Bros. (Dublin) v. Davidson* (H.C.) Unreported December 4, 1978, Costello J. held that, while the search in these cases is directed at discovering the intention of the parties, this will not prevent a court from disregarding any statement contained in the contract if it is in any way a fiction. There are a number of English cases which address the question of when and in what circumstances the "labelling" found in the contract should be considered by the courts but the general direction of this debate is uncertain.

Contract of Apprenticeship

If the apprentice is under 16 years of age, this contribution class is inapplicable. It is no longer necessary that the apprentice be remunerated to make him insurable but if no remuneration is provided then P.R.S.I. contributions can hardly be deducted: see the earlier case of *Minister for Industry and Commerce v. Ussher* [1948] I.R. 133.

Contract: written or oral, whether expressed or implied

It is not necessary that all, or any, of the contractual terms be reduced into writing to make the employee insurable. Contracts may be constituted by the parties through conduct, typically by the rendering of goods or services to a person who accepts them (*e.g. McEvoy v. Moore* (1902) 36 I.L.T.R. 99; *Minister for Industry and Commerce v. Higginbotham* [1932] I.R. 216).

Whether paid by the employer or some other person

This factor is directed at persons who are employed by a given employer but who are paid by someone else. This kind of arrangement may occur when a subcontractor's employees are paid by the main contractor, or vice versa, following an agreement between the subcontractor and main contractor. There can under such an arrangement be a transfer of responsibility which makes the employee an employee of the employer to whom the employee has become attached: *Smith v. Blandford Gee Cementation Co.* [1970] C.L.Y. 897. A related question arose in *Hearne v. O'Cionna, Mac Donnchadha, Whelan, O'Brien, trading as J.A. Kenny & Partners* (H.C.) Unreported, June 4, 1988. The plaintiff, the Collector General of the Revenue Commissioners, sought to obtain judgment against the defendants on the ground that, *inter alia*, arrears of P.R.S.I. contributions, admittedly due in respect of certain insured contributors, were outstanding. The defendant contended that the employed contributors were not employed by the defendants but, rather, by a limited company, Kenny International Limited, which had been formed by the defendants. The defendants had, due to somewhat lax financial control procedures in place in J. A. Kenny & Partners, made financial returns and paid the wages of Kenny International Limited employees. The defendants claimed that in these circumstances they had been "paymaster" on behalf of Kenny International Limited and it was throughout their intention to reclaim the money disbursed from Kenny International Limited. In contrast with P.A.Y.E. deductions, the Social Welfare Acts do not include a provision which deems a person paying emoluments to be the employer of the person receiving the emoluments. O'Hanlon J. refused to enter judgment against the defendants on this point and he directed that this issue should stand over for a full plenary hearing.

Whether one or more employers

A person can be an employee of one or more employers. Whether a person is insurable in respect of one or more employments is, however, resolved by reference to a variety of factors. If the employment is a subsidiary employment, or employment of inconsiderable extent, social insurance is inapplicable. If the employment is not excluded, *e.g.* X works for three employers for 10 hours each per week, X will become insurable. Regulations determine which employer is to deduct the social insurance contribution: in general, each employer is required to deduct P.R.S.I. on the usual percentage basis, that is, the employer will proceed on the basis that the employee is only employed in that particular employment.

Whether paid by time, piece, a combination, or not at all

The P.R.S.I. system requires that the employee receive a money payment. It seems to be impossible to conceive of a case where an employee who is paid either wholly or partly in kind will be insurable at a certain level of reference to a non-money element in the form of payment. Nevertheless, the improbability that payment in kind will constitute reckonable earnings for the purpose of determining what the percentage level of contribution is to be, does not prevent the employee from being technically insurable. In the case of persons who are in employment but who do not receive payment (*e.g.* persons who work for a charity on a volunteer basis), the problem of insurability is presumably solved by holding that there is no contract of employment in existence.

2. Employment (under a contract of the kind referred to under Part 1 Employments, No. 1 above):
   (a) as master or member of the crew of:
       (i) any ship registered in the State, or
       (ii) any other ship or vessel the owner of which, or if more than one owner, the managing owner or manager, resides or has his principal place of business in the State, or
   (b) as captain or a member of the crew of:
       (i) any aircraft registered in the State, or
       (ii) any other aircraft the owner of which, or, if there is more than one owner, the managing owner or manager, resides or has his principal place of business in the State.

Apart from noting that there are some marginal problems of definition (*e.g.* what is a ship or vessel (*McEurnan v. Leitrim C.C.* (1908) 42 I.L.T. 90)) this provision is self explanatory.

3. Employment in the Civil Service of the Government or the Civil Service of the State and employment such that the service therein of the employed person is, or is capable of being, deemed under section 24 of the Superannuation Act, 1936, to be service in the Civil Service of the Government or the Civil Service of the State.

4. Employment as a member of the Defence Forces.

5. Employment by any local or other public authority.

The phrase "public authority" is not defined. In the case of *General Medical Services (Payments) Board v. Minister for Social Welfare* (H.C.) Unreported November 30, 1976, the question arose whether employment by the Medical Services (Payments) Board, a body established by statutory instrument, was employment by a public authority. Hamilton J., noting that no adequate definition of this phrase existed in either statute law or case law, said: "Before deciding whether the plaintiff Board is or is not a public authority it is necessary to examine its nature, the manner in which it was created, its powers, duties and functions, the control to which it is subject and all matters relating thereto". The Board, established under the enabling provisions of section 11 of the Health Act, 1970 was required to assist in the administration of the health services. The Board possessed limited functions—to calculate and verify payments and compile statistics relating to these activities. It was a non-profitmaking body which, for certain purposes, had the status of a local authority even though it was generally under ministerial control. After citing a definition found in *Halsbury's Laws of England*: "a public authority is a body, not necessarily a County Council, Municipal Corporation or other Local Authority, which has public or statutory duties to perform and which performs these duties and carries out its transactions for the benefit of the public and not for private profit", Hamilton J. held the Board to be a public authority. Stressing the need to look to the functions and duties undertaken, Hamilton J. suggested that the test should be, does the body perform statutory duties imposed on it for the benefit of the public?

6. Employment as a court messenger under section 4 of the Enforcement of Court Orders Act, 1926. This category of insurable employment was added by S.I. No. 373 of 1952, following *I.I.C. v. Craig* [1916] 2 I.R. 59.

7. Employment as a trainee midwife, student midwife, pupil midwife, probationary midwife, trainee nurse, student nurse, pupil nurse or probationary nurse. In this paragraph "nurse" includes a nursery or children's nurse. This category of insurable employment was added in 1960 following two celebrated, but unacceptable, decisions in which persons engaged in trainee posts of this kind were held to be involved in a teacher-pupil relationship rather than an employer-employee relationship: *Sister Dolores v. Minister for Social Welfare* decided in 1957 but reported at [1962] I.R. 77, and *National Maternity Hospital v. Minister for Social Welfare* [1960] I.R. 74.

8. Employment by the Minister as manager of an employment office. However, there is an exemption in the case of such employment which is for a duration of less than 18 hours per week or where the manager is not mainly dependant on it for his livelihood: see below under *Expected Employments*. This category is necessary because of *O'Coindealbhain v. Mooney*, (H.C.) Unreported April 21, 1988.

9. Employment as a member of the Garda Síochana.

10. Employment where the employed person is a person in Holy Orders or other Minister of religion or a person living in a religious community as a member thereof.

The recognition of this category of insurable person has evolved slowly over the years. Section 15 of the 1972 Act started this process in the form of an enabling provision and it was first used in 1975 in order to bring certain Ministers of the Church of Ireland into social insurance, their employer being declared to be the Representative Church body of the Church of Ireland: S.I. No. 76 of 1975. The existing law was formulated in the shape of a 1988 Statutory Instrument in order to bring the religions into insurability regardless of means of payment or the view of the Church or other representative body in question.

11. Employment by An Post as a sub-postmaster remunerated by scale payment.
S.I. No. 72 of 1991 directs that such employment is part-time employment and that employees are insurable for occupational injuries.

Excepted Employments

Part II of the First Schedule sets out the categories of employment that are excepted employments for the purpose of social insurance contributions. These are:

1. Employment in the service of the husband or wife of the employed person.

2. Employment of a casual nature, otherwise than for the purposes of the employer's trade or business, and otherwise than for the purposes of any game or recreation where the persons employed are engaged or paid through a club.

3. Employment by a prescribed relative of the employed person, being either employment in the common home of the employer and the employed person, or employment specified by regulations as corresponding to employment in the common home of the employer and employed person. The regulations in question are S.I. No. 19 of 1953 and S.I. No. 348 of 1994.

4. Employment specified in regulations as being of such a nature that it is ordinarily adopted as subsidiary employment and not as the principal means of livelihood.

The regulations which specify the subsidiary employments are the Social Welfare (Subsidiary Employments) Regulations, 1995 (S.I. No. 80 of 1995) which specify that additional part-time employment taken up by a person mainly dependent for his livelihood on that other employment is exempt from Class A-rate subscriptions but is insurable in Class J for occupational injuries. This employment is employment in the service of his or her spouse, or by a prescribed relative, or employment insurable in the public sector at reduced rates, defence forces or Army Nursing Service. Employment as an examination attendant to Department of Education examinations, and occasional service by a returning officer during elections is also subsidiary employment.

5. Employment specified in regulations as being of inconsiderable extent.

The regulations which specify which employments are of inconsiderable extent are S.I. No. 72 of 1991, as amended by S.I. No. 76 of 1994. Part-time employment in which weekly reckonable earnings are less than £30 per week is included. Systematic short-term work is, however, not included in these regulations and such employment is insurable regardless of income levels. Social Employment Scheme employment is regarded as part-time employment and insurable for occupational injuries. The same is true for FAS trainees.

6. Employment under a scheme administered by An Foras Aiseanna Saothair and known as the Social Employment Scheme.

Employment contributions

10.—(1) (a) Employment contributions shall be paid by employed contributors and their employers in accordance with this section.

(b) Subject to paragraph (c) and to regulations under section 11, where in any contribution week a payment is made to or for the benefit of an employed contributor in respect of reckonable earnings of that employed contributor, there shall be payable a contribution by the employed contributor at the rate of 5.5 per cent. of the amount of reckonable earnings in excess of £50 in that week in respect of each employment (or the equivalent thereof in the case of an employed contributor remunerated otherwise than on a weekly basis) to which such payment relates [1995 Act, section 6].

(c) Where in a particular contribution year an employed contributor's reckonable earnings have amounted to the sum of £21,500 and the contributions payable under paragraph (b) have been paid in respect of those reckonable earnings, no further such contribution shall be payable in respect of any reckonable earnings of that employed contributor by the employed contributor in that contribution year. [1994 Act, section 7 & 1995 Act, section 7(c)].

(d) Subject to paragraphs (e) and (f) and to regulations under section 11, where in any contribution week a payment is made to or for the benefit of an employed contributor in respect of reckonable earnings of that employed contributor, there shall be payable a contribution by the employed contributor's employer—

(i) at the rate of 9 per cent. of the amount of the reckonable earnings in that week to which such payment relates where those reckonable earnings do not exceed £231, (or the equivalent thereof in the case of an employed contributor remunerated otherwise than on a weekly basis), and

(ii) at the rate of 12.2 per cent. of the amount of the reckonable earnings in that week to which such payment relates where those reckonable earnings exceed

£231, (or the equivalent thereof in the case of an employed contributor remunerated otherwise than on a weekly basis).

(e) Where in a particular contribution year an employed contributor's reckonable earnings have amounted to the sum of £25,800 and the contributions payable under paragraph (d) have been paid in respect of those reckonable earnings, no further such contribution shall be payable in respect of any reckonable earnings of that employed contributor by his employer in that contribution year.

(f) Where in a particular contribution year an employed contributor is employed by two or more employers concurrently (as defined in regulations under section 13), the provisions of paragraph (e) shall, in relation to contributions mentioned in paragraph (d), apply to the reckonable earnings from each of the employments separately. [1994 Act, section 7].

(2) (a) The Minister may be regulations vary the sums specified in paragraphs (c) and (e) of subsection (1) and such variation shall take effect from the beginning of the contribution year following that in which the regulations are made. [1994 Act, Schedule C]

(b) When making regulations under this subsection to vary the sum specified in subsection (1)(c) the Minister shall take into account any changes in the average earnings of workers in the transportable goods industries so recorded by the Central Statistics Office since the date by reference to which the sum specified in subsection (1)(c) was last determined. [1994 Act, Schedule C]

(3) The employer shall, as respects any employment contribution, be liable in the first instance to pay both the employer's contribution comprised therein and also, on behalf of and to the exclusion of the employed contributor, the contribution comprised therein payable by such contributor.

(4) An employer shall be entitled, subject to and in accordance with regulations, to recover from an employed contributor the amount of any contribution paid or to be paid by him on behalf of that contributor and, notwithstanding anything in any enactment, regulations for the purposes of this subsection may authorise recovery by deductions from the employed contributor's remuneration, but any such regulations shall provide that—

(a) where the employed contributor does not receive any pecuniary remuneration either from the employer or from any other person, the employer shall not be entitled to recover the amount of any such contribution from him, and

(b) where the employed contributor receives any pecuniary remuneration from the employer, the employer shall not be entitled to recover any such contribution otherwise than by deductions.

(5) Notwithstanding any contract to the contrary, an employer shall not be entitled to deduct from the remuneration of a person employed by him, or otherwise to recover from such a person, the employer's contribution in respect of that person.

(6) Any sum deducted by an employer from remuneration under regulations for the purposes of this section shall be deemed to have been entrusted to him for the purpose of paying the contribution in respect of which it was deducted.

(7) (a) Where but for this subsection, an employment contribution would be payable by and in respect of an employed contributor at the rates specified in paragraphs (b) and (d) of subsection

(1) the employed contributor shall, subject to regulations, be exempted from the employment contribution payable under subsection (1)(b) where his weekly reckonable earnings are below a prescribed amount. [1994 Act, Schedule C]

(b) Regulations under paragraph (a) may in particular and without prejudice to the generality of the foregoing specify—

    (i) the manner in which the amounts of weekly reckonable earnings are to be calculated for the purposes of that paragraph,

    (ii) the manner in which the provisions of that paragraph are to be applied in the case of an employed contributor who is employed by two or more employers concurrently, and

    (iii) the manner in which the provisions of that paragraph are to be applied in the case of an employed contributor remunerated other than on a weekly basis.

(8) An employer who, during the period commencing on the 19th day of October, 1992, and ending on the 19th day of September, 1993, employed additional employees under and by virtue of the scheme administered by the Department of Social Welfare known as the Employers' Pay-Related Social Insurance Exemption Scheme, shall not, during the period commencing on the 6th day of April, 1993, and ending on the 5th day of April, 1995, be liable to pay in respect of additional employees who constitute a net increase in the employer's workforce under the scheme above that applying on the 9th day of September, 1992, all or any of the following, namely—

(a) the contribution specified in section 10(1)(d) of this Act [1994 Act, Schedule C];

(b) the health contribution payable by an employer under section 5(1)(b) of the Health Contributions Act, 1979;

(c) the employment and training levy payable by an employer under section 16(c) of the Youth Employment Agency Act, 1981 (as extended by section 25 of the Labour Services Act, 1987).

(9) An employer who, during the period commencing on the 6th day of April, 1994, and ending on the 5th day of April 1995, employs additional employees under and by virtue of the scheme administered by the Department of Social Welfare known as the Employers' Pay-Related Social Insurance Exemption Scheme, shall not, during the period commencing on the 6th day of April, 1994, and ending on the 5th day of April, 1996, be liable to pay the contribution specified in section 10(1)(d) in respect of additional employees who constitute a net increase in the employer's workforce under the scheme above that applying on the 21st day of February, 1994. [1994 Act, section 10].

(10) Regulations may, subject to such conditions and in such circumstances as may be prescribed, exempt an employer who employs an employee under and by virtue of a scheme administered by the Department of Social Welfare known as the Employers' Pay-Related Social Insurance Exemption Scheme, from the liability to pay the contribution specified in section 10(1)(d) in respect of any such employee. [1995 Act, section 10].

DEFINITIONS

"contribution year": section 2(1).
"employment contributions": section 6(1)(a).
"employed contributor": section 9(1).
"reckonable earnings": section 2(1).

GENERAL NOTE

Subsection (1)

The obligation created by section 9(1)(a) of the Principal Act requires persons who are employed in any of the specified employments, that is, any of the employments set out in Part

1 of the First Schedule, to become an employed contributor upon reaching 16 years of age. That person must continue throughout his/her life to pay contributions until he/she reaches the pensionable age of 66 years or leaves insurable employment. There are several provisions in the Principal Act which allow the Minister, by regulation, to modify the provisions of Part II of the Act in relation to certain categories of insurable employment, for example, in the case of persons who have been employed outside the State while insured under Part II: section 25. Section 26 directs that regulations may modify the rates of employment or voluntary contributions. Regulations may also make exceptions from the liability to pay contributions for any specified periods. The basic position for employed contributors who fall within paragraph 1 of Part I of the First Schedule is as follows. Liability to make employment contributions is fixed by section 10 of the Principal Act. The employee's contribution is set at five-and-a-half per cent but an additional levy of one per cent (the health contribution) and a further one per cent Employment and Training Levy is extracted making the employee liable to pay seven-and-a-half per cent of earnings up to a statutory ceiling. The ceiling fixed by the Social Welfare Act, 1995 is set at £21,500 as from April 6, 1995. This means that where reckonable earnings exceed this figure, no further payments by way of P.R.S.I. will be made in that contribution year. Furthermore, the 1995 Act waives the first £50 of reckonable earnings: for full P.R.S.I. contributors: see S.I. No. 77 of 1995 for further "offsets". The employer of the insured contributor is also liable to make a contribution. The reckonable earnings ceiling for the employer is fixed by the Principal Act as from April 6, 1994, at £25,800. The employer is required to pay 12.2 per cent of all reckonable earnings but the 1995 Act improved the position for the employer by providing that if reckonable weekly earnings are £231 or less, the employer's contribution is nine per cent of reckonable earnings, in the case of a Class A contributor. When reckonable weekly earnings exceed £231, then the contribution of 12.2 per cent is fully payable.

Subsection (2)
The provisions which modify the statutory ceilings in respect of both employer and employee contributions are found in section 7 of the 1995 Act. Regulations are not in fact used to raise these ceilings.

Subsection (3)
This subsection places the onus upon the employer to pay both contributions, in the first instance.

Subsection (4)
The right of the employer to recover the amount paid over in the form of the employment contribution is governed by regulations: see S.I. No. 298 of 1989.

Subsection (7)
This enabling provision is intended to exempt certain categories of insured contributor from the liability to pay the employee's contribution when weekly reckonable earnings fall below a prescribed amount. Statutory Instrument No. 88 of 1990 set the level at £60 per week, or its equivalent when the contributor is remunerated on some other basis (*e.g.* fortnightly, monthly, daily). The employer's contribution is not affected by this subsection.

Subsection (8)
This subsection was present in section 18 of the Social Welfare Act, 1993, which is not to be confused with the Consolidation Act. This measure is intended to act as an incentive to employers to take on additional workers, by giving the employer an exemption from paying the employers' P.R.S.I. contributions. The Employers' Pay-Related Social Insurance Exemption Scheme requires employers to apply to the Department of Social Welfare before September 19, 1993 and obtain clearance to participate in the scheme. Once the employer is cleared to participate the employer will be exempted from paying employers' P.R.S.I. for the tax years 1993–4 and 1994–5 for that employee. The employee must constitute a net increase in the employer's workforce and the relevant period for recruitment is the period between October 19, 1992 and September 19, 1993. The Minister indicated that based upon the average industrial wage of £260 per week, the exemption grants amount to a subsidy of £31 per week or £1,647 per annum for each additional employee taken on.
The exemption also covers the employment and training levy and the health contribution when the employee holds a medical card.

Subsection (9)
This was added by the 1994 Act.

Subsection (10)
This was added by the 1995 Act.

Modified insurance

11.—(1) Regulations may modify the provisions of this Part in their application in the case of—

(a) persons employed in any of the employments specified in paragraphs 2, 3, 4, 5, 9 and 10 of Part I of the First Schedule, or

(b) persons employed in a statutory transport undertaking, or

(c) persons employed as teachers in comprehensive schools established by the Minister for Education, or

(d) persons employed as teachers in national schools under the Rules and Regulations for National Schools, or

(e) persons employed as teachers in training colleges recognised by the Minister for Education for teachers in national schools, or

(f) persons employed as teachers in secondary schools recognised by the Minister for Education under the Rules and Programme for Secondary Schools, or

(g) persons employed as teachers in domestic science training colleges recognised by the Minister for Education, or

(h) persons employed as members of the Army Nursing Service, or

(i) persons employed in voluntary hospitals to which grants are paid from moneys provided by the Oireachtas in recoupment of revenue deficits, or

(j) persons employed by voluntary organisations which are providing district nursing services, or

(k) persons employed in an employment which is an insurable (occupational injuries) employment pursuant to section 50.

(2) The provisions of this section are without prejudice to the generality of any other provision of this Part providing for regulations.

DEFINITIONS

"insurable (occupational injuries) employment": section 50.

GENERAL NOTE

Good insurance principles dictate that the category of contributors should be as widely drawn as possible. Nevertheless, Irish social welfare law does not meet this standard. Because of the selective nature of social insurance and the fact that the social insurance net has expanded over a period of many years, often on an *ad hoc* basis, the practice has been against including persons who do not always seem likely to be future "charges" upon the Social Insurance Fund. This has helped to weaken the principle of social solidarity and, in a practical sense, has starved the Social Insurance Fund of much-needed finance. In an administrative context, the willingness of various Governments to accede to special pleading by certain interest groups has created a proliferation of special categories of insurance contributor. There are presently nine compulsory employment contribution classes. Each of these contribution classes is further divided into three, so as to represent separate categories of person. While there is clear statutory authority for such distinctions, the designation of Contribution Classes by letter (*i.e.*, categories A–N) is of an administrative nature. The significance of the further subdivision, *e.g.* Category A contributors may be A0, A1 or A2 contributors, is as follows: A0 contributors pay the full five-and-a-half per cent employee's contribution but the employer pays 12.2 per cent. Anyone in the A1 category also pays the entire amount of the employee's contribution without any discount being available for the employer. A person in the A2 category will be a person who holds a medical card or is in receipt of either a survivor's contributory pension, deserted wife's benefit or allowance, injury or death benefit, single woman's allowance or unmarried mother's allowance, or a widow's pension obtained under the social security legislation of another E.C. State. A2 contributors do not pay the Health contribution or the employment or training levy. In such a case the employer is obliged to pay the one per cent health contribution and the one per cent employment and training levy that otherwise form part of the employee's portion of the employment contribution.

Class A

Class A employment corresponds with certain of the employments set out in Part I of the First Schedule of the 1981 Act, paragraphs 1, 2, 6 and 7. The Department of Social Welfare summarise those in Class A as people in industrial, commercial and service type employment, male and female agricultural workers, domestics and seamen who are E.C. nationals employed aboard ships flying the Irish flag and engaged on home trade.

The test for determining when a person is engaged in agricultural work is determined by reference to the nature of the enterprise in which that person is engaged: *Phillips v. Minister for Social Welfare* H.C. Unreported, February 28, 1974, distinguishing *Warner v. Minister for Industry and Commerce* [1929] I.R. 582. See also *Lydon v. Minister for Industry and Commerce* (1934) 68 I.L.T.R. 263. Domestic workers were defined in *Pile v. Minister for Industry and Commerce* [1942] I.R. 132, applying *Minister for Industry and Commerce v. Stewart and Lowry* [1930] I.R. 112. See also *French v. Minister for Industry and Commerce* (1945) 81 I.L.T.R. 96.

Class B

Persons within Class B are Garda Siochana, permanent and pensionable civil servants, as well as registered doctors and dentists employed in the Civil Service. Contributors in this class do not pay the full contribution rates payable by Class A contributors and are, accordingly, only entitled to qualify for a limited range of benefits, namely contributory widow's pension, contributory orphan's allowance, deserted wife's benefit, and a limited range of occupational injury benefits. The modified insurance for such persons was implemented by Part III of S.I. No. 87 of 1979. A gap in the insurance cover afforded to the Gardai was perceived in cases where members of the force were injured or contracted a disease whilst on duty. Should a member of the Garda suffer a malicious injury or death, then a case for compensation under the Garda Siochana (Compensation) Acts was available, but in no other case was statutory compensation available. The Garda were therefore added to contribution Class B, with effect from 1989. Insured contributors in this class receive limited occupational injuries benefits because the conditions of employment of such persons provide some injury payments for a period following the accident or injury. Thus, Class B contributors obtain half-rate disablement benefit starting 26 weeks after the accident or the contracting of the disease: see S.I. No. 72 of 1989.

Class C

Persons within Class C are the Commissioned Army Officers and members of the Army Nursing Service. Prior to section 18 of the Social Welfare Act, 1989, the Gardai were included in this category. Persons in Class C are entitled to claim contributory widow's pension, contributory orphan's allowance and deserted wife's benefit. The Army Nursing Service is defined in S.I. No. 106 of 1980.

Class D

Class D contributors are permanent and pensionable employees in the public service, other than those mentioned in classes B or C. This class is typically represented by employees of semi-public bodies such as the E.S.B., An Post, Telecom Eireann, teachers and third level educational staff. Class D1 contributors are eligible to claim only survivor's contributory pension, deserted wife's benefit, orphan's contributory pension, and the full range of occupational injury benefits. Like contributors in classes B and C, a percentage contribution of 3.15 per cent is payable by employees.

In the Report of the Commission on Social Welfare (1986), the Commission stated that some 310,000 employees in the public sector pay P.R.S.I. contributions and of these some 150,000 paid full P.R.S.I. Class A rates, while the remaining 160,000 paid a reduced rate in either category B, C or D. The Commission indicated that this situation was the result of historical circumstances and, in particular, a belief that the terms and conditions of employment have been an adequate source of income replacement, particularly through sick pay and contributory retirement schemes. Additionally, some risks have been seen as largely irrelevant to those in public sector employment, particularly the risk of involuntary unemployment. The Commission felt that P.R.S.I. should be fully extended to those in public sector employment on the grounds, first, that the social insurance system is an expression of the principle of social solidarity and citizenship and its risks, costs and benefits should be shared as widely as possible. Secondly, variable treatment of persons in employment, and variable treatment of similar organisations in respect of employment contributions is unjustified. Thirdly, variable treatment may lead to inhibitions in freedom of movement by a worker from one job to another. A common rate of social insurance would facilitate job mobility and deal with the problem of mixed insurance records, that is, persons who find eligibility impaired by the fact that their employment pattern has traversed two or more contribution classes or has included a period of non-insurable self employment. A fourth explanation advanced by the Commission for the need for integration involves the fact that some in low paid public sector employment may receive occupational pensions that are inadequate and at times are payable at considerably lower rates of pension than those available under the Social Welfare Acts.

These arguments, no matter how convincing they appear, have not been accepted by public service trade unions because no guarantee has been received that the full P.R.S.I. contribution of five-and-a-half per cent, if imposed on employees, would lead to an eligibility for full P.R.S.I. benefits, regardless of the availability of occupational health and retirement pensions to individual workers. The Commission avoided the really difficult technical issue of integration by declaring that "consequential problems would be a matter for discussion through the normal employer/labour channels". Indeed, the Commission evaded the issue of whether full contribution liability would result in full benefit eligibility by stating that the public sector worker in the reformed system would be "entitled to benefits as appropriate". Nevertheless, in the 1994 Budget, the Minister for Finance, Mr. Ahern, announced that as from April 6, 1995, all future recruits into Class D employment will pay the full five-and-a-half per cent contribution rate and be eligible for all benefits. S.I. No. 77 of 1995 implements this proposal.

Class E

Ministers of religion employed by the Church of Ireland representative body are insurable under Part I of the First Schedule, paragraph 10. E1 contributors pay 3.83 per cent of reckonable earnings subject to a £50 offset (S.I. No. 77 of 1995): the employer's contribution is 8.12 per cent. All benefits are payable except unemployment benefit and occupational injuries.

Class H

This contribution class comprises non-commissioned officers and enlisted personnel of the defence forces. The H1 employee's contribution is fixed at 7.65 per cent subject to a £50 offset (see S.I. No. 77 of 1995) and the employer's contribution at 11.30 per cent. Class H benefits include the full range of benefits and pensions with the exception of occupational injuries benefit.

Class J

This is a residual category of social insurance which applies normally to employed persons who have reached the age at which old age pension is payable, that is, 66 years of age. Others who fall within category J include persons employed on FAS and social employment schemes and persons whose employment is subsidiary employment or employment of inconsiderable extent, as defined in the Social Welfare Acts. No employee's contribution is payable and the only benefit available to class J "contributors" is occupational injury benefit, the employer being obliged to pay a contribution of 0.50 per cent, the employee contribution being 2.25 per cent (J1). The most recent additions to this category are people participating in Euroform, Horizon and new initiatives of the E.U.: S.I. No. 203 of 1993.

Class K

This category of contributor consists of persons who are not insurable for social welfare purposes at all but who are required to pay the health contribution and the employment and training levy. This class confers health cover only on the contributor. It is availed of by persons employed by their spouse, retired persons in receipt of occupational pensions, company directors paid on a fee basis only, and members of religious orders. Some holders employed in the public service are also insurable under class K, such as the judiciary and State Solicitors. The Commission on Social Welfare saw no reason why office-holders should be excluded from P.R.S.I. and recommended that they be fully included in the social welfare system.

Class M

This is a category confined to persons with no liability to make contributions (*e.g.* persons under 16 years of age).

Self-employed contributors

For the sake of completeness, these are as follows.

Class S

This contribution class, added in 1988 as a result of the implementation of Part III of the Social Welfare Act, 1988, which introduced partial P.R.S.I. liability for the self-employed, applies to self-employed persons such as farmers, members of the professions who are self-employed, and certain company directors not already included in social insurance because they are not paid on a fee only basis (see section 17 below).

Class P

This category was added in 1994 to deal with those self-employed in share fishing: see section 24D, added in 1993 by No. 32 of 1993 (Social Welfare (No. 2) Act, 1993).

Calculation of reckonable earnings

12.—(1) For the purposes of this Part, reckonable earnings may be calculated or estimated, either for a person or a class of persons, in such manner, by reference to such matters and on such basis as may be prescribed.

(2) Regulations may provide for the calculation of the amounts payable in respect of employment contributions in accordance with prescribed scales, and for adjustments of such amounts to facilitate computation and to avoid fractions of one penny in the amounts.

DEFINITION

"reckonable earnings": section 78.

GENERAL NOTE

See article 4 of S.I. No. 298 of 1989 for section 12(1). See article 11 of S.I. No. 298 of 1989 for section 12(1). For special contributors, see article 4 of S.I. No. 302 of 1989.

Employment by more than one employer

13.—Regulations may—

(a) provide for the determination of liability for the payment of employment contributions in the case of a person who works under the general control or management of a person who is not his immediate employer, and

(b) determine the circumstances in which a person is to be regarded for the purposes of section 10(1)(f) as being concurrently employed by two or more employers [1994 Act, Schedule C].

DEFINITION

"employment contributions": section 6(1)(a).

GENERAL NOTE

See S.I. No. 298 of 1989. In general, each employer deducts P.R.S.I. contributions up to the set ceiling without reference to the other employment. The employee can claim a refund of any overpayment but the employer is not so entitled.

Payment of contributions and keeping of records

14.—(1) Regulations may provide for—

(a) the time and manner of payment of employment contributions,

(b) the collection and the recovery of, and the furnishing of returns by employers in relation to, employment contributions,

(c) the charging of interest on arrears of employment contributions,

(d) the waiving of interest due on arrears of employment contributions,

(e) the estimation of amounts due in respect of employment contributions and appeals in relation to such estimates,

(f) the furnishing of returns by employers in relation to periods of insurable employment,

(g) the deduction by an employer from the reckonable earnings of an employed contributor of any employment contribution reasonably believed by the employer to be due by the contributor, and adjustment in any case of over-deduction, and

(h) any matter ancillary or incidental to any of the matters referred to in any of the preceding paragraphs of this subsection.

(2) Without prejudice to the generality of subsection (1), regulations under that subsection may provide for—

(a) the assignment of any function relating to any matter referred to in that subsection to the Collector-General or to such other person engaged under contract by the Minister, with the consent of the Minister for Finance, for this purpose,

(b) the assignment to the Collector-General of any function conferred on the Minister by section 224 and the modification for that purpose of any provision of that section,

   (c) the inspection by or on behalf of the Revenue Commissioners of records prescribed under subsection (5),

   (d) treating, for the purpose of any right to benefit, contributions paid after the due dates as paid on those dates or on such later dates as may be prescribed, or as not having been paid, and

   (e) treating as paid, for the purposes of any right to benefit, employment contributions payable by an employer in respect of an insured person which have not been paid, where the failure to pay such contributions is shown not to have been with the consent or connivance of the insured persons or attributable to any negligence on the part of the insured person.

(3) Nothing in any regulations under this section shall affect the liability of the employer under section 10(3) to pay employment contributions.

(4) The provisions of any enactment, regulation or rule of court relating to the inspection of records, the estimation, collection and recovery of, or the furnishing of returns by employers in relation to, income tax, or relating to appeals in relation to income tax, shall, with any necessary modifications, apply in relation to employment contributions which the Collector-General is obliged to collect as they apply in relation to income tax.

(5) For the purposes of this Part, regulations may require employers to keep such records as may be prescribed in relation to the earnings of persons employed by them and the periods during which the persons were employed, and to retain the records for prescribed periods.

DEFINITIONS

"Collector-General": section 2(1).
"employment contributions": section 6(1)(a).
"Minister": section 2(1).

GENERAL NOTE

This section is, in the main, an enabling section which empowers the Minister for Social Welfare to make regulations governing the payment of contributions and the keeping of records.

Subsection (1)

Paragraphs (a), (b) and (c). These details are set out in the Social Welfare (Contributions) Regulations, 1953–91 and the Social Welfare (Collection of Employment Contributions) Regulations, 1989. The Principal Regulations are S.I. No. 5 of 1953 and S.I. No. 298 of 1989 respectively.

Paragraph (d). This was added in section 9 of the 1988 Act to allow the Minister to waive interest on arrears of employment contributions as part of a tax amnesty scheme. See the instruments relevant to the 1988 and 1993 amnesties, namely S.I. No. 242 of 1988 and S.I. No. 208 of 1993.

Subsection (2)

This subsection makes provision for the making of regulations governing specific matters. Paragraph (a) provides that regulations can be made whereby collection and other functions can be assigned to the Collector-General or any other person engaged under contract by the Minister for such purposes: see S.I. No. 298 of 1989.

Paragraph (b) provides that regulations can be made whereby the Minister's powers to prosecute under section 224 can be assigned; the power includes a power to modify some of those provisions (*e.g.* the certification provision in subsection (4)) where necessary. See S.I. No. 298 of 1989.

Paragraph (c): see S.I. No. 298 of 1989.

Paragraph (d) deals with deeming late contributions to have been paid on the due date, on some later date, or not at all.

Paragraph (e) makes provision for allowing contributions which have not been paid over by an employer to be regarded as having been paid, thereby allowing a claim for benefit to be established.

Subsection (5)

This is one of a number of provisions designed to oblige employers, and others, to maintain employment records and retain these records for prescribed periods.

Priority debts to Social Insurance Fund in a company winding-up

15.—(1) For the purposes of section 285(2)(e) of the Companies Act, 1963—

    (a) the amount referred to in that subsection shall be deemed to include any amount—

        (i) which, apart from the provisions of Article 22 of the Regulations of 1988 (as amended by the Social Welfare (Collection of Contributions by the Collector-General) Regulations, 1989 (S.I. No. 72 of 1989)), or Article 22 of the Regulations of 1989, would otherwise have been an amount due at the relevant date in respect of sums which an employer is liable under Chapter 2 or 3 of Part II of this Act, and any regulation thereunder (other than the said Article 22 of the Regulations of 1988 or Article 22 of the Regulations of 1989) to deduct from reckonable earnings or reckonable emoluments, to which the said Chapters 2 and 3 apply, paid by him during the period of 12 months next before the relevant date, and

        (ii) with the addition of any interest payable under Article 23 of the Regulations of 1988 or Article 13 of the Regulations of 1989, and

    (b) the relevant date shall, notwithstanding the provisions of subsection (1) of section 285 of the Companies Act, 1963, be deemed to be the date which is the ninth day after the end of the income tax month in which the relevant date (within the meaning of the said subsection (1)) occurred.

(2) In this section—

"the Regulations of 1988" means the Social Welfare (Miscellaneous Provisions for Self-Employed Contributors) Regulations, 1988 (S.I. No. 62 of 1988);

"the Regulations of 1989" means the Social Welfare (Collection of Employment Contributions by the Collector-General) Regulations, 1989 (S.I. No. 298 of 1989).

GENERAL NOTE

Section 285(2)(e) of the Companies Act, 1963, gives unpaid P.R.S.I. contributions preferential status in the winding-up of a company. Section 45(2) of the 1990 Act was passed in order to ensure that any unpaid social insurance contributions, which would otherwise be treated as a preferential debt under the Companies Act, 1963, but for the fact that the employer was authorised by the Collector-General to make remittances of P.R.S.I. at intervals greater than the normal monthly interval, shall nevertheless be preferential.

Winding-up and bankruptcy

16.—(1) In this section "the Act of 1889" means the Preferential Payments in Bankruptcy (Ireland) Act, 1889.

(2) The assets of a limited company in a winding-up under the Companies Acts, 1963 to 1990, shall not include—

    (a) any sum deducted by an employer from such remuneration of an employee of his as was paid prior to the winding-up in respect of an employment contribution due and unpaid by the employer in respect of such contribution, or

    (b) any sum which would have been deducted from the remuneration of an employee in respect of an employment contribution for a period of employment prior to a winding-up had such remuneration been paid prior to such winding-up,

and in such a winding-up a sum equal in amount to the sum so deducted and unpaid or which would have been deducted and payable, shall notwithstanding anything in those Acts, be paid to the Social Insurance Fund in priority to the debts specified in section 285(2) of the Companies Act, 1963.

(3) A sum equal in amount to any sum deducted by an employer from the remuneration of an employee of his in respect of an employment contribution due by the employer and unpaid by the employer in respect of such contribution before the date of the order of adjudication or the filing of the petition for arrangement (as the case may be) shall not form part of the property of the bankrupt or arranging debtor so as to be included among the debts which under section 4 of the Act of 1889 are in the distribution of such property to be paid in priority to all other debts, but shall, before such distribution and notwithstanding anything in the Act of 1889, be paid to the Social Insurance Fund in priority to the debts specified in section 4 of the Act of 1889.

(4) Formal proof of a debt to which priority is given by this section shall not be required except where required by or under the Act of 1889 or the Companies Act, 1963.

(5) There shall be included among the debts which under section 4 of the Act of 1889 are, in the distribution of the property of a bankrupt or arranging debtor, to be paid in priority to all other debts, all employment contributions payable by the bankrupt or arranging debtor during the twelve months before the date of the order of adjudication in the case of a bankrupt or the filing of the petition for arrangement in the case of an arranging debtor, and that Act shall have effect accordingly, and formal proof of the debts to which priority is given under this subsection shall not be required except in cases where it may otherwise be provided by general orders made under that Act.

DEFINITIONS

"employment contribution": section 6(1)(a).
"Social Insurance Fund": sections 2(1) and 7.

GENERAL NOTE

This section sets out the general position of the Social Insurance Fund *vis-à-vis* employment contributions which have not been paid into the Social Insurance Fund prior to a winding-up or a bankruptcy.

Subsection (2) provides that the assets of a limited company shall not include either sums deducted from employee remuneration but not paid over prior to the winding-up, or sums which would have been deducted from remuneration, but for the fact that remuneration was not paid to the employee prior to the winding-up. The unpaid sums so deducted or deductible from remuneration take priority in the winding-up. This subsection was made necessary by the decision in *Castlemahon Poultry Products Ltd* [1987] I.L.R.M. 222.

Subsection (3) provides that an amount corresponding to any sum deducted from remuneration by an employer in respect of an employment contribution due and unpaid before the date of adjudication of bankruptcy, or the filing of a petition for arrangement, is not to form part of the property of the bankrupt or arranging debtor. The sum is payable into the Social Insurance Fund as a preferential debt.

Subsection (5) gives priority to all unpaid employment contributions payable to the Fund as employer contributions, by a bankrupt or arranging debtor. Priority is given in respect of such contributions payable 12 months prior to the date of adjudication of bankruptcy or the filing of the petition for arrangement.

CHAPTER 3

SELF-EMPLOYED CONTRIBUTORS AND SELF-EMPLOYMENT CONTRIBUTIONS

Self-employed contributors and insured persons
   17.—(1) Subject to this Act—

(a) every person who, being over the age of 16 years and under pensionable age (not being a person included in any of the classes of person specified in Part III of the First Schedule) who has reckonable income or reckonable emoluments shall be a self-employed contributor for the purposes of this Act, regardless of whether he is also an employed contributor,

(b) every person becoming for the first time a self-employed contributor shall thereby become insured under this Act and shall thereafter continue throughout his life to be so insured, and

(c) in the case of a person who, not having an employed contributor at any time, becomes for the first time a self-employed contributor the first day of the contribution year in which he becomes a self-employed contributor shall be regarded as the date of entry into insurance.

(2) Regulations may provide for—

(a) including among self-employed contributors classes of person or part of any such class of person specified in or included in Part III of the First Schedule,

(b) adding to the classes of person specified in Part III of the First Schedule,

(c) the modification of any of the provisions of this Act relating to self-employed contributors,

(d) the application (with or without modification) to self-employed contributors or self-employment contributions payable under paragraph (a), (b) or (c) of section 18(1) any provisions of this Act which apply to employed contributors or employment contributions.

DEFINITIONS

"contribution year": section 2(1).
"employment contributor": section 9(1).
"pensionable age": section 2(1).
"reckonable emoluments": section 2(1).
"reckonable income": section 2(1).
"self-employment contributions": section 6(1)(b).

GENERAL NOTE

The 1949 White Paper, *Social Security* (p. 9661) noted that the I.L.O., at the 26th session held in Philadelphia in 1944, suggested that social insurance should provide protection, in the contingencies resulting in loss of income to which they are exposed, to all employed or self-employed persons, together with their dependants, in respect of whom it is practicable (a) to collect contributions without incurring disproportionate administrative expenditure, and (b) to pay benefits with the necessary co-operation of medical and employment services and with due precautions against abuse. The White Paper recommended that the self-employed should not be brought within the social insurance net because there were doubts about the ability of many self-employed persons to make contributions, as well as considerable difficulty in collecting contributions, observing at paragraph 53: "an immediate extension of compulsory insurance to the independent worker would present problems which, in the interests of the community as a whole, would require such a measure of inspection and supervision as might be even more objectionable than the present means inquiries in assistance schemes which they would replace. It has, therefore, been decided that it is not practicable, all things considered, to extend social insurance on a compulsory basis outside the employee class".

The White Paper therefore envisaged that the self-employed would continue to depend on social assistance in the event of a contingency arising for which the self-employed person could not provide out of his or her own resources. The 1978 Green Paper, *Social Insurance for the Self-Employed*, (prl. 6772) reiterated the view that problems of administration would be substantial. The Green Paper did not, as a discussion document, make any specific recommendation, but the arguments presented in the Green Paper clearly favoured the extension of the existing social insurance framework to self-employed persons, with whatever modifications were needed. This subject was taken up by the Commission on Social Welfare in 1986. The Report recommended the extension of social insurance to the self-employed.

Although the Commission suggested that it was not necessary to pitch the level of insurance contribution in such a way as to meet the total amount needed in order to provide social insurance benefits to the self-employed, the Commission did not provide any convincing scientific evidence to support the view that the self-employed should contribute at the rate of five-and-a-half per cent or a flat rate contribution of £10 per week: see pl.3851, at p. 236. The Commission suggested that the self-employed contributor should only be eligible for certain long-term payments, specifically invalidity pension, old age pension and widow's pension. The nettle of social insurance for the self-employed was ultimately grasped in January 1988 when the Minister for Finance, Mr. McSharry, announced that, as from April 6, 1988, the majority of self-employed persons would become insurable. The Social Welfare Act, 1988, accordingly, inserted into the Principal Act of 1981 a new Chapter, Chapter 1A, which made specific provision for self-employed contributors and the levying and collection of self-employment contributions.

Subsection (1) of section 17 sets out the categories of person obliged to pay S.I. self-employment contributions. These persons must be aged between 16 years and 66 years and have reckonable income or emoluments. In essence, these are, first, Schedule D taxpayers with reckonable income. Reckonable income is defined as aggregate income from all sources. The term therefore includes unearned income (income from rents and investments such as dividends and interest) subject to capital allowances being available. Secondly, Schedule E taxpayers who are not employed under a contract of service. These Schedule E taxpayers are proprietary directors of companies who are taxable as Schedule E taxpayers on earned and unearned income. There were estimated to be 40,000 persons who fell into this category in 1988.

These two categories bring into social insurance around 130,000 people who were previously outside social insurance. However, there are a substantial number of exemptions considered below under subsection (2). It should be noted that the Act provides that, in general terms, the fact that a self-employed person is also an employed contributor does not prevent that person from being liable to pay self-employment contributions. Of course, a person in self-employment, who is also an employed contributor, will not be liable to make any further P.R.S.I. payments if the income ceiling is reduced *vis-à-vis* the employed contributor contributions levied against that person. In other cases, the person with dual liability will have to come within one of the exemptions if liability to pay self-employment contributions is to be avoided. There is no provision for voluntary "contracting out" of social insurance on the ground that existing social insurance or private or occupational insurance schemes provide adequate cover to a particular individual or class of self-employed person. The net effect of the creation of this distinct category of self-employed person, on commencement of these provisions on April 6, 1988 was to make persons in each class insurable in so far as, on that day, the self-employed person was not already a voluntary contributor. Any person who came into insurable self-employment after that date became effectively insured from the first day of the contribution year (*i.e.* the tax year) in which self-employment begins. The obligation to pay self-employment contributions will end if, prior to reaching pensionable age, self-employment ceases.

Part III of the First Schedule, "Excepted Self-Employed Contributors", sets out the categories of self-employed person who are exempted from the requirement that they contribute self-employment contributions to the Social Insurance Fund. These are:

(i) A prescribed relative of a self-employed contributor, where the prescribed relative participates in the business and performs the same tasks or ancillary tasks. S.I. No. 62 of 1988 defines a prescribed relative as "father, mother, grandfather, grandmother, stepfather, stepmother, son, daughter, grandson, granddaughter, stepson, stepdaughter, brother, sister, halfbrother, halfsister, husband or wife of the self-employed contributor".

(ii) Persons in receipt of unemployment assistance. Two categories of self-employed person who are likely to be eligible for unemployment assistance are proprietors of small shops located in rural areas and small holders. These persons are not only not insurable, they may, by virtue of their right to unemployment assistance, be eligible for credited contributions which may ultimately help establish a right to social insurance old age (contributory) pension.

(iii) Persons in receipt of pre-retirement allowance.

(iv) Persons with an income below a prescribed amount. The income limit established by regulation is currently £2,500 p.a. The obligation to pay a flat rate contribution of £250 p.a., mentioned below, is therefore qualified by the requirement that income reach a minimum level of £2,500.

(v) Employed contributors who receive an occupational pension, or an occupational survivor's pension resulting from a deceased spouse's former employment, and who have other income under Schedule D as unearned income.

(vi) Persons in modified social insurance contribution classes, where contributions are reckonable only for the purpose of widow's (contributory) pension, deserted wife's benefit or orphan's contributory allowance. These persons are persons employed in the public service but who also have alternative sources of income in the form of self-employed earnings. In justifying the exclusion of these persons, the then Minister for Social Welfare, Dr. Woods, said that these persons, who are already pensionable "could, for a relatively small additional contribution, acquire entitlement to a contributory pension additional to their occupational pension": 378 *Dáil Debates* Col. 2054.

(vii) Persons not resident in Ireland with income from investments who are employed contributors, such income from investments being the only liability such persons have to Schedule D taxation.

Subsection (2) is an enabling provision which allows the Minister to either include exempted persons on a class, or part of a class, basis, or add to the list of exempted persons. While the list of exempted persons in Part III of the First Schedule has been amended by primary legislation rather than under subsection (2), there have been provisions in the regulations which have been passed in reliance upon subsection (2).

Rates of self-employment contributions and related matters

18.—(1) Self-employment contributions shall be paid by self-employed contributors in accordance with the following provisions—

(a) Subject to paragraphs (b), (d) and (h), where in any contribution year a self-employed contributor has reckonable income there shall be payable by him a self-employment contribution which shall be of an amount equal to 5 per cent of the reckonable income in excess of £520 or the amount of £230, whichever is the greater [1995 Act, section 7].

(b) Where for any contribution year a self-employed contributor is informed by the Revenue Commissioners that he is not required to make a return of income within the meaning of section 48(1) of the Finance Act, 1986, self-employment contributions shall be paid by the self-employed contributor (whether by instalments or otherwise as may be prescribed) amounting to £124 in respect of that contribution year.

(c) Subject to paragraphs (d) and (h), where in any contribution year a payment is made to a self-employed contributor in respect of reckonable emoluments of that self-employed contributor, there shall be payable by him a self-employment contribution which shall be of an amount equal to 5 per cent. of reckonable emoluments in excess of £520 or the amount of £230, whichever is the greater [1995 Act, section 7].

(d) Contributions under paragraph (a) or (c) shall not be payable in any contribution year on so much (if any) of the reckonable income or reckonable emoluments for that year of a self-employed contributor as is in excess of £21,500 [1995 Act, section 7].

(e) Subject to regulations under section 19, where a self-employment contribution has been paid by a self-employed contributor of not less than the amount that he is liable to pay under paragraph (a) or the amount specified in paragraph (b), whichever is appropriate, he shall be regarded as having paid contributions for each contribution week in that contribution year and, where the contribution paid is less than the appropriate amount aforesaid, no contribution shall be regarded as having been paid by the self-employed contributor in respect of any week of that contribution year.

(f) The Minister may by regulations vary the sum specified in paragraph (d) and such variation shall take effect from the beginning of the contribution year following that in which the regulations are made.

(g) Subject to subsection (3) of section 23, self-employment contributions shall be disregarded in determining whether the contribution conditions for any benefit other than old age (contributory) pension, survivor's pension or orphan's (contributory) allowance are satisfied [1995 Act, Schedule D].

(h) A person who but for this paragraph would be liable for contributions of £230 under both paragraph (a) and paragraph (c) shall be liable only for a single contribution of £230.

(2) Regulations may provide for adjustments in the calculation of amounts payable in respect of self-employment contributions to facilitate computation and for the elimination from self-employment contributions of amounts of not more than 5p and for the rounding up of amounts of more than 5p but less than 10p to 10p.

DEFINITIONS

"contribution year": section 2(1).
"Minister": section 2(1).
"reckonable income": section 2(1).
"self-employment contribution": section 6(1)(b).

GENERAL NOTE

This section sets the rates of self-employment contribution and other related matters.

Subsection (1) directs that if the self-employed contributor has reckonable income in a given year, the contribution rate will be five per cent of reckonable income which exceeds £520, or the sum of £230, whichever is the greater. This is subject to the ceiling of £21,500. If the self-employed contributor is in receipt of very low income, in particular, if earnings come within section 48(1) of the Finance Act, 1986 and the Revenue Commissioners have indicated that no return of income need be made, then a flat-rate contribution of £124 for the contribution must be made. The method of payment is dealt with by way of regulations.

The Minister, by regulations, has the power to amend the ceiling, although this has most recently been done by primary legislation, *i.e.* section 7 of the 1995 Act. Self-employed contributors are in general only able to claim old age (contributory) pension, survivor's pension or orphan's (contributory) allowance.

Subsection (2)

These rounding regulations are found in Article 30 of S.I. No. 62 of 1988.

REGULATION

S.I. No. 62 of 1988.

Regulations providing for determination of contributions payable

19.—(1) Subject to subsection (2), regulations may provide for the determination of the contributions payable, the amount or rates of such contributions, and the contribution weeks in respect of which such contributions shall be regarded as having been paid, in the case of a person who—

(a) becomes for the first time a self-employed contributor,
(b) ceases to be a self-employed contributor,
(c) is both an employed contributor and a self-employed contributor whether concurrently or not,
(d) in any contribution year has reckonable emoluments but does not have reckonable income,
(e) in any contribution year has both reckonable emoluments and reckonable income, or
(f) in any contribution year has reckonable emoluments which relate to a period less than the full year.

(2) Regulations made under subsection (1) shall not cause an insured person to pay contributions on the excess over the amount specified in section 18(1)(d) of the aggregate of his total reckonable earnings, reckonable emoluments and reckonable income in any contribution year.

(3) The Minister may by regulations specify circumstances in which contributions payable by a self-employed contributor may be treated as paid.

(4) For the purposes of this section "contributions" means employment contributions payable under section 10 and self-employment contributions payable under section 18.

DEFINITIONS

"contribution week": section 2(1).
"contribution year": section 2(1).
"reckonable emoluments": section 2(1).
"reckonable income": section 2(1).
"self-employed contributor": section 17.

GENERAL NOTE

This is an enabling section.

Subsection (1) provides for a Ministerial power to make regulations governing points of detail on when contributions are payable, the amount or rate of contribution and the contribution weeks in which contributions may be deemed to have been paid. In relation to paragraph (a), article 3 of S.I. No. 62 of 1988 (as amended by S.I. No. 121 of 1991) is the governing regulation. In relation to paragraph (b), article 4 of S.I. No. 62 of 1988 (as amended by S.I. No. 121 of 1991) is the governing regulation. In relation to paragraph (c), articles 5 and 6 of S.I. No. 62 of 1988 (as amended by S.I. No. 121 of 1991) are the governing regulations. In relation to paragraph (e), article 7(1) of S.I. No. 62 of 1988 (as amended by S.I. No. 121 of 1991) is the governing regulation.

Subsection (2) provides a statutory rôle which limits the aggregate amount that an individual self-employed contributor may pay by way of reckonable earnings, emoluments and income to the statutory ceiling of £21,500.

Subsection (3) empowers the Minister, by regulations, to provide that in certain circumstances contributions payable by self-employed contributors may be treated as paid. In explaining this amendment to the original contributions rules by way of section 23 of the 1989 Act, the Minister said that some difficulties had arisen in relation to self-employed contributors who had made P.R.S.I. contributions but were not regarded as contributors because income tax problems over the previous two-year period had not been resolved.

Regulations for collection of self-employment contributions, etc.

20.—(1) For the purposes of self-employment contributions payable under section 18(1)(b) and (c), regulations may provide for—

(a) the time and manner of payment of self-employment contributions,

(b) the collection and the recovery of and the furnishing of details in relation to self-employment contributions,

(c) the charging of interest on arrears of self-employment contributions,

(d) the waiving of interest due on arrears of self-employment contributions,

(e) the estimation of amounts due in respect of self-employment contributions and appeals in relation to such estimates,

(f) the furnishing of returns by employers in relation to periods of insurable self-employment,

(g) the deduction by an employer from the reckonable emoluments of a self-employed contributor of any self-employment contribution reasonably believed by the employer to be due by the contributor, and adjustment in any case of overdeduction, and

(h) any matter ancillary or incidental to any of the matters referred to in any of the preceding paragraphs of this subsection.

(2) Without prejudice to the generality of subsection (1), regulations under that subsection may provide for the assignment of any function relating to a matter referred to in that subsection to the Collector-General or to such person as may be specified.

(3) The provisions of any enactment or instrument made under statute relating to the estimation, collection or recovery of income tax or the inspection of records for those purposes or relating to appeals in relation to

income tax shall with any necessary modifications apply in relation to self-employment contributions in respect of reckonable emoluments that the Collector-General is obliged to collect as they apply in relation to income tax.

(4) Self-employment contributions payable by a self-employed contributor for a contribution year under section 18(1)(a) in respect of reckonable income shall be assessed, charged and paid in all respects as if they were an amount of income tax and they may be stated in one sum (hereafter in this subsection referred to as the "aggregated sum") with the income tax contained in any computation of or assessment to income tax made by or on the self-employed contributor for the year of assessment (within the meaning of the Income Tax Acts) which coincides with the contribution year and for this purpose the self-employed contributions may be so stated notwithstanding that there is no amount of income tax contained in the said computation or assessment and all the provisions of the Income Tax Acts, other than any such provisions in so far as they relate to the granting of any allowance, deduction or relief, shall apply as if the aggregated sum were a single sum of income tax.

(5) Where an election made or deemed to be made under section 195 of the Income Tax Act, 1967, has effect for the year of assessment the self-employment contributions payable by a wife shall be charged, collected and recovered as if they were the contributions of her husband provided that the question as to the amount of the self-employment contributions so payable in respect of the husband or the wife shall not be affected by the provisions of this subsection.

(6) In any proceedings instituted by virtue of this Act, a certificate purporting to be signed by the Collector-General or by any officer duly appointed by the Minister in that behalf which certifies that an amount in respect of employment or self-employment contributions is due and payable by the defendant shall be evidence until the contrary is proved that that amount is so due and payable.

DEFINITIONS

"Collector-General": section 2(1).
"reckonable emoluments": section 2(1).
"self-employment contribution": section 6(1)(b).
"self-employed contributor": section 17.

GENERAL NOTE

Subsection (1) relates to the collection of self-employment contributions and enables the Minister, by regulation, to provide for a number of administrative matters set out in paragraphs (a)–(h). The matters addressed in subsection (1) are dealt with in Parts V and VI of S.I. No. 62 of 1988.

Subsection (2) permits regulations to be made in which the Minister assigns certain of the functions found in subsection (1) to the Collector-General or any other person contracted to discharge those functions.

Subsections (3), (4), (5) and (6) integrate the self-employed contribution collection system into the income tax code, in so far as, inter alia, the estimation of liability, inspection of records, the charging of liability, joint assessment of couples and evidentiary matters are concerned.

REGULATIONS

S.I. No. 62 of 1988.
S.I. No. 65 of 1988.
S.I. No. 121 of 1991.
S.I. No. 137 of 1993.

CHAPTER 4

VOLUNTARY CONTRIBUTORS AND VOLUNTARY CONTRIBUTIONS

Voluntary contributors

21.—(1) Subject to this Act, where a person ceases to be—
(a) an employed contributor, or
(b) a self-employed contributor,
otherwise than by reason of attaining pensionable age and he has qualifying contributions in respect of not less than 156 contribution weeks, he shall, on making application in the prescribed manner and within the prescribed period, be entitled to become an insured person paying contributions under this Act voluntarily (in this Act referred to as "a voluntary contributor").

(2) The occupational injuries insurance of any person shall be disregarded in determining his right to become, or to continue to be, a voluntary contributor and the rate of voluntary contribution payable in any case shall not be affected by such insurance.

(3) A voluntary contributor shall—
(a) if he becomes an employed contributor, cease to be a voluntary contributor except insofar as is provided in section 22(2), or
(b) if he becomes a self-employed contributor, cease to be a voluntary contributor.

DEFINITIONS

"contribution weeks": section 2(1).
"employed contributor": section 6(1)(b).
"insured person": section 2(1).
"occupational injuries insurance": section 49(2).
"pensionable age": section 2(1).
"qualifying contributions": section 2(1).
"self-employed contributor": section 17.
"voluntary contribution": section 22.

GENERAL NOTE

Under the 1952 Act, prior to 1974, certain categories of worker were liable to fall in and out of insurance (*e.g.* non-manual workers whose earnings exceeded a set figure). Further, a person who was in insurable employment who decided to become self-employed ceased to be insurable at all. These events were unwelcome for the individuals concerned, they constituted substantial impediments to freedom of movement of labour, as well as creating anomalies and injustices when long-term pensions were ultimately claimed. One attempt to alleviate and rationalise the law was made in the 1978 Act, which developed the category of the voluntary contributor. The 1988 Act expanded the concept so as to include self-employed contributors as well as insured contributors.

Subsection (1) provides that when a person ceases to be either an employed contributor or a self-employed contributor (*e.g.* ceases employment, is living on savings or certain kinds of investment income or is dependent on a spouse), is below 66 years of age and has made at least 156 weekly qualifying contributions, that person may opt to become a voluntary contributor. The decision to elect and the circumstances in which the election may be made are set out in S.I. No. 119 of 1979, as amended, and S.I. No. 62 of 1988.

Subsection (2) is a necessary provision precluding persons insurable for occupational injuries purposes only from being considered to be employed contributors. But for this provision such persons could opt for voluntary contributor status.

Subsection (3) terminates voluntary contributor status if the voluntary contributor becomes an employed contributor, unless the exception noted in section 22(2) below is applicable. That exception was a consequence of the abolition of the earnings ceiling for non-manual workers as from April 1, 1974. Voluntary contributor status is also lost if the voluntary contributor becomes a self-employed contributor.

Voluntary contributions by former employed contributors

22.—(1) (a) Subject to paragraph (c), a contribution (in this Act referred to as a "voluntary contribution"), in the case of a person who becomes a voluntary contributor by virtue of paragraph (a) of section 21(1) and who is under pensionable age, shall be payable in each contribution year at such time or times and in such manner as the Minister shall prescribe—

    (i) at a percentage rate (as set out in paragraph (b)) of the amount of the reckonable income of the contributor in the preceding contribution year, or

    (ii) where there was no such income or such income did not exceed such amount as may be prescribed, at a percentage rate of such amount as the Minister shall prescribe.

  (b) A percentage rate for the purpose of paragraph (a)(i) shall be—

    (i) in the case of a voluntary contributor who, immediately before ceasing to be an employed contributor, was employed in employment in respect of which the employment contributions payable are not reckonable for the purposes of old age (contributory) pension, 2.6 per cent.,

    (ii) in the case of a voluntary contributor who, immediately before ceasing to be an employed contributor, was employed in employment in respect of which the employment contributions payable are reckonable for the purposes of old age (contributory) pension, 6.6 per cent., and

    (iii) in the case of a person to whom subsection (2) applies and who, by virtue of compliance with that subsection, continues to be a voluntary contributor, 4.0 per cent.

  (c) A contribution under paragraph (a) shall not be payable in respect of reckonable income in any contribution year which exceeds the sum specified in section 10(1)(c) [1994 Act, Schedule C].

  (d) "Reckonable income" for the purposes of this subsection means, subject to regulations, income derived from any employment, including any trade, business, profession, office or vocation.

(2) In the case of a person who, on the 31st day of March, 1974, was a voluntary contributor entitled to pay voluntary contributions and who became an employed contributor in respect of whom special rate contributions were payable under section 17(1) of the Social Welfare Act, 1975, such a person shall, notwithstanding section 21(3), continue to be entitled to be a voluntary contributor upon applying to the Minister in writing for such entitlement.

(3) Voluntary contributions paid pursuant to subsection (2) by a person to whom that subsection applies shall be disregarded in determining whether the contribution conditions for any benefit other than old age (contributory) pension, retirement pension or death grant are satisfied.

(4) Notwithstanding any other provision of this Act, but subject to subsection (5), a voluntary contributor shall not be entitled to disability benefit, unemployment benefit, maternity benefit, invalidity pension or treatment benefit and, if any voluntary contributions paid by him are at the percentage rate for the time being payable under subsection (1)(b)(i), they shall be disregarded in determining whether the contribution conditions for old age (contributory) pension, retirement pension or death grant are satisfied.

(5) Notwithstanding subsection (4), any benefit mentioned in that subsection may be granted to a voluntary contributor in such circumstances and subject to such limitations as may be prescribed.

(6) A voluntary contribution paid under subsection (1)(a) shall be regarded, where the contribution relates to a full contribution year, as having been paid for each contribution week in that contribution year or, where the contribution relates to a shorter period, as having been paid for each contribution week in that period.

DEFINITIONS

"contribution year": section 2(1).
"employment contributions": section 6(1)(a).
"employed contributor": section 9(1)(b).
"pensionable age": section 2(1).
"voluntary contributor": section 21.

GENERAL NOTE

Subsection (1) provides that a former employed contributor who has elected to become a voluntary contributor, and who is under pensionable age, is liable to pay a contribution in accordance with prescribed conditions as either a percentage of reckonable income or, in the absence of income not reaching a particular figure, at a prescribed percentage rate of a prescribed figure.

The percentage rate of voluntary contribution is set in paragraph (b) and the rate differs as between classes of voluntary contribution. If the former employment did not qualify the voluntary contributor for old age contributory pension (*e.g.* B, C, D employed contributors), then the rate is 2.6 per cent of reckonable income, as defined in paragraph (d), and the ceiling set in section 10(1)(d) is also the ceiling for voluntary contributions. In the case of former employment which did qualify the voluntary contributor for old age (contributory) pension, the percentage rate is 6.6 per cent of reckonable income, subject to the ceiling. In the case of voluntary contributors who come within (b)(ii) of this subsection, the prescribed threshold is £4,750.

Section 22(1)(b)(iii) is explained in subsection (2) below.

Subsection (2) applies to certain voluntary contributors, who were voluntary contributors on March 31, 1974, and who the day after became employed contributors upon abolition of the income ceiling for certain classes of worker. These persons were given concessionary treatment and this subsection continues this by, firstly, continuing eligibility to be entitled to be a voluntary contributor. The percentage rate for such persons is four per cent of reckonable earnings subject to the section 10(1)(d) ceiling of £21,500. In this case subsection (3) directs that such voluntary contributions entitle the contributor to old age (contributory) pension, retirement pension or death grant.

Subsection (4) directs that voluntary contributors are not entitled to disability benefit, unemployment benefit, maternity benefit, invalidity pension, or treatment benefit. In the case of the 2.6 per cent voluntary contributor, entitlement to old age (contributory) pension, retirement pension and death grant cannot be established by way of these contributions. Such persons are therefore only covered for widow's and orphan's (contributory) pensions and deserted wife's benefit.

Subsection (5), however, allows the general restriction in subsection (4) to be modified by regulation.

Voluntary contributions by former self-employed contributors

23.—(1) A voluntary contribution, in the case of a person who becomes a voluntary contributor by virtue of paragraph (b) of section 21(1), shall be at the rate of £230 in a contribution year payable at such time or times and in such manner as the Minister may prescribe.

(2) Subject to subsection (3), voluntary contributions paid by a person under subsection (1) shall be disregarded for all benefit other than old age (contributory) pension, survivor's pension and orphan's (contributory) allowance [1995 Act, Schedule D].

(3) Self-employment contributions paid by a person who, being a voluntary contributor becomes a self-employed contributor on or after the

6th day of April, 1988, and any subsequent voluntary contributions paid by such persons, shall also be reckonable for—

(a) in the case of a person whose rate of voluntary contribution, immediately before ceasing to be a voluntary contributor, was determined under section 22(1)(b)(i), deserted wife's benefit,

(b) in the case of a person whose rate of voluntary contribution, immediately before ceasing to be a voluntary contributor, was determined under section 22(1)(b)(ii), retirement pension, deserted wife's benefit and death grant, and

(c) in the case of a person whose rate of voluntary contribution, immediately before ceasing to be a voluntary contributor, was determined under section 22(1)(b)(iii), retirement pension and death grant.

(4) A voluntary contribution paid under subsection (1) shall be regarded as having been paid for each contribution week in that contribution year.

DEFINITIONS

"contribution year": section 2(1).
"Minister": section 2(1).
"voluntary contribution": section 22.
"voluntary contributor": section 21.

GENERAL NOTE

Subsection (1) provides that where the voluntary contributor becomes so insured as a result of former self-employed contributor status, the rate of contribution shall be at the rate of £230, payable at times and in the manner prescribed (section 9 of the 1995 Act).

Subsection (2) provides that voluntary contributions paid under subsection (1) make the voluntary contributor eligible for old age (contributory) pension, survivor's pension and orphan's (contributory) allowance. Notwithstanding subsection (2), however, subsection (3)(a) allows section 22(1)(b)(i) voluntary contributors who become self-employed contributors to also claim deserted wife's benefit. Subsection (3)(b) allows voluntary contributors who were contributing at 6.6 per cent and who then become self-employed contributors, to claim retirement pension, deserted wife's benefit and death grant, while by virtue of subsection (3)(c) the section 22(1)(b)(iii) four per cent voluntary contributor who then becomes a self-employed contributor is entitled to retirement pension and death grant.

Calculation of voluntary contributions

24.—Regulations may provide for the calculation of the amounts payable in respect of voluntary contributions in accordance with prescribed scales, and for adjustments of such amounts to facilitate computation and to avoid fractions of one penny in the amounts.

GENERAL NOTE

The regulations in question are S.I. No. 119 of 1979, as amended.

CHAPTER 4A

OPTIONAL CONTRIBUTORS AND OPTIONAL CONTRIBUTIONS

GENERAL NOTE

The main purpose behind this new Chapter is to implement a scheme whereby share fishermen may be insurable for short-term social insurance benefits, specifically unemployment benefit and disability benefit. This legislation was necessary because of the cumulative effect of two High Court decisions, *D.P.P. v. McLoughlin* [1986] I.L.R.M. 493 and *The Minister for Social Welfare v. Griffiths* [1992] I.L.R.M. 667. In the first of these cases Costello J. held that the skipper of a fishing vessel and the crew employed on that vessel on the basis that they would be remunerated by way of a share in the proceeds of the catch, were not to be regarded as employer and employees respectively, but rather, were to be regarded as partners in a joint venture. As such, the defendant skipper could not be convicted of certain revenue offences in respect of employees. While this decision did not directly confront the issue of the insurability of share fishermen for PRSI purposes, the decision threatened to undermine the then existing state of the law, under which share fishermen had been regarded as fully insurable under the Social Welfare (Consolidation) Act, 1981. In Part 1 of the First Schedule, share fishermen were regarded as being in insurable employment, but the law was not entirely clear on this because the governing provision in the 1981 Act was section 5(1)(a), which defines an employed contributor as being a "person who, being over the age of 16 years and under pensionable age, is employed in any of the [Part 1 of the First Schedule] employments". In order to try and resolve this ambiguity in favour of insurability, the Minister for Social Welfare, through the Social Welfare (Collection of Employment Contributions for Special Contributors) Regulations, 1989 (S.I. No. 302 of 1989), sought to collect social welfare PRSI contributions from the employer of the share fishermen in question, defining an employer as the bailee of the vessel (in cases of hire-purchase), the lessee (in cases of leasing) or the owner of the vessel (in all other cases). However, in *The Minister for Social Welfare v. Griffiths* (supra.), the accused, the owner of a vessel, was charged with three offences under the Act arising from the non-payment of special contributions in respect of share fishermen employed on his vessel. A case stated for the High Court by the Circuit Court asked whether the accused was the employer of one of these fishermen, one Eugene Pepper, within the meaning given in the 1989 regulations, and, if so, were the regulations insofar as they define the word "employer", *ultra vires* the Social Welfare Acts? Blayney J. found that there was no relationship of employer and employee as between the accused and Eugene Pepper. Not only was there no contract of employment between them (a point conceded by counsel for the Minister), the regulations in question were based upon the premise that an employment relationship, in the traditional sense, exists. The judge went on to conclude that Eugene Pepper was not employed in any sense by anyone. In the opinion of Blayney J., paragraph 6 of Part 1 to the First Schedule did not provide the Minister with an intelligible argument: "The share in the profits of the working of the [vessel] which he received were not received by him as an employed person but as a partner. He was not employed by the accused or by anyone else. He was in partnership with the accused and with the other men who worked the boat from time to time" ([1992] I.L.R.M. 667 at 673). While this interpretation may have followed on from the distinction between a contract of employment and a partnership, and have been a reasonable one to place on ambiguously drafted statutory rules within the context of a criminal prosecution, the effect on the income support rights of this very specialised sector of the community was catastrophic. Given the fact that the ability of the share fisherman to earn a living was dependent upon a number of factors, such as the willingness of the skipper to engage the share fisherman's services, the weather, and E.C. tie-up Regulations, the need to provide income maintenance in times of unemployment or illness were important matters that could not be addressed through social insurance for the self-employed, because the self-employed are eligible only for widow's, orphan's and old age contributions and retirement pensions. This Chapter provides, therefore, an optional contribution scheme through which the share fisherman can obtain limited cover for unemployment benefit and disability benefit. The precarious nature of the industry has been underlined recently by the announcement of a multi-million pound aid package to the fishing industry in order to compensate fishermen for losses experienced as a result of the weather conditions in 1993/4 (see *The Irish Times*, April 1 and 2, 1994).

Optional contributors and contributions

24A—(1) A person engaged in share fishing shall, subject to such conditions as may be prescribed, be entitled to opt to become an insured person ('optional contributor') paying contributions under this Chapter ('optional contributions') which shall be payable in each contribution year with effect from the contribution year ending on the 5th day of April, 1994 at such time and in such manner as may be prescribed.

(2) An optional contributor shall cease to be an optional contributor if he—

    (a) ceases to be a person engaged in share fishing,

    (b) ceases to be a self-employed contributor, or

    (c) fails, in any contribution year, to pay an optional contribution which by virtue of being an optional contributor, he is liable to pay.

GENERAL NOTE

Section 24A(1) of the Principal Act provides that regulations may prescribe the conditions under which a share fisherman may be entitled to opt to become an optional contributor. As share fishermen are compulsorily self-insurable if they have income which reaches £2,500 per annum, a share fisherman is not eligible to be an optional contributor if his income falls below this level or share fishing is not the principal means of livelihood for such a person, *i.e.* the Act does not apply to "part-time" fishermen.

As presented initially to Dáil Eireann, the Social Welfare (No. 2) Bill, 1993 utilised the contribution year 1994 to 1995. At Report Stage in Dáil Eireann, the operative date for making optional contributions payable was moved forward one day, to April 5, 1994, thereby utilising the contribution year 1993 to 1994. This has the effect of allowing optional contributors to make one payment of £250 during the 1993 to 1994 contribution year (or within three months under regulations) in order to obtain benefits under the scheme commencing on January 1, 1995. As initiated, benefits would not commence until January 1, 1996, and in the face of comments by the IFO and many deputies, the Minister amended the Bill in this way. Section 24A(1) also makes it possible to prescribe the method of collecting optional contributions. The regulations are the Social Welfare (Optional Contribution) Regulations, 1994 (S.I. No. 53 of 1994). These regulations make provision for the furnishing of information to an officer of the Minister and provide for the payment of optional contributions before the end of the relevant contribution year. There is no exception when an optional contributor first elects to contribute. If the contribution is paid within three months of the end of the contribution year in which the election was made, then the payment is to be treated as having been paid within the contribution year. The regulations also allow for payments to be made, by arrangement, in instalments. In the year of election, the payment needed to obtain benefits under the optional scheme is £230: S.I. No. 79 of 1995. Contributions paid under the PRSI scheme prior to the *Griffiths* decision (supra.) may also be credited for the purpose of the optional scheme (see regulation 11 of S.I. No. 53 of 1994).

Rates of optional contributions and related matters

24B—(1) Optional contributions shall be payable by optional contributors in accordance with the following provisions—

(a) Subject to paragraph (b), an optional contributor shall pay an optional contribution of an amount equal to 5 per cent. of his reckonable income in excess of £520 in the preceding contribution year, or the sum specified in section 18(1)(h), whichever is the greater [1995 Act, section 8(1)].

(b) An optional contribution shall not be payable in respect of so much (if any) of the reckonable income of an optional contributor in any contribution year which exceeds the sum specified in section 18(1)(d).

(2) Subject to regulations under section 24C, where an optional contribution has been paid by an optional contributor of not less than the amount that he is liable to pay under subsection (1), he shall be regarded as having paid contributions for each contribution week in that contribution year and, where the contribution paid is less than the appropriate amount aforesaid, no contribution shall be regarded as having been paid by the optional contributor in respect of any week of that contribution year.

(3) Regulations may provide for adjustments in the calculation of amounts payable in respect of optional contributions to facilitate computation and for the elimination from optional contributions of amounts of not more than 5p and for the rounding up of amounts of more than 5p but less than 10p to 10p.

(4) Optional contributions shall be disregarded in determining whether the contribution conditions for any benefit other than disability benefit (excluding disability benefit payable by virtue of sections 53 or 56), unemployment benefit or treatment benefit are satisfied:

Provided that the contribution conditions for the said benefits shall not be regarded as being satisfied unless all optional contributions payable by an optional contributor in accordance with the provisions of this Chapter have been paid [1995 Act, Schedule E].

GENERAL NOTE

Section 24B(1) of the Principal Act as amended by the 1995 Act provides that the optional contributor will pay five per cent of reckonable income in excess of £520, up to the limit of £20,000, or the sum of £250, whichever is the greater amount. Section 24B(4) was amended at Report Stage in Dáil Eireann in order to include treatment benefits. As introduced, the Bill only made provision for unemployment and disability benefits. Because adult dependants are also eligible for optical and dental benefits under the treatment benefit scheme, this was universally welcomed.

Matters concerning the calculation and refunding of optional contributions are dealt with by regulations 8–10 of S.I. No. 53 of 1994.

Regulations providing for determination of optional contributions payable and related matters

24C—Regulations may provide for—

(a) the determination of optional contributions payable, the amount or rates of such contributions, and the contribution weeks in respect of which such contributions shall be regarded as having been paid, in the case of a person who—

(i) becomes for the first time an optional contributor,

(ii) ceases to be an optional contributor, or

(iii) in any contribution year has reckonable earnings and reckonable income,

and

(b) any matter ancillary or incidental to any of the matters referred to in the preceding paragraph of this section. [1993 (No. 2) Act, section 4].

GENERAL NOTE

These issues are addressed in S.I. No. 53 of 1994, in particular regulation 11 which deals with contribution weeks.

Cesser of Optional Contributor Status

The Minister of State at the Department of Social Welfare, Ms. Burton, indicated that in the light of representations made by the IFO and share fishermen, many of whom wished to acquire full insurability through the status of an employee, it was possible for contractual arrangements to be devised between skippers and crews which would avoid the *Griffiths* decision: "I wish to make it known that, following consultations with the Office of the Attorney General, guidelines aimed specifically at share fishermen as to what constitutes employment under contract of service will be made available. The advantage of this approach is that it will meet the needs of those skippers who wish to be treated as employers without having to enact legislation which might be challenged at some future date".

CHAPTER 5

GENERAL

Employment outside State

25.—(1) Regulations may modify the provisions of this Part and the First Schedule in their application in the case of persons who are or have been outside the State while insured under this Part.

(2) The modifications which may be made by regulations for the purposes of subsection (1) shall, in particular, include the deletion of "in the State" in paragraph 1 of Part I of the First Schedule.

(3) The provisions of this section are without prejudice to the generality of any other provision of this Part providing for regulations.

GENERAL NOTE

This is an enabling section which permits the Minister to modify the law relating to social insurance and the law relating to insurable employments and excepted employments in relation to persons who have been outside the State while insured under Part II of the Act. The power of modification includes the power to make the general insurability obligation applicable to employments under paragraph (1) of Part I of the First Schedule, even if the employment is not within the State.

Regulations varying rates and amounts of contributions

26.—Regulations may alter the rates or amounts of employment, self-employment or voluntary contributions.

Exceptions and credits

27.—Regulations may provide for—
  (a) making exceptions from the liability to pay contributions for any specified periods, and
  (b) crediting contributions to insured persons for any specified periods, including, in particular—
      (i) periods for which there is an exception from the liability to pay contributions by virtue of paragraph (a), and
      (ii) the period between the beginning of the contribution year last preceding that in which they become insured persons and their entry into insurance.

DEFINITIONS
"contribution year": section 2(1).
"insured person": section 2(1).

GENERAL NOTE
This is an enabling provision which allows the Minister, to make regulations which exclude persons from the obligation to pay contributions, or giving the Minister the power to credit contributions to insured persons. Social insurance schemes require the applicant for that particular insurance benefit to establish entitlement by proving that social insurance contributions have been made which entitle the applicant to social insurance payments. Social insurance contributions for employed contributors fall into two categories. Generally, if a claim is to be successful, two contribution conditions must be satisfied. The first contribution condition requires that there must be a minimum level of *paid* qualifying contributions in respect of the applicant. Qualifying contributions are somewhat unhelpfully defined in section 2(1) as "appropriate employment contribution" paid in respect of the insured person. This effectively means that the contribution class must be a contribution class that entitles a member of that class to claim a particular social insurance payment. This first contribution condition is the basis of the social insurance principle: by analogy with an insurance contract, payment of the contribution is payment of a "premium" which entitles the insured person to compensation in the event of the risk materialising. However, the social insurance contribution system adds a further contribution condition. The concept of entitlement to social insurance requires the system to be equitable and fair for all contributors and, as a result, there is a further requirement that the insured person establish an enduring link with the social insurance system. If the first contribution condition were the sole test of eligibility then many persons with only an incidental or passing acquaintance with social insurance could establish entitlement, because the first contribution condition only fixes the period within which the insurance payment will be made, if at all, and also serves to establish the worker within the social insurance scheme. In order to ensure that the Fund is not depleted by claims made by persons who have no record of a consistent involvement or commitment to social insurance, the second qualifying contribution was added to social insurance in the Social Insurance Act, 1952 following recommendations in the 1949 White Paper, *Social Security*, paragraph 99. This requires the applicant to satisfy a requirement that paid qualifying contributions or credited contributions be made by the applicant over an extended period. Where the benefit claimed is a short-term benefit, such as unemployment benefit or disability benefit, the period is reasonably short and proximate to the date of the claim, that is, the last complete contribution year before the benefit year in which the claim is made. Where the payment is long-term, such as a deserted wife's benefit or retirement pension, the period is

longer. The applicant must show an extended link with the social insurance fund by satisfying a minimum average contribution record over a prescribed period. For deserted wife's benefit the average is 39 contribution weeks of paid or credited contributions in either the three or five years prior to desertion, if four years or more have elapsed since entry into insurance and the claim. In the alternative, if an average of at least 48 contribution weeks of paid or credited contributions can be shown since entry into insurance, deserted wife's benefit will be payable. For a retirement pension to be payable, the yearly average cannot fall below 24 contribution weeks of paid or credited contributions since 1953 or the year of entry into insurance, if later than 1953.

Credited Contributions

For the purpose of satisfying the second contribution requirement, the payment of qualifying contributions is given the same practical value as obtaining credited contributions. Satisfying the second contribution requirement by a mixture of both paid and credited contributions is a quite normal and acceptable method of establishing the necessary degree of consistency of insurance record over a period of time. The advent of credited contributions in Irish social policy seems to pre-date the second contribution condition. The 1949 White Paper does not refer to credited contributions as a *condition of entitlement*, but it did envisage that the second contribution condition, to be satisfied by paid or credited contributions, would have to be satisfied in order to obtain full benefit (p. 9661). The Social Welfare Act, 1952, however, made satisfaction of the second contribution condition a condition of entitlement in the strict sense: some minimum yearly average of paid or credited contributions over the requisite period would have to be established. The White Paper did not provide any real explanation as to why credited contributions were to be allowed in the reformed system. The White Paper simply states: "credits, as may be provided by regulations, will be granted for periods when no contributions are payable. In particular, they will be allowed during periods of unemployment and of incapacity for work due to sickness". Yet the explanation for the existence of credited contributions is not hard to find: indeed the rationale exists within the second contribution condition itself. It is hardly equitable to impose an obligation to satisfy the second contribution by way of paid qualifying contributions in the appropriate period (generally, the whole or part of the previous contribution year or a given number of contribution years), when that person had no link with employment, either as an employee or as a self-employed person. To the extent that it would be unfair to require that both contribution conditions should be satisfied by reference to paid qualifying contributions only, the Oireachtas in section 27 of the Principal Act has recognised that the second contribution requirement can be met by exempting persons from the obligation to pay qualifying contributions and crediting those persons with contributions. Ogus and Barendt, in a paragraph cited with approval by the Commission on Social Welfare, at page 223 of the Report, state: "the system of crediting contributions is designed to assist those who are already established in the scheme but, for reasons beyond their control, have been unable to continue to make the requisite payments, sufficient to satisfy the second condition".

Sickness

The most obvious circumstances in which persons would not be required to continue to pay contributions and would expect to have credited contributions registered in order to assist them in claiming future social insurance benefits, are where employment is interrupted by sickness or unemployment. Article 4(1) of the Principal Regulation (which is S.I. No. 5 of 1953, as amended by S.I. No. 135 of 1979) directs that an employment contribution shall be credited to an insured person in respect of any contribution week of duly notified incapacity for work, although the credited contribution may not be effective for the purpose of all insurance benefits if the insured person was last an employed contributor at a reduced rate. With the introduction of social welfare occupational injuries benefits and the fact that persons can be insured solely against occupational injuries benefit, S.I. No. 89 of 1967 provides that a person solely insured for the purpose of occupational injury benefits is not to receive a credited employment contribution under article 10 of S.I. No. 5 of 1953 unless he or she subsequently becomes an employed contributor for the purpose of the social insurance scheme. A person solely insured for occupational injury purposes only, however, will obtain credited contributions in respect of periods of incapacity for work resulting from occupational injury or disease. When employment is interrupted by pregnancy and the claimant is entitled to maternity benefit, credits are available, which are reckonable for all benefits, for any week in which maternity benefit is payable. Credits are not awarded for any other week in which a woman takes statutory rights to extended maternity leave, however, if she does not, for that week, successfully claim disability benefit. Persons in receipt of invalidity pension or retirement pension will obtain credited contributions under S.I. No. 222 of 1970, which will be of assistance in satisfying the second contribution condition in respect of treatment benefit: section 117 of the Principal Act of 1993.

Unemployment

Article 4(1) of the Social Welfare (Contributions) Regulations, 1953 provides that an employment contribution shall be credited to an insured person in respect of any contribution week of proved unemployment. Article 4 also directs a credit in respect of days of incapacity for work. Article 5 of that regulation, however, deals with the break in the employment pattern by providing that where there is no contribution paid or credited during two successive contribution years, any subsequent employment contribution is not to be credited in respect of any contribution week of proved unemployment until 26 employment contributions have been paid in respect of that person. The onus is upon the claimant to show that he is entitled to a credited contribution by proving the day is a day of proved unemployment within the Acts and that on that day the claimant was not incapable of work and was available for employment. To this end, the claimant must furnish the Minister with such evidence as the Minister may require.

Pre-Entry Credits

There are pre-entry credits available to persons who become employed contributors. Article 10 of the Principal Regulation (S.I. No. 5 of 1953, as amended by S.I. No. 107 of 1980), states that contributions shall be credited for the period before entry into insurance. If a person enters into insurance in a given contribution year then, in respect of the two previous contribution years, that person shall obtain credited contributions. These credited contributions are available from the beginning of the second last contribution year and the date of entry into insurance, so that if a person enters into insurance just before the end of a particular contribution year, credit contributions for almost three years will accrue to that person. Pre-entry credits therefore ensure that a person will obtain short-term benefits, that is, unemployment benefit, disability benefit, and maternity benefit, when that person has paid 39 qualifying contributions. Credits may also be obtained when an insured person moves from one contribution category to another due to changing employment: regulations provide that if an employed contributor was insurable at a reduced rate (*e.g.* public sector employment) and takes up new employment in which the contributor is insurable for old age contributory pension purposes, credits will be awarded for the current contribution year up to the date of commencement of the new employment. These credits, which are awarded once only, are reckonable for old age (contributory) pension, retirement pension and death grant only: S.I. No. 135 of 1979. However, if a person who is incapable of work or unemployed has not been an insured contributor, credits cannot be awarded. Further, if a period of two years—two consecutive full contribution years—has intervened between the last paid or credited contribution, this will break the link with social insurance and crediting will only be possible after the insured person has paid 26 reckonable contributions (*i.e.* has worked in insurable employment for six months).

Student Credits

Students who are participating in a course of full-time education, defined by S.I. No. 107 of 1980, the controlling regulation, as a course of full-time instruction by day at any university, college, school or other educational establishment, may, at an earlier date, have worked in insurable employment. As a result of this employment, *e.g.* employment over the summer months prior to going to university, the student will have been given pre-entry credits. Because these credits are given only once, a student who takes up employment when the course of study has ended would be penalised when subsequently claiming short-term benefits, if the ability to satisfy the second contribution condition is determined by reference to the pre-entry credits obtained several years before the application for benefit. The pre-entry credits, at least when the course of study is of several years duration, would be "spent" and the student, who would not have been insurable whilst a student, could not satisfy the second contribution condition by way of paid qualifying contributions.

To rectify this, employment contributions, reckonable only for disability benefit, employment benefit, maternity benefit and death grant, are credited to all insured persons who, during a course of education or during an interval between such courses, were engaged in insurable employment and who, at the end of the course, re-entered insurable employment for which contributions in respect of old age (contributory) pension are payable. These credits are awarded from the beginning of the second last contribution year to the date of re-entry into insurable employment after having ceased to attend a course of full-time education. The regulation provides that credits are not available if, upon commencement of the educational course, the student was 23 years old or more, or where the student had been given credits in relation to an earlier course of study. Because the regulation refers to "ceased to attend" rather than "ceased to be registered on, or participate in", a student who has unsuccessfully completed the course of study is entitled to those credits, even if the student intends to resit examinations at some time in the future.

Training and Work Experience

The recent spate of training and work experience programmes have produced policy issues with regard to the crediting of contributions: is a person who participates in a scheme to be considered to have re-entered employment (even though there may be no long-term assurance that training or employment will continue), or does the ephemeral nature of the programme in question mean that participants must be regarded as being less than employed? If the former attitude is to prevail, then credited contributions should not be available. This of course would seriously damage the appeal of many training schemes in that unemployed persons may be dissuaded from participating in the scheme partly because the credited contributions obtained while registered as unemployed will cease. In practice, the response to this problem has been a rather pragmatic one. Ever since AnCo was founded under the Industrial Training Act, 1967, AnCo trainees have been entitled to a credited contribution for any week during the whole or part of which that person attends a course of training provided or approved by AnCo when an employment contribution (other than an occupational injuries contribution payable by the employer) is not payable. The credits obtained are reckonable for the same range of benefits as were covered by the contribution payable when the trainee was last in insurable employment. These credits are not available when the gap between a paid or credited contribution having been recorded and the commencement of training exceeds two consecutive contribution years. While AnCo has been dissolved and replaced by a new training and retraining agency, An Foras Aiseanna Saothair, under the provisions of the Labour Services Act, 1987, that Act does not extend the life of S.I. No. 1 of 1968 to programmes of training and retraining provided by An Foras. Credited contributions will also be awarded to insured persons who undertake training provided or approved by the Youth Employment Agency (YEA), a statutory body established under the Youth Employment Agency Act, 1981. Persons so engaged (the maximum age for entry into youth training, set by the 1981 Act at 25 years of age, has been abolished by the Labour Services Act, 1987) are given credited contributions when an employment contribution, other than an occupational injuries contribution payable by the employer, is not payable. The credits obtained are reckonable for the same range of benefits as were covered by the contribution payable when the trainee was last in insurable employment. These YEA credits are not available if the insured person's record shows a gap of two consecutive contribution years between the date on which an employment contribution was paid or credited and entry into YEA training.

S.I. No. 179 of 1983

The Enterprise Allowance Scheme, a non-statutory scheme which is administered by the Department of Labour, aims to provide assistance to unemployed persons who wish to start a business venture. Insured participants in the Enterprise Allowance Scheme are awarded credits under S.I. No. 224 of 1984 for a maximum period of 52 weeks (being the maximum duration of Enterprise Allowance Scheme entitlements) when an allowance is paid by the Department. S.I. No. 224 of 1984 credits are also awarded to insured persons who receive a loan from the Youth Employment Agency under the Agency's Youth Self-Employment Programme. Those credits may be awarded for up to 156 weeks. Again, credits are referable to the range of benefits for which the insured person was covered in the last period of insurable employment and the two-year break in paid or credited contributions means that credited contributions will not be registered. Should the Enterprise Allowance Scheme participant be a voluntary contributor or formerly a permanent and pensionable public sector worker (within article 7 of S.I. No. 87 of 1979), these Enterprise Allowance Scheme credited contributions are referable to survivor's pension and deserted wife's benefit only, or to widow's contributory pension, deserted wife's benefit, retirement pension, old age (contributory) pension and death grant, respectively. Article 4(2) of S.I. 224 of 1984 also enables persons to maintain their social insurance record through the crediting of contributions for the duration of involvement in the Social Employment Scheme, a programme providing work for the long-term unemployed and administered by the Department of Labour: S.I. No. 101 of 1985. Some Department of Labour and Department of Social Welfare training, education and work experience schemes, however, do not attract credited contributions even though some of these schemes, namely the Alternance Scheme, the Teamwork Scheme, the Part-Time Job Allowance Scheme and the Educational Opportunities Scheme have been recognised by the Oireachtas for other purposes: see 42(5) of the Principal Act.

Credits for Persons engaged in Beneficial Activities

There are specific provisions dealing with insured contributors who experience a break in their employment record or availability for employment as the case may be. If a carer, on cessation of payment of the prescribed relative's allowance in respect of the care provided by that carer, returns to employment or availability for employment, then a credited contribution will be made in respect of each week in which prescribed relative's allowance (PRA) was payable, as long as the carer had an employment contribution paid or credited in either of the two complete contribution years immediately preceding the date when PRA was payable: Social Welfare (Contributions) (Amendment) (No. 3) Regulations, 1972 (S.I. No. 344 of 1972). The award of credits in these circumstances recognises the obligations, legal and moral, which members of a family owe to one another and, at the same time, provides the carer with some assurance that the discharge of these obligations will not be financially costly. In general, the credited contributions system requires that the insured person be able to demonstrate some enduring link with the social insurance system if credits are to be forthcoming. In this context the employment record, past and present, is the relevant reference point. There are exceptional situations in which credits may be granted in respect of interruptions or gaps in an individual's contribution record if they are the result of some laudable or altruistic action, even though there seems to be a clear "break" with the Irish social insurance system. The case of volunteer development workers who leave Ireland to work in Third World countries is just such an exceptional situation. If these persons are paid local rates of pay they may be given credited contributions (S.I. No. 161 of 1985) for the period spent abroad, for up to five years, the credits being referable to the contribution paid during the last period of insurable employment in Ireland. While other persons may spend time abroad for educational or training purposes, *e.g.* au pairs, these persons are not seen in the same light as volunteer development workers, for obvious reasons.

Assessment of Credited Contributions

The Commission on Social Welfare pointed out that while the system of awarding credited contributions involves a cost factor—in a time of recession more people establish entitlement through credits rather than by paid contributions—it is probable that the Exchequer costs which result are not high because many persons who could not, but for credits, obtain social insurance payments, would be entitled instead to means-tested assistance payments. Indeed the argument can be taken further by pointing out that the increased Exchequer costs which result from claimants receiving insurance payments, rather than the lower assistance payments, are largely illusory. The Social Insurance Fund meets social insurance claims: the Fund is sustained by the Exchequer to the extent that 30 per cent of the annual cost of maintaining it is met by Exchequer subvention, the balance being met by employer and insured contributors in the form of P.R.S.I. contributions. Because social assistance disbursements are met almost entirely from the Exchequer, it is in the interest of the Exchequer to have claims for social welfare payments met, whenever possible, by social insurance rather than social assistance. This begs the question, is it just and equitable to give certain persons credited contributions when others may be denied? Some persons indeed register as unemployed, not in order to obtain unemployment benefit or assistance, but solely in order to obtain insurance credits for long term social insurance pensions — around five per cent of the live register, primarily married women without an adequate insurance record and who cannot obtain unemployment assistance because of the aggregation with their husband's earnings: *Commission Report* pp. 223 and 244. The Commission on Social Welfare took the view (pl. 3851 p. 224) that the "real and substantial" justification for awarding credits to the unemployed and those in receipt of disability benefit "is fairly clear cut". The Commission added "we also support the granting of credits in the various other circumstances to which this facility has been extended." Any further credits will, it seems, be added in a piecemeal fashion, as before, when the necessary justification can be made out.

Return of contributions paid in error

28.—Regulations may provide for the return, subject to any conditions, restrictions and deductions specified in the regulations, of any sums paid in error by way of employment, self-employment or voluntary or optional contributions [1993 (No. 2) Act, section 6].

DEFINITIONS

"employment contribution": section 6(1)(a).
"self-employment contribution": section 6.
"voluntary contribution": section 22.

Return of contributions where entry into insurance occurs after specified age

29.—(1) Regulations shall provide for the return, subject to any conditions, restrictions and deductions specified in the regulations, of so much of any employment contribution paid by an employed contributor or voluntary contribution payable under section 22 by a voluntary contributor whose entry into insurance occurred—

(a) after he had attained the age of 60 years,

(b) after he had attained the age of 58 years in the case of a person who attained the age of 57 years on or after the 1st day of July, 1974.

(c) after he had attained the age of 57 years in the case of a person who attained the age of 56 years on or after the 1st day of April, 1975, or

(d) after he had attained the age of 56 years in the case of a person who attained the age of 55 years on or after the 1st day of October, 1977,

as is determined in accordance with the regulations to have been paid in respect of old age (contributory) pension.

(2) (a) In the case of a person who attained the age of 56 years on or after the 1st day of April, 1975, subsection (1)(b) shall not apply on his attaining the age of 57 years.

(b) In the case of a person who attained the age of 55 years on or after the 1st day of October, 1977, subsection (1)(c) shall not apply on his attaining the age of 56 years and subsection (1)(b) shall not apply on his attaining the age of 57 years.

(3) For the purposes of this section, the entry into insurance of an employed contributor or a voluntary contributor by virtue of section 21(1)(a) shall, subject to subsection (6), be deemed to have occurred after he had attained the appropriate age under subsection (1) if after the time of such attainment he became for the first time an employed contributor in respect of whom contributions reckonable for the purposes of the contribution conditions for an old age (contributory) pension are payable and he had not been an employed contributor under the National Health Insurance Acts, 1911 to 1952, before attaining that age.

(4) Regulations shall provide for the return, subject to any conditions, restrictions and deductions specified in the regulations, of so much of any self-employment contribution paid by a self-employed contributor or a voluntary contribution payable under section 23 by a voluntary contributor, who entered into insurance for the purposes of section 84(1) after he had attained the age of 56 years, as is determined in accordance with regulations to have been paid in respect of old age (contributory) pension.

(5) Regulations shall provide for the return, subject to any conditions, restrictions and deductions specified in the regulations, of so much of any employment contribution paid by an employed contributor or voluntary contribution payable under section 22 by a voluntary contributor who entered into insurance for the purposes of section 89(1) after he had attained the age of 55 years as is determined in accordance with the regulations to have been paid in respect of retirement pension.

(6) For the purposes of this section in the case of a relevant person as defined in section 83(3) "entry into insurance" shall have the meaning assigned to it by section 83(4) or (5).

DEFINITIONS

"employment contribution": section 6(1)(a).
"employed contributor": section 9(1).
"voluntary contribution": section 22.
"voluntary contributor": section 21.

CHAPTER 6

DESCRIPTION OF BENEFITS

Description of benefits

30.—(1) Benefits under this Part shall be of the following descriptions and are so described in this Act—

(a) disability benefit,
(b) maternity benefit,
(bb) health and safety benefit [S.I. No. 25 of 1995],
(bbb) adoptive benefit [1995 Act, section 11(2)],
(c) unemployment benefit,
(d) occupational injuries benefit [1995 Act, Schedule E],
(e) pay-related benefit,
(f) old age (contributory) pension,
(g) retirement pension,
(h) [Repealed by 1994 Act, section 13(1)(a)],
(i) invalidity pension,
(j) survivor's pension [1995 Act, Schedule D],
(k) orphan's (contributory) allowance,
(l) deserted wife's benefit, and
(m) death grant.

(2) Subject to section 117 and so long as that section remains in force, benefit shall, in addition to including the benefits referred to in subsection (1), also include treatment benefit under that section.

(3) Benefit shall be paid or provided for out of the Social Insurance Fund.

GENERAL NOTE

For the Social Insurance Fund see the General Note to section 7.

CHAPTER 7

DISABILITY BENEFIT

Entitlement to benefit

31.—(1) Subject to this Act, a person shall be entitled to disability benefit in respect of any day of incapacity for work (in this Act referred to as "a day of incapacity for work") which forms part of a period of interruption of employment, if—
(a) he is under pensionable age on the day for which the benefit is claimed, and
(b) he satisfies the contribution conditions in section 32.

(2) A person shall not be entitled to disability benefit for the first three days of any period of incapacity for work.

(3) For the purposes of any provision of this Act relating to disability benefit—
(a) a day shall not be treated in relation to an insured person as a day of incapacity for work unless on that day he is incapable of work,
(b) "day of interruption of employment" means a day which is a day of incapacity for work or of unemployment,
(c) any three days of interruption of employment, whether consecutive or not, within a period of six consecutive days shall be treated as a period of interruption of employment and any two such periods not separated by a period of more than 13 weeks shall be treated as one period of interruption of employment.
(d) any three days of incapacity for work, whether consecutive or not, within a period of six consecutive days shall be treated as a period of incapacity for work and any two such periods not separated by more than three days shall be treated as one period of incapacity for work:

Provided that a period of incapacity for work shall be deemed to include any day or days of unemployment in the period of three consecutive days preceding the 1st day of incapacity for work, but any such day of unemployment shall not be a day of incapacity for work to which section 81(2) applies,

(e) Sunday or such other day in each week as may be prescribed shall not be treated as a day of incapacity for work or of unemployment and shall be disregarded in computing any period of consecutive days,

(f) a day shall not be treated in relation to an insured person as a day of incapacity for work if, in respect of that day, the insured person is being paid by his employer in respect of holiday leave,

(g) any two periods of incapacity for work separated by a period in respect of which an insured person is being paid by his employer in respect of holiday leave shall be treated as one period of incapacity for work.

(4) Regulations may make provision (subject to subsection (3)) as to the days which are or are not to be treated for the purposes of disability benefit as days of incapacity for work or of unemployment.

(5) The amount payable by way of benefit for any day of incapacity for work shall be one-sixth of the appropriate weekly rate, subject to the total amount being paid at any time by virtue of this subsection being rounded up to the nearest 10p where it is a multiple of 5p but not also a multiple of 10p and being rounded to the nearest 10p where it is not a multiple of 5p or 10p.

(6) A person who was in receipt of maternity benefit under section 37 on any of the three days prior to the day in respect of which a claim for disability benefit is made shall not be entitled to disability benefit for the first three days of incapacity for work in respect of such claim.

DEFINITIONS

"insured person": section 2(1).
"pensionable age": section 2(1).

GENERAL NOTE

Disability benefit, in its existing form, goes back to 1952 but there is a substantial history of legislation, made on an insurance basis, that should be addressed.

Historical Introduction

The most important early legislative insurance scheme directed at the sick combined the element of compulsory insurance and the philosophy of self-help, in so far as administration of the scheme was charged to existing Approved Societies which, in the main, existed as a result of voluntary action by workers. Inspired by the German sickness insurance schemes, Lloyd George and Churchill pushed through the National Insurance Act, 1911, an important part of which provided cash benefits to the sick. Persons covered at the outset of the legislation were all manual workers and non-manual workers earning less than £160 a year. A weekly contribution of 4d for men and 3d for women was levied on the worker. On proof of incapacity for work, the insured would be entitled to 10 shillings per week (male) or 7 shillings and 6d per week (female) for a maximum of 26 weeks. If the incapacity continued beyond this time, disablement benefit would be paid until such time as the incapacity ceased, but benefit rates were half those payable for the first six months of incapacity. Contribution conditions were quite onerous. The 1911 Act was something of a pantomime horse. At the front, the insurance principle suggested a uniformity of approach that, in reality, was subverted by the rear end of the beast. While the "Approved Societies" (Friendly Societies, Trade Unions and Insurance Societies) were not expected to operate from a profit motive, the legislation gave a considerable degree of autonomy to each Approved Society in regard to recruitment of members and the provision of benefits additional to the statutory rates. Membership could sometimes be refused if, for example, the applicant was in high risk employment and, in any event, many of the societies were confined to persons in particular occupations, some of which would be "low risk" in insurance terms. Factors of this kind led to significant differences in the wealth held by each society. The considerable surpluses collected by some societies were not channelled off to assist in meeting claims made in respect of other high-risk occupations (as an insurance principle would require) but were distributed to the members (as the self-help principle was thought to require). The task of supervising and granting approval to each society was vested in the Irish Insurance Commissioners. The first valuation made after the foundation of Saorstat Eireann, in 1923, revealed that there were 72 societies and 20 branches with a membership of 378,821. These societies and branches collectively produced a surplus. In contrast, seven societies with a membership of 29,213 showed a substantial deficit. This dichotomy continued until the early 1930s. The Government, in 1933, acting on the 1925 and 1927 Reports of the Committee of Inquiry into Health Insurance and Medical Services, decided that reform was needed, especially in the light of estimates which indicated that the societies in deficit would have to impose reduced benefits on members if they were to be actuarily sound, when, in contrast, the other societies could increasingly provide additional benefits to their members. In introducing amending legislation, the Minister for Local Government and Public Health, Mr. O'Kelly, said: "the direct cause of this anomalous position is that insured persons instead of being units in a single national insurance scheme were allowed to group themselves at will under all kinds of heads which had no concern with insurance, and that as a result of this policy the character of the membership varies from societies with good lives and with good conditions of employment, to societies with bad or indifferent lives and an undue proportion of unemployment" (47 *Dáil Debates* Col. 106).

The National Health Insurance Act, 1933, accordingly created a Unified Society (Cumann an Arachais Naisunta ar Shlainte) to take over the assets, liabilities, functions and responsibilities of the various societies. The desire to keep health insurance entirely divided from any form of commercial insurance was an important policy objective. This legislation functioned until 1952 when it was repealed by the Social Welfare Act, 1952. However, the creation of the Department of Social Welfare in 1947 resulted in the transfer to the Department of the functions and responsibilities of the Unified Society..

The 1949 White Paper

The White Paper, *Social Security* (p. 9661) addressed the question of whether the existing schemes were sufficiently comprehensive. The White Paper noted that, despite the obvious case for similarity of treatment of persons who suffer loss of income due to unemployment or ill health, there had developed substantial differences in regard to benefit rates. Dependant additions of 7s 6d per week for an adult dependant and 2s 6d for each child dependant were payable under the unemployment scheme, but no dependant additions were payable under the sickness scheme. A juvenile rate of benefit for those of 16–18 years of age was payable under the unemployment scheme but there was no comparative provision for sickness benefit. Sickness benefit was payable at two distinct rates: a low rate was payable after six months; while unemployment benefit was payable at the same rate throughout. Contribution conditions were also significantly different. The number of contribution conditions for minimum sickness benefit was 26, as against 12 in relation to unemployment benefit. Six waiting days had to be served for unemployment benefit, but only three in relation to sickness benefit. Maximum periods of eligibility differed significantly: 156 days in each year for unemployment benefit, while sickness benefit could, in certain circumstances, be payable for as long as the sickness lasted, up to the age of 70. These, and other anomalies, led the authors of the White Paper to suggest unification of the unemployment and sickness schemes. The White Paper, however, indicated that a departure from the philosophy behind the 1911 Act was necessary. The insurance scheme should be applicable to cash benefits only, because the Department of Health was the appropriate body to control the area of health and the presentation and care of sickness. Nor would benefits be cut after a period of time had elapsed. The decision not to extend benefits to non-cash schemes was defended by the authors of the White Paper, at para. 74, who noted that apart from sanatorium benefit (abolished in 1929) and treatment benefits, the subject of improving general public health had not been attempted. While two quite different attempts were made to implement several of the proposals in the White Paper on the question of sickness benefit, the 1950 Bill, introduced by the Minister, Mr. Norton, and the later Fianna Fáil Bill, introduced in 1951 by Dr. Ryan, were substantially the same. A uniform sickness and unemployment benefit scheme was introduced by sections 15–17 of the Social Welfare Act, 1952. A disability benefit claimant, if insured and incapable of work, could receive disability benefit of 24 shillings per week (with additions for adult and child dependants) for as long as the claimant was sick and able to certify this condition. However, if the claimant had less than 156 contributions paid, disability benefit would expire after 312 days, entitlement only resuming by requalifying through the payment of another 13 contributions. There were transitional provisions in the 1952 Act in respect of National Health Insurance claimants. Despite these improvements, the shortcomings of the 1952 reforms are obvious. Except for those in employment for more than three years, disability benefit was effectively a short-term benefit. Only when invalidity pensions were introduced in 1970 could the insurance system be said to recognise effectively long-term disability, *ipso facto*, as a risk worthy of affording protection against. The failure to make any provision for those who were sick or suffered disability and were outside the insurance for the workmen's compensation scheme is a further shortcoming. While this is in part due to the division of functions *vis-à-vis* health and social welfare and was not addressed in the 1949 White Paper, an adequate social assistance scheme for the disabled has yet to be implemented, although the transfer of disabled person's maintenance allowance to the Department of Social Welfare from the health boards in late 1995 has been widely welcomed: see *Irish Times* of March 16, 1995.

Entitlement to Disability Benefit under section 31

Subsection (1) creates a right to disability benefit in respect of any day of incapacity for work which forms part of a period of interruption of employment if the claimant is under pensionable age of 66 years on the day for which benefit is claimed and the contribution conditions are satisfied. The two central concepts involved are "incapacity for work" and "interruption of employment". Because disability benefit is payable on a daily basis the claimant, to be able to qualify for benefit for each day of incapacity, must, according to subsection (3), be incapable of work. However, the claimant must be able to demonstrate that the day of incapacity forms part of a period of interruption of employment. The cost of isolated days of sickness must be borne by the claimant or the claimant's employer in the form of remuneration lost, or paid out despite absence from employment, as the case may be. A claimant who is to successfully establish entitlement to disability benefit must show that the day is part of a period of interruption of employment within subsection (3), that is, each day is either a day of incapacity for work or a day of unemployment. The linkage provision, found in relation to unemployment benefit, also operates here. If a claimant is absent from work due to sickness and upon recovery the claimant returns to the place of employment but is not re-engaged (*e.g.* is dismissed or laid off), a day of incapacity or day of unemployment can form part of one period of interruption of employment. So, in the example just given, the claimant would immediately obtain unemployment benefit, because section 42(3) directs that the three waiting days are only to be served for the first three days of any period of interruption of employment, and in the example just given, the claimant will have served the three waiting days *vis à vis* the first three days of incapacity for work. The converse however is not true. If the claimant is in receipt of unemployment benefit, but the claim is interrupted by sickness, the three waiting days served at the commencement of the period of unemployment do not function as the three waiting days in respect of days of disability occurring within one period of interruption of employment because section 42(3), in contrast with subsection (2), directs that three waiting days must be served for the first three days of "incapacity for work": section 42(3) refers to the first three days of interruption of employment. The linkage provision in subsection (3)(c) provides that any three days of interruption of employment, falling within six consecutive days, Sunday being excluded, shall be one period of interruption of employment; and any similar period, not separated by more than 13 weeks, shall be treated as one period of interruption of employment. This provision is clearly designed to thwart the possibility of short periods of employment (in the case of a worker with recurring periods of ill health) breaking the continuity of the claim and requiring new waiting days to be served before entitlement is established. This is in keeping with the situation *vis à vis* unemployment benefit. There is however one important difference. Subsection (3)(d) sets out an additional requirement. If three days of incapacity for work, consecutive or not, occur within a period of six consecutive days, that is to be a period of incapacity for work. However, a further period of three more days of incapacity for work can only be treated as one period of incapacity if it occurs within three days of the first period. This has the effect of enabling disability benefit to be payable, free of a second waiting days requirement if a person becomes ill while unemployed or again becomes ill, *e.g.* suffers a relapse, within three days of returning to work. When this provision was introduced, the Minister indicated that it was designed to counteract abuse by workers who claimed disability benefit in respect of unnecessarily short absences from work; those workers exploiting the fact that the linkage rule removed the waiting days requirement if the second period of absence from employment occurred within three months of the first: 318 *Dáil Debates* Col. 1757. Subsection (3)(f), inserted first by section 10 of the Social Welfare Act, 1986, provides that a day in respect of which an insured person is in receipt of holiday pay from that person's work is not to be treated as a day of incapacity for work. If, however, there are two periods of incapacity for work separated by a period for which the claimant is in receipt of holiday pay, subsection (3)(g), added by section 16(1) of the Social Welfare (No. 2) Act, 1987, directs that those two periods will still be one period of incapacity for work. In other words, if a claimant is continuously incapacitated and the disability benefit claim is interrupted by paid holiday leave, the claimant will not have to serve a further three waiting days before disability benefit payments can resume. Prior to section 16(1)(b) of the No. 2 Act of 1987, women who transferred to disability benefit upon exhaustion of entitlement to maternity benefit were not required to serve a further three waiting days: section 18(2) of the Principal Act did not apply to such a claimant. As from April 4, 1988, a woman who claims disability benefit in such circumstances will have to serve three waiting days. It was estimated in 1988 that over 50 per cent of women in receipt of maternity benefit claimed disability benefit immediately afterwards. The fact that in such a case of virtually automatic "transfer" to disability benefit no waiting days are served was described by the Minister as an "anomaly". It was calculated that this provision would save around £500,000 per annum: per Dr. Woods at 118 *Seanad Debates* Cols. 326–339. The provision is repeated in subsection (6).

Certification of disability under subsection (4)

The application for disability benefit must be made in a prescribed manner under S.I. No. 417 of 1994; this means that the application must be made in writing and proof of incapacity for work must be provided in accordance with these regulations. The proof of incapacity will be furnished by a doctor in most cases, although the Department of Social Welfare has also recognised letters of certification of disability by some paramedicals. Recently (*Irish Times* October 10, 1987), a controversy arose at a conference organised by the Irish Medical Organisation about the Department practice of recognising letters certifying disability written by bonesetters. Difficulties had arisen because some employers refused to recognise bonesetters as competent to certify sickness. The I.M.O. was critical of this *ad hoc* arrangement and instead urged the Minister to consider allowing other medical and paramedical persons— radiographers and public health nurses, for example—to issue certificates of disability. The medical profession has been critical of the certification procedure on a number of grounds. Because doctors are asked to verify the presence of a disease or condition, particularly when there is no obvious physical evidence of disability, the classic example being a patient who complains of a pain in the back, the doctor is placed in an invidious position. The doctor who refuses to issue the certificate harms the relationship between doctor and patient. If the doctor gives the certificate when there is little or no medical evidence to validate presence of the condition, the doctor is generally only offering the opinion that the patient's veracity should not be questioned in this matter. In either event, many members of the medical profession feel that certification brings the profession generally into disrepute. In 1983, the Medical Union urged the Minister for Social Welfare to introduce a system of self-certification whereby the claimant would certify that he or she is incapable of work, such certificate being effective for up to seven days. The advantages of self-certification for short-term absence from employment, apart from the obvious, are that it will no longer take up the time of medical practitioners who would be more usefully engaged on other matters. Statistical evidence in the U.K. and elsewhere suggests that self-certification can lead to a greater sense of personal responsibility by workers because it is the individual worker rather than an intermediary, the doctor, who must justify the certificate. Although self-certification has not been rejected as a possible development, most discussions about disability benefit reform tend to centre on the possibility of requiring employers to provide sick pay for short-term sickness.

Incapable of Work

In order to avoid loss of benefit the claim should, under S.I. 417 of 1994, be made within seven days of incapacity commencing, or recurring. Upon making the claim, the claimant is required to show incapacity for work. This is defined by section 2(1) of the Principal Act of 1993 as "incapable of work by reason of some specific disease or bodily or mental disablement or deemed, in accordance with regulations, to be so incapable". Whether the claimant's condition comes within this definition is an issue of fact, resolved by reference to the medical evidence addressed, both written and oral. If the reason for the incapacity is not medical but due to personal circumstances, *e.g.* a desire to look after children or engage in unpaid voluntary work, then the fact that the claimant is, coincidentally, sick will not be relevant and the claimant will not be able to prove incapacity. Alcoholism and other forms of drug addiction may be a "specific disease", but the origins of the disease may lead to disqualification, although the present writer understands that absence from work as a result of such a condition does not always result in disqualification from sickness benefit. While pregnancy is catered for by way of maternity benefits, there are possible issues of entitlement for women who experience pregnancy-related difficulties before or after the period of confinement. In principle, there would seem to be no objection to a woman who is certified to be incapable of work because she is threatening to miscarry being entitled to disability benefit. Women who experience medical complications following childbirth may certainly be entitled to disability benefit, if the condition continues after entitlement to maternity allowance ends. The definition of a disease favoured by the statutory authorities in the U.K. is "a departure from health capable of identification by its signs and symptoms, an abnormality of some sort": *CS* 221/49, [1983] J.S.W.L. 306. Pregnancy *ipso facto* does not fall within this definition but medical complications that result from this condition, if they prevent a woman from doing her work, would fall within it.

The U.K. decisions distinguish between being capable of work and being capable of getting to the workplace by reason of bodily disablement. In Social Security Decision No. *R(S) 8/53* the claimant had his right leg amputated just below the thigh: he wore an artificial leg—a prothesis. Due to a heavy fall of snow and the resultant icy conditions, he could not get to his place of work. His doctor certified he was incapable of work because of "prothesis— impossible for him to attend work because of snow". The claim was disallowed. If work could have been brought to him, or he could have been transported to his workplace, he could have done the work. He was prevented by circumstances outside his control from attending his workplace, but he was still capable of work.

The issue of medical disablement due to some mental condition has produced some fine distinctions. The statutory authorities in the U.K. attempt to distinguish between mental conditions that prevent the claimant from being capable of work as against a condition making the claimant unwilling to work because the claimant fears that he or she is ill. English social security case-law indicates that, where the issue centres on disablement and personality disorders which allegedly make the claimant mentally disabled, the crucial distinction is between a mental condition which means the claimant cannot work as against a voluntary attitude of workshyness which means the claimant can but will not work: [1983] J.S.W.L. 306. The fact that both conditions may produce the same external manifestations is not conclusive. In the best known of these U.K. decisions (Social Security Decision No. *R(S) 6/59*) a long distance lorry driver was suffering from Munchausen's Syndrome, a condition which induced a desire to be the centre of attention, a craving for medication and a desire to deceive doctors and obtain free board and lodging for the night, despite the risk of investigation and treatment of the condition. The medical evidence indicated that the motives behind the claimant's assertion that he suffered from a kidney infection—for which there was no supporting medical evidence—was some "strange twist of personality". The claimant was, however, found to be aware of the fact that the imaginary ailment did not exist and, as such, this distinguished him from the psychotic who is not really aware of the true condition. In any event, the condition did not prevent the claimant from being able to drive his lorry. He drove it long distances in the intervals between hospital admissions. Even if there was a disabling condition, the condition was the result of a defect of character—a refusal to accept medical directions, for whatever motive—and was not a disease or mental disablement. Other U.K. decisions point out that it can be difficult to establish entitlement by way of a mental disablement leading to unwillingness to work: [1982] J.S.W.L. 48, noting *C.S. 1/81*.

In most cases the claimant is not incapable of work in the literal sense. The claimant who is physically disabled could presumably do light work or work of a mental or intellectual nature, *e.g.* serve in a shop or add up columns of figures. Does this limited capacity mean that the claimant is capable of work and therefore not entitled to disability benefit? A variety of situations may arise. A claimant may be disabled and incapable of discharging some of the physical or skilled tasks that are an essential part of the job description but he could still supervise the work of others. A management executive may be confined to bed and incapable of attending the marketplace but would be able to do some paperwork. Are these persons incapable of work? A commonsense approach would indicate that the phrase is not to be interpreted literally and a variety of factors are relevant. If the work is part-time work, *i.e.* the same tasks can be discharged, but the medical condition requires less hours be worked, then the claimant may be found capable of work. If the work is light work of a negligible kind and is work which an employer would not be willing to pay for, these factors would tend to point away from the claimant being held capable of work. Some decisions in the U.K. indicate a concern to encourage recuperative activity without a resulting loss of benefit. In one recent case a man, recuperating from illness, worked behind the bar in his local bowling club for some hours on a regular basis. The Social Security Commissioner, noting that a claimant is not expected to sit around the house all day, indicated that this activity could not be considered work, probably because of the limited time spent and the limited economic value of the activity in question (*CSS 61/83*) noted in [1986] J.S.W.L. 55.

The test of "capable of work" in the U.K. is generally directed at work the claimant can do without training, not work the claimant could do if the claimant were retrained. Again, a commonsense approach to the matter of limited capacity, in cases where the claimant is shown to be capable of tasks that normally fall outside the claimant's usual occupation, is to distinguish short-term illness and long-term disability. If the indications are that the claimant's condition is short-term and that recovery will occur reasonably soon, it is unreasonable to require the claimant to take up an alternative career. If there is no immediate prospect of recovery, and the claimant could take up alternative employment, even if not available in the area, the claimant is capable of work. The fact that the work may be of lower status, or that the claimant's eduction makes the claimant overqualified for the work, do not of themselves indicate the claimant is not capable of the work in question.

Deemed incapable of work

There are provisions which govern the circumstances in which a claimant is deemed to be incapable of work (article 11 of S.I. No. 417 of 1994): "(1) A person who is not incapable of work shall, if it is so decided under the provisions of the Principal Act, be deemed to be incapable of work by reason of some specific disease or bodily or mental disablement for any day when (a) he is under medical care in respect of such a disease or disablement and it is certified by a registered medical practitioner that by reason of such disease or disablement he should abstain from work and he does not work; or (b) he is a probable source of infection with a disease specified in regulations under the Health Act, 1947 (No. 28 of 1947), to be an infectious disease and he abstains from work in pursuance of a written order or of written advice of a registered medical practitioner. (2) A person who at the commencement of any day is or thereafter on that day becomes incapable of work by reason of some specific disease or bodily or mental disablement and does not work on that day shall be deemed to be so incapable throughout that day".

Diseases that are infectious diseases under section 29 of the Health Act, 1947 are specified in the Schedule to the Infectious Diseases Regulations (see S.I. Nos. 380 of 1981 and 268 of 1985). There is no reason why a claimant who satisfies the deemed "incapable of work" requirement could not be disqualified for up to nine weeks for some other reason, principally the misconduct provision, discussed below.

Day of incapacity for work

Regulations provide that certain days are deemed not to be days of incapacity for work. These are found in S.I. No. 417 of 1994: (1) Days when a person (i) fails to prove to the satisfaction of the Minister that he is incapable of work, or (ii) does any work other than work of the nature specified in Rule 5 of the Rules of Behaviour specified in Schedule A. (2) The nightworker's regulation in Article 13 of S.I. No. 417 of 1994 applies to disability benefit claimants as well as unemployment benefit claimants. (3) For the limited purpose of calculating a day of interruption of employment only, a day in which a woman obtains maternity allowance is to be treated as a day of incapacity for work.

Duration of entitlement

Because disability benefit is a short-term insurance benefit, it is payable on a daily basis, for any day of incapacity for work, at a daily rate of one-sixth of the appropriate weekly rate. Benefit is not payable for any of the first three days of any period of incapacity for work. As from April 4, 1988, a maternity benefit recipient who is transferred to disability benefit upon exhaustion of maternity benefit must serve three waiting days before disability benefit will be payable: subsection (6).

Once entitlement is established, disability benefit is payable for as long as the disability lasts, up to the age of 66 years, if the claimant's contribution record shows 260 qualifying contributions between entry into insurance and the day of incapacity for work, in relation to periods of incapacity for work which commence on or after July 4, 1988. If the period of incapacity begins before that date, the contribution conditions are less onerous for the claimant. However, if the claimant cannot satisfy the requirement, *i.e.* in respect of a post July 4, 1988 new claimant, the contribution record shows more than 26 qualifying contributions but less than 260 such contributions, entitlement will end on the 312th day of entitlement. When entitlement is exhausted, the disability benefit claimant may either be transferred to an invalidity pension or disabled pension's maintenance allowance. The former is unlikely in the case of a claimant failing to qualify for payment of disability benefit for an unlimited period because invalidity benefit conditions of entitlement are much the same. The second option, transfer to disabled person's maintenance allowance, is not attractive because the allowance is strictly means tested and rates are thus often less attractive.

Conditions for receipt

32.—(1) The contribution conditions for disability benefit are—

(a) that the claimant has qualifying contributions in respect of not less than 39 contribution weeks in the period between his entry into insurance and the day for which the benefit is claimed, and

(b) that the claimant has qualifying contributions or credited contributions in respect of not less than 39 contribution weeks, of which at least 13 must be qualifying contributions, in the last complete contribution year before the beginning of the benefit year which includes the day for which the benefit is claimed, and

(c) that the claimant has—
   (i) prescribed reckonable weekly earnings, or
   (ii) in the case of a person who qualifies for disability benefit by virtue of having paid optional contributions, prescribed reckonable weekly income,

in excess of a prescribed amount in the prescribed period. [1993 (No. 2) Act, section 7]

(2) In the case of any claim for disability benefit where the period of interruption of employment commenced before the 6th day of April, 1987, subsection (1)(a) shall be construed as if "26" were substituted for "39".

(3) Regulations may provide for entitling to disability benefit, subject to such conditions as may be prescribed, such class or classes of persons as would be entitled thereto but for the fact that the requirement in paragraph (b) of subsection (1) that there must be qualifying contributions in respect of at least 13 contribution weeks in the last complete contribution year before the beginning of the benefit year which includes the day for which the benefit is claimed is not satisfied.

(4) Where a person has been entitled to payment of disability benefit in respect of any day which is on or after the 3rd day of January, 1981, or would but for the provision of section 31(2) or 36(1) have been so entitled, then, as respects disability benefit, the benefit year which includes the 1st such day in every period of incapacity for work which is, or is deemed to be, a separate period of incapacity shall, for the purpose of the condition contained in paragraph (b) of subsection (1), be regarded as continuing for each day of incapacity for work in that period in respect of which the person's right to such benefit has not been exhausted up to and including the 312th day in that period in respect of which such benefit has been paid.

(5) Regulations may provide for modifications of the contribution conditions set out in subsection (1).

(6) Subject to subsection (7), regulations may provide for entitling to disability benefit persons who would be entitled thereto but for the fact that the condition set out in subsection 1(c) is not satisfied.

(7) Regulations for the purposes of subsection (6) shall provide that benefit payable by virtue thereof shall be payable at a rate less than that specified in the Second Schedule, and the rate specified by the regulations may vary with the extent to which the condition set out in subsection (1)(c) is satisfied.

(8) The requirement contained in subsection (1)(b) that there must be qualifying contributions in respect of at least 13 contribution weeks in the relevant contribution year shall not apply to any period of incapacity for work commencing before 1st day of July, 1992.

(9) The requirement contained in subsection (1)(c) that the claimant must have prescribed reckonable weekly earnings in excess of a prescribed amount in the prescribed period shall not apply in the case of a claim for disability benefit made by a person in the benefit year in which that person, having been a volunteer development worker, returns to the State from a developing country or in the next succeeding benefit year. [1993 (No. 2) Act, section 12]

GENERAL NOTE

Disability benefit is, in general terms, a short-term insurance cash benefit which is available to insured workers who satisfy the conditions of eligibility. It was introduced by the Social Welfare Act, 1952 and is the successor to National Health Insurance. Payment is made on the basis of the insurance record of the claimant and the origin of the incapacity is normally irrelevant unless the incapacity is the result of "misconduct", in which case benefit is denied, or the incapacity is occupational in origin, in which case occupational injuries benefits will be payable.

Contribution Conditions for Disability Benefit

Due to the historical and conceptual link with unemployment benefit, the contribution conditions closely mirror those applicable to unemployment benefit applications. Indeed the authors of the White Paper of 1949 used the differences that operated *vis-à-vis* contribution conditions as a compelling argument favouring unification of these benefits. Section 32(1) of the Principal Act of 1993 sets out three contribution conditions. These are, firstly, that the claimant has qualifying contributions in respect of not less than 39 contribution weeks in the period between his entry into insurance and the day for which benefit is claimed. Despite the philosophy underlining the 1952 reforms, particularly the view that unemployment benefit and disability benefits should be unified, there are some classes of contributor who are covered for disability benefit but not full unemployment benefit. These are contributors in classes E and P. The second contribution condition requires the claimant to have paid or credited contributions in the preceding contribution year, of which at least 13 are paid contributions. The regulations governing the award of credits, particularly for the newly-insured, students, the unemployed and sick will, in the main, result in the second contribution requirement being met if the first is satisfied. Credited contributions are considered in detail in the General Note to section 27. If, however, the claimant is not able to satisfy the second contribution condition while the claimant can satisfy the first, section 32(3) enables the Minister, by regulations, to direct that reduced rates of benefit will be payable. In relation to the first contribution condition, section 32(2) provides that if the period of incapacity for work began before April 6, 1987, the minimum number of contributions paid or credited in the last complete contribution year must be not less than 26. The requirement that at least 13 of the 39 contributions must be paid was introduced in 1992. In announcing this provision, the Minister, Mr. McCreevy, said: "At present to qualify for disability benefit a person must have a minimum number of paid contributions at any time since entry into insurance—39 for short-term disability benefit or 260 for long-term disability benefit—and a minimum of 39 contributions paid or credited in the governing contribution year. It is now proposed that, with certain exceptions to be specified in regulations, at least 13 of the 39 contributions in the governing contribution year will have to be paid rather than credited. The basis for this proposal is that the disability benefit scheme is essentially for people who have recently been at work and paying PRSI contributions and who then fall sick. The requirement to have a minimum number of paid contributions in the governing contribution year is designed to establish a recent attachment to the workforce for people applying for disability benefit. Under present arrangements, it is possible for a person to qualify for disability benefit on the basis of credited contributions even though he has not been in employment for a very long time, has effectively lost any attachment to the workforce and perhaps has no intention to seek paid employment. The revised condition will have the effect of directing the scheme more effectively at those for whom it was intended" (417 *Dáil Debates* Cols. 1340–41).

When pressed on the question of what will happen to claimants who do not satisfy the contribution condition, the Minister indicated that the regulations to be passed would provide flexibility. The new condition will apply at the initial stage of qualification only. If unemployed persons become ill, then the recent contributions used to obtain unemployment benefit will be available to establish entitlement to disability benefit. Social assistance in the form of supplementary welfare seems to be the only payment available under the Social Welfare Acts. Disabled person's maintenance allowance may not be available given the nature of the eligibility conditions laid down for this Health Board payment. The Minister, in Seanad Eireann, promised to look at the situation of social assistance claimants and illness payments: 132 *Seanad Debates* Col. 289. In fact, the order passed allows entitlement to be established if 13 paid contributions have been established in either of the two preceding contribution years (S.I. No. 417 of 1994) or the claimant was in receipt of long-term unemployment assistance, pre-retirement allowance, or invalidity pension (see article 19). Subsection (8) prevents this condition from operating retrospectively.

The third contribution condition requires the claimant to have earnings which exceed a prescribed reckonable weekly earnings limit. This third requirement became necessary in order to reconcile the rights of part-time workers to social welfare benefits when those workers could theoretically be insurable when working for one day a week and claim benefits for five other days on the basis of such a modest insurance record. Accordingly, S.I. No. 417 of 1994 prescribes £69.99 per week as the minimum amount of reckonable weekly earnings.

Subsection (5)

The regulations which modify the contribution conditions in subsection (1) are S.I. No. 417 of 1994.

Subsections (6) and (7)

The regulations which entitle persons to receive disability benefit who do not satisfy the minimum earnings figures are S.I. No. 417 of 1994. For current rates see S.I. No. 146 of 1995.

Subsection (9)

Subsection (9) (added by section 12 of the 1993 (No. 2) Act) cancels out the third contribution condition for volunteer development workers.

Under the Social Welfare Consolidation Act 1993, section 27, volunteer development workers have been permitted to claim credited contributions in respect of periods of time spent abroad on voluntary work. This provision was first devised in 1987 in the aftermath of the Ethiopian famine and it was both a popular and an enlightened provision. However, with the introduction of the earnings limit in order to prevent part-time workers with low earnings from establishing social welfare entitlements, many returning volunteer development workers found that entitlement could not be established because payments made in the overseas country of placement, in accordance with local conditions, were too low to meet the threshold set for full eligibility (currently set at £69.99 weekly by the Principal Act). Accordingly, the weekly earnings limit in respect of disability benefit claimants, as found in subsection (1)(c), does not apply where the claimant is a volunteer development worker and the claim is made in the benefit year when the worker returns to the State, or in the following benefit year.

Rate of benefit

33.—Subject to this Act, the weekly rate of disability benefit shall be as set out in column (2) of part I of the Second Schedule.

GENERAL NOTE

Benefit is payable on a daily basis at one sixth of the weekly rate.

Increases for adult and child dependants

34.—(1) The weekly rate of disability benefit shall be increased by the amount set out in column (3) of Part I of the Second Schedule for any period during which the beneficiary has an adult dependant, subject to the restriction that, except where regulations otherwise provide, a beneficiary shall not be entitled for the same period to an increase of benefit under this subsection in respect of more than one person. [1995 (No. 2) Act, section 10]

(2) The weekly rate of disability benefit shall be increased by the amount set out in column (4) of Part I of the Second Schedule in respect of each qualified child who normally resides with the beneficiary.

(3) Any increase of disability benefit payable pursuant to subsection (2) in respect of a qualified child who normally resides with a beneficiary and with the spouse of a beneficiary shall be payable at the rate of one-half of the appropriate amount in any case where the spouse of the beneficiary is not an adult dependant, and subsection (2) shall be construed and have effect accordingly.

DEFINITIONS

"adult dependant": section 2(2).
"normally resides": S.I. No. 417 of 1994.
"qualified child": section 2(3).

GENERAL NOTE

Subsection (1) limits "adult dependant" additions to one person during one particular period of time.

Subsections (2) and (3) limit the qualified child addition to one half of the appropriate amount where the spouse of the claimant also resides with the claimant but is not an adult dependant (*e.g.* is in specified employment or entitled to unemployment benefit in their own right).

Duration of payment

35.—(1) Where a person—
(a) has qualifying contributions in respect of less than 260 contribution weeks in the period between his entry into insurance and any day of incapacity for work, and
(b) before that day has been entitled, in respect of any period of interruption of employment (whether including that day or not) during the period beginning on the date one year immediately prior to that day, to disability benefit for 312 days,

he shall not be entitled to disability benefit for that day unless since the last of the said 312 days and before that day he has requalified for benefit.

(1A) Disability benefit paid by virtue of sections 53 and 56 shall be disregarded for the purposes of section 35 in determining whether a person has been entitled to disability benefit for 312 days. [1994 Act, section 20]

(2) In the case of any claim for disability benefit which was made before April 5, 1993 subsection (1)(b) shall be construed as if "three years" were substituted for "one year".

(3) Notwithstanding subsection (1), where in any period a person has exhausted his entitlement to disability benefit he shall not requalify therefor unless he satisfies the conditions set out in subsection (4).

(4) Where a person has exhausted his right to disability benefit—
(a) he shall requalify therefor when he has qualifying contributions in respect of 13 contribution weeks begun or ended since the last day for which he was entitled to benefit, and
(b) on his requalifying therefor, subsection (1) shall again apply to him but, in a case where the period of interruption of employment in which he exhausted his right to benefit continues after his requalification, as if the part before and the part after his requalification were distinct periods of interruption of employment.

(5) For the purposes of this section, any period in respect of which a person is disqualified for receiving disability benefit by virtue of subsection (1) of section 36 shall be treated as though it were a period in respect of which disability benefit was paid.

(6) Regulations may provide for treating a person for the purposes of this section as having been entitled to benefit for any day if he would have been so entitled but for any delay or failure on his part to make or prosecute a claim:

Provided that a person shall not be so treated where he shows that he did not intend, by failing to acquire or establish a right to benefit for that day, to avoid the necessity of requalifying for benefit under this section.

(7) Where a person has qualifying contributions in respect of not less than 260 contribution weeks on the 312th day on which benefit is paid in respect of a period of incapacity for work, and he would be entitled to disability benefit but for the fact that the contribution condition set out in subsection (1)(b) of section 32 is not satisfied, he shall be deemed to satisfy that contribution condition in respect of every subsequent day of incapacity in that period of incapacity for work.

(8) In the case of any claim for disability benefit where the period of interruption of employment in respect of incapacity for work beyond 312 days commenced before the 6th day of April, 1987, subsection (1)(a) shall be construed as if "156" were substituted for "260".

(9) In the case of any claim for disability benefit where the period of interruption of employment in respect of incapacity for work beyond 312 days commenced on or after the 6th day of April, 1987 and before the 4th day of January, 1988, subsection (1)(a) shall be construed as if "208" were substituted for "260".

(10) Subsections (8) and (9) shall not apply to any claim for disability benefit where the period of incapacity for work commenced on or after the 4th day of July, 1988.

DEFINITIONS

"day of incapacity for work": section 31(1).
"qualifying contribution": section 2(1).

GENERAL NOTE

Subsection (1)

Payment of disability benefit is normally limited to a maximum of 312 days of incapacity for work. However, the old linkage rule in the Principal Act of 1981 meant that where a period of incapacity for work occurred within six years of another period of incapacity for work these could be linked together and benefit would cease to be payable after days of incapacity if the two linked periods aggregated 312 days. The Principal Act of 1981 was eased, under section 55 of the Social Welfare Act, 1991, through the reduction of the six-year period to three years. This subsection reduces the linkage to a period of one year between the periods of incapacity for work.

Subsection (2) provides that if the claimant was entitled to disability benefit before the commencement of the new one-year linkage rule on April 5, 1993, the old three-year linkage rule will apply (see above subsection (1)).

Subsection (3) prevents the claimant from benefiting from subsection (1) when entitlement has been exhausted (*i.e.* by 312 days of incapacity for work accruing).

Subsection (4) provides that following upon exhaustion of entitlement, a claimant requalifies for benefit upon payment of 13 qualifying contributions if those qualifying contributions have been paid after disability benefit payments ended.

Subsection (5) provides that the disqualification from receiving disability benefit for up to nine weeks will have the effect of deeming disability benefit to have been paid, thereby partly exhausting entitlement earlier than heretofore. In cases where the claimant is entitled to continue to receive disability benefit after day 312 of the claim, because the claimant has 260 paid contributions to PRSI, the provision in this subsection is not operative.

Subsection (6): the regulations which allow a late claim to be made are found in S.I. No. 417 of 1994.

Subsection (7) relaxes the contribution conditions that must be satisfied if a disability benefit claimant is to continue to receive disability benefit after day 312 of a period of interruption of employment, that is, after one year of receiving the benefit. The contribution conditions imposed in respect of a period of incapacity for work required the claimant, on day 312, to show 260 contributions (paid) since entry into insurance and the commencement of the claim, and 39 contributions (paid or credited) in the qualifying year on which entitlement is calculated. The Minister explained that this second requirement, in section 19(1)(b) of the Principal Act of 1981, was "particularly harsh in its application to some persons": 397 *Dáil Debates* Col. 768. The current section amends section 32(1)(b) contribution conditions in relation to persons who would otherwise qualify to be eligible to receive disability benefit, deeming them to satisfy also the second contribution requirement.

Subsection (8) reduces the number of qualifying contributions needed to ensure the continuation of disability benefit after day 312 of incapacity for work to 156 contributions when the period of incapacity commenced before April 6, 1987 (subject to subsection 10).

Subsection (9) reduces the number of qualifying contributions needed to ensure the continuation of disability benefit after day 312 of incapacity to work to 208 contributions when the period of incapacity occurred between April 6, 1987 and January 4, 1988 (subject to subsection 10). S.I. No. 146 of 1985 prevents disability benefit from being payable concurrently with health and safety benefit: section 41A.

Duration of payment (optional contributors)

35A.—(a) Notwithstanding section 35, where in any period of interruption of employment a person, having satisfied the contribution conditions contained in section 32 by virtue of having paid optional contributions, has been entitled to disability benefit for 312 days, he shall not be entitled to the said benefit for any subsequent day of incapacity for work unless before that day he has requalified for benefit in accordance with paragraph (b).

(b) Where a person to whom paragraph (a) applies has paid optional contributions in the contribution year following the benefit year which includes the said 312th day, he shall requalify for disability benefit in the benefit year subsequent to the contribution year in respect of which the said optional contributions have been paid. [1993 (No. 2) Act, section 7]

Disqualifications

36.—(1) Regulations may provide for disqualifying a person for receiving disability benefit for such period not exceeding nine weeks as may be determined under the provisions of this Part if—

(a) he has become incapable of work through his own misconduct, or

(b) he fails without good cause to attend for or to submit himself to such medical or other examination or treatment as may be required in accordance with the regulations, or to observe any prescribed rules of behaviour.

(2) Regulations may also provide for imposing in the case of any class of persons additional conditions in relation to the receipt of disability benefit and restrictions on the rate and duration thereof if, having regard to special circumstances, it appears to the Minister necessary so to do for the purpose of preventing inequalities or preventing injustice.

(3) Regulations may also provide for disqualifying a person for the receipt of disability benefit if he fails, on becoming or again becoming incapable of work, to make a claim within the prescribed time, but any such regulations may provide for extending, subject to any prescribed conditions, the time within which the claim may be made.

DEFINITIONS

"incapable of work": section 2(1).

GENERAL NOTE

Irish social welfare law has explicit provisions which recognise that disability benefit should not be payable where the contingency is brought about by the claimant's own deliberate act or where there is substantial basis for believing that the claimant is not acting *bona fide* in relation to the claim, particularly in cases where the claimant's actions impede recovery. The National Insurance Act, 1911 authorised the approved societies to adopt rules which would suspend members from eligibility for sickness benefits in the event of non-compliance. The general impact of these provisions was carried over in amended form by statutory instrument when the National Health Insurance legislation was superseded by disability benefit under the Social Welfare Act, 1952. The statutory instrument in question, the Schedule to S.I. No. 417 of 1994 remains important because the rules of behaviour, discussed below, are still in force and are located, in amended form, in that statutory instrument. The Principal Act of 1993, however, sets out the basic position *vis-à-vis* disqualification in section 36(1).

Misconduct

The most obvious example of misconduct, and a significant factor in the high rate of absenteeism in Ireland, is where sickness and/or addiction results from alcohol abuse. Ogus and Barendt indicate that the only reported English decision indicates that an incapacity due to alcoholism will be misconduct and that the inference of misconduct will only be removed if the addiction impairs the willpower of the claimant to the extent that the claimant could not voluntarily moderate his or her consumption of alcohol. The emphasis on voluntary as against involuntary behaviour is, however, a very uncertain basis upon which to predicate the disqualification. Is a motorist to be denied disability benefit for severe injuries suffered in a motor accident simply because it is suggested that had a belt been worn the injuries would have been much less severe? Examples of this kind are not as fanciful as may first appear, due to the fact that there is no guidance at all on the meaning of "misconduct". If the disablement is brought about by voluntary and wilful conduct, *e.g.* the injury is caused by fighting, drunkenness or disorderly behaviour, then the immoral, and probably criminal, nature of the conduct of the claimant would probably cause the statutory authorities to consider that the Social Insurance Fund should not be called upon to meet the cost of conduct of this kind. Where, however, no moral or legal opprobrium attaches to the claimant, *e.g.* the injury results from some sporting activity, the fact that an injury is a foreseeable result of some voluntary activity, does not amount to misconduct. Delicate issues of policy have traditionally arisen under the National Insurance Act, 1911 on whether sexual activity which results in sickness or disability can be misconduct. Certainly, sexually transmitted diseases, principally venereal disease, would be considered to be a condition obtained *via* misconduct. If this remains the policy in Ireland, then the statutory authorities will have to adopt some fairly subtle distinctions, particularly when facing up to the question of enabling an AIDS victim to claim entitlement to disability benefit. Because this illness can be contracted in circumstances in which misconduct cannot be imputed, the disease being transmitted via blood products, for example, not all AIDS victims could be disqualified. But what of cases where the disease is contracted via intravenous drug abuse or sexual activity? If the Department are unwise enough to venture into areas of personal morality in order to defend the Social Insurance Fund, difficult issues will arise. Will it be necessary to distinguish, in the first case, between drug abuse and legitimate but unhygienic use of hypodermic needles? More importantly, if the disease is contracted by sexual activity, are the statutory authorities to distinguish between modes of transmission. If the victim is married is there to be a presumption that the condition was transmitted by that person's spouse? To what extent will inquiries by the statutory authorities infringe the constitutional right to marital privacy, if at all? These complex, and at times, value judgment issues are not addressed by the legislation and it would perhaps be prudent to either provide guidance on the scope of the misconduct disqualification or at least direct (preferably by statutory instrument) the statutory authorities on the circumstances in which drink and drug abuse, for example, may result in disqualification.

Failure to attend or submit to a medical examination or treatment
It is an established practice for the Department of Social Welfare to require a claimant to attend and submit to a medical examination by a medical referee, particularly where the claim lasts for some weeks. The procedure set down by S.I. No. 417 of 1994 involves giving the claimant not less than three clear days notice in writing that the claimant must submit to examination at a time and place specified in the notice. Reasonable travelling and subsistence expenses are payable to the claimant in connection with the examination. In 1985 some 6,000 persons who failed to attend a medical inspection lost benefit under this provision. The operation of the medical referee system in relation to both disability benefit and invalidity pension has proved controversial, and in a recent study the Coolock Community Law Centre highlighted both the high percentage of persons found capable of work in 1992 (12,052 out of 50,492), the somewhat cursory nature of the examination, and the high percentage of success when appeals were made on behalf of claimants by the Centre. The study, *Fit for Work—Who Decides?* recommends a number of changes, including more notice of the examination in order to facilitate the claimant in compiling evidence of sickness. Another factor that is of interest is the high percentage of persons who fail to attend for examination—around 20 per cent—although non-attendance will not necessarily involve disqualification if good cause for not attending or submitting to examination or treatment can be shown. Obvious examples would include cases where the letter of notice is lost or arrives late or where the claimant relies on public transport and a strike by transport workers prevents the claimant from making the journey. Perhaps a direction by the claimant's G.P. that the claimant must not travel would be good cause. Note that the claimant's doctor is also served with a notice of the impending medical examination. If the claimant refuses to submit to examination or treatment on religious grounds—the claimant is a Christian Scientist, for example—English case law indicates that the refusal may be good cause as long as the statutory authorities are persuaded that the claimant is convinced that personal religious beliefs require the claimant not to comply with the directive: Social Security Decision No. *R(S)9/51.*

Rules of Behaviour
These are set out in Schedule A to S.I. No. 417 of 1994. There are five rules. The first two are: 1. He shall obey any instructions, relating to his behaviour or any other matter concerning his incapacity, of a doctor attending on him or on whom he has attended for medical or other examination in accordance with article 15(2) of the Schedule.
2. He shall refrain from behaviour which is likely to retard his recovery.
The "misconduct" provision in the Principal Act is a separate ground for disqualification. Considerations of misconduct will involve events before or at the time the disability manifests itself. These first two rules of conduct will involve the claimant's actions at the time or after the submission of the claim. Rule 2 seems to be broad enough to overlap with much of rule 1. Again "good cause" is a defence. If, for example, the treatment is having no effect or, perhaps, has very serious side effects on the claimant, a refusal to obey the instructions of the doctor in attendance may constitute refusal with good cause.

The next rule, like the second part of rule 1 is a control of abuse measure.

3. He shall not be absent from his place of residence without leaving word where he may be found.

Again, "good cause" may excuse non-observance of this rule. If the attending physician directs the claimant to go immediately into hospital or a nursing home, or perhaps away from the claimant's residence for a short holiday, good cause may be shown, particularly where non-observance of the directive may produce disqualification under rules 1 and 2. This rule of behaviour has its counterpart in the U.K. The U.K. provision was considered in Social Security Decision No. *R(S)7/83*, noted in [1983] J.S.W.L. 308. The Social Security Commissioner there held that place of residence means the place where a person usually lives and sleeps. It follows that some people do not have a place of residence, *e.g.* a homeless person who sleeps rough wherever this is possible. If this be so, that person cannot be disqualified under this rule because the legislation does not imply that a person *must* have a place of residence.

The fourth rule is self-explanatory.

4. He shall not refuse unreasonably to see an officer of the Minister and he shall answer any reasonable enquiries by any such officer relating to his claim.

The rule originally provided that women claimants shall not be visited otherwise than by women. This was deleted in 1986 by S.I. No. 237 of 1986.

Rule 5 directs that the claimant shall not engage in work unless it be (a) light work for which no remuneration is, or would ordinarily be, payable, or (b) work undertaken primarily as a definite part of his treatment while he is a patient in or out of a hospital sanatorium, or other similar institution and his weekly earnings in respect of that work do not exceed £33.30, or (c) work under a scheme that is in the opinion of the Minister charitable in character and purpose and his weekly earnings in respect of that work do not exceed £33.30.

There is a considerable overlap between this rule of behaviour and the initial concept of the claimant being "incapable of work". If the claimant is found "capable of work" the benefit is withheld altogether. Under these rules of behaviour infraction leads to a nine-week loss of benefit. Further, if the claimant does work with a substantial physical content (*i.e.* work that falls outside the definition of "light work") it may be that, despite the fact that the work undertaken bears no relation to the sphere of employment the claimant is normally engaged in, the maximum nine-week disqualification results. Take the example of a person suffering from some mental disability who undertakes demanding physical labour, on a friend or relative's farm, for example. Even if that person is normally employed as an office worker, the conditions of rule 5(a) would appear to be applicable because the work is work of a kind for which "remuneration is, or would ordinarily be payable". So, if the work has some economic value, which would normally be the subject of payment, in cash or in kind, the rule is satisfied, even if the claimant renders the service *gratis*. It may be that a claimant in such a position could make out a "good cause" defence if the work undertaken could not possibly aggravate the disability and if the claimant, or his doctor, considered the work therapeutic in nature.

Rule 5 can be flexible in so far as the Minister can exempt a person from rule 5 for such period as the Minister thinks fit if, firstly, the work is part-time work and is undertaken by way of rehabilitation or occupational therapy, or secondly, the claimant has become incapable of following the claimant's usual occupation and is undergoing training with a view to taking some other occupation: see Article 16(3) of S.I. No. 417 of 1994. Disqualification will also result from the claimant being absent from the State or undergoing penal servitude: section 211 below.

Late Applications and Subsection (3)

The regulations governing late applications are found in S.I. No. 417 of 1994.

CHAPTER 8

MATERNITY BENEFIT

Entitlement to and duration of benefit

37.—(1) Subject to this Act, a woman shall be entitled to maternity benefit if—

    (a) it is certified by a registered medical practitioner or otherwise to the satisfaction of the Minister that it is to be expected that she will be confined in a week specified in the certificate (hereafter in this section referred to as "the expected week of confinement") not being more than the prescribed number of weeks after that in which the certificate is given, and

(b) it is certified by her employer that she is entitled to maternity leave under section 8 of the Maternity Protection Act, 1994, and [1995 Act, section 13(1)(a)]

(c) she satisfies the contribution conditions in section 38.

(1A) The requirement in subsection (1)(c) shall not apply in the case of a claim for maternity benefit made by a woman who was in receipt of health and safety benefit under section 41A at any time during the pregnancy as a result of which it is expected that she will be confined. [S.I. No. 25 of 1995]

(2) Regulations may provide for entitling to maternity benefit, subject to such conditions and in such circumstances as may be prescribed, such class or classes of women who would be entitled thereto but for the fact that the contribution conditions in section 38 are not satisfied. [1995 Act, section 13(1)(b)]

(3) (a) Subject to this Act, where it is certified by his employer that a man, who satisfies the contribution conditions in section 38, is entitled to leave under section 16 of the Maternity Protection Act, 1994, he shall be entitled to benefit under this Chapter as if he was a woman who was entitled to maternity leave under section 8 of the said Act and the provisions of this Chapter (other than section 40(b)) shall apply in all respects in the case of such a man.

(b) In this Act, a reference to maternity benefit shall be construed as including a reference to benefit payable to a man under this subsection. [1995 Act, section 13(1)(c)]

(4) Subject to this Chapter, maternity benefit shall be payable to—

(a) a woman, for the period of maternity leave she is entitled to under section 8 of the Maternity Protection Act, 1994 (including any extension of that period by virtue of section 12 of that Act), or

(b) a man, for the period of leave he is entitled to under section 16 of the Maternity Protection Act, 1994:

Provided that where the beneficiary dies, the benefit shall not be payable for any subsequent day. [1995 Act, section 13(1)]

(5) Regulations may modify subsections (1) and (4) in relation to cases where—

(a) it is certified by a registered medical practitioner or otherwise to the satisfaction of the Minister that a woman has been confined, and

(b) no such certificate as is referred to in subsection (1)(a) has been given.

(6) For the purposes of this section, a Sunday shall not in any week be treated as a day of entitlement to maternity benefit and, accordingly, the amount payable by way of such benefit for any other day of a week shall be one-sixth of the appropriate weekly rate, subject to the total amount being paid at any time by virtue of this subsection being rounded up to the nearest 10p where it is a multiple of 5p but not also a multiple of 10p, and being rounded to the nearest 10p where it is not a multiple of 5p or 10p.

(7) Where the employment ceases (whether due to the death of the employer or otherwise) during the period for which maternity benefit is payable in accordance with subsection (4), the beneficiary shall continue to be treated as if the event which caused the cesser of employment had not occurred. [1995 Act, section 13(1)]

(8) Regulations may provide for requiring an employer to furnish such information as may be required for the purposes of determining a claim for maternity benefit.

GENERAL NOTE

Historical Introduction

The payment of an insurance-based maternity benefit (the original scheme) dates back to the National Insurance Act, 1911 and it has formed an essential element in the Irish social welfare system ever since. The existing scheme dates back to the Maternity (Protection of Employees) Act, 1981 and it supplanted the original scheme in 1992: thus, between 1981 and 1992, the State operated two separate schemes providing two distinct maternity payments to women.

This situation arose because the original scheme provided a flat rate payment (which could be topped up by pay-related benefit) to women based upon their insurance records. Because eligibility could be established on the basis of credited contributions, many women registered as unemployed, signing for credits, even though benefits or assistance payments were not payable (*i.e.* because these women were held in many cases not to be available for employment). Thus, eligibility for the original scheme could be established even though these women had a tenuous or, in many cases, no link with employment other than employment in the home. Conversely, the flat rate scheme, even when the claimant was in full-time employment was seen as being inadequate in many respects, and it was decided to develop a specific scheme for women whose link with employment was substantial and likely to endure beyond the outcome of the pregnancy. The 1981 legislation was seen as part of a broader perspective which sought to give women both security of employment and adequate leave and income support rights upon pregnancy.

The Report of the Commission on Social Welfare, at pp. 246–248, examined the two schemes and concluded that the existence of both schemes could be justified, although the Commission recommended that a "recent employment" condition should be inserted into the original scheme and that benefit entitlement should be for 14, not 12, weeks, as in the 1981 scheme.

Notwithstanding this recommendation, the 1992 Act abolished the original scheme and transferred the 1981 scheme into social welfare law, rather than allowing it to remain a Department of Labour responsibility (as it then was). Abolition of the old scheme is thought to have affected around 100 women annually, for the employment condition found in the 1981 scheme effectively precludes entitlement for women who do not have any prospect of returning to work when the pregnancy ends. The Maternity Protection Act, 1994 now supersedes and replaces the 1981 Act and the link with employment-based maternity leave is underlined in section 13 of the Social Welfare Act, 1995.

Subsection (1)

There are three conditions of entitlement in this subsection. First, a woman shall be entitled to maternity benefit if a registered medical practitioner certifies that she is expected to be confined in a week certified in the certificate within 16 weeks of the certificate being given: article 20(1) of S.I. No. 417 of 1994. Even if the procedural element is not satisfied (*e.g.* the woman discovers very late in her pregnancy the she is in fact pregnant), entitlement can be established under the regulations by way of a medical certificate stating that the woman has had a baby (article 20(2) of S.I. No. 417 of 1994). In such a case the 14-week period of entitlement is to be fixed by a deciding officer.

The second condition has been simplified by section 13 of the 1995 Act. The employer must certify that the woman is entitled to maternity leave under the Maternity Protection Act, 1994.

The third condition requires the claimant to satisfy the contribution condition set in section 38, save in cases where the claimant received health and safety benefit during this particular pregnancy.

Subsection (2)

This power has been exercised in relation to volunteer development workers who are located overseas and who return to Ireland in order to have their babies. Both the contribution and the employment conditions would not normally be satisfied by such persons. Statutory Instrument No. 201 of 1993 (now S.I. No. 417 of 1994) provides entitlement under separate criteria. The volunteer development worker must have qualifying contributions in respect of 39 weeks between the date of entry into insurance and the first day of maternity leave. The same requirement is imposed upon persons who cease to be volunteer development workers in either the benefit year or the next benefit year in which they return to Ireland.

Subsection (3)

This subsection, introduced by the 1995 Act, allows a father who has been given employment leave following upon the death of the mother within 14 weeks of a child's birth, to receive a payment which is the equivalent of maternity benefit. The contribution conditions and payments are the same as for maternity benefit.

Subsection (4)
Entitlement lasts for 14 weeks although an extension for a further period of up to four weeks may be made in the case of a late birth.
A man's entitlement under the preceding subsection is to last for 14 weeks.

Subsection (5)
See S.I. No. 417 of 1994, article 20(2).

Subsection (6)
Maternity benefit is payable as a daily payment, payable at one-sixth of the appropriate weekly rate, Sunday being excluded by this subsection. The rate of payment is rounded in accordance with this subsection.

Subsection (7)
This provision preserves entitlement, even if an event occurs which makes resumption of employment impossible by reason of the cesser of employment (*e.g.* the contract is frustrated or discharged).

Subsection (8)
The regulations in question are found in article 101(3) of S.I. No. 417 of 1994.

Conditions for receipt

38.—(1) The contribution conditions for maternity benefit are—
   (a) (i) that the claimant has qualifying contributions in respect of not less than 39 contribution weeks in the period beginning with her entry into insurance and ending immediately before the relevant day, and
       (ii) that the claimant has qualifying contributions or credited contributions in respect of not less than 39 contribution weeks in the last complete contribution year before the beginning of the benefit year in which the relevant day occurs or in a subsequent complete contribution year before the relevant day, or
   (b) that the claimant has qualifying contributions in respect of not less than 39 contribution weeks in the 12 months immediately preceding the 1st day of maternity leave.

(2) Regulations may provide for modifications of the contribution conditions set out in subsection (1).

(3) In subsection (1) 'the relevant day' means the first day for which maternity benefit is claimed. [1995 Act, section 13(2)]

GENERAL NOTE

The minimum contribution conditions fixed by this section are either (a) qualifying contributions for 39 weeks from entry into insurance to the first day of maternity entitlement, as well as 39 qualifying or credited contributions in the last complete contribution year before the beginning of the benefit year in which maternity entitlement starts (qualifying or credited contributions in the current contribution year may also be used); or (b) 39 qualifying contributions in the 12-month period preceding the first day of maternity leave.

Condition (a) above benefits women who have been *bona fide* registered as unemployed and who have less recent links with the social insurance system than those under (b). The employment contribution will preclude eligibility for women with no link with insurable employment.

Rate of benefit

39.—(1) Subject to this Act, the weekly rate of maternity benefit shall be an amount equal to—
   (a) 70 per cent. of the reckonable weekly earnings of the woman to whom the benefit is payable in the income tax year prescribed for the purposes of this section, or

(aa) the amount of disability benefit, including any increases thereof, which the woman would otherwise receive if she was entitled to the said benefit, or [1994 Act, section 17]

(b) such amount as shall be prescribed,

whichever is the greater.

(2) The percentage specified in subsection (1)(a) may be varied by regulations having regard to—

(a) movements in the annual average earnings of women, and

(b) the imposition or variation of statutory deductions from or charges on earnings.

(3) In this section "reckonable weekly earnings" means the average amount, calculated in accordance with regulations, of reckonable earnings and such other income as may be prescribed, received in a week up to such limit as may be prescribed.

GENERAL NOTE

One of the innovative features of the 1981 scheme, which is retained by way of the 1992 reform, is the provision of maternity benefit as an income-related payment rather than a flat-rate universal payment, thus strengthening the short-term employment related aspects of this scheme. Subsection (1)(a) makes the payment an amount equal to 70 per cent of the claimant's weekly earnings in the governing contribution year. The method of calculating a woman's reckonable weekly earnings under subsection (3) is determined by S.I. No. 417 of 1994 by reference to the woman's relevant annual earnings, divided by the number of qualifying contributions in that contribution year, up to a maximum of £232.60.

Alternatively, the claimant may receive a minimum of £75.70 per week, if this is greater than the figure produced by the calculation of 70 per cent of reckonable weekly earnings: S.I. No. 417 of 1994, as amended by S.I. No. 146 of 1995, article 7.

Disqualifications

40.—Regulations may provide for disqualifying a woman for receiving maternity benefit if—

(a) during the period for which the benefit is payable, she engages in any occupation other than domestic duties in her own household, or

(b) she fails, without good cause, to attend for or to submit herself to any medical examination that may be required in accordance with the regulations.

GENERAL NOTE

The regulations in question are found in articles 24 and 25 of S.I. No. 417 of 1994.

Article 24 provides that where any question arises as to the correctness, or otherwise, of a certificate given by a doctor which relates to the pregnancy, the claimant is required to submit herself to a medical examination in accordance with the requirements of that article.

Article 25(b) provides for disqualification for non-compliance without good cause, although the disqualification cannot pre-date the day upon which the failure occurred. Should confinement actually occur, the disqualification will not operate for that day or any day after the day of confinement.

Article 25(a) of S.I. No. 417 of 1994 gives effect to the disqualification for engaging in any occupation other than household duties, although the disqualification only operates in respect of an occupation which takes place prior to the actual day of confinement.

In each case a deciding officer is to determine the period of disqualification, subject to the restrictions found in article 25 of S.I. No. 417 of 1994.

Supplementary provisions

41.—(1) In this Chapter—

(a) "confinement" means labour resulting in the issue of a living child, or labour after 24 weeks of pregnancy resulting in the issue of a child whether alive or dead, and "confined" shall be construed accordingly, and

(b) references to the date of the confinement shall be taken as referring, where labour begun on one day results in the issue of a child on another day, to the date of the issue of the child or, if a woman is confined of twins or a greater number of children, to the date of the issue of the last of them.

(2) In deciding whether or not to make an order under section 21A (inserted by the Status of Children Act, 1987) of the Family Law (Maintenance of Spouses and Children) Act, 1976, in so far as any such order relates to the payment of expenses incidental to the birth of a child, the Circuit Court or the District Court, as the case may be, shall not take into consideration the fact that the mother of the child is entitled to maternity benefit.

GENERAL NOTE

This is a definition section. Subsection (1)(a) makes it clear that the benefit is to be payable if, after a pregnancy of 24 weeks, the claimant delivers a stillborn child. For a discussion on the law relating to the registration of stillbirths, where a period of 24 weeks is the relevant standard, see the Stillbirths Registration Act, 1994.

Subsection (2) directs that, where there is an application under section 21A of the Family Law (Maintenance of Spouses and Children) Act, 1976, in respect of birth or funeral expenses (or expenses incidental thereto), any lump sum so awarded is not to be assessed in the light of the mother's eligibility for maternity benefit.

CHAPTER 8A

HEALTH AND SAFETY BENEFIT

Entitlement to benefit

41A—(1) In this Chapter—

"confined" and "confinement" have the meanings respectively assigned to them by section 41;

"relevant period" has the meaning assigned to it by section 18(6) of the Maternity Protection Act, 1994 (No. 34 of 1994).

(2) Subject to this Act, a woman shall be entitled to health and safety benefit, if—

(a) it is certified by a registered medical practitioner or otherwise to the satisfaction of the Minister that it is to be expected that she will be confined or that she has been confined, as the case may be in a week specified in the certificate,

(b) it is certified by her employer, in accordance with section 18(2) of the Maternity Protection Act, 1994, that she has been granted leave under section 18 of the said Act (hereafter in this Chapter referred to as "health and safety leave"), and

(c) she satisfies the conditions in section 41B.

(3) For the purposes of this Chapter—

(a) any two periods of health and safety leave arising in a relevant period shall be treated as one period of health and safety leave, and

(b) a Sunday shall not in any week be treated as a day of entitlement to health and safety benefit and, accordingly, the amount payable by way of such benefit for any other day of a week shall be one-sixth of the appropriate weekly rate, subject to the total amount being paid at any time by virtue of this subsection being rounded up to the nearest 10p where it is a multiple of 5p but not also a multiple of 10p, and being rounded to the nearest 10p where it is not a multiple of 5p or 10p.

GENERAL NOTE

This new section, first inserted by the European Communities (Social Welfare) Regulations, 1994 (S.I. No. 312 of 1994) under the powers given to the Minister for Social Welfare by section 3 of the European Communities Act, 1972, gives effect to Council Directive 92/85/EEC of October 19, 1992. The Directive provides an allowance for pregnant workers and workers who have recently given birth or who are breastfeeding.

Section 41A is the definition section. Most of the provisions relating to women who have recently given birth are aligned with the existing provisions on maternity benefit. The real benefits for claimants relate to women who are pregnant, who are breastfeeding, or who, having given birth, are nightworkers, as defined in S.I. No. 446 of 1994.

S.I. No. 25 of 1995 repeals S.I. No. 312 of 1994 and replaces those regulations.

The regulations governing applications and other matters are S.I. No. 26 of 1995, as amended by S.I. No. 146 of 1995.

Subsection (2)

This subsection sets out the classes of beneficiary:

(1) women who are pregnant and for whom a due date of confinement has been certified by a registered medical practitioner;

(2) woman who have, within 14 weeks of the certificate, given birth or who have delivered a stillborn child after 24 weeks of pregnancy;

(3) women who are breastfeeding up to 26 weeks after giving birth.

The woman in question should also be an employed contributor immediately before her absence from work.

In the case of a pregnant woman, the practitioner certificate of expected confinement will entitle the woman to the new health and safety benefit, subject to the requirement that a health risk is perceived to exist. In the case of a woman who is pregnant or breastfeeding, the employer must certify that a risk to health or safety, or a possible effect on pregnancy or breastfeeding, exists and that the risk cannot be removed or suitable alternative work cannot be allocated to the woman. If the woman is engaged in nightwork, as defined, and her employer certifies that suitable alternative work is not available, then such a woman should be given benefit for a period of absence from work. Note that the definition of "woman who is required to perform nightwork" requires a certified risk to be present before the woman is eligible for the benefit: See S.I. No. 446 of 1994. The reduced rates referred to in subsection (4) and set out in S.I. No. 146 of 1995.

Conditions for receipt

41B.—(1) The conditions for health and safety benefits are—

(a) (i) that the claimant has qualifying contributions in respect of not less than 13 contribution weeks in the 12 months immediately preceding the expected date of confinement or the actual date of confinement, as the case may be, or

    (ii) (A) that the claimant has qualifying contributions in respect of not less than 39 contribution weeks in the period beginning with her entry into insurance and ending immediately before the 1st day for which health and safety benefit is claimed, and

        (B) that the claimant has qualifying contributions or credited contributions in respect of not less than 39 contribution weeks in the last complete contribution year before the beginning of the benefit year which includes the 1st day for which health and safety benefit is claimed, and

(b) that the claimant has prescribed reckonable weekly earnings in excess of a prescribed amount in a prescribed period.

(2) The requirement in subsection (1)(a) shall not apply in the case of a claim for health and safety benefit which is made in a relevant period where

the claimant was previously in receipt of maternity benefit under section 37 in that relevant period.

(3) Subject to subsection (4), regulations may provide for entitling to health and safety benefit a woman who would be entitled thereto but for the fact that the condition in subsection (1)(b) is not satisfied.

(4) Regulations for the purposes of subsection (3) shall provide that benefit payable by virtue thereof shall be payable at a rate less than that specified in the Second Schedule, and the rate specified by the regulations may vary with the extent to which the condition set out in subsection (1)(b) is satisfied.

GENERAL NOTE

Contribution conditions are essentially the same as for maternity benefit under section 38. The prescribed amount of reckonable weekly earnings is £69.99: see S.I. No. 26 of 1995. Note Section 41B(3) which allows continuation of eligibility notwithstanding noncompliance with the first contribution condition.

The regulation which implements section 41C is S.I. No. 26 of 1995. The provisions on claims and payments are also set out in S.I. No. 26 of 1995.

Duration of payment

41C.—(1) Subject to this Chapter, health and safety benefit shall be payable from the day immediately following the last of the 21 days of health and safety leave in respect of which the claimant is entitled to receive remuneration from her employer under the provisions of section 18(4) of the Maternity Protection Act, 1994 and regulations made thereunder and shall continue to be payable for the period of health and safety leave granted to the claimant under Part III of the Maternity Protection Act, 1994:

Provided that health and safety benefit shall not be payable for any day in respect of which maternity benefit under section 37 is payable.

(2) If the woman who is entitled to health and safety benefit dies, the benefit shall not be payable for any subsequent day.

GENERAL NOTE

Health and safety benefit is payable from the first day of the fourth week of a woman's certified absence from work, for as long as the statutory conditions remain in place. Entitlement ends when the woman becomes entitled to maternity benefit, where applicable, or 14 weeks after the birth, or the end of 26 weeks following birth in the case of a breastfeeding woman.

Rate of benefit

41D.— Subject to this Act, the weekly rate of health and safety benefit shall be as set out in column (2) of Part I of the Second Schedule.

GENERAL NOTE

Rates of health and safety benefit correspond with those payable for short-term insurance payments such as disability benefit.

The conditions of entitlement, in terms of health and safety risks, are set out in the Safety Health and Welfare at Work (Pregnant Employees) Regulations, 1994 (S.I. No. 446 of 1994).

Increases for adult and child dependants

41E.—(1) The weekly rate of health and safety benefit shall be increased by the amount set out in column (3) of Part I of the Second Schedule for any period during which the beneficiary has an adult dependant, subject to the restriction that a beneficiary shall not be entitled for the same period to an increase of benefit under this subsection in respect of more than one person.

(2) The weekly rate of health and safety benefit shall be increased by the appropriate amount set out in column (4) of Part I of the Second Schedule in respect of each qualified child who normally resides with the beneficiary.

(3) Any increase of health and safety benefit payable pursuant to subsection (2) in respect of a qualified child who normally rsides with a beneficiary and with the spouse of a beneficiary shall be payable at the rate of one-half of the appropriate amount in any case where the spouse of the beneficiary is not an adult dependant, and subsection (2) shall be construed and have effect accordingly.

Disqualifications

41F.—A woman shall be disqualified for receiving health and safety benefit during any period in which she engages in any occupation other than domestic activities in her own household.

GENERAL NOTE

Disability benefit cannot be payable for days in respect of which health and safety benefit is payable: S.I. No. 146 of 1995.

CHAPTER 8B

ADOPTIVE BENEFIT

Entitlement to and duration of adoptive benefit

41G.—(1) In this Chapter, 'adopting parent' has the meaning assigned to it in section 2(1) of the Adoptive Leave Act, 1995.

(2) Subject to this Act, an adopting parent shall be entitled to adoptive benefit if—

(a) it is certified by the adopting parent's employer that the adopting parent is entitled to adoptive leave under the Adoptive Leave Act, 1995, and

(b) the adopting parent satisfies the contribution conditions in section 41H.

(3) Regulations may provide for entitling to adoptive benefit, subject to such conditions and in such circumstances as may be prescribed, such class or classes of adopting parents who would be entitled thereto but for the fact that the contribution conditions in section 41H are not satisfied.

(4) Subject to this Chapter, adoptive benefit shall be payable for the period of adoptive leave which the adopting parent is entitled to under section 6, 9 or 42, as the case may be, of the Adoptive Leave Act, 1995:

Provided that, where the beneficiary dies, the benefit shall not be payable for any subsequent day.

(5) For the purposes of this section, a Sunday shall not in any week be treated as a day of entitlement to adoptive benefit and, accordingly, the amount payable by way of such benefit for any other day of a week shall be

one-sixth of the appropriate weekly rate, subject to the total amount being paid at any time by virtue of this subsection being rounded up to the nearest 10p where it is a multiple of 5p but not also a multiple of 10p, and being rounded to the nearest 10p where it is not a multiple of 5p or 10p.

(6) Where the employment ceases (whether due to the death of the employer or otherwise) during the period for which adoptive benefit is payable in accordance with subsection (4), the beneficiary shall continue to be treated as if the event which caused the cesser of employment had not occured.

GENERAL NOTE

Adoptive benefit, introduced by section 11 of the 1995 Act, gives an adopter with eligibility for adoptive leave under the Adoptive Leave Act, 1995 a 10-week payment which is based upon maternity benefit contribution conditions and is payable at the same percentage of earnings rate as maternity benefit.

The Adoptive Leave Act, 1995 was brought into operation as from March 20, 1995 by S.I. No. 64 of 1995. S.I. No. 94 of 1995, as amended by S.I. No. 146 of 1995, makes provision for the information to be provided at the date of making a claim.

Conditions for receipt

41H.—(1) The contribution conditions for adoptive benefit are—

   (a) (i) that the claimant has qualifying contributions in respect of not less than 39 contribution weeks in the period beginning with the claimant's entry into insurance and ending immediately before the relevant day, and

     (ii) that the claimant has qualifying contributions or credited contributions in respect of not less than 39 contribution weeks in the last complete contribution year before the beginning of the benefit year in which the relevant day occurs or in a subsequent complete contribution year before the relevant day, or

   (b) that the claimant has qualifying contributions in respect of not less than 39 contribution weeks in the 12 months immediately preceding the relevant day.

     (2) In subsection (1), 'relevant day' means that first day for which adoptive benefit is claimed.

     (3) Regulations may provide for modifications of the contribution conditions set out in subsection (1).

Rate of adoptive benefit

41I.—(1) Subject to this Act, the weekly rate of adoptive benefit shall be an amount equal to—

   (a) 70 per cent. of the reckonable weekly earnings of the person to whom the benefit is payable in the income tax year prescribed for the purposes of this section, or

   (b) the amount of disability benefit, including any increases thereof, which the person would otherwise receive if entitled to the said benefit, or

   (c) such amount as shall be prescribed,

whichever is the greater.

     (2) In this section, 'reckonable weekly earnings' means the average amount, calculated in accordance with regulations, of reckonable earnings and such other income as may be prescribed, received in a week up to such limit as may be prescribed.

GENERAL NOTE

See S.I. No. 146 of 1995 for minimum and maximum rates.

Disqualification

41J.—Regulations may provide for disqualifying an adopting parent for receiving adoptive benefit if, during the period for which the benefit is payable, the adopting parent engaged in any occupation other than domestic activities in that parent's own household. [1995 Act, section 11]

CHAPTER 9

UNEMPLOYMENT BENEFIT

Entitlement to benefit

42.—(1) Subject to this Act, a person shall be entitled to unemployment benefit in respect of any day of unemployment (in this Part referred to as "a day of unemployment") which forms part of a period of interruption of employment, if—
  (a) he is under pensionable age on the day for which the benefit is claimed,
  (b) he proves unemployment in the prescribed manner,
  (c) he satisfies the contribution conditions in section 43, and
  (d) other than in the case of a person engaged in casual employment, he has sustained a substantial loss of employment in any period of six consecutive days. [1994 Act, section 19]

(1A) The circumstances in which a person is to be regarded, for the purposes of subsection (1), as being engaged in casual employment shall be specified in regulations. [1994 Act, section 19]

(2) The circumstances in which a person is to be regarded, for the purposes of this Chapter, as having sustained a substantial loss of employment shall be specified in regulations, and different circumstances may be specified for different provisions of this Chapter.

(3) A person shall not be entitled to unemployment benefit for the first three days of any period of interruption of employment.

(4) For the purposes of any provision of this Act relating to unemployment benefit—
  (a) a day shall not be treated in relation to an insured person as a day of unemployment unless on that day—
    (i) he is capable of work,
    (ii) he is, or by reason of his participation in an activity prescribed for the purposes of this subsection and subject to such conditions as may be prescribed, is deemed to be, or is exempted from being required to be, available for employment, and
    (iii) he is genuinely seeking, but is unable to obtain, employment suitable for him having regard to his age, physique, education, normal occupation, place of residence and family circumstances,
  (b) "day of interruption of employment" means a day which is a day of unemployment or of incapacity for work,
  (c) any three days of interruption of employment, whether consecutive or not, within a period of 6 consecutive days shall be treated as a period of interruption of employment and any two such periods not separated by a period of more than 13 weeks shall be treated as one period of interruption of employment,
  (d) Sunday or such other day in each week as may be prescribed shall not be treated as a day of unemployment or of incapacity for work and shall be disregarded in computing any period of consecutive days.

(4A) Notwithstanding subsection (4)(c), where in respect of any day of unemployment (referred to in this subsection as 'the relevant day of unemployment') which forms part of a period of interruption of employment a person has not, before the relevant day of unemployment, been entitled to unemployment benefit in respect of a day of unemployment within the period of two years prior to the relevant day of unemployment, that day shall be treated as the first day of unemployment in a separate period of interruption of employment. [1994 Act, section 19]

(5) Notwithstanding anything contained in subsection (4), any period, not exceeding one year duration, of—

(a) employment under a scheme administered by An Foras Áiseanna Saothair and known as Community Employment [1995 Act, section 18].

(b) participation in a scheme administered by An Foras Áiseanna Saothair and known as the Enterprise Allowance Scheme,

(c) participation in a scheme administered by An Foras Áiseanna Saothair and known as the Alternance Scheme,

(d) attendance at a training course provided or approved of by An Foras Áiseanna Saothair,

(e) [repealed: 1995 Act, section 18].

(f) participation in a scheme administered by the Minister and known as the Part-Time Job Incentive Scheme, or

(g) participation in a scheme administered by the Minister for Education and known as the Vocational Training Opportunities Scheme,

shall be disregarded in treating, pursuant to subsection (4)(c), any two periods of interruption of employment not separated by more than 13 weeks as one period of interruption of employment.

(6) Regulations may make provision (subject to subsection (4)) as to the days which are or are not to be treated for the purposes of unemployment benefit as days of unemployment or of incapacity for work.

(7) The amount payable by way of benefit for any day of unemployment shall be one-sixth of the appropriate weekly rate, subject to the total amount being paid at any time by virtue of this subsection being rounded up to the nearest 10p where it is a multiple of 5p but not also a multiple of 10p and being rounded to the nearest 10p where it is not a multiple of 5p or 10p.

(8) Notwithstanding subsection (1), the number of days of unemployment in respect of which a person engaged in short-time employment shall be entitled to unemployment benefit in any week shall be limited so that the total of the number of days in respect of which such benefit is paid and the number of days worked shall not exceed 5, and in such a case the amount payable by way of such benefit for any day of unemployment in that week shall, notwithstanding subsection (7), be one-fifth of the appropriate weekly rate, subject to the total amount being paid at any time by virtue of this subsection being rounded up to the nearest 10p where it is a multiple of 5p but not also a multiple of 10p and being rounded to the nearest 10p where it is not a multiple of 5p or 10p.

DEFINITIONS

"pensionable age": section 2(1).
"short-time employment": section 2(1).

GENERAL NOTE

Entitlement to benefit in respect of a day of unemployment is governed by section 42.

Subsection (1)

Subsection (1)(a) requires the claimant to be under 66 years of age on the day for which benefit is claimed. In terms of result subsection (1)(b) requires unemployment to be proved in accordance with S.I. No. 417 of 1994.

Subsection (1)(d) requires the claimant to show a substantial loss of employment in a period of six consecutive days. This provision was added to the law in 1992. The extension of unemployment benefit and other benefits to part-time workers, as from April 6, 1991, had the effect that employees who earned in excess of £25 became insurable from that date and entitled to benefit as from January 1993. However, in cases of part-time employment it was realised that workers could be engaged in part-time employment, and obtain unemployment benefit for those parts of the working week in which they did not work, even though no loss of employment was concerned *i.e.* the part-time worker was engaged on that basis. Under this new subsection unemployment benefit will be payable by reference to the employment that the part-time worker has lost, as distinct from the employment the worker was unable to secure. So, if a worker was normally employed for three days and then lost employment, benefit would be payable by reference to the three days normally worked and not the six days the part-time worker was generally available for employment. This is achieved by the introduction of condition (d), that the claimant has sustained a substantial loss of employment in any period of six consecutive days. This subsection gives the Minister the power to specify when a substantial loss of employment has occurred and different circumstances may be specified for different provisions in this regard. Article 31 of S.I. No. 417 of 1994 provides that a person will be regarded as having suffered a substantial loss of employment if that person has lost at least one day of insurable employment in any week. The 1994 Act, however, exempted those in casual employment, which is defined in article 33 of S.I. No. 417 of 1994.

Subsection (2)
See S.I. No. 417 of 1994.

Subsection (3)
These three days are known as waiting days.

Subsection (4)
This is probably the most complex provision in the entire Act. The constituent parts of this subsection are examined below in considerable detail.

Introduction
Unemployment benefit is payable "in respect of any day of unemployment (in this Part referred to as 'a day of unemployment') which forms part of a period of interruption of employment". The key concept "day of unemployment" is not defined in the Act but rather the Act specifies certain circumstances in which the applicant will or will not be regarded as unemployed. The Commission on Social Welfare pointed out (p. 344) that the conditions which attach to unemployment benefit are more rigorous than in the case of other contingencies because the claimant, when unemployed, is not prevented from working: that person may engage in activities which may constitute work without forfeiting entitlement. The difficulties arise, it must be said, in relation to whether the work in question is done voluntarily, without hope or expectation of remuneration. Conversely, the fact that a person is not in employment does not lead to the conclusion that that person is unemployed. There may be no evidence of an attachment to the labour force: indeed, a refusal to take up an offer of employment or training may lead to the inference that an unemployed person is no longer to be regarded as unemployed. Because the law has to resolve these difficult and complex issues of human behaviour and motivation, the statutory conditions provide a great deal of assistance in deciding when a person should be regarded as "unemployed" but, in contrast with British social security law, there is a dearth of legislative guidance on several crucial issues surrounding the concept of unemployment.

Section 42(4) of the Principal Act of 1993 sets out the circumstances within which a day of unemployment may be established. The history of this provision is not without interest. Before the 1986 Act amended section 29(4)(a) of the Principal Act of 1981, it was by no means clear what the claimant had to establish before entitlement to unemployment benefit would result. It was clear that if the claimant was not capable of work *e.g.* through accident or illness, the claimant would not be entitled to unemployment benefit. It was also clear that the claimant was required to establish availability for employment, but neither the Unemployment Insurance Act, 1920, the 1952 Act, nor the 1981 Act, required the claimant to prove active steps have been taken to find suitable employment. As we shall see, there is a considerable amount of evidence to support the view that social welfare officers have interpreted the law as if such a requirement has always been part of Irish law. The 1986 Act put the issue of proof beyond doubt. Section 19 of the Social Welfare Act, 1986 amended section 29(4)(a) of the Principal Act of 1981 by substitution; further amendments to this section were made by section 28(1) of the Act of 1989 and section 25(1) of the Act of 1993 in order to broaden the powers of the Minister to allow unemployed persons to engage in educational or other activities without losing unemployment payments.

Definition of Terms
This complex provision must be broken down into its constituent elements.

Day
Any part of a day worked, subject to a *de minimis* rule, prevents that day from being a day of unemployment.

Capable of work
This requirement makes it clear that the cause of interruption in employment must be unemployment, not illness.

Is or is deemed . . . available for employment
The statutory requirement whereby the insured person must establish that he or she is, or is deemed in accordance with regulations to be, available for employment is imposed in order to distinguish between claimants whose unemployment is voluntary and involuntary. Certain activities which the applicant may participate in for the benefit of the community generally may nevertheless prejudice a claim for unemployment benefit. Part-time or full-time charitable or voluntary work carried on by the applicant may lead the Department of Social Welfare to conclude that the applicant is not available for work. In the U.K., persons who voluntarily participate in certain worthwhile activities—crewing a lifeboat, serving in a firebrigade, emergency rescue work and charitable community service—may automatically satisfy the availability condition. Problems of this kind make the following observation of the Commission on Social Welfare pertinent to this exposition: "Perhaps the most contentious of the [entitlement] conditions, and the most difficult to implement, is that of availability for employment. It implies that the person is free and willing to take up full-time employment without placing unreasonable conditions on the type or location of the employment".

A person who refuses to work more than a given number of miles from the town in which that person resides because it may prevent that person from participating in a part-time emergency mountain rescue team raises an interesting problem: does the voluntary activity, undoubtedly of benefit to society in general, in any sense legitimate what would otherwise be an unreasonable restriction on that person's availability to take up employment? While the Social Insurance Fund should not be seen as a method of subsidising or effecting socially progressive or economically worthwhile policies that are unrelated to job creation schemes, many may take the view that persons in such a situation should be eligible for benefit. However, it is unlikely that activities of this kind are compatible with the statutory test. The claimant is not given a power to declare the circumstances in which he or she is available for employment.

Administrative Procedures and "genuinely seeking . . . employment"
There are some indications that the "available for work" criterion has contained more than a requirement that the claimant be ready and willing to accept an offer of suitable employment if it were to be offered to the claimant. Such a hypothesis, particularly in a country which has one of the highest unemployment rates within the E.U., would be administratively and legally meaningless: the prospect of an offer of suitable employment being made is too hypothetical to offer any meaningful method of distinguishing between those unemployed due to adverse employment conditions and those who remain unemployed due to other factors. Although there are no legislative requirements in relation to registration with various Government agencies as a condition of entitlement to benefit, a failure to observe certain procedures may lead to the conclusion that a person is not available for employment. The Commission on Social Welfare set out at p. 335–6 the various administrative procedures involved. First, at the initial claim stage, there are questions on the claim form which refer to the type of work and hours (or days) in respect of which employment is sought. The applicant is also asked what steps have been taken to find work. This latter question implies that, as a condition of entitlement, the applicant must actively seek, and continue to seek, work. The Commission point out that the Department continuously monitor the availability for employment requirement. Those aged under 25 are automatically registered with FAS once they have been on the Live Register for six months. Older claimants are advised to register. Non-registration is taken into account in deciding whether the claimant is available for work: The Commission, however, indicate that the registration requirement goes further than this: registration "is nevertheless taken into account in assessing whether an individual is genuinely seeking work". It is through this shift in language that we see the "available for employment" requirement being interpreted in such a way as to require the claimant to demonstrate an initial and continuous search for employment, as a condition for eligibility. The Commission also stress that failure to attend for interview with the Manpower Service Scheme in connection with a job referral or training programme can also lead to disqualification. The Jobsearch Scheme also attracted much public discussion and reinforces the point that with

"available for employment", the statutory test can be interpreted restrictively: if a claimant cannot show a recent history of job applications, there is an argument to be made in favour of the view that the applicant is not available for work. Such an argument however is not a logical, nor a necessarily, sound one. A failure on the part of the claimant to show that he or she has recently sought employment may just as well reflect the claimant's past experience: a pessimistic view of the claimant's own prospects of finding work is common, particularly if the claimant is middle-aged and unskilled, living in an area of high unemployment. Nevertheless, the broadening of the "available for employment" condition so as to expressly require the claimant to prove he or she is genuinely seeking employment makes it clear that this controversial requirement will prove to be a decisive one. The Commission on Social Welfare pointed out that mass unemployment has resulted in a relaxation of the administrative measures devised to ensure that persons are available for employment. These include the following:

    (1) Signing-on conditions have been relaxed at most employment exchanges and other signing centres. Most claimants in urban areas now sign on once weekly. Daily signing and twice weekly signing is still required but only where the claimant lives near to the exchange or signing centre.

    (2) Since 1984 claimants may take an annual two-week holiday within the State, without loss of benefit.

The Commission welcomed these measures and recommended they be extended to allow the more widespread adoption of fortnightly, and even monthly, signing and the development of a more diverse range of payment methods. Signing-on and cash payment of unemployment benefit have traditionally been seen as methods of testing availability for employment. The Commission recommend greater use of cheque payments and electronic funds transfers to bank accounts, suggesting that random interviewing rather than daily or weekly signing would provide a more accurate test of determining the claimant's availability for work. The introduction of pre-retirement allowance has also extended this trend.

Jobsearch

The 1987 Budget led to a programme called Jobsearch, which was a mixture of abuse-control measures and interview and training exercises intended to motivate the unemployed into renewing efforts to find a job. Although Jobsearch was devised after the Commission Report was published, the Report contains an implicit criticism of these kind of procedures: "the requirement to be available for employment pre-supposes the availability of employment procedures. In a period of prolonged recession it is questionable whether this condition should be strictly enforced". With respect, the issue appears to be not whether the statutory condition should be "strictly enforced" but whether it should be interpreted in this way: "available for employment" need not mean available and seeking employment. It may just as easily be interpreted to mean available to take employment immediately, if offered. The Commission went on to note that certain administrative procedures connected to the statutory condition *vis-à-vis* availability have been relaxed, particularly the conditions relating to daily signing on at exchanges and the two-week holiday scheme. Further administrative changes were recommended by the Commission, the most important of which relates to educational courses and is considered below.

Availability for Employment and Parent Claimants

The claim form requests information on childminding arrangements if the claimant indicates that he or she has child dependants. If the claimant is unable to provide a satisfactory explanation on the arrangements which will apply when employment is secured, then it may be that the claimant will be held not to be available for employment. The operation of this administrative procedure has proved to be extremely controversial. The experience of many married women with dependant children has been that the Department police the availability for employment criteria unduly rigorously: the female claimant was traditionally asked questions on childminding and other domestic arrangements, *e.g.* who will make the husband's lunch or tea if the claimant finds a job? These questions were not asked when the applicant was male with dependant children. Not only are such administrative practices sexist in nature, they can prove intimidating. Official policy is against this kind of questioning but traditional attitudes cannot be expunged so easily.

The Council Directive on the Implementation of the Principle of Equal Treatment for men and women in matters of Social Security

This Directive, implemented in Ireland by the Social Welfare (No. 2) Act, 1985, makes such discriminatory administrative practices unlawful. In commenting on the interpretation of the "available for employment" requirement an Oireachtas Joint Committee on Women's Rights (pl. 3204) referred to the need for new guidelines for social welfare officers, indicating what questions are permissible under the Directive of all claimants, regardless of sex.

Restrictions upon availability for employment—the claimant

Subsection 4(a)(iii) makes it clear that the claimant does not have to seek and take up any offer of employment, regardless of its nature or location. The claimant is entitled to narrow-down the search for employment to jobs that are suitable for the claimant's circumstances and talents. Of course if the claimant narrows down the focus too much (*e.g.* part-time in an office in the street next to his or her place of residence) there will be appropriate grounds for concluding that the claimant is not genuinely seeking employment. If the restrictions are due to factors that, objectively speaking, can be attributed to age, health, or any other factor personal to the claimant, the claimant may be held to have placed reasonable restrictions on the employment sought. The Act sets out several connecting factors. Although there are structural differences between Irish law and the corresponding U.K. legislation governing the assessment of whether personal idiosyncrasies prevent a claimant from being available for employment, the decisions of the Social Security Commissioners and their predecessors are of value in coming to terms with this important notion of when a person is available for employment.

The initial application for benefit is regulated by S.I. No. 417 of 1994. At this stage the applicant for unemployment benefit will be asked about the kind of work, the hours of work and the location of employment which the claimant is prepared to accept. All restrictions placed by the claimant will reduce the claimant's prospects but it would be incorrect to conclude that a claimant who specifies that only employment of a particular kind is acceptable is necessarily placing restrictions on their availability for employment. The claimant may only be providing an indication of past employment or may be providing a realistic assessment of the range of employment which the claimant may reasonably expect to take up. The claimant's past employment record will provide a valuable indication of whether the claimant is really available for employment.

Age

Subsection (4)(a)(iii) indicates that the age of the claimant may be a reasonable explanation for the claimant's failure to find suitable employment. The section seems to refer to age or ageism as an explanation for the claimant's failure to obtain employment (because of an employer's reluctance to engage a person in their middle or late years, preferring to take on a youthful person) as well as the claimant's own reluctance to apply for employment in a particular workplace. A woman in her early sixties may have many years experience in the retail clothing trade as a salesperson, but if she specifies that she would not like to take up a job in a boutique catering exclusively for girls and young women, this may reflect the fact that she is unlikely to secure employment in such a shop.

Physique

This requirement seems to involve questions of physical strength. A person may not hold themselves available for hard manual labour because of his or her own perception of personal physical inadequacy for such work. Physical build may be a condition upon which an employment offer is dependent *e.g.* the police force, and it may be relevant to other jobs *e.g.* security personnel.

It may also be in doubt whether a man whose height and build are substantially below the average for the rest of the population should be expected to be available for employment as a security guard or dance-hall bouncer. The test set out in the section—the word "physique" is used—may be too narrow. It should surely be broadened to encompass the physical or mental health of the claimant. In a leading decision, Social Security Decision No. *R(U)6/72*, the National Insurance Commissioner in England held that a claimant who suffered from a heart condition—he was aged 62—could restrict his availability to employment for which he was qualified in the locality in which he resided. The crucial factors were his age and his physical health, which together could legitimately allow him to restrict the geographical area to his home town and its surrounding environs. This case points up the need for the word "physique" to be given an extended meaning.

Education

This factor would appear to be self-evident. A person who is educated to a level which allows that person to have a reasonable expectation of employment in a given field may restrict availability for employment unduly in specifying that certain fields of employment are not acceptable *e.g.* a mathematics graduate who declines to be available for employment as a computer programmer. A person who insists that employment in the nuclear physics field is the only career acceptable would probably unduly restrict availability for employment.

Normal occupation

This factor will probably be the most important factor of all in determining availability for employment. A claimant's previous employment record will prove an invaluable reference point in determining availability. Indeed in the U.K. the existing regulations were reviewed in 1980 in a joint D.H.S.S./Department of Employment Report. The existing rules were seen as cumbersome and rarely applied by the authorities because of pressure of work in other areas. A more vigorous and yet simplified system was recommended, the central factor being a new test of availability. If the claimant is prepared to take up employment in a position similar to their last employment then the claimant, the Review Team recommended, should be regarded as available for employment for the first three months following the claim. After three months the claimant must be more flexible—non-manual workers must accept any non-manual work within their capabilities and manual workers must accept any manual work within their capabilities. The proposal has not been implemented but, in any event, a similar mechanism can operate in relation to disqualification for refusing suitable employment, considered below.

The "normal occupation" test, at first sight, would suggest that if the claimant refuses to make himself or herself available for employment of a type normally carried on by the claimant, the application for benefit will fail. This need not follow. The claimant may refer to other factors that warrant this restriction: poor health or an industrial accident in previous employment may make the claimant unsuitable to resume a job or career in that field. The claimant may well have left the area in which he or she previously resided, making it impossible, or extremely difficult, for the claimant to travel to take up a job in that trade or industry, particularly if the industry is geographically based. A balance has to be struck between a policy of protecting skilled workers from wasting their talents or diminishing their employability by accepting work of an inferior standard, and a desire to discourage voluntary unemployment. However, the fact that a claimant does not wish to take up employment in their former job area may not be fatal to a claim for unemployment benefit. In *CU 305/1985* ([1985] J.S.W.L. 201), the claimant, a married woman, had worked in the retail industry, an essential part of which requires the worker to work on Saturdays. Her husband had formerly looked after the children but his job made this increasingly difficult to arrange at weekends. When claiming benefit, she indicated that she would be available for clerical work: she explained that she could not work on Saturday because she wished to spend that day with her young daughter while she settled in at a new school. She was held to be unavailable for employment. On appeal, the Commissioner upheld the decision *vis-à-vis* Saturdays, but held that the central issue, namely, did the restriction mean the claimant had no reasonable prospect of securing employment, had to be answered in her favour. Most offices and creches are closed on Saturdays. The Commissioner contrasted this with shop work and held that, in initially disallowing the claim, the local tribunal had concentrated too much on her previous employment.

Place of Residence

As *R(U)6/72* indicates, a restriction placed on the area of employment may be acceptable, particularly if there are other factors such as age, ill-health, transport difficulties and the like.

Family circumstances

As with ill-health, this factor may prove a double-edged sword for many claimants. A claimant in poor health may be so indisposed as to lead to the conclusion that the claimant is not capable of work and thus liable to be disqualified on that ground. A claimant who seeks unemployment benefit because family circumstances require them to look after children, or some other relative, may not be available for work due to this circumstance. A restriction that is designed to allow the claimant to meet family responsibilities and take up employment may be too narrow. In *Dennehy v. Minister for Social Welfare* (Unrep. H.C. 1984) the plaintiff was deserted by his wife, leaving him with the custody of the children of the marriage. He left his employment as a bus driver to look after the children. His claim before the High Court in regard to a deserted wife's claim for unemployment benefit was untenable because, by taking on the job of rearing the children, he was not available for employment. If the restriction is limited, as in *CU 305/1985*, then entitlement may not be impeded. There remains the possibility that some other insurance or assistance payment will be available, particularly prisoner's wife's allowance, deserted wife's benefit or assistance, single woman's allowance and prescribed relatives' allowance.

Penal Detention

If a claimant becomes involved in proceedings which involve the claimant being detained in prison it follows that the claimant is no longer "available for employment". In the Canadian case of *Gouland v. Canadian Employment and Immigration Commission* (1985) 23 DLR (3d) 393, a person released from custody, but liable to be returned to prison at any time, was held not to be "available for employment".

Participation in an Educational Course

When a person is in full-time education this, without more, is regarded as preventing that person from satisfying the "available for employment" requirement in regard to unemployment benefit and unemployment assistance. Nor can this interpretation be sidestepped by making an application for supplementary welfare allowance. The Principal Act expressly excludes such persons from receipt of this allowance, although members of families headed by persons in full-time education are entitled and, in exceptional cases, even the person in full-time education may receive supplementary welfare allowance.

Until recently there were no statutory guidelines on the kinds of educational course that is regarded as incompatible with availability for employment. In 1986 the Commission on Social Welfare commented that this matter "is determined in the particular circumstances of each case". The Commission explained that where the course involves a high degree of commitment, such as a full-time college course, the student will not be held to be available for employment. The Commission on Social Welfare, while generally accepting that the full-time student should not be regarded as unemployed, suggested that a distinction between short-term and part-time courses, on the one hand, and long-term courses on the other, should be used as the basis of operating the available for employment requirement. A course of six months or less duration should not prevent participants from taking up employment at any stage. Where the course is of longer duration the claimant should be removed from the Live Register and supported by way of training or educational grants provided by the agency involved, *e.g.* CERT, FAS, I.D.A. The Commission also seem to have envisaged that training and skills courses should entitle participants to obtain maintenance grants administered by some unspecified body. In any event the Commission were clearly correct to stress that the unemployed should be encouraged to participate in education and training courses that enable them to maintain and enhance their skills and thus improve employment prospects. Statutory Instrument No. 328 of 1989 builds upon the recommendations of the Commission by allowing persons aged over 21 to continue to be eligible for unemployment assistance when attending a second level course approved by the Minister. This in effect allows students to pursue Leaving Certificate courses while continuing to be eligible for unemployment assistance, because entitlement to unemployment benefit ends after 15 months in any event. Some unemployed persons do receive unemployment assistance while on training or educational courses on the basis of non-statutory pilot schemes.

Day of unemployment—calculation of benefit

For the purpose of calculating entitlement, the working week is judged on the basis of a six-day week: Sunday is not normally regarded as a day of unemployment. Therefore any day which is not "a day of unemployment" does not secure for the claimant payment of unemployment benefit in respect of that day and the weekly rate of benefit is reduced, by $\frac{1}{2}$ of the weekly amount, for each day for which the claimant is not unemployed. For unemployment benefit to be payable, the day of unemployment must form part of a period of "interruption of employment".

"Period of interruption of employment"

If benefit was payable for each and every day on which a person became unemployed there would be a significant administrative burden placed upon the Department of Social Welfare. A person leaving employment with X Ltd. on Friday, taking up a new job with Y Ltd. the following Monday could seek unemployment benefit for the intervening Saturday even though Saturday would normally be an idle day. The considerable administrative costs that would result from making a successful claim for an isolated day of unemployment could not really be supported on a cost-effective basis. For this reason the policy of imposing on an unemployed person the initial cost of self-support when unemployed was devised. This policy is implemented by requiring the day of unemployment to link up with other days of unemployment or a day of incapacity for work. Subsection (4)(c) states "any three days of interruption of employment, whether consecutive or not, within a period of six consecutive days shall be treated as a period of interruption of employment and any two such periods not separated by a period of more than 13 weeks shall be treated as one period of interruption of employment".

This provision means that unless a day of unemployment is linked to at least two other days of unemployment in the period Monday to Saturday inclusive, benefit cannot be paid for that day. Allied to this requirement is the three waiting days rule: benefit cannot be obtained for the first three days of a period of interruption of employment. However, subsection (4)(c) mitigates the effect of this prohibition for those claimants who are affected by intermittent periods of unemployment: where unemployment takes the form of temporary lay-offs and short-time working it would be unconscionable to require three waiting days to elapse, at the beginning of each period of unemployment, before benefit could be paid. In the case of a worker on short-time (*e.g.* three days on and three days off), it might mean benefit would never be paid. To overcome this, a linkage rule operates: any three days of unemployment out of six continuous days can form one period of interruption of employment and, as long as the next three days of interruption of employment occur within 13 weeks, the two periods are linked and benefit is payable as from day one in the second period.

Two examples should clarify this seemingly complex position:
  (i) Tom is put on a three day week as from Monday June 1. He works on Monday, Wednesday and Saturday but does not work on Tuesday, Thursday and Friday. On Monday June 8, Tom goes back to work on his normal six-day schedule. Seven weeks later Tom is again put on the same three-day week. Because three days have been days of unemployment during the first week of June they form a period of interruption of employment. Because the next period of interruption of employment (*i.e.* at the end of July) commences within 13 weeks of the first, the two periods are linked. Thus the days in June are days of unemployment and also serve as the three waiting days. Tom collects unemployment benefit for each "day of unemployment" that occurs after the onset of unemployment in July.
  (ii) Same facts as above, except that the second three-day week commences in December of that year. The linkage rule does not operate and the first "three days of unemployment" occurring in December are "waiting days".
  However, recent legislative changes have been introduced to mitigate the effects of a break in the continuity of a period of interruption of employment. In order to encourage the long-term unemployed to avail of job training and other work experience schemes section 42(5) provides that the claimant's participation, for a period of not more than one year, in any of the schemes set out in the section, shall not break the continuity of the period of unemployment. So, a person who receives benefit for 12 months and is then placed upon one of the schemes in question, may, upon becoming unemployed again, receive unemployment benefit until entitlement lapses without having to serve another three waiting days. The schemes in question are the Social Employment Scheme, the Enterprise Allowance Scheme, the Alternance Scheme, FAS training, the Teamwork Scheme, the Part-Time Job Incentive Scheme and the Vocational Training Opportunities Scheme. With effect from September 20, 1994, section 42(4A) further relaxes the linkage rule. Two years without benefit leads to a new period of interruption of employment beginning. See S.I. No. 283 of 1994.

Days which are not "days of unemployment"
A day upon which the claimant is employed is not a "day of unemployment".
Both the Act and S.I. No. 7 of 1953 make it clear that, unless the claimant is available for employment on that particular day, the day cannot be a day of unemployment. The Act does not define "employment", but it is clear that the term is not to be confined to the concept of availability to take up a contract of service for reward. If a person takes up any activity, with a view to generating an income or profit therefrom, that person cannot be said to be unemployed. It is irrelevant whether the status of that person is that of employee, partner or self-employed, *vis-à-vis* that activity. An "employed person" has been defined as "a person engaged in employment under a contract of service whether paid by time or piece" by Kennedy C.J. in *Graham v. Minister for Industry & Commerce* [1933] I.R. 159, in the context of defining insurability. A person who claims unemployment benefit for a day when that person has secured gainful employment would not be eligible. Payment in any form would defeat the claim, whether in cash or kind. Any earnings obtained from the activity in question will generally be fatal to any assertion that the earner was unemployed on the day in question. This proposition is reinforced by the subsidiary employment regulation which declares that any day on which any person follows any occupation from which any remuneration or profit is derived, cannot be a day of unemployment, unless it comes within the subsidiary employment exceptions, considered below. The use of the phrase "remuneration or profit" also makes it clear that the amount earned is of no significance: if the claimant works all day gathering potatoes for £1 then the claimant is employed, subject to the subsidiary employment exception. Indeed, the Court of Appeal in England has provided a definitive statement on the word "remunerative" in the case of *Perrot v. Supplementary Benefits Commission* [1980] 3 All E.R. 110. The plaintiff was in receipt of supplementary benefit. She began a translation agency. In the first year of trading, net losses were £1,123. In the second year a trading net loss of £309 was returned. She continued to receive supplementary benefit in these two years. During her third year she was disqualified under the legislation because she was held to be in "remunerative full-time work". Her appeal to the Court of Appeal against disqualification was dismissed. In the judgment of Brightman L.J. "remunerative" could not, in this context, be "profitable" or "broadly profitable". A secondary, if unusual interpretation was preferred, that is, work which brings remuneration or work which is paid for. This decision is very pertinent to Irish conditions because the phrase found in the subsidiary employment regulation is "any remuneration or profit". If however the claimant has worked, not for profit or remuneration, but, rather, for personal satisfaction or gratification, payment being made to cover travelling

expenses only, the claimant would not be prevented from claiming that such a day is nevertheless a day of unemployment, although the onus of proof would still rest on the claimant to prove that the nature of the payment falls outside remuneration or profit. The claimant is not required to abstain from physical or mental activity as a condition of entitlement. However, problems may arise where the claimant, on a particular day, engages in an activity which would prevent the claimant from taking up employment if it were offered. An unemployed person in receipt of benefit who travels by bus from Dublin to Killarney and back to attend a funeral could not, on that day, show availability for employment and, similarly, an unemployed person in receipt of benefit who stays at home all day in order to look after a sick partner or child might have the greatest difficulty in proving availability for employment on that particular day. Yet it would seem harsh indeed to deprive that person of benefit for the day in question. A distinction should perhaps be drawn between an activity which, while absorbing most of the working hours of a particular day, is not going to occur on a regular basis, and activities which will form a pattern of activity which would preclude acceptance of full-time employment, if offered. This distinction is implicit in the way in which benefit is administered for married persons with children. There are, however, circumstances in which an unemployed person may take up employment without forfeiting all rights to unemployment benefit. Because benefit is calculated on a daily basis, a person who works for up to three days in a particular week can still retain entitlement to benefit for each of the other three days in the working week, because those three remaining days form a period of interruption of employment. While there will be some difference in the rate of benefit paid if the claimant is held to be working on a systematic short-time basis, discussed below, it matters not whether the claimant works during that week for the same employer (or indeed is self-employed) on each of those days in which he is not available for employment, because the claimant is in remunerative or profitable employment. The social employment scheme and other work experience schemes are a logical development of the existing legislative position for persons who seek for one or more days of the working week.

Exceptions

Subsidiary Employments. A day of unemployment may also be prescribed by regulation: the most obvious example of this is found by way of regulations which stipulate that certain kinds of employment are not to lead to the conclusion that a day on which such employment occurs cannot be a day of unemployment. The general rule is found in article 26 of S.I. No. 417 of 1994:

"a day shall not be treated as a day of unemployment if an insured person:
   (a) fails to prove to the satisfaction of the Minister that he is unemployed, capable of work and available for employment, or
   (b) follows any occupation from which he derives any remuneration or profit, unless such occupation could ordinarily have been followed by him in addition to his usual employment and outside the ordinary working hours of that employment and either—
      (i) the remuneration or profit therefrom for any such day does not exceed £10, or, where the remuneration or profit is in respect of a period longer than a day, such remuneration or profit does not on the daily average exceed that amount, or
      (ii) not less than 117 employment contributions have been paid in respect of him in respect of either the period of 3 years immediately preceding that day or in respect of the last three complete contribution years immediately preceding that day".

The subsidiary employment exception to the prohibition on employment and entitlement to benefit was examined by the Commission on Social Welfare. The Commission said the provision applied mainly to farmers and small shopkeepers claiming unemployment benefit. In the view of the Commission, the employment contribution provision was anomalous in that it allowed persons to obtain substantial earnings and still be eligible for unemployment benefit. The Commission recommended that the exception should be abolished. On the general question of whether claimants should be able to work on a part-time basis and continue to receive unemployment benefit, earnings up to a prescribed limit being disregarded, the Commission came down against such changes on the ground that this would tend to be administratively difficult to police, as well as produce conceptual confusion on the nature of unemployment: pp. 339–40.

Rehabilitation training. A further exception to the provision which declares that benefit is not available for a day in which a person follows any occupation for which he derives any remuneration or profit, is found in Article 26 of S.I. No. 417 of 1994. Any person undergoing a course of rehabilitation training provided by approved organisations may be deemed for unemployment benefit purposes, to be unemployed and available for employment.

"Deemed" days of unemployment. Regulations made under section 42 of the Principal Act envisage that certain days will be deemed to have been days of unemployment. This enables the Minister to resolve difficult problems where a worker may only be employed for a short period of any one day, such employment being nevertheless capable of preventing that day from being a day of unemployment. British social security legislation has been interpreted in such a way as to provide a *de minimus* rule, but the rule is hardly generous: 15 minutes has been disregarded but 20 minutes has been held a sufficient period to prevent the day upon which it was worked from being a day of unemployment. Where a claimant's working hours span two calendar days—(*e.g.* shiftworker, fisherman, nightbaker) any period of unemployment or short-time working may produce complications by virtue of the fact that the social welfare system tends to keep "office hours". The Nightworkers Regulation (article 27 of S.I. No. 417 of 1994) provides:

"(1) Where a person is employed to work continuously from a time on any day until a time on the next following day, that person shall be regarded for the purpose of unemployment benefit, as being, by virtue of such employment, employed—

    (a) in case the first day is a Monday, Tuesday, Wednesday, Thursday or Friday and the employment on the first day is longer than that on the second, or in the case the first day is a Saturday—only on the first day, which day shall not be treated as a day of unemployment, or

    (b) in any other case he shall be regarded as being employed only on the second day, and that day shall not be treated as a day of unemployment.

(2) Where by virtue of the provisions of sub-article (1) a person—

    (a) is to be treated as having been employed on 1 day only of 2 days, and

    (b) throughout that part of the other of those 2 days during which that person is not employed, or is deemed in accordance with regulations to be available for employment, that person shall . . . be deemed . . . to be so available for employment, throughout that other of those 2 days".

Unemployment and Compensated days

Compensated Days during the currency of the Contract of Employment. It is not a necessary precondition for entitlement to unemployment benefit that the claimant prove that the contractual relationship between the claimant and the claimant's employer is at an end. If this were a requirement, it would mean that a claimant whose contract of employment continues, but who cannot obtain employment because of lay-off or short-time working, or even because of industrial action, would be deprived of unemployment benefit. It is clear that a person who is in employment will generally fail to satisfy the available for employment criteria and will therefore not be able to show that there is a period of interruption of employment. However, what is the position of a claimant who receives payment from an employer but does not work on a particular day? There are a variety of circumstances in which this could occur. The employee may be absent from employment while on holiday or may be suspended from work while an allegation of misconduct is investigated by the employer. The employee may have been dismissed from employment and given wages in lieu of the statutory or contractual entitlement to notice. In these, and many other situations, the employer may make payments which are intended to provide an income for the employee. Can any of those days be days of unemployment, entitling the worker to claim unemployment benefit? While specific regulations in the U.K. stipulate that a day in respect of which a payment is made, in lieu of notice or remuneration, prevent that day from being a day of unemployment there is surprisingly little guidance on these "compensated days" in Ireland. There appears to be no provision in the regulations which prohibits a compensated day from also being a day of unemployment. The subsidiary employment regulation, which confirms the general rule declaring that a day in which a person is employed cannot be a day of unemployment does not refer to the issue of payment at all, other than as a factor in determining whether work undertaken is "employment". But what if a person does not work on a particular day but receives a payment which is referable to that day? The question of whether the contract of employment is terminated or not is not always of significance. In Social Security Decision No. *R(U)11/73(T)* the claimant, a factory worker, worked on a basic five-day week in normal circumstances. A strike made it necessary to restructure factory hours. As a result, the claimant worked for six days in a period of two weeks but he did not work on any other day in that period. He received his basic pay for the hours worked in the two week period. He claimed unemployment benefit for five days on which he did not work. It was understood that the claimant was entitled to seek employment elsewhere and that he was not at the disposal of the employers except on the six work days. The claimant was paid a lump sum: he was not required to stand by and be at the disposal of the employer: in these circumstances the claimant was held to be unemployed on the days when he did not work. As the Commissioner said:

"unfortunately the word "unemployed" is ambiguous. Sometimes it is used to describe a person who on the day in question has no work or perhaps no work and no pay; sometimes to describe one who has no contract of employment or in whose case there is no subsisting relationship of employer and employee. If an hourly paid worker never works on Saturday few people would on Saturday describe him in ordinary language as being "unemployed" on that day or his employment as having been terminated. But he may well be unemployed".

In this case, and other similar U.K. decisions, the change in hours worked during emergency periods—strikes, power failures and the like—often meant that the worker obtained the same or a similar level of remuneration but, nevertheless, was still held unemployed on days not worked. The concept of "unemployed" in the U.K. is broad enough to cover situations where remuneration is obtained even though work is not undertaken. Payments made to employees under suspension or required to stand idle on a particular day are regarded in the U.K. as days when the claimant is employed and, in policy terms, it would be sound to apply the same reasoning in Ireland. The crucial factors will be whether the worker is required to remain on call for the employer, whether he is required to abstain from other work, or whether he is required to refuse an offer of employment elsewhere if incompatible with the requirements of the employer. The problem of deciding whether a person is unemployed on a day when no work is done arises in several kinds of employment. Part-time professional footballers do not play competitive matches every day but they are given payment by way of wages. Are they considered employed only on the days a match is played? Are they considered to be employed when the contract of employment stipulates a requirement to attend for training sessions?

This kind of issue arose in *Louth and Others v. Minister for Social Welfare*, H.C. Unrep. April 9, 1992. The 27 plaintiffs were engaged as dockers by a stevedoring company in the Port of Drogheda. As was the custom within the port, the dockers were engaged on rotation depending upon available work, but, in order to balance out earnings, the workers agreed amongst themselves that they would pool their earnings. Payments made exceeded the average industrial wage. For the days upon which they did not work, each docker sought unemployment benefit but, as from 1988, the Department refused to accept that these persons were at any stage unemployed, a view that the appeals officer upheld on the basis that the work pattern here was a full normal week and that these workers were not casual workers. The appeals officer wrote, "whilst the men do not physically perform work [on certain days] they are remunerated as if they had done the work. I cannot see how they may be regarded as unemployed." On appeal, Barron J. held that the appeals officer should not have considered the level of earnings but, rather, whether on a given day a person was to be regarded as unemployed. These dockers, the judge found, were employed by the stevedore under contracts of service and the pooling arrangements, with which that employer had no involvement, could not alter the legal position of the plaintiffs so far as unemployment or employment was concerned. The plaintiffs were thus held to be entitled to claim that they were unemployed on days which they did not work. While this may be a correct result on the facts, such a situation makes the evolution of a new compensated days rule very desirable.

Compensated days after the contract has been terminated. Although the regulations do not indicate that the termination of a contract of employment has any vital significance for the issue of entitlement to unemployment benefit, it is submitted that the question of whether the contract of employment remains in existence will be a vital consideration when the claimant is compensated after the contract of employment appears to have ended. Before we consider termination, an intermediate position must be considered. What if the employee leaves the workplace but does not irrevocably leave employment? Where an employee avails of a career break or takes leave of absence from employment while at the same time agreeing, for a cash payment, that at the end of the break or leave that person will return to that employment, can that person be said to be unemployed for this time? The contract of employment, in such a case, would, in all probability, be held to have been suspended and not terminated. The argument in favour of holding that, despite a cash payment, the worker is entitled to do whatever he or she likes during the period of absence are formidable. If the employer cannot require the worker to discontinue this period of absence and return to employment then, by analogy with workers laid off as a result of an industrial dispute which they are not financing, participating or directly interested in, the claimant on leave of absence should be regarded as unemployed. On the other hand, if the unemployment is voluntary (*i.e.* the worker has sought leave of absence), one of the basic tenets governing payment of unemployment benefit is flouted. This is not, however, an absolute principle because the claimant in such a case is "guilty" of voluntarily leaving employment, the appropriate sanction for which is disqualification for nine weeks under section 47. A consistent pattern of employment, in which earnings are high but there are substantial rewards (*e.g.* oil rig workers who work two weeks on and two weeks off) should be regarded as amenable to special treatment. Existing legislation does not deal with such patterns of employment and it may be suggested that regulations be laid which deem employment patterns which structurally provide for extensive periods of work followed by extensive periods of rest to be periods of continuous employment. If the payment made by the employer on termination of the contract is of a charitable or gratuitous kind it should be ignored. If the payment is made in recognition of past service or is a redundancy payment (statutory or otherwise), in principle it would seem to be improper to regard that as remuneration. Such payments are regarded as being referable to past employment services or the loss of a property "right" — a proprietary interest in one's job. Lump sum payments which are retrospective in nature cannot be remuneration as to future days on which the worker may not be in remunerative or profitable employment. The issue is dealt with in the contribution section through an amendment inspired by the fact that compensated days do not in general prevent benefit from being payable. This is considered in the General Note to section 43.

There are other post-termination means of compensating a worker, most notably compensation for unfair dismissal or wrongful dismissal. Again there is no direct authority on this point. There is Canadian authority for the proposition that damages awarded for wrongful dismissal may be classified as "income arising out of any employment:" *A.G. for Canada v. Walford* (1979) 93 DLR (3d) 748. If there is a contractual right to a review of, or appeal against, a dismissal this may be held to be an integral part of the process of dismissal, but even in such a case the effective date of dismissal remains the original date of dismissal unless the appeal is successful. In Ireland, the Constitutional guarantee as to fair procedures, however, may lead to the conclusion that the exercise of a common law power—such as summary dismissal in a manner that infringes a citizen's constitutional rights—is itself wrongful, by analogy with *Meskell v. CIE* [1973] I.R. 121. If this were held to prevent the contract of employment from terminating, upon notice being given, it is conceivable that the payment made could prevent following days from being "days of unemployment", but even this argument would be speculative and incompatible with the view that once an employee is free to take up employment elsewhere, a payment received in respect of that day does not prevent the day from being a day of unemployment. This large void in Irish statute law, coupled with the fact that the Employment Appeal Tribunal, in granting compensation under the Minimum Notice and Terms of Employment Act, 1963, do not deduct social welfare payments, means that substantial overlap in payments can follow dismissal.

Subsection (5)
See above, note to subsection (4).

Subsection (6)
See above, note to subsection (4).

Subsection (7)
See above, note to subsection (4).

Subsection (8)
Under section 29 of the Principal Act of 1981, an insured contributor could work for three days in a normal working week and claim unemployment benefit for any other day in that week which is a day of unemployment sustained in a period of interruption of employment. A period of interruption of employment is made up of any three days, whether consecutive or not, within a period of six consecutive days. Because Sunday will not normally be a day of unemployment, a worker laid off for three days could collect unemployment benefit and pay-related benefit for three days, prior to the 1983 reforms discussed below. This procedure is quite unobjectionable when the claimant works a six-day week, but such patterns of employment tend to be the exception rather than the rule. For workers who work a four or five day week the pre-1983 position could produce anomalies. A worker who was laid off due to work shortages for two out of the normal five worked could receive 60 per cent of wages normally earned and 50 per cent of the weekly benefit payable to the full-time unemployed. This operated to the advantage of many claimants who found that short-time working could provide a higher income than that available through full-time employment. It mattered not that the worker did not normally work on one or two of the "days of unemployment": in the absence of something approaching the "normal idle day" rule found in the U.K., the actual working pattern of many unemployed persons was irrelevant in calculating the rate of unemployment benefit payable. The failure of the law to take account of changing industrial practices and work patterns led to allegations of abuse but, it is submitted, the problem, while it existed, was not in any legal sense an abuse of the social security system. Employers and unions no doubt devised their lay-off procedures to take advantage of the unreformed law: the real difficulty lay in the failure of the Oireachtas to respond to changes in industrial practices. In 1982 an interdepartmental committee was appointed to review the law on social welfare benefits for workers on short-time.

The Committee recommended changes to be made and these recommendations were implemented in the Social Welfare Act, 1983. These recommendations went beyond the immediate problem at hand, namely the failure of Irish law to acknowledge the generality of the five-day week, extending into the entire question of an appropriate level of unemployment benefit compensation for those on short-time. The view that structural problems were exacerbated by the availability of pay-related benefit was widely accepted by the major political parties. Employers were able to use the Social Insurance Fund to provide an employment subsidy for the workforce. Workers were able in many cases to obtain a higher net income by being partially employed than fully employed. The deleterious effects on industrial efficiency and the work ethic were to be deprecated.

The solution adopted in 1983 accepts that irregularities are inevitable and, rather than attempt to create rules that operate equitably, attempts to minimise the anomalies that result by adjusting benefit levels according to circumstance. This is achieved by limiting the maximum number of days of unemployment in respect of which a short-time worker can receive unemployment benefit and wages in a week to five. Thus, for each day of unemployment in a period of interruption of employment which occurs in a period of short-time working, the claimant will get unemployment benefit at a daily rate of one fifth of the weekly rate. "Short-time employment" is defined in section 2(1) of the Principal Act (inserted by section 5 of the Social Welfare Act, 1983 and now found in section 42(8) of the Act of 1993).

The effect of the short-time working rule can be illustrated:

(i) S works Monday to Friday. S is put on short-time, working on Thursday, Friday and Saturday. The unemployment benefit payable will be for two out of the three remaining working days, Sunday not being a day of unemployment. One of the days he normally works, but is unemployed on, cannot be compensated because the aggregate of five is reached.

(ii) T works Monday to Saturday. T is put on short-time, working Monday and Tuesday only. The unemployment benefit payable will be for three of the four remaining days of his normal working week.

In both of the above examples, benefit is calculated at one fifth and not one sixth of the weekly rate, which goes some way towards easing the loss of one day of unemployment, the loss being a very real one in (ii) above. There are cases in which the worker who genuinely works a six-day week may suffer hardship as a result of this measure. Suppose X works a six-day week, Wednesday being the day off. If the employer puts X on short-time, working on Thursday, Friday, Saturday and Sunday, X will only receive unemployment benefit for one day. While Monday, Tuesday and Wednesday will form a period of interruption of employment, X has worked on four days. X can only add one day on to that in respect of which benefit is payable, despite the fact that X is not working on two of the days he is normally employed.

The short-time working provision, devised in part as a response to collusive agreements between employers and workers which sought to exploit the Social Insurance Fund as a kind of employment subsidy, is not itself immune from abuse. Systems could be devised which would amount to short-time working which would not be caught by the 1983 reform:

(1) X works a three-day week with two days of unemployment in respect of which benefit would be payable. If the employer were to restructure X's work pattern *e.g.* instead of requiring X to work three eight-hour shifts per day if X were to work on two days, working two six-hour shifts per day, X would work the same number of hours but three days of unemployment could now be compensated by way of unemployment benefit. Further, each of those days of unemployment would be compensated at one fifth of the appropriate weekly rate.

(2) Suppose X works a short-time pattern which consists of one week on, one week off, the contract of employment being suspended when work did not take place. X, for each day of unemployment, would collect unemployment benefit at one sixth of the weekly rate. Further, pay-related benefit would also be available. The definition of short-term employment refers to a period of a week: it cannot operate where there is systematic short-term working over longer periods such as a fortnight or a month.

While these avoidance tactics may be difficult to implement in practice, the examples above show that many of the Irish provisions on short-time working are as deeply flawed as the "normal idle day" and "full extent normal" rules in the U.K. There is no statistical evidence that suggests abuse is widespread.

Condition for receipt (optional contributors)

42A.—(1) It shall be a condition for the receipt of unemployment benefit in respect of any day by a person engaged in share fishing that—

(a) it is not a day on which he is engaged in share fishing and it is a day in respect of which he makes reasonable efforts to obtain such work, and

(b) there was no work on, or in connection with, the fishing vessel of which he is a member of the crew avaiable for him on that day for the reason that—

    (i) as a consequence of weather conditions, the fishing vessel could not reasonably have put to sea for the purposes of fishing, or

    (ii) the fishing vessel was undergoing repairs or maintenance, not being repairs or maintenance constituting work within the meaning of subsection (2).

(2) For the purposes of subsection (1), work includes any work done to the fishing vessel or its nets or gear by way of repairs (including running repairs) or maintenance, or in connection with the laying up of nets and gear or their preparation for fishing which at the time of its performance is necessary for the safety or reasonable efficiency of the fishing vessel, or is likely to become so necessary in the near future, and which it is the duty of a person engaged in share fishing (whether by agreement, custom, practice or otherwise) to undertake without remuneration other than by way of a share in the profits or the gross earnings of the working of the fishing vessel, but any other work done to the fishing vessel or its nets or gear, shall be disregarded.

GENERAL NOTE

The provision found in section 42A(1) of the Principal Act is an additional qualifying condition which applies to share fishermen who under the Act are seeking unemployment benefit by virtue of their status as optional contributors. The day of unemployment for an optional contributor must not be a day on which the optional contributor is engaged in share fishing or associated work, such as the maintenance of the vessel or its nets or gear. One senator, a share fisherman himself, explained this provision very well:

"It is traditional for fishermen to maintain their boats, usually at Easter, because there is a high tide at that time. Fishermen will lay their boats up and carry out general repairs, scrub the bottom of the boat and paint it. According to the Bill, fishermen would not draw unemployment benefit while carrying out such work. However, if a boat was tied up in a boat yard and professional people were employed to work on it, fishermen would be idle and should qualify for unemployment benefit" (Senator Fitzgerald, 138 *Seanad Debates* Col. 1545).

The Minister for State, Ms. Burton, went on to explain that the section was intended to catch routine maintenance—which is regarded as part and parcel of the share fisherman's work—and exceptional repairs. In the latter case unemployment benefit is payable:

" . . . this condition is not a new one and Senator Fitzgerald is probably aware of this. It was introduced in 1964 when share fishermen first became insured as employees and entitled to unemployment benefit. It has been in operation for 28 years and is also in operation in the U.K. It has not caused problems for individual share fishermen or the organisations that represent them. The scheme has always worked well and has been operated fairly by the Department of Social Welfare. There is a general understanding between the Department, the industry and individual fishermen as to what constitutes being engaged in repair work and what qualifies as periods when they may apply for unemployment benefit".

Conditions for receipt

43.—(1) The contribution conditions for unemployment benefit are—

(a) that the claimant has qualifying contributions in respect of not less than 39 contribution weeks in the period between his entry into insurance and the day for which the benefit is claimed,

(b) that the claimant has qualifying contributions or credited contributions in respect of not less than 39 contribution weeks in the last complete contribution year before the beginning of the benefit year which includes the day for which the benefit is claimed, and

(c) that the claimant has—
  (i) prescribed reckonable weekly earnings, or
  (ii) in the case of a person who qualifies for unemployment benefit by virtue of having paid optional contributions, prescribed reckonable weekly income,

in excess of a prescribed amount in the prescribed period. [1993 (No. 2) Act, section 8]

(2) In the case of any claim for unemployment benefit where the period of interruption of employment commenced before the 6th day of April, 1987, subsection (1)(a) shall be construed as if "26" were substituted for "39".

(3) Where a person under 65 years of age has been entitled to payment of unemployment benefit in respect of any day or would but for the provisions of section 42(3), 47(1) or 47(4) have been so entitled then, as respects unemployment benefit, the benefit year which includes the 1st such day in every period of interruption of employment, which is, or is deemed to be, a separate period of interruption or employment, shall, for the purpose of the condition contained in subsection (1)(b), be regarded as continuing so long as the period of interruption of employment continues.

(4) Regulations may provide for modifications of the contribution conditions set out in subsection (1).

(5) Subject to subsection (6), regulations may provide for entitling to unemployment benefit persons who would be entitled thereto but for the fact that the condition set out in subsection (1)(c) is not satisfied.

(6) Regulations for the purposes of subsection (5) shall provide that benefit payable by virtue thereof shall be payable at a rate less than that specified in the Second Schedule, and the rate specified by the regulations may vary with the extent to which the condition set out in subsection (1)(c) is satisfied.

(7) The requirement contained in subsection (1)(c) that the claimant must have prescribed reckonable weekly earnings in excess of a prescribed amount in the prescribed period shall not apply in the case of a claim for unemployment benefit made by a person in the benefit year in which that person, having been a volunteer development worker, returns to the State from a developing country or in the next succeeding benefit year. [1993 (No. 2) Act, section 13]

GENERAL NOTE

Subsection (1)

The first contribution condition for unemployment benefit is that the claimant must have paid qualifying contributions in respect of 39 weeks in the period since entry into insurance and the day for which the benefit is claimed (the first contribution condition). Of those insured persons who are liable to pay a social insurance contribution, only those in contribution classes A, D, H and P pay qualifying contributions for the purpose of an award of unemployment benefit. The exclusion of other insured contributors from eligibility for unemployment benefit has traditionally been explained on the ground that the risk of unemployment for persons in other contribution classes is not such as to make this an insurance risk worth covering, particularly for public servants, civil servants, gardai, and commissioned army officers. The Commission on Social Welfare recommended full cover for, and that full employment contributions be levied on, these contributors.

The exclusion of the self-employed from social insurance, recently ended by bringing the self-employed into social insurance for a limited range of benefits, continues in regard to unemployment benefit for a variety of reasons. In the U.K., Beveridge pointed out that social insurance for the self-employed would be simply too difficult to administer, particularly in relation to the question of whether the self-employed are gainfully occupied. The Department of Social Welfare in the 1978 Discussion Paper (Prl. 6772) examined this question in some detail:

"the question as to whether self-employed persons might appropriately be insured against unemployment must be looked at in the light of the different circumstances of employees and self-employed persons. An employee by definition supports himself and his dependants on his earnings from employment. Loss of employment, which in his care occurs generally as a result of a decision by his employer, means that he is in need of income maintenance and this is supplied through the unemployment benefit scheme in the social insurance system. In the case of a self-employed person, however, the day-to-day or week-to-week earnings may not be the relevant factor in regard to his need for income maintenance, but rather his overall income position and thus his position between "jobs" or contracts could hardly be regarded as unemployment in the sense in which that term applies to employees. It does not follow that, during intervals between jobs, a self-employed person is necessarily in need of income maintenance and, therefore, it is more appropriate in his case to make available a means-tested payment where that need would be explicitly established. Furthermore, an important feature of insurance against unemployment is that the period of unemployment covered should be no longer than it takes to find another suitable employment and the conditions of such schemes are framed with this in mind, availability for work being one of the conditions for receipt of benefit. This condition could not be realistically applied in the case of certain self-employed classes, *e.g.* traders, professional and other groups of self-employed, the nature of whose occupations would scarcely allow of their being genuinely available for other employment. This may not be true to the same extent in the case of certain crafts and services workers for whom transfer from self-employment to employee status would not present the same difficulty. Again, however, administrative control would not be an easy matter. Taken all-in-all, the nature of self-employment does not lend itself to the adoption of a system of social insurance against unemployment."

The Commission on Social Welfare agreed that unemployment benefit cover for the self-employed would not be appropriate, recommending that long-term insurance benefits only be provided for the self-employed through P.R.S.I. (Pl. 3851 p. 232).

The second contribution condition, that the claimant has 39 paid or credited contributions in the preceding contribution year, is not as forbidding as it first appears. The regulations governing the award of credits will, in the case of the newly-insured, former students, the unemployed and sick, result in the second condition being satisfied if the first contribution condition is met.

In relation to the second contribution condition, regulations provide that where entitlement would be established but for the fact that less than 39 paid or credited contributions have been registered in the last complete contribution year, reduced rates of benefit will be payable.

The third contribution condition requires the claimant to have reckonable weekly earnings in excess of a prescribed figure. This provision was inserted to ensure that part-time workers who became insurable in 1991 could not obtain unemployment benefit on the basis of a somewhat tenuous link with the social insurance system, *e.g.* work for one day and claim benefit for the five other days in the week. The prescribed amount, under S.I. No. 417 of 1994 is £69.99 per week.

Subsection (2)

This is a transitional measure which is attributable to the fact that the contribution conditions were amended in 1987 to increase the minimum number of qualifying contributions from 26 to 39.

Subsections (5) and (6)

Reduced rates of benefit are payable on a graduated basis under S.I. No. 417 of 1994.

Rate of benefit

44.—Subject to this Act, the weekly rate of unemployment benefit shall be as set out in column (2) of Part I of the Second Schedule.

GENERAL NOTE

Despite the recommendations of the Commission on Social Welfare, which supported the insurance principle and sought to maintain a payment differential of 10 per cent in favour of insurance based payments, the tendency in recent years has been to increase long-term assistance payments, so much so that unemployment assistance payments for the long-term unemployed are now higher, at least where nil means are established, than unemployment benefit scale rates. Statutory Instrument No. 166 of 1989 allows a claimant who is entitled to either unemployment benefit or unemployment assistance to elect which payment he or she wishes to receive. If assistance is chosen, the election can only be revoked if the unemployment assistance payment is reduced (*e.g.* as a result of an increase in means). This is now found in article 35 of S.I. No. 417 of 1994.

Increases for adult and child dependants

45.—(1) The weekly rate of unemployment benefit shall be increased by the amount set out in column (3) of Part I of the Second Schedule for any period during which the beneficiary has an adult dependant, subject to the restriction that except where regulations otherwise provide a beneficiary shall not be entitled for the same period to an increase of benefit under this subsection in respect of more than one person. [1995 (No. 2) Act, section 10]

(2) The weekly rate of unemployment benefit shall be increased by the amount set out in column (4) of Part I of the Second Schedule in respect of each qualified child who normally resides with the beneficiary. [1995 Act, Schedule F]

(3) Any increase of unemployment benefit payable pursuant to subsection (2) in respect of a qualified child who normally resides with a beneficiary and with the spouse of a beneficiary shall be payable at the rate of one-half of the appropriate amount in any case where the spouse of the beneficiary is not an adult dependant, and subsection (2) shall be construed and have effect accordingly.

GENERAL NOTE

See the General Note to section 34.

Duration of payment

46.—(1) A person who, in respect of any period of interruption of employment, has been entitled to unemployment benefit for 156 days shall not thereafter, subject to subsection (3), be entitled to that benefit for any day of unemployment (whether in the same or a subsequent period of interruption of employment) unless before that day he has requalified for benefit or unless, in the case of a person over 65 years of age, he has qualifying contributions in respect of not less than 156 contribution weeks in the period between his entry into insurance and the day for which unemployment benefit is claimed.

(2) Where a person entitled to unemployment benefit for 156 days has exhausted his right to unemployment benefit—

    (a) he shall requalify therefor when he has qualifying contributions in respect of 13 contribution weeks begun or ended since the last day for which he was entitled to that benefit, and

    (b) on his requalifying therefor, subsection (1) shall again apply to him, but, in a case where the period of interruption of employment in which he exhausted his right to that benefit continues after his requalification, as if the part before and the part after his requalification, as if the part before and the part after his requalification were distinct periods of interruption of employment.

(3) Subsection (1) shall, in respect of a person who is over the age of 18 years, have effect as if "390 days" were substituted for "156 days".

(4) Where a person entitled to unemployment benefit for 390 days has exhausted his right to that benefit—

    (a) he shall requalify therefor when he has qualifying contributions (other than optional contributions) [1995 Act, section 17] in respect of 13 contribution weeks begun or ended since the last day for which he was entitled to that benefit, and

    (b) on his requalifying therefor, subsections (1) and (3) shall again apply to him, but, in a case where the period of interruption of employment in which he exhausted his right to benefit continues after his requalification, as if the part before and the part after the exhaustion were distinct periods of interruption of employment.

(4A) Notwithstanding the provisions of this Chapter, in the case of a person who satisfies the contribution conditions contained in section 43 by virtue of having paid optional contributions—

(a) where he has been entitled to unemployment benefit for 78 days in any benefit year he shall not thereafter be entitled to the said benefit in respect of any day of unemployment in that benefit year, and

(b) the first day of unemployment in any benefit year shall be treated as the commencement of a separate period of interruption of employment. [1993 (No. 2) Act, section 8]

(5) Regulations may provide for treating a person for the purposes of this section as having been entitled to benefit for any day if he would have been so entitled but for any delay or failure on his part to make or prosecute a claim:

Provided that a person shall not be so treated where he shows that he did not intend, by failing to acquire or establish a right to benefit for that day, to avoid the necessity of requalifying for benefit under this section.

(6) For the purposes of this section, any day in respect of which a person receives unemployment assistance while he is entitled to unemployment benefit shall be treated as though it were a day in respect of which unemployment benefit was paid.

(7) For the purposes of this section, any period in respect of which a person is disqualified for receiving unemployment benefit by virtue of subsection (4) of section 47 shall be treated as through it were a period in respect of which unemployment benefit was paid.

(8) Where, in any period of interruption of employment, a person was in receipt of unemployment benefit on the 11th day of April, 1991 for more than 155 days, subsection (4)(a) shall be construed as if a reference to "since the 156th day for which he was entitled to that benefit" was substituted for the reference to "since the last day for which he was entitled to that benefit".

GENERAL NOTE

Subsection (1) limits the duration of entitlement for a person aged under 18 to 156 days of unemployment. A person aged over 65 is similarly limited unless that person has qualifying contributions for an aggregate of three years since entry into insurance and the day for which benefit is claimed. Subsection (3) invalidates subsection (1) if the claimant is aged over 18 years, in which case benefit is payable for 390 days (*i.e.* 15 months) of unemployment.

Subsections (2) and (4) provide that re-qualification occurs upon payment of 13 qualifying contributions. Entitlement is then re-established, subject to subsection (1), or subsections (1) to (3). However, there is no linkage and the second period of entitlement stands apart from the first period. Re-qualification requires the claimant to pay these contributions at the end of the period of entitlement rather than dating the currency of the claim. However, this is relaxed by subsection (8) for claimants entitled to benefit on April 11, 1991. The previous rule was that re-qualification could be established from qualifying contributions made after day 156 in a 390-day period of entitlement. Optional contributions do not count for these purposes: 1995 Act, section 17.

Subsection (5) relaxes the rule which requires a claim to be made promptly. In relation to unemployment benefit the governing regulation is S.I. No. 417 of 1994.

Subsections (6) and (7) provide that entitlement periods continue to run, notwithstanding a decision to opt for unemployment assistance under S.I. No. 417 of 1994 or a disqualification under section 47(4) respectively.

Disqualifications

47.—(1) A person who has lost employment by reason of a stoppage of work which was due to a trade dispute at the factory, workshop, farm or other premises or place at which he was employed shall be disqualified for receiving unemployment benefit so long as the stoppage of work continues, except in a case where he has, during the stoppage of work, become *bona fide* employed elsewhere in the occupation which he usually follows or has become regularly engaged in some other occupation:

Provided that the foregoing provisions of this subsection shall not apply to a person who is not participating in or directly interested in the trade dispute which caused the stoppage of work.

(2) Where separate branches of work which are commonly carried on as separate businesses in separate premises or at separate places are in any case carried on in separate departments on the same premises or at the same place, each of those departments shall, for the purposes of subsection (1), be deemed to be a separate factory, workshop or farm or separate premises or a separate place, as the case may be.

(3) A person shall be disqualified for receiving unemployment benefit during any week in which he is employed under a scheme administered by An Foras Áiseanna Saothair and known as Community Employment. [1995 Act, section 18]

(4) A person shall be disqualified for receiving unemployment benefit for such period not exceeding nine weeks as may be determined under the provisions of this Act if he—

(a) has lost his employment through his own misconduct or has voluntarily left his employment without just cause,

(b) has refused an offer of suitable employment,

(c) has without good cause refused or failed to avail himself of any reasonable opportunity of receiving training provided or approved of by An Foras Áiseanna Saothair as suitable in his case,

(d) has failed or neglected to avail himself of any reasonable opportunity of obtaining suitable employment, or

(e) being a person under the age of 55 years who, in accordance with the Redundancy Payments Acts, 1967 to 1991, has been dismissed by his employer by reason of redundancy, has received or is entitled to receive any moneys, in excess of a prescribed amount, in respect of that redundancy under the said Acts or under an agreement with his employer,

and the period of disqualification shall commence on the day on which the loss or leaving of employment, refusal, failure, neglect or redundancy (as the case may be) occurred.

(5) Regulations may also provide for imposing in the case of any class of persons additional conditions with respect to the receipt of unemployment benefit and restrictions on the rate and duration thereof, if, having regard to special circumstances, it appears to the Minister necessary so to do for the purpose of preventing inequalities or preventing injustice.

(6) For the purpose of this section, employment shall not be deemed to be suitable employment in the case of any person if it is—

(a) employment in a situation vacant in consequence of a stoppage of work due to a trade dispute,

(b) employment in the district where he was last ordinarily employed at a rate of remuneration lower, or on conditions less favourable, than those which he habitually obtained in his usual employment in that district, or would have obtained had he continued to be so employed, or

(c) employment in any other district at a rate of remuneration lower, or on conditions less favourable, than those generally observed in that district by agreement between associations of employers and of employees or, failing such agreement, than those generally recognised in that district by good employers.

GENERAL NOTE

Subsection (1)

The trade dispute disqualification. The availability of social welfare payments to persons who are unemployed as the result of a trade dispute is an issue that generates a greater range of opinion, and perhaps uninformed comment, than any other in the entire field of social welfare law. The reasons for this are obvious: there are complex issues of industrial and social policy at stake here and in most cases of industrial conflict there are powerful industrial forces at odds with each other, to say nothing of the interest that the State has in ensuring the continuity of essential goods and services as well as economic production which will be vital to the economic well-being of the nation. Within this context it will be obvious that any normative structure that addresses (or fails to recognise) the effect that industrial conflict has on normal employment patterns, will be accused by one of the interest groups as being biased or partial. As will be seen, Irish law attempts to steer some kind of middle course in an attempt to meet the merits of each case and at the same time ensure that important principles and procedures, which are an essential part of good industrial relations, are fostered and encouraged.

There are two general theories which, from time to time, are used to explain why persons prevented from working by a trade dispute should not be eligible for social welfare payments. The first, and least satisfactory, is predicated on the view that the worker is, in such a situation, voluntarily unemployed. This theory does not hold water, because it would be necessary to distinguish between cases where the unemployment results from a strike by workers as against a lock-out or even a dismissal following a work-to-rule. Even under the Elizabethan poor law and its nineteenth century accretions, the manner in which a worker became unemployed was irrelevant to questions of entitlement to poor relief: Jennings 46 L.Q.R. 225. This position has been carried forward into legislation governing unemployment benefit.

In one English case (noted at p. 147 of Calvert, *Social Security Law*), a group of workers who were originally on strike indicated to their employer that they were prepared to return to work on a given date. The employer refused to allow them to return on that date. A National Insurance Tribunal held that after that date it could not be said that it was the fault of the men that work did not resume until a much later date. The Commissioner reversed the decision of the Tribunal, saying that the legislation is "not directed to disqualification on the ground of fault". The Commissioner referred to previous decisions in which the disqualification had been imposed to prevent the insurance fund from providing finance to employees during strikes *or lock-outs*. This proposition has led to the formulation of a second explanation for the non-availability of social welfare payments to strikers. The reason why the cause of the stoppage of work is not relevant is attributable to the neutrality theory. While neutrality has various nuances, the central issue is a reluctance to allow state payments to influence the outcome of a dispute, not simply because the insurance fund or the Exchequer would be depleted in sponsoring an economically wasteful activity, but because it is feared that if state support for strikers were widely available then industrial conflict could be encouraged or precipitated. Rather than attempt to investigate the legal, economic and industrial relations issues that lie beneath each dispute, it is more convenient for the statutory authorities to shelter behind the sham of a "neutrality" theory. The theory, loosely drawn from international law, is singularly inappropriate because it does not compare like with like: it is only the unemployed workers who are seeking, or eligible for, state payments. The theory is also quite unreal when the state is effectively the employer, or where the underlying conflict is the result of government policies on pay or redundancies.

Historical Background. The provisions in Irish social welfare law governing financial support for strikers and their families closely resemble those that have evolved in the U.K., although legislation in recent years has resulted in very significant differences, particularly in the U.K. where recent changes indicate that an overtly partisan approach is now in vogue. This traditional unity of approach is hardly surprising, given the historical relationship between the two jurisdictions. Indeed, section 87(1) of the National Insurance Act, 1911, the foundation upon which the trade dispute disqualification was subsequently built, was in force in Ireland when the Irish Free State came into being in 1922. Both the National Insurance Act, 1911 and the Unemployment Insurance Act, 1920, also in force in the Irish Free State, were repealed by section 66 of and Schedule 5 to the Social Welfare Act, 1952.

Until 1967, however, the trade dispute disqualification was not altered in any way, the 1952 Act simply re-enacting the original trade dispute disqualification of 1920. The disqualification was in the following terms:

> "A person who has lost employment by reason of a stoppage of work which was due to a trade dispute at the factory, workshop, farm or other premises or place at which he was employed shall be disqualified for receiving unemployment benefit so long as the stoppage of work continues, except in a case where he has, during the stoppage of work, become *bona fide* employed elsewhere in the occupation which he usually follows or has become regularly engaged in some other occupation".

The trade dispute disqualification operated harshly as all the statutory authority had to show in order to effect the disqualification was that the worker was unemployed due to a stoppage of work within the place where he or she worked. The geographical test (see Gennard, *Financing Strikers*, p. 15) failed to discriminate between workers involved in the dispute and others who were merely caught up in the dispute. This was amended in 1924 in the U.K. The effect of the 1924 amendment was to narrow down the general disqualification by permitting workers to show that if they were not financing, participating in or directly interested in the outcome of the trade dispute then they should be entitled to unemployment benefit. Even this amendment was unsatisfactory because, as the General Strike of 1926 illustrated, workers who were laid-off in one industry in one part of the country could be disqualified under the "grade or class" provision if members of that grade or class were "financing" the dispute, notwithstanding the fact that those workers were members of another trade union opposed to the interests of those laid-off. Despite the difficulties associated with the 1924 amendment effected in the U.K., it was something of an improvement on the original disqualification. During the Committee Stage of the Unemployment Insurance Bill, 1924 an amendment was tabled in Dáil Eireann to the trade dispute disqualification contained in the 1920 Act, the effect of which would have been to give benefit to a worker who was not participating in the trade dispute if that worker did not belong to a grade or class of workers, members of which were participating in the trade dispute. The Minister for Industry and Commerce, Mr. McGilligan (7 *Dáil Debates* Col. 2557) rejected this amendment because he could not agree with such a breach of the neutrality principle: "if it gives the opportunity for the use of unemployment benefit to aid either party to a trade dispute, I cannot accept it".

Further attempts to relax the disqualification were made *via* trade union pressure over many years, a fact acknowledged in the Dáil Debates relating to the general issue of disqualification for unemployment benefit under what ultimately became the Social Welfare Act, 1952. It seems, however, that the difficulty of framing legislation resolving the issues in a satisfactory manner induced a kind of paralysis in Irish legislators: indeed, the complexity of the issue seems to have prevented the unions from forming any very clear picture of what form legislative amendment of the 1920 Act should take. The Oireachtas in 1967 eventually implemented a proviso to the disqualification. The "geographical test" was amended by the Social Welfare (Miscellaneous Provisions) Act, 1967, which added the following proviso to section 17(2) of the 1952 Act:

"Provided that the foregoing provisions of this subsection shall not apply to a person who (a) is not participating in or financing or directly interested in the trade dispute which caused the stoppage of work, and (b) does not belong to a grade or class of workers of which, immediately before the commencement of the stoppage, there were members employed at his place of employment any of whom are participating in or financing or directly interested in the dispute".

This 1967 Act meant that Irish law on unemployment benefit for strikers was, at this time, virtually identical to that which operated within the U.K. Nevertheless the 1967 reforms were not to be the final solution to the trade dispute disqualification. It is somewhat ironic that the trade dispute disqualification was brought into line with the U.K. model at exactly the same time as the Royal Commission on Trade Unions and Employers Associations 1965–68 (Cmnd. 3623) (Donovan) reported, *i.e.* June 1968. The trade dispute disqualification, the Royal Commission felt, was in need of quite substantial amendment. The Royal Commission were particularly critical of the "financing" and "grade or class" provisions. Of the "financing" provision, the Royal Commission pointed out that workers laid off could be deprived of benefit simply because their union made funds available to other workers (or their union) who were disqualified for involvement in the trade dispute: see Cmnd. paras. 983–991. The "financing" provision is discussed by Calvert, *Social Security Law* (2nd ed.) pp. 166–170. The Royal Commission also attacked the "grade or class" provision as resting on a "fallacious" notion of community of interest amongst all workers and, further, said the provision was capable of producing "considerable injustice". Both these provisions were deleted from the U.K. statute book by section 111(1) of the Employment Protection Act, 1975 (see now section 44 of the Social Security Act, 1986). In Ireland both the "financing" and "grade or class" provisions have attracted academic and trade union hostility: see Kerr & Whyte, *Irish Trade Union Law* (1985) pp. 365–9 and Clark, *Towards the Just Strike?* (1985) 48 M.L.R. 659 at 676–7. The Ombudsman, commenting on the outcome of one adjudication by the Social Welfare Tribunal, recommended the repeal of the "grade or class" provision: see (1985) M.L.R. 659 at 669–70.

Section 13 of the No. 2 Act of 1987 repealed both the "financing" and "grade or class" provisions.

The disqualification. Although the trade dispute disqualification has not been considered by the ordinary counts either in Britain or in Ireland, other than on a few occasions, the few judicial decisions that do exist, allied to the considerable number of decisions made by the statutory authorities charged with interpreting the disqualification, indicate that the disqualification throws up issues of considerable complexity. Many of the decisions seem contrary to both common sense and lack any sound policy basis, a fact acknowledged even by the judges and Commissioners involved!

Stoppage of work. One preliminary issue that can arise is this: does the term "stoppage of work" cover only cases where workers cease to work, thereby halting production at the premises or place of employment, or does the term simply refer to a stoppage of work by workers, regardless of whether or not production at the workplace is affected. The Tribunal and Commissioner decisions in the U.K. are considered at pages 149–151 of Calvert, *Social Security Law* who points out that the tendency is to find that a "stoppage of work" takes place even if production at the factory is not brought to an end (*e.g.* by a handful of workers doing extra duties normally carried out by others who have withdrawn their labour), as long as there is a significant interference with work at the premises or place of employment. It has also been decided in the U.K. that while a work-to-rule does not amount to a "stoppage of work" other industrial action that precipitates a dismissal can fall within the term "stoppage of work". A lock-out that follows a "go- slow" may constitute "a stoppage": the vital element here is the dismissal by the employer of the workforce. Seen in this context, the High Court decision of McMahon J. in *State (Kearns) v. Minister for Social Welfare* (February 11, 1982) illustrates that a similar approach is taken in Ireland. Clover Meats had two meat-processing plants, one processing beef and the other processing pig meat. Due to diminishing orders and supplies of material, the company decided to close the beef factory and lay off workers from that plant. The union claimed that layoffs should depend on seniority of position in each plant. The company refused to accept the inconvenience and additional costs such a course of action would involve and rejected this submission. All employees were accordingly dismissed. The workers were refused unemployment benefit by a deciding officer and an appeals officer on the ground that there was a trade dispute which had led to a stoppage of work. No industrial action had commenced or been threatened. McMahon J. upheld these decisions. It seems that the learned judge viewed the disagreement and failure to agree on a redundancy plan as a "trade dispute" and the dismissals were in turn a "stoppage of work". Calvert, however, indicates that there have been cases in which workers have refused to work but, notwithstanding this, the impact on the workplace has not been profound enough to lead to a "stoppage of work".

In the U.K., legislation has amended the trade dispute disqualification to cover situations where an employee withdraws his labour as a result of a trade dispute with the employer but no stoppage of work results. Section 44(1) of the Social Security Act, 1986 substitutes a new section 19(1) for the old provision contained in the Social Security Act, 1975. This new section provides, *inter alia*, that an employed earner who has withdrawn his labour in furtherance of a trade dispute is disqualified for any day on which his labour remains withdrawn.

The disqualification may end if the stoppage of work, while initially caused by a trade dispute, continues but for some other reason. The test advanced in English Commissioner decisions, as approved by the Divisional Court in *R. v. Chief National Insurance Commissioner, ex p. Dawber* [1981] J.S.W.L. 304, is directed towards considering whether the intervening act breaks the chain of causation. In order for the event not to break the chain of causation, the occurrence must be the natural and probable result of the dispute and must be reasonably foreseeable by the parties to the dispute. Thus in *Dawber,* a stoppage of work at a glassworks was initially the result of a stoppage of work caused by a trade dispute. This created an unsafe situation *vis-à-vis* the furnace and some workers returned to "hold" the furnace but the roof of the furnace fell in. The management wrote to all workers that the strike had caused the collapse of the furnace roof. Remedial work had to be undertaken and all staff were laid-off for several weeks. At around this time the dispute was settled. Forbes J. refused to interfere with the Commissioner's decision to disqualify the claimants on the ground that the stoppage never ceased to be due to the trade dispute.

Trade dispute. Section 2(1) of the Principal Act defines a trade dispute as

"any dispute between employers and employees, or between employees and employees, which is connected with the employment or non-employment or the terms of employment or the conditions of employment of any persons, whether employees in the employment of the employer with whom the dispute arises or not."

This statutory definition is identical with the corresponding provision in the U.K. and is based on the definition of trade dispute set out in the Trade Disputes Act, 1906. As Ogus and Barendt point out in *The Law of Social Security* (Butterworths), the use of a statutory definition intended to provide nguidance on the question of immunity from legal liability in tort in a quite different context, has produced some curious decisions in the context of entitlement to unemployment benefit. Wedderburn also comments on the pragmatic position the claimant will have to adopt when industrial conflict breaks out: for the purpose of protection from tortious liability *via* the immunity under the 1906 Act the claimant must urge a wide construction upon a court, but when the same person seeks to claim social security he must argue for "a narrow construction that might allow him to escape the net of disqualification": *per* Wedderburn, *The Worker and the Law* (Penguin), p. 677.

Notwithstanding this, the statutory authorities have invoked the cases governing the statutory immunity, holding them applicable to the social security issue. Thus a worker who does not work after being persuaded by pickets placed outside his or her place of work (even though the pickets are not in dispute with the employer carrying on work at the place picketed) may be disqualified. In such a case it has been held that there is a trade dispute between the pickets and the claimant even though the pickets are not employed by the claimant's employer. To this extent it was irrelevant that at no time was there any dispute between the claimant and his own employer, although the Commissioner said that it was certainly arguable that there was a dispute between the pickets and the claimant himself: see Social Security Decision No. *R(U) 1/74.*

It is also likely that subtle differences of approach will emerge on whether there is a necessary link between the dispute and "the employment or non-employment or the terms of employment or the conditions of employment of any persons". The neutrality principle has traditionally prevented the statutory authorities from investigating the underlying causes of the trade dispute in order to rule on the appropriateness of state support for workers who may be coerced into agreeing to less favourable terms and conditions of employment. A lock-out may therefore be invoked by an employer in an attempt to force the workforce to accept a variation, unilateral or otherwise, in their terms and conditions of employment. While one may feel little sympathy for workers who refuse to accept new work practices and, in doing so, throw the employment of others into jeopardy, it is unfortunate that unjustifiable coercion or duress by an employer is ignored under the traditional features of the trade dispute disqualification. The Irish judiciary adopt, as Kerr and Whyte point out in *Irish Trade Union Law* at p. 274, a very restrictive approach to the "trade dispute" immunity under the Trade Disputes Act, 1906. Whether this means that persons who find themselves unemployed as a result of politically motivated action escape the trade dispute disqualification for the purposes of social security on the ground that no "trade dispute" exists is pure conjecture, although Kerr and Whyte suggest that in logic this result would follow from the immunity cases.

Separate place of business. Section 47(2) must be distinguished from the proviso to subsection (1). Section 47(2) directs that if there is a separate business in progress, this will be sufficient to enable the claimant to obtain unemployment benefit without having to resort to the proviso.

In the U.K. it has proved difficult to satisfy the "separate business" requirement. It is not enough to show that separate trades or activities are carried on in the workplace. There should be distinct and separate industrial or manufacturing processes involved, each of which is capable of being carried on as a separate business and, further, it must be shown that the trade or activity is commonly carried on elsewhere.

In one of the most influential of the National Insurance Commissioner's decisions, workers in a trim shop were laid off as a result of a trade dispute at the Ford Motor Company Dagenham works. The Dagenham operation was carried on at three plants on the estate. It was held that the estate was, for national insurance purposes, a factory for the production of vehicles and not merely a number of distinct factories producing components. Alternatively, the three plants constituted one factory rather than three distinct factories. It was not sufficient to hold that the trim shop in one plant was a distinct department. Evidence that trim could be obtained from one other source was not evidence of a separate business or process of trim manufacture being recognised as a distinct industrial or commercial activity: Social Security Decision No. *R(U)1/70.*

Bona fide employed elsewhere. Compliance with this requirement is the only way in which a person disqualified for receipt of unemployment benefit can obtain benefit at some time during the future while the stoppage of work continues. Upon commencement of the stoppage of work a member of the workforce may find employment elsewhere than in their normal place of employment. If it is intended as a temporary measure, to tide the worker over until such time as the stoppage of work is at an end, then the worker will not satisfy the *bona fide* part of the statutory provision. If, however, the claimant intends to break with the former employer, then the fact that the employment taken is for a limited period of time does not necessarily lead to the conclusion that the employment is not *bona fide* employment elsewhere. The *bona fide* employment elsewhere does not apply where the claimant loses employment due to a stoppage of work but who regains employment at the normal place of employment (*e.g.* by passing pickets) only to lose employment again for some other reason: *Cartlidge v. Chief Adjudication Officer* [1986] 2 All E.R. 1.

The proviso to subsection (1). The proviso involves a very important temporal problem. The tense employed is the present tense—"is not participating etc.". The Social Security Commissioners have taken the view that the proviso can only apply to persons who have never been disqualified by virtue of the trade dispute provision *vis-à-vis* the current stoppage of work. Once the claimant has been rightly disqualified, the fact that some new or intervening event can, as a matter of causation, be shown to be the reason why the claimant is not currently in employment (*e.g.* redundancy or illness) is regarded as irrelevant. The words "is not participating" refer to a requirement that the claimant show that, *on the day in question*, the claimant is not participating in, financing or directly interested in the outcome of the dispute, notwithstanding a determination that, at the time of the initial stoppage, the claimant was so involved in the dispute. While this conclusion is not an inevitable or even a natural interpretation of the proviso, it is justified on the ground that if the law were otherwise, the "*bona fide* employed elsewhere" exception would be redundant. While there are conflicting decisions on this point, the decision of the Court of Appeal in *Cartlidge v. Chief Adjudication Officer (supra)* puts the question beyond doubt in the U.K. Cartlidge was employed as a mineworker by the National Coal Board. On March 10, 1984 Cartlidge was given 12 weeks' notice of termination of his employment in pursuance of an application made by him with regard to voluntary redundancy. On March 23 there was a stoppage of work at his place of employment as part of a national coalworkers' strike over wages and colliery closures. Cartlidge did not support the strike but was prevented from working because of violent mass picketing for eight days. After that time Cartlidge did gain access to his place of employment save for a further eight-day period. Despite the stoppage of work Cartlidge worked at his place of employment on those days. On June 2, 1984 the 12-week period of notice expired. Cartlidge applied for unemployment benefit on June 5 but both the adjudication officer and the Tribunal of Commissioners held that the disqualification was to operate for as long as the stoppage of work at his place of employment lasted. The fact that the stoppage of work commenced after Cartlidge began to work his period of notice, which expired during the currency of the stoppage, did not displace the fact that Cartlidge had lost his employment due to a stoppage of work. Nor did the disqualification cease when Cartlidge resumed his employment at his place of work. The Court of Appeal, unanimously, but with regret, found that the words of the statute were clear and felt that previous decisions of the Tribunal of Commissioners, notably Social Security Decision No. *R(U)12/72,* were not incorrectly decided. Once the stoppage of work commences the fact that a worker subsequently, but during the currency of the stoppage, finds employment, is only relevant to the *bona fide* elsewhere exception if the employment is employment elsewhere. As Lincoln J. said, "the obstinate fact remains that the court cannot construe the phrase 'employed elsewhere' as if it read 'employed anywhere' ". *Cartlidge v. Chief Adjudication Officer* is no longer effective after section 44 of the U.K. Social Security Act, 1986 but the decision would be persuasive in Ireland.

Participating. Although there are no Irish cases involving the notion of participating in the trade dispute that caused the stoppage of work, it is safe to say that one participates in the trade dispute if one knowingly does or abstains from doing something that contributes to the onset or continuance of the stoppage of work. This proposition is illustrated by Social Security Decision No. *R(U)41/56,* cited by Calvert *Social Security Law* at p. 165. A worker was contractually bound to carry out two kinds of work when directed. He usually worked as a repairer but could be required to work as a brusher. When a strike was called by brushers the employer directed that he take on this work but the worker declined so to do. This refusal was held to make the worker a participant in the stoppage of work. Calvert indicates that this result may also follow if a worker declines to take on alternative work created by a stoppage of work by others, even if there is no finding that the worker was contractually bound to take on this work. Presumably this proposition hinges on a requirement that the contract of employment requires a worker faithfully to serve the employer, although it is submitted that the task directed must be closely related to that worker's usual occupation.

Many of the British cases involve the circumstances surrounding the calling of a stoppage of work. Failure to attend a union meeting where a decision to call a strike is made has been held not to amount to participation on the ground that abstention does not amount to participation: Social Security Decision No. *R(U)5/66.* This line of authority, according to U.K. precedents, is a narrow one. If the claimant votes to continue or prolong the strike, the claimant participates. Indeed, a claimant who votes to end the strike may also participate if it is clear that, notwithstanding the claimant's opposition, the claimant will abide by the decision of the majority: Social Security Decision No. *R3/68 UB.* Within the context of this distinction between participating in the process whereby the stoppage of work is commenced or prolonged and disassociating oneself from the stoppage or trade dispute, guidance has been given in Social Security Decision No. *R(U)2/85,* a decision of Social Security Commissioner J. G. Mitchell. A trade dispute arose out of the employer's proposal to implement compulsory redundancies when a programme of voluntary redundancies failed to shed a required number of workers from employment. The claimant was not selected for compulsory redundancy and was not therefore "directly interested". He did however attend two mass meetings to vote in support of opposition to these redundancies, but he opposed and disassociated himself from later action, including a factory occupation which was led by shop stewards and forced the stoppage of work. The claimant informed his employer he would work at any other factory after the stoppage occurred. Commissioner Mitchell held that the issue of participation is to be decided in the context of the initial stoppage of work. At that time clear evidence of disassociation is needed and this claimant could not prove disassociation from the mere fact that he did not join in the occupation and that the mass meetings which he did attend did not direct the shop stewards to initiate the occupation which caused the stoppage of work.

Directly interested. In cases where a group of workers are participating in a strike which has the effect of laying off another group of workers until such time as the strike ends, it is possible to hold that, in an extended sense, the workers laid off are directly interested in the dispute because their own prospects of returning to employment depend on the resolution of the strike or trade dispute. The statutory authorities in Britain have refused to accept this extended meaning of "directly interested", because to do so would render the proviso, in the words of one National Insurance Commissioner, "otiose and impossible of application" (*Social Security Decision No. R(U)3/69*). Instead, the statutory authorities have attempted to distinguish between cases where the workers laid off are indirectly and those where they are directly interested in the outcome of the dispute, a distinction which the Donovan Commission characterised as "notoriously difficult". The Donovan Commission declined to provide a definition, preferring to leave the matter to the courts as a matter of interpretation. If the worker laid off stands to benefit from the industrial action taken by others—where a bonus payment or an improved physical work environment will enure to that worker, as well as those striking in order to secure this concession—then that worker will be directly interested, particularly if the contractual terms of employment between the strikers and those laid off are identical *vis-à-vis* the employer. In the absence of a formal contractual link of this kind the statutory authorities must predict the consequences for worker A if a strike between the employer and workers B and C is resolved, in favour of either a change in or an affirmation of existing conditions of employment. The decision of the House of Lords in *Presho v. Insurance Officer* [1984] 1 All E.R. 97 is a definitive statement on when a worker is directly interested in the trade dispute. The claimant, a production worker, was laid off as a result of a strike by maintenance staff at the factory where she was employed. The dispute, about pay increases, was settled by the maintenance staff's trade union (AUEW) a few days later. Presho meanwhile had been refused unemployment benefit on the ground that she was directly interested in the outcome of the trade dispute, notwithstanding the fact that she was a member of another trade union (USDAW) which had not submitted a similar pay demand. The House of Lords, acting on a finding that if the AUEW demand was conceded it would automatically be conceded to USDAW workers as well, indicated that the fact that the extension of the pay agreement to USDAW workers might only follow after formal negotiations between USDAW and the employer did not prevent the claimant from being directly interested in the trade dispute. In giving the leading judgment in the House of Lords, Lord Brandon said:

"I would hold that, where different groups of workers, belonging to different unions, are employed by the same employers at the same place of work and there is a trade dispute between the common employers and one of the unions to which one of the groups of workers belong, those in the other groups of workers belonging to other unions are directly, and not merely indirectly, interested in that trade dispute provided that two conditions are fulfilled. The first condition is that, whatever may be the outcome of the trade dispute, it will be applied by the common employers not only to the group of workers belonging to the one union participating in the dispute, but also to the other groups of workers belonging to the other unions concerned. The second condition is that this application of the outcome of the dispute 'across the board', as it has been aptly described, should come about automatically as a result of one or other of three things: first, a collective agreement which is legally binding; or, second, a collective agreement which is not legally binding; or, third, established industrial custom and practice at the place of work concerned."

Thus, in *Cartlidge v. Insurance Officer (supra)* the Court of Appeal, applying Lord Brandon's approach, held that a claimant who was both opposed to the stoppage and serving out his notice when a stoppage of work occurred (his notice and employment expiring during the currency of the stoppage) could nevertheless be directly interested in the trade dispute. The possibility of retrospective payment being made to all workers was held to prevent the claimant from satisfying the proviso.

The Social Welfare Tribunal. Unemployment payments for persons affected by an industrial dispute or stoppage of work may, notwithstanding section 47, be available following a decision by the Social Welfare Tribunal that claimants have been unreasonably deprived of employment. This issue is examined in depth in the General Notes to sections 274–6 below.

Subsection (4)

Disqualification under subsection (4).

A claimant may satisfy the contribution conditions and the condition that he or she be unemployed and yet may be disqualified from receipt of unemployment benefit. Apart from the trade dispute disqualification, considered separately above, there are several circumstances in which the claimant will be denied benefit because unemployment is perceived to be attributable to the claimant's own conduct. In this wider sense unemployment is seen as voluntary even though the claimant may not have anticipated or desired unemployment to result from the claimant's actions. The disqualification provision currently found in Irish social welfare law is contained in section 47(4) of the Principal Act. Section 87(2) of the National Insurance Act, 1911 contained a not dissimilar provision and the Unemployment Insurance Act, 1920 carried this on so that, at the foundation of the State in 1922, voluntary unemployment, within the relevant statute, was a ground for disqualification from receipt of unemployment benefit. Amendments to the disqualification provision were made in 1952, 1967 and 1992.

Subsection (4)(a)

Lost his employment through his own misconduct. As Ogus and Barendt point out in *The Law of Social Security* (Butterworths),misconduct as a ground for disqualification has been an essential part of unemployment law since the inception of unemployment insurance in 1911, but the exact policy basis for this disqualification has never been made wholly explicit. Ogus and Barendt invoke three alternative theories:

(i) *Punishment.* The first, that of punishment, is predicated on the view that a person dismissed for misconduct is not a worthy recipient of support from the insurance fund. This rationale, Ogus and Barendt point out, has been rejected in the U.K. but it is still an operative factor in some American jurisdictions. There are other common law jurisdictions in which moral opprobrium that attaches to unethical behaviour may produce similar practical consequences.

(ii) *Unsuitability.* According to this theory the claimant should be disqualified where the claimant's own actions disclose unsuitability for the job. Only persons who lose employment through external circumstances, rather than their own lack of ability, should receive unemployment compensation. This proposition enables the statutory authorities to determine, on an objective basis, that the claimant's behaviour or professional incompetence is an adequate basis upon which to disqualify the claimant from benefit. This theory is a convenient one because it overcomes many of the difficulties associated with the subjectively-based third possibility, that of voluntary unemployment. However, the unsuitability theory does not always readily explain all situations in which a claimant may be dismissed for misconduct and subsequently disqualified from unemployment benefit.

(iii) *Voluntary unemployment.* The public purse, or social insurance fund, as the case may be should be protected from claims made for financial support by persons who know or should be expected to know that their conduct was reasonably likely to result in dismissal. This theory does provide a very attractive basis for explaining many of the decisions. Ogus and Barendt point out that there are difficulties with this theory, however, because it depends on proof as to the mental state of the employee and that because the mental state of the employee is determined by reference to subjective factors, the voluntary unemployment theory seems difficult to apply. Ogus and Barendt conclude that the suitability theory is perhaps the most satisfactory way of explaining the majority of the cases.

Lewis, at [1985] J.S.W.L. 145 rejects these arguments and doubts whether a misconduct rule is required.

The meaning of "misconduct". Some guidance on the meaning to be attached to the word misconduct, which, for social security purposes, is nowhere defined in Irish or English law, can be found in the cases which decide when and in what circumstances an employer may be entitled to terminate the contract of employment for misconduct by the employee. The common law power to dismiss summarily (*i.e.* dismiss an employee without giving the common law or statutory notice normally required to terminate the contract of employment) may be exercised in a variety of circumstances. In the view of the Court of Exchequer in *Kean v. Fitzgerald* (1894) 28 I.L.T. 620, a master is justified in dismissing his servant without previous notice if the conduct of the servant is inconsistent or incompatible with the due or faithful discharge of his duty to his master; or if the servant wilfully disobeys any lawful order of his master, or is guilty of such moral misconduct, or such a violation or non-performance of any express or implied obligation, undertaking, or duty imposed on him by or involved in his contract of service, as is either prejudicial to his master, or is likely to render his continuance in the service prejudicial to his master. Despite the fact that this proposition is almost one century old a recent study of English law indicates that existing tribunal decisions suggest it is directly relevant today: Lewis [1985] J.S.W.L. 145. Normally, the misconduct is associated with the employment. In *Harrington v. Gleeson* (1897) 31 I.C.T. 429, a farm worker was summarily dismissed because he could not adequately operate a threshing machine. The employer was held entitled to dismiss because there was an implied condition that the plaintiff would be fit to do the work required. However, it is doubtful whether a dismissal for incompetence will be followed by a determination that, for benefit purposes, the claimant is guilty of misconduct. In the U.K. the misconduct concept is somewhat narrower than the test in *Kean v. Fitzgerald*. An employer may be entitled to protect the economic viability of a business by dismissing an incompetent worker, even though the worker may be attempting to meet the employer's expectations. The fact that the worker is simply not able to discharge adequately his or her contractual duties will entitle the employer to dismiss. When the dismissed employee claims unemployment benefit, the issue of misconduct will not be resolved simply by holding that the employer was entitled to dismiss. Blameworthiness must be proved. In the U.K. a distinction is drawn between mere carelessness (*e.g.* incompetence, fecklessness, indolence) and "the more deliberate or the more serious type of carelessness": Social Security Decision No. *R(U)8/57*. Dismissal due to negligence in the discharge of contractual duties seems to mark the boundary between misconduct in the sense intended by the legislature and carelessness. One National Insurance Commissioner expressed the view that behaviour which falls within the definition of misconduct *is* behaviour which is "blameworthy, reprehensible and wrong": Social Security Decision No. *R(U)2/77*. For this reason the National Insurance Commissioner there held that British Railways workers, who lost their jobs because they refused to accept, as a condition of their continued employment, that they were bound to join a trade union under a post-entry closed-shop agreement struck between the employer and railway unions, had been dismissed for misconduct. The applicants lost their employment, not because they refused to satisfy their contracts of employment but because the employer wished to carry out obligations owed to third parties, namely the unions. The fact that after *Meskill v. C.I.E.* [1973] I.R. 121, such conduct would be an actionable conspiracy, designed to ensure that a worker abstains from exercising an implicit constitutional right not to join a trade union, suggests that the position in Ireland would be the same *vis-à-vis* the question of dismissal for misconduct. Most cases of dismissal involve a deliberate act on the part of the employee in circumstances in which the employee's behaviour arises out of, or is connected with, the employment. A refusal to follow orders given by the employer (*Brewster v. Burke* H.C. February 8, 1978), swearing at the employer in a deliberately offensive manner (*Pepper v. Webb* [1969] 2 All E.R. 216), and assaulting the employer or the customers or clients of the employer would clearly fall within the notion of misconduct, as would some acts of carelessness. Not all actions however will *ipso facto* entitle the employer to dismiss. In *Power v. Binchy* [1929] 64 I.L.T.R. 35, it was held that non-attendance at work on one occasion does not constitute misconduct so as to justify dismissal. The Employment Appeal Tribunal has also held that not all cases of breach of the employee's duty to serve faithfully an employer automatically entitle the employer to dismiss. In *Mullen v. C.I.E. UD 54/1979*, a CIE bus driver worked in his leisure hours as a coach driver for a private bus company. The Tribunal held that this alone would not justify summary dismissal. The driver should be warned as to future conduct and if at some future time another breach of the duty occurs the employee may then be dismissed.

Some cases of misconduct may also involve issues of qualification or competence. A driver who loses his or her driving licence following conviction for a criminal offence does something "reprehensible, blameworthy and wrong" in order to attract such a punishment, even though some road traffic offences may be strict liability offences. While most cases of misconduct will be related to the contractual setting, a conviction for a criminal offence, which is not directly related to the contract of employment, may constitute misconduct, especially if the contractual relationship is prejudiced by a conviction for sex offences (Social Security Decision No. *R(U)1/71*) or dishonesty (*Singh v. LCBS* [1976] I.R.L.R. 176). When the dismissal follows from conduct which is related to the claimant's way of life there may be difficult issues to resolve. The courts have tended to allow the employer an inordinate power to require employees to conduct themselves in a manner which enures to the benefit of the employer, both inside and outside the workplace. In *Kean v. Fitzgerald* it was said that dismissal may follow from conduct likely to render the servant's continuance in the service prejudicial to his master. Such a residual test broadens the basis for dismissal beyond "misconduct" in any readily definable sense and reserves for the employer the power to dismiss if it is felt that the employee's conduct, although not criminal, insubordinate or in any way indicative of an inability to discharge contractual duties, is prejudicial to the employer's interests. The cases which illustrate this point involve persons whose lifestyle is such that it conflicts with certain values held by the employer to be ethical imperatives. Dismissal may be permitted here despite the citizen's constitutional right to privacy. In *Flynn v. Sr. Power and the Sisters of the Holy Faith* [1985] I.L.R.M. 336 the appellant, a teacher in a convent school, was dismissed after she became pregnant by a married man with whom she was living. There were several interviews between the appellant and the principal of the Order, who managed and controlled the school, in which the appellant was warned that her liaison with her friend caused disquiet amongst parents and staff and that she would be dismissed if she did not terminate her association. Shortly after her pregnancy became known she was dismissed. Costello J., affirming the decision of the Employment Appeal Tribunal and Circuit Court, held that the appellant's sexual conduct, because it was capable of damaging the reputation of her employer and subverting norms of behaviour and certain religious tenets propounded in the school, was a substantial ground for dismissal.

Other Proceedings. Conduct which entitles the employer to dismiss without being liable for breach of contract or under statutory minimum notice legislation, does not always constitute misconduct. It is harsh to hold that a person is to be denied unemployment benefit for incompetence or inability to perform certain duties when there is no evidence of bad faith or deliberateness on the employee's part. So a finding in the Employment Appeal Tribunal or any other Tribunal should not be dispositive of the issue of misconduct for social welfare purposes. Conversely, the fact that criminal or other proceedings are not completed, or even contemplated, may not be compelling proof that there has been no misconduct. The statutory authorities are required to decide issues under the Social Welfare Acts and must not merely decide that a related matter (*e.g.* the outcome of criminal proceedings or a civil action) should be conclusive on the question of disqualification from entitlement due to misconduct. Many employers who dismiss an employee for theft do not place the matter in the hands of the police for a variety of reasons, principally of course the fear of attendant bad publicity which may be detrimental to the business itself. Yet the statutory authorities would be entitled to disqualify the claimant for misconduct and the authorities have acted in appeals where the disqualification was upheld even though no prosecution was contemplated. There are circumstances in which the statutory authorities would give the fact of a conviction or acquittal, or the outcome of a civil action, some probative value but caution is necessary. Sometimes the issues raised in related proceedings are entirely different. In unfair dismissal cases the Unfair Dismissals Act, 1977 requires the Employment Appeal Tribunal or Circuit Court to decide whether the employer acted reasonably in dismissing the employee. This is a quite different issue from that raised by the "misconduct" question in social welfare cases, for the 1977 Act closely controls the presumptive, evidential and factual issues at hand and ultimately requires the Employment Appeal Tribunal or Circuit Court to decide if the employer had a reason for dismissal and if, in dismissing, the employer acted reasonably. Nevertheless, there will be cases where both the Unfair Dismissals Act, 1977 and the misconduct issue will be resolved against the claimant as in *Higgins v. McNaughton Trustees Reinforcements Ltd.* The Employment Appeal Tribunal *(UD 155/1978)* held that the applicant had not been unfairly dismissed by his employer when the employer discovered that the claimant had been in receipt of disability benefits for four years when, during that time, he had been working in their employment. The applicant, through his conduct, was held to have breached the confidence and trust placed in him by his employer and the dismissal was not unfair.

Fair Procedures. Principles of natural justice and the Constitution require that fair procedures be adopted before any allegation of wrongdoing is followed by action which is prejudicial to the suspected or accused person. This principle clearly applies within the context of the contractual issue between employer and employee, as in *Glover v. B.L.N.* [1973] I.R. 388, when the Supreme Court, affirming Kenny J. at first instance, held that an employer who learns that an employee may have been guilty of wrongdoing, must, under article 40 of the Constitution, give the employee a full account of the allegations and afford him the opportunity to meet these charges in full. Further, if the charges are considered by a disciplinary panel or tribunal the composition of the panel or tribunal must be an impartial group of persons: *McConnell v. N.E.E.T.U. (No. 1 and No. 2)* [1983] J.I.S.L.L. 97. If the initial decision to dismiss is made in circumstances which breach these requirements, the statutory authorities would be in difficulty if a decision to disqualify the claimant from unemployment benefit was predicated on bare allegations made against the accused person in the absence of a reply or explanation or proof that the accused person was given the opportunity to respond. Furthermore, the Constitution has direct consequences for the statutory authorities themselves. The exercise of a power to disqualify a claimant from a statutory entitlement is itself surrounded by constitutional guarantees for the citizen. In *State (Hoolahan) v. Minister for Social Welfare* (H.C. Unrep. July 23, 1986) it was held that before a claimant in receipt of deserted wife's benefit could be disqualified by a deciding officer for alleged cohabitation, there must be a detailed account of the allegations made against the claimant to which the claimant may respond. This decision would lend support to the view that the statutory authorities must disclose to the claimant an account of the allegations of misconduct made by the former employer before reaching any decision on the question of disqualification.

Voluntary leaving without just cause. The National Insurance Act, 1911 contained an express provision disqualifying the claimant for voluntarily leaving employment without just cause and while this provision initially meant that the claimant was disqualified from receipt of unemployment benefit for six weeks in all cases, the Unemployment Insurance Act, 1920 modified this provision to enable the statutory authorities to impose a lesser period up to a maximum of six weeks. Ogus and Barendt indicate, in *The Law of Social Security* (Butterworths), that in the U.K. the tribunals hold that the disqualification is imposed because, where the claimant unjustifiably left employment, the unemployment was caused by the claimant rather than by force of external circumstances.

Leaving. It is not necessary that the contract of employment be terminated. Any temporary break in the employment relationship may constitute leaving employment. Absenteeism, for whatever reason, will satisfy the "leaving" criteria. The question of whether the claimant can prove a justifiable basis for absenting himself or herself from employment is relevant to the "just cause" aspect of the "voluntary leaving" rule.

Voluntary. In the normal course of events the employee will resign from employment. Even if resignation does not occur but the conduct of the employee brings about termination of the contract of employment, the employee may be held to have voluntarily left employment. There are several cases involving wrongful and unfair dismissal claims in which the employee has been held to have voluntarily left employment rather than to have been dismissed.

With just cause. If the employee leaves employment for a specific reason, that reason may be used to explain or justify the claimant's behaviour in a general sense. Good faith by the claimant is not enough (*Attorney General for Canada v. Moura* [1982] 2 F.C. 93); nor is it enough to show that the employee acted reasonably in pursuit of self interest or the interests of a third party. An employee is free to terminate a contract of employment in a lawful manner but if a claim for support from the Social Insurance Fund is to be made reference must be made to the interests of the community as a whole, rather than the interests of the claimant alone. The statutory authorities should balance these interests by asking whether, in all the circumstances of the case, it can be said that the claimant left with good cause.

In the U.K. a pressing and urgent matter has been held to be a basis for holding that the employee left employment with just cause. Severe ill-health of the claimant or a member of the claimant's household is most typically involved here. Similarly, where one spouse resigns employment because the other spouse has been transferred from one place of employment to another this may also be "good cause", even if following the transfer the claimant discovers that employment prospects in the new location are poor. The need to keep the family together will be seen as worthy of support. It would be prudent however to attempt to secure employment in the area where relocation is to take place before resigning from employment: Social Security Decision No. R(U) 20/64 (extracted in Calvert, *Cases and Materials on Social Security Law* (1979) p. 133).

If the employee leaves employment because of a dispute with the employer over conditions of employment, this too may prove to be a resignation for good or just cause. If the employer proposes to breach the contract of employment—by imposing new work practices in breach of contract, by refusing to provide a safe system of work or safety equipment, or some other measure which is substantially prejudicial to the employee — the employee may be justified in leaving employment. If the matter is trivial or if the employee acts precipitously by resigning before a dispute procedure or before trade union representatives have been given the opportunity to reach an accommodation, this procedural irregularity may deprive the employee of the "just cause", no matter how substantial the reason for leaving. This conclusion follows from several U.K. tribunal and commissioner decisions (*e.g.* Social Security Decision No. *R(U) 18/57*). In *Coveney v. Blackwater Ltd* (October 1, 1984) the claimant's union had negotiated new working practices in 1982. The employer sought to modify the agreement while retaining the basic principles involved. The union resisted and directed Coveney and others not to operate the 1982 agreement. Coveney was suspended when he refused to follow the 1982 agreement. The Social Welfare Tribunal held that even though the union was disappointed that the 1982 agreement was now under review by the employer, there were approaches open to the union other than withdrawal of normal working. In these circumstances it could not be said that Coveney, in following his union's instructions, had been unreasonably deprived of his employment.

If an employee leaves employment in order to take up employment elsewhere or possibly to take up a place on an educational course, the job offer or the place on the course subsequently being withdrawn, this would seem to be within the "good cause" test. However, either the job must be offered at the time of leaving, or the claimant must use the prospect of finding employment reasonably soon after resignation as one of several factors (housing difficulties or travel difficulties in the existing job) which together provide a cumulative method of either showing just cause or reducing the period of disqualification (Social Security Decision No. *R(U) 1/71*).

The period of disqualification in voluntary leaving cases. One point of interest arises from the "voluntary leaving" disqualification, which does not feature in relation to misconduct. If an employee leaves employment for a reason that is clearly in the "public interest" in the widest sense, it may be appropriate to reduce the period of disqualification to take account of this. In a recent U.K. case, Social Security Commissioner Monroe was asked to consider a social science graduate who had left his clerical post in the civil service in order to take up social work on a voluntary basis. This voluntary work in turn led to full-time social work with the mentally handicapped. The claimant argued that, in giving up a post for which there were many applicants in order to take up work which few people would undertake, he had operated in the public interest. While *Crewe v. Social Security Commissioner* [1982] 2 All E.R. 745 meant that the argument could not justify the voluntary leaving, it was appropriate to substitute a disqualification of one week for the six-week disqualification imposed by the local tribunal: *CU/032/1986*, noted [1987] J.S.W.L. 203.

In many of these cases, the "voluntary leaving" disqualification seems to be another way of explaining the concept of a repudiatory breach of contract. If the employee acts in such a manner as to indicate an intention not to be bound by the terms of the contract, then the employer may elect to terminate the contract of employment: *Industrial Yarns Ltd v. Greene* [1984] I.L.R.M. 15; Kerr [1984] M.L.R. 30. These cases may be regarded as instances of dismissal for misconduct. The increasing availability of jobsharing schemes, early retirement and career breaks suggests that the voluntary leaving disqualification will be invoked against many unemployed claimants during the initial stages of unemployment. In *Crewe v. Social Security Commissioner* [1982] 2 All E.R. 745 a local education authority sought to reduce the number of schoolteachers it employed. The authority wished also to encourage younger teachers to remain in employment, and to balance these objectives it was decided to offer older teachers a generous financial inducement to take early retirement. Crewe, a man of 61, took up the offer. He was held by the Court of Appeal to have left without just cause. Donaldson L.J. in his judgment accepted that the community interest may be best served by promoting and encouraging young teachers but this, the Lord Justice said, was not the issue. The community interest that is at issue is the interest of the community as "insurance underwriters" of the insurance fund. In a later decision it was held that where the premature retirement scheme is designed to retire people on structural grounds or limited efficiency, and the claimant is asked to retire, then the claimant does not voluntarily leave employment at all. In such a case "just" cause does not arise. It may be that disqualification may be limited to a short period, as in *CU/032/1986* ([1987] J.S.W.L. 203).

Subsection (4)(b)
Refusal of an offer of suitable employment. This separate ground for disqualification was added to the "misconduct" and "voluntary leaving" provisions contained in the Unemployment Insurance Act, 1920 by section 17 of the Social Welfare Act, 1952. Prior to the 1952 enactment, refusal to take employment was seen as proof that the claimant was not available for employment and the claimant was disentitled altogether. This meant that in certain cases of voluntary unemployment, the claimant was disqualified for up to six weeks, while in other situations the claimant was held not entitled at all for failure to satisfy one of the statutory conditions. While an offer which is declined out of hand will clearly activate the disqualification, it is also established that if a claimant responds to an offer by asserting new terms of employment which the employer resists, the making of this counter-offer has the same effect as a refusal. Most of the attention will focus, however, on the question of whether the offer is an offer of suitable employment. The 1981 Act, in particular in s.47(6), provides some guidance on unsuitability, but as we shall see, there is still considerable room for the statutory authorities to decide that employment is not suitable for the claimant in question.

The only real difficulty with this subparagraph is to determine when the employment offered is suitable. The provision, although based on the corresponding U.K. provision, is much wider in one significant respect. Under the U.K. provision an unemployed person may decline to accept an offer of employment if the offer does not involve employment in that person's usual occupation, regardless of whether the remuneration and conditions of employment are as favourable as those habitually obtained in previous employment. Only if unemployment lasts for some time does the claimant, under the U.K. legislation, have to take employment outside the sphere of the claimant's normal occupation or lose entitlement to benefit. In Ireland, however, the claimant is required to be more flexible from the outset. Refusal to accept a job offer to work in the district where last employed on equally favourable terms and remuneration, because the occupation is of a kind which the claimant does not have any experience of, does not necessarily lead to disqualification. All section 47(6) does is to indicate employment which is *not* suitable. It is a *non sequitur* to interpret subsection (6) as if it, by implication, indicates that all other offers are offers of suitable employment. It remains possible to argue that circumstances may throw up examples of unsuitable employment which are not governed by section 47(6). A recently unemployed skilled worker may argue legitimately that an offer of unskilled employment may not be "suitable employment" if that claimant may reasonably expect an offer in the claimant's usual occupation in the near future. It is also possible to envisage situations where the skilled worker may prejudice any chance of getting employment in that worker's area of specialisation if the claimant is required to take unskilled work under threat of losing benefit. It is essential that section 47(6) is seen as not being comprehensive and all embracing on the question of suitable employment, not least of all because there are personal circumstances which may render an offer of employment unsuitable for a particular claimant. An offer may not be suitable within the context of the claimant's resources, beliefs or aspirations. A refusal to take employment because of illness or family circumstances (e.g. difficulties with childminding) would perhaps invite disqualification and also the prospect of being held not to be available for employment. If the refusal is due to transport difficulties, however, then the refusal may be permissible because the employment is not suitable. Ethical factors too may arise. An offer of employment in a particular supermarket by an unemployed shopworker may be refused because of a particular policy adopted by the employer, or because the shop may stock "objectionable" goods, such as contraceptive devices. Does this make an offer of employment to an opponent of apartheid in the first example and a devout Roman Catholic in the second "unsuitable"? Employment offered to a claimant when the employer in question discourages the workforce from joining a trade union may nevertheless be considered to be suitable, given the protection afforded by the Unfair Dismissals Act, 1977. The U.K. tribunal decisions indicate that a refusal to take up work on the Sabbath, for religious reasons, is justifiable *(R2 63 (U.B.))*. Presumably employment that requires the employee to break the criminal law would not be suitable employment.

Subsection (4)(c)

FAS Training. Refusal to participate in a training programme provided or approved by An Foras Aiseanna Saothair, the statutory successor to An CO, is a ground for disqualification. It is not necessary that An Foras provide the training programme. All that is necessary is that An Foras approve the programme and, if this occurs, then it seems impossible for the statutory authorities established by the Social Welfare (Consolidation) Act, 1981 to rule that the training course is not *per se* suitable. Thus CERT training, Jobsearch training and other training programmes recognised by An Foras must be taken up if the claimant is not to lose unemployment benefit. While a refusal means loss of unemployment benefit under section 47(4) for up to nine weeks, the period of disqualification could be indeterminate if the claimant refused to take up approved training if and when offered again at the end of a period of disqualification and this went on *ad infinitum*. The claimant may, however, challenge the suitability of training within the context of the claimant's circumstances, if the claimant can show "good cause". In a leading U.K. decision *(2/57 U.B.)*, a National Insurance Commissioner indicated that there are several issues that the social security authorities may consider, notwithstanding certification that the programme of training is suitable. These issues include in the view of the Commissioner:

(i) "Whether the claimant has without good cause refused or failed to avail himself" of an opportunity of such training.

(ii) Whether the claimant has, in fact, "refused or failed to avail himself" of the opportunity. This would involve consideration of the terms of the offer, how it was communicated to the claimant, if so communicated at all, and his response or reaction to any such offer.

(iii) Whether any opportunity given was "reasonable" in all the circumstances. To some extent, I think, consideration of this issue may overlap (i) and (ii) above, but in my opinion it clearly involves consideration also whether, first of all, there was intelligible communication to the claimant of an offer of the training, given in time for him to avail himself of it and in a proper manner; and, secondly, whether it was otherwise "reasonable". Even, for example if it had been approved by the Ministry in relation to the claimant an offer of training might not be considered "reasonable" if it were made on a day when the claimant was unwell or was being interviewed for work by an employer."

Subsection (4)(d)

Failed or neglected to avail of any reasonable opportunity of obtaining suitable employment. This ground for disqualification will operate if, at a stage prior to the claimant being offered employment, the claimant makes it unlikely that such an offer will be made. A variety of situations could lead to this provision being invoked. It is conceivable that unemployed persons who refuse to participate in programmes that are designed to improve employment prospects (*e.g.* involvement in mock interviews, letter writing and typing courses run as part of Jobsearch) would fall within this provision although it is worthy of note that refusal to participate in the Social Employment Scheme (now known as Community Employment) run by the Department of Labour does not lead to disqualification from entitlement to unemployment benefit or assistance. A failure to attend an interview for a vacancy notified to the claimant by Manpower would also be grounds for disqualification, as long as there is a reasonable opportunity to take up the opening (*e.g.* the interview is not to be held many miles from the claimant's district) and the employment is "suitable" (discussed above) for that particular claimant. Decisions on the corresponding U.K. provision indicate that disqualification follows if the claimant turns up for a job interview in a dishevelled and unshaven state in order to discourage the employer from making an offer to him. In contrast, a conscientious objection to the work in prospect (*e.g.* a dedicated vegetarian refusing to work in an abattoir) may not lead to disqualification because the work may not be suitable employment for that person. In one case *(R(U) 5/7)*, it was said by a National Insurance Commissioner that a person's attitude towards some aspect of prospective employment may render it not "suitable" in that person's case.

Subsection (4)(e)

This provision was added to the Social Welfare Code in 1992. There was substantial evidence that redundancy and other severance packages were being put together on the basis that the employee would, upon being let go, be entitled to unemployment benefit for the entire period of entitlement. It was decided to discourage this kind of misuse of the Social Insurance Fund by disqualifying persons aged under 55, who received a redundancy payment, from entitlement to benefit for a period of up to nine weeks when the redundancy payment exceeds a set amount. Statutory Instrument No. 128 of 1994 sets this figure at £15,000.

The Period of Disqualification

While the National Insurance Act, 1911, section 87(2) provided that the period of disqualification was to be six weeks in all cases of misconduct and voluntary leaving, calculated from the day the claimant lost employment, the Unemployment Insurance Act, 1920, section 8(2) modified this somewhat by permitting this disqualification to be six weeks, or such shorter period, being not less than one week, from the date the claimant lost or left employment. The maximum six-week period was extended to nine weeks in 1992. This subsection to the Act provides a convenient solution to a difficult factual issue: in what circumstances can it be said that the action, which is deemed to be the cause of the claimant's voluntary unemployment, is no longer the effective cause of unemployment? This does not of course mean in all case of voluntary leaving, for example, that a period of disqualification will be followed by entitlement. The deciding officer may conclude that the claimant left work in order to discharge some task or duty (*e.g.* to look after children) in circumstances where it is reasonable to conclude that the claimant is not available for employment.

Evidence on the proper period of disqualification is not found in the legislation, despite the opening sentence of subsection (4) which could lead one to believe that the Act contains specific provisions on this point. The words "as may be determined under the provisions of this Act" refer instead to the statutory rôle of the deciding officer and the appeals officer in deciding questions raised under the Social Welfare Acts. The fact that the legislation confers upon the officer in question a discretion, does not mean that the discretion is to be exercised by the officer in question in whatever manner he or she sees fit, or not at all (*i.e.* a blanket nine-week disqualification policy in every case would be improper, at least if the decision were made or upheld by an appeals officer regardless of the facts of the case at hand). Appeals officers are quasi-judicial officers who must act judicially and, as such, a failure by an appeals officer to exercise a discretion could be challenged in the courts through *certiorari* and *mandamus*. In *The State (Kershaw) v. Eastern Health Board* [1985] I.L.R.M. 235 a claim for supplementary welfare allowance (S.W.A. — a statutory scheme which has concepts of legal entitlement and discretionary payments running throughout) was refused on the ground that the claimant was not included in the classes of claimant, set out in a Ministerial Circular, who were to be entitled to free fuel under S.W.A. The decision was quashed by way of *mandamus*.

In the U.K. there was a practice of imposing the maximum disqualification unless the claimant could show that special circumstances existed which made a six-week disqualification inappropriate. In 1974 this approach was rejected by a Tribunal of National Insurance Commissioners on the ground that such an approach would constitute an improper restriction of the discretion. Rather, the issue of the period of the disqualification should be exercised by reference to the statutory language, "regarding each case as one in which a sensible discretion has to be exercised in such manner as the justice of the case requires" (Ogus and Barendt). Such a broad common-sense approach requires the disqualification to be tailored to the facts of each case. If the claimant narrowly fails to justify a "voluntary leaving" this may be appropriate for a week or a two-week disqualification, as in Social Security Decision No. *R(U) 20/64*. A police sergeant left the force because he was transferred away from his place of residence. He reasonably anticipated that he would find employment shortly after resignation and had taken steps to find employment prior to tendering his resignation. A two-week disqualification was substituted for the maximum six-week disqualification. In contrast, if the claimant has lost employment due to misconduct—theft from the employer for example—it is the author's experience, as a claimant advisor, that the maximum disqualification will be imposed, even if a parallel criminal sanction has been imposed or is pending. A more compassionate approach may be urged upon the deciding officer if hardship is likely to result. If the claimant has found employment shortly after making the claim, Social Security Decision No. *R(U) 20/64* suggests that a more lenient approach should be taken: immediate efforts to find new employment may "purge" the initially voluntary unemployment of its self-induced aspect.

One further issue arises from the final sentence in section 47(4): "the period of disqualification shall commence on the day on which the loss or leaving of employment, refusal, failure or neglect (as the case may be) occurred." This provision, included in the Social Welfare Act, 1952 by way of Government amendment at Committee stage in the Dáil, was said by the Minister for Social Welfare to be designed to safeguard the claimant (131 *Dáil Debates* Col. 1236). The disqualification must begin to run immediately after the voluntary unemployment occurs: otherwise the Minister could come along some months later and penalise the claimant for something that had occurred in the past. Other Deputies took the contrary position. Practice in the Department is to consult the employer and if misconduct, for example, is alleged then disqualification is imposed automatically on the word of the employer. One Deputy suggested that a more equitable system would allow the claimant to receive benefit and disqualify him or her when there had been a thorough investigation of the complaint, the claimant being notified of the allegations made against him or her. It is arguable that this provision and the way it is automatically invoked is unconstitutional as being in breach of the principles of natural justice and constitutional justice. Statutory authorities are required to exercise powers that affect the citizen in a fundamental manner in a reasonable way.

CHAPTER 10

OCCUPATIONAL INJURIES BENEFITS

Preliminary

Interpretation

48.—(1) In this Chapter, save where the context otherwise requires—
"apprentice" means a person undergoing full-time training for any trade, business, profession, office, employment or vocation;
"claimant" means a person claiming occupational injuries benefit and also includes an applicant for a declaration that an accident was or was not an occupational accident, and reference to a claim shall be construed accordingly;
"the deceased" means, in relation to death benefit, the person in respect of whose death the benefit is claimed or payable;
"disablement gratuity" has the meaning specified in section 54(7);
"disablement pension" has the meaning specified in section 54(8) or (9);
"medical examination" includes bacteriological and radiographical tests and similar investigations, and references to being medically examined shall be construed accordingly;
"medical treatment" has the meaning specified in section 72(1);
"occupational accident" has the meaning specified in section 69;
"period of injury" means, in relation to any accident, the period of 156 days (Sundays being disregarded) beginning with the day following the

accident, or the part of that period for which, under section 54(2), disablement benefit in respect of the accident is not available to the insured person; [1994 Act, section 20]

"relevant accident" and "relevant injury" mean respectively, in relation to any benefit, the accident and injury in respect of which the benefit is claimed or payable;

"relevant loss of faculty" means the loss of faculty resulting from the relevant injury.

(2) References in this Chapter to loss of physical faculty shall be construed as including references to disfigurement, whether or not accompanied by any actual loss of faculty.

GENERAL NOTE

This is the definition section in relation to occupational injuries benefits.

Insurable Employment

Occupational injuries insurance

49.—(1) Subject to this Part, every person, irrespective of age, who is employed in insurable (occupational injuries) employment shall be insured under this Part against personal injury caused by accident arising out of and in the course of such employment.

(2) Any reference in this Act to occupational injuries insurance shall be construed as a reference to the insurance provided for by this section.

(3) Notwithstanding subsection (1), regulations may provide for entitling to such and so many of the benefits which comprise occupational injuries benefits, as may be prescribed, subject to such conditions and circumstances as may be prescribed, such class or classes of persons as may be prescribed. [1994 Act, section 31]

GENERAL NOTE

Historical background

The passage through the Westminster Parliament of legislation creating a workmen's compensation scheme in the final years of the 19th century underlines a significant historical and conceptual development in the evolution of principles of accident compensation in these islands. The impact of the statutory reform of 1897 was to extend further afield and the 1897 Act, flawed as it was, became a model for legislative measures in many of the American states, the first effective state legislation being the New York legislation of 1910. Many Commonwealth jurisdictions adopted workmen's compensation legislation although other jurisdictions, particularly Australia and New Zealand, have, in a theoretical sense, overtaken the British in terms of providing innovative legislation in respect of accident compensation. The Workmen's Compensation Act, 1897 was something of a forerunner for the generally no-fault system of industrial injuries benefit provided through state social insurance from 1946 in the U.K. and in Ireland some 20 years later. However, before we turn our attention to the impact of the 1897 Act it is worthwhile to consider briefly the common law and statutory background which made the 1897 Act such a pioneering statute.

At common law the employee could only establish a right to compensation if the employer could be shown to have been negligent, or in breach of contract, by not providing proper equipment, or by employing other workers who were not competent to discharge their duties, such failure being the cause of the accident. If the employer was, under statute, obliged to fence machinery or other equipment, failure to observe this obligation could perhaps lead to compensation being available if the worker could establish a cause of action for breach of statutory duty, *e.g.* under the Factories Acts. When the employee in question was able to establish a cause of action, and somehow find the means to finance an action before the courts, the employer could defeat the claim in most instances by way of one of three defences: contributory negligence, *volenti non fit injuria* or common employment.

Contributory negligence. If the accident could in some way be regarded as having been, in whole or in part, "caused" by some act or omission by the employee, then the employer could defeat the tort action by pleading contributory negligence. The successful plea was a complete defence. Even if negligence by the employer was a further causal element, the courts permitted contributory negligence to operate so as to exonerate the employer entirely from any obligation to provide compensation. The Civil Liability Act, 1961, section 60, however, now allows the courts to reduce the damages to such an amount as the court thinks just and equitable.

Volenti non fit injuria. This concept has been described as being nothing more nor less than contributory negligence by another name. Where it operates, the tort victim is prevented from recovering damages because the victim is said to have "consented". The express or implied assumption of risk, in employment contract cases, is frequently a policy determination by the courts rather than a deduction that can be made from any objective analysis of the intention of the parties, or even one of them.

Common employment. If two workers were employed under a contract of service, the doctrine of common employment provided that where one worker negligently injured another worker whilst engaged on some employment task, the employer was in no way responsible under the doctrine of vicarious liability.

The workmen's Compensation Act, 1897 and subsequent developments

Rather than attempt to take on these judicially created methods of frustrating a workman's action in tort, Parliament adopted, in 1897, a radically different approach to these issues. The removal of these defences would not fundamentally overcome the evidentiary hurdle of proving negligence.

Liability under the Workmen's Compensation Act, 1897, to quote the *Report of the Commission on Workmen's Compensation* (1962 pr. 6525, chaired by Judge Shannon) was instead based "on an entirely new principle. [The Act] imposed a liability upon the employer to pay compensation to a workman injured by an accident arising out of, and in the course of, employment, or to the dependants of such a workman who was killed, irrespective of any question of negligence on the part of the employer or any person employed by him": para. 16. Cover was extended only to dangerous employments: heavy engineering, railways, quarries and mines, factories and some construction works. Compensation was provided by weekly payments which were pitched at the level of one half of pre-accident earnings, up to a statutory ceiling of £1 per week in the case of accidents causing injury. If the accident resulted in the death of the workman, a lump sum of £150 or three years wages, whichever was the larger, was payable, subject to a ceiling of £300. The 1897 Act required waiting days which amounted to three weeks. The limited nature of the compensation in accidental injury cases meant that the risk of injury was effectively shared between employer and workman: the three weeks waiting-day rule meant that, in the case of industrial injuries which healed relatively quickly the cost was borne largely, if not exclusively, by the workman. Some degree of contracting out of the scheme altogether was available if the worker contracted into an equally effective scheme. If the injury was an injury which lasted for longer than six months the County Court could authorise redemption of the continuing obligation to pay weekly benefit through the payment of a lump sum. The 1897 Act allowed workers to run an orthodox tort action at the same time as making a claim under the Act: the workman could not, however, recover on two fronts and an election was necessary as between the two remedies. The legislation of 1934 and 1953 ultimately allowed the workman to pursue a tort action and seek workmen's compensation but the workman could not obtain payments from both sources. There were significant improvements made to the statutory scheme. In non-fatal cases the percentage of pre-accident weekly earnings normally payable in the form of compensation was increased to 75 per cent and dependant additions were subsequently payable (weekly supplemental allowances) under the 1953 Act. Many other changes, *e.g.* the relaxation of the waiting-day rules, were progressive in nature but despite periodic reviews, most notably those undertaken and published in 1925 and 1930 by the Departmental Commission on Workmen's Compensation, the basic tenets of workmen's compensation law remained unaltered until 1966.

The criticisms levelled at the workmen's compensation scheme by Beveridge in Britain were also influential in Ireland. Beveridge, in *Social Insurance and Allied Services* (1942 Cmd. 6406) conceded that the existing law provided workmen's compensation for most workers without serious difficulty or unreasonable delay. Nevertheless, Beveridge identified several disadvantages which could be eliminated by adopting a social insurance system. These factors were mainly:

(i) The scheme ultimately depended on the threat of, or resort to, litigation rather than friendly and informal arbitration between the parties.

(ii) The absence of machinery to assist workers in prosecuting the claim, a factor which produced a sense of injustice amongst workers.

(iii) In some cases, the worker did not obtain compensation because insurance cover was not, in general, compulsory on the part of employers.

(iv) There was no guarantee of continuity of income. The practice of bargaining to compromise a claim, in return for a lump sum payment, meant that no permanent and regular income for the permanently disabled existed in many cases.

(v) The basic principle behind the compulsory Act, the fixing of liability on individual employers, was unsound. In industrial disease cases, where the onset of the disease and its final manifestation can occur over several years, employers discharged workmen in order to avoid liability. More fundamentally the scheme did nothing to restore the employee to productive and remunerative capacity.

Beveridge went on to condemn the Workmen's Compensation Scheme: "The pioneer system of Social Security in Britain was based on a wrong principle and has been dominated by a wrong outlook. It allows claims to be settled by bargaining between unequal parties, permits payment of socially wasteful lump sums instead of pensions in cases of serious incapacity, places the cost of medical care on the workman or on charity or poor relief, and over part of the field range in the numbers covered, though not in the proportion of the total compensation paid, it relies on expensive private insurance" (para. 80).

Beveridge recommended adoption of compulsory social insurance as the most effective method of providing income maintenance and medical benefits to those affected by industrial injury and disease and these recommendations were adopted in 1946.

The Commission on Workmen's Compensation

The Department of Social Welfare White Paper of October 1949 (P. 9661) dealt with the issue of workmen's compensation reform by indicating that the Department could not resolve the problems that clearly existed in relation to rehabilitation of accident victims or eliminating accidents in the workplace. The White Paper conceded that reform was necessary but after listing three options the authors of the White Paper commented that there was much to be said for and against each of the courses of reform canvassed. The White Paper indicated that no decision had been taken at that time. Eventually a Government Commission on Workmen's Compensation was appointed in December 1955. The Commission, chaired by Mr Justice Shannon, reported in 1962. The members of the Commission could not agree on the way forward: the majority favoured a series of measures aimed at fine-tuning the existing system. After examining the U.K. compulsory social insurance model the majority felt that the advantages of such a system over a reformed workmen's compensation scheme were not made out and the majority confessed to being "strongly influenced by the arguments in favour of the preservation of the status quo and the undesirability of interfering with the established private enterprise system unless substantial advantages could thereby be achieved". The minority report, on the other hand, recommended the implementation of compulsory occupational injury insurance cover and that the scheme be administered by the Department of Social Welfare. The Irish Congress of Trade Unions favoured this approach and, after a review of the Report, the Government, in 1965, opted to implement a social insurance scheme. In introducing the Social Welfare (Occupational Injuries) Bill, 1965, the Minister for Social Welfare, Mr Boland, indicated that even if the majority report were to be implemented, the Workmen's Compensation Scheme would still be unsatisfactory in several respects. The Scheme proved far too contentious *vis-à-vis* the employer and workman and the employer and insurance company. This, and the attendant threat or use of litigation, disrupts the employment relationship and retards the employee's recovery. Mr Boland said that under the new scheme "compensation for employment injury will henceforward be a social service rather than an obligation on an individual employer". The 1965 Bill was not only a more efficient method of providing income maintenance, it provided the necessary emphasis on health care, rehabilitation and retraining. It was suggested that administrative costs would be in the region of 10 per cent, *i.e.* benefits would constitute 90 per cent of expenditure, and this compared very favourably with workmen's compensation which forwarded less than 50 per cent of insurance premiums paid by employers to private insurance companies, to workmen in the form of cash payments. In fact the Department of Social Welfare calculated that in 1984 the cost of administering the social welfare services generally is around four per cent of estimated expenditure: no figures are available which allow one to estimate whether occupational injury administrative costs are higher than this figure. Experience from other countries would suggest that the figure, as a percentage, would be higher than the median four per cent.

The industrial preference

Beveridge himself noted that there was no rational basis upon which there should be a distinction between injuries caused at the workplace and injuries that have no link with employment, if social insurance as a unified system is adopted. Beveridge gave as an example the case of a worker who loses a leg: the needs of that worker are the same regardless of whether the worker loses the leg in an accident at a factory or in the street. Beveridge, however, gave three reasons why it is felt necessary to make special provision for industrial accidents and industrial diseases. First, many industries that are vital to the community are especially dangerous. Persons should not be deterred from taking on such work by a fear that, if killed or injured, compensation levels will not make special reference to earnings and simply provide subsistence income levels. Secondly, a person injured in employment is normally acting under orders: this is less likely where the injury is caused by sickness or a non-work related accident. Thirdly, only if special provision is made for those who suffer industrial injury, irrespective of negligence, would it appear possible to limit the employer's liability at common law to the results of actions for which he is factually and morally responsible, not simply by virtue of legal principle. Beveridge found the first argument to be the strongest but he also found the other two difficult to disregard. These arguments, however, have not been supported by everyone. Ogus and Barendt, for example, favour the view that there is no logic in differentiating between income maintenance awards on the ground of the origin of the industry. The Royal Commission on Civil Liability and Compensation for Industrial Injury (1978) under the chairmanship of Lord Pearson, felt that the Beveridge arguments "carry a good deal less weight now". The Royal Commission pointed out that the industrial injuries scheme applies to all industries, whether dangerous or not, and felt that it was not possible to endorse the industrial preference in principle. Opposition to abolition of the industrial preference has, in Britain and Australia, come from trade unions who wish to uphold a concept which is clearly advantageous to the industrial workforce, a large number of whom will be trade union members.

Irish commentators have also been critical of the industrial preference. According to Casey, writing in (1969) 4 Ir.Jur. 234 at 235: "the higher rate of benefit for occupational injury cases is an anomaly, impossible to justify upon rational grounds. The real reason for its existence would appear to be simply the force of tradition".

Notwithstanding comments of this kind there was a marked reluctance on the part of the Barrington Commission on Health and Safety at Work (1983) to recommend the abolition of the industrial preference. The Commission suggested further research on the entire question of accident compensation was necessary. The Commission on Social Welfare was supportive of the industrial preference, observing that the method of financing occupational injuries benefits, from employer's contributions only, marked the scheme as something separate from the rest of the social welfare system.

On May 1, 1967, the date when the Occupational Injuries Scheme became operative, the maximum rate of injury benefit (short-term benefit payable in respect of a person aged over 18 years who was not a married woman living with her husband) was 115 shillings (£5.75) weekly. The comparable rate of disability benefit was 52½ shillings (£2.51). While differing contribution and eligibility criteria make a straightforward comparison somewhat misleading, this figure indicates that the industrial preference had a striking effect on the levels of benefit paid. This factor of over 100 per cent increases substantially if one bears in mind the possibility that the occupational injury benefit recipient could also obtain supplemental payments, e.g. in cases where constant attendance is required. In some cases during the early years the normal figure of 40 shillings (£2) weekly could be doubled. In recent years this differential fell dramatically because across the board increases in social insurance benefits have not taken account of the industrial preference.

Under the Social Welfare Act, 1988, disability benefit for a person over 18 years of age was payable at the rate of £43.60 weekly. Injury benefit for such a person was a maximum of £59.60. The difference, while still significant, shows that as a proportion of disability benefit rates, injury benefit fell from over 100 per cent to less than 50 per cent in the 22 years following introduction of occupational injuries benefit.

The industrial preference was abolished by section 35 of the 1992 Act. Rates for injury benefit and disability benefit were aligned for new claimants as from April 6, 1992. Statutory Instrument No. 82 of 1992 directed a similar alignment for persons aged under 16 years as from that same date. The net effect for the Exchequer was a happy one; injury benefit rates were reduced from £65 per week to £50 per week.

The amended section 53 of this Act, introduced by section 20 of the Act of 1994, further this integration by directing that persons in occupational injuries employment are to be entitled to disability benefit when incapable of work, notwithstanding the contribution conditions in section 32.

Section 49(3) inserted by section 31 of the 1994 Act should be noted. This is an enabling provision which empowers the Minister to make regulations which extend entitlement to occupational injuries benefits. These powers will be used to extend cover to certain categories of sub-contractor on construction sites who, as self-employed persons, are not covered by occupational injuries benefit.

Insurable (occupational injuries) employment

50.—(1) Any reference in this Act to insurable (occupational injuries) employment shall, subject to the following subsections, be construed as a reference to any employment for the time being specified in Part I of the First Schedule, not being an employment specified in Part II of that Schedule.

(2) (a) For the purposes of this section, the following employments shall be taken as being added to the employments specified in Part I of the First Schedule—

(i) employment in the State in plying for hire with any vehicle, vessel, aircraft, machine or animal, the use of which is obtained under any contract of bailment (other than a hire purchase agreement) in consideration of the payment of a fixed sum or a share in the earnings or otherwise,

(ii) employment under any contract of service or apprenticeship entered into in the State (otherwise than as captain, master or a member of the crew) on board a ship or aircraft, being employment for the purpose of the ship or aircraft or of any passengers or cargo or mails carried by the ship or aircraft, and

(iii) employment in the State as a member or as a person training to become a member of any such fire brigade, rescue brigade, first-aid party or salvage party at a factory, mine or works, as may be prescribed, or of any such similar organisation as may be prescribed.

(b) In paragraph (a)(ii)—
"ship" means—

(i) any ship registered in the State, or

(ii) any other ship or vessel of which the owner or, if there is more than one owner, the managing owner or manager, resides or has his principal place of business in the State;

"aircraft" means—

(i) any aircraft registered in the State, or

(ii) any other aircraft of which the owner or, if there is more than one owner, the managing owner or manager, resides or has his principal place of business in the State.

(3) For the purposes of this section, the following employments shall be taken as being added to the employments specified in Part II of the First Schedule—

(a) employment as a member of the Defence Forces,

(b) employment, which is neither wholetime as may be defined in regulations nor under contract of service, as a member of the crew of a fishing vessel where the employed person is wholly remunerated by a share in the profits or the gross earnings of the working of the vessel,

(c) employment under any local or other public authority in the execution of any contract for services,

(d) employment, otherwise than under contract of service, specified in paragraph 10 of Part I of the First Schedule.

(4) For the purposes of this section, paragraph 2 of Part II of the First Schedule shall be taken as not including employment of a casual nature for the purposes of any work in or about the residence of the employer.

(5) For the purposes of this section, a pilot to whom the Pilotage Act, 1913, applies shall, when employed on any ship as defined in subsection (2)(b), be deemed to be a member of the crew of that ship.

(6) The Minister may, in relation to paragraphs 4 and 5 of Part II of the First Schedule, by regulations provide that an employment specified as being subsidiary employment or an employment specified as being of inconsiderable extent shall be taken for the purposes of this section as not being so specified.

(7) The Minister may by regulations provide that any specified employment under any local or other public authority shall be taken for the purposes of this section as being added to Part II of the First Schedule.

(8) Where it appears to the Minister—

(a) that the nature or other circumstances of the service rendered or the work performed in any employment which, apart from this subsection, is insurable (occupational injuries) employment and in any employment which, apart from this subsection, is not such employment (whether by reason of the fact that it is an excepted employment or otherwise) are so similar as to result in anomalies in the operation of this Part, and

(b) that either—

(i) the first-mentioned employment can conveniently be included among the excepted employments, or

(ii) the second-mentioned employment can conveniently be included among the insurable (occupational injuries) employments,

the Minister may by regulations provide that the employment shall be so included.

(9) The Minister may by regulations modify the provisions of this Part in its application in the case of persons employed in employments specified in subsection (2)(a)(ii).

(10) A person who is unemployed shall, while in attendance at such course as may be prescribed and provided by such person as may be prescribed, be deemed, for the purposes of this Part, to be in insurable (occupational injuries) employment and to be employed by the person by whom the course is being provided.

(11) A person employed under a scheme administered by An Foras Áiseanna Saothair and known as Community Employment [1995 Act, section 18] shall be deemed, for the purposes of this Part, to be in insurable (occupational injuries) employment.

GENERAL NOTE

Subsections (1) and (2)

Section 50(1) of the Principal Act of 1993 requires that every person, irrespective of age, who is in insurable (occupational injuries) employment shall, subject to the Act, be insured against personal injury caused by accident arising out of and in the course of employment. Insurable (occupational injuries) employment is interpreted as being any of the employments specified in Part I of the first Schedule, as long as it is not employment specified in Part II of that Schedule: see Section 51 of the Principal Act. This effectively means that if an employed person is insurable as an employed contributor under section 9 of the Principal Act, then that person is also likely to be in insurable (occupational injuries) employment. There are, however, exceptions to this general rule, as provided by subsection (2). First, persons who are included in insurable (occupational injuries) employment include persons employed in the State in plying for hire with any vehicle, vessel, aircraft, machine or animal, the use of which is obtained under a contract of bailment. Taxi drivers and others in this category are thus insurable, even if paid on a profit sharing basis by the owner of the means of conveyance. Similarly, persons employed under a contract of service entered into in the State to serve on board a ship or aircraft (other than as captain, master or crew member), the ship or aircraft being operated to transport passengers, cargo or mail, are also in insurable (occupational injuries) employment. A further category of insurable (occupational injuries) employment is provided in respect of persons who are members of or who are training within the State to become a member of a fire brigade or other rescue brigade group. Employment which is specified as subsidiary employment or employment of inconsiderable extent is nevertheless insurable (occupational injuries) employment: see subsection (6). Unemployed persons on a FAS training course are also within the scope of insurable (occupational injuries) employment (see subsection (11)), a provision which has been amended by substitution to also include CERT trainees. Persons employed on the Social Employment Scheme (now known as Community Employment) by the Department of Enterprise and Employment are also to be considered to be in insurable (occupational injuries) employment.

There is an overlap between subsections (1) and (10). Section 29 of the 1988 Act amended section 38(11) of the Principal Act of 1981 so as to provide that persons participating in FAS, ACOT or CERT training courses, could still be regarded as in insurable (occupational injuries) employment. Section 26 of the 1993 Act broadened the scope of the provision by giving the Minister the power, by statutory instrument, to deem certain persons to be in insurable (occupational injuries) employment. The Minister indicated that the power will be exercised so as to include Euroform, Horizon and NOW training courses: see S.I. No. 177 of 1993.

Subsection (3)

Conversely, there are some categories of insurable employment which do not constitute insurable (occupational injuries) employment. Employment as a member of the Defence Forces, employees of local or public authority independent contractors and certain ministers of religion are all outside the scope of insurable (occupational injuries) employment. Those excluded by Part II of the First Schedule include those in subsidiary employments: see S.I. No. 80 of 1967 and S.I. No. 83 of 1992.

Extension of meaning of references to accidents arising out of and in course of employment

51.—(1) An accident arising in the course of an insured person's employment shall be deemed for the purposes of this Part, in the absence of evidence to the contrary, also to have arisen out of that employment.

(2) An accident shall be treated for the purposes of this Part, where it would not apart from this section be so treated, as arising out of an insured person's employment if—

(a) the accident arises in the course of the employment,

(b) the accident—

  (i) either is caused by another person's misconduct, negligence or misbehaviour, or by steps taken in consequence of any such misconduct, negligence or misbehaviour or by the behaviour or presence of an animal (including a bird, fish or insect), or

  (ii) is caused by or consists in the insured person's being struck by any object or by lightning, and

(c) the insured person did not directly or indirectly cause or contribute to the happening of the accident by his conduct outside the employment or by any act not incidental to the employment.

(3) An accident shall be deemed for the purposes of this Part to arise out of and in the course of an insured person's employment, notwithstanding that he is at the time of the accident acting in contravention of any statutory or other regulations applicable to his employment, or of any orders given by or on behalf of his employer, or that he is acting without instructions from his employer, if—

(a) the accident would have been deemed for the purposes of this Part so to have arisen had the act not been done in contravention as aforesaid or without instructions from his employer, as the case may be, and

(b) the act is done for the purposes of and in connection with the employer's trade or business.

(4) An accident happening to an insured person while travelling to or from his place of work shall, subject to such conditions as may be prescribed, be deemed for the purposes of this Part to arise out of and in the course of his employment.

(5) An accident happening to an insured person in or about any premises at which he is for the time being employed for the purposes of his

employer's trade or business shall be deemed for the purposes of this Part to arise out of and in the course of his employment if it happens while he is taking steps, in an actual or supposed emergency at those premises, to rescue, succour or protect persons who are, or are thought to be or possibly to be, injured or imperilled, or to avert or minimise serious damage to property.

(6) An accident happening to an insured person, who is an apprentice, while he is in attendance at a technical school or other place for training or instruction (whether during ordinary hours of employment or otherwise), shall be deemed for the purposes of this Part, in the absence of evidence to the contrary, to have arisen out of and in the course of his employment if his attendance at that school or place is with his employer's consent or is required by direction of his employer or under his contract or apprenticeship.

GENERAL NOTE

For an insured person to receive an occupational injury payment there must be a personal injury, caused by an accident (or a prescribed disease) which arises out of and in the course of employment.

The provisions in this section considerably ease the difficulties of causation and proof that would otherwise confront the insured person. In order to understand the significance of this section it is necessary to address a wealth of caselaw produced by the Workmen's Compensation Acts, which established a statutory formula by which to test the presence or absence of an industrial injury.

The statutory formula: "personal injury by accident"

"*Personal injury*". It is well established that there must be actual harm done to the body or mind of an individual. If the physical injury induces mental instability there is personal injury according to *Gilmore v. Belfast Corporation* [1942] 76 I.L.T.R. 182. A workman suffered an injury to his finger at the workplace. The finger turned septic and severe pain caused the workman to become mentally unsound. The finger was amputated. Six weeks after the accident the workman committed suicide. The logic established by *Marriott v. Mattby Main Collier Co. Ltd.* (1920) 13 B.W.C.C. 353, holds that if the victim of an accident suffers shock this can be a "personal injury" within the statutory formula. If there is resultant neurosis, or insanity, it follows that a personal injury results even though there be no actual "structural injury" capable of detection.

An accident that results in incapacity does not *ipso facto* lead to the "personal injury by accident" formula being satisfied. In a recent English case a worker was incapable of discharging his contractual duties because a metal plate fell and scratched the lens of his spectacles. The Social Security Commissioner held that there had not been "a personal injury". Cases have arisen on the question of whether damage done to a prosthesis, *e.g.* an artificial hand or limb, which prevents the worker from discharging contractual duties until the item is repaired or replaced, can be a personal injury, and it is established that the injury need not be an injury to living tissue for a claim to be successful. In the leading case of *R(I) 8/81* a Social Security Commissioner indicated that if the "item" damaged is so intimately linked with the body that it can be said to be a part of the body, then a personal injury may have been suffered. This may be easier to establish if the item is an "internal part" of the body, *e.g.* a heart pacemaker or replacement hip joint, than if it is a detachable and external item such as an artificial limb.

"*Accident*". The statutory formula requires that the personal injury must be caused by "accident". The formula found in the Principal Act of 1993 is in this respect identical with that contained in the Workmen's Compensation Acts. The case law on the meaning of the word "accident" makes it clear that the question of whether an "accident" has occurred is to be judged by reference to the plain and ordinary meaning of the word. However, the leading English appellate cases indicate that the judges are divided on the question of what precisely this meaning is. The early English cases indicated that the word "accident" meant an event which was "fortuitous and unexpected". No accident occurred, according to this view, if something happened which was intended, and an injury resulted. So, if a workman strained back muscles by attempting to lift a heavy object there was no accident because the act (lifting) was intended. This interpretation was the result of taking a literal approach to the phrase "injury by accident". Because the statute distinguished between the physical event and the physiological effects, so a technical approach developed. The House of Lords however took a different view for, as Viscount Haldane L.C. said in *Trim Joint District School v. Kelly*

[1914] 7 B.W.C.C. 274, "the common meaning of this word [accident] is ruled neither by logic nor by etymology, but by custom, and no formula will precisely express its usage for all cases". In *Fenton v. Thorley & Co.* [1903] A.C. 443 the House of Lords ruled that it was not acceptable to distinguish "personal injury" from "accident". So, in that case, a workman who strained his back in attempting to shift an unexpectedly heavy piece of machinery was able to recover compensation because he had suffered "personal accident by injury". In his judgment Lord MacNaghten indicated that the compound phrase "personal injury by accident" is qualified by the phrase, "accident arising out of and in the course of employment". Lord MacNaghten went on to say that "the expression 'accident' is used in the popular and ordinary sense of the word as denoting an unlooked-for mishap or an untoward event which is not expected or designed". In the celebrated case of *Trim Joint District School v. Kelly* the House of Lords, by a majority of 4 to 3 provided a more complete analysis of Lord MacNaghten's definition of the word "accident". In particular, the mishap or event must not be "designed" by the sufferer. Kelly was an assistant master at an industrial school. Part of his duties required him to superintend the boys in the school and to inflict punishment when appropriate. Kelly had on a previous occasion forbidden the boys from playing hurling and had caught one of them stealing. Two boys, in accordance with a pre-arranged plan, assaulted Kelly with heavy brushes, causing Kelly's death. The majority found that there was an accidental injury within Lord MacNaghten's test. The fact that death or injury results from an intentional act by another does not prevent the event from being within the notion of an accident. Only if the injury is self-inflicted by the design of the victim is a deliberate act excluded. It follows from this interpretation that an assault by strikers on workers called in to undertake tasks normally carried out by the strikers is an accident. A wages clerk who is shot by a robber during an attempt to take money which the clerk regularly carries, on behalf of his employer, suffers an accident as does a gamekeeper who is shot by poachers while engaged in the discharge of his duties. To similar effect is *Noble Ltd v. Carragher* (1923) 57 I.L.T.R. 137, a case in which compensation was paid to a carter who was shot dead while driving his lorry through an area where civil disturbances were taking place.

The "accident" must be proved to have occurred and the burden of proof, in this regard, rests on the claimant. The statutory formula overlaps in the sense that an illness or condition that manifests itself during employment may not lead to benefit being paid, either because there was no accident or because the injury did not "arise out of" the employment. In *O'Hara v. Hayes* (1910) 44 I.L.T.R. 71 a workman hurrying to a railway station with a parcel on behalf of his employer felt faint, collapsed and died shortly afterwards. Walker L.C., giving the judgment of the Court of Appeal, held that heart disease was the cause of death and that there was no "accident". Apart from instances of this kind where injury or death is the result of natural causes, it is often difficult to establish entitlement where the injury, or death, follows from contracting a disease. In *Finlay v. Guardians of Tullamore Union* [1914] 2 I.R. 233 a workman was employed, as part of his duties, to remove sewage from a machine. After having been employed for several years, he contracted typhoid fever and died. Medical evidence was adduced which showed that handling sewage could be a cause of typhoid but there was no evidence that removal of the sewage from the machine was the cause of this man's death.

If however the condition, or illness, can be attributed to an event, or a series of events, which are themselves external to the condition or illness involved, then it may be possible to show that there has been a "personal injury by accident". The test advanced by Lord Hanworth M.R. in *McFarlane v. Hutton Bros. Ltd* (1926) 20 B.W.C.C. 222 has been approved by English and Irish judges on several occasions: "if there is an unexpected personal injury arising from some physiological condition set up in the course of the work that may be described as an accident even though there is at the moment nothing unusual or particular which sets it up." *McFarlane's* case also establishes that in cases where the physiological condition already existed there may still be an accident even if the event that produces the condition is an ordinary and elemental part of the employment. However, in many of the cases, a physical event can be identified and fixed as an accident. In *Mooney v. Belfast S.S. Co.* (1904) 38 I.L.T.R. 195 a stevedore was struck on the chest by a cart when he was at work. A medical examination revealed that the worker had an advanced state of heart disease. He returned to work but could only do light work: he died nine days after the accident. It was held that, despite the heart disease, compensation could be payable if the incident involving the cart was the immediate cause of death. To similar effect is *Lavery v. Kelly Ltd* (1932) 66 I.L.T.R. 117, in which compensation was payable to a workman who suffered a cerebral haemorrhage. This case, like the leading English case of *Ismay, Imrie & Co. v. Williamson* [1908] A.C. 437 indicates that there may still be "personal injury by accident" notwithstanding the fact that the worker was in a weak or debilitated condition and was therefore less likely to withstand the task or physical conditions that brought on the physiological change. Some of the "physical strain" cases demonstrate a marked reluctance by the judiciary to adopt artificial distinctions. In the words of Lord Loreburn in *Clover, Clayton & Co. Ltd. v. Hughes* [1910] A.C. 242: "In each case the arbitrator ought to consider whether in substance, as far as he can judge on such a matter, the accident came from the disease alone, so that whatever the man had been doing it would probably have come all the same, or whether the employment contributed to it. In other words, did he die from the disease alone or from the disease and employment taken together, looking at it broadly? Looking at it broadly I say, and free from over-nice conjectures, was it the disease that did it, or did the work he was doing help in any material degree?" This dictum was applied by O'Dalaigh J. in the Supreme Court in *Larkin & Others v. C.I.E.* [1962–3] Ir. Jur. Rep. 73. A workman came on duty as a railway shunter complaining of chest pains. He operated a points lever in order to change the track. This required considerable effort and exertion by the workman. Immediately thereafter he fell down dead: post mortem revealed advanced cardiac disease and death by thrombosis. While medical evidence conflicted on the causative element the Supreme Court found that there was personal injury by accident: moving the points lever was described as "the precipitating factor".

In cases where death or injury is the result of disease the courts initially refused to hold that there could be "personal injury by accident" in such circumstances. In the famous case of *Brintons v. Turvey* [1905] A.C. 230 a workman contracted anthrax while employed in a wool factory. The bacillus had entered the workman's body via his eye. In many cases where a disease results there can be a specific incident that fits into the concept of an accident. In *Walker v. Mullins* (1908) 42 I.L.T.R. for example, a gardener contracted tetanus when a nail pierced his boot. Clearly the injury itself could constitute an accident, the entry of the tetanus virus being a consequence of the injury but, to go back to *Brintons v. Turvey*, it seems odd to hold that entry of the germ into the body is the accident for, if this be the case, all diseases would satisfy the "personal injury by accident" test. There are however Irish cases in which work-related diseases have been compensatable even though no physical injury or physical event, other than entry of the germ or virus, occurs. An extreme example of this is found in *Maguire v. Brownlee* [1952] Ir. Jur. Rep. 35. A farm labourer contracted ringworm while employed as a cowherd. Given the incubation period of the virus the date of entry into the labourer's body was fixed approximately at August 12, 1952. The Circuit Court judge held that cows pushing against the labourer, a possible source of infection, could constitute a series of "accidents". Similarly, when a gardener contracted a species of jaundice commonly transmitted via rat droppings, proof that rats had been seen in the garden seem to have provided the "accident" necessary to satisfy the statutory formula: *McCarthy v. Lillingston* (1943) 77 I.L.T.R. 59. While these cases demonstrate an admirable willingness on the part of some judges to provide compensation for work-related conditions, reasoning of this kind produces an inherent contradiction, for no real accident occurs. There is simply a physical change or illness, which is no doubt attributable to employment, but there is no real evidence of an accident occurring.

The English courts began to develop the distinction between medical conditions that were the result of a specific and identifiable event and those that were clearly work-induced but which did not satisfy the notion of personal injury by accident. The distinction is between an accident and a process. Lead poisoning of a workman by a gradual process, caused by repeated exposure to lead, was held not to be compensatable because no specific incident could be shown, given the nature of the condition, or attributed as the date when the condition was contracted. Two Irish cases illustrate this distinction. In *Kelly v. Cement Ltd* [1940] I.R. 84 a workman was employed to fill bags with cement by using a packing machine. The machine was fitted with a fan and exhaust pipe, and the workman was supplied with a respirator and mask, but nevertheless the workman inhaled cement dust during the 11-month period he was so employed. During the last six months of employment he had developed a chronic cough and was expelling the dusty deposit from his throat and nose. He developed pleurisy. The Circuit Court held that the workman had suffered "personal injury by accident". The Supreme Court, by a majority of 2 to 1, held that there was no accident. Sullivan C.J. indicated that it was reasonably well-established, by reference to English appellate case law, that the expression personal injury by accident was designed to exclude idiopathic disease. In this particular case the workman, like the workman in *Williams v. Guest, Keen, and Nethefolds* [1905] 2 K.B. 232, had over a protracted period simply inhaled the dust produced by the activity in which he was engaged. Sullivan C.J. dissented vigorously, remarking that *Steel v. Cammell, Laird & Co.* was not binding on the Supreme Court and that to require the workman to be able to show a "precise time" at which the "mischief" arose—the language used by Lord Collins M.R. in *Cammell, Laird & Co.*—is not only unwarranted by the objectives behind the Act but "have only led to confusion and a conflict of authority".

In contrast stands the Northern Ireland case of *Swan v. Dorman Long & Co.* [1934] N.I. 158. A workman employed for six months in compression conditions excavating the Foyle bridge suffered decompression sickness on one occasion when he left the decompressor. There seems to have been no real evidence that the time spent in the decompressor was less than that normally endured. The evidence was that the decompressor had been ineffective. Despite the fact that there were grounds for believing, on the evidence, that the decompressor was ineffective because of prolonged exposure to decompression, the Court of Appeal allowed compensation for a personal injury by accident. The distinction between "accident" and "process" is too well established now to be displaced. In the Northern Ireland case of *Reg* (Curry) v. National Insurance Commissioner [1974] N.I. 89 Lord Lowry C.J. explained how the courts began to mark the boundary between these two concepts. After examining the judicial interpretation of accident, the Lord Chief Justice went on: "in time the courts grafted onto these simple ideas a new concept: if a workman as a result of a series of incidents consisting of accidental occurrences (each of which may have been insignificant if viewed in isolation) suffered injury, he was regarded as having suffered personal injury by accident. One would still expect that each incident must qualify to be regarded as an 'accident' before the cumulative effect of the series of incidents could be held to have produced injury by *accident*, because, if a workman is injured by a series of incidents none of which was an accident he could not properly be said to have been injured by accident." After examining the caselaw Lord Lowry concluded that no clear line of authority could be found. He was therefore thrown back onto a process of statutory interpretation of the words "injury by accident" in order to find their "ordinary meaning". In his view a series of everyday and somewhat routine incidents, *e.g.* industrial noise or vibrations generated by a machine, the emission of dust or fumes from a machine or by an industrial process, are incidents, but, without more, such incidents or series of incidents cannot be called an accident or series of accidents. In the case concerned the applicant suffered injury as a result of the high pitched noise emitted by a saw over a continuous period. Each occasion on which noise assailed his ears could not be described as an accident although some exceptional incident or series of incidents would fit into the notion of an accident as an unlooked-for mishap or untoward event which is not expected or designed. Lord Lowry noted that if, the saw had emitted unwarranted noises due to lack of maintenance then an injury by accident would be likely to occur. Unless the working conditions are themselves harmful, Lord Lowry reasoned, an everyday incident which progressively brings on a physiological change in a worker does not occur via an "accident". It may be that where the injury occurs to a worker a short time after commencing that particular employment, even if the work conditions are normal, this temporal factor may persuade the statutory authorities that "injury by accident" has occurred. It matters not that the worker was particularly susceptible to being affected by the working conditions in question as long as an incident, capable of constituting an accident, occurred.

The statutory formula: "arising out of and in the course of"

In order for an industrial injury to be compensable under the occupational injuries scheme, the claimant must satisfy the statutory authorities that the relevant injury is a "personal injury . . . by accident arising out of and in the course of his employment". This phrase was an integral part of the Workmen's Compensation Acts and, as a phrase, it is commonly held to have provoked more litigation than any other statutory provision in the common law world. More importantly, the phrase, and its constituent parts, endeavours to traverse the most complicated and difficult issues of risk, causation and fault imaginable, so it is hardly surprising that the law reports are laden with cases that are simply irreconcilable. No wonder one English Lord of Appeal, in a celebrated dictum, a mere 23 years after the statute was passed, was forced to admit that "the language of the Act of Parliament and the decisions upon it are such as that I have long since abandoned the hope of deciding any case upon the words "out of and in the course of" upon grounds satisfactory to myself or convincing to others": Lord Wrenbury in *Armstrong Whitworth & Co. v. Redford* (1920) 13 B.W.C.C. 89. More recently, Lawton L.J., in *R. v. National Insurance Commissioners ex p. Michael* [1977] 2 All E.R. 420 at 429 remarked that "In the long history of English law there probably has been no group of words more often construed than personal injury caused by accident arising out of and in the course of employment". Irish judges have made similar observations on the unhappy and litigious effects of the formula in Irish caselaw. In the report of *Kelly v. Cement Ltd* [*supra*] Sullivan C.J. mentioned that one English judge in the Court of Appeal had, in 1925, confessed that he found it impossible to say what was an accident. O'Sullivan C.J. remarked that he doubted whether a review of the cases decided after that date would have removed the learned judge's difficulty in this regard.

In the view of those responsible for the majority report submitted by the 1962 Commission on Workmen's Compensation, the word "accident" and the statutory formula "arising out of and in the course of employment" had been the subject of so much litigation that the meaning to be extracted from each is well settled. The majority and minority reports agreed that the most appropriate response to problems of defining which injuries should be employment risks would require retention of these existing concepts, in preference to alternative and sometimes vaguer expressions, while at the same time making provision for complimentary statutory provisions to broaden the scope of the employment risk so as to embrace incidents that fall outside the statutory formula. Many commentators feel that this pragmatic approach is deeply flawed and recommendations for alternative statutory definitions of compensatable industrial injury are sometimes canvassed. In one telling phrase Mr Justice Cardozo described the phrase as a "serbonian bog". Ogus and Barendt comment that the problem of defining when an injury is to be classified as an employment risk is itself the source of the difficulty: the language employed is not of itself the cause of difficulties in establishing the connection between work and the accident. The decision to continue to utilise the formula "arising out of and in the course of employment" has not been widely welcomed. Casey (1969) 4 Ir.Jur. 235 comments that both the majority and minority reports failed to address the essential issues posited by the phrase. The same commentator notes that the phrase encourages legalism and can give rise to uncertainty of application (notwithstanding the opportunities that have arisen *via* case law to tease out the implications of this phrase) and that, even when the meaning to be attributed is clear, the result is not always desirable. As we shall see, many of the criticisms levelled at the implications of retaining this formula have been defused by pragmatic legislative qualifications (*e.g.* in relation to travelling) but there are still many commentators who favour adopting other approaches to the vexed question of determining when a work-related injury is to bring the sufferer within the industrial compensation scheme. The traditional approach to the formula has been to regard the phrase "arising out of and in the course of employment" as having two distinct elements. The words "out of" indicate that the injury must have occurred as the result of the employed person being engaged in employment: there must be some causal link, an employment risk, that distinguishes the employed person from other members of the public. The words, "in the course of employment", on the other hand, indicate that, for the injury to be within the formula, the employed person must have suffered the injury while engaged in doing something which is a part of the employee's contract of employment or is an incidental element thereof. Lord Wright in *Craig v. Dover Navigation Co. Ltd* (1939) 32 B.W.C.C. 300 summed up this distinction, with characteristic clarity, thus: "what arises 'in the course' of the employment is to be distinguished from what arises 'out of the employment' ". The former words relate to time conditioned by reference to the man's service, the latter to causality".

"*In the course.*" If the statutory formula is to be satisfied, the accident by injury must occur "in the course of employment". At first sight this should be easy to determine. If it is possible to identify what the hours of employment are, then an accident occurring within these set hours should be sufficient to comply with this formula. However, it is not quite so simple. First of all, the cases show that many workers do not have set hours. This is particularly true of persons in domestic employment and persons who have limited mobility, even when "off-duty", *e.g.* mariners, oil rig workers. Secondly, geographical considerations may intervene. The worker may suffer the injury in a place where the public may also have rights of access, *e.g.* the highway. This may defeat the employment risk element which the statutory formula is designed to accommodate. Thirdly, the accident may occur within working hours, at a place where the worker is contractually obliged to be, but it may occur when the worker is engaged in an activity that may not fall within the worker's contractual duties or be reasonably incidental thereto. The case law throws up a series of tests and distinctions that at times indicate a failure by many judges to bear in mind the strictures of the House of Lords on the purpose behind the legislative scheme and how this should influence the process of statutory interpretation. The view that the word accident should be given a liberal interpretation because the legislation is intended to function on an insurance rather than fault basis appears in many cases, on the ground that the words "arising out of and in the course of employment" are to locate the risk to be insured against. But, it is submitted, the emphasis laid by some judges on fault, reasonable contemplation and the onus of proof resting on the claimant, reveals that, in interpreting the statutory formula, many judges seem to have lost sight of the fact that the Workmen's Compensation Acts were not essentially about establishing a breach of duty by the employer.

The classical definition. In a frequently cited speech on the question of when an accident occurs in the course of employment Lord Loreburn said, in *Moore v. Manchester Liners Ltd* (1910) 3 B.W.C.C. 527: "to sum it up, I think an accident befalls a man 'in the course of' his employment, if it occurs while he is doing what a man so employed may reasonably do within a time during which he is employed, and at a place where he may reasonably be during that time." If the worker has fixed hours of work, and the accident occurs during these hours, then few difficulties will arise as long as the worker is on the employer's premises in pursuance of some duty owed to the employer. Difficulties about what precisely the employee was doing at the time the injury happened can sometimes lead to the conclusion that the injury did not occur in the course of employment but, in general, issues about the activity are best considered under the "arising out of" part of the statutory formula, particularly when one bears in mind the "reasonably incidental" aspect of the "course of employment" portion of this phrase. Difficulties can arise where the worker has no fixed hours of employment and the injury occurs when the worker has arguably embarked on an activity that seems primarily to benefit the worker, or at least, someone other than the employer. In *O'Rourke v. Woods* [1959] Ir. Jur. Rep. 55 an agricultural worker was injured while cutting boughs from trees on his employer's land. The accident occurred on a church holiday. Evidence was allowed to show that some weeks earlier the worker had been instructed to cut the boughs, as a matter of good husbandry. Although the wood was to be used by the worker as firewood, the instruction given earlier, and the flexible working hours normally anticipated in employment of this kind, meant that the injury occurred "in the course of employment". Domestic servants and hotel workers who "live in", have often been considered to be within the statutory formula when an injury befalls them on the employer's premises, especially when discharging a duty owed to the employer (*e.g.* in keeping their accommodation clean or aired) but even when resting. If, however, the worker is injured and the employment is not continuous the accident will not occur "in the course of employment" if the accident occurs at the end of the day, or occurs in sleeping accommodation provided by the employer, the worker being under no obligation to use the accommodation: see *Daly v. Limerick County Council* [1962–3] Ir. Jur. Rep. 42 when compensation was not payable in respect of injuries caused when a gas fire caused an explosion in sleeping accommodation provided by the employer. Seamen who are injured while on board the vessel are also able to establish that the injury occurs in the course of employment, even if engaged in legitimate recreational activities and certainly while undertaking duties. While in many of the early cases where a mariner disappeared from on board ship, the worker's body being found subsequently in the water near to where the person in question was last seen, this initially caused difficulties of proof for dependants of the deceased mariner, the English Courts and later the Irish Supreme Court adopted a more reasonable position in relation to unexplained accidents. Accordingly, if a workman is on board ship, or other workplace where he is authorised to be, and is not seen again until the worker's body is recovered nearby, sometime later, in the absence of anything else it may reasonably be inferred that the worker was killed while engaged in contractual duties and therefore as a result of an accident arising out of and in the course of employment. Indeed, this proposition may also function in cases where an injury occurs in the workplace and the worker cannot give an explanation of how the injury occurred, *e.g.* as a result of shock.

When the worker leaves the place of employment, by order of the employer, and injury results, the fact that the worker was ordered to leave the place of employment for some purpose may be conclusive. So, where a bricklayer returned to his place of employment after being ordered to collect his wages from the works depot and was struck by a passing cart when alighting from a tram, a majority of the Court of Appeal held that the accident occurred in the course of employment. In *Cummins v. Irish Insurance* (1940) 74 I.L.T.R. 161 a full-time insurance agent was injured in a garage premises when he arrived to inspect repair work on his motor car. Upon evidence that the employer expected the employee's motor vehicle to be used in discharging contracting duties the statutory formula was held to have been satisfied. In cases such as these the fact that the worker is in a place other than where the worker is expected to be, or is in the workplace at a time the worker is not contractually bound to be there, or is engaged in an activity that falls outside the worker's job-description, does not preclude the worker from satisfying the courts, or the statutory authorities, that the accident occurred in the course of employment. On the time factor *McKenna v. Higgins* (1935) 69 I.L.T.R. is instructive. A nurse, prior to going on duty, began to comb her hair and generally attend to her appearance while looking in a mirror over a fireplace. Her clothes caught fire and she was burned. Compensation was payable. Even if the employee was not bound to be in the place of employment, *e.g.* the employee arrives early for work in order to be thoroughly prepared for employment, or when a shift has ended in order to clean tools or machinery, the accident will occur in the course of employment. On the other hand, attending a criminal trial in order to give evidence favourable to the employer is not an activity which occurs in the course of employment.

If the worker leaves the place of employment for personal reasons there is a danger that any accident "occurring off the premises" will not be an employment risk. Cases in which mariners leave their ship in order to go ashore for various purposes illustrate these difficulties. According to Lord Dunedin in *Davidson v. McRobb* [1918] A.C. 304, when a sailor is leaving his ship by the provided access, or has reached provided access on his return, he has not left the course of his employment in the first case, and in the second he has returned to it. Thus a sailor, leaving or returning to his ship may be within the statutory formula if he falls from a gang plank or vertical ladder on the side of a quay provided by the employer or a docks authority. If no reasonable access is provided and the sailors are to get ashore by traversing other vessels an accident occurring on another vessel will be within the statutory formula. The leading Irish case is *Toner v. Dublin Trawling Ice & Cold Storage Co.* [1945] I.R. 459. A crewman left his ship one night entirely for his own purposes. It was dark because of the "black-out" imposed during World War II. Access to shore was gained by propping a movable ladder against the jetty. The crewman got to the top of the ladder, mounted the jetty but then fell onto a slipway and was severely injured. The Supreme Court held the accident did not occur in the course of employment. The question may of course be complicated if we consider the purpose behind the sailor's visit ashore. Here, two factors may coincide. The fact that a sailor goes ashore to a public place, thereby exposing himself only to the dangers that any member of society generally may face, is outweighed by the activity in appropriate cases. If the visit ashore is due to an instruction by the employer which the sailor is obliged to carry out then an accident befalling that employee is of course, in a different position. There the accident would not have occurred to that employee but for the contract of employment requiring him to be in the public place where the accident happened. Even if the worker leaves the workplace entirely for his own purposes, if the reason for the absence is reasonably contemplated, a later injury may still occur in the course of employment. Where the employer fails to provide adequate toilet facilities and the employee leaves the premises in order to go to the toilet in a place, and by a route, expressly or tacitly assented to by the employer, subsequent death or injury will occur in the course of employment. Absence from the workplace for meal or refreshment breaks or to go to the toilet are within the reasonable contemplation test. However, in a leading English case dealing with an injury that occurred to a worker while overstaying or abusing an authorised or statutory employment interval of this kind, Lord Denning M.R. addressed the question of whether an employee who interrupts employment for some personal matter not incidental to the employment may still act in the course of employment. In *R. v. N.I.C. ex parte A.E.U.* [1966] L.Q.B. 31, he said "I would agree that in the ordinary way if a man, while at his place of work, during his hours of work, is injured by a risk incidental to his employment, then the right conclusion usually is that it is an injury which arises out of and in the course of the employment, even though he may not be doing his actual work but chatting to a friend or smoking or doing something of that kind. But he may take himself out of it if he does something of a kind entirely different from anything he was employed to do."

In recent years several English judges have found it necessary to distance themselves from the "reasonably incidental" test, at least in the sense that reasonably incidental activities are referable to the *work* that the claimant is engaged to carry out, as against the somewhat broader notion of "reasonably incidental to the employment". In *R. v. National Insurance Commissioner ex p. Michael* [1967] 2 All E.R. 420 a police constable was seriously injured while playing football for the Gwent Constabulary. The match during which the injury was sustained took place on a "rest day". Participation in sporting activities of this kind was encouraged by his superiors as being good for force morale as well as helping to keep officers fully fit. The force recognised such participation by granting participating officers with eight hours per month "duty time" so, to that extent, Constable Michael was "on duty" even while playing on his rest day. The Court of Appeal unanimously held that the injury did not occur in the course of employment. "The appellant was employed as a police officer. It was no part of his work as a police officer to play football for his force team, even though his superiors expected that he would play for that team and every encouragement was given to him to do so". However, the Court of Appeal indicated that injuries sustained while engaged in recreational activities could possibly be compensatable when the activity is part of a training course or physical fitness course which is designed to better equip the employee for arduous duties: see [1982] J.S.W.L. 179. Recreational activities that help ensure continued physical fitness in difficult climatic conditions can also fall within this category: *Reinhardt v. Irish Shipping* [1964] Ir. Jur. Rep. 43.

Arising "out of". The statutory formula requires that the accident must not only occur within the context of the employment contract but also that the accident must be linked, as a matter of cause and effect, to some risk related to the work in which the claimant is legitimately engaged. In this context the requirements of the statutory formula have been given a broad interpretation. It is, for example, not necessary to show that the employment risk in question was uniquely run by the employee. In a leading case decided on the Workmen's Compensation Acts, a sailor perished after contracting yellow fever while serving on a ship in West Africa, the area being infested with mosquitoes carrying the disease. Viscount Maugham had this to say of the question of whether the accident arose out of the employment (*Craig v. Dover Navigation Co.* (1939) 32 B.W.C.C. 300): "the words connote a certain degree of causal relation between the accident and the employment. It is impossible exactly to define in positive terms the degree of that causal connection but certain negative propositions may I think be laid down. For example, we are bound, I think, to hold that the fact that the risk is common to all mankind does not prove that the accident does not arise out of the employment." So in the case at bar, the sailor was required to proceed by ship to West Africa as a part of his employment. Thirteen of the crew of 24 contracted yellow fever, seven of them dying as a result. Factors of this kind made it relatively easy for the House of Lords to hold that being on this particular vessel at the time in question was a dangerous place and a place to which his employment had taken him.

Some risks, however, are not employment risks at all: [1984] J.S.W.L. 59. One of the tests often advanced to distinguish between employment-related risks and accidental events that are considered to be the ordinary perils that individuals in society must generally endure is this: was it within the reasonable contemplation of the parties that the accident would occur in the manner in which it actually occurred? The cases involving assault and wrongful actions by third parties are particularly instructive in this context. Clearly, an assault by pupils on a teacher charged, *inter alia*, with enforcing discipline amongst pupils would be within the test of contemplated employment risks: *Trim Joint District School v. Kelly* (*supra*). Similarly, a gamekeeper or fisheries inspector could anticipate physical attack when confronting poachers. Wages clerks or security guards and workers responsible for making important decisions and enforcing discipline amongst workers in particularly "hard" trades and industries could envisage physical assault during the course of employment. A night-watchman who is assaulted when properly protecting his employer's property would also be within the reasonable contemplation test. However, in *Leslie v. O'Hara* (1951) 85 I.L.T.R. 141 a headgardener was struck on the nose by another gardener during a disagreement about the laying out of flowerbeds. The blow caused a cerebral haemorrhage. The injury was held not to arise out of the employment because an event of this kind was not something the nature of which the employment contract would envisage as an employment risk. Similarly in *Byrne v. Tyner* (1944) 78 I.L.T.R. 149, the death of a domestic servant who was shot by a fellow employee who had become insane was held not to arise out of the employment. In *Kelly v. Weatherwell Ltd* [1959] Ir. Jur. Rep. 67 the driver of a small motor vehicle used to transport goods around a factory premises was injured when an overhead door was partially lowered by an unknown person and the driver reversed into the doorway believing the door to be completely raised. The injury suffered by hitting an obstruction while driving the vehicle was held to be an employment risk. The Supreme Court held that the cause of the injury (an unauthorised act by a third party) did not break the chain of causation. McGuire C.J. indicated that the case was within Lord Loreburn's example in the *Trim* case of boys putting logs on a railway line, thereby causing a collision and injuries to the driver of a railway engine.

If the injury results from a practical joke or horseplay between workers then the injury is unlikely to be, as a matter of causation, an accident "arising out of employment." In *Kelly v. Weatherwell Ltd* the Supreme Court were at pains to point out that the evidence before the Circuit Court fell short of a finding that the injury was caused by "larking". The general situation where "larking" is present is illustrated by *Dunne v. Dublin & Alliance Consumers Gas Co.* (1938) 72 I.L.T.R. 59. One worker took the opportunity afforded by the absence of the foreman and threw a heavy object at another worker thereby injuring him. The accident was held to occur in the course of employment although it did not arise from the employment. Allowances are made however for the mischievous tendencies of young boys: *Clayton v. Hardwick Colliery Co.* (1915) 9 B.W.C.C. 136.

The workmen's compensation case law also throws up other examples of accidents that occur during the course of employment but which fail to satisfy the causal requirement. If the injury is the result of natural phenomena there is a likelihood that the injury will not be held to be an employment risk. The leading Irish case is *Kelly v. Kerry County Council* (1908) 42 I.L.T.R. 23. A workman employed to clean out storm gullets by the roadside was struck dead by lightning. The workman was held not to be exposed to a greater risk than any other person within the area of the storm. If the employment brings the worker into contact with adverse conditions on a continuous basis or if the employment required the worker to be in a place of greater exposure, *e.g.* on top of a high building or scaffold then the answer may well be different. In cases where the injury is caused by an insect or animal, similar considerations arise. The fact that a worker was bitten or stung during the course of employment did not satisfy both limbs of the statutory formula. If the injury occurs while the victim is in a place where he or she would not have been but for the employment, *e.g.* on board ship in the tropics or in a stable yard where the farmyard dog or cat bites the worker.

The distinction between risks common to humanity and risks peculiar to employment creates borderline cases like *Byrne v. Campbell* [1923] 2 I.R. 106. A farm labourer was forking hay and kicked an object out of his way. The object, a detonator, left in the shed probably by combatants during the Civil War, exploded causing injury. The Court of Appeal held that the injury arose out of the employment. In contrast stands *Dixon v. Tipperary County Council* [1931] 66 I.L.T.R. 77. A workman found an object on his employer's premises and out of curiosity he chose to examine it. The object, a mills bomb, exploded. Because the examination or movement of the object was not directly for the employer's purpose, no compensation was awarded since the injuries caused by the explosion did not arise out the employment. Other activities that have been held to be activities engaged in for purposes outside the reasonable contemplation of the parties at the time the contract of employment was formed include firing a shotgun at crows without permission, notwithstanding that the crows would harm the potato crop and therefore the act was for the benefit of the employer: *Loughrey v. Morrison* [1930] I.R. 93.

Where the claimant suffers personal injury in the course of employment but the injury is in part attributable to some pre-existing medical condition, there may be difficult issues of causation to resolve. Many of the issues addressed earlier in relation to the distinction between an "accident" and "injury" are again relevant. If the injury is the result of some physiological change or, indeed, physical incident, then it may be that the chain of causation is not broken by proof that the claimant had some pre-existing condition that made the disability or injury more likely to occur. In *Coughlan v. Sheehan* (1933) 67 I.L.T.R. 235 a domestic servant, sitting by a fire after dinner, was seized by an epileptic fit. She fell into the hearth and was severely burned. The fit did not disentitle her from recovering workman's compensation. Physical injuries which induce depression or further mental or physical sickness may also be held to "arise out of" the employment, as long as it can be shown that the injury actually claimed for, as a matter of causation, would not have occurred so soon but for the accident: *Masterson v. Longford C.C.* (1954) 88 I.L.T.R. 127. The statutory authorities however must adjudicate on the issue of medical causation by reference to the documentary or parole evidence lawfully adduced. Once the medical opinion relied upon by the statutory authorities to decide against the claimant is rebutted by written or oral evidence at the appeal, the medical assessor has no rôle to play and the appeals officer, in the absence of further evidence from the deciding officer, cannot rule that the accident did not "arise out of" employment: *Kiely v. Minister for Social Welfare* [1977] I.R. 267.

Statutory modification of the onus and burden of proof

Subsection (1)

The reader will readily appreciate that the Workmen's Compensation Acts threw up a series of borderline, not to say irreconcilable, decisions on what risks were to be considered to be employment risks. The strict theoretical position which the courts were required to take, allied to the evidentiary difficulties that faced the dependants of workers who had died with no explanation of the circumstances in which the accident occurred, did not produce an intelligible jurisprudence, even though some judges began to grapple with these issues in a creative way. The Commission on Workmen's Compensation recommended that the statutory formula be retained but that an accident arising in the course of shall be deemed, in the absence of proof to the contrary, also to have arisen out of that employment. This recommendation, based on the U.K. legislation on industrial injuries, was adopted in 1966 and is now found in section 51(1) of the Principal Act of 1993.

In the U.K. the identical provision has been narrowly construed. The onus still rests on the claimant to show that the accident occurred in the course of employment and more seriously, any evidence (rather than speculation) that the accident may not have arisen out of the employment will defeat the presumption, *e.g.* evidence that an employee is later found with a head wound consistent with either assault or the possibility that the employee's head struck something when losing consciousness as a result of a medical condition.

Subsection (2)

Section 51(2) of the Principal Act of 1993, also originally implemented in 1966, deals with the problem of industrial injury that is the result of natural phenomena, third party intervention or contributory negligence by the employee that is nevertheless within the contract of employment. Unlike section 51(1), this provision is not tentative: once the claimant comes within section 51(2) there can be no question of other evidentiary matters defeating the claim for occupational injury benefits.

Problems which arose from the added peril or contravention of orders doctrines were also addressed by the Commission on Workmen's Compensation. The Commission felt it to be unjustifiable to allow accidents which occur in contravention of statutory regulations, or when the employee has not received instructions to act in a particular manner, to be compensatable employment risks unless death or serious physical disablement results. The Commission basically recommended the retention of section 15(2) of the Workmen's Compensation (Amendment) Act, 1934. Notwithstanding this recommendation the 1966 legislation adopted the provision governing the added peril and contravention of orders provisions, thus broadening the range of insurable work-related activities beyond those formally anticipated by the contract of employment.

Subsection (3)

Despite the apparent breadth of this provision the courts have drawn a distinction between acting in contravention or without orders *vis-à-vis* employment tasks as against doing things the employee was never employed to do at all. In *R. v. D'Albuqerque ex p. Bresnahan* [1966] 1 Lloyds Rep. 69, the deceased was employed as a "hooker on" in Liverpool docks. He was employed as a general labourer. Some pallets had been left on the dockside and because these objects interfered with the unloading of a vessel the deceased drove a forklift truck in an effort to move the pallets. The deceased overshot the quay and was drowned. The Divisional Court held that the accident did not come within the deeming provision above. In order to come within that provision it is not enough that the task be undertaken for the benefit of the employer. The act in question must be an act of a kind which the worker is engaged to do. The deceased was not employed to drive forklift trucks. This work was entrusted to special drivers. The question of whether a prohibition exists or not is irrelevant to this issue: see [1984] J.S.W.L. 59 for more recent English case law on this point.

Subsection (4)

"Travelling" under the Workmen's Compensation Acts. The question whether personal injury by accident may be compensatable as an industrial accident because it comes within the statutory formula has produced a voluminous amount of case law. The position established through case law, in particular on the question of whether injury sustained while travelling can occur "in the course of" employment, proved to be so unsatisfactory that two specific attempts have been made by the Oireachtas in order to mitigate the worst effects of Workmen's Compensation Acts litigation. If the injury was the result of the worker travelling from one place to another in order to carry out the instructions of the employer than a personal injury that results would be within the statutory formula. In *Ivory v. Finnegan* (1936) 70 I.L.T.R. 194 a maid cycled home in order to get aprons. Her employer gave her permission to make this journey. She was injured when she was knocked off her bicycle in the street. Sullivan P. declared that when an employee is injured, not on the employer's premises but in the street, the employee must be "in the place of accident in discharge of a duty to his employer imposed by his contract of service." In this context it is necessary to note that there are two qualifications to be added. First, the notion of the employer's premises had an extended meaning and was generally understood to cover a place where an employer has a right of way or, at the very least, a place to which the public have no right of access: *Sullivan v. Kerry C.C.* [1954] I.R. 120. Secondly, if the injury occurred during working hours and the employee was injured while doing something the employee was not employed to do, *e.g.* collecting food from a nearby shop or visiting adjacent premises to use a toilet when no such facility existed at the workplace, the employee did not go outside the course of employment if still under orders and the accident occurred outside the workplace or the accident occurred upon return to the place of employment: *Malorey v. Irish Button Co.* (1966) 100 I.L.T.R. 213; *Hetherington v. Dublin and Blessington Ry. Co.* [1927] I.R. 75. The type of activity for which the worker was employed may also have been material. If the accident occurred in a public place and the worker suffered the injury, it being in essence a matter of being in the wrong place at the wrong time, there was often no real basis upon which that injury could be an employment risk unless the employment, by its very nature, envisaged public places to be the workplace of the employee in question. So, porters and messengers injured on the street or other public place may have been injured in the course of employment, particularly when the contract required the employee to constantly cross and recross the street rather than proceed along a footpath or thoroughfare: *Cooper v. Healy* [1916] 2 I.R. 33. The issue of risk in these cases was determined, in many cases, on entirely subjective factors. Why should a cattleherder cycling between the two farms on which he was employed, on a public road, not be injured in the course of employment see: *Greene v. Shaw* [1912] 2 I.R. 430. If the employment envisaged that the worker would travel between places in order to carry out the contract of employment and the use of transport was envisaged as a proper and convenient way of getting around, then compensation could result following an accident: *Heffernan v. Secretary for War* [1918] 2 I.R. 267. These cases were clearly so haphazard and contradictory that no intelligible principle emerged.

In the next set of circumstances the principle was absolutely clear but the consequences that followed quite objectionable. When the employee began a journey to or from the place of employment, however, the employee was, in general, not held to act in the course of employment. Should the journey homeward involve carrying out an errand for the employer *en route*, the employee being free after the task was completed, then the course of employment was not ended upon leaving the employer's premises: *Redmond v. Bolger* [1957] Ir. Jur. Rep. 8. When the employee used a method of transport which the parties envisaged to be the most likely method of transport it could reasonably be supposed that the "course of employment" was not at an end, but the Workmen's Compensation Acts case law suggested a quite different result. In the leading case of *St Helens Colliery Co. Ltd. v. Hewitson* [1924] A.C. 59 a collier, injured whilst travelling on a special train provided for colliers by arrangement between his employers and the railway company, failed in his action because there was only a right, and no obligation, for the collier to travel on the train. Some of the decisions thrown up by such a test were horrific. In *Carroll v. Irish Steel* [1945] 79 I.L.T.R. 151 the plaintiff was a steelworker employed on Haulbowline Island by the defendant company. He got to work by travelling from the mainland by motor launch. The service provided by the motor launch was not exclusive to steelworkers but the employer had obtained a preferential rate, the launch company being paid by the defendants who deducted the fare from wages. One evening, upon returning to the ferry after completing his day's work, the plaintiff slipped while trying to get access to the launch and was injured. There was no obligation to use this particular boat and thus the accident did not occur in the course of employment. The cases show that the concept of an implied contractual term, an implicit obligation to use the transport in question, was not easily satisfied. In *Doran v. Kellet* (1936) 70 I.R.L.R. 237, a worker injured when the car he was driving home crashed was not injured in the course of employment even though his employer expressly allowed him to take the car. The distinction between the employer's consent and the employee's obligation was strictly maintained.

Statutory modification of the "travelling" rule. A consideration of the case law from the Workmen's Compensation Acts helps to illustrate why it became necessary for statute to modify the rigours of the cases, particularly the contractual obligation found in section 39(4) of the Principal Act of 1981 which went back to the original 1966 legislation when it provided: "An accident happening while an insured person is, with the express or implied permission of his employer, travelling as a passenger by any vehicle to or from his place of work shall, notwithstanding that he is under no obligation to his employer to travel by that vehicle, be deemed for the purposes of this Part to arise out of and in the course of his employment, if: (a) the accident would have been deemed for those purposes so to have arisen had he been under such an obligation; and (b) at the time of the accident, the vehicle—(i) is being operated by or on behalf of his employer or some other person by whom it is provided in pursuance of arrangements made with his employer, and (ii) is not being operated in the ordinary course of a public transport service. An identical provision has been criticised in the U.K.: (see [1986] J.S.W.L. 194), but this subsection went some way towards mitigating the effects of decisions such as that in *Carrol v. Irish Steel.* The subsection however is difficult to satisfy in several respects. The only case that clearly comes within it would be a situation where a works bus or a taxicab is provided *by an employer* in order to transport workers to or from their place of employment and the accident occurs while travelling in the vehicle, even though the worker was not contractually obliged to travel in the vehicle. If the accident occurs in circumstances that fall outside this somewhat limited set of facts then the subsection may not be satisfied. If the service in question is provided by a public transport service, even as a result of a specific request by that employer, the subsection would not be satisfied if the route is accessible to members of the public generally. Workers who travel to and from work by a mode or transport that the employer has in no way arranged *e.g.* car-pooling by employees, are completely outside the subsection.

The limited nature of section 39(4) led to it being replaced, by substitution, by section 12 of the Social Welfare Act, 1986. This is now section 51(4) of the Principal Act of 1993 which, at first sight, would appear to resolve the issue. In the absence of regulations which limit the general scope of the "deeming" provision, any accident whilst travelling with be an industrial injury. It is clear that the statutory authorities cannot hold section 51(4) to be all embracing for it is extremely narrowly drawn. Suppose the journey to or from work includes a substantial break in the journey, *e.g.* to visit relatives or a public house? The intent behind the reform is clearly not to include broken journeys of any kind. This raises another issue: are the statutory authorities free to hold that an injury that occurs to a worker on the way into work or on the journey home has been the result of an accident arising out of and in the course of employment, under section 51(1) for example, even though there is no possibility of it being "deemed" under section 51(4)? No real debate accompanied the 1986 reform of section 39(4) of the 1981 Act: Parliamentary debates are silent on whether an accident whilst travelling can still come within the formula in the ordinary way or whether what is now section 51(4) is the sole determinant.

Section 51(4) is an enabling provision and its impact is based on the provisions of S.I. No. 81 of 1986, set out below. The relevant statutory instrument suggests that any interruption in the journey will prevent the accident from being deemed to occur in the course of, and arise from, the employment. The regulations provide that section 51(4) is satisfied in two instances:

"(1) the insured person, in the case of an accident while travelling to work, shall be engaged in travelling to his place of employment at the time with a view to carrying out the duties of his employment, such journey being an unbroken journey from his normal place of residence.

(2) the insured person in the case of an accident while travelling from work, shall be engaged in travelling directly, after he has completed the duties of his employment, from his place of employment in an unbroken journey to his normal place of residence."

The travelling to work requirement seems particularly narrow. Suppose the insured is travelling to the place of employment for a purpose other than carrying out his duties of employment, *e.g.* is going to clean equipment or tools which would normally be done by others, or outside the workplace. Similarly, a worker who is proceeding to the workplace to collect wages during a holiday period would not seem to be within the deeming provision. Similarly, if the journey is broken, *e.g.* the worker stops off to buy a morning newspaper or breakfast, does this interruption prevent the deeming provision from operating *at all*? Does the break in continuity only render the deeming provision inoperative if the injury occurs within the break in the journey? Even more marginal situations could arise. If the insured stops at the filling station to buy petrol for the car in which the journey is undertaken is the journey still "unbroken"? Does the notion of a broken journey only arise when the break is for the sole benefit of the employee or does a "reasonably incidental to the employment" test function here? Even more ludicrous still, the deeming provision is not available if the journey commences from a place other than the insured's normal place of residence, *e.g.* the insured stays overnight in a hotel in order to attend a business meeting and is injured when *en route* the following morning or where the insured is a lorrydriver or commercial traveller who habitually starts the working day from hotel accommodation. Similar factors could apply when the accident occurs after the employment has, in spatial terms, apparently ended. If the employee is injured after stopping off on the way home to visit a public house, this break in the journey would appear to be fatal to a claim. Suppose, however, the journey is broken for purposes related to the employment, *e.g.* the employee delivers a letter, or has a meeting with a person relevant to the employer's business. Suppose the accident occurs on a Friday evening, shortly after leaving the place of employment while *en route* to a weekend cottage which is not the employee's normal place of residence. The deeming provision in section 51(4) is not satisfied. In reality section 51(4) is really only relevant to travelling cases when the worker is commuting to or from the workplace. The older case law on "accident arising out of and in the course of" will remain of cardinal importance if the accident occurs during working hours or where the journey is undertaken or broken for purposes which are related to the employee's contractual duties or purposes incidental to the contract of employment. Specific provisions have been made for persons who are employed on ships or aircraft: S.I. No. 87 of 1979, as modified by S.I. No. 81 of 1986. If these persons suffer an accident by travelling to work on their ship or aircraft by means of another ship or aircraft the accident is deemed to arise out of and in the course of employment.

Subsection (5)

When the employment risk run was clearly the result of an emergency that required a response by the employee, the fact that no contractual duty could be imposed on an employee did not defeat a claim under the Workmen's Compensation Acts if the worker acted, and was injured, whilst acting in the interests of the employer: *Stephen v. Cooper* [1929] A.C. 570. The emergency need not be the result of some physical event such as a fire or flood at the workplace: it could just as easily be an exceptional or undesirable occurrence during the process of production, *e.g.* an expensive machine jamming or another worker being absent from the workplace, events which endanger life or result in damage to property and which induce a response by a worker who is, as a result, injured. The recognition by the courts of the emergency exception was followed by the Oireachtas in 1966 by a provision which is now section 51(5) of the Principal Act of 1993. It is worth noting that, in one respect, this "emergency" provision is narrower than that developed by the courts. In the case of *Tobin v. Hearn* [1910] 2 I.R. 639 Cherry L.J. indicated that the emergency concept could embrace an unauthorised act by an employee which is designed to further the business generally (*e.g.* undertaking work because another worker is absent). On the other hand the statutory emergency provision in subsection (5) applies to injuries sustained in or about premises he is employed at for the purposes of the employer's trade or business.

Subsection (6)

Workmen's compensation case law generally prevented recovery by apprentices while engaged in educational training, day release and the like. This subsection reverses the onus by way of a "deeming" provision.

Accidents in illegal employment and accidents outside State

52.—(1) Where a claim for occupational injuries benefit is made under this Part in respect of any accident or of any disease or injury prescribed for the purposes of section 66, or an application is made thereunder for a declaration that any accident was an occupational accident or for a corresponding declaration as to any such disease or injury, the Minister may direct that for the purposes of this Part the relevant employment shall, in relation to that accident, disease or injury, be treated as having been insurable (occupational injuries) employment, notwithstanding that, by reason of a contravention of or non-compliance with some provision contained in or having effect under any enactment passed for the protection of employed persons or of any class of employed persons, the contract purporting to govern the employment was void or the employed person was not lawfully employed therein at the time when or in the place where the accident happened or the disease or injury was contracted or received.

(2) In subsection (1) "relevant employment" means, in relation to an accident, the employment out of and in the course of which the accident arises and, in relation to a disease or injury, the employment to the nature of which the disease or injury is due.

(3) Except where regulations otherwise provide, an occupational injuries benefit shall not be payable in respect of an accident happening while the insured person is outside of the State.

GENERAL NOTE

Subsection (1)

Under the general law of contract, illegal contracts of employment normally preclude recovery on the contract by either party: see generally, Clark, *Contract Law in Ireland* (3rd ed.) Ch. 14. Specifically, in workmen's compensation actions, the illegal contract precluded recovery of compensation: *McHugh v. Ministry of Labour* [1940] N.I. 174.

This subsection empowers the Minister to direct that an accident, disease or injury occurring in either illegal employment or in void employment shall, nevertheless, be treated as in insurable employment.

Subsection (3)

This general prohibition against occupational injuries benefit being payable when an accident occurs outside the State has been relaxed by regulations, particularly in respect of volunteer development workers.

Benefits

Disability benefit

53.—(1) Subject to this Act, an insured person who suffers personal injury caused on or after the 1st day of May, 1967, by accident arising out of and in the course of his employment, being insurable (occupational injuries) employment, shall notwithstanding the contribution conditions contained in section 32 of Chapter 7 of Part II, be entitled to disability benefit in respect of any day on which, as a result of the injury, he is incapable of work during a period of injury:

Provided that an insured person shall not be entitled to disability benefit in respect of the first three such days.

(2) For the purposes of this section, a day shall not be treated in relation to an insured person as a day of incapacity for work if, in respect of that day, the insured person is being paid by his employer in respect of holiday leave.

(3) A person under the age of 16 years shall not be entitled to disability benefit under subsection (1) except in so far as may be provided for by regulations. [1994 Act, section 20]

(4)–(6) [repealed by 1994 Act, Section 31].

GENERAL NOTE

The integration of short-term injury benefit with disability benefit following the abolition of the industrial preference (see the General Note to section 49 above) was completed by the 1994 Act which effectively abolished both injury benefit and unemployability supplement, subject to the transitional provisions in section 56, as similarly amended by the 1994 Act.

For current rates of injury benefit for persons under 16, see S.I. No. 137 of 1995.

Disablement benefit

54.—(1) Subject to this Act, an insured person who suffers personal injury caused on or after the 1st day of May, 1967, by accident arising out of and in the course of his employment, being insurable (occupational injuries) employment, shall be entitled to disablement benefit if he suffers as a result of the accident from loss of physical or mental faculty such that the extent of the resulting disablement assessed in accordance with the following provisions of this section amounts to not less than 1 per cent.; and, for the purposes of those provisions, there shall be deemed not to be any relevant loss of faculty when the extent of the resulting disablement, if so assessed, would not amount to 1 per cent.

(2) Disablement benefit shall not be available to an insured person until after the 3rd day of the period of 156 days (Sundays being disregarded) beginning with the day of the relevant accident, nor until after the last day, if any, of that period on which he is incapable of work as a result of the relevant accident:

Provided that, if he is not so incapable on any day, being the 4th or a later day after the relevant accident, before the end of that period, he may claim, and if otherwise entitled, be awarded disablement benefit as from that day, but in that event the fact that he is or may be so incapable on a subsequent day of the period shall be disregarded for the purposes of this subsection.

(3) For the purposes of this section, the extent of disablement shall be assessed, by reference to the disabilities incurred by the claimant as a result of the relevant loss of faculty, in accordance with the following general principles—

(a) save as hereafter provided in this subsection, the disabilities to be taken into account shall be all disabilities (whether or not involving a loss of earning power or additional expense) to which the claimant may be expected, having regard to his physical and mental condition at the date of the assessment, to be subject during the period taken into account by the assessment as compared with a person of the same age and sex whose physical and mental condition is normal;

(b) any such disability shall be treated as having been incurred as a result of the relevant loss of faculty except that, subject to the provisions of any regulations made under subsection (4), it shall not be so treated in so far as the claimant either—

(i) would in any case have been subject thereto as the result of a congenital defect or of an injury or disease received or contracted before the relevant accident, or

(ii) would not have been subject thereto but for some injury or disease received or contracted after, and not directly attributable to, that accident;

(c) the assessment shall be made without reference to the particular circumstances of the claimant other than age, sex and physical and mental condition;

(d) the disabilities resulting from such loss of faculty as may be prescribed shall be taken as amounting to 100 per cent. disablement and other disabilities shall be assessed accordingly.

(4) Provision may be made by regulations for further defining the principles on which the extent of disablement is to be assessed, and such regulations may in particular direct that a prescribed loss of faculty shall be treated as resulting in a prescribed degree of disablement; and, in connection with any such direction, nothing in subsection (3)(c) shall be taken as preventing the making of different provision, in the case of loss of faculty in or affecting hand or arm, for right-handed and for left-handed persons.

(5) The period to be taken into account by an assessment of the extent of a claimant's disablement shall be the period (beginning not earlier than the end of the period of injury and limited by reference either to the claimant's life or to a definite date) during which the claimant has suffered and may be expected to continue to suffer from the relevant loss of faculty:

Provided that, if on any assessment the condition of the claimant is not such, having regard to the possibility of changes therein (whether predictable or not), as to allow of a final assessment being made up to the end of the said period—

(a) a provisional assessment shall be made, taking into account such shorter period only as seems reasonable having regard to his condition and the said possibility, and

(b) on the next assessment the period to be taken into account shall begin with the end of the period taken into account by the provisional assessment. [1995 Act, Schedule E]

(6) An assessment shall state the degree of disablement in the form of a percentage and shall specify the period taken into account thereby and, where that is limited by reference to a definite date, whether the assessment is provisional or final:

Provided that—

(a) the said percentage and period shall not be specified more particularly than is necessary for the purpose of determining in accordance with this section the claimant's rights as to disablement benefit, and

(b) a percentage between 20 and 100 which is not a multiple of 10 shall be treated—

(i) if it is a multiple of 5, as being the next higher percentage which is a multiple of 10, and

(ii) if it is not a multiple of 5, as being the nearest percentage which is a multiple of 10.

(7) (a) Where the extent of the disablement is assessed for the period taken into account as amounting to less than 20 per cent., disablement benefit shall be a gratuity (in this Chapter referred to as "a disablement gratuity")—

(i) of an amount fixed, in accordance with the length of the said period and the degree of disablement, by a prescribed scale, but not in any case exceeding the amount set out in Part II of the Second Schedule,

(ii) payable, if and in such cases as regulations so provide, by instalments.

(b) The scale prescribed for the purposes of paragraph (a) shall be the same for all persons.

(8) Where the extent of the disablement is assessed for the period taken into account as amounting to 20 per cent. or more, disablement benefit shall be a pension (in this Chapter referred to as "a disablement pension") for that period at the weekly rate set out in column (2) of Part III of the Second Schedule appropriate to the degree of disablement:

Provided that where the period is limited by reference to a definite date, the pension shall cease on the death of the beneficiary before that date.

(9) (a) Where, apart from this subsection, a gratuity would fall to be paid under subsection (7) in a case in which the period taken

into account by the assessment of disablement is the period of the claimant's life or a period exceeding seven years and the extent of disablement is assessed as amounting to not less than 10 per cent. and not more than 19 per cent., the following provisions shall have effect if the claimant opts, before the gratuity is paid, for the substitution of a pension for the gratuity—
  (i) the gratuity shall not be paid,
  (ii) the disablement benefit shall be a pension (in this Chapter also referred to as "a disablement pension") at the weekly rate appropriate in accordance with a prescribed scale,
  (iii) the disablement pension shall be for the period taken into account by the assessment of disablement:
      Provided that, where that period is limited by reference to a definite date, the pension shall cease on the death of the beneficiary before that date.
(b) The following provisions shall apply in relation to the scale prescribed for the purposes of this subsection—
  (i) the scale shall be the same for all persons,
  (ii) different amounts may be specified in relation to the different percentages under 20 per cent., but each such amount shall not be less than the amount which bears to the appropriate amount of disablement pension (set out in Part III of the Second Schedule) for a degree of disablement of 20 per cent., the same proportion as the percentage with respect to which it is specified bears to 20 per cent.

(10) In the case of an assessment of disablement where the period to be taken into account by the assessment commenced before the 1st day of May, 1990, subsection (9)(a) shall be construed as if the reference to "and the extent of disablement is assessed as amounting to not less than 10 per cent. and not more than 19 per cent." were deleted.

GENERAL NOTE

Most industrial injuries and diseases are not so serious that the worker concerned will suffer from permanent incapacity or death. After a relatively short period of time the worker will, on average, be able to return to employment. The award of injury benefit for a maximum period of 156 days recognises that the income maintenance needs of the injured worker can largely be met by regular cash payments until the worker resumes employment. However, there are many accident or disease victims who cannot be accommodated by regular cash payments made whilst recovering from the deleterious consequences of an employment risk. The worker may not be incapable of work and may continue to perform contractual tasks for the employer even though an injury has been sustained. The worker may nevertheless require medical treatment. The worker is likely to have suffered some degree of pain and suffering, indeed the worker may be disfigured. The worker may never fully recover from the accident or disease. Some recognition of the difference between an injury from which the victim will recover and an injury that has permanent consequences for the victim insofar as the injury will impair what would otherwise have been that person's physical or mental capabilities in the future, is built into the occupational injuries scheme in the form of disablement benefit. It is perhaps unfortunate that the British model should have been adopted, however, because those workers who suffer long-term or permanent disability do not receive a disablement pension that is in any way related to the past earnings or future earning potential of the individual worker concerned. In reality, the worker who is the victim of an industrial injury or industrial process is still compelled, in many instances, to resort to the courts to establish breach of contract or negligence by the employer if that worker is to establish a realistic level of compensation for a work-related disability. The British and Irish occupational injury schemes are, in this regard, out of step with most other jurisdictions in the West in failing to provide disablement pensions that are indexed to the pre-accident earnings of the person who suffers the injury. We should recall that workmen's compensation was payable by reference to a proportion of pre-accident earnings. In the U.S., where workmen's compensation schemes are still in force, payment is made by reference to pre-accident earnings, the disability payment traditionally being fixed at between 50 per cent to 66 and two thirds per cent. Some states control payments by reference to minimum and maximum amounts and by reference to the number of dependants the claimant has. Because pay-related benefit has never been seen as a long-term social welfare payment it is irrelevant to this discussion. If the occupational injury scheme provides a disabled person with a level of income that would approximate to the level that could have been expected but for the accident, this is a matter of good fortune rather than good planning. It is surprising that neither the Green Paper on Services for Disabled People (Pl. 2264) or the Commission on Social Welfare (Pl. 3851) drew attention to the shortcomings of a flat-rate system of income maintenance for the long-term disabled.

If a claim for disablement benefit is to be successful, the claimant must establish that the claimant has suffered a loss of physical or mental faculty which is assessed at not less than one per cent. Loss of faculty has been judicially interpreted as "loss of power or function of an organ of the body". The same judge stressed that it is unhelpful to consider whether there has been a loss of faculty in isolation from other factors for it is only the intermediate link in a chain of causation that consists of "personal injury", "loss of faculty" and "disablement": Lord Diplock in *Jones v. Secretary of State* [1972] 1 All E.R. 145 at 185.

If no loss of faculty is established or if the degree of loss does not reach one per cent then disablement benefit is not payable. Disfigurement is not expressly included as an incapacity in the Act. The list of prescribed conditions, however, makes specific reference to severe facial disfigurement as a disablement. Whether this is, strictly speaking, consistent with the idea that a disablement is an impairment of the body or the mind must, in the absence of amending legislation, be a moot point. It is clearly unsatisfactory that there is no legislative guidance on so fundamental an issue. In any event, the tariff does not indicate that severe disfigurement of the skin, *e.g.* serious burns or scars to the leg or arm is to be compensated. Section 54(3) of the Principal Act of 1993 sets out a series of general principles. First, the disabilities to be taken into account are determined objectively but it is irrelevant that the disability may or may not result in loss of earning power or medical expenses. The relevant disabilities are "all disabilities . . . to which the claimant may be expected, having regard to his physical and mental condition at the date of the assessment, to be subject [during the assessment period] as compared with a person of the same age and sex whose physical and mental condition is normal". The emphasis on providing compensation for impairing the "wholeness" of the accident victim, as a human being, is progressive enough, but it is at odds with the fact that the reference point is not the specific individual concerned but some idealised "average" human being. It is also curiously out of step with the basic premise upon which accident compensation for occupational injury has rested, namely a desire to provide economic security when an employment risk has produced insecurity.

Secondly, the claimant is generally able to benefit from a provision whereby the loss of faculty is deemed to produce the disability unless the claimant would have suffered this disability as a result of a congenital defect, injury or disease received or contracted before the accident, or would not have received the disability but for some injury or disease received after, and not attributable to the accident. The working of this second principle is somewhat problematic. It is directed at issues that arise when the victim suffers an injury which is not work-related but which, when added to the work injury, the resulting disability could produce a much higher assessment had both injuries been work-related *e.g.* a worker who has already lost sight in one eye via a detached retina loses the other eye in a work accident. Is the assessment to be 100 per cent or 40 per cent? The effect of the first of the two sub-rules would arguably seem to require separate assessments to be made. The statutory authorities are then to disregard the first disability, insofar as it is to be discounted or offset against the global assessment of disablement. In the statutory tariff, loss of sight in both eyes through an industrial accident is a 100 per cent disablement; loss of one eye counts as a 40 per cent disablement. If the Irish statutory authorities were to follow the U.K. practice, according to section 54(3)(b)(i) the statutory authorities are not to make an assessment based on total disability but a disability "in so far as the claimant . . . would in any case have seen subject thereto" by way of a congenital disease or prior injury. It is necessary therefore to make an assessment of the non-work-related disability (in this example, 40 per cent) and deduct that 40 per cent from the 100 per cent initial calculation, leaving a disablement benefit estimate of 60 per cent. The U.K. system seems much more reasonable. To simply calculate that loss of an eye is a 40 per cent disablement, ignoring that the injury to a partially sighted person is of greater significance would be harsh indeed. Article 5(3) of the Occupational Injuries Regulations (S.I. No. 77 of 1967) provides some guidance. The adjustment to be made is not as mathematical as the U.K. formula set out above. The regulation provides that where a person has suffered an injury set out in the First Schedule but, because of the physical or mental condition of the victim, he may be expected to be subject to greater disabilities than would be normal in such cases of injury, or if the part of the body injured was not functioning normally, then the loss of faculty is to be assessed against the degree of disablement set out in the second column "subject to such adjustment as may be reasonable in the circumstances of the case". The same flexible rule can apply to cases where the injury is not specified in the First Schedule.

Thirdly, and this is related to the first point, the assessment is to be made without reference to the particular circumstances of the claimant other than the age, sex, physical or mental condition of that person. In the case of the individual who is in good health at the time of the accident the statutory authorities may use the prescribed degrees of disablement laid down by S.I. No. 77 of 1967. Loss of both hands is fixed at 100 per cent disablement, as is the loss of both eyes and very severe facial disfigurement. Loss of one eye is fixed at 40 per cent. The loss of an index finger is set at 14 per cent. The loss of two phalanges of that finger is set at 11 per cent. A guillotine amputation of the tip without loss of bone is set at five per cent. It is by no means clear whether the prescribed degrees of disablement can be adjusted by the statutory authorities by using article 5(3) of these occupational injuries rules generally. It is submitted that no discretion exists save where the degree of disablement is not prescribed, *e.g.* loss of bodily functions not associated with amputation, such as motor or neurological damage as a result of spinal or head injuries. The assessment can be a final or provisional assessment. The latter will be made when there is a possibility that the condition may change. The conditional assessment will be for such period as is reasonable, the period in question being specified in the assessment itself. There are rounding provisions. If a multiple of 10 is not involved (if it is a figure between 20 and 100) the following rules apply. If the figure is a multiple of five then the assessment will be rounded to the nearest higher 10 per cent, *e.g.* if the assessment is 35 per cent then there will be a rounding up to 40 per cent. If the figure is not a multiple of 5 per cent there will be a rounding to the nearest multiple of 10, *e.g.* a 22 per cent assessment will be rounded to 20 per cent an assessment of 28 per cent will be rounded to 30 per cent. Impairment of sexual functions is not mentioned at all. Where a final assessment is made, any improvement in the condition of the pensioner does not lead to a reduction in the disablement pension.

It is doubtful whether the statutory authorities have the power to adjust later the pension payable because some later, but not work-related, injury or disease makes the initial disability more serious for the pensioner, *e.g.* a worker loses an eye in an industrial accident and loses the other eye in an accident in the home.

If the degree of disablement is assessed at below 20 per cent than a gratuity in the form of a lump payment can be made. The payment can, under the regulations, be made in instalments. See S.I. No. 137 of 1995 for current rates. Where a disablement gratuity is to be paid in respect of a prescribed condition in the First Schedule and the period of assessment is not less than seven years, the amount of the gratuity is set by the Schedule. If the period of assessment is less than seven years it is to be paid *pro rata*. While it is clear that the payment of the gratuity is in part a matter of administrative convenience, the legislation recognises that it may be appropriate to give a small but regular income rather than a lump sum to the long-term disabled. Where the disablement is assessed to continue for seven years or more and a disablement gratuity would be paid, the claimant can opt for a disablement pension, to be paid at a rate fixed by statutory instrument.

Increase of injury benefit and disablement pension for adult and child dependants

55.—[Repealed by the 1994 Act, section 20(9)].

GENERAL NOTE

This section was repealed by section 20(9) of the 1994 Act although the repeal has yet to be brought into force.

Increase of disablement pension on account of unemployability

56.—(1) Subject to this Act, a person in receipt of a disablement pension shall, notwithstanding the contribution conditions contained in section 32 of Chapter 7 of Part II, be entitled to disability benefit if, as a result of the relevant loss of faculty, the beneficiary is incapable of work and is likely to remain permanently so incapable. [1994 Act, section 20]

(2) (a) For the purposes of this section, a person may be treated as being incapable of work and likely to remain permanently incapable of work, notwithstanding that the loss of faculty is not such as to prevent him being capable of work, if it is likely to restrict him to earning not more than such amount as may be prescribed.

(b) In paragraph (a) the reference to "earning" includes a reference to receiving any remuneration or profit derived from gainful occupation.

(3) Disability benefit payable by virtue of this section shall be payable for such period as may be determined at the time it is granted, but may be renewed from time to time. [1994 Act, section 20]

GENERAL NOTE

Prior to the 1994 Act, unemployability supplement was payable in order to compensate for loss of faculty. Such a disablement pensioner is now eligible for disability benefit if the loss of faculty renders that person likely to be permanently incapable of work.

For definitions of "permanently incapable", see *R. v. National Insurance Commissioners, ex p. Steele* [1978] 3 All E.R. 78.

Transitional provisions are found in section 20(5) of the 1994 Act which was not inserted into this Act by substitution.

Increase of disablement pension where constant attendance is needed

57.—(1) Where a disablement pension is payable in respect of an assessment of 100 per cent., then, if as a result of the relevant loss of faculty the beneficiary requires constant attendance, the weekly rate of the pension shall be increased by an amount determined in accordance with regulations by reference to the extent and nature of the attendance required by the beneficiary, subject to the limitation that such amount shall not exceed the amounts specified in Part IV of the Second Schedule.

(2) An increase of pension under this section shall be payable for such period as may be determined at the time it is granted, but may be renewed from time to time;

Provided that no such increase shall be payable in respect of any period during which the beneficiary is receiving medical treatment as an in-patient in a hospital or similar institution.

GENERAL NOTE

If a 100 per cent disablement pension has been assessed then, if as a result of the relevant loss of faculty the pensioner requires constant attendance, the pension is to be increased, by reference to regulations, to the extent and nature of the attendance required by that person. There are several reference points, found in section 46, S.I. No. 77 of 1967 and S.I. No. 255 of 1986. These can be summarised as follows. First, the claimant may only be in need of part-time attendance as against full-time attendance. Secondly, there may be a case of exceptionally· severe disablement which requires a greater amount of attendance by virtue of that disablement. Thirdly, the exceptionally severe disablement may be expected to last for a substantial period—in excess of six months. In these circumstances the weekly rate of constant attendance allowance may increase accordingly with the degree and length of the constant attendance required. A slightly higher rate is payable to disablement pensioners aged 66 years and over.

For current rates see S.I. No. 137 of 1995.

Adjustments for successive accidents

58.—(1) Where a person suffers two or more successive accidents against which he is insured by occupational injuries insurance—

(a) the person shall not for the same period be entitled (apart from any increase of benefit such as is mentioned in subsection (2)) to receive benefit, either by way of disability benefit payable by virtue of section 53 and any disablement pension or pensions or by way of two or more disablement pensions, at an aggregate rate exceeding the amount equivalent to the appropriate maximum rate of disablement pension payable under section 54(8),

(b) regulations may provide for adjusting—

(i) disability benefit payable by virtue of section 53 or disablement benefit, or the conditions for the receipt thereof, in any case where the person has received or may be entitled to, a disablement gratuity,

(ii) any increase of benefit such as is mentioned in subsection (2), or the conditions for the receipt thereof.

(2) The increases of benefit referred to in subsection (1) mean increases in respect of an adult dependant or qualified child in the rate of disability benefit payable by virtue of section 53 and in the case of disablement pension, disability benefit payable by virtue of section 56 and an increase under section 57. [1995 Act, Schedule E]

GENERAL NOTE

Section 58 enables the Minister, by regulation, to adjust the rates of industrial injuries benefits when there have been successive accidents to persons who are in receipt of occupational injury benefits. Section 58(1)(a) directs that the claimant is not to be entitled to payments (other than disability benefit dependency increases, or constant attendance allowance) at an aggregate rate which exceeds the rate appropriate to the degree of disablement found in the Second Schedule to the Principal Act. The claimant cannot therefore divide up each accident and disability and produce a degree of disablement and loss of faculty that exceeds the appropriate disablement pension payment appropriate for the net degree of disablement.

If the claimant, at the time of the application for injury benefit or disablement pension, is in receipt of, or entitled to, a disablement gratuity (the claimant may not have applied for a gratuity if the injury is not serious) then the injury benefit or disablement pension can be adjusted according to S.I. No. 77 of 1967 by the statutory authorities who are to regard the initial loss of faculty as if it had been caused by the later accident for which disablement pension is payable. Where an existing disablement pension is paid or entitlement can be established for the life of the pensioner and a later accident resulting in further loss of faculty occurs, for which a disablement gratuity would be payable, then aggregate assessments are to be made on the degree of disablement. If the pensioner so elects, prior to the final assessment being made the pensioner can receive, in lieu of the gratuity, a disablement pension at a rate equal to the difference between the higher pension rate and the existing pension. So, if a disablement pension is paid at 30 per cent and a later disablement gratuity of 16 per cent is assessed as a consequence of a later accident, the disablement pension will be, all things being equal, increased to a 36 per cent disablement pension. The increase is not however payable if the disablement pension is already paid in respect of 100 per cent assessment or if the total payable would exceed 100 per cent.

Subsection (2)

Subsection (2), inserted by the 1994 Act, directs that the additions are adult and child dependant additions under sections 53, 56, and 57.

Entitlement to death benefit

59.—Subject to this Act, where an insured person dies as a result of personal injury caused on or after the 1st day of May, 1967, by accident arising out of and in the course of his employment, being insurable (occupational injuries) employment, death benefit shall be payable as provided for in sections 60 to 63.

GENERAL NOTE

This section provides that death benefit shall be payable when an insured person dies, after May 1, 1967, by an accident arising out of and in the course of employment as long as the insured was in insurable (occupational injuries) employment. The question of to whom death benefit is payable is answered in later sections of the Act.

Death benefit for widows and widowers and increases for qualified children, etc.

60.—(1) The widow of the deceased shall be entitled to death benefit if at his death she either was living with him or was being, or would but for the relevant accident have been, wholly or mainly maintained by him.

(2) In the case of a widow, death benefit shall be a pension at the weekly rate set out in column (2) of Part I of the Second Schedule, and if she has attained pensionable age and is living alone that rate shall be increased by the amount set out in column (6) of that Part. [1995 Act, Schedule F]

(3) A pension under subsection (2) shall not be payable for any period after the remarriage of the widow.

(4) A widow shall be disqualified for receiving a pension under this section if and so long as she and any person are cohabiting as husband and wife.

(5) The widower of the deceased shall be entitled to death benefit if at her death he was being wholly or mainly maintained by her or would, but for the relevant accident, have been so maintained.

(6) In the case of a widower who was, at the death of the deceased, incapable of self-support by reason of some physical or mental infirmity and likely to remain permanently so incapable, death benefit shall be a pension at the weekly rate set out in column (2) of Part I of the Second Schedule and if he has attained pensionable age and is living alone that rate shall be increased by the amount set out in column (6) of that Part. [1995 Act, Schedule F]

(6A) A pension under subsection (6) shall not be payable for any period after the remarriage of the widower.

(6B) A widower shall be disqualified for receiving a pension under this section if and so long as he and any person are cohabiting as husband and wife. [1995 No. 2 Act, section 2]

(7) In the case of any other widower, death benefit shall be a gratuity of the amount set out in Part II of the Second Schedule.

(8) A pension under subsection (6) shall not be payable for any period after the person to whom it is payable ceases to be incapable of self-support by reason of some physical or mental infirmity.

(9) The weekly rate of pension under subsection (2) or (6) shall be increased by the amount set out in column (4) of Part I of the Second Schedule in respect of each qualified child who normally resides with the beneficiary. [1995 Act, Schedule F]

(10) In this section—
(a) a reference to a widow or a widower shall include a reference to a person who would otherwise be a widow or a widower but for the fact that the person's marriage has been dissolved, being a dissolution that is recognised as valid in the State, and
(b) 'the deceased' in relation to a widow or a widower who has been married more than once, refers only to the widow's or widower's last spouse and for this purpose spouse shall be construed as including a party to a marriage that has been dissolved, being a dissolution that is recognised as valid in the State. [1995 No. 2 Act, section 2]

GENERAL NOTE

Under this section, the Persons entitled to death benefit are as follows:
(i) *Widows.* If the widow of the deceased was, at the death of the deceased, living with him and but for the accident would have been wholly or mainly maintained

by him, she is entitled to death benefit, payable in the form of a pension. The pension ceases to be payable upon remarriage and cohabitation by the widow leads to disqualification.

(ii) *Widower.* A widower does not obtain death benefit simply upon the death of his wife following an industrial injury or disease occurring after May 1, 1967. For the widower to receive such a pension the widower must have been wholly or mainly maintained by her at her death, or would have been so dependent but for the accident. If, however, this fact of dependency is established, a further requirement is imposed before death benefit will be payable in the form of a pension. The widower, at the death of his spouse, must show that he was incapable of self-support by reason of some physical or mental infirmity and that he is likely to remain permanently incapable of self-support. If the widower cannot satisfy this requirement then death benefit takes the form of a gratuity. No cohabitation rule applies, however, to a widower.

The 1995 (No. 2) Act. The new subsections (6A) and (10) provide both for equality of treatment and the continuing entitlement of spouses following divorce. Subsection (6A) provides for the disqualification of a widower upon remarriage or cohabitation with another party. Subsection (10) provides that upon the death of a former spouse, a divorced person may qualify for death benefit, notwithstanding the fact of the divorce. These new provisions are not yet in force.

Death benefit—parents

61.—(1) A parent of the deceased shall be entitled to death benefit if, at the deceased's death, the parent was being wholly or mainly maintained by the deceased, or would but for the relevant accident have been so maintained.

(2) Subject to subsections (3) and (4), the death benefit shall be a pension at the weekly rate set out in column (2) of Part I of the Second Schedule, increased, in the case of a person who has attained pensionable age, by the amount set out in column (7) of that Part I of the Second Schedule where the beneficiary is living alone.

(3) Subject to subsection (4), the weekly rate of pension payable to a parent shall be—

    (a) at the reduced weekly rate, where the deceased was at death a married person,

    (b) at the maximum weekly rate, where the deceased was at death a widower, a widow or a single person—

        (i) in any case where the parent is the father and was, at the death of the deceased, incapable of self-support by reason of some physical or mental infirmity and likely to remain permanently so incapable,

        (ii) in any case where the parent is the mother, having been, at the death of the deceased, a widow or having thereafter become a widow, or

        (iii) in any case where the parent is the mother, not being a widow. and a pension at the maximum weekly rate is not payable to her husband,

    (c) at the reduced weekly rate in any other case.

(4) Where a person, to whom the provisions of subparagraph (i) of subsection (3)(b) apply, ceases at any time to be incapable of self-support by reason of some physical or mental infirmity, the pension shall thereafter be payable at the reduced weekly rate and, if at that time the provisions of subsection (3)(b) apply to his wife, that pension shall thereafter be payable at the maximum weekly rate.

(5) In this section—

"reduced weekly rate" means the reduced weekly rate of death benefit by way of parent's pension as set out in column (2) at reference 2(b)(i) in Part I of the Second Schedule;

"maximum weekly rate" means the maximum weekly rate of death benefit by way of parent's pension as set out in column (2) at reference 2(b)(ii) in Part I of the Second Schedule.

(6) Where a parent was partly maintained by each of two or more insured persons who have died as a result of accidents arising out of and in the course of their employments, being insurable (occupational injuries) employments, the parent may be treated for the purposes of this section as having received from the last of those insured persons to die contributions to the maintenance of the parent equal to the aggregate amount which those insured persons were together contributing before the first of the accidents happened, and has having received nothing from the other or others.

(7) A pension under this section payable to a woman who, at the deceased's death, was a widow or an unmarried woman shall not be payable for any period after her remarriage or marriage.

(8) A widow or an unmarried woman shall be disqualified for receiving a pension under this section if and so long as she and any person are cohabiting as husband and wife.

(9) For the purposes of subsections (1) and (6) "parent", if the deceased was adopted pursuant to the provisions of the Adoption Acts, 1952 to 1991, shall be taken as referring to the adopters or the adopter, and includes a step-parent.

GENERAL NOTE

Apart from the preceding section, a parent of the deceased may be entitled to death benefit if, at the child's death, the parent was being wholly or mainly maintained by the child, or would have been so maintained but for the accident. If the parent is eligible then payment takes the form of a pension. If the parent at the child's death was a widow or an unmarried woman, payment ceases upon remarriage or marriage respectively. Cohabitation by a widow or unmarried woman will lead to disqualification. Parent will include adoptive parents and step-parents.

Under subsection (3) differential rates of death benefit are payable, depending upon the circumstances of the parent. If the parent is the deceased's father then if he is incapable of self-support a maximum rate will be payable, as it will if the parent is a widow under section 61(3)(ii) or, if married, her husband is not incapable of self-support. This maximum rate is only payable if, at the time of death, the deceased was a widower, widow or single person. In such a case the mother receives the maximum rate of pension while the father receives a reduced rate pension. If the father is incapable of self-support then he will also receive the maximum rate of death benefit. In all other cases (e.g. the deceased was married) a reduced rate of pension is payable. There is a cohabitation rule for women and entitlement ends for a widow upon remarriage.

Death benefit—orphans

62.—(1) Death benefit shall be payable in respect of an orphan who is a child or step-child of the deceased and in respect of an orphan who was wholly or mainly maintained by the deceased at the date of his death.

(2) In the case of an orphan death benefit shall be a pension at the weekly rate set out in column (2) of Part I of the Second Schedule.

(3) Section 109 shall apply to a pension under this section as it applies to an orphan's (contributory) allowance.

GENERAL NOTE

Children orphaned as a result of occupational injuries are also eligible in the case of a wholly or mainly maintained child or step-child of a deceased person who dies as a result of industrial accident or disease, suffered after May 1, 1967. This is payable in the form of a weekly pension. For the purpose of this payment a child is a person under the age of 18 years, or, if over that age, is under 21 and receiving full-time instruction by day at any university, college, school, or other educational establishment. The Minister may pay the pension to the guardian of the orphan or some other person, determined by the Minister, for the benefit of the orphan: section 109.

Death benefit—funeral expenses

63.—(1) Death benefit by way of a grant in respect of funeral expenses shall be payable in respect of the death of the deceased.

(2) Subject to subsection (3), the grant shall be the amount set out in Part II of the Second Schedule.

(3) In any such case as may be specified by regulations, the grant shall be such lesser amount as may be specified by the regulations for that case.

(4) Except where regulations otherwise provide, a grant under this section shall not be payable in respect of a death occurring outside the State.

GENERAL NOTE

Where an insured worker dies as a result of an occupational accident or disease, a funeral grant is payable under the death benefit provisions of section 63. When the death benefit funeral grant was introduced in 1967 the grant stood at a maximum of £50. It was increased to £60 in 1971, to £100 in 1972, to £115 in 1978, to £175 in 1980, and to £220 in 1982. The Social Welfare Act, 1988 increased the funeral grant to a £230 maximum and it now stands at £300. Although this maximum amount will not be payable whenever funeral expenses do not reach this level it must be impossible to conceive of funeral expenses falling below this statutory maximum figure. Even though the funeral grant has increased almost fivefold in 27 years, benefit levels and income levels generally have risen at a rate which far outstrips this increased percentage, particularly in recent years when the funeral grant has not increased significantly. On average, around 35 funeral grants are awarded each year.

The regulations governing the making of claims and payments for funeral grant stipulate that the application may be made by the personal representative of the deceased, or in the absence thereof, the husband or wife or any next of kin or by any other person claiming to be entitled: this latter phrase seems to refer to creditors or, formerly, illegitimate children of the deceased. The Minister is given wide powers to determine whether payment should be made. Funeral grant may be paid in respect of a death occurring outside the State if the deceased was, immediately before death, employed in insurable (occupational injuries) employment, or entitled to and not disqualified from injury benefit or disablement benefit: S.I. No. 85 of 1967.

Supplements to workmen's compensation payments

64.—(1) Regulations shall provide for conferring on persons who—

(a) are or have been on or after the 1st day of October, 1965, entitled in respect of any injury or disease to weekly payments by way of compensation under the Workmen's Compensation Acts, and

(b) as the result of the injury or disease are, or could for the purpose of the provisions of this Chapter relating to disability benefit payable by virtue of section 56 to be treated as being, incapable of work and likely to remain permanently so incapable,

the like right to payments under this Chapter by way of disability benefit payable by virtue of section 56 and the like right to payments under this Chapter in respect of a child or adult dependant as if the injury or disease were one in respect of which a disablement pension were for the time being payable.

(2) Regulations shall also provide for conferring on persons who—

(a) are or have been on or after the 1st day of October, 1965, entitled in respect of any injury or disease to weekly payments by way of compensation under the Workmen's Compensation Acts, and

(b) as the result of that injury or disease require constant attendance,

the like right to payments under this Chapter in respect of the need of constant attendance as if the injury or disease were one in respect of which a disablement pension were for the time being payable in respect of an assessment of 100 per cent.

(3) Such regulations may further provide for applying, in relation to payments under this section, the provisions of this Part relating to benefit and to the making of claims and the determination of claims and questions in so far as those provisions apply in relation to a disability benefit payable by virtue of section 56, to an increase of a disablement pension in respect of a child or adult dependant, or to an increase of a disablement pension in respect of the need of constant attendance, as the case may be, subject to any additions or modifications. [1995 Act, Schedule E]

(4) All payments under this section shall be paid out of the Social Insurance Fund.

GENERAL NOTE

Persons incapable of work who were in receipt of weekly payments of workmen's compensation on October 1, 1965 are entitled to unemployability supplement and the relevant dependant additions under articles 19 and 21 of S.I. No. 77 of 1967.

Cost of medical care

65.—(1) Subject to this section, the cost of medical care which, in the opinion of the Minister, is reasonably and necessarily incurred by an insured person as a result of an injury or disease against which, when it was sustained or contracted, he was insured under this Part, shall be payable out of the Social Insurance Fund to the extent that such cost is not met under the Health Acts, 1947 to 1979, or the Mental Treatment Acts, 1945 to 1966, or regulations made under section 117.

(2) Where an insured person is eligible to avail himself of services provided under the Health Acts, 1947 to 1979, or the Mental Treatment Acts, 1945 to 1966, or treatment benefit under regulations made under section 117 but does not do so, the amount payable under this section shall not exceed that which would have been payable had he availed himself of such services or benefit.

(3) Where an insured person receives medical care during any period in which he is an in-patient in a hospital or similar institution, the amount payable under this section in respect of such care shall not exceed—

(a) the maximum amount which would be chargeable under section 53 of the Health Act, 1979, to an insured person to whom the institutional services provided under that section are made available for that period, or

(b) the maximum amount which would be chargeable under section 231A of the Mental Treatment Act, 1945, (inserted by section 71 of the Health Act, 1953) to an insured person to whom mental hospital assistance is made available for that period,

as may be appropriate.

(4) The amount payable under this section in respect of medical care provided otherwise than during a period in which the insured person is an in-patient in a hospital or similar institution shall be such sum as is, in the opinion of the Minister, reasonably appropriate to the care afforded, having regard to the reasonable necessity for such care and the customary charge therefor.

(5) Where an insured person requires medical care as a result of an injury or disease against which, when it was sustained or contracted, he was insured under this Part, he or such other person as may be prescribed shall, within such period as may be prescribed, give notice in writing to the Minister of the care required by him, and shall furnish such particulars as may be required of such care, and no payment under this section shall be

made unless the notice is given and, where any particulars are required as aforesaid, those particulars are furnished.

(6) Where notice is given under subsection (5), the insured person may be required to submit himself to medical examination for the purpose of establishing that the medical care is necessary as a result of the relevant accident or disease and that it is reasonable in his case, and no payment shall be made under this section if he fails to comply with the requirement.

(7) Payments under this section shall be made to such persons as the Minister thinks fit and, in particular, where the cost of the medical care payable under this section is due to a health board, payment may be made to that board.

(8) Regulations may provide for applying in relation to payments under this section any of the provisions of this Part relating to benefit and to the making of claims, subject to any additions or modifications.

(9) For the purposes of this section medical care shall comprise, subject to any additions which may be made by regulations—

(a) general practitioner and specialist care, including domiciliary visiting,

(b) nursing care at home except where the cost is met by an increase under section 57 in respect of constant attendance, and nursing care and maintenance in hospitals, convalescent homes, sanatoria or other medical institutions,

(c) pharmaceutical and other medical or surgical supplies, including prosthetic and aural appliances, prescribed by a registered medical practitioner, kept in repair and replaced where necessary,

(d) dental and optical treatment and appliances,

(e) the care furnished, on the prescription of a registered medical practitioner, by members of professions allied to the medical profession, including physiotherapists and chiropodists, and

(f) conveyance to and from the place where medical care as specified in this subsection is provided.

GENERAL NOTE

If the claimant has suffered industrial injury or disease and has incurred medical costs that are not met under the Health Acts or the Mental Treatment Acts, then, if the Minister certifies that these additional costs have been reasonably and necessarily incurred by an insured person as a result of an injury or disease against which the claimant was insured under the Act, these costs shall be payable by way of Occupational Injuries benefits. If the insured person fails to make use of these other statutory benefits, or treatment benefit under section 117 below, the Fund is not to be debited *vis-à-vis* those costs that could have been so deferred elsewhere. Medical care under this provision can include in-patient and out-patient services, as well as general practitioner and specialist care, most nursing care, pharmaceutical and other supplies. Section 65(9) contains a complete list of the range of services and equipment available under the scheme. There are control provisions to counter abuse or false claims. Notice of medical care required must be made within six weeks from commencement of the care, subject to a good cause for failure provision. Should the beneficiary be unable to act, or is under 16 years of age, then the Minister may appoint a person to deal with the medical care costs allowed on the claimant's behalf. Provision is also made by regulations for dealing with the sums due should the claimant die before payment of these medical care costs be made: see the Social Welfare (Occupational Injuries) (Medical Care) Regulations, 1967 (S.I. No. 92 of 1967).

Prescribed Diseases

Insurance against prescribed diseases and injuries not caused by accident

66.—(1) Subject to this section, a person who is insured under this Part against personal injury caused by accident arising out of and in the course of his employment shall be insured also against any prescribed disease and against any prescribed personal injury not so caused, being a disease or injury due to the nature of that employment and developed on or after the 1st day of May, 1967.

(2) A disease or injury shall be prescribed for the purposes of this section in relation to any insured persons, if the Minister is satisfied that—

(a) it ought to be treated, having regard to its causes and any other relevant considerations, as a risk of their occupations and not as a risk common to all persons, and

(b) it is such that, in the absence of special circumstances, the attribution of particular cases to the nature of the employment can be established or presumed with reasonable certainty.

(3) Regulations prescribing any disease or injury for the purposes of this section may provide that a person who developed the disease or injury on or at any time after a date specified in the regulations, being a date before the regulations came into force but not before the 1st day of May, 1967, shall be treated for the purposes of this section, subject to any prescribed modifications, as if the regulations had been in force when he developed the disease or injury.

(4) Provision may be made by regulations for determining the time at which a person is to be treated for the purposes of this Part as having developed any disease or injury prescribed for the purposes of this section, and the circumstances in which any such disease or injury is, where the person in question has previously suffered therefrom, to be treated as having recrudesced or as having been contracted or received afresh.

(5) The benefit payable pursuant to this section in respect of a prescribed disease or injury, and the conditions for the receipt of such benefit, shall be the same as in the case of personal injury by accident arising out of and in the course of a person's employment, subject, however, to the power to make different provision by regulations as respects any matter which is to be prescribed and to the following provisions of this section.

(6) Regulations may provide, in relation to prescribed diseases and injuries, for modifying the provisions of this Chapter relating to disability benefit payable by virtue of section 53 and disablement benefit and for adapting references in this Chapter to accidents, and for modifying the provisions of this Part in their application in relation to claims for benefit and in relation to questions arising in connection therewith or with an award of benefit on any such claim. [1995 Act, Schedule E]

(7) Without prejudice to the generality of subsection (6), the said regulations may in particular include provision—

(a) for presuming any prescribed disease or injury–

(i) to be due, unless the contrary is proved, to the nature of a person's employment where he was employed in any prescribed occupation at the time when, or within a prescribed period or for a prescribed length of time (whether continuous or not) before, he developed the disease or injury,

(ii) not to be due to the nature of a person's employment unless he was employed in some prescribed employment at the time when, or within a prescribed period or for a prescribed length of time (whether continuous or not) before, he developed the disease or injury;

and

(b) for such matters as appear to the Minister to be incidental to or consequential on provisions included in the regulations by virtue of the foregoing provisions of this section.

(8) Nothing in this section shall affect the right of any person to benefit in respect of a disease which is a personal injury by accident within the

meaning of this Chapter except that a person shall not be entitled to benefit in respect of a disease as being an injury by accident arising out of and in the course of any employment if at the time of the accident the disease is in relation to him a prescribed disease by virtue of the occupation in which he is engaged in that employment.

GENERAL NOTE

As was discussed in the General Note to section 50 above, when the Workmen's Compensation Act, 1897 was first implemented there was no real attempt to deal with occupational disease. The statutory formula required an individual incident, or series of incidents, causing physiological damage, before compensation was permitted. Disease, it was felt, should be regarded as amenable to general health insurance cover. This approach proved unrealistic, particularly when universal health cover was an aspiration and not a reality. The Workmen's Compensation Act, 1906, section 8, amended the 1897 Act by enabling certain industrial diseases to be certified as industrial diseases which, if contracted by workmen in the course of their employment, could give rise to compensation. These scheduled diseases were narrow in scope and the determining factor, in relation to inclusion as a scheduled disease, was whether the disease was of such a nature that it was improbable that it could be contracted outside the working environment of the workman. Generally speaking, this restrictive approach still has a degree of influence. If the disease was not a scheduled disease the workman was required to bring the condition within the notion of "accident". As we have already discovered this produced several innovative decisions, the courts whenever possible finding that "accident" had an extensive meaning. Some of the cases involving invasion of the body by a virus contracted, in all likelihood, in the course of employment are plainly correct because a specific event or accident caused the invasion of the body, *e.g.* tetanus invading the body when the workman stepped on a nail which pierced his boot and his foot. Other decisions, while decided in favour of the workman, are more dubious. In some cases, however, a work-related disease was not compensatable at all. This was particularly hard on the victim if the disease was the result of an industrial process. The implementation of the prescribed occupational disease system as part of the occupational injuries scheme in 1967 was a considerable advance but, as we shall see, there is still room for improvement.

Section 66 of the Principal Act of 1993 now provides that an insured person in insurable (occupational injuries) employment shall, apart from the question of insurability against personal injury by occupational accident, be insured against any prescribed disease and any prescribed personal injury not caused by an accident within the meaning of that word. The Act gives the Minister the power to prescribe diseases as occupational diseases if the Minister thinks it ought to be treated as a risk to which persons in particular occupations are exposed and not a risk common to all persons and that the causal link with the employment can be established or presumed with reasonable certainty. The methodology employed involves the creation of a list of diseases and injuries which can be occupational in origin. If the claimant contracts this disease or condition and the claimant can show that, at the relevant time, the claimant had been employed in an occupation which the list acknowledges to be causally linked, then the claimant will be entitled to occupational injury benefit. For example, if the claimant has contracted glanders, the disease will be prescribed if the claimant has had contact with equine animals or their carcasses. The employment should have commenced after May 1, 1967 and the claimant must have been so employed on, or within one month of,the date when the claimant began to develop the disease if the claimant is to take the benefit of a presumption that the disease or injury is due to employment. The one-month linking requirement does not apply to certain conditions which do not necessarily manifest themselves during or immediately after employment, such as dust, liquid or vapour irritation of respiratory passages, non-infective dermatitis, occupational deafness or byssinosis, tuberculosis or pneumoconiosis. In these cases either no limit, or a more extended limit, is placed by the regulations. Normally the presumption will be conclusive: the onus is on the statutory authorities to prove that the disease or injury was not of occupational origin once the presumption operates. The principal regulations are the Social Welfare (Occupational Injuries) (Prescribed Diseases) Regulations, 1983 (S.I. No. 392 of 1983).

If the claim is brought within the occupational disease or injury provisions the benefits payable are generally identical to those payable in respect of an industrial accident. In the first instance injury benefit will be payable once the condition is established to be an occupational disease. If the condition is not held to be occupational in origin disability benefit may be payable. At the end of the injury benefit period, if the disease continues to render the claimant incapable of work or if a loss of faculty is established, the disablement benefit will be payable. If, however, the condition develops but the claimant is not incapable of work, then disablement benefit will be payable from the date of development, the need for an injury benefit period to precede the claim being inapplicable. In relation to a claim for injury benefit the date of development of the disease is the first day on which the claimant was incapable of work. If the claim is for disablement benefit the date of development is the date when a loss of faculty results. If the claim is for death benefit the date of commencement is the date on which death occurs.

Part V of S.I. No. 392 of 1983 sets out special provisions relating to pneumoconiosis, byssinosis, occupational asthma and occupational deafness. Injury benefit is not payable in relation to these conditions, the claimants being instead entitled to seek disablement benefit. There are special conditions in relation to pneumoconiosis and byssinosis. If the assessment of loss of faculty falls below 20 per cent, the disablement gratuity is not payable: rather, the claimant is entitled to a disablement pension. If byssinosis is contracted the disablement pension will only be payable if it is likely to last permanently. If the claim is brought in respect of occupational asthma the claim should normally be brought within 10 years of the cessation of employment, if applicable, unless a prior claim for disablement benefit has been allowed. The maximum time limit within which a claim for disablement benefit may be made in relation to occupational deafness is five years from cessation of employment. The regulations also provide for later claims when minimum hearing loss is not established: S.I. No. 77 of 1967. In the event of an application for injury or disablement benefit being permitted in respect of an occupational disease, there can be difficulties if the disease is of a recurring nature. It may be necessary to decide wither the disease is a fresh attack or a recurrence of the first attack. This issue will be a matter for the medical referees and the claimant's own doctor. If the decision is that the disease is a fresh attack, a new injury benefit period will commence. If, however, the condition is held to be a recurrence, entitlement to benefit will depend on whether the claimant is still in the injury benefit period or is in receipt of disablement pension. A review of the disablement pension can be made to take account of these new physiological circumstances.

The List

The original 1967 position as set out in the Schedule to the relevant statutory instrument was based on the development of the U.K. occupational disease scheme. It was in fact two lists. Part I set out general diseases and injuries and the corresponding occupations which would lead to the disease or injury being prescribed. Part II set out the list of occupations in respect of which pneumoconiosis is prescribed. Part I was extended in 1973 to include persons employed in some occupations who contract adeno carcinoma of the nasal cavity, brucella abortus infection, chlome poisoning and acrylamide monomer poisoning. In 1977 persons in certain specified occupations who contracted viral hepatitis were added to the list in Part I. The most significant event since the occupational disease list was established in 1967 is undoubtedly the extension of disablement benefit to those in specified employment who suffer from occupational deafness. The inclusion of occupational deafness, occupational asthma, occupational vitiligo, angiosarcoma of the liver, osteolysis of the terminal phalanges of the fingers, infection by streptococcus suis and non-cirrhotic portal fibrosis mean that the Social Welfare (Occupational Injuries) (Prescribed Diseases) Regulations, 1983 are both innovative and consolidatory regulations. The list was extended again in 1985 to cover vibration induced white finger, ulnar nerve neuritis, non-endemic infections or parasitic diseases. The poisoning provisions in the list were also extended in 1985: S.I. No. 102 of 1985.

The listing method has advantages for the claimant. The claimant is able to rely on the presumption once the disease or injury manifests itself and the burden of difficult issues of proof is thrown upon the statutory authorities, who must disprove that the occupation was the likely cause of the injury. But there are also several drawbacks. If the disease is not on the list, or if the occupation in which the worker was employed is not a prescribed employment, then the worker will have to fall back on to the "personal injury by accident" provision and show that there was an accident, as distinct from a process. Invariably the law will lag behind medical science in this regard. The tendency in Ireland seems to require recognition that a disease is an occupational disease by the I.L.O. and the E.C. before it will be added to the list. It should be pointed out that in the U.K. the statutory authorities listed occupational vitiligo a full three years before the condition was added to the list in Ireland. Indeed, some diseases and injuries that were added in 1984 in Britain have yet to be added to the Irish list. In Northern Ireland lung cancer contracted by a worker exposed to asbestos in industry was added as a prescribed disease in 1985, but it has not been added in the Republic. Despite revision of the list to include more diseases as prescribed diseases, there are some cases where a disease is contracted but occupational injury benefit will be denied because the disease or occupation is not of a type listed in the schedule. An example is infection by leptospira. In Ireland two types of leptospira are listed. In the U.K. it has been recognised that this is too restrictive and since 1979 all forms of infection by leptospira are prescribed diseases in relation to persons in occupations which involve being placed in locations where the virus is likely to be. Critics of the list system point out that there is a great reluctance (certainly in Britain, but the criticism is equally valid in Ireland) to deal comprehensively with illnesses that often have their origins in environmental factors, the most obvious being lung cancers, arthritis, bronchitis and rheumatism. No attempt has been made to deal with stress-related conditions or mental illnesses that often have their origin in the working environment or job description. For these workers, unless an accident, or series of accidents, can be demonstrated, the only state compensation is disability benefit. In the U.K. the Industrial Injuries Advisory Council recommended in 1981 that the list system should be retained but a complementary system of proving occupational disease should be permitted. Under this system the worker could be allowed to show that a disease, *e.g.* resulting from an industrial process, should be regarded as an occupational disease even if it is not a scheduled disease or the employment was not a scheduled employment. The worker would be able to prove the case but would not have the benefit of a presumption, as is the situation under the list system. The Industrial Injuries Advisory Council, however, suggested sweeping exclusions and for this reason this dual approach, if implemented, would not have a substantial impact. This dual approach functions in many of the individual states in the U.S., where catch-all clauses are tacked on to the end of the list. The Ohio clause, for example, provides "All other occupational diseases: a disease peculiar to a particular industrial process, trade or occupation and to which an employee is not ordinarily subjected or exposed outside or away from his employment."

In Ireland there is no real movement at all towards creating a residual test whereby a court or tribunal could ask, did the occupation in which the employee was engaged, or the working environment in which the employee was situated, have any substantial causal link, in a clinical sense, with the disease or injury suffered? In 1983 the then Minister for Social Welfare was asked whether the revision of the prescribed diseases list would allow disablement or death benefits to be paid if medical evidence could establish that a person suffered a disease as a result of that person's work, regardless of whether it was on the list or not. Mr Desmond replied negatively. He said (346 *Dáil Debates* Col. 1329) that he "could not in any circumstances accept a proposition of that nature. That would be a licence to print money to be handed over to the medical profession". With respect, it would be for the statutory authorities to be convinced of the link, on the evidence. Some movement along these lines would, in the view of the present writers, be extremely desirable. The list system, as the sole determinant, is too inflexible and at times is entirely arbitrary and capricious in its results: see further Wilson (1982) 11 I.L.J. 141; Lewis [1983] J.S.W.L. 11; Mesher [1984] J.S.W.L. 253.

Occupational Accidents

Notice of accidents

67.—(1) Regulations may provide for requiring the prescribed notice of any accident in respect of which occupational injuries benefit or any amount under section 65 may be payable to be given within the prescribed time by the insured person or, where within that time his death results from the accident, by such other person as may be prescribed, to the insured person's employer or another prescribed person.

(2) In a case of failure without good cause to give the prescribed notice referred to in subsection (1) (including, in the case of a claim for death benefit, a failure on the part of some other person to give the prescribed notice of the relevant accident), regulations may provide for disqualification for receipt for occupational injuries benefit or any amount under section 65 for such period as may be determined in accordance with the regulations.

GENERAL NOTE

This is an enabling provision which requires claimants to meet prescribed conditions concerning the giving of notice of an accident which may lead to occupational injuries benefits or medical care benefits being payable. The regulations are S.I. No. 85 of 1967. See also the General Notes to sections 68 and 69 below.

Reporting of accidents by employers

68.—Regulations may provide for requiring employers—

(a) to make reports, to such person and in such form and within such time as may be prescribed, of accidents in respect of which occupational injuries benefit or any amount under section 65 may be payable,

(b) to furnish to the prescribed person any information required for the determination of claims for occupational injuries benefit or of questions arising in connection with claims for or awards of that benefit, and

(c) to take such other steps as may be prescribed to facilitate the giving of notices of accidents in respect of which occupational injuries benefit or any amount under section 65 may be payable, the making of claims for that benefit and the determination of claims for that benefit and of questions arising in connection with claims for or awards of that benefit.

GENERAL NOTE
The regulations in question are found in S.I. No. 85 of 1967.

Declaration that accident is an occupational accident

69.—(1) Where, in relation to any claim for occupational injuries benefit, it is decided that the relevant accident was or was not an occupational accident, an express declaration of that fact shall be made and recorded and (subject to subsection (3)) a claimant shall be entitled to have the question whether the relevant accident was an occupational accident decided notwithstanding that his claim is disallowed on other grounds.

(2) Subject to subsection (3), any person suffering personal injury by accident shall be entitled, if he claims that the accident was an occupational accident, to have that question decided, and a declaration made and recorded accordingly, notwithstanding that no claim for occupational injuries benefit has been made in connection with which the question arises, and the provisions of this Act shall apply for that purpose as if the question had arisen in relation to a claim for occupational injuries benefit.

(3) Notwithstanding anything contained in subsections (1) and (2), the deciding officer or appeals officer, as the case may be, may refuse to determine the question whether an accident was an occupational accident if satisfied that it is unlikely that it will be necessary to decide the question for the purposes of any claim for occupational injuries benefit, but any such refusal of a deciding officer shall, on notice of appeal being given to the Chief Appeals Officer within the prescribed time, be referred to an appeals officer.

(4) Subject to this Act as to appeal and revision, any declaration under this section that an accident was or was not an occupational accident shall be conclusive for the purposes of any claim for occupational injuries benefit in respect of that accident, whether or not the claimant is the person at whose instance the declaration was made.

(5) For the purposes of this section, an accident whereby a person suffers personal injury shall be deemed, in relation to him, to be an occupational accident if—

(a) it arises out of and in the course of his employment,

(b) that employment is insurable (occupational injuries) employment, and

(c) payment of occupational injuries benefit is not precluded because the accident happened while he was outside the State,

and reference in other sections of this Chapter to an occupational accident shall be construed accordingly.

GENERAL NOTE
Once an industrial accident has occurred it is within the best interests of the employee to ensure that the correct statutory procedures are met. Indeed, once the accident occurs it may

be that no obvious physiological change takes place, *e.g.* there may be an accident in the sense of an "unlooked for mishap" but the personal injury may only manifest itself later. Obvious examples would include cases where radiation or a noxious substance escaped into the workplace with the danger that a subsequent illness or condition may result. It is prudent, in cases of this kind, for the claimant to seek a declaration, under section 69(2), that an accident was or was not an occupational accident. If such a declaration is given, and if occupational injuries benefit is not at the same time sought, the statutory authorities have a discretion to refuse to determine the question. The declaration is conclusive in respect of later claims in respect of that accident. This is so even if the declaration is given and the subsequent claim is made in respect of a person other than the person seeking the declaration, *i.e.* the claim is made by another worker involved in the accident but not a party to the original declaration (section 69(4)). In a recent English case ([1984] J.S.W.L. 58) a declaration was granted where a claimant had, by mistake, walked in front of an antenna dish which was part of radio transmitting equipment at a military establishment. The claimant had not at that time suffered any detectable injury but was anxious that the effect might emerge in the future. The Social Security Commissioner granted the declaration sought, holding that there was a specific event from which there could emerge some personal injury, physical or mental.

The distinction between "accident" and "personal injury" raised by section 69 leads to a further difficulty: if there is no immediate sign of a personal injury and the employee fails to inform the employer that an accident has occurred, can this prejudice the claimant? Section 67, an enabling provision, may require claimants to meet prescribed conditions as to the giving of notice of an accident occurring where occupational injuries benefit or section 65 (medical care) payments may be payable. These prescribed conditions require notification to the employer, not after the accident occurs, but after the claimant suffers personal injury by accident. Failure without good cause may lead the statutory authorities to suspend payments until the time that the notice was given. Obviously if death results from the accident, notice given by any other person will suffice. This Act and regulations in S.I. No. 85 of 1967 also impose upon an employer the obligation to investigate the accident and provide the Minister with such information as may be required. Non-compliance with these obligations is, curiously enough, not a specific offence under the Principal Act but is made an offence by statutory instrument. The penalty for non-compliance is set as a fine not exceeding £10 for an offence and £10 for each day on which the offence continues.

Miscellaneous

Disqualifications for disability benefit payable by virtue of section 53 or disablement benefit and suspension of proceedings

70.—(1) Regulations may provide for disqualifying a person for receiving disability benefit payable by virtue of section 53 or disablement benefit for any period not exceeding nine weeks, or for suspending proceedings on any claim for, or on any payment of, injury benefit or disablement benefit, if the person fails without good cause—

(a) to submit himself from time to time to medical examination for the purpose of determining the effect of the relevant accident, whether the accident has resulted in a loss of faculty, at what degree the extent of disablement resulting from a loss of faculty is to be assessed and what period is to be taken into account by the assessment, or the treatment appropriate to the relevant injury or loss of faculty,

(b) to submit himself from time to time to appropriate medical treatment for the relevant injury or loss of faculty.

(c) to attend at such places and times as may be required for the purposes of the said medical examination or treatment, or

(d) to observe any prescribed rules of behaviour. [1995 Act, Schedule E]

(2) Regulations under this section shall provide for payment to any person attending for medical examination or treatment as aforesaid of such amount as may be determined by the Minister as the amount of the reasonable and necessary travelling and other expenses (including any

expense consisting of loss of remunerative time) incurred by the person in respect of the attendance.

GENERAL NOTE

This is an enabling provision dealing with grounds for disqualification of claimants. In the case of section 70(1)(a) the relevant regulations are article 18(2) of S.I. No. 77 of 1967, as amended by Part III of S.I. No. 81 of 1986. There are also specific regulations dealing with the prescribed rules of behaviour mentioned in section 70(1)(d); these are contained in S.I. No. 77 of 1967, as amended by S.I. No. 237 of 1986, and are as follows:

"1. He shall obey the instructions of the doctor in attendance and answer any reasonable enquiries by the Minister or his officers relating to his claim.

2. He shall refrain from behaviour which is likely to retard his recovery.

3. If he absents himself from his place of residence he shall leave word as to where he may be found.

4. He shall not refuse unreasonably to see the Minister's sickness visitor.

5. In the case of a person claiming or in receipt of injury benefit, he shall do no work unless it be—

(a) light work for which no remuneration is, or would ordinarily be, payable, or

(b) work undertaken primarily as a definite part of his treatment while he is a patient in or of a hospital, sanatorium, or other similar institution and his earnings in respect of that work do not, on the average, exceed twenty-four pounds a week, or

(c) work under a scheme that is, in the opinion of the Minister, charitable in character and purpose, and his earnings in respect of that work do not, on the average, exceed twenty-four pounds a week.

6. In the case of a person claiming or in receipt of an increase of disablement pension by way of unemployability supplement, he shall do no work unless it be work in respect of which his earnings do not, on the average, exceed eighteen pounds a week."

There are, under S.I. No. 85 of 1987, procedural requirements which, if not met, can mean a loss of injury benefit. Disqualification from receipt of injury benefit will also follow from neglect or failure by the claimant to provide medical or other satisfactory evidence of incapacity, if the neglect lasts for longer than six months. The disqualification lasts for any part of the period for which injury benefit would otherwise have been payable if there had been no such neglect or failure. A similar disqualification can apply if there is a neglect or failure to provide evidence to show that the disability continues; again the omission by the claimant must run for six months if the claimant is to be deprived of injury benefit altogether. There is provision whereby the Minister may extend the period within which the evidence may be submitted, for good cause, but injury benefit is not to be payable for any period in excess of six months before the actual submission of the evidence.

Treating person as incapable of work, etc.

71.—Regulations may provide for treating a person for the purposes of this Chapter as incapable of work as the result of an accident or injury when he would not be so treated apart from the regulations, and may also make provision—

(a) as to the days which, in the case of a person who at any time is, or is to be treated as, incapable of work as the result of an accident or injury, are or are not to be treated for the purpose of occupational injuries benefit as days of incapacity for work, and

(b) as to the day which, in the case of night workers and other special cases, is to be treated for the purpose of occupational injuries benefit as the day of the accident.

GENERAL NOTE

If the claimant is to receive injury benefit it is necessary to show that the day is a day of incapacity for work. The claimant may be deemed to be incapable of work if the claimant can satisfy the following conditions:

(a) be under medical care in respect of a disease or disablement in respect of which a registered medical practitioner certifies the claimant should not work; and

(b) be suffering from an infectious disease: S.I. No. 77 of 1967.

Should the claimant do any work on that day, other than work done earlier in the day the accident occurred, or work that comes within rule 5 of the Rules of Behaviour, that day cannot be regarded as a day of incapacity for work. A day for which the claimant receives holiday pay cannot be a day of incapacity for work. Should the claimant not seek injury benefit or be disqualified on a day from receipt of benefit, that day is not to be regarded as the day of incapacity for work. That day will, however, be regarded as a day of incapacity for the limited question of eligibility for disablement benefit 156 days after the occurrence of the accident. The usual provision exists in relation to night workers: S.I. No. 77 of 1967.

Application for injury benefit is made by way of the prescribed procedure found in the regulations. Application for benefit (including a declaration under section 69) should be made within 21 days of the first day of incapacity. If a section 60 declaration is sought then, of course, the reference should be within 21 days of the accident. This time limit can be extended by the Minister if good cause for failure to make the claim can be shown. Failure to make the application within the prescribed time however will disqualify the claimant from receiving injury benefit for any period greater than 21 days before the application was made. This disqualification may not be imposed if good cause for the failure is shown. The claimant is deemed to have good cause for failure to make the claim within the prescribed time if the Minster is satisfied that the claimant has been a hospital in-patient and the claim is made within three weeks of discharge from hospital or 13 weeks following first entry into hospital after the accident, whichever period is the shorter. In any event, injury benefit will not be payable for any day of incapacity which is more than six months before the date of the actual making of the claim: S.I. No. 374 of 1952.

Medical treatment

72.—(1) For the purposes of this Chapter "medical treatment" means medical, surgical or rehabilitative treatment (including any course of diet or other regimen), and references in this Chapter to "a person receiving or submitting himself to medical treatment" shall be construed accordingly.

(2) Regulations may provide that where a person receives medical treatment as an in-patient for two or more distinct periods separated by an interval or intervals of less than a specified duration, he shall be treated for the purposes of this Chapter as receiving it continuously from the beginning of the first period until the end of the last.

Rehabilitation

73.—(1) The Minister may make, towards the cost of rehabilitation services (including rehabilitation services provided under section 68 of the Health Act, 1970) for persons entitled to disablement benefit, such contributions as he may, with the consent of the Minister for Finance, determine.

(2) The amounts required for any contributions under this section shall be paid out of the Social Insurance Fund.

Research

74.—(1) The Minister may promote research into the causes, incidence and methods of prevention of—
(a) accidents and injuries against which occupational injuries insurance is provided, or
(b) diseases against which such insurance is provided or which it is contemplated may be prescribed for the purposes of section 66,
either by himself employing persons to conduct the research or by contributing to the expenses of, or otherwise assisting, other persons engaged in the research.

(2) The Minister may pay to persons so employed such salaries or other remuneration, and such travelling or other allowances, as he may, with the consent of the Minister for Finance, determine.

(3) The amounts required for any payments under this section shall be paid out of the Social Insurance Fund.

Taking of benefit into account in assessing damages

75.—(1) Notwithstanding section 2 of the Civil Liability (Amendment) Act, 1964, and section 236 of this Act, in an action for damages for personal injuries (including any such action arising out of a contract) there shall in assessing those damages be taken into account, against any loss of earnings or profits which has accrued or probably will accrue to the injured person from the injuries, the value of any rights which have accrued or will probably accrue to him therefrom in respect of disability benefit payable by virtue of section 53 (disregarding any right in respect of the said disability benefit payable by virtue of section 210, after the death of the injured person) or disablement benefit (disregarding any increase thereof under section 57 in respect of constant attendance) for the five years beginning with the time when the cause of action accrued. [1995 Act, Schedule E]

(2) The reference in subsection (1) to assessing the damages for personal injuries shall, in cases where the damages otherwise recoverable are subject to reduction under the law relating to contributory negligence or are limited by or under any Act or by contract, be taken as referring to the total damages which would have been recoverable apart from the deduction or limitation.

(3) Notwithstanding section 50 of the Civil Liability Act, 1961, in assessing damages in respect of a person's death under Part IV of that Act, account may be taken of any death benefit, by way of grant under section 63 of this Act in respect of funeral expenses, resulting from that person's death.

(4) Notwithstanding the Garda Síochána (Compensation) Acts, 1941 and 1945, there shall in assessing compensation be taken into account, against—

(a) any loss of earnings or profits which has accrued or probably will accrue to the injured person from the injuries,

(b) the detrimental effect which the injuries might reasonably be expected to have on the future earnings power generally of the injured person and in particular (if the injuries do not preclude the injured person from continuing to be a member of the Garda Síochána), on his future career in that force, and

(c) the pain and suffering occasioned by the injuries to the injured person and also to any disease or tendency to disease caused by the injuries,

the value of any rights which have accrued or will probably accrue to him therefrom in respect of disablement benefit (disregarding any increase thereof under section 57 in respect of constant attendance) for the five years beginning with the time when the cause of action accrued.

(5) Notwithstanding the Garda Síochána (Compensation) Acts, 1941 and 1945, in assessing compensation under those Acts in respect of—

(a) a person's death, account may be taken of any death benefit by way of grant under section 63 of this Act in respect of funeral expenses, resulting from that person's death, and

(b) any medical or surgical expenses incurred or likely to be incurred by the injured person in respect or in consequence of the injuries, account may be taken of any medical care payment under section 65 of this Act, resulting from those injuries for the five years beginning with the time when the cause of action accrued.

(6) Subsections (4) and (5) shall not apply to any proceedings instituted for compensation under the Garda Síochána (Compensation) Acts, 1941 and 1945, before the 6th day of April, 1989.

GENERAL NOTE

This disregard was present in the original 1966 Act. Its rationale is considered in Clark, *Damages and the Social Welfare Overlap* (1984) 19 Ir.Jur. 40.

See, generally, the General Note to section 236 below.

Saver for repeal of Workmen's Compensation Acts

76.—The Workmen's Compensation Acts, as amended by Part V of the Civil Liability Act, 1961, shall continue to apply to cases to which they would have applied if the Social Welfare (Occupational Injuries) Act, 1966, had not been passed, being cases where a right to compensation arose in respect of employment before the 1st day of May 1967, except where, in the case of a disease or injury prescribed for the purposes of section 66, the right did not arise before that date and the workman, before it arose, has been insured under this Chapter against that disease or injury.

Construction of certain references in Local Government (Superannuation) Act, 1956

77.—The references to the Social Welfare (Occupational Injuries) Act, 1966, in—

(a) the definitions of "service day" and "wages" in section 2 of the Local Government (Superannuation) Act, 1956 as amended by section 42 of the first-mentioned Act, and

(b) section 43 of the said Local Government (Superannuation) Act, 1856, as so amended,

shall be construed as references to this Chapter.

CHAPTER 11

PAY-RELATED BENEFIT

Interpretation

78.—In this Chapter—

"reckonable earnings" means, subject to regulations under this Chapter, earnings derived from insurable employment in respect of which employment contributions are payable in accordance with section 10(1);

"reckonable weekly earnings" means the average amount, calculated in accordance with regulations, of reckonable earnings received in a week;

"relevant income tax year" means, in relation to pay-related benefit payable in respect of any particular day, such year of assessment within the meaning of the Income Tax Acts as may be prescribed in relation to such benefit.

GENERAL NOTE

Pay-related benefit was introduced in 1973 with the intention of providing benefits as a supplement to certain flat-rate insurance payments, namely maternity, unemployment and disability benefits and some occupational injuries benefits. This supplement would bring these income maintenance payments into line with the claimant's pre-illness or pre-unemployment earnings and this acts as a buffer between the claimant and substantial income loss occasioned by a short-term insurance contingency. However, the provision of pay-related benefit was expensive and a policy reversal against the provision of pay-related benefit occurred in the 1983 legislation, with successive governments progressively eroding pay-related benefits. This process was hastened by the Report of the Commission on Social Welfare in which the Commission reviewed the arguments for and against pay-related benefits, concluding that, while the goal was a laudable one, pay-related benefit was an imperfect mechanism for achieving it, and that a better approach to adopt would be the improvement of basic payment rates to all recipients: Pl. 3851, pages 203–5.

When introduced in the 1973 Act, there were four tiered rates of 40 per cent, 30 per cent, 25 per cent and 20 per cent, depending on circumstances. The 1983 Act reduced the rates to two rates of 25 per cent and 20 per cent respectively. The 1987 Act reduced the rate to 12 per cent throughout the period of eligibility. The 1987 (No. 2) Act terminated eligibility for pay-related benefit for maternity allowances, in respect of new claims, from April 4, 1988. The 1992 Act terminated entitlement for disability and occupational injury recipients, thereby making pay-related benefit available only to those in receipt of unemployment benefit: see S.I. No. 99 of 1992. The regulations which assist in defining the terms "reckonable earnings" and "reckonable weekly earnings" are S.I. No. 141 of 1979, as amended by S.I. No. 188 of 1987 and S.I. No. 253 of 1991.

Entitlement to benefit

79.—(1) Subject to this Act, a person who had reckonable earnings in the relevant income tax year shall be entitled to pay-related benefit in respect of any day which—

(a) is a day of unemployment which forms part of a period of interruption of employment where the first day of unemployment in that period commenced before the 21st day of July, 1994 and in respect of which the person is entitled to unemployment benefit and which is not earlier than the 19th day of unemployment in the said period of interruption of employment, or [1994 Act, section 21(1)]

(b) is a day of incapacity for work which forms part of a period of interruption of employment in respect of incapacity for work which commenced before the 6th day of April, 1992, in respect of which the person is in receipt of disability benefit (or would be in receipt of disability benefit but for the fact that injury benefit is payable to the person).

(2) Notwithstanding subsection (1), a person engaged in—

(a) short-time employment, or

(aa) share fishing, or [1993 (No. 2) Act, section 9]

(b) employment in a period of interruption of employment, in which for the time being, a number of days is systematically worked in a period of four consecutive weeks, which is less than the number of days which was normal in the employment concerned prior to the reduction in the number of days of employment;

Provided that the number of days worked is equal to, or exceeds half of the number of days which would have been normally worked in that four week period,

shall not be entitled to pay-related benefit for any day in respect of which he is entitled to unemployment benefit.

DEFINITIONS

"day of unemployment": section 42.
"day of incapacity for work": section 31(1).
"short-time employment": section 2(1).

GENERAL NOTE

Subsection (1)

Subsection (1)(a) provides that a person entitled to unemployment benefit shall be entitled to pay-related benefit as from day 19 in the period of interruption of employment. Following upon the abolition of entitlement for new disability benefit claimants in the 1992 Act, entitlement is preserved in respect of disability benefit claims that commenced before April 6, 1992: subsection (1)(b).

Subsection (2)

Subsection (2) dates back to the Act of 1992. This subsection is designed to counteract a method whereby workers on short-time employment were able systematically to evade the provisions previously found in section 7 of the Social Welfare Act, 1983. When workers were required to work during a week on short-time (*e.g.* three days in a six-day week), they were, prior to the 1983 Act, able to obtain unemployment benefit for each of the three remaining days of unemployment, even if such workers habitually only worked for five days in a week. The 1983 Act closed this loop-hole by providing that benefit is payable in such cases at one-fifth of the weekly rate for each day of unemployment. However, the Act did not address week on–week off practices. This section addresses this anomaly by providing that in cases of this kind pay-related benefit is not to be payable along with unemployment benefit. The proviso requires that systematic short-time working is to be measured over a period of four consecutive weeks and that the disentitlement depends on the number of days actually worked being equal to, or in excess of, half of the days that would normally have been worked in that four-week period.

Rate of benefit

80.—(1) The weekly rate of pay-related benefit payable to a person in any period of interruption of employment shall be for any part of that period up to the 393rd day of unemployment (or in the case of a person to whom section 79(1)(b) applies, for any part of that period up to the 393rd day of incapacity for work) an amount equal to 12 per cent. of the part (if any) of his reckonable weekly earnings for the relevant income tax year that exceeds £97.50 but does not exceed such limit as stands prescribed for the time being, subject to such conditions as may be prescribed to restrict the total amount of benefit payable under this Part to the person in respect of any week.

(2) In the case of any entitlement to pay-related benefit payable in respect of a period of interruption of employment where—
  (a) the period of interruption of employment commenced before the 8th day of April, 1991, subsection (1) shall be construed as if "£72" were substituted for "£97.50",
  (b) the period of interruption of employment commenced on or after the 8th day of April, 1991 but before the 6th day of April, 1992, subsection (1) shall be construed as if "£75" were substituted for "£97.50", and
  (c) the period of interruption of employment commenced on or after the 6th day of April, 1992 but before the 6th day of April, 1993, subsection (1) shall be construed as if "£78" were substituted for "£97.50". [1994 Act, section 21(3)]

GENERAL NOTE

Subsection (1) provides that any person entitled to pay-related benefit shall receive that benefit at the rate of 12 per cent of reckonable weekly earnings for the relevant income tax year, as long as those earnings exceed the minimum earnings floor of £97.50. The maximum figure of reckonable weekly earnings is set at £220 by S.I. No. 298 of 1989.

Subsection (2) simply reinstates the minimum ceiling figure in place at the time when a claim for unemployment benefit commenced in lieu of the current figure of £97.50.

Duration of payment

81.—(1) In any period of interruption of employment a person shall not be entitled to pay-related benefit in respect of any day of unemployment after the 393rd day of unemployment in that period.

(2) In calculating for the purposes of section 80 and this section whether, in a period of interruption of employment, a person has had a specified number of days of unemployment, account shall be taken of only the first

18 days of unemployment in that period and any day of unemployment in that period in respect of which that person was entitled to pay-related benefit or would have been so entitled but for any condition prescribed for the purposes of section 80.

(3) In subsection (2), day of unemployment shall be construed as including a day of incapacity for work in the case of a person to whom section 79(1)(b) applies.

GENERAL NOTE

Entitlement to pay-related benefit is to expire after 393 days of unemployment, as calculated under this section.

Payment of benefit

81A.—Notwithstanding the provisions of this Chapter, pay-related benefit shall not be payable to a person in respect of any day of unemployment or of incapacity for work on or after the 1st day of November, 1995, unless he is in receipt of the said benefit on that day in which case benefit shall continue to be payable for the duration of his continuous entitlement up to the 393rd day of unemployment or of incapacity for work. [1994 Act, section 21(4)]

GENERAL NOTE

Section 81A, added by section 21 of the 1994 Act, provides that pay-related benefit will not be payable for a new claim after July 20, 1994, or in the case of a claim linked with an earlier period of unemployment, after November 1, 1995.

Regulations

82.—(1) The Minister may by regulations provide for—

(a) the calculation or estimation of the amount of the reckonable earnings and the amount of the reckonable weekly earnings of a person or class of persons for the purposes of this Chapter, in such manner, by reference to such matters and on such basis as may be specified;

(b) the calculation of the amounts payable in respect of pay-related benefit in accordance with prescribed scales and for such adjustments of the amounts as may be necessary to facilitate the computation of the amounts and avoid multiples of other than 10p in the amounts;

(c) the application of this Chapter to persons employed in such class or classes of employment as may be specified in the regulations and may by such regulations make such modifications in the provisions of this Chapter as may appear to him to be necessary for that purpose;

(d) the exclusion from the application of this Chapter of persons employed in employment of such class or classes as may be specified in the regulations;

(e) the modification of any of the conditions for receipt of pay-related benefit in the case of any claim to such benefit arising during the period which began on the 8th day of April, 1974, and ending on such date as may be specified in the regulations; and

(f) requiring employers for the purposes of pay-related contributions and pay-related benefit, to keep such records as may be specified in the regulations of the earnings of persons employed by them and to retain the records for such periods as may be prescribed.

(2) Notwithstanding section 79, the Minister may make regulations providing that, for the purposes of a scheme administered by An Foras

Áiseanna Saothair and known as the Enterprise Allowance Scheme, a person accepted into that Scheme who, if he had continued to be unemployed, would be entitled to continue to receive pay-related benefit, shall be entitled, subject to such conditions as may be specified in the regulations, to receive such benefit in the form of a lump sum equivalent to the amount which he would otherwise have received in respect of the unexpired portion (subject to a maximum of 26 weeks) of the relevant period of interruption of employment.

(3) A class of employment may be specified in regulations under subsection (1)(c) or (d) in such manner and by reference to such matters as the Minister thinks appropriate.

GENERAL NOTE

Regulations under this section are as follows:
Social Welfare (Pay-Related Benefit) Regulations, 1979 (S.I. No. 141 of 1979).
Social Welfare (Pay-Related Benefit) (Enterprise Allowance) Regulations, 1987 (S.I. No. 65 of 1987).
Social Welfare (Pay-Related Benefit) (Amendment) Regulations, 1987 (S.I. No. 188 of 1987).
Social Welfare (Pay-Related Benefit) Regulations, 1991 (S.I. No. 253 of 1991).

CHAPTER 12

OLD AGE (CONTRIBUTORY) PENSION

Entitlement to pension

83.—(1) Subject to this Act, a person shall be entitled to old age (contributory) pension if he has attained pensionable age and satisfies the contribution conditions in section 84.

(2) In this Chapter—
"yearly average" means, in relation to any claimant, the average per contribution year of contribution weeks in respect of which that claimant has qualifying contributions, voluntary contributions or credited contributions in the period commencing either—
  (a) on the 5th day of January, 1953, in case the claimant is a man, or on the 6th day of July, 1953, in case the claimant is a woman, or
  (b) at the beginning of the contribution year in which the claimant's entry into insurance occurred (if after the 5th day of January, 1953, in the case of a man, or the 6th day of July, 1953, in the case of a woman),
(whichever is the later) and ending at the end of the last complete contribution year before the date of his attaining pensionable age;
"alternative yearly average" means, in relation to any claimant, the average per contribution year of contribution weeks in respect of which that claimant has qualifying contributions, voluntary contributions or credited contributions in the period commencing on the 6th day of April, 1979, and ending at the end of the last complete contribution year before the date of his attaining pensionable age.

(3) In this Chapter, "relevant person" means—
  (a) a person who first becomes—
    (i) an insured person by virtue of section 9(1) insured for old age (contributory) pension purposes, or
    (ii) an insured person by virtue of section 17,

on or after the 6th day of April, 1991, or
(b) a person who fails to satisfy the contribution condition set out in subsection (1)(c) of section 84 and had periods in which he had been—
    (i) employed mainly in one or more of the employments specified in Article 5(1), 6(1) or 7(1) of the Social Welfare (Modifications of Insurance) Regulations, 1991 (S.I. No. 94 of 1991), and
    (ii) an employed contributor, a self-employed contributor or a voluntary contributor in respect of whom contributions, reckonable for the purposes of the contribution conditions for entitlement to old age (contributory) pension were paid in respect of or credited to him.

(4) For the purposes of this Chapter, in the case of a relevant person—
"entry into insurance" means, subject to section 83(7), in relation to any person whichever occurs first—
    (a) the date on which he first becomes an insured person by virtue of section 9(1), except where he becomes an insured person by virtue of paragraph (b) of subsection (1) of the said section 9 only, or
    (b) the date on which he first becomes an insured person by virtue of section 17,
and that that date shall be regarded as the date of entry into insurance for the purposes of paragraphs (a) and (c) of section 84(1).

(5) Notwithstanding subsection (4) regulations may provide that the date on which a relevant person first becomes an employed person or a self-employed person, insurable for old age (contributory) pension purposes under the legislation of another Member State, or under the legislation of any other State with which the Minister has made a reciprocal arrangement under the provisions of section 238, may be regarded as the date of entry into insurance.

(6) Notwithstanding subsections (4) and (5), regulations may provide that where a date of entry into insurance occurs before a date to be prescribed, that day may be regarded as the date of entry into insurance.

(7) For the purposes of this Chapter, in the case of a person who became a self-employed contributor on the 6th day of April, 1988, and who at any time prior to that date was an employed contributor, the date on which the person first entered into insurance or the 6th day of April, 1988, whichever is the more favourable to him, shall be regarded as the date of entry into insurance:

Provided that where a date other than that on which the claimant first entered into insurance is so regarded, that date shall be regarded as the date of entry into insurance for the purposes of paragraphs (a) and (c) of section 84(1).

GENERAL NOTE

Prior to the Social Welfare (Amendment) Act, 1960, the only provision made for old age pensions was the old age (non-contributory) pension that dated back to 1908. The introduction of an insurance-based pension was seen as a priority for the majority of workers who did not have access to occupational pensions and who deserved a more adequate level of income than the means-tested non-contributory pension could provide.

Debate in the last 20 years has centred around three issues: firstly, the adequacy of State pension payment levels with particular reference to the possibility of a State earnings-related pension; secondly, the provision of State pensions for the self-employed; and, thirdly, the legal protection of persons who are members of occupational pension schemes. These issues have been resolved in a variety of ways. The Commission on Social Welfare came out against an earnings-related system, preferring instead to target resources at improvements in benefit and pension levels for all, rather than by targeting specific categories, as was canvassed in the 1976 Green Paper on Pensions. The self-employed were brought into the State pension system in 1988, thereby providing State pensions after 10 years of qualifying contributions for a large number of persons who otherwise had no State entitlement. The regulation of occupational pensions has been secured under the provisions of the Pensions Act, 1990, as amended.

Subsection (1) provides statutory entitlement to an old age (contributory) pension to persons who have reached 66 years of age who satisfy the contribution conditions fixed in section 84.

Subsection (2) provides for alternative methods of calculating the yearly average contributions paid or credited to an applicant seeking to establish entitlement to an old age (contributory) pension at the maximum rate of pension. The qualifying contribution rule is designed to establish an enduring link between the contributor and the social insurance system and, heretofore, the test was whether the contributor had an average of 48 contributions, paid or credited, from 1953 or entry into insurance, if that was later than 1953. Where this test was not satisfied, the pension would be payable at various tiered reduced rates as long as the average did not fall below 20.

The yearly average test produced a considerable number of hard cases, particularly in situations where the contributor may have been insurable in 1953, fell out of the insurance net, and then came back into insurance in recent years. In such a case the yearly average would be low, despite a significant volume of recent contributions.

The alternative test provides that the alternative yearly average is the average number of contributions paid or credited commencing on April 6, 1979, that is, the date when the PRSI scheme began to function. The period ends at the close of the last complete contribution year prior to the contributor's reaching 66 years of age.

This alternative test is only to be utilised to consider whether the maximum pension is payable. If the test results in the average being lower than 48 (*e.g.* 40 contributions) the test becomes irrelevant and the reduced rate of pension will be calculated by reference to the older test (*i.e.* yearly average since 1953 or entry into insurance, if later).

Social welfare contributions made prior to 1953 are not considered for contributory pension purposes because this pension was only introduced in 1961. The decision to allow contributions before 1953 and 1961 is a concession not to be extended. Further anomalies in relation to pension contributions were highlighted in Dáil Eireann at Committee Stage: 417 *Dáil Debates* Cols. 1871–1893.

The definition in subsection (3) is necessary in order to allow persons with mixed insurance records to qualify for old age (contributory) pensions when entitlement under the full or reduced rate contributory pensions cannot be satisfied. The term "relevant person" was inserted into Irish social welfare law by section 36(5) of the Act of 1993. This subsection indicates the categories of person eligible for old age (contributory) pension. "Relevant persons" are:

     (i) employed contributors under section 9(1) insured for such pensions (in effect category A, H, E and voluntary 'S' contributors);

    (ii) self-employed contributors under section 17 when either of the above first became so insured after April 6, 1991;

   (iii) a person who fails to satisfy section 84(1)(c) and had periods of modified insurance within S.I. No. 94 of 1991 and had been an employed person, voluntary contributor or self-employed contributor for whom qualifying contributions had been paid or credited.

Subsections (4), (5) and (6) introduce into the legislation a flexible method of devising when a person entered into insurance for the purpose of calculating the average contribution of a person.

Subsection (4) directs that this date will be either the date on which that person first became insured (save in section 9(1)(b) instances) or when that person became a self-insured contributor, whichever happened first. However, subsection (5) now allows the period to be abridged by providing that regulations may stipulate that if a person became insurable in another E.C. Member State, or in another State with whom Ireland has reciprocal arrangements then the date of entry into insurance abroad may be regarded as the date of entry into insurance in Ireland. Of course the reverse may also occur and in such a case subsection (6) will allow the Minister to state that the date of entry into insurance may be prescribed by regulations.

Subsection (7) is intended to avoid a repetition of the situation that arose after the extension of social insurance to non-manual workers in 1974, an anomalous situation that attracted much publicity and unfavourable comment from the Ombudsman and the Commission on Social Welfare. Under the terms of this subsection a person who, on April 6, 1988 came into social insurance as a self-employed contributor may, if that person has a social insurance record as an employed contributor, declare that April 6, 1988 is to be regarded as the date of entry into insurance, rather than the previous date upon which contributions as an employed contributor commenced. This will enable the claimant for an old age (contributory) pension to establish entitlement to a pension, or a higher rate of pension, because the average of contributions paid each year will be higher than would otherwise be the case. This provision is not available if the claimant was not a self-employed contributor on April 6, 1988. Take a person in insurable employment on April 6, 1988 who gives up insurable employment and after an interval abroad, returns to Ireland. If that person takes on self-employed contributor status he cannot take advantage of this subsection. The date of entry into insurance as a self-employed contributor will not determine the average but, rather, this will be determined by the earlier date of entry into insurable employment.

Conditions for receipt

84.—(1) The contribution conditions for old age (contributory) pension are—

    (a) subject to subsection (2), that the claimant has entered into insurance before attaining the age of 56 years,

    (b) that the claimant has qualifying contributions in respect of not less than 156 contribution weeks since his entry into insurance, and

    (c) that the claimant has a yearly average or in the case of a person who attains pensionable age on or after the 6th day of April, 1992, an alternative yearly average of not less than 48.

(2)   (a) In the case of a person who attained the age of 57 years before the 1st day of July, 1974, subsection (1)(a) shall be construed as if "60" were substituted for "56".

    (b) In the case of a person who attained the age of 57 years on or after the 1st day of July, 1974, subsection (1)(a) shall be construed as if "58" were substituted for "56".

    (c) In the case of a person who attained the age of 56 years on or after the 1st day of April, 1975, subsection (1)(a) shall be construed as if "57" were substituted for "56" and paragraph (b) of this subsection shall not apply on his attaining the age of 57 years.

    (d) In the case of a person who attained the age of 55 years on or after the 1st day of October, 1977, paragraph (c) shall not apply on his attaining the age of 56 years and paragraph (b) shall not apply on his attaining the age of 57 years.

(3)   (a) A person who attained the age of 69 years on or after the 1st day of July, 1974, but before the 5th day of January, 1976, may have his entitlement to old age (contributory) pension determined under the provisions of the Acts relating to social welfare in operation prior to the 1st day of July, 1974, if that would be to his advantage.

    (b) A person who attained the age of 69 years before the 1st day of July, 1974, and has been awarded an old age (contributory) pension under the provisions of the Acts relating to social welfare in operation prior to that date shall on and after that date have a right to such pension at the rate for the time being payable by reference to a yearly average equal to the yearly average calculated in his case under those provisions.

(4)   (a) A person who attained the age of 68 years on or after the 1st day of April, 1975, but before the 3rd day of January, 1977, may have his entitlement to old age (contributory) pension determined under the provisions of the Acts relating to social welfare in operation prior to the 1st day of April, 1975, if that would be to his advantage.

    (b) A person who attained the age of 68 years before the 1st day of April, 1975, and has been awarded an old age (contributory) pension under the provisions of the Acts relating to social welfare in operation prior to that date shall on and after that date have a right to such pension as the rate for the time being payable by reference to a yearly average equal to the yearly average calculated in his case under those provisions.

(5) (a) A person who attained the age of 67 years on or after the 1st day of October, 1977, but before the 1st day of January, 1979, may have his entitlement to old age (contributory) pension determined under the provisions of the Acts relating to social welfare in operation prior to the 1st day of October 1977, if that would be to his advantage.

(b) A person who attained the age of 67 years before the 1st day of October, 1977, and has been awarded an old age (contributory) pension under the provisions of the Acts relating to social welfare in operation prior to that date shall, on and after that date, have a right to such pension at the rate for the time being payable by reference to a yearly average equal to the yearly average calculated in his case under those provisions.

(6) Regulations may provide for modifications of the meaning of yearly average contained in section 83(2) or of the contribution conditions set out in this section.

(7) Subject to subsection (8), regulations may provide for entitling to old age (contributory) pension a claimant who would be entitled thereto but for the fact that he has a yearly average of less than 48.

(8) Regulations under subsection (7) shall provide that old age (contributory) pension payable by virtue thereof shall be payable at a rate less than that specified in the Second Schedule, and the rate specified by the regulations may vary by reference to the yearly average so calculated, but any increase of that pension payable under section 87(1) or section 87(2) shall be the same as if the claimant had a yearly average of not less than 48.

(9) Contributions paid or credited under this Part, or paid, excused or deemed to be or treated as paid under the National Health Insurance Acts, 1911 to 1952, (other than, in the case of a person who is not a relevant person, contributions paid by or in respect of a person during which such person is or was employed mainly in one or more of the employments specified in Article 5(1), 6(1) or 7(1) of the Social Welfare (Modifications of Insurance) Regulations, 1991 (S.I. No. 94 of 1991)), shall be taken into account in such manner and subject to such conditions and limitations as may be prescribed for the purpose of the satisfaction of the contribution conditions for old age (contributory) pension.

(10) Regulations under subsection (9) may also provide for modifications, in the case of persons who were insured under the National Health Insurance Acts, 1911 to 1952, or who were absent from the State before the 3rd day of October, 1960, of any of the contribution conditions for old age (contributory) pension.

(11) Where a person, other than in the case of a relevant person, becomes an employed contributor by virtue of paragraph (b) of section 9(1) and would not, apart from that paragraph be an employed contributor, his entry into insurance by virtue thereof shall be deemed not to be an entry into insurance for the purposes of subsection (1) of this section and for those purposes his entry into insurance shall be deemed to occur when he first becomes an employed contributor by virtue of paragraph (a) of section 9(1).

(12) Subject to subsection (13), regulations may provide for entitling to old age (contributory) pension a person who would be entitled thereto but for the fact that the contribution condition set out in subsection (1)(c) is not satisfied where that person, having earlier ceased to be an employed contributor became, as a consequence and at the time of the coming into operation of section 12 of the Social Welfare Act, 1973, an employed

contributor in respect of whom contributions reckonable for the purposes of the contribution conditions for entitlement to old age (contributory) pension were payable.

(13) Regulations for the purposes of subsection (12) shall provide that old age (contributory) pension payable by virtue thereof shall be payable at a rate less than that specified in the Second Schedule, and the rate specified by the regulations may vary with the extent to which the contribution condition set out in subsection (1)(c) is satisfied.

(14) Regulations may provide, subject to subsection (15), for entitling to old age (contributory) pension a relevant person who would be entitled thereto but for the fact that the contribution condition set out in subsection (1)(c) is not satisfied and who does not have an entitlement to an old age (contributory) pension by virtue of Regulation (EEC) No. 1408/71 of the Council of the European Communities,[1] or by virtue of a reciprocal arrangement under the provisions of section 238 and who in respect of any period has been employed mainly in one or more of the employments specified in Article 5(1), 6(1) or 7(1) of the Social Welfare (Modifications of Insurance) Regulations, 1991 (S.I. No. 94 of 1991).

(15) Regulations for the purposes of subsection (14) shall provide that old age (contributory) pension payable by virtue thereof shall—

(a) be payable at a rate less than that specified in the Second Schedule, and the rate specified by the regulations may vary in relation to the proportion to which the number of—
  (i) employment contributions paid in respect of or credited to the insured person, and
  (ii) self-employment contributions paid by him, and
  (iii) voluntary contributions paid by him,
  reckonable for old age (contributory) pension purposes bears to the total number of such employment contributions, self-employment contributions and voluntary contributions, but any increase of pension in respect of a qualified child shall be paid at the rate specified in the Second Schedule, and
(b) where the amount calculated in accordance with paragraph (a) is not a multiple of £2, be increased to the next multiple of £2.

GENERAL NOTE

Subsection (1)

The contribution conditions set by subsection (1) are first, that the claimant enters into insurance before reaching 56 years of age. Secondly, that the claimant has paid at least 156 qualifying contributions since first becoming insured. Thirdly, that the claimant has a yearly average of at least 48 paid or credited contributions since 1953 or when first becoming insured, whichever is the later, in the last complete contribution year before reaching 66. In the alternative, a yearly average, in the case of a person who reaches 66 on or after April 6, 1992, of at least 48 paid or credited contributions between April 6, 1992 and the last complete contribution year prior to reaching 66 years of age. Department practice is to look at a claimant's contribution record since 1979 in order to establish eligibility. It is only when this insurance record is insufficient for this purpose that post-1953, or the date of entry into insurance, contributions are looked at in order to establish maximum entitlement: Department of Social Welfare Guide p. 16.

Subsections (2) (3) (4) and (5)

These provisions operate in respect of older pensioners so as to allow entitlement not to be prejudiced by changes in the law or to operate in case of the pensioner, *e.g.* subsections (4) and (5).

Subsection (6)

S.I. No. 235 of 1994 directs that years spent as a homemaker looking after young children or an incapacitated person are to be disregarded in calculating a person's yearly average number of contributions.

[1]O.J. No. L149 of 5.7.1971.

Subsections (7) and (8)

A person who fails to qualify for a maximum pension because their contribution average falls below 48 paid or credited contributions but above 20 paid or credited contributions is entitled to a reduced rate pension under article 38 of S.I. No. 417 of 1994.

See S.I. No. 146 of 1995 for payment rates.

Subsection (9)

See article 37 of S.I. No. 417 of 1994.

Subsections (12) and (13)

This subsection is an enabling provision which allows certain contributors who fell out of insurance prior to April 1, 1974, but who fell back into insurance upon the abolition of the earnings limit by section 12 of the Act of 1973, to receive an old age (contributory) pension. These persons found that their average could fall below 20 because of the operation of the earnings limit prior to that date. In 1974 the distinction between manual and non-manual workers was abolished for social insurance purposes, thus bringing into social insurance most non-manual workers employed under a contract of employment, regardless of remuneration levels. Non-manual workers found, prior to 1974, that as income and the prescribed level of remuneration both fluctuated, they often came into and out of social insurance at certain times. If the non-manual worker came into social insurance prior to 1974 this had quite an important consequence. A condition of entitlement is that the insured has a minimum level of average contributions, paid or credited, over the period between entry into insurance and the date when the insured seeks old age (contributory) pension. If, after initial entry into insurance, there are gaps in the insurance record then this contribution condition (currently section 79(1)(c) of the Principal Act) will not be satisfied in many cases. This situation is made worse by the case of a person who first came into insurance in April 1974, following abolition of the manual/non-manual worker distinction. Even though such a person may have less contributions actually paid into the Social Insurance Fund than a person with an earlier and longer record of insurance, the section 79(1)(c) contribution condition will be more easily met by such a person. Widespread public concern at this situation was heightened by critical observations by the Ombudsman, *e.g. Annual Report of the Ombudsman Ireland* (1984) p. 18 (Pl. 2909) and the *Report of the Commission on Social Welfare* p. 232 (Pl. 3851).

An average of five paid or credited contributions since 1953 or entry into insurance is necessary.

Regulations

S.I. No. 235 of 1994.
S.I. No. 417 of 1994.
S.I. No. 146 of 1995.

Subsection (14)

This subsection deals with claimants who spent part of their working lives in modified insurance. If such a person does not qualify for one of the reduced rate pensions under subsection (7) above, is not entitled to a pension from some other E.C. state under Regulation 1408/71, or under a reciprocal arrangement with another State, and that person has a total of 260 paid or credited contributions, or 208 paid contributions since 1953 or when first being insured (whichever is the later), then a pro-rata old age pension will be payable. See Schedules C and D of S.I. No. 417 of 1994.

Regulations

S.I. No. 417 of 1994.

Disregard of self-employment contributions in certain cases

85.—(1) In the case of a person who, having been a self-employed contributor, makes a claim for old age (contributory) pension on or after the 6th day of April, 1995, the contribution conditions contained in section 84 shall not be regarded as having been satisfied unless, in accordance with section 18—

(a) he has paid self-employment contributions in respect of at least 1 contribution year before attaining pensionable age, and

(b) all self-employment contributions payable by him have been paid.

(2) Notwithstanding subsection (1), the Minister may, if he is satisfied that in all the circumstances of the case it would be appropriate to do so, direct that subsection (1) shall not be applied in that case. [1995 Act, section 19].

GENERAL NOTE

This section governs entitlement to old age (contributory) pension in circumstances where the contributor is a self-employed contributor. If the claim for a pension is made after April 6, 1993, the contribution conditions will not be deemed to have been satisfied unless all self-employment contributions payable by the claimant have actually been paid.

This provision may be relaxed by the Minister in each particular case: this does not require a statutory instrument to be made before this power to exempt may be exercised by the Minister and it is exercised in hardship cases.

As from April 5, 1995, the self-employed contributor must have paid at least one year's contributions between April 5 in one year and April 4 in another year.

Rate of pension

86.—Subject to this Part, the weekly rate of old age (contributory) pension shall be as set out in column (2) of Part I of the Second Schedule.

Increases (including increases for adult and child dependants)

87.—(1) The weekly rate of old age (contributory) pension shall be increased by the amount set out in column (3) of Part I of the Second Schedule for any period during which the beneficiary has an adult dependant, subject to the restriction that, except where regulations otherwise provide, a beneficiary shall not be entitled for the same period to an increase of pension under this subsection in respect of more than one person. [1995 (No. 2) Act, section 10]

(2) The weekly rate of old age (contributory) pension shall be increased by the amount set out in column (4) of Part I of the Second Schedule in respect of each qualified child who normally resides with the beneficiary. [1995 Act, Schedule F]

(3) Any increase of old age (contributory) pension payable pursuant to subsection (2) in respect of a qualified child who normally resides with a beneficiary and with the spouse of a beneficiary shall be payable at the rate of one-half of the appropriate amount in any case where the spouse of the beneficiary is not an adult dependant, and subsection (2) shall be construed and have effect accordingly.

(4) The weekly rate of old age (contributory) pension shall be increased by the amount set out in column (6) of Part I of the Second Schedule where the beneficiary is living alone. [1995 Act, Schedule F]

(5) The weekly rate of old age (contributory) pension shall be increased by the amount set out in column (7) of Part I of the Second Schedule where the beneficiary has attained the age of 80 years. [1995 Act, Schedule F]

CHAPTER 13

RETIREMENT PENSION

Entitlement to pension

88.—(1) Subject to this Act, a person who has attained the age of 65 years shall be entitled to retirement pension for any period of retirement if he satisfies the contribution conditions in section 89.

(2) The periods which shall be regarded for the purposes of this section as periods of retirement shall be specified by regulations.

(3) In this Chapter—

"yearly average" means, in relation to any claimant, the average per contribution year of contribution weeks in respect of which that claimant has qualifying contributions, voluntary contributions or credited contributions in the period commencing either—

(a) on the 5th day of January, 1953, in case the claimant is a man, or on the 6th day of July, 1953, in case the claimant is a woman, or

(b) at the beginning of the contribution year in which the claimants entry into insurance occurred (if after the 5th day of January, 1953, in the case of a man, or the 6th day of July, 1953, in the case of a woman),

(whichever is the later) and ending at the end of the last complete contribution year before the date of his attaining the age of 65 years;

"alternative yearly average" means, in relation to any claimant, the average per contribution year if contribution weeks in respect of which that claimant has qualifying contributions, voluntary contributions or credited contributions in the period commencing on the 6th day of April, 1979, and ending at the end of the last complete contribution year before the date of his attaining the age of 65 years.

(4) In this Chapter, "relevant person" means—

(a) a person who first becomes—

(i) an insured person by virtue of section 9(1) insured for old age (contributory) pension purposes, or

(ii) an insured person by virtue of section 17,

on or after the 6th day of April, 1991, or

(b) a person who fails to satisfy the contribution condition set out in subsection (1)(c) of section 89 and had periods in which he had been—

(i) employed mainly in one or more of the employments specified in Article 5(1), 6(1) or 7(1) of the Social Welfare (Modifications of Insurance) Regulations, 1991 (S.I. No. 94 of 1991), and

(ii) an employed contributor, a self-employed contributor or a voluntary contributor, in respect of whom contributions, reckonable for the purposes of the contribution conditions for entitlement to old age (contributory) pension were paid in respect of or credited to him.

(5) For the purposes of this Chapter, in the case of a relevant person "entry into insurance" means in relation to any person whichever occurs first—

(a) the date on which he first becomes an insured person by virtue of section 9(1), except where he becomes an insured person by virtue of paragraph (b) of subsection (1) of the said section 9 only, or

(b) the date on which he first becomes an insured person by virtue of section 17,

and that that date shall be regarded as the date of entry into insurance for the purposes of paragraphs (a) and (c) of section 89(1).

(6) Notwithstanding subsection (5), regulations may provide that the date on which a relevant person first becomes an employed person or a self-employed person, insurable for retirement pension purposes under the legislation of another Member State, or under the legislation of any other State with which the Minister has made a reciprocal arrangement under the provisions of section 238, may be regarded as the date of entry into insurance.

(7) Notwithstanding subsections (5) and (6), regulations may provide that where a date of entry into insurance occurs before a date to be prescribed, that day may be regarded as the date of entry into insurance.

GENERAL NOTE

Subsection (1)

Retirement pensions were introduced into Irish social welfare law through the 1970 Act. The pension is payable to persons aged 65 who satisfy the retirement condition. The retirement condition is tied to an age requirement and the Report of the Commission on Social Welfare considered that a more flexible retirement scheme was both socially useful and worthy of introduction, when resources permit (pp. 328–329). No movement has been made in this direction as yet.

Subsection (2)

The retirement condition is set by regulation as being satisfied if an employee does not have earnings of £30 per week or more, or self-employment earnings of £2,500 or more per annum. See article 46 of S.I. No. 417 of 1994.

Subsection (3)

This definition subsection parallels that found above in section 83(2) in relation to old age (contributory) pension in order to provide two standards by which a fair and reasonable contribution average can be established in the individual circumstances of retirement pensioners, particularly in the case of retirement pensioners falling in and out of insurance prior to abolition of the earnings limit in 1974.

Subsection (4)

See the General Note to section 83(3). This section identifies persons who are eligible for a retirement pension.

Subsection (5)

This section defines the term "entry into insurance" and makes provision for allowing modifications of the date under regulations.

Conditions for receipt

89.—(1) The contribution conditions for retirement pension are—

   (a) that the claimant has entered into insurance before attaining the age of 55 years,

   (b) that the claimant has qualifying contributions in respect of not less than 156 contribution weeks since his entry into insurance, and

   (c) that the claimant has a yearly average or in the case of a person who attains the age of 65 years on or after the 6th day of April, 1992, an alternative yearly average of not less than 48.

(2) Regulations may provide for modifications of the meaning of yearly average contained in section 88(3) or of the contribution conditions set out in this section.

(3) Contributions paid under the National Health Insurance Acts, 1911 to 1952, by or in respect of an employed contributor may be taken into account in such manner and subject to such conditions and limitations as may be prescribed for the purpose of the satisfaction by him of the contribution conditions for retirement pension.

(4) Subject to subsection (5), regulations may provide for entitling to retirement pension a claimant who would be entitled thereto but for the fact that he has a yearly average of less than 48.

(5) Regulations under subsection (4) shall provide that retirement pension payable by virtue thereof shall be payable at a rate less than that specified in the Second Schedule, and the rate specified by the regulations may vary by reference to the yearly average so calculated, but any increase of that pension payable under section 91(1) or section 91(2) shall be the same as if the claimant had a yearly average of not less than 48.

(6) Regulations may provide, subject to subsection (7), for entitling to retirement pension a relevant person who would be entitled thereto but for the fact that the contribution condition set out in subsection (1)(c) is not satisfied and who does not have an entitlement to a retirement pension by virtue of Regulation (EEC) No. 1408/71 of the Council of the European

Communities, (O.J. No. L149 of 5.7.1971.) or by virtue of a reciprocal arrangement under the provisions of section 238 and who in respect of any period has been employed mainly in one or more of the employments specified in Article 5(1), 6(1) or 7(1) of the Social Welfare (Modifications of Insurance) Regulations, 1991 (S.I. No. 94 of 1991).

(7) Regulations for the purposes of subsection (6) shall provide that retirement pension payable by virtue thereof shall—

(a) be payable at a rate less than that specified in the Second Schedule, and the rate specified by the regulations may vary in relation to the proportion to which the number of—

(i) employment contributions paid in respect of or credited to the insured person, and

(ii) voluntary contributions paid by him,

reckonable for retirement pension purposes bears to the total number of such employment contributions, self-employment contributions and voluntary contributions, but any increase of pension in respect of a qualified child shall be paid at the rate specified in the Second Schedule, and

(b) where the amount calculated in accordance with paragraph (a) is not a multiple of £2, be increased to the next multiple of £2.

GENERAL NOTE

The entitlement conditions set for a retirement pension at full rate are found in subsection (1). The claimant must have first entered into insurance before reaching 55, the claimant must have 156 qualifying contributions or more since entry into insurance, and maintain a yearly average, or alternative yearly average of 48 contributions paid or credited.

National Health Insurance Act contributions are reckonable for the purpose of satisfying the 156 qualifying contribution condition on the basis that two such contributions count as three under S.I. No. 417 of 1994. For persons who fail to satisfy either of the yearly average provisions, subsections (4) and (5) allow reduced rates of retirement pension to be payable as long as a minimum yearly average of 24 contributions paid or credited can be shown. For rates of retirement pension see S.I. No. 417 of 1994, Schedule E. For persons who have spent part of their working life in modified insurance which did not levy contributions which were qualifying contributions for retirement pensions, subsection (6) permits such persons to be eligible for pro-rata retirement pensions as long as those persons do not qualify for a retirement pension under Regulation 1408/71 or a reciprocal arrangement with some other member state. The pro-rata pension is payable if at least 260 paid or credited contributions have been registered, at least 208 of which are paid qualifying contributions, since 1953 or entry into insurance, whichever is the most recent event. For rates see S.I. No. 146 of 1995.

Regulations
S.I. No. 417 of 1994.

Rate of pension

90.—Subject to this Part, the weekly rate of retirement pension shall be as set out in column (2) of Part I of the Second Schedule.

GENERAL NOTE

See the Social Welfare Act, 1995 for current rates of pension.

Increases (including increases for adult and child dependants)

91.—(1) The weekly rate of retirement pension shall be increased by the amount set out in column (3) of Part I of the Second Schedule for any period during which the beneficiary has an adult dependant, subject to the restriction that, except where regulations otherwise provide, the beneficiary shall not be entitled for the same period to an increase of pension under this subsection in respect of more than one person [1995 (No. 2) Act, section 10]

(2) The weekly rate of retirement pension shall be increased by the amount set out in column (4), of Part I of the Second Schedule in respect of each qualified child who normally resides with the beneficiary. [1995 Act, Schedule F]

(3) Any increase of retirement pension payable pursuant to subsection (2) in respect of a qualified child who normally resides with a beneficiary and with the spouse of a beneficiary shall be payable at the rate of one-half of the appropriate amount in any case where the spouse of the beneficiary is not an adult dependant, and subsection (2) shall be construed and have effect accordingly.

(4) The weekly rate of retirement pension shall be increased by the amount set out in column (6) of Part I of the Second Schedule where the beneficiary has attained pensionable age and is living alone. [1995 Act, Schedule F]

(5) The weekly rate of retirement pension shall be increased by the amount set out in column (7) of Part I of the Second Schedule where the beneficiary has attained the age of 80 years. [1995 Act, Schedule F]

DEFINITIONS
"adult dependant": S.I. No. 417 of 1994.
"qualified child": section 2(3).
"normally resides": S.I. No. 417 of 1994.

CHAPTER 14

SURVIVOR'S BENEFIT

[Repealed by 1994 Act, section 13]

GENERAL NOTE
Survivor's Benefit was integrated with the widows contributory pension by the 1994 Act to form a new payment, survivor's pension. See sections 100–105 above.

CHAPTER 15

INVALIDITY PENSION

Entitlement to pension

95.—(1) Subject to this Act, a person shall be entitled to invalidity pension if—
(a) he is permanently incapable of work, and
(b) he satisfies the contribution conditions in section 96.

(2) The conditions under which a person shall be regarded for the purposes of this section as being permanently incapable of work shall be specified by regulations.

(3) Regulations may provide for disqualifying a person for receiving invalidity pension if he fails without good cause to observe any prescribed rules of behaviour.

GENERAL NOTE
Unless the accident that caused the disability was work-related, in which case the injured person may have been entitled to workmen's compensation or, latterly, occupational injury

benefit, a long-term disabled person who, effectively, became incapable of work for an extensive period, or perhaps became permanently incapacitated, had no State pension entitlement prior to 1970. If the claimant's contribution record was substantial enough (effectively the claimant had been paying qualifying contributions for three years) then disability benefit would be payable until pensionable age or until the end of the incapacity. If the contribution record fell below this standard, in the absence of requalification, social assistance was available in the form of home assistance. The emphasis placed on the social insurance model by politicians who, at the same time, stressed that universal social insurance was not compatible with Irish conditions, inevitably meant that whatever reforms were implemented would tend to ignore categories of substantially deprived individuals. This lack of perception also afflicted those responsible for devising a coherent and integrated system of social welfare. The 1949 White Paper *Social Security* (P. 9661) recommended and proposed changes in the sickness scheme which would include provision for the new disability benefit to be payable for as long as the sickness lasted, but only if 156 contributions had been paid. Persons unable to meet these contribution conditions would have to depend on social assistance. There was no real perception that the income maintenance needs of the long-term sick and disabled were more dependant on State payments than those on short-term insurance payments, nor was there any real appreciation that social assistance for the sick and disabled, short-term and long-term, was completely inadequate. It can be said that, even today, both these points have not been fully addressed and that further reform is urgently needed. Given that entitlement to disability benefit and invalidity pension are based on identical contribution conditions and that, when initially introduced in the Social Welfare Act, 1970, scale rates were identical, the rationale behind the creation of a distinct invalidity pension was not then apparent on the face of the legislation. The Minister for Social Welfare Mr Brennan gave two reasons. First, medical certification of invalidity would be unnecessary "except on rare occasions". Secondly, payment would be made on pension conditions. Pension order books would ensure easier access to social welfare payments for these could be cashed at Post Offices: 248 *Dáil Debates* Col. 996. However, since the creation of invalidity pension, significant differences in the scale rates have developed. In 1979 the basic weekly rate was increased to £16.65 for an invalidity pensioner while a claimant on basic disability benefit received £16.05. This differential has continued to develop. Under the Social Welfare Act, 1988 the basic rate of disability benefit stood at £43.60. Invalidity pension for a person below 66 years of age was £50 weekly. Thus, under the 1988 Act a claimant with an adult dependant and two qualified children then received £105.60 weekly on invalidity pension, while a disability benefit claimant in the same circumstances then received £92.00. Under the 1994 Act the position of such a family on invalidity pension and disability benefit would be £134.30 and £110.80 respectively. Some other benefits will be available to an invalidity pensioner but not a claimant on disability benefit. These additional benefits include prescribed relative allowance. Benefits-in-kind consist of free travel, free electricity allowances, free television licence, free telephone rental, free bottled gas and other free fuel schemes. It is therefore obvious that considerable financial benefit can be derived from the claimant being allowed, at the end of one year of incapacity, to change from disability benefit to invalidity pension. There remain a substantial number of long-term disabled persons who remain eligible for disability benefit only because medical prognosis of the disability is that the claimant will be capable of work within two years of the incapacity occurring, a prognosis that will prevent the claimant from being classified as "permanently incapable of work".

Subsection (2)
The regulations which direct the circumstances in which a person is classified as being "permanently incapable of work" are found in the regulations of 1994 (S.I. No. 417 of 1994). "Incapable of work" is defined as being "incapable of work by reason of some specific disease or bodily or mental disablement". The U.K. case law on this phrase has already been examined during discussion on section 31 above, disability benefit.
Under article 52 of the 1994 regulations the persons who are deemed to be permanently incapable of work fall into two categories:

   (a) a person is to be regarded as permanently incapable of work if for the period of one year, immediately before the date of claim for a pension, he had been continuously incapable of work, and it is shown to the satisfaction of a deciding officer or an appeals officer that the person is likely to continue to be incapable of work for at least a further year;

   (b) in the alternative, if a person is incapable of work and it is established to the satisfaction of the deciding officer or appeals officer that the incapacity is of such a nature that the likelihood is that the person will be incapable of work for life.

Condition (b) above represents a sensible easing of the qualifying conditions necessary for invalidity pension. It should be noted that (a) above does not require the pension applicant to have been in receipt of disability benefit (*i.e.* even if the claimant had previously been paid a salary during absence from employment by his employer) as a condition of eligibility.

Subsection (3)

Disqualification under this subsection is perceived by the Department to be an important anti-abuse measure. The regulations in question are article 53, Schedule F, to S.I. No. 417 of 1994.

There are four Rules of Behaviour. Disqualification for non-compliance is not linked to the maximum of nine weeks applicable in relation to disability benefit.

Rule 1 requires the claimant to submit to any medical or other examination the Minister shall require. Seven days notice of the time and place of the examination must be given. Despite the polite language in rule 1 the "request" is really a direction. The person so directed may obtain payment of reasonable and necessary travelling and other expenses incurred under article 9 of S.I. No. 417 of 1994. Rule 2 requires the claimant to obey the instructions of the attending doctor, or the doctor undertaking a medical examination consequent on rule 1, in relation to his behaviour or any other matter concerning his incapacity. Rule 3 requires the claimant not unreasonably to refuse to see the Minister's sickness visitor officer and requires the claimant to answer any reasonable enquiries by the Minister's officers in relation to the claim. Rule 4 directs that the claimant shall not engage in work whether on his own account or on behalf of any other person. Rule 4 may be relaxed in appropriate cases under article 54(2) of S.I. No. 417 of 1994.

Conditions for receipt

96.—(1) The contribution conditions for invalidity pension are—

(a) that before the relevant date the claimant has qualifying contributions in respect of not less than 260 contribution weeks since his entry into insurance, and

(b) that before the relevant date the claimant has qualifying contributions or credited contributions in respect of not less than 48 contribution weeks in the last complete contribution year before that date.

(2) In this section "relevant date" means—

(a) any date subsequent to the completion of one year of continuous incapacity for work, or

(b) such lesser period as may be prescribed, subject to such conditions and in such circumstances as may be prescribed,

where the insured person has entered into a continuous period of incapacity for work and he is subsequently proved to be permanently incapable of work.

(3) In the case of person who is in receipt of invalidity pension where—

(a) the period of entitlement to invalidity pension commenced before the 6th day of April, 1987, or

(b) the period of entitlement to invalidity pension commenced on or after the 6th day of April, 1987 but before the 4th day of January, 1988 and who, immediately before that date, had been in receipt of disability benefit for a period greater than 312 days,

subsection (1)(a) shall be construed as if "156" were substituted for "260".

(4) In the case of person who is in receipt of invalidity pension where—

(a) the period of entitlement to invalidity pension commenced on or after the 6th day of April, 1987, and before the 4th day of January, 1988, or

(b) the period of entitlement to invalidity pension commenced on or after the 4th day of January, 1988 and who, immediately before that date, had been in receipt of disability benefit for a period greater than 312 days,

subsection (1)(a) shall be construed as if "208" were substituted for "260".

(5) Subsections (3) and (4) shall not apply to any claim for invalidity pension where the period of incapacity for work commences on or after the 7th day of July, 1988.

(6) Regulations may provide for modifications of the contribution conditions set out in subsection (1).

GENERAL NOTE

The contribution conditions for eligibility for invalidity pension are identical with those that must be satisfied if the claimant is to be continuously eligible for disability benefit for a period in excess of 312 days. The claimant must therefore have (where a claim is made in respect of invalidity pension for a period of incapacity for work commencing after July 7, 1988) 260 qualifying contributions since entry into insurance and the date the application is made. The claimant must also, before that latter date, have not less than 48 paid or credited contributions in the last complete contribution year before that date. It is possible to take account of national health insurance contributions for the purpose of establishing entitlement to disability benefit and invalidity pension: article 10 of S.I. No. 417 of 1994.

Subsection (2)

This is the basis upon which S.I. No. 417 of 1994 has currently relaxed the definition of permanently incapable of work. See the General Note to section 95.

Subsection (3)

The 1987 (No. 2) Act increased the contribution conditions now found in section 96(1)(a) from 156 contributions to 260 contributions. This subsection provides that where the invalidity claim pre-dated implementation of this change then the old contribution requirement shall apply.

Subsection (4)

This subsection governs the number of paid contributions necessary for invalidity pension entitlement when the initial period of entitlement came within the dates fixed in the subsection. Section 8 of the 1987 Act set contributions at 208 rather than the 156 contributions necessary before commencement of that section.

Subsection (5)

This makes it clear that claims commencing after July 7, 1988 require the 260 contributions paid requirement to be satisfied.

Contributions paid under National Health Insurance Acts

97.—Contributions paid under the National Health Insurance Acts, 1911 to 1952, by or in respect of an employed contributor may be taken into account in such manner and subject to such conditions and limitations as may be prescribed for the purpose of the satisfaction by him of the contribution conditions for invalidity pension.

GENERAL NOTE

See article 10 of S.I. No. 417 of 1994.

Rate of pension

98.—Subject to this Part, the weekly rate of invalidity pension shall be as set out in column (2) of Part I of the Second Schedule.

Increases (including increases for adult and child dependants)

99.—(1) The weekly rate of invalidity pension shall be increased by the amount set out in column (3) of Part I of the Second Schedule for any period during which the beneficiary has an adult dependant, subject to the restriction that, except where regulations otherwise provide, a beneficiary shall not be entitled for the same period to an increase of pension under this subsection in respect of more than one person. [1995 (No. 2) Act, section 10]

(2) The weekly rate of invalidity pension shall be increased by the amount set out in column (4) of Part I of the Second Schedule in respect of

each qualified child who normally resides with the beneficiary. [1995 Act, Schedule F]

(3) Any increase of invalidity pension payable pursuant to subsection (2) in respect of a qualified child who normally resides with a beneficiary and with the spouse of a beneficiary shall be payable at the rate of one-half of the appropriate amount in any case where the spouse of the beneficiary is not an adult dependant, and subsection (2) shall be construed and have effect accordingly.

(4) The weekly rate of invalidity pension shall be increased by the amount set out in column (6) of Part I of the Second Schedule where the beneficiary has attained pensionable age and is living alone. [1995 Act, Schedule F]

(5) The weekly rate of invalidity pension shall be increased by the amount set out in column (7) of Part I of the Second Schedule where the beneficiary has attained the age of 80 years. [1995 Act, Schedule F]

GENERAL NOTE

Invalidity pension rates are payable at higher income rates than disability benefit because the invalidity pension is a long-term payment.

Additions in respect of qualified children and spouses. Where the pensioner has reached 66 years of age and is living alone, an additional payment will be made. A further addition is payable if the beneficiary is aged 80 or over.

CHAPTER 16

SURVIVOR'S PENSION

Interpretation

100.—In this Chapter—

'relevant time' means—

(a) if the contribution conditions are being satisfied on the survivor's insurance record—

(i) the date of the spouse's death, or

(ii) if the survivor attained pensionable age before the date of the spouse's death, the date on which he attained that age,

or

(b) if the contribution conditions are being satisfied on the deceased spouse's insurance record—

(i) the date on which the spouse attained pensionable age, or

(ii) if the spouse died before attaining pensionable age, the date of his death;

'spouse', in relation to a survivor who has been married more than once, refers only to the survivor's last spouse and for this purpose that last spouse shall be construed as including a party to a marriage that has been dissolved, being a dissolution that is recognised as valid in the State;

'survivor' means a widow, or a widower or a person who would otherwise be a widow or a widower but for the fact that the person's marriage has been dissolved, being a dissolution that is recognised as valid in the State; [1995 No. 2 Act, section 3]

'yearly average' means the average per contribution year of contribution weeks in respect of which the survivor or deceased spouse (as the case may be) has qualifying contributions, voluntary contributions or credited contributions in the appropriate period specified in section 102 (1) (b).

GENERAL NOTE

This section, and the four sections that follow, are inserted into the Principal Act by section 11 of the 1994 Act, by substitution, to provide a gender-free survivor's pension, thereby supplanting widow's (contributory) pension which had been introduced in 1935, and survivor's benefit (see Chapter 14 of Part II).

This section is the definition section. For definitions of "pensionable age", "contribution year", "contribution week", "qualifying contributions", "voluntary contributions" and "credited contributions": see section 2.

The definition of "spouse" and "survivor" were broadened by way of substitution in the 1995 (No. 2) Act, so as to make it clear that these words include a former spouse, or spouses, of the survivor, when the survivor has divorced a spouse, or spouses.

COMMENCEMENT

October 28, 1994: S.I. No. 321 of 1994.

Entitlement to pension

101.—(1) Subject to this Act, a survivor shall be entitled to survivor's pension—

(a) if the contribution conditions set out in section 102 are satisfied on either the insurance record of the survivor or that of his deceased spouse.

(b) if the survivor's spouse was entitled to an old age (contributory) pension or a retirement pension which included an increase in respect of him by virtue of section 87(1) or section 91(1) in respect of a period ending on the spouse's death, or [1995 (No. 2) Act, section 3]

(c) if his spouse would have been entitled to an old age (contributory) pension or a retirement pension at an increased weekly rate by virtue of section 87(1) *or* section 91(1), but for the receipt by that survivor of an old age (non-contributory) pension, a blind pension or a carer's allowance in his own right, in respect of a period ending on his death.

(2) A survivor's pension shall not be payable to a survivor for any period after his remarriage.

(3) A survivor shall be disqualified for receiving a survivor's pension if and so long as he and any person are cohabiting as husband and wife.

(4) A woman who becomes a widow while she is in receipt of or entitled to deserted wife's benefit shall, on becoming a widow, be entitled to a survivor's pension at the same rate as that of the deserted wife's benefit payable to her, whether or not the relevant contribution conditions for entitlement to such pension are satisfied in her case.

(5) For the purposes of subsection (4), a reference to a widow shall include a reference to a woman who would otherwise be a widow but for the fact that the woman's marriage has been dissolved, being a dissolution that is recognised as valid in the State. [1995 (No. 2) Act, section 3]

DEFINITIONS

"spouse": section 100.
"survivor": section 100.

GENERAL NOTE

Under subsection (1), entitlement to a survivor's pension is established by being a survivor, that is, a widow or a widower, as long as the contribution conditions in section 102 are satisfied, or the survivor's spouse was entitled to a widow's (contributory) pension or retirement pension with an adult dependant's addition being payable, or such an addition would have been paid but for the survivor's entitlement to old-age (non-contributory), blind pension or carer's allowance in the survivor's own right.

Under subsection (2) entitlement ceases upon re-marriage. Subsection (3) imposes a cohabitation disqualification. The leading Irish case on the meaning of cohabitation is *Foley v. Moulton* [1989] I.L.R.M. 169. The entitlement of a deserted wife's benefit recipient to a survivor's pension upon the death of her spouse, at the same rate, is discriminatory as a result of historical circumstances but it is probably not unconstitutional: see *Lowth v. Minister for Social Welfare* H.C. Unrep. December 16, 1993.

The 1995 (No. 2) Act

Subsections (1)(b) and (5)

Because of the amended definition of spouse, in the preceeding section, a divorced person is to be entitled to a survivor's pension on the basis of a divorced spouse's insurance record. More importantly, subsection (5) makes it clear that a divorced woman is to be entitled to a survivor's pension, notwithstanding the fact of her being divorced from a former husband, when that former husband dies if she has been in receipt of deserted wife's benefit immediately prior to that former husband's death.

The 1995 (No. 2) Act provisions are not yet in force.

Conditions for receipt

102.—(1) The contribution conditions for survivor's pension are—

(a) that the survivor has qualifying contributions in respect of not less than 156 contribution weeks in the period beginning with his entry into insurance and ending immediately before the relevant time, and

(b) that, if at the relevant time, 4 years or longer has elapsed since the survivor's entry into insurance—

(i) the yearly average for the 3 contribution years, of (if warranted by his insurance record) 5 contribution years, ending with the end of the last complete contribution year before the relevant time is not less than 39, or

(ii) the yearly average in respect of the period commencing at the beginning of the contribution year in which his entry into insurance occurred and ending at the end of the last complete contribution year before the relevant time is not less than 48,

but, if those conditions are not satisfied on the survivor's insurance record, they may be satisfied on his deceased spouse's insurance record (the survivor's insurance record being disregarded).

(2) Regulations may provide for modifications of the meaning of yearly average contained in section 100 or of the contribution conditions set out in this section.

(3) Subject to subsection (4), regulations may provide for entitling to survivor's pension a person who would be entitled thereto but for the fact that the contribution condition set out in subsection (1) (b) is not satisfied.

(4) Regulations for the purposes of subsection (3) shall provide that survivor's pension payable by virtue thereof shall be payable at a rate less than that specified in the Second Schedule, and the rates specified by the regulations may vary with the extent to which the contribution condition set out in subsection (1) (b) is satisfied, but any increase of pension payable under section 104 (1) shall be the same as if that condition had been fully satisfied.

(5) Subject to subsection (6), regulations may provide for entitling to survivor's pension a person who would be entitled thereto but for the fact that the contribution condition set out in subsection (1) (b) is not satisfied by reference to the insurance record of a person where that person, having earlier ceased to be an employed contributor became an employed contributor as a consequence of the coming into operation of section 12 of the Social Welfare Act, 1973.

(6) Regulations for the purposes of subsection (5) shall provide that survivor's pension payable by virtue thereof shall be payable at a rate less than that specified in the Second Schedule, and the rates specified by the

regulations may vary with the extent to which the contribution condition set out in subsection (1) (*b*) is satisfied.

(7) Where a person becomes an employed contributor by virtue of paragraph (*b*) of section 9 (1) and would not, apart from that paragraph, be an employed contributor, his entry into insurance by virtue of that paragraph shall be deemed not to be an entry into insurance for the purposes of subsection (1) and for those purposes his entry into insurance shall be deemed to occur when he first becomes an employed contributor by virtue of paragraph (*a*) of section 9 (1).

(8) In the case of a person who became a self-employed contributor on the 6th day of April, 1988, and who at any time prior to that date was an employed contributor, the date on which the person first entered into insurance or the 6th day of April, 1988, whichever is more favourable, shall be regarded as the date of entry into insurance for the purposes of subsection (1) (*b*).

GENERAL NOTE

The contribution conditions in subsection (1) require qualifying contributions totalling three years to have been paid since entry into insurance and the relevant time (defined in section 100) as well as an average of 39 qualifying contributions in the three or five year period preceding the last complete contribution year before the relevant time. Alternatively, the average requirement can be satisfied if the yearly average since entry into insurance and the relevant time is not less than 48 qualifying contributions. The relevant time is essentially the date of death of the spouse or when the survivor reaches 66 years of age. These requirements can be met on the insurance record of either the survivor or the deceased spouse, but aggregation of insurance records is not possible.

Despite subsection (2), article 55 of S.I. No. 417 of 1994 confines the meaning of yearly average to that found in section 100. On rounding up, see article 59 (*ibid.*). Subsections (3) and (4) are given effect by article 56 of S.I. No. 417 of 1994 which provides a reduced rate of survivor's pension when the yearly average does not fall below 24. S.I. No. 146 of 1995 sets out a sliding scale of survivor's pension but section 104 additions are payable at the full rate. Subsection (5) implements a policy that has progressively evolved to deal with persons who have a "mixed" insurance record because of the operation of the earnings ceiling which, although abolished under section 12 of the 1973 Act, meant that some persons passed in and out of insurability prior to abolition, thereby making their contribution average very low indeed. These special partial survivor's pensions are provided for in article 57 of S.I. No. 417 of 1994, as long as the average does not fall below 5. Schedule H of these regulations set out the reduced rates that are thus payable under subsection (6). Subsection (7) provides that entry into insurance as a self-employed contributor is not to satisfy subsection (1) unless prior to April 6, 1988 (the date when self-employed insurance commenced) that person had earlier been an employed contributor, in which case either that date or the earlier date of entry is to be regarded as the date of entry into insurance (whichever is the more favourable): subsection (8).

Rate of pension

103.—Subject to this Act, the weekly rate of survivor's pension shall be as set out in column (2) of Part I of the Second Schedule.

GENERAL NOTE

For reduced rates, and the special partial survivor's pension rates, see Schedules G and H of S.I. No. 417 of 1994.

Increases (including increases for child dependants)

104.—(1) The weekly rate of survivor's pension shall be increased by the amount set out in column (4) of Part I of the Second Schedule in respect of each qualified child who normally resides with the beneficiary.

(2) The weekly rate of survivor's pension shall be increased by the amount set out in column (6) of Part I of the Second Schedule where the beneficiary has attained pensionable age and is living alone.

(3) The weekly rate of survivor's pension shall be increased by the amount set out in column (7) of Part I of the Second Schedule where the beneficiary has attained the age of 80 years.

DEFINITIONS

"normally resides": article 7 of S.I. No. 417 of 1994.
"pensionable age": section 2.
"qualified child": section 2(3).

Disregard of self-employment contributions in certain cases.

105.—(1) In the case of any claim for survivor's pension made on or after the 6th day of April, 1995, where the insurance record of a person, who, having been a self-employed contributor, is being used to establish entitlement to survivor's pension, the contribution conditions contained in section 102 shall not be regarded as having been satisfied unless, in accordance with section 18—

(a) he has paid self-employment contributions in respect of at least 1 contribution year before the relevant time, and

(b) all self-employment contributions payable by him have been paid.

(2) Notwithstanding subsection (1), the Minister may, if he is satisfied that in all the circumstances of the case it would be appropriate to do so, direct that subsection (1) shall not be applied in that case. [1995 Act, section 19]

GENERAL NOTE

This provision prevents survivor's pension from being payable if a self-employed contributor's insurance record is the basis upon which entitlement is being established unless contributions for one contribution year have been made and all self-employment contributions have been paid. In the case of employed contributors who find that their employer has not paid over contributions, entitlement is generally possible notwithstanding non-payment as long the employee did not participate in the fraud: section 14(2)(e).

In hardship cases the Minister may decide not to operate this provision under subsection (2).

Certain claims

105A.—(1)(a) Entitlement to survivor's pension which is due to be determined by reference to the insurance record of a person who attained the age of 69 years before the 5th day of January, 1976, may be determined under the provisions of the Acts relating to social welfare in operation prior to the 1st day of July, 1974, if this would be to the advantage of the widow.

(b) A widow who, under the provisions of the Acts relating to social welfare in operation prior to the 1st day of July, 1974, has been awarded a survivor's pension on the basis of her own or her spouse's insurance record at the date on which she or he attained the then pensionable age shall on and after the 1st day of July, 1974, have a right to such pension at the rate for the time being payable by reference to a yearly average equal to the yearly average calculated in her case under those provisions.

(2)(a) Entitlement to survivor's pension which is due to be determined by reference to the insurance record of a person who attained the age of 68 years before the 3rd day of January, 1977, may be determined under the provisions of the Acts relating to social welfare in operation prior to the 1st day of April, 1975, if this would be to the advantage of the widow.

(*b*)   A widow who, under the provisions of the Acts relating to social welfare in operation prior to the 1st day of April, 1975, has been awarded a survivor's pension on the basis of her own or her spouse's insurance record at the date on which she or he attained the then pensionable age shall on and after the 1st day of April, 1975, have a right to such pension at the rate for the time being payable by reference to a yearly average equal to the yearly average calculated in her case under those provisions'.

(3)(*a*)   Entitlement to survivor's pension which is due to be determined by reference to the insurance record of a person who attained the age of 67 years before the 1st day of January, 1979, may be determined under the provisions of the Acts relating to social welfare in operation prior to the 1st day of October, 1977, if this would be to the advantage of the widow.

(*b*)   A widow who, under the provisions of the acts relating to social welfare in operation prior to the 1st day of October, 1977, has been awarded a survivor's pension on the basis of her own or her spouse's insurance record at the date on which she or he attained the then pensionable age shall on and after the 1st day of October, 1977, have a right to such pension at the rate for the time being payable by reference to a yearly average equal to the yearly average calculated in her case under those provisions. [1994 Act, Part IV].

GENERAL NOTE

These provisions remain in the legislation because they represent transitional provisions that benefited widow's (contributory) pension claimants who could avail of more favourable contribution rules under earlier legislation where this would stand to their benefit: see section 93(7) of the 1981 Consolidation Act and section 101(6) of this Act.

Note also article 58 of S.I. No. 417 of 1994 which gives widow's and orphan's pension contributions added value under the new survivor's pension rules.

CHAPTER 17

ORPHAN'S (CONTRIBUTORY) ALLOWANCE

Entitlement to allowance

106.—Subject to this Act, orphan's (contributory) allowance shall be payable in respect of an orphan if the contribution condition in section 107 is satisfied.

GENERAL NOTE

The orphan's (contributory) allowance was introduced in 1935 as part of a general package of contributory and non-contributory widow's and orphan's pension schemes.

An orphan is defined in section 2(1) of the Principal Act of 1993 as amended by section 20 of the 1995 Act.

Condition for receipt

107.—(1) The contribution condition for orphan's (contributory) allowance is that one of the following persons has qualifying contributions for not less than 26 contribution weeks—

(a) a parent of the orphan,
(b) a step-parent of the orphan.
(2) Regulations may provide for modifications of the contribution condition set out in this section.

GENERAL NOTE

Obviously the orphan is unlikely to be an employed contributor in most cases, so insurability will relate to a person other than the beneficiary. The contribution conditions therefore require 26 qualifying contributions to have been paid by either a parent of the orphan or a step-parent of the orphan. Contribution classes which currently cover Orphan's (Contributory) Allowance are A, B, C, D, H, E and S. It should be noted that contribution classes do change so the SCOPE section of the Department will be able to verify whether at any stage a parent or step-parent had paid qualifying contributions.

Rate of allowance

108.—Subject to this Part, the weekly rate of orphan's (contributory) allowance shall be as set out in Part I of the Second Schedule.

Payment of allowance

109.—(1) Subject to subsection (2), orphan's (contributory) allowance shall be paid to the guardian of the orphan in respect of whom the allowance is payable.

(2) An orphan's (contributory) allowance may, if the Minister thinks fit, instead of being paid to the guardian of the orphan in respect of whom the allowance is payable, be paid to some other person for the benefit of the orphan.

GENERAL NOTE

This procedure is an informal one which depends upon the discretion or judgement of the Minister and Departmental officials: it will be exercised in situations where the guardian is *likely* to use the allowance for purposes other than the proper maintenance of the orphan.

CHAPTER 18

DESERTED WIFE'S BENEFIT

Entitlement to benefit

110.—(1) Subject to this Act, deserted wife's benefit shall be payable to a woman who—
(a) has been deserted by her husband,
(b) if she is less than 40 years of age, has at least one qualified child residing with her,
(c) in the case of a claim made on or after the 31st day of August, 1992, does not have an aggregate of reckonable income and reckonable earnings in excess of a prescribed amount in the last compete income tax year or in such subsequent period as a deciding officer or an appeals officer may consider appropriate,
(d) satisfies the contribution conditions in section 111, and
(e) satisfies such other conditions as may be prescribed.
(2) The circumstances in which a woman is to be regarded for the purposes of this section as having been deserted by her husband shall be specified in regulations.

(2A) Subject to this Chapter, a woman who has been deserted by her husband shall, for the purposes of this Chapter, continue to be regarded as a deserted wife where her marriage has been dissolved, being a dissolution that is recognised as valid in the State.

(2B) A deserted wife's benefit shall, subject to this Chapter, continue to be payable to a woman unless she remarries and in such a case the benefit shall cease as and from her remarriage [1995 No. 2 Act, section 4].

(3) A woman shall be disqualified for receiving deserted wife's benefit if and so long as she and any person are cohabiting as husband and wife.

(4) In this Chapter—

"husband" in relation to a woman who has been married more than once, refers only to her last husband and for this purpose that last husband shall be construed as including the man to whom, but for the fact that the marriage has been dissolved, being a dissolution that is recognised as valid in the State, she would be married; [1995 No. 2 Act, section 4]

"relevant time" means—

(a) the date on which the husband attained pensionable age or the date before he attained that age on which he and his spouse are determined to have commenced living apart from one another, or

(b) if the conditions are being satisfied on the woman's insurance record—

(i) if she attained pensionable age before the date on which she is determined to have commenced living apart from her husband, the date on which she attained that age, or

(ii) the date on which she is determined to have commenced living apart from her husband;

"yearly average" means the average per contribution year of contribution weeks in respect of which the husband (or claimant) has qualifying contributions, voluntary contributions or credited contributions in the appropriate period specified in section 111(1)(b).

GENERAL NOTE

Historical Introduction

The introduction of deserted wife's benefit in 1970 was an important part of the development of family-centred benefits in Ireland. Prior to this scheme, the deserted wife was required to seek support from her deserting spouse or seek income maintenance from the health boards in the form of public assistance, the precursor to supplementary welfare allowance. While the 1970 scheme was carried over into the 1981 Consolidation, there has been substantial modification of the Scheme, particularly in the guise of the earnings limit introduced in 1992. The context within which deserted wife's benefit operates at the present time has altered substantially. The Family Law (Maintenance of Spouses and Children) Act, 1976 began a process of improving private law income support mechanisms in cases of family breakdown, and the trend towards enforcing liable relative provisions (see Part IX) made recourse against the deserting husband a much more realistic option. Furthermore, State income support measures, in the shape of supplementary welfare allowance (1975) and lone parent's allowance (1990) have produced broader, non-judgemental schemes of social assistance for one-parent families.

Subsection (1)

The factual basis upon which a woman is eligible for deserted wife's benefit has been a matter of controversy since the scheme was introduced in 1973. The requirement in subsection (1)(a), desertion, has proved particularly contentious: desertion is often distinguished from instances where the parties have separated and agreed to live apart, the male partner perhaps agreeing to meet certain financial commitments, under a separation agreement for example. Also, the emphasis placed upon desertion as being present when the husband left the family home of his own volition could preclude eligibility if the husband was not present in the family home because a barring order had been granted. The Commission on Social Welfare saw the desertion factor as being an undesirable contingency for a person to insure against, and it recommended that for deserted wife's payments, the "own volition" test should be discontinued. Indeed, the Commission took the view that it's primary concern was that income support should be available to a woman, regardless of the circumstances surrounding marital breakdown. The situations in which desertion will be established are considered below under subsection (2).

The requirement in subsection (1)(b), while arbitrary, is intended to distinguish between women who may be expected to find self-support less difficult when they are relatively young and child-free, from women who would find self-support more difficult because of age and other circumstances, such as lack of recent contact with the employment market. The requirement in subsection (1)(c) is of recent origin. As an insurance-based payment, deserted wife's benefit was based upon the insurance record and other circumstances, regardless of income. In 1992 it was decided to impose a means test of sorts upon the ground that benefit was often payable to women who had substantial earnings from employment and who could not be said to need the benefit.

The amount prescribed as the income limit beyond which benefit will not be payable is £14,000: S.I. No. 417 of 1994. Reduced rates of benefit are payable to women who have income levels below this figure and annual income above £10,000: see section 111 below.

The additional conditions referred to in subsection (1)(e) are found in article 62 of S.I. No. 417 of 1994. The woman shall make, and continue to make, reasonable efforts, in the particular circumstances, to obtain maintenance from her husband. This provision, while supported by the Commission on Social Welfare as being correct in principle, is controversial and at times difficult to operate if the husband has left the jurisdiction, is otherwise untraceable, or unlikely to be able to provide for his children for financial reasons. In practice, proof of reasonable efforts can be provided by way of letters from a solicitor, clergyman or Department of Social Security (U.K.). There have been recent efforts to move either towards non-adversarial means of maintenance recovery (e.g. mediation) or to allow the Department to proceed under the liable relative provisions found in sections 284–299 of this Act. The other condition originally stipulated under S.I. No. 237 of 1992 is now set out in subsection (3) of this section.

Subsection (2)

Article 61 of S.I. No. 417 of 1994 provides:

A woman is to be regarded for the purposes of section 110 as having been deserted by her husband if—

(a) her husband has of his own volition left her, or his conduct has resulted in her leaving him with just cause, and

(b) she is not being maintained by her husband, or if she is being so maintained, the weekly amount of maintenance received is less than the rate of benefit applicable to that woman under the Act.

(c) she and her husband have lived apart from one another for a continuous period of at least three months immediately preceding the date of her claim for benefit.

Paragraph (a), the volition test, is retained despite criticism by the Commission on Social Welfare: the second part of the paragraph sets out constructive desertion by the husband as an alternative method of showing desertion. Paragraph (c) has been a part of the qualifying conditions since inception of the scheme in 1973, in order to distinguish isolated or intermittent acts of desertion. During such a three-month period, the woman should seek supplementary welfare allowance.

Subsection (3)

Cohabitation is nowhere defined in Irish law. The only case on cohabitation to examine the issue from a procedural perspective is *State (Hoolahan) v. Minister for Social Welfare*, H.C. Unrep. 23/7/86. The leading case is *Foley v. Moulton* [1989] I.L.R.M. 169. In the U.K. there are a substantial number of judicial and administrative decisions on the meaning of the concept of cohabiting, or living together, as husband and wife. See *Crake v. SBC* and *Butterworth v. SBC* [1982] 1 All E.R. 498 and the discussions in the 1981, 1984 and 1985 issues of the *Journal of Social Welfare Law* at pp. 372, 123 and 382 respectively.

Subsection (4)

This subsection defines two expressions necessary in order to allow the calculation of contributions to be made.

The 1995 (No. 2) Act

Subsection (4) was amended to provide a definition of husband, thereby providing that upon divorce a woman who was in receipt of deserted wife's benefit would continue to be eligible notwithstanding the divorce. Of course, if she remarries or cohabits then entitlement will end.

This provision is not yet in force.

Conditions for receipt

111.—(1) The contribution conditions for deserted wife's benefit are—

(a) that the husband had qualifying contributions in respect of not less than 156 contribution weeks in the period beginning with his entry into insurance and ending immediately before the relevant time, and

(b) that, if at the relevant time, four years or longer has elapsed since the husband's entry into insurance—

(i) the yearly average for the three contribution years, or (if warranted by his insurance record) five contribution years, ending with the end of the last complete contribution year before the relevant time is not less than 39, or

(ii) the yearly average in respect of the period commencing at the beginning of the contribution year in which his entry into insurance occurred and ending at the end of the last complete contribution year before the relevant time is not less than 48,

but, if the foregoing conditions are not satisfied on the husband's insurance record, they may be satisfied on the woman's insurance record (the husband's insurance record being disregarded).

(2) Regulations may provide for modifications of the meaning of yearly average contained in section 110(4) or of the contribution conditions in this section.

(3) Subject to subsection (4), regulations may provide for entitling to deserted wife's benefit a woman who would be entitled thereto but for the fact that—

(a) she has an aggregate of reckonable income and reckonable earnings, in excess of an amount prescribed for the purposes of section 110(1)(c) in the last compete income tax year or in such subsequent period as a deciding officer or an appeals officer may consider appropriate, or

(b) the contribution condition set out in subsection (1)(b) is not satisfied.

(4) Regulations under subsection (3) shall provide that deserted wife's benefit payable by virtue thereof shall be payable at a rate less than that specified in the Second Schedule and the rate specified by the regulations may vary with the extent to which—

(a) the claimant has an aggregate of reckonable income and reckonable earnings in excess of the amount prescribed for the purposes of section 110(1)(c) but not in excess of the amount prescribed for the purposes of this subsection, in the last complete income tax year or in such subsequent period as a deciding officer or an appeals officer may consider appropriate, and

(b) the contribution condition set out in subsection (1)(b) is satisfied,

but any increase of the benefit payable under section 113(1) shall be the same as if the conditions set out in section 110(1)(c) and in subsection (1)(b) had been fully satisfied.

(5) (a) Entitlement to deserted wife's benefit which is due to be determined by reference to the insurance record of a person who attained the age of 69 years before the 5th day of January, 1976, may be determined under the provisions of the Acts relating to social welfare in operation prior to the 1st day of July, 1974, if this would be to the advantage of the claimant.

(b) A deserted wife who, under the provisions of the Acts relating to social welfare in operation prior to the 1st day of July, 1974, has been awarded deserted wife's benefit on the basis of her own or her husband's insurance record at the date on which she or he attained the then pensionable age shall, on and after the 1st day of July, 1974, have a right to such benefit at the rate for the time being payable by reference to a yearly average equal to the yearly average calculated in her case under those provisions.

(6) (a) Entitlement to deserted wife's benefit which is due to be determined by reference to the insurance record of a person who attained the age of 68 years before the 3rd day of January, 1977, may be determined under the provisions of the Acts relating to social welfare in operation prior to the 1st day of April, 1975, if this would be to the advantage of the claimant.

(b) A deserted wife who, under the provisions of the Acts relating to social welfare in operation prior to the 1st day of April, 1975, has been awarded deserted wife's benefit on the basis of her own or her husband's insurance record at the date on which she or he attained the then pensionable age shall, on and after the 1st day of April, 1975, have a right to such benefit at the rate for the time being payable by reference to a yearly average equal to the yearly average calculated in her case under those provisions.

(7) (a) Entitlement to deserted wife's benefit which is due to be determined by reference to the insurance record of a person who attained the age of 67 years before the 1st day of January, 1979, may be determined under the provisions of the Acts relating to social welfare in operation prior to the 1st day of October, 1977, if this would be to the advantage of the claimant.

(b) A deserted wife who, under the provisions of the Acts relating to social welfare in operation prior to the 1st day of October, 1977, has been awarded deserted wife's benefit on the basis of her own or her husband's insurance record at the date on which she or he attained the then pensionable age shall, on and after the 1st day of October, 1977, have a right to such benefit at the rate for the time being payable by reference to a yearly average equal to the yearly average calculated in her case under those provisions.

(8) Subject to subsection (9), regulations may provide for entitling to deserted wife's benefit a person who would be entitled thereto but for the fact that the contribution condition set out in subsection (1)(b) is not satisfied by reference to the insurance record of a person where that person, having earlier ceased to be an employed contributor became an employed contributor as a consequence of the coming into operation of section 12 of the Social Welfare Act, 1973.

(9) Regulations for the purposes of subsection (8) shall provide that deserted wife's benefit payable by virtue thereof shall be payable at a rate less than that specified in the Second Schedule, and the rate specified by the regulations may vary with the extent to which the contribution condition set out in subsection (1)(b)(ii) is satisfied.

GENERAL NOTE

Deserted wife's benefit is unusual in that eligibility can be determined by reference to the claimant's insurance record or that of her spouse, but not through the aggregation of both records. In practice, most successful claims are based upon the record of the deserting spouse, thus throwing the entire scheme open to the charge that Irish social welfare law makes it possible for a husband to insure himself against a contingency, that is, in the main, based upon an act of volition—desertion. In any event, the contribution conditions are found in subsection (1).

Subsection (1)
  (a) If the husband has at least 156 qualifying contributions since entry into insurance and either commencement of desertion or his reaching the age of 66, there should be less than four years since entry into insurance. In the likely event that more than four years have elapsed since entry into insurance and either the husband reaching 66 or desertion commencing, the husband should also have either
      (i) a yearly average of 39 paid or credited contributions over either the three or five years that preceded his reaching 66 or commencement of desertion, or
      (ii) a yearly average of 48 paid or credited contributions between entry into insurance or the last complete contribution year before he reached 66 or desertion commenced.
  (b) If the husband's insurance record is insufficient for the purposes of (a) above, the wife may invoke her own insurance record in order to satisfy the above contribution conditions. However, there can be no aggregation of records.

Subsection (2)
This subsection allows regulations to modify the contribution conditions in respect of women who do not satisfy the yearly average provisions found in relation to section 110(4). Article 64 of S.I. No. 417 of 1994 allows this where the yearly average falls below 48 but not below 24. Benefit rates correspond to the average contributions which are fixed in bands. Thus, S.I. No. 417 of 1994, Schedule I, fixes two bands of 36 to 47 contributions and 24 to 35 contributions and weekly benefit rates are £63.40 and £61.60 respectively (1994 figures).

Subsections (3) and (4)
These subsections deal with the situation of women whose earnings fall between a minimum figure of £10,000 (in which case maximum benefit is payable) and £14,000 (in which case no benefit is payable). In fact, the regulations in question distinguish between three groups of women:
      (i) women who satisfy the contribution conditions for maximum benefit but fall foul of the income limits;
      (ii) women who satisfy the reduced range of contribution conditions (*i.e.* a yearly average of between 24 and 47) but fall foul of the income limits;
      (iii) women who satisfy the mixed contribution conditions that resulted from the abolition of the earnings limit (*i.e.* a yearly average of five to 23 contributions) but fall foul of the income limits.
S.I. No. 146 of 1995 sets out the applicable reduced benefit payments, but child dependant additions are payable at the full rate.

Subsections (5) to (7)
These provisions are intended to allow persons whose insurance record preceded the introduction of deserted wife's benefit and the specific qualifying contributions applicable thereto, to utilise their insurance contributions, notwithstanding the fact that these contributions are not qualifying contributions or are not such as to satisfy the yearly average provisions above.

Subsections (8) and (9)
The mixed insurance records that occurred as a result of the 1974 abolition of the earnings limit for non-manual workers also had a prejudicial effect on many contributors who found it impossible to maintain even the 24 contribution average necessary for reduced benefit. Article 65 of S.I. No. 417 of 1994, accordingly, modifies the yearly average rule for persons who came back into insurance following the implementation of section 12 of the 1973 Act (on April 1, 1974). As long as the yearly average comes within one of the three bands of 18 to 23 contributions, 12 to 17 contributions or 5 to 11 contributions, reduced rates of benefit are payable under S.I. No. 417 of 1994. See also the commentary on subsections (3) and (4).

Rate of benefit
    112.—Subject to this Part, the weekly rate of deserted wife's benefit shall be as set out in column (2) of Part I of the Second Schedule.

Increases (including increases for child dependants)
    113.—(1) The weekly rate of deserted wife's benefit shall be increased by the amount set out in column (4) of Part I of the Second Schedule in

respect of each qualified child who normally resides with the beneficiary. [1995 Act, Schedule F]

(2) The weekly rate of deserted wife's benefit shall be increased by the amount set out in column (6) of Part I of the Second Schedule where the beneficiary has attained pensionable age and is living alone. [1995 Act, Schedule F]

(3) The weekly rate of deserted wife's benefit shall be increased by the amount set out in column (7) of Part I of the Second Schedule where the beneficiary has attained the age of 80 years. [1995 Act, Schedule F]

DEFINITIONS

"pensionable age": 66 years.
"qualified child": section 2(3).

CHAPTER 19

DEATH GRANT

Entitlement to grant

114.—(1) Subject to this Act, a death grant shall be payable, to such person or persons as may be prescribed, on the death of—

(a) an insured person,

(b) the wife or husband of an insured person,

(c) the widow or widower of a deceased insured person, or

(d) a qualified child,

if the contribution conditions in section 115 are satisfied, but only one death grant shall be paid by virtue of this section on any one death.

(2) In this Chapter—

"relevant insured person" means—

(a) in case the deceased person was a qualified child—

(i) the father or mother of such deceased person,

(ii) the person with whom such deceased person at the date of death is determined, in accordance with regulations made under section 3(5), to have been normally residing or with whom he would have been normally so residing if he had not been committed to a reformatory or an industrial school, or

(iii) the spouse of the person referred to in subparagraph (ii),

(b) in any other case, the deceased person or the spouse of the deceased person;

"relevant date" means the date of death of the deceased person or the date of death of the relevant insured person or the date of attainment of pensionable age of the relevant insured person, whichever occurs first, whether the deceased is the relevant insured person or not;

"yearly average" means the average per contribution year of contribution weeks in respect of which the relevant insured person has qualifying contributions, voluntary contributions or credited contributions in the appropriate period specified in section 115(1)(b)(ii).

(3) In this Chapter and in Part V of the Second Schedule "qualified child" means a person—

(a) who is under the age of 18 years at the date of death,

(b) who is ordinarily resident in the State on that date, and

(c) in respect of whose death the relevant contribution conditions for death grant are not satisfied by such person's insurance or the insurance of such person's wife or husband.

GENERAL NOTE

The death grant was introduced in 1970. The grant is a lump sum payment which is intended to assist in the funeral expenses incurred by a family following the death of an insured person, the wife or husband of an insured person or a child under 18 years of age, of an insured person. The Commission on Social Welfare commented that the one-off nature of the grant made it somewhat unique in a social insurance context. The Commission noted that the levels of grant were low and, on balance, recommended that it should be reshaped as a social assistance payment, to be paid in respect of a recipient, spouse or child dependant of a social assistance recipient. This has not been implemented.

Conditions for receipt

115.—(1) The contribution conditions for a death grant are—
(a) that before the relevant date the relevant insured person has qualifying contributions in respect of not less than 26 contribution weeks since his entry into insurance or since the 1st day of October, 1970, (whichever is the later), and
(b) that either—
    (i) the relevant insured person has qualifying contributions, voluntary contributions or credited contributions in respect of not less than 48 contribution weeks in the last complete contribution year before the beginning of the benefit year in which the relevant date occurs, or
    (ii) the yearly average in respect of the period commencing at the beginning of the contribution year in which his entry into insurance occurred or the beginning of the contribution year next following the 1st day of October, 1970, (whichever is the later) and ending at the end of the last complete contribution year before the beginning of the benefit year in which the relevant date occurs is not less than 48.

(2) Regulations may provide for modifications of the contribution conditions for receipt of death grant.

(3) Subject to subsection (4), regulations may provide for entitling to death grant persons who would be entitled thereto but for the fact that the contribution condition set out in subsection (1)(b) is not satisfied.

(4) Regulations under subsection (3) shall provide that death grant payable by virtue thereof shall be of an amount less than that specified in Part V of the Second Schedule, and the amount specified in the regulations may vary with the extent to which the relevant contribution condition set out in subsection (1)(b) is satisfied.

(5) Regulations may provide for modifications of the contribution conditions for death grant in the case of a person who was an insured person on the 1st day of October, 1970, and who, during the year subsequent to that date, was absent from the State for any period or was credited with contributions in respect of any period of unemployment, incapacity for work or retirement or is or becomes a voluntary contributor paying contributions at the rate specified in section 22(1)(b)(ii).

GENERAL NOTE

The contribution conditions to be satisfied in respect of the relevant insured person, that is, the person whose insurance record is to measure eligibility, are that at least 26 qualifying contributions have been paid since entry into insurance or October 1, 1970, whichever is the later date, and that 48 paid or credited contributions have been made in the last complete contribution year before the beginning of the benefit year in which the death occurs.

Alternatively, if the relevant insured person has an average of 48 paid or credit contributions between entry into insurance, or October 1, 1970 (whichever is the later event) and the beginning of the last complete contribution year before the beginning of the benefit year in which death occurs. If these contribution conditions cannot be met then subsection (3) allows the Minister to modify the contribution conditions relating to the yearly average to be met.

The Social Welfare (Death Grant) Amendment Regulations, 1982 (S.I. No. 91 of 1982), which amend S.I. No. 98 of 1971, provide reduced rates of grant to persons whose yearly average under both tests stands at 26 or more.

Amount of grant

116.—Subject to this Act, the amount of death grant shall be as set out in column (2) of Part V of the Second Schedule.

GENERAL NOTE

Death grant payment levels have not been increased since 1982: for reduced rates of grant see S.I. No. 91 of 1982.

CHAPTER 20

TREATMENT BENEFIT

General provisions as to benefit

117.—(1) A person shall, subject to satisfaction of the prescribed conditions, be entitled to such treatment benefit as may be specified by regulations.

(2) The regulations for the purposes of this section may specify the payment of the whole or any part of the cost of any of the following—
(a) dental treatment,
(b) optical treatment and appliances,
(c) hearing aids,
(d) any other benefits of the same character as any of those mentioned in the foregoing paragraphs.

(3) The payments referred to in subsection (2) shall not exceed in the aggregate such sums as may from time to time be agreed upon between the Minister and the Minister for Finance.

(4) This section shall remain in force until the day appointed under subsection (5) and shall then expire.

(5) The Minister may by order appoint a day to be the day on which this section expires.

GENERAL NOTE

Treatment benefits appear in the arena of social welfare as a matter of "historical chance": Commission on Social Welfare, p. 375. The provision of additional benefits by the approved societies which were responsible for operating sickness and workmen's compensation schemes in the early years of the Irish State constitute the basis upon which these health benefits become available to income maintenance recipients when several of the functions of these approved societies were transferred to the Department of Social Welfare in 1950. The Commission on Social Welfare recommended that treatment benefits should be administered by the Department of Health so as to secure more efficient administration, particularly when there is a degree of duplication between treatment benefits and the general medical services scheme, available to medical card holders.

Subsection (1)

The prescribed conditions are found in the Social Welfare (Treatment Benefit) Regulations 1954 to 1994. The principal regulations are S.I. No. 156 of 1954. The main condition is that the employed contributor be in employment in respect of which qualifying contributions are paid (*i.e.* A, H, E and P employments). The contributions required depend on age and, roughly, for those under 25, 39 contributions are needed; for those over 25, 260 contributions are needed: see S.I. No. 187 of 1992, which also makes provision for a relaxation of these contribution requirements for those under 66 years of age. Since 1992 there has been an earnings limit. The current limit means that if the employed contributor earns over £35,000 treatment benefit cannot be claimed on his or her behalf.

The spouse of the employed contributor is eligible for treatment benefit as long as the employed contributor's income does not exceed £70,000: S.I. No. 129 of 1994. Specific contribution conditions are provided for volunteer development workers: S.I. No. 187 of 1992, article 5. Since 1992, dependant spouses are also eligible, subject to the contribution conditions and the above income limits.

Subsection (2)

The principal treatment benefits are dental benefits, which include extractions, fillings, dentures and cleaning treatments. Payment is made to any dentist participating in the scheme according to rates negotiated by the Department with the Irish Dental Association. Optical benefits include optical treatment and glasses, and medical appliances are provided by way of contact lenses and hearing aids in cases of medical need.

PART III

SOCIAL ASSISTANCE

CHAPTER 1

DESCRIPTION OF SOCIAL ASSISTANCE

Description of assistance

118.—(1) Assistance under this Part shall be of the following descriptions and is, in each case, so described in this Act—

(a) unemployment assistance,
(b) pre-retirement allowance,
(c) old age (non-contributory) pension,
(d) blind pension,
(e) widow's and orphan's (non-contributory) pensions,
(f) deserted wife's allowance,
(g) prisoner's wife's allowance,
(h) lone parent's allowance,
(i) carer's allowance, and
(j) supplementary welfare allowance.

(2) Assistance shall be paid out of moneys provided by the Oireachtas.

CHAPTER 2

UNEMPLOYMENT ASSISTANCE

Interpretation

119.—(1) In this Chapter—

"beneficiary" means a person entitled to unemployment assistance;
"weekly means" shall, subject to Rule 1(6) of Part I of the Third
Schedule, be the yearly means divided by 52:

Provided that the amount so calculated shall be rounded up to the
nearest £1 where it is a multiple of 50p but not also a multiple of £1
and shall be rounded to the nearest £1 where it is not a multiple of
50p or £1. [1995 No. 2 Act, section 11]

(2) In this Chapter references to means shall be construed as references
to means as calculated in accordance with the Rules contained in Part I of
the Third Schedule.

(3) Where, immediately before the 29th day of July, 1992, a person was
entitled to or in receipt of unemployment assistance, any decision by a
deciding officer or an appeals officer in relation to the means of that person
for the purposes of his qualifying for a qualification certificate shall be
deemed to be a decision under section 120(1)(f).

GENERAL NOTE

Historical Introduction

The passage of the Unemployment Assistance Bill, 1933 has to be seen in the context of the
mass unemployment that affected Ireland in the 1920s and 1930s. Provision for the relief of
the unemployed took various forms. Unemployment Insurance was available to insured
workers if the claimant was insured. Benefit was payable at the rate of one week's benefit for
every six contributions paid. No matter how long the claimant was unemployed, the claimant
could not receive more than 26 weeks' benefit in any one year. Given that large sectors of the
workforce were not insured—agricultural workers, for example—the insurance model was
doubly deficient. If the claimants' entitlement, if any, was exhausted, then recourse to the local
authority for poor relief was available. If the applicant was destitute then the authority could
grant relief, at its discretion. While local authorities were able to provide relief from the poor
rate, the stigma of pauperism and the generally discretionary nature of the relief can be
illustrated by reference to the Poor Relief (Dublin) Act, 1929. This Act enabled the guardians
of any Union situated, in whole or in part, in the County or County Borough of Dublin, to
provide relief, at their discretion, to a person even though they were not inmates of the
workhouse. Certain residence requirements had to be met and the guardians could require
work to be done before relief would be afforded: if work was not required the guardians could
declare the relief would be by way of loan and the sums recoverable under the Poor Relief
(Ireland) Acts 1838 to 1914. *Ad hoc* relief by way of Parliamentary votes to provide money for
the organisation of public works in various parts of Ireland was also attempted although these
measures were not thought to be efficient or effective: see 49 *Dáil Debates* Col. 1651.

In introducing the 1933 Bill to Dáil Eireann, the Minister for Industry and Commerce,
Mr Lemass, described the principle behind the Bill as resting on the view that:

"all able-bodied persons who are involuntarily unemployed and have either no means at all
or insufficient means to maintain themselves and their dependants, should be given a
statutory right to assistance in the manner in which the Bill proposes".

This right was to be implemented by giving every person who satisfied statutory conditions,
a right to apply for a qualification certificate. This certificate, while valid, would be lodged by
the holder at the employment exchange and it would represent a certificate of entitlement to
unemployment assistance. At this time a similar procedure operated in relation to unemployment benefit. The certificate was issued if the male applicant met the conditions set out in
section 10(3) of the 1933 Act, *i.e.* the applicant was a national of Saorstát Eireann, was
between 18 and 70 years of age and had annual means below £52 (County Borough or Dun
Laoghaire Borough) or £39 (elsewhere in Saorstát Eireann). Female applicants had to meet
additional requirements. A married woman was entitled to a qualification certificate if her
husband was a dependant of her or, if living apart from her husband, she had one or more
dependants. A widow or spinster was eligible for a qualification certificate if she had one or
more dependants. This provision survived until repealed by the Social Welfare Act, 1982.
Under the 1933 Act, a widow or spinster without a dependant had to show that 52
contributions under the Unemployment Insurance Acts had been made in the previous four
years if she was to be eligible for a certificate. The 52 contributions requirement for single
women, although reduced to 26 by the Social Welfare Act, 1977, was, in fact, inserted at
Committee Stage in order to allow women with a link with the workforce to establish
eligibility. As initially drafted single women without dependants were not entitled at all
because, the Minister said, there was concern that single women in the west of Ireland, for

whom there was no work in the area in which they resided, could otherwise establish entitlement and cause the scheme to be twice as expensive to operate: 49 *Dáil Debates* Col. 1772. The Act provided, in section 4(3), for a power to make employment period orders, which, if operated, would prevent persons in those areas from eligibility. This was designed to deal with smallholders who did work in an area for an employer, or for himself, from being entitled to unemployment assistance while an opportunity for such supplementary employment was thought to be available during the summer months.

Because the 1933 Act was designed to create entitlement as of right it was necessary to provide for maximum scale rates; rates differed, depending on whether the applicant resided in an urban or rural area, as defined in the Act. A statutory means test was laid down in the Act. Financing of the scheme, estimated as costing £1 million per annum, was by Exchequer payments to each local authority, although each urban area local authority was obliged to remit part of the rate raised in the locality, to the Minister for Industry and Commerce, to be paid or remitted by the Minister to the Exchequer. A deliberate attempt to integrate the unemployment assistance schemes into the existing legislative and bureaucratic framework that governed the unemployment insurance scheme was made. In general, entitlement depended on satisfying the test of being unemployed and available for work. Disqualifications from assistance mirrored the provisions on unemployment insurance. Claims were made in the same place and manner for assistance as was the case in relation to unemployment insurance: the unemployment assistance officer was in reality also an insurance officer under the Unemployment Insurance Acts. Appeals against adverse assistance decisions were made to Unemployment Assistance Committees, bodies modelled, by and large, on the Old Age Pensions Committees established by the Old Age Pensions Act, 1908. Amending legislation in 1935, 1937 and 1940 dealing specifically with unemployment assistance was followed by *ad hoc* amendments in several of the Social Welfare Acts—the functions of administering unemployment assistance being transferred to the Department of Social Welfare on its establishment in 1947. These various provisions remained in force until the 1981 Consolidation Act repealed the Unemployment Assistance Acts. The process of revision remains constant however: several important amendments to the unemployment assistance scheme have been made since the 1981 Consolidation Act was passed: probably the most significant feature has been recognition, by administrations of different party political composition, of the need to provide greater resources for the long-term unemployed. Higher scale rates for the long-term unemployed were introduced in 1983. In the 1988 Budget the percentage income to long-term unemployment assistance recipients was increased by over 11 per cent, eight per cent higher than the increase allowed for, *inter alia*, unemployment benefit recipients.

The most significant recent reforms relate to the abolition of the qualification certificate procedure in the 1992 Act. As presently constituted, unemployment assistance is a much more streamlined assistance programme than previously: under the 1981 Consolidation Act there were 21 sections in the Act devoted to unemployment assistance; the 1993 Act has eight sections on unemployment assistance.

Subsections (1) and (2)

Unemployment assistance is payable to persons who satisfy eligibility conditions and whose statutory weekly means fail to meet the minimum standards setout in the Fourth Schedule to Part I, as the appropriate income level for an unemployed person in that position. Subsections (1) and (2) define "weekly means" and provide a reference to the appropriate statutory means test.

Subsection (3)

The 1992 Act amended and consolidated existing provisions on unemployment assistance, in particular abolishing the qualification certificate procedure which determined the basis of eligibility for a beneficiary. This subsection provides that a reference to a decision by a deciding officer or appeals officer on a qualification certificate shall be regarded as a decision on whether the beneficiary satisfies the statutory means test specified in Chapter 2 of Part III.

Entitlement to assistance

120.—(1) Subject to this Act, a person shall be entitled to unemployment assistance in respect of any day of unemployment in a continuous period of unemployment if—

(a) he has attained the age of 18 years and has not attained pensionable age,

(b) he proves unemployment in the prescribed manner,

(c) he is capable of work,

(d) he is, or by reason of his participation in an activity prescribed for the purposes of this subsection and, subject to such conditions as may be prescribed, is deemed to be, or is exempted from being required to be, available for employment,

(e) he is genuinely seeking, but is unable to obtain, employment suitable for him having regard to his age, physique, education, normal occupation, place of residence and family circumstances, and

(f) he satisfies the conditions as to means specified for the purposes of this Chapter.

(2) (a) A person shall not be entitled to unemployment assistance for the first three days of unemployment in any continuous period of unemployment.

(b) No unemployment assistance shall be paid for any period less than one day.

(c) For the purposes of this section, any period prior to the relevant date of application for unemployment assistance shall not be reckoned as, or as part of, a continuous period of unemployment.

(d) Any period during which a person is disqualified for receiving unemployment assistance shall not be reckoned in the computation of any continuous period of unemployment of such person.

(3) For the purposes of this Chapter, any three days of unemployment, whether consecutive or not, within a period of six consecutive days shall be treated as a continuous period of unemployment, and any two such periods not separated by more than 52 weeks shall be treated as one continuous period of unemployment, and references in this Chapter to being continuously unemployed or continuous unemployment shall be construed accordingly.

(4) Sunday shall not be treated as a day of unemployment and shall be disregarded in computing any period of consecutive days.

(5) Notwithstanding subsection (3), any period of continuous—

(a) employment under a scheme administered by An Foras Áiseanna Saothair and known as Community Employment [1995 Act, section 18].

(b) participation in a scheme administered by An Foras Áiseanna Saothair and known as the Enterprise Allowance Scheme,

(c) participation in a scheme administered by An Foras Áiseanna Saothair and known as the Alternance Scheme,

(d) attendance at a training course provided or approved by An Foras Áiseanna Saothair,

(e) [repealed 1995 Act, section 18].

(f) participation in a scheme administered by the Minister and known as the Part-Time Job Incentive Scheme,

(g) participation in a scheme administered by the Minister for Education and known as the Vocational Training Opportunities Scheme, or

(h) participation in, employment under or attendance at a prescribed scheme or course,

shall be disregarded in treating, pursuant to subsection (3) of this section, any two continuous periods of unemployment not separated by more than 52 weeks as one continuous period of unemployment.

(6) Regulations may make provision as to the days which are or are not to be treated for the purposes of unemployment assistance as days of unemployment.

(7) Subsection (2)(a) shall not apply in relation to the payment of unemployment assistance to a person who ceased, not earlier than 52 weeks

before the day in respect of which his application for unemployment assistance is made, to be entitled to unemployment benefit—

    (a) by reason of having, by virtue of section 46, exhausted his entitlement to such benefit, or

    (b) if the person is of or over 65 years of age, by reason of having failed to satisfy the contribution set out in section 43(1)(b).

(8) The amount payable by way of unemployment assistance for any day of unemployment shall be one-sixth of the appropriate weekly rate, subject to the total amount being paid at any time by virtue of this subsection being rounded up to the nearest 10p where it is a multiple of 5p but not also a multiple of 10p and being rounded to the nearest 10p where it is not a multiple of 5p or 10p.

GENERAL NOTE

Many of these provisions mirror those found in relation to unemployment benefit and the meaning to be attached to them has been considered above, particularly in the General Note to section 42. However, specific matters are dealt with under S.I. No. 417 of 1994.

Subsection (1)

This subsection sets out the principal conditions of eligibility. The beneficiary should be between 18 and 66 years of age and prove unemployment in the prescribed manner. Article 70 of S.I. No. 417 of 1994 provides that this is done by attending at a local office of the Department, or other appointed place, and signing a declaration of unemployment. A day of unemployment is there defined as a day to which the prescribed method of proving employment relates and a day when the beneficiary does not work for wages or other remuneration, whether paid in money or otherwise. The beneficiary must be capable of work (*i.e.* not physically or mentally incapacitated) and available for employment. This latter provision can be relaxed by way of a ministerial order which exempts certain persons from the need to prove availability for employment. Articles 72 and 73(1) of S.I. No. 417 of 1994 make provision in respect of nightworkers where the working day spans two days of the week. Article 73(4) provides that persons who are in approved second level or third level education, are attending an Area Partnership course, or some other applied course, and prior to attendance that person has met certain provisions about being long-term unemployed, those days are deemed days in which the beneficiary is available for employment. Article 73(3) similarly treats days of rehabilitation training approved by the Minister for Health. Article 74 of S.I. No. 417 of 1994 allows mature students, as defined, engaged on a Vocational Training Opportunities Scheme/Third level Allowance Scheme or Area Partnership Scheme under the PESP also to be deemed available for employment. In this latter situation, Area Partnership participants do not have to meet any age criteria, but under the other programmes minimum ages of 21 or 23 apply.

Subsections (2), (3) and (4)

A continuous period of employment, is any period of three days of unemployment, within six days, Sundays being excluded, even if not continuous. Two periods not separated by more than 52 weeks form one period of unemployment. Because the first three days of unemployment cannot be compensated, this linkage rule is important in providing unemployment assistance in respect of periodic or intermittent unemployment. Fractions of a day are not to be days of unemployment, nor are days which pre-date the claim or periods of disqualification.

Subsection (5)

This provision relaxes the 52-week linkage rule in respect of continuous employment, participation or attendance (as the case may be) in a Social Employment Scheme, Enterprise Allowance Scheme, Alternance Scheme, FAS Course, Teamwork or Part Time Job Incentive Scheme, Vocational Training Opportunities Scheme, or other prescribed scheme or course. It was realised that if a long-term unemployed person took up a course which did not lead to a job, that person would not only have to serve three waiting days but would lose higher long-term assistance rights. This subsection presents the linkage rule in subsection (3) from having this consequence. Subsection (7) further relaxes this rule.

Subsection (6)

See S.I. No. 417 of 1994.

Subsection (7)

Despite the three waiting days rule in subsection (2)(a) unemployment assistance will be payable as from the first day of unemployment if the beneficiary claims within 12 months of exhaustion of entitlement to unemployment benefit. Also if the beneficiary is 65 years old and cannot satisfy the contribution condition of 39 paid or credited contributions in the contribution year prior to the beginning of the benefit year in which the claim was made, unemployment assistance will be payable.

Subsection (8)
Multiples of five pence are rounded up: multiples of less than that are rounded down.

Rates of assistance and effect of means on rates

121.—(1) Subject to this section and to sections 122 and 124, the rate (in this Chapter referred to as "the scheduled rate") of unemployment assistance shall be—

(a) in the case of a person who—
  (i) in any continuous period of unemployment, as construed in accordance with section 120(3), has been in receipt of unemployment benefit or unemployment assistance for not less than 390 days, or
  (ii) immediately before the day for which unemployment assistance is claimed, was in receipt of lone parent's allowance, but has ceased to be entitled to such allowance by virtue of his no longer being regarded as a lone parent within the meaning of section 157(1),

the weekly rate set out in column (2) at reference 1(a) in Part I of the Fourth Schedule," [1995 Act, section 16(1)].

(b) in any other case, the weekly rate set out in column (2) at reference 1(b) in Part I of the Fourth Schedule,

increased by—
  (i) the amount set out in column (3) of that Part opposite that reference for any period during which the claimant or beneficiary has an adult dependant, subject to the restriction that, except where regulations otherwise provide, the claimant or beneficiary shall not be entitled for the same period to an increase of assistance under this subparagraph in respect of more than one person, and
  (ii) the appropriate amount set out in column (4) of that Part opposite that reference in respect of each qualified child who normally resides with the claimant or beneficiary. [1995 (No. 2) Act, section 10]

(2) Unemployment assistance shall be payable where—
(a) the weekly means of the claimant or beneficiary are less than £1, at the scheduled rate,
(b) such weekly means are equal to £1, at the scheduled rate reduced by £1, and
(c) such weekly means exceed £1, at the scheduled rate, reduced by £1 for each amount (if any) of £1 by which those weekly means exceed £1:

Provided that, if the weekly means of the claimant or beneficiary are equal to or exceed the scheduled rate, no unemployment assistance shall be payable.

(3) Notwithstanding paragraph (c) of subsection (2), where the sole means of a claimant for unemployment assistance, who is not one of a couple, are assessed under Rule 1(5) of Part I of the Third Schedule and where the rate of assistance payable to or in respect of such claimant, as calculated in accordance with paragraph (c) of subsection (2), would be a weekly amount which is 10p or more, but less than £25, such person shall be entitled to payment of unemployment assistance at the weekly rate of £25. [1995 Act, section 16(2)]

(4) (a) In subsection (3) "couple" means a married couple who are living together or a man and a woman who are not married to each other but are cohabiting as husband and wife.

(b) For the purposes of Rule 1(5) of Part I of the Third Schedule, when applied to subsection (3), "spouse" means each person of a couple in relation to the other.

(5) In the application of the provisions of subsection (2) in the case of such persons or classes of persons as may be prescribed, regulations may provide for disregarding, in such manner as may be prescribed, any part of the weekly means of a claimant or beneficiary up to an amount not exceeding £2.

(6) The Minister may, notwithstanding the provisions of regulations made pursuant to subsection (5) providing for weekly means of up to £2 in the case of certain persons or classes of persons to be disregarded, apply the provisions of subsection (2) to such persons or classes of persons at any time.

(7) Any regulations made under subsection (5) may apply to the whole State or to a specified part or parts of the State.

GENERAL NOTE

Subsection (1)

The scheduled rate of unemployment assistance refers to the maximum scale rate of assistance payable under Part I of the Fourth Schedule. The rate payable to persons who have been continuously employed for 15 months (390 days) is higher, in recognition of the fact that the long-term unemployed are more likely to have depleted other resources than a recently unemployed person. This differential was introduced by S.I. No. 268 of 1983 and has been integrated into the Principal Act ever since.

The adult dependant addition referred to in subsection (1)(i) depends upon compliance with the definition of adult dependant in section 2(2) and S.I. No. 417 of 1994. The terms qualified child and normal residence are defined in section 2(3) and S.I. No. 417 of 1994.

Subsection (2)

When the beneficiary has no means, or means below £1 weekly, under the means test, full payment is made at the scheduled rate. When a weekly means figure is calculated, this will be offset against assistance scheduled rates on the basis of £1 of means resulting in a £1 loss of assistance until such a stage when the means of the beneficiary are equal to, or exceed, the scheduled rate.

Subsection (3)

If the minimum assistance payment is below £25 weekly, then this subsection allows for a payment of £25 to be paid, notwithstanding subsection (2) as long as the beneficiary is neither one-half of a married or cohabiting couple and the beneficiary has had assistance reduced solely by reference to the benefit or privilege rule in rule 1(5) of the Third Schedule. The figure in the 1993 Consolidation Act was raised from £5 to £10 by section 22 of the 1994 Act and to £25 by section 16(2) of the 1995 Act, as from June 7, 1995.

Subsections (5), (6) and (7)

These subsections have been used to provide that where a person aged between 55 and 66 has been continuously unemployed for not less than 390 days, and he is receiving assistance at less than the scheduled rate, assistance will be payable at the scheduled rate if his weekly means do not exceed £2: the £1 for £1 disregard is increased to a £2 for £2 disregard: see article 9 of S.I. No. 364 of 1993.

Total amount payable to couple

122.—(1) In the case of a couple, both of whom are entitled to be paid unemployment assistance, the total amount payable to them pursuant to this Chapter shall not exceed the amount which would be payable if only one of them was entitled to be paid unemployment assistance and the other was an adult dependant, and each of them shall be entitled to be paid one-half of the amount which would be payable to him if the other were his adult dependant.

(2) Where the spouse of a claimant for unemployment assistance is not an adult dependant, the unemployment assistance payable to the claimant shall be at a rate equal to the scheduled rate reduced by £1 for every £2 or part of £2 of his means.

(3) Subsection (2) shall not apply in any case where the spouse is living apart from the claimant.

(4) Where one of a couple is entitled to disability benefit, unemployment benefit, disablement pension, old age (contributory) pension, old age (non-contributory) pension, retirement pension or invalidity pension and the other is entitled to unemployment assistance, the total of the amount payable to them by way of such benefit or pension, as the case may be, and such unemployment assistance (in this subsection referred to as "the relevant amount") shall not exceed the total amount of benefit or pension, as the case may be, or the total amount of unemployment assistance, whichever is the greater (in this subsection referred to as "the greater amount"), that would be payable if only one of the couple were in receipt of benefit, pension or unemployment assistance, as the case may be, and the benefit, pension or unemployment assistance included an increase in respect of the other as his adult dependant; and, if the relevant amount would but for this subsection exceed the greater amount, the amount of unemployment assistance payable to the spouse who is entitled to such unemployment assistance shall be reduced by the amount of the excess.

(5) In this section "couple" means a married couple who are living together or a man and woman who are not married to each other but are cohabiting as husband and wife.

(6) In this section "spouse" means each person of a couple in relation to the other.

(7) For the purposes of this section, a reference to "unemployment assistance" shall be construed as including a reference to pre-retirement allowance.

(8) This section shall not apply in the case of a person who was entitled to or in receipt of pre-retirement allowance before the 2nd day of April, 1993. [1994 Act, section 27]

GENERAL NOTE

The resolution of the problem of how to treat married and cohabiting couples has proved legislatively difficult. Recognition by the Irish social welfare code of heterosexual relationships outside marriage first took place, at least within the context of unemployment assistance rates, with section 12 of the 1985 (No. 2) Act, which directed that while married couples could not obtain two separate scheduled rates, and the couple would only receive reduced rates, the same rate did not apply to a cohabiting couple. This legal reform, made in the context of the Third Equality Directive, was criticised at the time by several Deputies (360 *Dáil Debates* Cols. 291–298) but the Minister defended it on the ground that the Directive only referred to discriminatory laws and administrative practices on the basis of sex. The Directive does not apply to situations where national laws discriminate against persons on the ground of marital status. The Attorney General (perhaps surprisingly) advised this section was constitutional; 360 *Dáil Debates* Col. 294.

However, the High Court struck down section 12 of the 1985 (No. 2) Act in *Hyland v. Minister for Social Welfare* (H.C.) Unrep. May 9, 1989, later confirmed by the Supreme Court.

The existing provisions repair the defect by making the beneficiary who claims unemployment assistance, but does not claim an adult dependant addition in respect of their spouse or partner, the spouse or partner seeking to claim either unemployment assistance or pre-retirement allowance in his or her own right, liable to receive one half of the aggregate payable to a married person claiming an adult dependant addition. The spouse or partner receives the other share of the married couple/adult dependant rate.

Subsection (2)

This subsection gives a beneficiary the benefit of a £1 for £2 of earnings disregard, in relation to means where a spouse is not an adult dependant, as long as they are not living apart (subsection (3)).

Subsection (4)

Where a beneficiary claims unemployment assistance and their spouse or partner is receiving disability, unemployment or injury benefit, or any of the pensions mentioned therein, the aggregate amount payable to the couple is limited to the greater amount that could be claimed if the beneficiary obtained an adult dependant allowance, or the beneficiary's spouse obtained an adult dependant addition in respect of the beneficiary. Regardless of the issue of whether the insurance payment or the unemployment assistance payment is the higher amount, the assistance payment is reduced to being the amount payable below the applicable limit.

Subsection (7)

This subsection is directed at putting on to a legislative basis the administrative practice that had evolved in order to deal with the situation of a person who is in receipt of a pre-retirement allowance and who has a spouse or partner who is also in receipt of unemployment assistance, a social insurance payment, or old age contributory pension. In the case of a person who is in receipt of unemployment assistance, legislation limits the payment made to the couple to the rate of payment appropriate for a married couple. Under the pre-retirement allowance means test the income derived by the claimant's spouse or partner from a long-term social assistance or insurance payment should, strictly, be used to reduce the pre-retirement allowance, but if this were done, the claimant would be left with less than the adult dependant addition. Administrative practice was to treat the couple in the same way as if the pre-retirement allowance claimant was seeking unemployment assistance. This section makes the procedure legislatively sound.

Subsection (8)

This was inserted by section 27 of the 1994 Act. Section 122 of the Principal Act limits the entitlements of couples in cases where one party is entitled to pre-retirement allowance and the other is entitled to another social welfare payment. This subsection provides that this limitation will not apply in instances where the pre-retirement allowance was paid prior to April 2, 1993, the effective date when this provision came into effect under the Principal Act. This provision is presumably necessary following advice on the constitutional propriety of removing accrued entitlements to certain claimants.

Certain claims

123.—(1) A person who, on or after the 9th day of May, 1989, claims or has claimed, in respect of a period before the 7th day of June, 1989, unemployment assistance of an amount to which he would not be entitled if section 122 were applicable shall be entitled to be paid such assistance only in accordance with section 122.

(2) (a) A person who has not, before the 9th day of May, 1989, specifically claimed, in respect of a period before the 7th day of June, 1989, any additional amount for unemployment assistance being an amount to which he would not be entitled if section 122 were applicable shall not be entitled to be paid the additional amount.

(b) In paragraph (a) of this subsection "claimed" means claimed in writing from the Minister or claimed in proceedings instituted against the Minister in any court.

(3) An amount properly paid to any person before the 7th day of June, 1989 by way of unemployment assistance which as a result of the Social Welfare (No. 2) Act, 1989 would be recoverable by the Minister shall not be so recoverable.

GENERAL NOTE

This section is inserted to continue to offset the consequences of the *Hyland* decision in the 1989 (No. 2) Act.

Subsections (1) and (2)

This section provides, in subsection (1) for the retrospective application of the Act, back to the date of the *Hyland* decision, to all claims for unemployment assistance and also limits, in subsection (2), the retrospective effect of that decision. Subsection (1) provides that claims for unemployment assistance made *after* the date of the decision (May 9, 1989) shall be determined in accordance with section 122. Subsection (2) applies to claims for an additional amount of unemployment assistance made *before* May 9, 1989, in anticipation of the ultimate ruling, and provides that such claimants shall only be entitled if the claim was made in writing to the Minister or in the context of legal proceedings against the Minister in any court.

Whereas it is perfectly lawful, in the light of *Murphy v. A.G.* [1982] I.R. 241, to limit the retrospective effect of the Supreme Court decision in *Hyland*, it is doubtful whether the Oireachtas can constitutionally provide for the retrospective application of the amended section. It is clear that, as a result of the Supreme Court decision, there was no lawful basis for applying the restriction on the payment of unemployment assistance to married claimants to any claimant prior to the enactment of the new provision on June 7, 1989.

Subsection (3)

This applies to cohabiting claimants who, prior to the passing of the Act, received unemployment assistance in accordance with the former, and, for them, more generous provisions of the welfare code. This section in essence provides that, notwithstanding the retroactive application provided for, a cohabiting claimant who received unemployment assistance in accordance with previous practice shall not be obliged to refund any amount of that assistance to which they are no longer entitled in the light of the new provision.

The net effect is to continue the favourable treatment of cohabiting claimants for a further four weeks after the date of the Supreme Court decision until June 7, 1989, the date of enactment of the 1989 (No. 2) Act. *Quaere* whether this is constitutionally valid?

Amount of increases payable in respect of qualified child in certain cases

124.—(1) Any increase of unemployment assistance payable pursuant to section 121(1) in respect of a qualified child who normally resides with the claimant or beneficiary and with the spouse of the claimant or beneficiary shall be payable at the rate of one-half of the appropriate amount in any case where the spouse of the claimant or beneficiary is not an adult dependant, and section 121(1) shall be construed and have effect accordingly. [1995 Act, section 16(4)]

(2) [repealed 1994 Act, section 30(1)].

DEFINITIONS

"adult dependant": section 2(2).
"qualified child": section 2(3).

GENERAL NOTE

When a beneficiary's spouse is not an adult dependant (*e.g.* is working and receiving more than £60 per week in wages) the child dependant addition is payable at 50 per cent of the scale rate, if the spouse is living with the beneficiary.

Disqualifications

125.—(1) A person shall be disqualified for receiving unemployment assistance while he is—

(a) an inmate of an institution maintained wholly or partly out of public moneys or by a local authority,

(b) entitled to or in receipt of unemployment benefit under Part II, or

(c) employed during any week under a scheme administered by An Foras Áiseanna Saothair and known as Community Employment [1995 Act, section 18].

(2) Notwithstanding subsection (1), regulations may provide, subject to such conditions as may be prescribed, that a person who is entitled to or in receipt of unemployment benefit under Part II shall not be disqualified for receiving unemployment assistance:

Provided that any such regulations shall not cause a person to receive both unemployment benefit and unemployment assistance or to receive both unemployment assistance and pay-related benefit in respect of the same day or days.

(3) A person who has lost employment by reason of a stoppage of work which was due to a trade dispute at the factory, workshop, farm or other premises or place at which he was employed, shall be disqualified for receiving unemployment assistance so long as the stoppage of work continues, except in the case where he has, during the stoppage of work, become *bona fide* employed elsewhere in the occupation which he usually follows or has become regularly engaged in some other occupation:

> Provided that the foregoing provisions of this subsection shall not apply to a person who is not participating in or directly interested in the trade dispute which caused the stoppage of work.

(4) Where separate branches of work which are commonly carried on as separate businesses in separate premises or at separate places are in any case carried on in separate departments of the same premises or at the same place, each of those departments shall, for the purposes of subsection (3), be deemed to be a separate factory, workshop or farm or separate premises or a separate place, as the case may be.

(5) A person shall be disqualified for receiving unemployment assistance for such period as may be determined by a deciding officer, but in any case not exceeding nine weeks, if he—

    (a) has lost his employment through his own misconduct or has voluntarily left his employment without just cause,

    (b) has refused an offer of suitable employment,

    (c) has without good cause refused or failed to avail himself of any reasonable opportunity of receiving training provided or approved by An Foras Áiseanna Saothair as suitable in his case, or

    (d) has failed or neglected to avail himself of any reasonable opportunity of obtaining suitable employment,

and the period of disqualification shall commence on the day on which the loss or leaving of employment, refusal, failure or neglect (as the case may be) occurred.

(6) For the purpose of this section, employment shall not be deemed to be suitable employment in the case of any person if it is employment in a situation vacant in consequence of a stoppage of work due to a trade dispute.

(7) Unemployment assistance and unemployment benefit shall not both be payable in respect of the same day or days.

GENERAL NOTE

With the exception of subsections (1) and (2), these disqualifications mirror those found in section 47 above. These grounds for disqualification have been exhaustively discussed in the General Note to section 47.

Subsection (1)(a)

This disqualification covers publicly-funded hospitals, nursing homes, as well as rehabilitation and treatment centres.

Subsections (1)(b) and (2)

The policy here is to oblige the social insurance fund to provide income maintenance, wherever possible. However, following the decision by successive governments in the late 1980s to increase long-term unemployment assistance rates as against unemployment benefit rates, it is possible for some unemployed claimants to be entitled to more in the way of assistance than benefit. S.I. No. 166 of 1989 allows the claimant to opt for whichever scheme is more beneficial in the claimant's particular circumstances.

Subsection (1)(c)

Persons engaged on a Social Employment Scheme, organised by FÁS receive an allowance which in October 1994 was paid at the single person's rate of £79.30 per week.

Disqualifications (continued)

126.—(1) A person shall not be entitled to receive unemployment assistance while attending a course of study, other than in such circumstances and subject to such conditions and for such periods as may be prescribed.

(2) In this section—

"academic year" means a period in which a course of study commences in one year and finishes in the next following year and includes term vacations;

"a course of study" means, subject to subsection (3), a full-time day course of study, instruction or training at an institution of education;

"institution of education" means—

(a) a school,

(b) a university,

(c) a college of a university,

(d) any institution which the Minister for Education has designated in regulations made pursuant to section 1 of the Higher Education Authority Act, 1971, as an institution of higher education for the purposes of that Act,

(e) any institution to which the National Council for Education Awards Act, 1979, applies,

(f) any institution established under the Regional Technical Colleges Act, 1992,

(g) any institution incorporated under the Dublin Institute of Technology Act, 1992,

(h) any institution which is not an institution for the purposes of paragraphs (a) to (g) and to which the Local Authorities (Higher Education Grants) Acts, 1968 to 1992, apply, or

(i) such other institution as may be prescribed.

(3) For the purposes of this section, a person shall be regarded, subject to regulations made under subsection (1), as attending a course of study—

(a) for the period of three months immediately following the completion or the leaving by that person of second level education or the completion of the Leaving Certificate Examination of the Department of Education, (whichever is the later),

(b) for the duration of an academic year, or

(c) for the period immediately following the completion of one academic year, other than the final academic year of a course of study, up to the commencement of the following academic year.

GENERAL NOTE

This section was inserted into the 1981 Consolidation Act by section 14 of the 1993 Act and it is carried over into the 1993 Consolidation in order to deny students a right to unemployment assistance during vacation periods.

The provision was perhaps the most controversial measure in the Social Welfare Act, 1993. Under section 136 of the Principal Act, persons aged between 18 years and 66 years were entitled to unemployment assistance as long as they satisfied statutory conditions and the statutory means test. One of the statutory conditions found in section 138 was that the claimant be capable of work and available for and genuinely seeking work. This provision was traditionally interpreted so as to preclude students attending educational courses from claiming unemployment assistance during term, but during vacations the student was considered to be available for employment and, where the student satisfied the requirement that he or she be capable of, and seeking employment, unemployment assistance was payable. In the case of students who did not live with their parents (who therefore were not likely to find their assistance payments reduced under the benefit or privilege rule) the student also sought supplementary welfare from the health boards in order to cover rent. Such was the volume of claims made by students (over 10,000 claims in the summer of 1991 and over 12,000 in the summer of 1992) that it was decided to terminate eligibility for unemployment assistance and supplementary welfare allowances to students.

In supporting this measure, the Minister for Social Welfare explained that because unemployment assistance was then payable to persons who were available for full-time employment, it followed, in his view, that students in full-time education were not properly to be regarded as available for full-time employment during their summer holidays (135 *Dáil Debates* Col. 1077). This is of course a very weak argument which implicitly suggests that student claims have hithertofore been made fraudulently, and several opposition Deputies were critical of smearing student claimants with the imputation of fraud.

A number of exceptions to this measure must be noted. First, mature students and students in "second chance" education are not affected by this measure: see section 120(1)(d). Students who are part of a family unit which is dependant on social welfare payments will either be entitled to workplace or unemployment assistance if the student applies from the parental home. Nor does the provision which disentitles the student from seeking supplementary welfare allowance affect the right of a student to claim supplementary welfare allowance in respect of adult or child dependants.

The end of eligibility for unemployment assistance has been replaced by a scheme of workfare. The student may now apply for a placement on a scheme of work which will ensure that the student will receive payment which approximates to the lost unemployment assistance payment. This section also limits the availability of unemployment assistance to students aged 18 years or more, who leave second level education without any intention of remaining in the educational system. The section prevents a school-leaver from being able to claim unemployment assistance within three months of leaving school or completing the leaving certificate examination. The Minister explained that students in such a situation would be encouraged immediately to seek FÁS placements. Section 2(3) of the 1993 Consolidation Act allows the parents of children who leave school in such circumstances to receive social welfare child dependant allowances (notwithstanding that the child is aged 18 years at least) for the three-month period during which the "qualified child" is disqualified from claiming unemployment assistance as of right. Previously, only parents receiving long-term payments could obtain child dependant additions for children aged 18 years who were in full-time education. Now short-term payments will also attract this additional payment. (Such a person cannot be classified as an adult dependant under section 2(2) of the Principal Act).

The workfare scheme, or scheme of summer work for students, is non-statutory. The work does not have a commercial basis but is community group and voluntary group based. The scheme allows a student to claim up to 10 weeks work for a weekly wage of £40. However, eligibility and the income derived from such work is means tested.

S.I. No. 364 of 1993 exempts certain students from disqualification, *e.g.* a mature student, participants in the Vocational Training Opportunities Scheme and Third Level Allowance Scheme, and participants in Area Partnership Training Schemes. Students who have an insurance record may still be eligible to claim unemployment benefit.

CHAPTER 3

PRE-RETIREMENT ALLOWANCE

Entitlement to allowance

127.—(1) Subject to this Act an allowance (in this Chapter referred to as "pre-retirement allowance") shall, subject to regulations, be payable in respect of any period of retirement to a person—

(a) who has attained the age specified by regulations but has not attained pensionable age,

(b) who has been in receipt of unemployment benefit or unemployment assistance for not less than 390 days for any continuous period of unemployment in the immediately preceding period as construed in accordance with section 120(3),

(c) whose weekly means, subject to subsection (2), calculated in accordance with the Rules contained in Part I of the Third Schedule do not exceed the amount of pre-retirement allowance set out in column (2) in Part I of the Fourth Schedule, increased by so much of the amount set out in the said Part as would be payable to him if he had an adult or child dependant.

(2) Where the spouse of a claimant for pre-retirement allowance is not his adult dependant, the means of the claimant shall be taken to be one-half the means calculated in accordance with the Rules contained in Part I of the Third Schedule.

GENERAL NOTE

The question of a flexible retirement system for those in employment was, cautiously, approved by the Commission on Social Welfare which reported in 1986. The pre-retirement scheme, while confined to persons who are unemployed, is rooted in the same kind of philosophy as flexible retirement. The Minister for Social Welfare Dr Woods explained the thinking behind the pre-retirement scheme in the following terms when introducing the pre-retirement allowance by way of the Social Welfare Act 1988 (119 *Seanad Debates* Col. 355).

"[P]rovision is being made ... to cater for one group, namely, the older long-term unemployed. The pre-retirement scheme is intended to provide more flexible arrangements for older unemployed people many of whom are in fact semi-retired and not really members of the labour force. At present, these people are required to sign on each week at their local office where they receive their cash payments. This new scheme would relieve claimants of the necessity of attending the local office while, at the same time, providing them with alternative arrangements for receiving their basic income maintenance entitlement. . . . The scheme will be optional. those who qualify for the allowance will be paid by pension order book which can be cashed weekly at their local post office and they will not have to attend the local office to sign on. However, they will be asked periodically to confirm that they are still, in fact, retired. Initially, the scheme will be confined to persons over 60 years of age who are entitled to the maximum rate of unemployment assistance".

Pre-retirement allowance is a form of social assistance and is based on satisfying a means test. It is intended that the rate of the allowance be equivalent to the rate of unemployment assistance, subject to regulations. It was initially a condition of entitlement that the claimant be eligible for unemployment assistance but this was dropped in 1989 so as to allow persons who fall ill to continue to be eligible, even though such a person is not available for work and thus not entitled to unemployment assistance.

Subsection (1)(a)
The prescribed age is 55: article 75 of S.I. No. 417 of 1994.

Subsection (1)(b)
Some unemployment benefit claimants may opt to take unemployment assistance if assistable rates are higher for that claimant than benefit rates. Such a decision runs down the claimant's entitlement to unemployment benefit. After 390 days, unemployment benefit entitlement runs out. Thus, an unemployed person aged over 55 will be switched to pre-retirement allowance in such a case.

Subsection (1)(c)
The means test of pre-retirement allowance is the same as that to establish entitlement to unemployment assistance.

Subsection (2)
Where the claimant's spouse is not an adult dependant, the claimant's means are half of those that would be calculated under the applicable means test (*i.e.* the joint means of the couple are halved for means test purposes).

Rate of allowance (including increases for adult and child dependants)

128.—(1) Subject to this section and section 122, the rate of pre-retirement allowance (in this Chapter referred to as "the scheduled rate") shall be the weekly rate set out in column (2) of Part I of the Fourth Schedule increased by—

(a) the amount set out in column (3) of that Part for any period during which the claimant or beneficiary has an adult dependant, subject to the restriction that, except were regulation otherwise provide, the claimant or beneficiary shall not be entitled to an increase under this paragraph in respect of more than one person, and

(b) the appropriate amount set out in column (4) of that Part in respect of each qualified child who normally resides with the claimant or beneficiary. [1995 (No. 2) Act, section 10]

(2) Pre-retirement allowance shall be payable where—

(a) the weekly means of the claimant or beneficiary do not exceed £2, at the scheduled rate, and

(b) such weekly means exceed £2, at the scheduled rate reduced by £2 for each amount (if any) of £2 by which these weekly means exceed £2, any fraction of £2 in those weekly means being treated for this purpose as £2:

Provided that, if the rate calculated pursuant to this paragraph at which, but for this proviso, the pre-retirement allowance would be payable is—

(i) equal to or greater than 10p but less than £1, the allowance shall be payable at the weekly rate of £1, and

(ii) less than 10p, the allowance shall not be payable.

(3) Any increase of pre-retirement allowance payable pursuant to paragraph (b) of subsection (1) in respect of a qualified child who normally resides with the claimant or beneficiary and with the spouse of the claimant or beneficiary shall be payable at the rate of one-half of the appropriate amount in any case where the spouse of the claimant or beneficiary is not an adult dependant and paragraph (b) of subsection (1) shall be construed and have effect accordingly.

DEFINITIONS

"adult dependant": section 2(2).
"qualified child": section 2(3).

GENERAL NOTE

Adult and child dependant additions are payable at the scheduled rate except where the spouse is not an adult dependant (*e.g.* in work, earning in excess of £60 per week). In such a case half the scheduled rate is payable.

Where means are assessed, any weekly means below £2 are ignored. Means which exceed this are used to offset the statutory rates at a £2 for £2 offset rate.

Regulations

129.—The Minister may make regulations for the purpose of giving effect to this Chapter and such regulations may, in particular and without prejudice to the generality of the foregoing—

(a) specify the age for the purposes of section 127(1)(a),

(b) specify the periods which shall be regarded as periods of retirement for the purposes of this Chapter,

(c) vary the weekly rate of pre-retirement allowance under section 128, but any such variation shall not reduce the weekly rates applicable immediately before the commencement of such regulations.

STATUTORY INSTRUMENTS

Regulations made under this section are:
S.I. No. 76 of 1990.
S.I. No. 94 of 1991.
S.I. No. 164 of 1992.
S.I. No. 417 of 1994.
Regulations governing claims are S.I. No. 417 of 1994.

Integration of single woman's allowance scheme with pre-retirement allowance scheme

130.—(1) Notwithstanding this Chapter and regulations made hereunder, where, immediately before the 5th day of November, 1992 (in this Chapter referred to as "the appointed day") a woman, who had not attained pensionable age, was in receipt of single woman's allowance, pre-retirement allowance shall be payable to her from the appointed day at the same rate as the said single woman's allowance which was payable to her immediately before the said day:

Provided that she continues to satisfy the conditions as to means in accordance with section 127(1)(c).

(2) For the purposes of subsection (1) a woman who was in receipt of single woman's allowance immediately before the appointed day shall be deemed—

(a) to be retired within the meaning of regulations made for the purposes of section 129(b), and

(b) to have complied with the requirement contained in section 127(1)(b).

(3) Any decision made by a deciding officer or by an appeals officer in relation to the award of a single woman's allowance to a woman prior to the appointed day shall be deemed to be a decision to award pre-retirement allowance to such person on and from the said day.

(4) In this Chapter a reference to "single woman's allowance" means single woman's allowance which was payable by virtue of section 198 (repealed by section 37 of the Social Welfare Act, 1992) of the Social Welfare (Consolidation) Act, 1981, and regulations made thereunder.

GENERAL NOTE

This section is intended to integrate the single woman's allowance, payable to women who are in late middle age and are not realistic contenders for a place in the workforce due to lack of work experience (see the *Report of the Commission on Social Welfare* at p. 44), with the pre-retirement allowance. As from the commencement of this section, women who are in receipt of single woman's allowance shall be entitled to the pre-retirement allowance and it is payable at the same rate as the single woman's allowance previously paid. The appointed day for commencement of this section, was November 5, 1992.

Subsection (2) removes any difficulties that such a person may have experienced in satisfying the qualifying conditions for pre-retirement allowance.

Single woman's allowance—transitional provisions

131.—(1) Where, immediately before the appointed day, a woman had applied for a single woman's allowance, and that application had not been finally determined, pre-retirement allowance shall be payable to her at the same rate as the single woman's allowance which, but for section 37 of the Social Welfare Act, 1992, would have been payable to her.

(2) Where, on the appointed day, a single woman was of or over the age of 56 years and under the age of 58 years, she shall, if she had not already qualified for pre-retirement allowance, be deemed for the purposes of the pre-retirement allowance—

(a) to be retired within the meaning of regulations made for the purposes of section 129(b), and

(b) to have complied with the requirement contained in section 127(1)(b),

when she attains the age of 58 years.

CHAPTER 4

OLD AGE (NON-CONTRIBUTORY) PENSION

Interpretation

132.—In this Chapter—

"spouse", subject to section 3(12), includes—
  (*a*) a party to a marriage that has been dissolved, being a dissolution that is recognised as valid in the State, or
  (*b*) a man and woman who are not married to each other but are cohabiting as husband and wife; [1995 (No. 2) Act, section 10]
"weekly means" shall be the yearly means divided by 52.

GENERAL NOTE

This is the definition section; other terms are defined in section 2. The definition of spouse includes a married couple even if the parties live apart. However, the meaning of spouse changes in relation to section 138, the dependant additions section, making it clear that in such a context the spouses must be living together. The 1995 (No. 2) Act also includes divorced persons although this part of the definition is not yet in force.

Entitlement to pension

133.—Subject to this Act, every person in whose case the conditions laid down by this Chapter for the receipt of an old age (non-contributory) pension (in this Chapter referred to as statutory conditions) are fulfilled, shall be entitled to receive such a pension under this Chapter so long as those conditions continue to be fulfilled, and so long as he is not disqualified under this Chapter for the receipt of the pension.

GENERAL NOTE

This section sets out the statutory right of persons to receive an old age (non-contributory) pension as long as the statutory conditions are satisfied and the person is not disqualified under Chapter 4 of Part III.
  The statutory conditions include a means test. The principal provisions of the means test, as set out in Part II of the Third Schedule, are as follows:
  (a) The capital value of property (excluding the family home and other property personally used or enjoyed) or savings is given a notional value: the first £200 is disregarded, the next £315 is assessed at one twentieth or five per cent of the capital producing an income, while the balance is assessed at 10 per cent. This results in an annual income which is divided by 52 to produce a weekly means figure.
  (b) all income in cash which that person may expect to receive in the year, excluding income from the investment or profitable use of property, health board and social welfare payments, gaeltacht grants, £104 of annual earnings from employment for each dependant child, and redundancy payments payable under statute.
  (c) the net cash income of the proceeds of the sale of a house can be disregarded. The agreed sale price of the residence, or, if the pensioner purchases other accommodation such as sheltered housing, the difference between the sale price of the former residence and the agreed purchase price of the purchased residence is exempt where it falls below a fixed amount; in the present situation, a purchase price of £75,000: S.I. No. 180 of 1993.
       The exemption does not apply to moneys obtained by way of profitable use of the moneys such as deposit interest. Of the use of the proceeds of sale or a principal residence, the Minister said "We should say that the sum should not be taken into account in means assessment and the seller can do what he likes with it—go to Cheltenham, Aintree or anywhere else" (132 *Seanad Debates* Col. 236).
       Thus, while the motivation behind the exemption is to encourage pensioners to take on manageable accommodation arrangements, the utilisation of the moneys is in fact for the sole discretion of the pensioner.
  (d) Maintenance payments paid by either spouse under a separation order are exempted from the assessment of the payer's means for the purposes of old-age (non-contributory) and blind pensions and carer's allowance. This is intended to improve the chance of a separation order being met by giving the paying spouse a kind of allowance.

Statutory conditions

134.—The statutory conditions for the receipt of an old age (non-contributory) pension by any person are—
  (a) the person must have attained pensionable age; and
  (b) the means of the person as calculated in accordance with the Rules contained in Part II of the Third Schedule do not exceed the appropriate highest amount of means at which pension may be paid to that person in accordance with section 136.

GENERAL NOTE

This section states the statutory conditions which are:
  (a) the person must have attained 66 years of age,
  (b) the means of that person must not exceed the highest amount of means at which the pension may be paid. Part II of the Third Schedule sets out the applicable means test.
Regulations governing the making of a claim are Part VI of S.I. No. 417 of 1994.

Special conditions for receipt of pension

135.—Where a person who has attained pensionable age is in receipt of or entitled to deserted wife's benefit, survivor's pension or old age (contributory) pension or is a person in respect of whom an increase of the latter pension is payable by virtue of section 87(1) and would but for section 139 be qualified for the receipt of an old age (non-contributory) pension—
  (a) the person may, notwithstanding anything contained in the said section 139, be paid the old age (non-contributory) pension for any period during which the rate of pension payable would be greater than the rate of deserted wife's benefit, survivor's pension, old age (contributory) pension or the increase thereof, as the case may be, payable, and
  (b) in any case where the old age (non-contributory) pension is so paid, entitlement to deserted wife's benefit, survivor's pension, old age (contributory) pension or the increase thereof, as the case may be, shall continue but the amount of any such benefit, pension or increase payable during any such period—
    (i) shall not be paid to or in respect of the person, and
    (ii) shall be paid out of the Social Insurance Fund to the Exchequer.
    [1995 Act, Schedule D]

GENERAL NOTE

This section provides that where someone aged 66 or more is in receipt of, or entitled to, deserted wife's benefit, widow's (contributory) pension or old age (contributory) pension, or is a person in respect of whom an adult dependant addition has been paid in connection with an old-age (contributory) pension, the section 139 disqualification is not to prevent that person from obtaining old-age (non-contributory) pension when the rate of payment exceeds the payment due under the social insurance payment referred to. In that case the non-contributory old-age pension is paid to that person but the social insurance payment is to be made from the Social Insurance Fund to the Exchequer.

Rate of pension and increases for child dependants

136.—(1) The rate (in this Chapter referred to as "the scheduled rate") of old age (non-contributory) pension shall be the weekly rate set out in column (2) of Part I of the Fourth Schedule increased, by the appropriate amount set out in column (4) of that Part in respect of each qualified child who normally resides with the claimant or beneficiary.

(2) The pension shall be payable where—

(a) the weekly means of the claimant or beneficiary do not exceed £6, at the scheduled rate, and

(b) such weekly means exceed £6, at the scheduled rate reduced by £2 for each amount (if any) of £2 by which those weekly means exceed £6, any fraction of £2 in those weekly means being treated for this purpose as £2:

Provided that, if the rate calculated pursuant to this paragraph at which, but for this proviso, the pension would be payable is less than £2, the pension shall not be payable.

GENERAL NOTE

Subsection (1)

This subsection increases the rate of old-age (non-contributory) pension in cases where a child dependant (section 2(3)) normally resides with the pensioner: see article 7 of S.I. No. 417 of 1994 for the meaning of "normally resides". Section 138 however halves this addition in the circumstances set out in section 138.

Subsection (2)

Where weekly means fall below £6 the scheduled rate is payable in full. Weekly means in excess of £6 are deductible at the rate of £2 for £2, subject to the proviso that if the pension payable is less than £2, the pension shall not be payable.

Increases (including increase for one of a couple)

137.—The weekly rate of old age (non-contributory) pension payable in accordance with section 136 shall be increased—

(a) by the amount calculated in accordance with Part II of the Fourth Schedule where the beneficiary is living with, or is wholly or mainly maintaining, his spouse and the spouse is not in receipt of any benefit, pension, assistance or allowance under Part II or this Part, subject to the restriction that, except where regulations otherwise provide, the beneficiary shall not be entitled for the same period to an increase of pension under this paragraph in respect of more than one person,

(b) by the amount set out in column (6) of Part I of the Fourth Schedule where the beneficiary has attained pensionable age and is living alone, and

(c) by the amount set out in column (7) of Part I of the Fourth Schedule where the beneficiary has attained the age of 80 years. [1995 No. 2 Act, section 10]

GENERAL NOTE

Subsection (a)

This provision, in its present form, goes back to the 1985 (No. 2) Act and section 17 of the 1992 Act. It should be recalled that section 132 above defines "spouse", for the purpose of these pensions so as to include "a man and woman who are not married to each other but are cohabiting as man and wife". In these circumstances an eligible pensioner who claims and satisfies the Department that the pensioner is one-half of a cohabiting couple, will be entitled to adult and child dependant additions in the same way as a married pensioner is *vis-à-vis* a married spouse living with that pensioner.

Normally, issues of cohabitation arise in a negative context, that is, the issue of cohabitation may arise as a basis for disqualification of the claimant (*e.g.* widow's pensions or deserted wife's payments). This section raises cohabitation as a means of entitlement.

On the issue of proof, the then Minister for Social Welfare, Mr McCreevy, said "If people say they are cohabiting we accept that. That is not a problem": 132 *Seanad Debates* Col. 245. Nevertheless, cohabiting, while undefined in the legislation, is a term of art and issues will no doubt arise about whether two persons who share a house or flat are cohabiting.

However, the proviso limits the additional payment to one person only for the same period, thereby eliminating the prospects of multiple payments, for example, if X is married to Y but is also cohabiting with Z at the same address.

Subsection (b)
This makes provision for an additional payment to a pensioner who lives alone.

Subsection (c)
This makes provision for an additional payment to a pensioner aged 80 years or more, normally on the assumption that such a person has extra heating needs.

Amount of increases payable in respect of qualified child normally resident with beneficiary

138.—The increase payable pursuant to subsection (1) of section 136 in respect of a qualified child who normally resides with the beneficiary and the spouse of the beneficiary shall be payable at the rate of one-half of the appropriate amount in any case where the spouse of the beneficiary is entitled to any benefit, assistance, allowance (other than supplementary welfare allowance) or any other pension under this Act or to disabled person's maintenance allowance.

GENERAL NOTE

See General Note to section 136(1).

Disqualifications

139.—(1) Except as provided in section 135, receipt of old age (contributory) pension by a person shall be a disqualification for the receipt by that person of old age (non-contributory) pension.

(2) A person to whom benefit under section 92 is payable or in respect of whom the weekly rate of old age (contributory) pension payable to another person is increased by virtue of section 87(1) shall, except as provided in section 135, be disqualified, for any period in respect of which the said benefit under the said section 92 is payable to him or the weekly rate of such pension payable to such other person is so increased, for receiving old age (non-contributory) pension.

(3) A person who has attained pensionable age and is in receipt of a survivor's pension or deserted wife's benefit shall, except as provided in section 135, be disqualified for receiving old age (non-contributory) pension for any period in respect of which she is in receipt of the survivor's pension or deserted wife's benefit. [1995 Act, Schedule D]

GENERAL NOTE

This section is a disqualification provision which is intended to prevent parallel social insurance payments being payable as well as old-age (non-contributory) pension. Section 135 however relaxes the disqualification where the old-age (non-contributory) pension exceeds the social insurance payment or social insurance addition—see the General Note to section 135.

Pensions of persons in certain mental institutions

140.—(1) Subject to subsection (2), the whole of any amounts payable on foot of old age (non-contributory) pension to a person while the person is detained in a district or auxiliary mental hospital within the meaning of the Mental Treatment Act, 1945, or while he is detained in any place as an eligible patient, within the meaning of that Act, or in the Central Mental Hospital, shall be appropriated towards the cost of maintenance of the person in the place where he is being detained.

(2) Where the old age (non-contributory) pension of a person is appropriated under subsection (1), the person in charge, within the meaning of the said Act, of the place where the person is detained, or, if the person is detained in the Central Mental Hospital, the Resident Physician and Governor thereof may, in his absolute discretion, do either or both of the following—

(a) pay to the person for his own use such portion of the pension as he considers proper in the particular circumstances, if, in his opinion, the person is capable of making proper use of the portion so paid,

(b) make out of the pension all or part of such of the following payments as the person in charge thinks proper in the circumstances to make and fall to be made by the person, that is to say, rent, ground rent, rates (including water rates), land purchase annuities, payments in respect of charges or mortgages, cottage purchase annuities, instalments payable under hire purchase or credit sale agreements and insurance or assurance premiums.

CHAPTER 5

BLIND PERSON

Entitlement to pension

141.—(1) Subject to this Act, every blind person who has attained the age of 18 years shall be entitled to receive and to continue to receive such pension (in this Act referred to as a blind pension) as under Chapter 4 he would be entitled to receive if he had attained pensionable age; and the provisions of Chapter 4 shall apply in all respects in the case of such person subject to the modification that, for the statutory condition contained in section 134(a) there shall be substituted the conditions that the person must be a person who has attained the age of 18 years and that he is so blind that he either cannot perform any work for which eyesight is essential or cannot continue his ordinary occupation.

(2) A blind person in respect of whom a pension is payable under this section shall not be a qualified child for the purposes of this Act.

GENERAL NOTE

Old-age (non-contributory) pensions and blind persons pensions have been linked together since the original Acts of 1908 and 1920 created these payments.

The eligibility criteria for the means-tested blind persons pension are the same as those which operate in relation to an old age (non-contributory) pension, save for the requirement that the blind person be of pensionable age—66 years or more — and the requirement that the person be aged 18 years and "so blind that he either cannot perform any work for which eyesight is essential or cannot continue his ordinary occupation". The earnings disregards available to a person who comes within the test for eligibility are greater than those available in respect of old age (non-contributory) pension, for additional disregards of employment or self-employment earnings of £312 per annum, or £6 per week for the pensioner and £208 per annum, or £4 per week for an adult dependant. The Regulations governing the making of a claim are S.I. No. 417 of 1994.

CHAPTER 6

WIDOW'S AND ORPHAN'S (NON-CONTRIBUTORY) PENSIONS

Interpretation

142.—(1) For the purposes of this Chapter—

"husband", in relation to a woman who has been married more than once, refers only to her last husband, and for this purpose that last husband shall be construed as including the man to whom, but for the fact that the marriage has been dissolved, being a dissolution that is recognised as valid in the State, she would be married; [1995 (No. 2) Act, section 5]

"pension" means a widow's (non-contributory) pension or an orphan's (non-contributory) pension, as the case may require;

means shall be calculated in accordance with the Rules contained in Part II of the Third Schedule;

"weekly means" shall be the yearly means divided by 52.

"widow" means a widow or a woman who would otherwise be a widow but for the fact that her marriage has been dissolved, being a dissolution that is recognised as valid in the State. [1995 (No. 2) Act, section 5]

(2) Where a widow has remarried she shall not for the purposes of this Chapter be regarded as the widow of her former husband.

GENERAL NOTE

The introduction of a social assistance pension in 1935 in respect of the premature death of a husband coincided with an insurance-based payment which arose upon the occurrence of the same contingency. These parallel schemes were necessary because of the fact that at this time only 32 per cent of the male population were within social insurance: see the Report of the Commission on Social Welfare, p. 34. This parallel system continued until 1994 when section 11 of the 1994 Act replaced widow's (contributory) pension with a gender-free survivor's pension. Male persons who are bereaved and unable to continue to work in order to look after dependant children have had difficulty in finding an appropriate social assistance payment although, since 1990, Lone Parent's Allowance has been available.

Subsection (1) is a definition section. The definition of husband makes it clear that in the case of a woman who has remarried following a foreign divorce, only the death of her last husband will trigger eligibility. Subsection (2) terminates a widow's entitlement following remarriage.

The 1995 (No. 2) Act

The amended definition of husband and the definition of widow inserted by the 1995 (No. 2) Act make it clear that upon a valid divorce, a woman who has not remarried or is not cohabiting will be able to obtain a widow's (non-contributory) pension following on the death of her former spouse.

This provision is not yet in force.

Entitlement to pension

143.—(1) Subject to this Act, widow's (non-contributory) pension shall be payable to a widow.

(2) Subject to this Chapter, a woman who becomes a widow while she is in receipt of or entitled to deserted wife's allowance shall, on becoming a widow, be entitled to widow's (non-contributory) pension at the same rate as that of the deserted wife's allowance payable to her. [1995 (No. 2) Act, section 5]

(3) A widow's (non-contributory) pension payable to a widow shall, subject to this Chapter, continue to be payable unless she remarries and in such a case the pension shall cease as on and from her remarriage.

GENERAL NOTE

Subsection (2)

This subsection deals with the situation of a deserted wife who is entitled to deserted wife's allowance on the date of her husband's death. She will continue to receive the same rate of social assistance notwithstanding her technical transfer under this subsection to widow's (non-contributory) pension. Because the means tests are the same, it is difficult to see why this provision is necessary.

The 1995 (No. 2) Act

Because of the definition of widow in the previous section, a woman who is in receipt of deserted wife's allowance will be entitled to a widow's non-contributory pension upon the death of her former spouse, even if she is divorced from him. Her remarriage or cohabitation will prevent such a payment however.

This provision is not yet in force.

Rate of pension

144.—(1) The rate (in this section referred to as "the scheduled rate") of widow's (non-contributory) pension shall be the weekly rate set out in column (2) of Part I of the Fourth Schedule.

(2) A widow's (non-contributory) pension shall be payable where—

(a) the weekly means of the claimant or beneficiary do not exceed £6, at the scheduled rate, and

(b) such weekly means exceed £6, at the scheduled rate reduced by £2 for each amount (if any) of £2 by which those weekly means exceed £6, any fraction of £2 in those weekly means being treated for this purpose as £2:

Provided that, if the rate calculated pursuant to this paragraph at which, but for this proviso, the pension would be payable is less than £2, the pension shall not be payable.

GENERAL NOTE

The scheduled rate of the pension is payable when the weekly means of the pensioner do not exceed £6. Means above that figures are deducted at the rate of £2 of the pension for each £2 of means subject to the proviso which states that if the net pension payable is less than £2, the pension is not payable.

Note that dependant child additions are not payable for either widow's (non-contributory) or deserted wife's allowance. In each case the claimant must seek child dependant additions by way of lone parent's allowance.

Increases

145.—The weekly rate of pension payable in accordance with section 144 shall be increased—

(a) by the amount set out in column (6) of Part I of the Fourth Schedule where the beneficiary has attained pensionable age and is living alone, and

(b) by the amount set out in column (7) of Part I of the Fourth Schedule where the beneficiary has attained the age of 80 years.

GENERAL NOTE

Additions are payable when the widow has reached 66 years of age and is living alone, and a further addition is payable when the widow reaches the age of 80.

Disqualifications

146.—A widow shall not, if and so long as she and any person are cohabiting as husband and wife, be entitled to and shall be disqualified for receiving payment of widow's (non-contributory) pension.

GENERAL NOTE

There is no statutory definition of cohabitation. However, see the General Note to section 110(3) and *Whyte* (1989) 11 D.U.L.J. 187, in which the learned author considers the leading case of *Foley v. Moulton* [1989] I.L.R.M. 169.

Provisions against double pensions

147.—(1) Where, under this Chapter, a widow would, but for this subsection, be entitled to both survivors pension and a widow's (non-contributory) pension, the widow's (non-contributory) pension shall not be payable except insofar as is provided by regulations under section 209.

(2) Not more than one survivors pension or widow's (non-contributory) pension shall be payable to any one widow. [1995 Act, Schedule D]

GENERAL NOTE

The Overlapping Benefits Regulations are considered under section 209 of this Act.

Orphan's Pension

Entitlement to pension

148.—(1) Subject to this Act, an orphan's (non-contributory) pension shall be payable in respect of an orphan.

(2) Not more than one pension shall be payable in respect of any one orphan.

(3) A pension shall not be payable in respect of an orphan in respect of whom an increase under section 105(1) or 159(1) is claimable.

GENERAL NOTE

This section establishes entitlement to an orphan's (non-contributory) pension, but limits the pension to one pension (*i.e.* to deal with deaths of parents and step-parents) and provides, that when an addition is made in respect of survivor's pension or a lone parent's allowance then no orphan's (non-contributory) will be payable.

For the definition of an orphan, see section 2(1).

Rate of pension

149.—(1) The weekly rate (in this Chapter referred to as "the scheduled rate") of orphan's (non-contributory) pension shall be the weekly rate set out in column (2) of Part I of the Fourth Schedule.

"(2) An orphan's (non-contributory) pension shall be payable where—
  (a) the weekly means of the claimant or beneficiary do not exceed £6 at the scheduled rate, and
  (b) such weekly means exceed £6, at the scheduled rate reduced by £2 for each amount (if any) of £2 by which those weekly means exceed £6, any fraction of £2 in those weekly means being treated for this purpose as £2:
       Provided that, if the rate calculated pursuant to this paragraph at which, but for this proviso, the pension would be payable is less than £2, the pension shall not be payable.". [1995 Act, section 20].

GENERAL NOTE

The rate of orphan's (non-contributory) pension is calculated by reference to the means test in Part II of the Third Schedule. It is the orphan's means which are relevant and not the guardian of the orphan. The rate of pension is payable at the maximum rate when weekly means are below £2; means above that figure are offset against the pension at the rate of £2 for £2 of pension. If the pension payable falls below £2, the proviso to subsection (2)(b) prevents any pension being payable.

Civil proceedings

150.—Where, in any civil proceedings in any court, it is shown to the satisfaction of the court that pursuant to a claim of or on behalf of a person a pension was allowed or awarded or that the amount of a pension payable to or in respect of a person was varied and that the pension as so allowed or awarded or as so varied was at any time in course of payment to the person to whom the pension was payable, that person shall, in each case, be presumed, unless the contrary is shown, to have been in receipt of a pension of the amount so allowed or awarded or as so varied, as the case may be, from the date on which the pension of the amount so allowed or awarded or as so varied, as the case may be, became payable until the date, if any, on which the amount of the pension is varied or further varied, as the case may be, or the date on which the pension ceases to be payable, whether by reason of the death of the person or otherwise, whichever should first occur.

GENERAL NOTE

This section constitutes a statutory presumption. If a person was allowed or awarded a pension, or a pension was varied, it shall be presumed, unless the contrary is shown, that the pension was actually paid from the date of initial calculation, until such time as it is later varied, or ceases to be payable, whichever is the former. This presumption is to apply when the pensioner has issued civil proceedings (*e.g.* an accident compensation claim arising from the death of a parent), the pension being deductible under the Civil Liability Acts, for example.

Payment of pension

151.—(1) Subject to this section, orphan's (non-contributory) pension shall be paid to the guardian of the orphan in respect of whom such pension is payable.

(2) The Minister may, if he considers it advisable so to do, direct that a pension shall, in lieu of being paid to the guardian of the orphan in respect of whom such pension is payable, be paid to some other person for the benefit of the orphan.

GENERAL NOTE

The pension is normally payable to the guardian of the orphan. The Minister may direct payment to be made to some other person where this is appropriate (*e.g.* in cases of temporary absence from the state of the guardian, to the guardian's spouse with whom the orphan may be residing). It is not necessary to use the Payments to Appointed Persons Regulations for this purpose.

CHAPTER 7

DESERTED WIFE'S ALLOWANCE

Entitlement to allowance

152.—(1) Subject to this Act and regulations, deserted wife's allowance shall be paid to a woman who—

(a) has been deserted by her husband,
(b) is 40 years of age or over, and
(c) satisfies the conditions as to means calculated in accordance with the Rules contained in Part II of the Third Schedule.

(2) The rate of deserted wife's allowance shall be the same as the rate of the widow's (non-contributory) pension which would be payable to the woman under Chapter 6 if she were a widow.

(3) Subject to this Chapter, a woman who has been deserted by her husband shall, for the purposes of this Chapter, continue to be regarded as a deserted wife where her marriage has been dissolved, being a dissolution that is recognised as valid in the State. [1995 (No. 2) Act, section 6]

(4) A deserted wife's allowance shall, subject to this Chapter, continue to be payable to a woman unless she remarries and in such a case the allowance shall cease as and from her remarriage. [1995 (No. 2) Act, section 6]

(5) For the purposes of this Chapter, "husband" in relation to a woman who has been married more than once, refers only to her last husband and for this purpose that last husband shall be construed as including the man to whom but for the fact that the marriage has been dissolved, being a dissolution that is recognised as valid in the State, she would be married. [1995 (No. 2) Act, section 6]

GENERAL NOTE

The introduction of deserted wife's allowance in 1970 was directly related to the inadequate nature of means-tested payments which were available at that time. While many improvements have been made since 1970, in particular the introduction of supplementary welfare allowance and lone parent's benefit, deserted wife's allowance remains an important income support measure.

Subsection (1)

The desertion requirement found in subsection (1)(a) has been considered above in relation to deserted wife's benefit (see above section 111). Pending the three-month desertion requirement in S.I. No. 364 of 1993 the wife may claim supplementary welfare allowance.

The means test stipulated by Part II of the Third Schedule is the same means test which operates *vis-à-vis* old-age (non-contributory) pension.

Additional conditions for disability are laid down by regulations.

It should be noted that the positions of a deserted wife's allowance claimant and a lone parent's allowance claimant were recently reviewed in Constitutional terms by Costello J. In *Lowth v. Minister for Social Welfare* H.C. unrep. December 16, 1993.

The 1995 (No. 2) Act

The provisions of subsections (3) to (5) ensure that the allowance will continue to be payable notwithstanding a valid divorce as between the eligible woman and her husband. Her remarriage or cohabitation under section 154 will terminate her entitlement.

Regulations

153.—The Minister may make regulations in relation to deserted wife's allowance and the regulations may, in particular and without prejudice to the generality of the foregoing, specify the circumstances in which a woman is to be regarded for the purposes of this Chapter as having been deserted by her husband.

GENERAL NOTE

S.I. No. 417 of 1994 provides, in article 77, the necessary definitions. Claims and payments regulations are also stated therein.

Disqualification

154.—A deserted wife shall not, if and so long as she and any person are cohabiting as husband and wife, be entitled to and shall be disqualified for receiving payment of deserted wife's allowance.

GENERAL NOTE

On the meaning of cohabitation see the General Notes to sections 110(3) and 146 above.

CHAPTER 8

PRISONER'S WIFE'S ALLOWANCE

Entitlement to allowance

155.—(1) Subject to this Act and regulations, prisoner's wife's allowance shall be paid to a woman—

(a) whose husband, being a prisoner, has been committed in custody to a prison or place of detention for a period of not less than 6 months,

(b) who is 40 years of age or over, and

(c) who satisfies the conditions as to means calculated in accordance with the Rules contained in Part II of the Third Schedule.

(2) The rate of prisoner's wife's allowance shall be the same as the rate of the widow's (non-contributory) pension which would be payable to the woman under Chapter 6 if she were a widow.

(3) A prisoner's wife's allowance shall continue to be paid for a period of 4 weeks after the release of the prisoner from a prison or place of detention.

(4) A prisoner's wife's allowance shall, subject to this Chapter, continue to be payable to a woman unless she remarries and in such a case the allowance shall cease as and from her remarriage.

(5) Subject to this Chapter, a woman whose husband, being a prisoner, has been committed in custody to a prison or place of detention for a period of not less than 6 months, shall, for the purposes of this Chapter, continue to be regarded as a prisoner's wife where her marriage has been dissolved, being a dissolution that is recognised as valid in the State.

(6) For the purposes of this Chapter, "husband" in relation to a woman who has been married more than once, refers only to her last husband and for this purpose that last husband shall be construed as including the man to whom, but for the fact that the marriage has been dissolved, being a dissolution that is recognised as valid in the State, she would be married.
[1995 (No. 2) Act, section 7]

GENERAL NOTE '

Prisoner's wife's allowance was introduced in 1974. The eligibility conditions require the applicant's husband to have been committed to prison or a place of detention for not less than six months. The applicant must be aged 40 years or over and satisfy the same means test as that imposed in respect of widow's (non-contributory) pension. Rates of allowance are identical to those payable to a widow under widow's (non-contributory) pension.

Apart from cases where a sentence of six months or more has been passed, it is also possible to receive the allowance if the applicant's husband has been remanded in custody for six months (*e.g.* while awaiting trial): see article 78 of S.I. No. 417 of 1994.

It is curious to note that, despite the opening words of section 155(1), there is no provision under Chapter 8 for the making of regulations, whereas, under section 196(5) of the 1981 Consolidation Act, a specific power was included in the legislation.

The 1995 (No. 2) Act

Subsection (5) provides that if a prisoner is divorced from his wife whilst detained, the wife will continue to be eligible for the allowance notwithstanding the divorce.

Because of the definition of "husband", as inserted, subsection (6) provides that where a divorced man has been sentenced to detention for more than six months, his former spouse shall be entitled to the allowance (unless she has remarried) if the other conditions of entitlement are satisfied.

Disqualification

156.—A prisoner's wife shall not, if and so long as she and any person are cohabiting as husband and wife, be entitled to and shall be disqualified for receiving payment of prisoner's wife's allowance.

See the General Notes to sections 110(3) and 146 on the meaning of cohabitation.

CHAPTER 9

LONE PARENT'S ALLOWANCE

Interpretation

157.—(1) In this Chapter—

"lone parent" means, subject to regulations under section 162—
(a) a widow,
(b) a widower,
(c) a separated spouse,
(d) an unmarried person, or
(e) a person whose spouse has been committed in custody to a prison or place of detention for a period of not less than 6 months,

who has at least one qualified child normally residing with that person;

"allowance" means a lone parent's allowance;

"weekly means" means the yearly means divided by 52.

(2) For the purposes of this Chapter—

(a) means shall be calculated in accordance with the Rules contained in Part II of the Third Schedule, and

(b) a reference to a lone parent shall include a reference to a person who would otherwise be a lone parent but for the fact that the person's marriage has been dissolved, being a dissolution that is recognised as valid in the State. [1995 (No. 2) Act, section 8]

GENERAL NOTE

Section 12 of the 1990 Act was the most recent substantive change in an evolving pattern of providing income support to one-parent families, especially following marital breakdown. Early income support schemes tended to adopt a perspective which assumed that the adult with child-rearing responsibilities would be female and, while a Constitutional challenge to sexist legislation failed (see *Dennehy v. The Minister for Social Welfare* H.C. Unrep. July 26, 1984 at section 6 of the 1989 Act implemented a scheme of deserted husband's benefit. Section 12 of the 1990 Act brought some degree of coherence to the law. This section introduced a new category of social assistance payment, the lone parent's allowance, by way of substitution of this allowance for the widower's non contributory pension, and deserted husband's allowance, introduced by section 6 of the Social Welfare Act, 1989, and implemented by the Social Welfare (Widower's (Non Contributory) Pension and Deserted Husband's Allowance) Regulations, 1989 (S.I. No. 281 of 1989) now S.I. No. 417 of 1994. The substitution of lone parent's allowance however goes much further than providing a generic description of the two 1989 allowances. The new social assistance payment is intended to replace the existing social assistance payments made to the heads of all one parent families. In introducing this new scheme to the *Dáil* at Second Stage the Minister said it will "streamline all existing social assistance payments for lone parents. It will incorporate the existing schemes for unmarried mothers, widowers and deserted husbands. Women receiving widow's non contributory pension, deserted wife's allowance and prisoner's wife's allowance, who have child dependants will also be covered by the new scheme": 397 *Dáil Debates* Col. 758.

The Minister also pointed out that the scheme would be able to provide social assistance to others who would not previously have been able to claim any social welfare payment but would be obliged to seek a supplementary welfare allowance from the health boards, that is, separated spouses where desertion could not be established, single fathers and prisoners' husbands. The Act does not however abolish these other categories of social assistance save for widower's non contributory pension and deserted husband's allowance. There are still some instances in which these other assistance payments will be important; for example, a deserted wife over 40 years of age will be able to claim deserted wife's allowance, but not the lone parent's allowance if she has no child dependants. Similarly, there may be cases where an existing claimant will receive a higher rate of assistance on the current scheme he or she is receiving payments under, as against the new lone parent's allowance. In such a case the higher payment will continue to be payable.

Subsection (1) achieves this by making it a condition of entitlement for a person falling into one of the five categories (a) to (e) to have a qualified child normally resident with that person. For the definition of qualified child, see section 2(3). On the meaning of normal residence see S.I. No. 417 of 1994.

During the 1990 Bill's passage through the legislative process, the new lone parent's allowance scheme was widely welcomed in the Oireachtas, both as a simplifying measure, as a means of broadening social assistance to provide income support to some parents who had not been catered for, and also as a non-sexist and (in part) value-judgement free system of income support.

Subsection (1)

For any of the persons mentioned under this subsection to be eligible for the allowance they must have at least one qualified child normally resident with them. While (a) and (b) are categories of person already covered by social assistance allowances, the gender free nature of (c), (d) and (e) should be noted. Category (c) in particular is new for another reason: the existing social assistance payments refer not to separated husbands or wives but deserted husbands and deserted wives. It seems that separated is a broader category and it includes a person who has been deserted by their spouse as well as a person who has agreed to live apart from their spouse. Category (d), an unmarried person, replicates unmarried mother's payments but also includes an unmarried father who lives where the child is normally resident. Category (e) similarly broadens the allowance to cover cases where the *wife* is in penal detention for more than six months.

Subsection (2)

See S.I. No. 417 of 1994.

The 1995 (No. 2) Act

This amended definition of lone parent in the new subsection (1)(b) makes it clear that lone parent's allowance entitlement is not prejudiced by any divorce that has taken place.

Entitlement to allowance

158.—(1) Subject to this Act, lone parent's allowance shall be payable to a lone parent.

(2) A lone parent's allowance payable to a lone parent shall, subject to this Act, continue to be payable unless the lone parent marries or remarries, as the case may be, and in such a case the allowance shall cease as and from the date of marriage or remarriage, as the case may be.

GENERAL NOTE

This section provides that the allowance shall be payable as of right to a lone parent who satisfies the provisions of the Act and the regulations made thereunder. The marriage or remarriage of a lone parent's allowance recipient will lead to cesser of the allowance as and from the date of the marriage or remarriage: see articles 79–81 of S.I. No. 417 of 1994.

Rate of allowance and increases for child dependants

159.—(1) The rate (in this section referred to as "the scheduled rate") of lone parent's allowance shall be the weekly rate set out in column (2) of Part I of the Fourth Schedule increased by the appropriate amount set out in column (4) of that Part in respect of each qualified child who normally resides with the beneficiary.

(2) A lone parent's allowance shall be payable where—

(a) the weekly means of the claimant or beneficiary do not exceed £6, at the scheduled rate, and

(b) such weekly means exceed £6, at the scheduled rate reduced by £2 for each amount (if any) of £2 by which those weekly means exceed £6, any fraction of £2 in those weekly means being treated for this purpose as £2:
Provided that, if the rate calculated pursuant to this paragraph at which, but for this proviso, the allowance would be payable is less than £2, the allowance shall not be payable.

(3) The weekly rate of lone parent's allowance shall be increased—

(a) by the amount set out in column (6) of Part I of the Fourth Schedule where the person entitled to the allowance has attained pensionable age and is living alone, and

(b) by the amount set out in column (7) of Part I of the Fourth Schedule where the person entitled to the allowance has attained the age of 80 years.

GENERAL NOTE

The means test earnings disregard envisaged for lone parent's allowance is set at £6 per week. Opposition deputies were particularly critical of this figure, saying that when the figure of £6 as a disregard was used in 1975 in regard to widow's allowance it represented two thirds of the allowance. The Minister explained that the means test would operate in the following way:

"Both Deputy Ferris and Deputy Byrne referred to the £6 means test. This will be £6 for a parent and £6 for each child so *that it cannot be less than £12 for a start. If a person has four children it will be £24 for the children and £6 for the parent, which will make a total of £30 for a start, plus expenses for baby sitting and travelling to work* [emphasis added]. These are also provided for and can be brought together under the scheme. These people may hire somebody to mind their children for £30 or £40 per week. I am not saying that is what the figure should be—it happens to be the amount paid by quite a few people I know—and I do not want to get into an argument about what it should be. If a person pays £40 to someone to mind his children the reasonable expenditure in that area can be taken into account as well as the £30, which would give a total of £70. This means that a person can earn £70 plus reasonable travelling expenses to work. Of course, there would be limitations on these expenses but it means a person could earn £80 per week, hire somebody to mind their children and receive the full payment. The full payment for a person with five children will be the basic rate plus the payment for the five children." (397 *Dáil Debates* Col. 1685)

The disregard in relation to the sale of a principal residence is found in article 90 of S.I. No. 417 of 1994.

For rules on the residence of a qualified child see S.I. No. 417 of 1994 (article 82).

Disqualification

160.—A lone parent shall not, if and so long as he and any person are cohabiting as husband and wife, be entitled to and shall be disqualified for receiving payment of an allowance.

GENERAL NOTE

The cohabitation rule is gender neutral. However, in 1990 many deputies criticised the retention of a cohabitation rule on the ground that it was difficult to determine when cohabitation begins and because its vagueness gave the social welfare officer a broad and at times arbitrary power. It should be noted that in operating the cohabitation rule officials must observe principles of constitutional justice: see *State (Houlihan)* v. *Department of Social Welfare (supra)* and General Note to section 110(3) above.

Prisoner's spouses

161.—In the case of a person who qualifies for an allowance by virtue of being a prisoner's spouse, such allowance shall continue to be paid for a period of 4 weeks after the release of the prisoner from a prison or place of detention.

Regulations

162.—The Minister shall make regulations in relation to lone parent's allowance and the regulations may, in particular and without prejudice to the generality of the foregoing specify the circumstances in which, for the purposes of this Chapter—

(a) a person is to be regarded as being a separated spouse, and

(b) a person is to be regarded as being an unmarried person.

GENERAL NOTE

These details are found in the Social Welfare (Consolidated Payments Provisions) Regulations 1994 (S.I. No. 417 of 1994).

Under these regulations, a separated spouse is a person separated from his or her spouse for at least three months when children are not being supported by that person or are being supported at less than the scheduled rate of the allowance. An unmarried person must be the natural or adoptive parent of a child dependant. For the making of late claims see S.I. No. 417 of 1994. On overlapping benefits see S.I. No. 417 of 1994.

CHAPTER 10

CARER'S ALLOWANCE

Interpretation

163.—(1) Subject to this Act, in this Chapter—

"carer" means a person who resides with and provides full-time care and attention to a relevant pensioner;

"prescribed relative" means a prescribed relative within the meaning of the Social Welfare (Prescribed Relative Allowance) Regulations, 1989 (S.I. No. 361 of 1989);

"prescribed relative allowance" means an increase for a prescribed relative under section 50(11), 51(2)(a), 81(3), 86(3), 91(3), 95(2), 103(2), 162(1)(a) or 179(a) of the Social Welfare (Consolidation) Act, 1981 or under regulations applying the provisions of section 179(a) of that Act;

" 'relevant pensioner' means a person (other than a person in receipt of an increase of disablement pension under section 57 in respect of constant attendance) who is so incapacitated as to require full-time care and attention, and who—

(a) has attained pensionable age, or is in receipt of—

    (i) invalidity pension, or a payment corresponding to invalidity pension from a Member State (other than the State), or under the legislation of any other State with which the Minister has made a reciprocal arrangement under the provisions of section 238,

    (ii) blind pension, or

    (iii) disabled person's allowance, or

(c) is in receipt of retirement pension or who has attained the age of 65 years and is in receipt of a payment corresponding to retirement pension from a Member State (other than the State) or under the legislation of any other State with which the Minister has made a reciprocal arrangement under the provisions of section 238, where such person was, immediately prior to the receipt of such pension, in receipt of invalidity pension or a payment corresponding to an invalidity pension from a

Member State (other than the State) or under such a reciprocal arrangement;" [1995 Act, section 12(1)].

"weekly means" means the yearly means divided by 52.

(2) For the purposes of this Chapter, means shall be calculated in accordance with the Rules contained in Part II of the Third Schedule.

(3) For the purposes of subsection (1), a relevant pensioner shall be regarded as requiring full-time care and attention where—

(a) he is so disabled or invalided that he requires from another person—

    (i) continual supervision in order to avoid danger to himself, or

    (ii) continual supervision and frequent assistance throughout the day in connection with normal bodily functions, and

(b) he is so disabled or invalided as to be likely to require full-time care and attention for a period of at least 12 months.

GENERAL NOTE

The failure of the Irish social welfare system to make a direct payment to a person who is required to look after an incapacitated person was eventually addressed by the Oireachtas in the Act of 1990. This gap in the social assistance net was identified by the Commission on Social Welfare in their 1986 Report (p. 255), although the Commission recommended that cover should be available via a new integrated assistance scheme rather than by way of yet another *ad hoc* programme.

Following on recent reforms of the prescribed relative's allowance under section 30 of the 1989 Act whereby the allowance could be paid directly to the prescribed relative, a decision further to develop the financial support available to persons who undertake to care for the sick and disabled outside of an institutional context was implemented in 1990. In introducing the scheme to Dáil Éireann the Minister Dr Woods said that it was the most significant measure in the 1990 Bill. He continued:

"This new allowance, which I am particularly pleased to introduce, represents a milestone in the development of our social welfare services. For the first time in our legislation we are giving official recognition to the role of the carer who provides full time care for elderly people in the community. Many public representatives and voluntary groups have stressed the importance of the work of those who care for the elderly and the need for this work to be recognised. Such was the lack of recognition of these caring people, mainly women, that they have been referred to as the "forgotten army". Their selfless dedication has been of inestimable value to the community over the years. I am delighted to be able to recognise the dedication of carers with the introduction of this new allowance.

Better living standards and improved health care have increased life expectancy for all of us. The number of elderly people is increasing and will continue to increase. Some of these will need full-time care and attention. Where possible, this is best provided in the home. This is where carers have such an important role. I am anxious that this role be recognised and that carers are supported and encouraged. The new allowance represents much needed reform in this area." (397 *Dáil Debates* Col. 755).

Subsection (1)

This is the definition section. The following points are of importance in understanding how the new allowance will be administered.

Carer: the person must reside with and provide full-time care and attention to the relevant pensioner. Unlike prescribed relative's allowance no familiar link is necessary. Other matters of definition are dealt with under the regulations.

Relevant pensioner: the person requiring full-time care and attention must be in receipt of one of the social insurance and social assistance payments mentioned in this subsection if the carer is to be eligible for the carer's allowance. The occupational injuries constant attendance allowance is not included. As initially drawn up the Bill did not make the section 69, Health Act, 1970 payment, known as disabled person's maintenance allowance, a qualifying payment. Following opposition criticism the Bill was amended in Committee to include DPMA.

In the 1995 Act the definition was broadened to cover non-social welfare pensioners. In explaining this measure, the Minister of State, Mr Duncan, said (142 *Seanad Debates* Col. 1489) that the entitlement was:

"being extended to those caring for non-social welfare pensioners aged 66 years or over. That is an important improvement. This will bring 1,000 new carers into the scheme, at a cost of £3 million in a full year. The means test for the allowance is also being improved. The earnings disregard of £100 a week in respect of working spouses is being increased to

£150 a week, an increase of 50 per cent. Again, I emphasise the percentage increase in this case. The new earnings disregard will apply not only to earnings from work but to all types of income such as pensions and that is also an important aspect of that provision".

This second aspect of the 1995 reforms is to be found in section 12(2) of the 1995 Act, which amends the means test in Rule 4, Part II of the Third Schedule to allow regulations to be made. Article 8 of S.I. No. 146 of 1995 raises the disregard to £150 p.w.

Section 163(1)(b) was added to the legislation by section 8 of the 1991 Act.

Subsection (2)

For details of the means test, see section 169.

Subsection (3)

Section 8 of the 1991 Act added this definition. There is no Irish caselaw on the meaning of this provision. For English case law, see *R. v. N.I.C., ex p. Secretary of State for Social Services* [1981] 2 All E.R. 738 and *Woodling v. Secretary of State for Social Services* [1984] 1 All E.R. 593.

Entitlement to allowance

164.—Subject to this Act, an allowance (in this Act referred to as "carer's allowance") shall, in such circumstances and subject to such conditions as may be prescribed, be payable to a carer.

GENERAL NOTE

This section establishes the right of a carer who satisfies the prescribed conditions to be entitled to payment of the allowance. The allowance is not to be paid to the relevant pensioner. The prescribed conditions are set out in article 85 of the Social Welfare (Consolidated Payments Provisions) Regulations, 1994 (S.I. No. 417 of 1994).

The carer must be resident in the State and
  (a) not engaged in employment or self-employment outside his home;
  (b) be 18 or more;
  (c) not resident in an institution (defined as a hospital, convalescent home, or home for persons with physical or mental disability, or premises analogous thereto).

Under these regulations, carer's allowance is still payable if the relevant pensioner is temporarily in hospital or a similar institution for treatment for no longer than 13 weeks: article 86.

Rate of allowance

165.—(1) The rate, (in this Chapter referred to as "the scheduled rate") of carer's allowance shall be the weekly rate set out in column (2) of Part I of the Fourth Schedule increased by the appropriate amount set out in column (4) of that Part in respect of each qualified child who normally resides with the beneficiary.

(2) A carer's allowance shall be payable where—
  (a) the weekly means of the claimant or beneficiary do not exceed £6, at the scheduled rate, and
  (b) such weekly means exceed £6, at the scheduled rate reduced by £2 for each amount (if any) of £2 by which those weekly means exceed £6, any fraction of £2 in those weekly means being treated for this purpose as £2:
  Provided that, if the rate calculated pursuant to this paragraph at which, but for this proviso, the carer's allowance would be payable is less than £2, the allowance shall not be payable. [1994 Act, section 16].

(3) Notwithstanding subsection (2), where, immediately before the 1st day of November, 1990, a prescribed relative allowance was being paid to or in respect of a claimant for a carer's allowance, the carer's allowance shall be paid at a weekly rate corresponding to the rate of prescribed relative allowance specified in column (5) of Part I of the Fourth Schedule,

unless the weekly rate of carer's allowance as calculated in accordance with subsection (2) payable to that claimant is greater than the said specified rate, in which case the greater amount shall be paid.

(4) Any increase in carer's allowance payable pursuant to subsection (1) in respect of a qualified child who normally resides with a beneficiary and with the spouse of a beneficiary shall be payable at one-half of the appropriate amount.

GENERAL NOTE

Carer's allowance is payable at a scheduled rate with additions in respect of dependant children who come within the definition of qualified child in section 2(3) of the Act. Note the half-payment rule where the carer lives with a spouse: subsection (4). The allowance is payable at the usual rate: a £6 weekly disregard of means is permitted, with the allowance being reduced by £2 for each £2 of means. No allowance is payable if the weekly rate falls below £2.

Section 16(1) of the 1994 Act increased the earnings disregard to £6 per week. An even more significant adjustment to the means test was made in section 16(2) of the 1994 Act with effect from July 28, 1994.

If the carer is married and the carer's spouse is either earning a salary or is self-employed, then there will be a disregard of that spouse's earnings at a level which will be fixed by statutory instrument. The Department estimates that an extra 500 claimants whose spouses are earning will come into entitlement and some 1,750 existing recipients will obtain enhanced allowances (139 *Seanad Debates* Col. 1577).

In the 1995 Act the Minister announced an intention to legislate for a £150 income disregard.

Subsection (3)

While the intention is to phase-out prescribed relatives' allowance, this subsection is a necessary transitional measure. The means of the person providing care were not relevant to eligibility to prescribed relatives' allowance but they are for carer's allowance. This subsection directs that the move to carer's allowance will not lead to rates of the allowance falling below the figure previously payable under the prescribed relative scheme. However, where the means test favours the carer, the allowance is payable at that higher rate.

Payment of allowance

166.—Notwithstanding the provisions of this Chapter, only one carer's allowance shall be payable to a carer, and only one carer's allowance shall be payable in respect of the full-time care and attention being provided to a relevant pensioner.

GENERAL NOTE

This provision prevents multiple payments from being made (*e.g.* where a carer looks after both his/her aged and incapacitated parents).

Prescribed relative allowance

167.—(1) A prescribed relative allowance which, by virtue of the provisions of the Social Welfare (Consolidation) Act, 1981, and regulations made under or applying the provisions of that Act, is payable immediately before the commencement of this Act shall, subject to section 168, continue to be paid at the rate set down in column (5) of Part I of the Second Schedule or column (5) of Part I of the Fourth Schedule, as appropriate, for as long as—

(a) the beneficiary remains so incapacitated as to require full-time care and attention,

(b) there is residing with the beneficiary for the purpose of providing that care and attention a prescribed relative of the beneficiary, and

(c) the conditions contained in the Social Welfare (Prescribed Relative Allowance) Regulations, 1989 (S.I. No. 361 of 1989), continue to be fulfilled. [1995 Act, Schedule F]

(2) The Social Welfare (Prescribed Relative Allowance) Regulations, 1989, (S.I. No. 361 of 1989), shall continue to have effect for the purposes of this section.

GENERAL NOTE

This is a saver section which continues eligibility for prescribed relative allowance when that allowance was payable under the Consolidation Act of 1981 before the commencement of the 1993 Consolidation Act. For this purpose subsection (2) saves the prescribed relative allowance regulations (S.I. No. 361 of 1989). Apart from the conditions of eligibility set by sections 167(1)(a) and (b), the regulations make provision as to who is to be regarded as a prescribed relative and set conditions to be satisfied by the pensioner (*e.g.* living alone) and the prescribed relative (*e.g.* not employed outside the home).

However, section 168(2) directs that the allowance is not to be payable when a new claim was made on or after November 1, 1990, the date of commencement of carer's allowance under S.I. No. 242 of 1990.

Entitlement to prescribed relative allowance

168.—(1) A prescribed relative allowance shall cease to be paid to a relevant pensioner or prescribed relative, as the case may be, where the prescribed relative becomes entitled to and receives a carer's allowance.

(2) Notwithstanding anything contained in this Act, a prescribed relative allowance shall not be paid where a claim for such allowance is made on or after the 1st day of November, 1990.

GENERAL NOTE

Subsection (1) terminates entitlement of a relevant pensioner, or the prescribed relative, to a prescribed relative's allowance when the prescribed relative becomes entitled to, and receives, a carer's allowance.

Subsection (2) operates prospectively to terminate the legislative basis for payment of a prescribed relative's allowance when this Chapter of Part III commenced under S.I. No. 242 of 1990.

Regulations

169.—(1) The Minister shall make regulations for the purpose of giving effect to this Chapter.

(2) Regulations under this section may, in particular and without prejudice to the generality of subsection (1)—
   (a) provide for amounts paid in respect of prescribed relative allowance on or after the 1st day of November, 1990 to be treated as payment on account of carer's allowance,
   (b) provide for—
      (i) entitling to carer's allowance such class or classes of person as may be prescribed who would be entitled thereto but for the fact that the conditions as to means as calculated in accordance with the Rules contained in Part II of the Third Schedule are not satisfied, or
      (ii) entitling to carer's allowance at a rate higher than that calculated in accordance with subsection (2) of section 165 such class or classes of person as may be prescribed,
   and the rate of allowance so payable may vary in accordance with the claimant's means.

GENERAL NOTE

Subsection (2)

See Parts I to III of S.I. No. 242 of 1990. The provisions on claims and payments are contained in S.I. No. 417 of 1994.

CHAPTER 11

SUPPLEMENTARY WELFARE ALLOWANCE

Interpretation
170.—In this Chapter—
"the Act of 1939" means the Public Assistance Act, 1939;
"adult dependant" means—
(a) the spouse of the beneficiary who is being wholly or mainly maintained by him, or
(b) a person over the age of 16 years being wholly or mainly maintained by the beneficiary and having the care of one or more than one qualified child who normally resides with the beneficiary where the beneficiary is—
(i) a single person,
(ii) a widow,
(iii) a widower, or
(iv) a married person who is not living with and is neither wholly nor mainly maintaining, nor being wholly or mainly maintained by, such married person's spouse;
" 'child dependant' means, in relation to a beneficiary any child, not being an adult dependant, who is dependent on that beneficiary for support and who is under the age of 18 years or is of or over the age of 18 years and is regarded as attending a course of study within the meaning of section 126(3)(a);" [1994 Act, section 23].
"home assistance" means home assistance within the meaning of the Act of 1939;
"public assistance authority" means a public assistance authority within the meaning of section 8 of the Act of 1939, as extended by section 7 of the Health Authorities Act, 1960, and section 84 of the Health Act, 1970;
"supplementary welfare allowance" means an allowance in cash or in kind granted under this Chapter.

GENERAL NOTE

Historical introduction
   In terms of legislative history, the supplementary welfare allowance programme is the contemporary equivalent of the old poor laws. While the Elizabethan poor laws were not part of Irish law, the 19th century amendments to the poor law which were effected under the Poor Law (Amendment) Act 1834 provided the basis of a legislative measure which put the provision of poor relief in Ireland on a statutory footing under the Poor Relief (Ireland) Act 1838. However, relief was subject to the same legal requirements that applied in England and Wales, particularly the prohibition on outdoor relief and an obligation to enter a workhouse as a condition of relief. The horrors of the famine years of 1846 to 1850 made the relaxation of the ban on outdoor relief a feature of Irish law: see Burke, *The Irish Poor Law* (1986). The provision of poor relief from the poor law unions was based on discretion, not legal entitlement, as the decision of the Supreme Court, in *O'Connor v. Dwyer* [1932] I.R. 466 illustrates. An application brought by four paupers in which they sought a declaration to be entitled to poor relief, and a declaration that previous relief provided was inadequate, was upheld by Meredith J. in the High Court. The Supreme Court however overruled Meredith J. In his judgment, Murnaghan J. ruled that poor relief was not payable as of right, but as a matter of discretion. A *bona fide* exercise of a discretion could not, in the view of the court, be challenged, even if the paupers, as in this case, were physically disabled and therefore within the Elizabethan concept of being the "deserving" poor.
   While substantial advances were made in the area of social insurance and assistance, significantly through old age pensions and widow's and orphan's pensions in 1908 and 1935,

poor relief was still the primary means of income support for many infirm and destitute people. In 1939 the Public Assistance Act cleared away the old poor law but many of the discretionary and arbitrary features of the poor law survived in the guise of home assistance, provided by local authorities within their areas of competence.

The opening up of debate and public discussion on the nature and incidence of poverty in Irish Society through the Kilkenny Conference in 1971, and the work of Seamus O'Cinneide, made it apparent that a new social assistance programme, based upon the concept of legal entitlement, while at the same time possessing a degree of flexibility and responsiveness to social need, had to be developed. The Labour Deputy, Frank Cluskey, using as a legislative model the U.K. supplementary benefit scheme of 1966, was at the forefront in pushing through legislation establishing the supplementary welfare allowance in 1975, although the scheme only became operational in July 1977.

Definition section

This section is the definition section. The terms "adult dependant" and "qualified child" found in sections 2(2) and 2(3) above are inapplicable to supplementary welfare allowance.

The definition of "adult dependant" was inserted into the 1981 Consolidation Act by section 16 of the 1985 (No. 2) Act. The definition of "adult dependant", for the purpose of supplementary welfare allowance, is in one respect more extensive than that found in section 2(2) above, which defines "adult dependant" for the purpose of insurance and assistance payments. Spouses in employment or self employment or who are entitled to or in receipt of any other social welfare payment, may be adult dependants under this section but are excluded under section 2(2) for the purpose of obtaining other social welfare payments. This is necessary because of the position of supplementary welfare allowances in the welfare state hierarchy. It is often paid when persons eligible for other benefits or allowances have not had their claims processed and to exclude a wife's application for supplementary welfare because her husband is entitled to unemployment assistance would undermine the "fire brigade" or "emergency" role supplementary welfare allowance plays. In any event, where a married couple seek supplementary welfare allowance the position has always been one of equality; either spouse may apply and obtain an adult dependant addition for the other: see section 9(2) of the Social Welfare (Supplementary Welfare Allowances) Act, 1975 (No. 28), now section 177(2) of the Principal Act.

The definition of "public assistance authority" in effect means the Community Care Department of one of the eight health boards established under the Health Act, 1970.

The definition of "supplementary welfare allowance" makes it clear that payment can be in kind. Delivery of large domestic goods—beds, cookers and the like—are made under the urgent needs provisions under section 180.

The definition of "child dependant" was broadened to include persons aged 18 years or more, at school or who have left school or completed the leaving certificate examination not more than three months previously.

Entitlement to supplementary welfare allowance

171.—Subject to this Act, every person in the State whose means are insufficient to meet his needs and the needs of any adult or child dependant of his shall be entitled to supplementary welfare allowance.

GENERAL NOTE

The statutory right to supplementary welfare allowance, at rates fixed by the Oireachtas, is one of the characteristics that distinguishes this allowance from the earlier home assistance scheme. The statutory needs are the scale rates found in the Fourth Schedule, while the statutory means are found in Part III of the Third Schedule.

Exclusion of persons receiving full-time education

172.—(1) A person shall not be entitled to receive supplementary welfare allowance while attending a course of study within the meaning of section 126, other than in such circumstances and subject to such conditions as may be prescribed. [1994 Act, section 24].

(2) Subsection (1) is without prejudice to the entitlement of any person to receive supplementary welfare allowance in respect of a person referred to in that subsection who is his adult or child dependant.

(3) Notwithstanding subsection (1), supplementary welfare allowance may, in a case in which there are exceptional circumstances, be granted to a person who would be entitled to receive supplementary welfare allowance but for that subsection.

GENERAL NOTE

Subsection (1)
This section extends the disqualification imposed upon students from eligibility for unemployment assistance during a course of study or during vacation periods to entitlement to supplementary welfare allowance. For a discussion of this disqualification see the General Note to section 126 above.

Subsection (2)
The disqualification imposed upon a student by subsection (1) does not prevent the student with adult or child dependants from applying for supplementary welfare allowance and receiving the relevant dependant additions. *Quaere*: can the spouse of a student apply in his or her own right and receive an adult dependant addition for the student spouse?

Subsection (3)
This "exceptional circumstances" discretion is only likely to be exercised in cases of extreme hardship. The original health board guidelines gave as an example "an orphan who is head of a household and possibly caring for younger members of a family or a handicapped student with dependants whose disability precludes him from obtaining remunerative employment".

Exclusion of persons in full-time employment

173.—(1) Subject to subsections (2) and (3), a person shall not, other than in such circumstances and subject to such conditions as may be prescribed, be entitled to supplementary welfare allowance in relation to any period during which he is engaged in remunerative full-time work. [1994 Act, section 25].

(2) The Minister may by regulations provide for the postponement of the operation of subsection (1) in respect of any class of persons becoming engaged in remunerative full-time work until such period after the commencement of the engagement as may be specified in the regulations.

(3) Subsection (1) shall not apply in the case of any person engaged in remunerative full-time work where the earning power of such person is, by reason of any physical or mental disability, substantially reduced in comparison with the earning power of other persons engaged in similar work.

GENERAL NOTE

The prohibition on paying the allowance to persons engaged in remunerative full-time work is not as absolute as it first appears because of the exceptional need and urgency payments in sections 181 and 182.

The enabling provisions of subsection (2) have been exercised to allow persons who take up full-time employment to continue to be eligible for the allowance for a 15-day period (wages often being withheld by an employer until the end of the second week of employment, or later). The guidelines indicate that a 30-hour week is the threshold for deciding what is or is not full-time employment. Subsection (3) allows payment to be made to disabled persons with reduced earning capacity and the power is exercised in favour of persons on rehabilitation training or persons who are self employed "in a small way".

STATUTORY INSTRUMENT
S.I. No. 168 of 1977.

Persons affected by trade disputes

174.—(1) In any case where, by reason of a stoppage of work due to a trade dispute at his place of employment, a person is without employment for any period during which the stoppage continues, and such person has not, during that stoppage, become *bona fide* employed elsewhere in the occupation which he usually follows, or has not become regularly engaged in some other occupation, his needs for that period shall be disregarded for the purpose of ascertaining his entitlement to supplementary welfare allowance except in so far as such needs include the need to provide for his adult or child dependants.

(2) Subsection (1) shall not apply to any person who is not participating in or directly interested in the trade dispute which caused the stoppage of work.

(3) In this section, "place of employment" in relation to any person, means the factory, workshop, farm or other premises or place at which he was employed, but, where separate branches of work which are commonly carried on as separate businesses in separate premises or at separate places are in any case carried on in separate departments on the same premises or at the same place, each of those departments shall, for the purposes of this section, be deemed to be a separate factory or workshop or farm or separate premises or a separate place, as the case may be.

GENERAL NOTE

The trade dispute disqualification prevents the allowance from being payable in respect of a person caught by the disqualification, although child and adult dependant rates are payable in respect of a striker. Again, discretionary payments under sections 181 and 182 are payable in hardship cases. For an extensive discussion of the trade dispute disqualification, see the General Note to section 47, unemployment benefit.

Note that the Social Welfare Tribunal has no jurisdiction in relation to supplementary welfare allowance: section 274 of this Act.

Administration

175.—(1) Subject to the general direction and control of the Minister, each health board shall, in respect of its functional area, be responsible for the administration of the functions relating to supplementary welfare allowance and other functions performable under this Chapter.

(2) Every health board shall grant to every person in its functional area who is eligible therefor such supplementary welfare allowance as is determined, in accordance with this Chapter, to be due to such person.

(3) Any doubt or dispute as to which health board shall be responsible for the provision of supplementary welfare allowance to a particular person or to persons of a particular class shall be decided by the Minister.

GENERAL NOTE

This section gives the Minister for Social Welfare overall supervisory responsibility in respect of supplementary welfare allowance, with administrative responsibility devolving to each health board in respect of its functional area, the health board having a statutory duty to grant an allowance to eligible persons resident in that functional area.

The Commission on Social Welfare was very critical of the organisational structure of income maintenance schemes provided by health boards and the Department of Health, suggesting that these should be transferred to the Department of Social Welfare. This recommendation has not been acted upon. There is however a supplementary welfare allowance policy unit within the Department of Social Welfare.

Conditions for grant of supplementary welfare allowance

176.—(1) A health board may, subject to regulations made by the Minister under section 188, determine that a person shall not be entitled to supplementary welfare allowance unless—
  (a) he is registered for employment in such manner as the Minister may prescribe, and

27–234

(b) he makes application for any statutory or other benefits or assistance to which he may be entitled including such benefits or assistance from countries other than the State.

GENERAL NOTE

This is a permissive provision which enables a health board to require persons to register for employment as a condition of entitlement. Some evidence exists in the form of the judgment in *Dennehy v. Minister for Social Welfare* H.C. Unrep., July 25, 1985, to suggest that in cases of one-parent families this condition is not imposed if the single parent finds that household commitments make employment unrealistic. Statutory Instrument No. 168 of 1977 exempts persons over 66 and those incapable of work due to illness or disablement.

Because supplementary welfare is seen as a scheme of last resort, the health boards require applicants to explore all other entitlements before the allowance will be payable. However, where another payment or pension is payable from another state at rates which fall below Irish scale rates (*e.g.* U.K. old age pensions), the allowance will be payable so as to bring that person's income up to the scheduled rate of supplementary welfare allowance.

Calculation of supplementary welfare allowance

177.—(1) The amount of supplementary welfare allowance to which a person is entitled shall be the amount by which his means fall short of his needs, and for the purpose of ascertaining that amount—

(a) the weekly needs of a person shall, subject to any payment pursuant to section 179, be taken to be—
  (i) in the case of a person who has no means, the amount calculated in accordance with section 178, or
  (ii) in the case of a person who has means, the amount calculated in accordance with section 178 which would be appropriate in his case if he had no means, reduced by £1 per week for every £1 of his weekly means,
(b) the weekly means of any person for the purpose of ascertaining his entitlement to supplementary welfare allowance shall be calculated in accordance with the Rules contained in Part III of the Third Schedule.
  Provided that the amount so calculated shall be rounded up to the nearest £1 where it is a multiple of 50p but not also a multiple of £1 and shall be rounded to the nearest £1 where it is not a multiple of 50p or £1. [1994 Act, section 30]

(2) In calculating the amount of supplementary welfare allowance payable to any person, the following provisions shall apply—

(a) where—
  (i) a husband and wife, or
  (ii) a man and woman who are not married to each other but are cohabiting as husband and wife,
  are members of the same household, their needs and means shall be aggregated and shall be regarded as the needs and means of the claimant;
(b) in the case of a person with a child dependant his needs shall be taken to include the needs of that child dependant;
(c) where the needs of any person are taken into account in determining the entitlement of any other person to supplementary welfare allowance, only such other person shall be entitled to an allowance.

GENERAL NOTE

Subsection (1)

This subsection directs that the means test to be applied in respect of supplementary welfare allowance is that contained in Part III of the Third Schedule.

Subsection (2)

This subsection provides that where married or cohabiting couples are part of the same household, their needs and means are to be aggregated and treated as those of the claimant.

A similar aggregation occurs in relation to the needs of a child dependant. Subsection (2)(c) prevents a person whose needs have been taken into account in calculating another person's entitlement from being able to claim a separate allowance.

Weekly amounts of supplementary welfare allowance for persons of no means

178.—(1) In the case of a person who has no means as determined by this Chapter and subject to any payment pursuant to section 179, the weekly amount of supplementary welfare allowance payable shall be as set out in column (2) of Part I of the Fourth Schedule, increased by—

    (a) the amount set out in column (3) of that Part for any period during which the beneficiary has an adult dependant, and

    (b) the appropriate amount set out in column (4) of that Part in respect of each child dependant.

(2) For the purposes of this section, the definition of adult dependant in section 170 and column (4) of Part I of the Fourth Schedule shall be construed as if "child dependant" were substituted for "qualified child".

GENERAL NOTE

This section sets out the scheduled rate of payment for a claimant who has no means and makes provision for adult dependant and child dependant additions. "Adult dependant" and "child dependant" are defined in section 170.

Additions to weekly amount of supplementary welfare allowance and other income

179.—(1) Where the weekly amount of supplementary welfare allowance, if any, payable to a person pursuant to section 177, and any other income, including any payment under this Act or under any other statute, of that person, is not sufficient to meet his needs, then—

    (a) in any case where that person is in receipt of supplementary welfare allowance, the weekly amount of such allowance payable to that person may, subject to this section, be increased, or

    (b) in any other case, a weekly payment of supplementary welfare allowance may be made, subject to this section, to supplement that person's other income.

(2) The Minister may prescribe—

    (a) the circumstances under which a payment may be made to any person pursuant to subsection (1), and

    (b) the amounts of payments to be made either generally or in relation to a particular class of persons.

(3) Regulations under subsection (2) may provide for the granting of allowances in kind in relation to specified needs and for all matters ancillary to and consequent on the provision of such allowances.

GENERAL NOTE

The flexibility of payment which makes supplementary welfare allowance significantly different to other income maintenance schemes is largely illustrated by these provisions. Because of the "fire brigade" nature of the allowance, that is, it is a scheme to be used in emergencies and as a matter of last resort, the allowance may be payable to persons who are already in receipt of income in the form of social welfare payments including supplementary welfare allowance at scheduled rates.

In fixing supplementary welfare allowance payments at the inception of the scheme, it was decided to peg the allowance at a lower rate than that payable for other insurance and assistance payments and no really scientific analysis was made to determine whether this rate, or indeed other welfare rates, provided adequate income levels. While significant steps have been taken since then, particularly by raising supplementary welfare payments to short-term unemployment assistance levels, successive governments have not addressed the question of adequacy, particularly when a claimant has exceptional dietary, heating or medical needs, or the claimant has foreseeable needs such as mortgage or rental costs. Despite the recommendations of the Commission on Social Welfare which recommended substantial changes, including provision for a national housing benefit, supplementary welfare allowance still provides for these needs.

Article 6 of S.I. No. 168 of 1977, as amended, makes provision for four kinds of allowance increases:

    (i) for rental or mortgage costs which are in excess of a minimum figure, currently set at £6 or £4.50 per week by S.I. No. 231 of 1994, depending on status;

    (ii) persons living alone or only with dependants who have, by reason of ill-health or infirmity, exceptional heating requirements;

    (iii) persons who have special dietary needs due to a health condition;

    (iv) where, in certain other exceptional needs circumstances, the health board determine that the weekly payment is not sufficient to meet that person's needs.

Of these payments, the regulations provide that where rented accommodation is shared by persons other than dependants, rent can be calculated by reducing the rent by reference to that other person's reasonable share of this expense. The heating addition can specifically be in kind. The regulations also provide that persons in institutions can receive the rental allowance as well as payments for ongoing financial commitments and for personal expenses. There is a statutory limit on the maximum amount that can be paid without the consent of the Minister in the rent supplement which is currently set at £45 per week (S.I. No. 220 of 1992).

The use of these powers has proved to be a very controversial element in the supplementary welfare scheme, particularly when the rental allowance and the miscellaneous power in (iv) above are concerned. The volume of claims between 1977 and 1985 increased by 51.2 per cent. Most of the 8,821 persons in receipt of supplements on March 31, 1985 were obtaining rent supplements (66 per cent) with 27 per cent being for miscellaneous needs such as school uniforms for children and the like.

Allowances in kind

180.—(1) Whenever it appears to a health board that by reason of exceptional circumstances the needs of a person can best be met by the provision of goods or services instead of the whole or part of any payment to which he would otherwise be entitled under this Chapter, the health board may determine that such goods or services be provided for him under arrangements made by the board.

(2) In making a determination under this section to meet sudden and urgent need, the health board may dispense with inquiry into means or other circumstances and with compliance with any regulations made under this Chapter.

(3) In relation to any goods or services provided by a health board pursuant to subsection (1), references in this Chapter to the amount of supplementary welfare allowances shall be deemed to be references to the value of the goods or services so provided.

GENERAL NOTE

This section clarifies the discretionary power to provide the allowance in cash or kind by dispensing with a means test where the payment is most appropriately dealt with in kind.

Power to make single payment for exceptional need

181.—A health board may, in any case where it considers it reasonable, having regard to all the circumstances of the case, so to do, determine that supplementary welfare allowance shall be paid to a person by way of a single payment to meet an exceptional need.

GENERAL NOTE

In contradistinction to the preceding section, this section allows a single payment to be made in respect of exceptional needs. Because of the difficulties of budgeting on a low income, many social welfare claimants have found it necessary to avail of this provision at some stage. The Commission on Social Welfare's snapshot of the supplementary welfare allowance population as of March 31, 1985 produced the following table:

Exceptional Needs	Number	%
Electricity	879	45.8
Gas	116	6.0
Rent	69	3.6
Clothing	366	19.1
Furniture	81	4.2
Funerals	66	3.4
Other	343	17.9
	1.920	100.0

The Commission noted substantial criticism of the discretionary payments structures in place with regard to this section and the preceding one and recommended that the problem should be addressed by payment structure improvements in respect of levels of assistance payment as well as better long-term electricity and fuel allowances which would help to address this problem. There has been a significant development in respect of household budgeting particularly for those on short-term unemployment payments. Section 54 of the 1991 Act (now section 240 of the 1993 Consolidation) amends directed payments procedure so as to allow bills, with the consent of the claimant, to be met by way of direct payment from social welfare entitlements.

Grant of supplementary welfare allowance in cases of urgency

182.—(1) Nothing in section 172, 173 or 174 shall prevent the payment of supplementary welfare allowance in an urgent case and, in determining whether an allowance is payable by virtue of this section and the amount or nature of the allowance, the health board shall not be bound by anything contained in sections 176 to 179 and Part III of the Third Schedule or in any regulations made under this Chapter which appears to it inappropriate in the circumstances of the case.

(2) Where pursuant to subsection (1) supplementary welfare allowance is paid to a person who is engaged in remunerative full-time work, a health board may, if it is satisfied that in all the circumstances of the case it would be equitable so to do, determine that the whole or part of the allowance so paid shall be recoverable from the person to whom it is paid.

GENERAL NOTE

This discretionary power to meet the needs of a person in emergency situations—domestic fire or flood and theft of wages are examples—is untrammelled by any means test or other provisions such as the trade dispute disqualification.

It is understood that the power to recoup payments is rarely used.

Supplementary welfare allowance granted to persons in receipt of certain health board payments

183.—Where—

(a) in respect of any period a health board has granted supplementary welfare allowance to or in respect of a person and disabled person's maintenance allowance or infectious diseases maintenance allowance, including any increase thereof, subsequently becomes payable to or in respect of that person in respect of the period (or part thereof) for which supplementary welfare allowance was paid, and

(b) such supplementary welfare allowance is in excess of the amount which would have been granted to or in respect of such person if either of the said allowances, including any increase thereof, had been paid during such period,

such excess supplementary welfare allowance shall be treated as payment on account of the said allowances.

GENERAL NOTE

This provision was inserted into the legislation by the 1990 Act. The section allows a health board which has paid supplementary welfare allowance to a claimant who subsequently becomes entitled to disabled persons maintenance allowance or infectious diseases maintenance allowance, for all or part of the same period of time, to treat the overlapping supplementary welfare allowance payment to be a payment on account of the disabled person's maintenance allowance or infectious diseases maintenance allowance. Overlapping claims of this kind are common because supplementary allowance is payable often as an "emergency" or "fire brigade" payment.

Recoupment of supplementary welfare allowance

184.—Where—
(a) in respect of any period a health board has granted supplementary welfare allowance to or in respect of a person who, though entitled to any other benefit, pension, assistance, allowance or supplement under this Act (in this section referred to as "relevant payment"), is not in receipt of such relevant payment, and
(b) such supplementary welfare allowance is in excess of the amount which would have been granted to that person if he had been in receipt of such relevant payment, and
(c) the health board has certified to the Minister the amount (in this section referred to as "the excess") so paid in excess in respect of the said period by such health board,

the Minister may reduce any such benefit, pension, assistance, allowance or supplement, which is or may become payable to such person during the relevant continuous period of entitlement to the said benefit, pension, assistance, allowance or supplement, by the amount of the excess and such amount shall be treated as having been paid on account of the relevant payment.

GENERAL NOTE

This is a general recoupment provision in respect of the payment of supplementary welfare allowance by a health board to a claimant who later becomes entitled to a social welfare benefit, pension, assistance, allowance or supplement. The earlier supplementary welfare allowance is deemed to have been paid on account.

Recoupement of supplementary welfare allowance

184A.—Where—
(a) in respect of any period a health board has granted supplementary welfare allowance to or in respect of a person who, though entitled under the legislation of a Member State (other than the State) to a social security payment (in this section referred to as 'the relevant payment'), is not in receipt of such payment, and
(b) such supplementary welfare allowance is in excess of the amount which would have been granted to that person if he had been in receipt of the relevant payment, and
(c) the health board has certified to the competent institution of the relevant Member State the amount of supplementary welfare

allowance in excess of which he would have been entitled (in this section referred to as 'the excess') in respect of the said period by such health board,

the health board may request the said institution to deduct the amount of the excess from the relevant payment. [1995 Act, section 21]

GENERAL NOTE

The recoupement provisions in section 184 of the Social Welfare (Consolidation) Act, 1993 are hereby broadened to include cases where supplementary welfare allowance is payable whilst the claimant awaits payment of social security by another E.U. State. The new section 184A envisages that where the allowance is payable at a higher rate and exceeds the non-Irish social security payment, the difference between the two can be recouped by requesting the competent institution of the other State (*e.g.* the U.K. Department of Social Security) to pay over the excess to the relevant Irish health board. Many U.K. claimants resident in Ireland receive higher rates of supplementary welfare allowance while their U.K. claims are being processed. This mechanism allows the Irish Exchequer to obtain some reimbursement, although once the claim is processed in the other State an Irish resident can top up any social security payments which fall below supplementary welfare allowance scale rates by claiming a supplementary welfare allowance from a health board.

Arrangements for burials

185.—(1) A health board may provide for the burial of any of the following persons—

(a) a person who died within the functional area of the health board and in respect of whose burial suitable arrangements are not otherwise being made,

(b) a person who has been drowned and cast ashore within its functional area or who has otherwise perished and been found dead within that area and (in either case) whose body has not been claimed for burial.

(2) A health board may, in any case in which it thinks proper, bring into and bury in its functional area the body of a person eligible for supplementary welfare allowance who has died outside such functional area.

(3) A health board may defray all expenses necessarily incurred in the burial under this section of a person or in the bringing of the body of a person into its functional area for burial.

(4) Where a health board incurs under this section expenses in relation to the body of a deceased person, it may obtain repayment of such expenses from the estate of the deceased person or from any person who was liable to maintain the deceased person immediately before his death.

GENERAL NOTE

The power to arrange for the burial of destitute persons was an essential function of the old poor law guardians and this power is carried forward into Irish social welfare law. Note that under section 181 members of a decreased person's family were often able to obtain financial help to arrange a funeral for a family member.

Estimates of income and expenditure in respect of supplementary welfare allowance

186.—A health board shall submit estimates of income and expenditure in respect of supplementary welfare allowance to the Minister in such form, at such times and in relation to such periods as the Minister, with the consent of the Minister for Health, may direct and shall also furnish the Minister with any information he requires in relation to such estimates.

GENERAL NOTE

The power to call upon the health boards to submit estimates of income and expenditure is an essential feature of the rôle of the Minister for Social Welfare to supervise the actions of the health boards in providing supplementary welfare allowance.

Financing of health board expenditure

187.—(1) Every local authority which, immediately before the 1st day of July, 1977, was a public assistance authority shall pay to the health board in whose functional area the functional area of the local authority is included in respect of each year a sum representing—

(a) the total expenditure by such local authority on home assistance in the year ending on the 31st day of December, 1975, and

(b) a proportion of 40 per cent. of the amount by which the total expenditure by all health boards on supplementary welfare allowance in the year for which payment is due exceeds the total expenditure by all local authorities on home assistance in the year ending on the 31st day of December, 1975, the said proportion of 40 per cent. payable by such authority being that which the total expenditure on home assistance by that authority in the year ending on the 31st day of December, 1975, bears to the total expenditure by all local authorities on such assistance in that year.

(2) In determining the amount of expenditure on home assistance and supplementary welfare allowance for the purposes of subsection (1), the costs of administration shall be excluded.

(3) The expenditure of a health board on the administration of supplementary welfare allowance shall be paid by the local authorities which, immediately before the 1st day of July, 1977, were public assistance authorities having their functional areas in the functional area of the health board.

(4) Section 32 of the Health Act, 1970, which relates to the agreement or, the absence of agreement, the determination of the manner of the sharing of contributions between local authorities, shall with any necessary modifications apply to payments under subsection (3) in like manner as it applies to contributions under the said section 32.

(5) The Minister may by regulations specify the manner in which and the times at which payments shall be made by local authorities to health boards under subsection (1) and, where appropriate, any such regulations may provide for interim payments calculated in accordance with estimates furnished by a health board pursuant to section 186.

(6) (a) Where any sum is due and payable under this Chapter to a health board by a local authority, the amount of that sum may be deducted from any money payable to that local authority from funds provided by the Oireachtas for any purpose whatsoever.

(b) Every amount deducted pursuant to paragraph (a) shall be paid to the health board concerned and shall be credited in the accounts of that health board as a payment by the local authority concerned of the sum in respect of which the amount was so deducted.

(7) References to supplementary welfare allowance in this section shall be construed as including reference to the cost of burials pursuant to section 185.

(8) The Minister shall, out of moneys provided by the Oireachtas, make grants to health boards to defray so much of their expenditure on supplementary welfare allowance and costs of administration of that allowance as is not met by income under this section.

(9) Notwithstanding any other provision of this section—

(a) the total amount to be paid under subsection (1) by all local authorities referred to in that subsection in respect of each of the years ending on the 31st day of December, 1981, the 31st day of December, 1982, the 31st day of December, 1983, the 31st day of December, 1984, and the 31st day of December, 1985, and in respect of no other year, shall be such amount as may be prescribed for each such year by the Minister, after consultation with the Minister for the Environment, and the proportion of those amounts payable by each such local authority in respect of each such year shall be that which the total expenditure on home assistance in the year ending on the 31st day of December, 1975, bears to the total expenditure by all local authorities referred to in subsection (1) on home assistance in that year;

(b) the amount payable under subsection (3) by a local authority referred to in that subsection in respect of each of the years ending on the 31st day of December, 1982, the 31st day of December, 1983, the 31st day of December, 1984, and the 31st day of December, 1985, and in respect of no other year shall not exceed such amount as may be prescribed for that year by the Minister, after consultation with the Minister for the Environment and with the consent of the Minister for Finance.

(10) The Minister shall, out of moneys provided by the Oireachtas, make grants to health boards to defray all expenditure (including the costs of administration) of those boards on supplementary welfare allowance in the year ending on the 31st day of December, 1986, and in each year thereafter, and, accordingly, so much of the preceding subsections of this section, other than subsection (9), as refer to the financing of health board expenditure on supplementary welfare allowance shall, on or after the 27th day of March, 1986, cease to have effect.

GENERAL NOTE

Because of the historical link between the poor law, a system based upon local taxes collected and disbursed locally, and the 1975 supplementary welfare allowance programme, the 1975 legislation envisaged that funding would be provided from a mixture of local authority funding and funds from the Oireachtas. Even prior to the reforms effected in the mid-1980s, sharing the costs of payments and administration between the Exchequer and the local authorities, was long regarded as unsatisfactory. The abolition of rates levied on residential properties severely affected the capacity of local authorities to meet their share of the burden and in the Social Welfare Act, 1983, s.15, the Government made provision for changes to be made in the method of finance. For the year ended December 1985 the Government, by statutory instrument, provided a maximum amount that each local authority would be required to disburse in order to meet the local authority's share of the cost. Article 2 of the Social Welfare (Supplementary Welfare Allowances) Regulations, 1985 (S.I. No. 443 of 1985) fixed the total amount at £14,100,000. Further changes were made in section 16 of the 1980 Act.

The section provided that the full costs, including the cost of administration would be borne by the Exchequer by way of an annual Social Welfare Vote, as and from January 1, 1986. The Commission on Social welfare later in 1986 approved the movement towards direct Exchequer funding: p. 367–8.

Regulations

188.—(1) The Minister may make regulations for any purpose in relation to which regulations are provided for by any of the provisions of this Chapter.

(2) Without prejudice to any specific provision in this Chapter, any regulations made under this Chapter may contain such incidental or supplementary provisions as may appear to the Minister to be expedient for the purposes of the regulations.

STATUTORY INSTRUMENTS

Regulations in force are:
    S.I. No. 168 of 1977.
    S.I. No. 443 of 1985

S.I. No. 220 of 1992
S.I. No. 214 of 1994
S.I. No. 231 of 1994

Transfer of certain property

189.—(1) All property transferred by section 22 of the Social Welfare (Supplementary Welfare Allowances) Act, 1975, to a health board and which, immediately before the 1st day of July, 1977, was standing in the book of any bank or was registered in the books of any bank, corporation or company in the name of a public assistance authority shall, on the request of the health board, be transferred in the books by the bank, corporation or company into the name of the health board.

(2) Every chose-in-action transferred by the said section 22 to a health board may be sued on, recovered or enforced by the health board in its own name and it shall not be necessary for the board to give notice to the person bound by the chose-in-action of the transfer effected by that section.

(3) Every bond, guarantee or other security of a continuing character made or given by a public assistance authority in pursuance of its functions under the Act of 1939 to another person, or by any person to a public assistance authority in connection with those functions, which was in force immediately before the 1st day of July, 1977, and every contract or agreement in writing in connection with the said functions made between a public assistance authority and another person which was not fully executed and completed before that date shall be construed and have effect as if the name of the health board in whose functional area the functional area of the public assistance authority is included were substituted therein for the name of the public assistance authority, and the security, contract or agreement shall be enforceable by or against the health board accordingly.

GENERAL NOTE

This section is a transitional measure which directs that action assets and liabilities standing in the name of a public assistance authority should, as from commencement of the supplementary allowance scheme, be transferred to the name of the relevant health board.

Transfer of certain officers and enforceability of contracts

190.—(1) Any question arising as to whether a particular officer or officers of a particular class of a public assistance authority was or were transferred to a health board pursuant to section 23 of the Social Welfare (Supplementary Welfare Allowances) Act, 1975, shall be referred to and decided by the Minister after consultation with the Minister for Health or the Minister for the Environment, whichever is appropriate, and, if it is decided that any such officer was so transferred, then, for the purpose of any enactment relating to superannuation, his office under the public assistance authority shall be deemed not to have been abolished.

(2) Every contract of service, express or implied, which—

(a) was made between a public assistance authority and any person who was not an officer of that authority but was a person to be transferred to a health board pursuant to the said section 23, and

(b) was continued in force by subsection (6) of that section and was in force immediately before the 24th day of February, 1981,

shall continue in force and shall continue to be construed and have effect as if the health board were substituted therein for the public assistance authority, and every such contract shall be enforceable by or against the health board accordingly.

(3) Any question arising in relation to subsection (2) as to whether a particular person or persons of a particular class was or were a person or

persons to be transferred pursuant to the said section 23 shall be referred to and decided by the Minister after consultation with the Minister for Health or the Minister for the Environment, whichever is appropriate.

GENERAL NOTE

This provision continues the contracts of employment and powers and functions of officers who previously administered home assistance on behalf of a local authority by substituting the health board for the local authority.

Transitional provisions

191.—(1) The Minister may by regulations make, in respect of any statute, order or regulation in force on the 1st day of July, 1977, and relating to any matter or thing dealt with or affected by this Chapter, any adaptation or modification which appears to him to be necessary to enable such statute, order or regulation to have effect in conformity with this Chapter.

(2) Any proceedings for the recovery of a sum which, if the Social Welfare (Supplementary Welfare Allowances) Act, 1975, had not been passed, could have been taken by a public assistance authority may be taken by the health board in whose functional area the functional area of the public assistance authority was included immediately before the 1st day of July, 1977.

(3) Any proceedings for the enforcement, variation or revocation of an order under section 29 of the Act of 1939 for the payment of money which by virtue of section 189 is payable to a health board may be brought and maintained by the health board.

GENERAL NOTE

See S.I. No. 168 of 1977 (Schedule).

PART IV

CHILD BENEFIT

Qualified child

192.—(1) A child shall be a qualified child (in this Part referred to as "a qualified child") for the purposes of child benefit if—
(a) he is under the age of 16 years, or
(b) having attained the age of 16 years he is under the age of 19 years and—
   (i) is receiving full-time education, the circumstances of which shall be specified in regulations, or
   (ii) is, by reason of physical or mental infirmity, incapable of self-support and likely to remain so incapable for a prolonged period, and
(c) he is ordinarily resident in the State, and
(d) he is not detained in a reformatory or an industrial school and is not undergoing imprisonment or detention in legal custody.

(2) Notwithstanding subsection (1), a child who resides with a qualified person and such person's spouse while the qualified person or his spouse

(being a member of the Defence Forces or the civil service of the Government or the State) is in the service, outside the State, of the Government, the State or an international organisation, shall be a qualified child for the purposes of this Part. [1995 Act section 5]

GENERAL NOTE

Child benefit is a universal, non-means tested payment which is payable to the person with whom a qualified child normally resides.

Subsection (1)

This subsection defines a qualified child as someone who is aged under 16 (or if aged 16, 17 or 18 is in full-time education or incapable of self-support by reason of physical or mental infirmity), is ordinarily resident in the state and is not detained in a reformatory, industrial school, or in legal custody.

Subsection (2)

The ordinary resident within the State requirement has been relaxed since 1984 in respect of a child who resides with "a qualified person" (generally that child's mother) while such "qualified person" is outside the State. The qualified person must be a member of the Defence Forces or a civil servant deployed abroad by the Government, the State or an international organisation. International organisation is nowhere defined in the Social Welfare Acts. It is also Department practice to pay child benefit in respect of children resident outside the State, as a matter of Community law, when the parent is resident in another member state but is paying Irish social insurance contributions.

The amendments made by the 1995 Act to section 192(2) of the Social Welfare (Consolidation) Act, 1993 will allow child benefit to be payable while a member of the Defence Forces or a Civil Servant's spouse or partner is employed as such outside the State. Prior to this amendment, it was only when the qualified person was so employed that child benefit could be payable while the child was outside the State.

The Minister stated that the child benefit reforms implemented by this section represent a first step in the overhaul of child dependant provisions. This universal payment will be accompanied by a child benefit supplement which will be payable to all families whose income falls below a certain level, such as those in receipt of social welfare payments, or employment and self-employment earnings. It is intended that these payments will supercede family income supplements and child dependency allowances for social welfare recipients and they give effect to a commitment made in the Coalition Programme, *A Government for Renewal.* The issue of taxation of child benefits arose in the Seanad although the Minister for State, Mr Duncan, indicated that decisions of this kind had not been made (142 *Seanad Debates* Cols. 1681–1682).

Qualified person

193.—(1) A person with whom a qualified child normally resides shall be qualified for child benefit in respect of that child and is in this Part referred to as "a qualified person".

(2) For the purpose of subsection (1)—

(a) the Minister may make rules for determining with whom a qualified child shall be regarded as normally residing,

(b) a qualified child shall not be regarded as normally residing with more than one person, and

(c) where a qualified child is resident in an institution and contributions are made towards the cost of his maintenance in that institution, he shall be regarded as normally residing with the person with whom in accordance with the rules made under paragraph (a) he would be determined to be normally residing if he were not resident in an institution but, where the person with whom he would thus be regarded as normally residing has abandoned or deserted the child, the child shall be regarded as normally residing with the head of the household of which he would normally be a member if he were not resident in an institution.

GENERAL NOTE

This section sets out the criteria by which the person entitled to claim child benefit is to be identified. The rules which are referred to in subsection (1)(a) are found in S.I. No. 367 of

1986. One of the substantial changes made in 1986 was not only to substitute child benefit for the old children's allowance and tax allowance but also to weigh the balance of entitlement in favour of the mother of the qualified child as distinct from the father of that child. Even where the parents, or step-parents of the child are separated, payment will be made to the mother if the child is resident with, or in the custody of the mother. If the child is not living with either parent or a step-parent, *e.g.* is at boarding school or placed in some institutional care requiring payment of contributions, then the father will be the qualified person in most cases. In cases of *de facto* custody, the woman, or, in the absence of such a woman, the man who heads the household will be the qualified person.

Amounts of child benefit

194.—(1) Subject to this Act, a person who is qualified for child benefit shall, so long as he remains so qualified, be paid out of moneys provided by the Oireachtas a monthly benefit of the amount set out in column (1) of Part III of the Fourth Schedule in respect of each of the first 2 qualified children and, in addition, the amount set out in column (2) of that Part in respect of each qualified child (if any) in excess of 2. [1994 Act, section 5].

(2) Notwithstanding anything in this Part, the monthly benefit payable to a qualified person in respect of a qualified child whose birth was part of a multiple birth of 3 or more children of whom not less than 3 remain qualified shall be double the benefit that would have been payable if this subsection had not been enacted.

(3) Subject to this Act, a person who is qualified for child benefit shall be paid a grant in accordance with subsection (4) in respect of 2 or more qualified children where the birth of each child was part of the same multiple birth.

(4) The amount of the grant payable in accordance with subsection (3) shall be £200 if the qualified children are 2 in number, £300 where they are 3 in number and £400 if they exceed 3 in number.

(5) Subsection (3) of this section shall apply in the case of any multiple birth occurring on or after the 1st day of July, 1993.

(6) A grant under subsection (3) shall become payable on the date of birth of the last-born of the qualified children of the multiple birth.

(7) Payment of a grant under subsection (3) shall be in addition to any child benefit payable by way of a monthly benefit under this Part in respect of the children concerned.

GENERAL NOTE

Subsection (1)

Child benefit is a monthly benefit, payable under the Fourth Schedule (inserted by the 1994 Act) at £20 monthly for each of the first two children, and at £25 monthly for each child in excess of two.

As part of the focus on improving family benefits, the 1995 Act marks a very significant shift towards providing (as a universal payment) child benefit at greatly enhanced rates. The monthly rate is increased by £7 with effect from September 1, 1995. So as from that date each of the first two children will attract a child benefit of £27, while the amount for each child in excess of two will be £32. The cost of this measure is estimated at more than £100 million (45 *Dáil Debates* Col. 156).

Subsection (2)

The monthly benefit is doubled in respect of multiple births of triplets, or any higher number of children, as long as at least three children are classified as qualified children.

Subsections (3) (4) and (5)

An additional grant in respect of multiple births is payable at the rate of £200 for twins, £300 for triplets and £600 for a birth of four or more children, when the birth occurs on or after July 1, 1993.

Exclusion of child benefit for superannuation or pension purposes

195.—Income from child benefit shall not be reckoned for the purpose of any abatement provisions in any enactment relating to superannuation or pensions.

GENERAL NOTE

Child benefit is excluded from any abatement provisions in respect of statutory superannuation or pensions.

Payments to persons absent from State

196.—Where a qualified person is for the time being absent from the State, an application on his behalf in respect of child benefit may be accepted from such person as the Minister thinks fit.

GENERAL NOTE

This gives the Minister the power to determine if the application made on behalf of a qualified person while absent from the state is an appropriate one or not.

PART V

FAMILY INCOME SUPPLEMENT

Interpretation

197.—In this Part—

"child", in relation to a family, means a qualified child as defined in section 2(3) who normally resides with that family;

"family" means—

    (a) a person who is engaged in remunerative full-time employment as an employee,

    (b) where such person is living with or wholly or mainly maintaining his or her spouse, that spouse, and [1995 No. 2 Act, section 9]

    (c) a child or children;

"family income supplement" shall be construed in accordance with section 198;

"spouse" includes—

    (a) a party to a marriage that has been dissolved, being a dissolution that is recognised as valid in the State, or

    (b) a man and woman who are not married to each other but are cohabiting as husband and wife; [1995 No. 2 Act, section 9]

"weekly family income" means, subject to regulations under section 202, the amount of income received in a week by a family, less any income of a person who in respect of that family is a child.

GENERAL NOTE

Historical introduction

Family Income Support (F.I.S.) was introduced in 1984 in order to provide persons in low-paid employment with an additional incentive to remaining in employment, or to provide unemployed persons with additional income if they should take up low-paid work, instead of remaining on social welfare payments. When initially introduced, it was anticipated that some 35,000 families would benefit but low take-up rates have since been explained as being due to lack of adequate publicity about F.I.S. as well as an initial overestimate of those who would be eligible for F.I.S. Since 1984 there have been successive legislative amendments to broaden the base of the scheme, *e.g.* by broadening the definition of family, by improving standard rates and improving the earnings disregards. While critics of F.I.S. schemes both in the U.K. and Ireland have complained that these schemes have the unfortunate effect of actually locking persons deeper into the social welfare system, by facilitating employers who pay low wages in the knowledge that the state will, in effect, provide a wage subsidy, the Commission on Social Welfare came out in favour of expanding and improving F.I.S.

Family. The claimant will be able to obtain F.I.S. if he or she is in remunerative full-time employment, defined in S.I. No. 279 of 1991 as employment which is expected to last for six months at least and consist of 20 working hours per week. Married couples or cohabiting couples can combine their hours for this purpose under the provisions of Article 7. This definition goes on to specify that if a married couple are living together or, if apart, the claimant is wholly or mainly maintaining the spouse, the spouse is part of the family unit for F.I.S. purposes. If the couple are cohabiting, then the partner of the claimant is a member of the family. Dependant children normally residing with the claimant are also part of the family unit. While a one-parent family can claim F.I.S., there must be one dependant child in the family unit.

The 1995 (No. 2) Act

As a result of the 1995 (No. 2) Act, which deleted a reference to couples (which was necessary due to the fact that the family unit referred to in the legislation required the parties to be married to each other) the law has been simplified and broadened. A spouse is now defined so as to include a cohabiting party and also a person who has been divorced from his or her spouse. Thus, a divorced person who is supporting his or her former spouse is, on that basis, if no other, entitled to claim F.I.S. This will not affect the situation of a person supporting two family units, which, on low pay, is not a likely prospect.

Entitlement to supplement

198.—Subject to this Act, an allowance (in this Act referred to as 'family income supplement') shall be payable out of moneys provided by the Oireachtas in respect of a family where the weekly family income is less than—

(a) in the case of a family which includes only 1 child, £185,
(b) in the case of a family which includes 2 children, £205,
(c) in the case of a family which includes 3 children, £225,
(d) in the case of a family which includes 4 children, £245,
(e) in the case of a family which includes 5 children, £270,
(f) in the case of a family which includes 6 children, £290,
(g) in the case of a family which includes 7 children, £307, or
(h) in the case of a family which includes 8 or more children, £324.

(2) This section came into operation on the 28th day of July, 1994. [1994 Act, section 6]

GENERAL NOTE

It is now an annual practice to increase the income limits within which F.I.S. will be payable. The most recent adjustment was made in Section 6 of the 1994 Act.

The section increases the upper family income limits that determine the availability of family income supplement (F.I.S.) to family units where the principal bread-winner is in full-time employment but is in receipt of low pay. In the case of each family unit the limit is raised by £10 per week. Thus the family income limit for a family with four children will be £245 per week, as from July 28, 1994. The family income limit for a family with eight children will be £324 per week, as from that same date. Family Income Supplement is payable as a supplement to persons in employment, the level of the supplement being payable by reference to income levels and the number of children in the family unit. For example, if the family unit has four children, the upper limit of income if £245 per week. If reckonable earnings are £180, then the supplement payable is 60 per cent of the difference between those figures, *i.e.* £39.

At the Committee Stage in the Seanad, some interesting details about F.I.S. emerged. The scheme has been constantly reputed to be under-subscribed. The Minister indicated that the take-up since September 1993 had increased by 25 per cent, the increase being due to the substantial increase in upper income limits in the Social Welfare (Consolidation) Act, 1993 and the efforts of the Department to publicise F.I.S. in conjunction with employers. The Minister also gave a profile of those claiming F.I.S. Agricultural workers counted for three-and-a-half per cent of recipients, skilled workers in manufacturing 18.8 per cent., labourers and unskilled workers some 43.5 per cent, transport and communications workers 16.4 per cent., clerical workers 4.9 per cent, commerce, insurance and finance 9.4 per cent, and Garda and Defence Forces workers 1.7 per cent and 0.16 per cent respectively. The total cost of F.I.S. is £22 million annually (see 139 *Seanad Debates* Cols. 1556–1563).

Rate of supplement

199.—(1) Subject to this Part, the weekly rate of family income supplement shall be 60 per cent. of the amount by which the weekly family income is less than the amount appropriate in the particular case under section 198.

(2) In calculating the weekly rate of family income supplement pursuant to subsection (1), any fraction of £1 shall be treated as £1 and where the weekly rate so calculated is below a prescribed amount, the supplement shall be payable at the prescribed amount.

GENERAL NOTE

See the preceding General Note for an explanation of how the rate of supplement payable is calculated *vis-à-vis* reckonable earnings.

Period of payment

200.—(1) Family income supplement shall be payable for a period of 52 weeks (or such other period as may be prescribed) beginning on the date on which it is receivable in accordance with regulations and, except where regulations otherwise provide, the weekly rate of family income supplement payable shall not be affected by any change of circumstances during that period.

(2) Where family income supplement is payable in respect of a particular family for any period, no person who was included in that family at the beginning of such period shall be regarded as a member of any other family during that period.

GENERAL NOTE

In order to minimise administrative costs that result from minor adjustments in income levels, F.I.S. is intended to be payable for one year following the initial decision on eligibility. Claims and payments are governed by Part V of S.I. No. 417 of 1994.

Person to whom supplement is payable

201.—Family income supplement shall be payable to the member of the family (other than a child) who is engaged in remunerative full-time employment as an employee or, where there are 2 members of the family so engaged, to the member whose weekly income as calculated for the purposes of family income supplement forms the greater part of the weekly family income as so calculated.

GENERAL NOTE

The supplement is payable to the person engaged in remunerative full-time employment; however, where aggregation of hours has taken place then the person whose income has formed the greater proportion of reckonable weekly income will be the payee.

Regulations

202.—(1) The Minister may make regulations for the purpose of giving effect to this Part.

(2) Regulations under this section may, in particular and without prejudice to the generality of subsection (1)—

    (a) provide for the manner of calculation or estimation of weekly family income;

(b) provide, in calculating or estimating weekly family income, for the disregarding in whole or in part of any amount of that income from any source specified in the regulations;

(c) determine the circumstances in which a person shall be regarded as being engaged in remunerative full-time employment as an employee;

(d) require employers to furnish such information as the Minister may require for the purpose of determining a claim for family income supplement.

(3) The Minister may by regulations vary—

(a) the amounts specified in section 198, and

(b) the percentage rate specified in section 199(1),

but any such variation shall not reduce the amounts or the percentage rate applicable immediately before the commencement of such regulations.

GENERAL NOTE

The regulations in question are S.I. No. 179 of 1991.

Subsection 2(a)

See article 5 of S.I. No. 279 of 1991.

Subsection 2(b)

Particular note should be taken of the income disregarded under these regulations: see article 6:

(a) any sums received by way of death benefit, by way of orphan's pension, orphan's (contributory) allowance, orphan's (non-contributory) pension, carer's allowance, supplementary welfare allowance, child benefit or family income supplement under the Act;

(b) any sums received by way of allowance for domiciliary care of handicapped children under section 61 of the Health Act, 1970;

(c) any sums received by way of an allowance under regulations made under section 23 of the Housing (Private Rented Dwellings) Act, 1982;

(d) any sums from the investment or profitable use of property (not being property personally used or enjoyed by the person concerned);

(e) payments by a health board in respect of a child who is boarded out;

(f) in the case of a qualified applicant under a scheme administered by the Minister for the Gaeltacht and known as Scéim na bhFoghlaimeoirí Gaeilge, any income received under that scheme in respect of a person who is temporarily resident with the qualified applicant, together with any other income received in respect of such temporary resident;

(g) any moneys received from a charitable organisation being a body whose activities are carried on otherwise than for profit (but excluding any public or local authority) where one of whose functions is to assist persons in need by making grants of money to them;

(h) any income arising from employment of a casual rating by a health board as a home help.

Subsection (2)(c)

See article 7 of S.I. No. 279 of 1991.

Subsection (2)(d)

See article 11 of S.I. No. 279 of 1991.

Subsection (3)

No regulations have yet been made.

Receipt of claims

203.—(1) Regulations may provide for treating a claim for family income supplement as having been made on a date earlier than the date on which it is received, where it appears to the Minister that the claimant would have satisfied the conditions for entitlement to family income supplement during that period, but for the receipt by that person of unemployment benefit or unemployment assistance.

(2) Where—

(a) in respect of any period any unemployment benefit or unemployment assistance has been paid to or in respect of a person who, though entitled to family income supplement by virtue of subsection (1), is not in receipt of such supplement, and

(b) such benefit or assistance is in excess of the amount which would have been granted to that person if he had been in receipt of family income supplement,

the Minister may reduce any such supplement which is or may become payable to such person by the amount of the excess and such amount shall be treated as having been paid on account of the family income supplement.

GENERAL NOTE

This section was added by section 50 of the 1992 Act.

The section is a backdating provision applicable to a person who is concurrently working and in receipt of unemployment benefit or assistance. Where the income from employment was at such a low level that family income supplement would have been payable, then any supplement which is or becomes payable can be reduced by the excess amount of benefit or assistance, and the benefit or assistance paid will be treated as having been paid on account of the family income supplement.

Regulations under subsection (1) have not yet been made.

PART VI

GENERAL PROVISIONS RELATING TO SOCIAL INSURANCE, SOCIAL ASSISTANCE AND INSURABILITY

Preliminary

Definitions

204.—Except where otherwise provided, in this Part—

"benefit" means—

(a) any benefit described in section 30(1),
(b) any assistance described in section 118(1),
(c) child benefit, or
(d) family income supplement.

CHAPTER 1

CLAIMS AND PAYMENTS

Claims

205.—(1) It shall be a condition of any person's right to any benefit that he makes a claim therefor in the prescribed manner.

(2) Regulations may provide for disqualifying a person for the receipt of any benefit if he fails to make his claim for such benefit within the prescribed time, but any such regulations may provide for extending,

subject to such conditions as may be prescribed, the time within which the claim may be made.

(3) Regulations may provide for provisionally allowing a claim for benefit before the date on which the claimant will actually become entitled to such benefit, in such manner and subject to such conditions as may be prescribed.

(4) For the purposes of this Act, any claim or notice made or sent by post or by any other method shall be deemed to have been made or given on the date of receipt of such claim or notice by an officer of the Minister.

GENERAL NOTE

The regulations which govern the making of a claim for any benefit, as defined in section 204, are the Social Welfare (Consolidated Payments Provisions) Regulations, 1994 (S.I. No. 417 of 1994).

These regulations consolidate, *inter alia*, the pre-existing statutory instruments on claims and payments except insofar as the pre-existing statutory instruments relate to occupational injuries benefits.

Article 100 of S.I. No. 417 of 1994 require a claim for benefit to be made in the form approved by the Minister or in such other form as is accepted as being sufficient in the circumstances, this latter point being an issue of fact for the judgement of the Department. Article 101 goes on to require the claimant to provide necessary certificates, documents or information for the purpose of deciding the claim and the claimant may be required to attend at an office or other place in order for the claimant to establish eligibility. This provision is interpreted so as to require certain claimants (*e.g.* persons seeking unemployment payments) to attend local exchanges at regular intervals to declare availability for employment and the fact of unemployment.

Article 102 set out the prescribed time for making a claim:
- (a) for old-age (contributory) pension, retirement pension and invalidity pension, between three months prior to entitlement and three months after entitlement to the pension,
- (b) for unemployment benefit or assistance, pre-retirement allowance, old age (non-contributory) pension, blind pension and carer's allowance, the day in respect of which the claim is actually made,
- (c) for survivor's pension, orphan's (contributory) allowance, deserted wife's benefit, widow's (non-contributory) pension, deserted wife's allowance, prisoner's wife's allowance and lone parent's allowance, orphan's (non-contributory) pension, within three months of the day on which entitlement was established (save for the requirement to make a claim),
- (d) for disability benefit, within seven days of commencement of incapacity for work,
- (e) for maternity benefit, on the day of entitlement,
- (f) for death benefit, within three months of the death of the deceased.

Article 103 provides that where a claim for old-age (non-contributory) pension has been made prematurely (*i.e.* within three months prior to entitlement commencing) a provisional entitlement may be establishment to commence on the date of entitlement.

Should the prescribed time-limit for making a claim not be met, *i.e.* the claim is late, a general prohibition against payment for a day outside the actual date of claim operates. However, Article 104 relaxes this thereby allowing old-age (contributory) retirement, invalidity and widow's (contributory) pensions, as well as orphan's (contributory) allowances to be payable in respect of up to six months prior to the date of claim. In relation to unemployment and deserted wife's benefits, as well as most social assistance payments, the disqualification is a total disqualification while disability benefit claimants can establish entitlement for up to seven days prior to the actual claim. Article 9 grants extensions where not making the claim was due to a good reason but the limit is set at six months in all cases.

Article 105 sets out the statutory requirement that claimants furnish documents to establish entitlement and an obligation to inform the Minister of any change in circumstances pertinent to entitlement. Specific provisions are made in respect of giving notice of a change in means for social assistance purposes. The general requirement is to give notice within seven days, except for old-age and blind persons where the period is three months. Non-compliance is an offence: see article 107(2).

S.I. No. 417 of 1994 introduced a new provision whereby a decision on a late application is to be a function of a deciding officer rather than a ministerial function. This allows claimants to appeal to an appeals officer if the claimant is dissatisfied with the decision: see article 105.

STATUTORY INSTRUMENT

S.I. No. 417 of 1994 (Part VI).

Payments

206.—(1) Regulations may provide for—

(a) the time and manner of payment of benefit,

(b) the information and evidence to be furnished by a claimant or beneficiary when applying for payment of benefit, and

(c) in consultation with An Post, the payment of specified benefits through An Post.

(2) Regulations made under this section as to the time of payment of benefit may provide—

(a) notwithstanding anything contained in this Act—

    (i) in the case of specified benefits (other than child benefit), for adjusting the commencement and termination of such benefit, or for changes in the rate of such benefit, so that payments shall not be made in respect of periods less than a week or at different rates for different parts of a week,

    (ii) in the case of child benefit, for adjusting the commencement and termination of such benefit, or for changes in the rate of such benefit, so that payments shall not be made at different rates for different parts of a month,

(b) for extinguishing the right to any sum payable by way of benefit where payment thereof is not obtained within 6 months or such shorter period as may be prescribed from the time at which that sum is receivable in accordance with regulations.

GENERAL NOTE

Subsection (1)

The time and manner of payment of benefit is regulated by Part VI, Chapter 2 of S.I. No. 417 of 1994. Payment is made by way of an order at a post office designated generally by the claimant, by way of a cheque sent to the residence of the claimant, by way of a direct credit transfer to a nominated account, or in cash at a local employment office or post office or by a bank order. As a matter of administrative convenience, certain long-term pensions such as retirement and invalidity pensions are payable weekly in advance on Thursdays, while other payments such as old-age contributory and non-contributory pensions are payable weekly in advance on Fridays: see article 110 of S.I. No. 417 of 1994 for precise details. Short-term payments—unemployment benefit and assistance, disability benefit—are payable weekly in arrears, partly because certification of unemployment or disability must logically follow the event, *i.e.* that the claimant did not work on a particular day.

In relation to proof of entitlement, article 114 of the regulations empowers the Minister to make arrangements requiring proof of entitlement, specifically identity, when cashing an order. Orders remain the property of the Minister and specific provisions are in place to counteract some moneylenders' activities which result in order books being forceably taken from a claimant either to secure or redeem a moneylending contract: apart from section 227 of this Act, the Consumer Credit Bill, 1994 has been amended at Committee Stage to make possession of social welfare documents as part of a moneylending agreement a criminal offence: see "Credit Bill to make holding of documents an offence": *Irish Times* September 7, 1994 [see section 91].

In relation to payments by An Post, article 108(2) of S.I. No. 417 of 1994 is a general provision which adds little detail to the legislation: payments are made via agreed procedures rather than through detailed regulation.

Subsection (2)

There do not appear to be any regulations governing the adjustment of entitlement and termination of benefits for periods of less than a week.

Article 113 of S.I. No. 417 of 1994 extinguishes entitlement when benefit has not been obtained six months after benefit entitlement is established.

STATUTORY INSTRUMENT
S.I. No. 417 of 1994.

Payment to persons other than claimant or beneficiary

207.—(1) Regulations may provide—

(a) for enabling a person to whom benefit is payable to nominate another person to receive that benefit on his behalf,

(b) for enabling a person to be appointed to exercise, on behalf of a claimant or beneficiary who is under 16 years of age or who may be or become unable for the time being to act, any right or power which the claimant or beneficiary may be entitled to exercise under this Act and for authorising a person so appointed to receive and deal with any sum payable by way of benefit on behalf of the claimant or beneficiary,

(c) where it appears to the Minister that the circumstances so warrant, for enabling a person to be appointed to receive and deal with on behalf of a claimant or beneficiary—

(i) in respect of disability benefit, unemployment benefit, old age (contributory) pension, retirement pension, invalidity pension, unemployment assistance, pre-retirement allowance, old age (non-contributory) pension or blind pension, so much of the benefit, pension, assistance or allowance, as the Minister considers reasonable in the circumstances:

Provided that in no case shall the amount to be received and dealt with as aforesaid exceed the total amount payable less the amount payable by virtue of section 34(1), 45(1), 87(1), 91(1), 99(1), 121(1)(b)(i), 128(1)(a) or 137(a), as appropriate, [1994 Act, Schedule E]

(ii) in respect of survivor's pension or deserted wife's benefit, so much of the pension or benefit as is payable by virtue of section 104(1) or 113(1), as appropriate, or in respect of lone parent's allowance, so much of the allowance as is payable in respect of a qualified child by virtue of section 159(1),

(iii) in respect of disablement pension, child benefit or family income supplement, so much of the pension, benefit or supplement as the Minister considers reasonable in the circumstances,

(d) in connection with the death of any person, for enabling a claim for benefit to be made or proceeded with in his name, subject to such conditions as may be prescribed. [1994 Act, Schedule D]

(2) Regulations may also provide that probate or other proof of title of the personal representative of any deceased person may be dispensed with in the case of payment of any sum representing benefit, and that in any such case the sum may be paid or distributed to or among the persons appearing in the manner provided by the regulations to be entitled to receive the said sum or any part thereof, either as being persons beneficially entitled thereto under any testamentary instrument or as next of kin, or as being creditors of the deceased person, or to or among any one or more of such persons exclusive of the others.

GENERAL NOTE

Subsection (1)

Part VI of S.I. No. 417 of 1994 makes provision for the payment of benefits to persons other than the claimant.

Article 114 provides that the power to nominate another person is subject to the consent of the Minister and that consent, once given, may be withdrawn by the Minister. The article provides that the power of consent may be prescribed by the Minister and that the claimant may revoke this consent on giving notice to the Minister.

Article 115 of these Regulations provide that where a person is below 16 years of age, or is temporarily unable to act, the Minister may appoint someone to act on that person's behalf. In the latter situation, the power will be exercised in cases of illness and the article provides that the appointment is revoked when a committee of the estate of the claimant has been appointed.

Articles 116–117 deal with the power to appoint persons so as to deal with payments to specific benefits and allowances under section 207(1)(c). These powers are generally exercised in favour of the spouse of a claimant and specific provision is made in Article 117 to allow payments to be split as between the adult and child dependant payments, which can be paid to the Minister's nominee (*e.g.* claimant's spouse or partner) leaving the claimant to the adult dependant's rate. This power is frequently exercised when the claimant has demonstrated an inability to support dependants, *e.g.* a gambling or alcohol addiction.

Subsection (2)

Articles 118–123 of S.I. No. 417 of 1994 make detailed provision for payment of benefits to persons who act as personal representative of a deceased claimant.

STATUTORY INSTRUMENT
S.I. No. 417 of 1994.

Statutory declarations

208.—Regulations prescribing a form of application for any purpose may require that all or any of the statements made by the claimant in such form be verified by a statutory declaration and that such statutory declaration may be taken and received by a deciding officer or by any other officer of the Minister or such other person authorised by the Minister in that behalf.

GENERAL NOTE

No regulations have been made under this section.

CHAPTER 2

PROVISIONS RELATING TO ENTITLEMENT

Overlapping provisions

209.—(1) Where, but for this subsection, more than one of the following would be payable to or in respect of a person in respect of the same period, only one shall be paid—

(a) any benefit specified in section 30(1) other than pay-related benefit, death benefit by way of a grant in respect of funeral expenses or death grant,

(b) any assistance specified in section 118(1) other than supplementary welfare allowance,

(c) disabled person's maintenance allowance, or

(d) infectious diseases maintenance allowance.

(2) Where, but for this subsection, more than one of the following would be payable to or in respect of a qualified child in respect of the same period, only one shall be paid—

(a) any benefit specified in section 30(1) other than pay-related benefit, death benefit by way of a grant in respect of funeral expenses or death grant,

(b) any assistance specified in section 118(1) other than supplementary welfare allowance,

(c) disabled person's maintenance allowance,

(d) infectious diseases maintenance allowance,

(e) any increase in the said benefit in respect of an adult dependant,

(f) any increase in the said assistance in respect of an adult dependant,

(g) any increase in the said benefit in respect of a qualified child, or

(h) any increase in the said assistance in respect of a qualified child.

(3) For the purposes of this section—

(a) an increase of disabled person's maintenance allowance or an increase of infectious diseases maintenance allowance, may be regarded as a separate payment, and

(b) any payment specified in paragraph (a), (b), (c) or (d) of subsection (1) payable in respect of a person may be regarded as such specified payment payable to that person.

(4) Notwithstanding subsections (1) and (2), the Minister may make regulations enabling more than one of the payments specified in those subsections to be paid to or in respect of a person in respect of the same period.

(5) Regulations made under subsection (4) may provide for reducing the amount of any payments specified in subsections (1) and (2) (including the partial payment thereof).

(6) Where, but for this subsection, family income supplement and—

(a) unemployment benefit,

(b) retirement pension,

(c) unemployment assistance, or

(d) pre-retirement allowance,

would be payable to or in respect of a person in respect of the same period, only one shall be paid.

(7) Where, but for this subsection, family income supplement would be payable to a person in a period of incapacity for work in respect of which disability benefit is also payable to that person, family income supplement shall not be payable to that person for that part of the period of incapacity for work which exceeds 6 weeks.

(8) Where in respect of the death of a person, a death grant and death benefit by way of a grant in respect of funeral expenses would, but for this subsection, be payable, only one such grant shall be payable.

(9) Regulations may provide for treating any payment specified in subsection (1) or (2), which it is subsequently decided was not payable, as paid on account of any other payment specified in those subsections which it is decided was payable.

GENERAL NOTE

Subsection (1)

This sets out the basic prohibition against concurrent eligibility for social welfare and some health board payments both to a person and in respect of a person, *i.e.* entitlement as a claimant and entitlement to an adult dependant addition. If one or more of the following are payable by reference to a person, then only one of them shall be payable:

(a) a social insurance payment other than pre-related benefit, death grant or funeral grant;

(b) social assistance other than supplementary welfare allowance;

(c) disabled persons' maintenance allowance;

(d) infectious diseases maintenance allowance.

The prohibition attempts to preclude both multiple claims for entitlement as of right, as well as a person claiming entitlement in his or her own right, while at the same time allowing for adult dependant additions to be payable in respect of the claimant to another party (*e.g.* the claimant's spouse).

Subsection (2)
This subsection prevents multiple payments to or in respect of a qualified child, as defined in section 2(3) of this Act.

Subsections (4) and (5)
Subsection (4) is an enabling provision which allows the Minister to relax the prohibitions in subsections (1) and (2), thereby allowing more than one payment to be made to or in respect of a person in regard to the same period of time, subject to subsection (5) which allows for reduced rates of multiple payments to be payable under these regulations. The existing regulations are the Social Welfare (Consolidated Payments Provisions) Regulations 1994 (S.I. No. 417 of 1994), Part VI, Chapter 3.

These complex regulations direct when these payments may be made and when the payments can be deemed to have been paid on account.

Article 125(1) directs that where disablement benefit *and* any benefit or assistance (including increases) would be payable to, or in regard to, a person for the same period, then both payments shall be payable. However, additions such as adult dependant additions are not payable in respect of the disablement benefit: article 125(2).

Article 126(1) directs that where an orphan's (contributory) allowance, orphan's (non-contributory) pension or orphan's pension in the form of death benefit is payable, then any concurrent payment by way of disability benefit, maternity allowance, unemployment benefit, injury benefit, unemployability supplement, survivor's pension, widow's (contributory) pension, deserted wife's benefit, widow's (non-contributory) pension or lone parent's allowance, shall also be payable to, or in respect of, the orphan. However, if the orphan is also in receipt of a blind pension or one of the long-term payments, these short-term payments cannot be paid: see article 126(2).

Article 127(1) provides that where entitlement to short-term insurance payments, viz, disability benefit, maternity benefit, injury benefit, unemployment benefit or unemployability supplement, arises in respect of a person who is receipt of long-term payments specified in article 127(6) (*e.g.* deserted wife's benefit and widow's (non-contributory) pension) then the short-term payment shall also be payable at half rate of the personal rate.

Article 128 allows a blind pension and short-term assistance and insurance payments to be payable: see also *Harvey v. Minister for Social Welfare* [1990] I.L.R.M. 185.

Articles 129 and 130 allow for certain payments made to be deemed to have been paid "on account" for other subsequent entitlements.

Payments after death
   210.—(1) In this section—
"benefit" means—
   (a) disability benefit,
   (b) unemployment benefit (including any amount payable by way of pay-related benefit where appropriate),
   (d) old age (contributory) pension,
   (e) retirement pension,
   (f) invalidity pension,
   (g) unemployment assistance,
   (h) old age (non-contributory) pension and blind pension,
   (j) supplementary welfare allowance,
   (k) pre-retirement allowance,
   (l) survivors pension, [1995 Act, Schedule D]
   (m) lone parent's allowance,
   (n) deserted wife's benefit,
   (o) death benefit under section 60,
   (p) carer's allowance;
"relevant pensioner" has the meaning assigned to it by section 163(1).
   (2) Notwithstanding any provisions to the contrary in this Act—
   (a) where a person who is in receipt of a benefit specified in paragraphs (a) to (k) of subsection (1) which includes an increase in respect of an adult dependant, or which would include such an increase but for the receipt by that person's spouse of an old age (non-contributory) pension, a blind pension or a carer's allowance in his own right, dies,

payment of the benefit shall continue to be made for a period of 6 weeks after the date of death and shall, during that period, be made to such person and subject to such conditions as may be prescribed, and

(b) where a qualified child, in respect of whom an increase of a benefit is being paid, dies, the amount of such increase shall continue to be made for a period of 6 weeks after the date of death, and

(c) where an adult dependant in respect of whom an increase of benefit specified in paragraph (a) to (h) or (j) and (k) of subsection (1) is being paid, or in respect of whom such an increase would be payable but for the receipt by the adult dependant of an old age (non-contributory) pension, a blind pension or a carer's allowance in his own right, dies, payment of such increase shall continue to be made for a period of 6 weeks after the date of death, and [1994 Act, section 26].

(d) subject to paragraph (a), where a person is in receipt of carer's allowance and the relevant pensioner in respect of whom that carer is providing full-time care and attention dies and the carer is not the spouse of that pensioner, payment of the carer's allowance shall continue to be made for a period of 6 weeks after the death of the relevant pensioner, and

(e) subject to paragraph (a), where a person is in receipt of a carer's allowance and the relevant pensioner in respect of whom that carer is providing full-time care and attention, dies, and the carer is the spouse of that pensioner, any benefit payable under paragraph (a) shall include an increase in respect of an adult dependant provided that the person in receipt of the carer's allowance would otherwise have qualified as an adult dependant but for the fact that he was in receipt of the said allowance, and

(f) in any case where payment is made by virtue of paragraph (a) or (c), entitlement to survivors pension, widow's (non-contributory) pension, orphan's (contributory) allowance, orphan's (non-contributory) pension, death benefit under section 60 or 62 or entitlement to lone parent's allowance by virtue of being a widow or widower, shall not commence until after the expiration of the period of 6 weeks mentioned in paragraph (a) or (c) except and to the extent that regulations otherwise provide. [1995 Act, Schedule D]

(3) Subject to this section—

(a) payment of old age (non-contributory) pension shall continue to be made for a period of 6 weeks after the death of a beneficiary who had an increase under section 137(a), and

(b) where a spouse in respect of whom an increase of old age (non-contributory) pension under section 137(a) is payable, or in respect of whom such an increase would be payable, but for the receipt by the spouse of an old age (non-contributory) pension, a blind pension or a carer's allowance in his own right, dies, payment of such increase shall continue to be made for a period of 6 weeks after the date of death [1994 Act, section 26].

GENERAL NOTE

The expansion of payments to adult dependant persons who survive the beneficiary of one of the benefits listed in section 210(1) was made by legislative amendments to section 125 of the 1981 Consolidation Act in sections 9 and 10 of the 1991 and 1993 Acts respectively.

The amendments made in 1991 to section 125 of the Principal Act, by substitution, extended the scope of the payments made in respect of social welfare beneficiaries who, following the death of such a beneficiary, remained the subject of continuing payments for six weeks following death. This compassionate feature of the social welfare system operated in the context of the death of a claimant, benefits and pensions continuing to be payable for six weeks following the death of the claimant to any surviving spouse. The 1991 provisions extended the payment of the benefit or pension for six weeks following upon the death of the claimant if the claimant received an addition for an adult dependant, or would have done so but for the fact that the adult dependent was a spouse and received old age (non-contributory) pension, blind pension, or carer's allowance in his or her own right. Note that the range of benefits that the recipient must have been in receipt of is limited to those in categories (a) to (k) of subsection (1).

The 1991 Act also extended the after death payment to allow qualified child additions to be payable for six weeks following the death of that child: see now subsection (2)(b).

In recommending this change to Seanad Eireann, the Minister for Social Welfare, Dr. Woods, said that those provisions recognise "the burden which parents and widowed people have to endure following the sad loss of a child or spouse. It is intended to ease the adjustment in the early stages of bereavement": see 128 *Seanad Debates* Col. 501.

In cases where an adult dependant dies, the recipient of disability benefit, unemployment benefit, injury benefit, unemployment assistance or supplementary welfare allowance will receive credit dependant addition for as long as the addition was payable, or would have been payable, but for the fact that the deceased was receiving old-age (non-contributory) or blind pension in the deceased's own right: see subsection (2)(c).

The 1991 Act also addressed the issue of the continuation of eligibility for carer's allowance for the carer when the relevant pensioner died. If the carer was not the spouse of the deceased relevant pensioner, the 1991 Act provided that the carer's allowance only continued to be payable for six weeks: see now subsection (2)(d). The 1993 Act however provided that where the carer is the spouse of the deceased relevant pensioner, both the carer's allowance and the adult dependant increase are to be payable for six weeks following the death of the relevant pensioner: see subsection (2)(e). This entitlement exists as long as the adult dependant addition would have been payable during the life of the relevant pensioner but for the entitlement to carer's allowance.

Subsection (2)(f) provides that when the six-week extension is payable to the adult dependant, any subsequent entitlement to one of the pensions or payments that the death creates, will not commence until six weeks after the relevant death, unless entitlement is greater under the new pension or payment than the after death payment: see article 121 of S.I. No. 417 of 1994.

STATUTORY INSTRUMENTS

S.I. No. 417 of 1994.

Absence from State or imprisonment

211.—(1) Subject to section 192, a person shall be disqualified from receiving—

(a) any benefit (including any increase thereof) while that person is absent from the State or is undergoing penal servitude, imprisonment or detention in legal custody, or

(b) any increase of benefit payable in respect of that person's spouse for any period during which that spouse is absent from the State or is undergoing penal servitude, imprisonment or detention in legal custody.

(2) Notwithstanding subsection (1), the Minister may make regulations enabling payment of any benefit or assitance to be made, subject to such conditions and in such circumstances as may be prescribed, to or in respect of any person who is absent from the State or is undergoing penal servitude, imprisonment or detention in legal custody. [1995 Act, section 22].

(3) Regulations may provide for the suspension of payment to or in respect of any person during any such period as is mentioned in subsection (1) or (2) which is excepted from the operation of that subsection or which is payable otherwise than in respect of that period.

(4) Notwithstanding a disqualification by virtue of subsection (1) for receiving a benefit which includes an increase, the increase shall, in such cases as may be prescribed, be paid to the prescribed person.

(5) Regulations for the purposes of this section may be so framed as to make payment of death grant, invalidity pension and retirement pension subject to any specified conditions, limitations or restrictions and, in particular, in the case of persons absent from the State, may modify the periods which may be regarded for the purpose of section 88 as periods of retirement.

(6) A person shall be disqualified for receiving unemployment assistance or pre-retirement allowance while he is—

(a) resident, whether temporarily or permanently, outside the State, or

(b) undergoing penal servitude, imprisonment or detention in legal custody.

(7) Subject to subsection (8), a sum shall not be paid on account of an old age (non-contributory) pension or blind pension to any person while absent from the State.

(8) Where a person who takes up or has taken up residence in Northern Ireland was, immediately before the commencement of such residence, in receipt of old age (non-contributory) pension or blind pension, payment of the pension may, notwithstanding anything contained in subsection (7) be made until either—

(a) the expiration of a period of 5 years from the commencement of such residence during which the person was continuously resident in Northern Ireland, or

(b) the receipt by the person of a payment by way of old age pension or public assistance from the appropriate authority in Northern Ireland,

whichever should first occur.

(9) Where a person has been convicted of any offence and ordered to be imprisoned without the option of a fine or to suffer any greater punishment, he shall be disqualified for receiving or continuing to receive old age (non-contributory) pension or blind pension while he is detained in prison in consequence of the order.

(10) Except where regulations otherwise provide, a person shall be disqualified for receiving widow's (non-contributory) pension, deserted wife's allowance, prisoner's wife's allowance or lone parent's allowance, (including in the case of lone parent's allowance any increase for a qualified child) for any period during which he is undergoing penal servitude, imprisonment or detention in legal custody.

(11) Regulations may provide for the suspension of payment of pension or allowance, as the case may be, to or in respect of any beneficiary during any such period as is mentioned in subsection (10) which is excepted from the operation of that subsection or which is payable otherwise than in respect of that period.

(12) Notwithstanding a disqualification by virtue of subsection (10) for receiving a lone parent's allowance, an increase in respect of a qualified child, shall, in such cases as may be prescribed, be paid to the prescribed person.

(13) (a) Where during any period a person is resident outside the State, the following provisions shall have effect—

(i) a pension shall not be granted to or in respect of that person,

(ii) if a pension has been granted to or in respect of that person, no sum shall be payable during that period on account of that pension.

(b) Nothing contained in paragraph (a) shall operate to prevent, in the case of a person resident for any period outside that State—

(i) a pension being granted to or in respect of that person if a claim for that pension was made prior to that person becoming so resident, or

(ii) a pension granted by virtue of paragraph (a) being paid for any period prior to (but not after) that person becoming so resident, or

(iii) any arrears of a pension granted to or in respect of that person (being arrears due for a period prior to that person becoming so resident) being paid.

(c) In this subsection "pension" means a widow's (non-contributory) pension or orphan's (non-contributory) pension.

(14) A person shall be disqualified for receiving lone parent's allowance, deserted wife's allowance and prisoner's wife's allowance while he is resident whether temporarily or permanently, outside the State.

(15) Child benefit shall be paid only within the State.

GENERAL NOTE

Subsection (1)

This subsection provides for general disqualification from a Part II benefit—effectively all social insurance benefits—for any period in which the claimant is absent from the State or undergoing penal servitude, imprisonment or detention in legal custody. In some instances this general disqualification overlaps with other eligibility conditions, the most obvious being the requirement that an unemployment benefit claimant be available for employment.

The exceptions to this prohibition are found in European Union Legislation, most noteworthy being Council Regulation 1408/71 which allows Irish benefits to be available to persons who leave the State in order to look for employment in another member State.

Regulations which provide exceptions to these prohibitions include the Social Welfare (Absence from the State) Regulations 1988 (S.I. No. 154 of 1988).

Section 22 of the 1995 Act, which has yet to be implemented, replaces this subsection giving the Minister broad regulatory powers on this subject.

Subsection (2)

This subsection provides that where the claimant receives an additional payment for that claimant's husband or wife in regard to disability or unemployment benefit, injury benefit, old-age (contributory) pension, retirement pension, or invalidity pension, absence from the State or penal servitude, imprisonment or detention in legal custody will lead to the addition not being payable.

The terms husband or wife are specific terms which are not defined in the Acts. Because the word spouse as defined by these Acts is not used, the disqualification appears not to disqualify a cohabiting couple. This may be explained as a drafting error, the present section predating the broadening of social welfare law so as to equate cohabiting couples with married couples.

Section 22 of the 1995 Act, not yet in force, repeals this subsection, replacing it with a broader power to regulate this issue.

Subsection (3)

Where the disqualifications in subsections (1) and (2) have been relaxed, there may be the possibility of suspending the payment of benefit during the period of absence or lawful confinement.

Subsection (4)

Where a basic entitlement is not payable under subsection (1) any additional payment may nevertheless be payable, *e.g.* increases in child or adult dependant additions.

Subsection (5)

This subsection enables regulations to be made so as to modify eligibility for death grant, invalidity pension and retirement pension by adding specific conditions, limitations or restrictions. In particular, retirement pensioners who are absent from the State may find that retirement periods under section 88 are modified in regard to such periods of absence.

Subsection (6)

Unemployment assistance and pre-retirement allowances are not to be payable to a person who is absent from the State, whether temporarily or permanently, or is undergoing penal servitude, imprisonment or legal custody. This disqualification is harsher than that found in subsection (1) *vis-à-vis* unemployment benefit for there is no power, by regulation, to create exceptions thereto: *e.g.* sportspersons representing Ireland in international competition.

Subsections (7) and (8)
Old-age (non-contributory) and blind pensions are not to be payable to a person while absent from the State, particularly when residence outside the State is established. However, should the place of residence be Northern Ireland, entitlement will continue until a similar payment is made by the Northern Ireland Authorities or for a period of five years, whichever period is the shorter.

Subsection (9)
Old-age (non-contributory) or blind pensions are not payable when a person has been sentenced to imprisonment without the option of a fine. The disqualification lasts as long as imprisonment lasts so the pension becomes payable on release (*e.g.* on parole).

Subsection (10)
Disqualification for these four one-parent family benefits operates for as long as the lawful detention lasts.

Subsection (11)
Should regulations relax the subsection (10) disqualification, entitlement to payment may nevertheless be suspended.

Subsection (12)
Lone parent's allowance, child dependant additions may be payable to some other person, notwithstanding subsection (10).

Subsection (13)
Widow's (non-contributory) or orphan's (non-contributory) pension are not payable to a person who has been granted such a pension while absent from the State. Payments or arrears in respect of prior periods of entitlement are not affected by this prohibition: subsection (13)(b).

Subsection (14)
Temporary or permanent residence outside the State will disqualify a claimant from entitlement to lone parent's allowance, deserted wife's allowance and prisoner's wife's allowance.

Subsection (15)
Child benefits are payable, notwithstanding this subsection, when the child is outside the State in certain circumstances. The most obvious example being when E.U. law so requires.

CHAPTER 3

APPOINTMENT AND DUTIES OF SOCIAL WELFARE INSPECTORS

Social welfare inspectors
212.—(1) The Minister may appoint such and so many of his officers as he thinks proper to be social welfare inspectors for the purposes of such provisions of Parts II, III, IV, V, IX and this Part as he may determine in the case of such appointments.

(2) Every social welfare inspector shall investigate and report to the Minister upon any claim for or in respect of benefit and any question arising on or in relation to such benefit which may be referred to him by the Minister, and may, for the purpose of such investigation and report require—
  (a) a claimant or a beneficiary,
  (b) the spouse or any employer of the claimant or beneficiary,
  (c) in the case of child benefit, any person in charge of a child in respect of whom the claim is made,
  (d) a person liable to contribute under section 286(1) or any employer of any such person, and
  (e) the personal representative of a person who was at any time in receipt of any benefit,

to furnish him with such information and to produce to him such documents, within such period as may be prescribed, as he may reasonably require.

(3) A social welfare inspector shall, for the purposes of Parts II, III, IV, V, IX and this Part, have power to do all or any of the following—

    (a) to enter, without prior notification, at all reasonable times any premises or place liable to inspection under this section,

    (b) to make such examination and enquiry as may be necessary for ascertaining whether the provisions of Part II, III, IV, V, IX or this Part are being or have been complied with in any such premises or place,

    (c) to examine either alone or in the presence of any other person, as he thinks fit, in relation to any matters on which he may reasonably require information for the purposes of Part II, III, IV, V, IX or this Part, every person whom he finds in any such premises or place, or who he has reasonable cause to believe to be or to have been an insured person, and to require every such person to be so examined and to sign a declaration of the truth of the matters in respect of which he is so examined,

    (d) to exercise such other powers as may be necessary for carrying Parts II, III, IV, V, IX and this Part into effect.

(4) The occupier of any premises or place liable to inspection under this section, and any other person who—

    (a) is or has been employing—

        (ii) any person in insurable employment or insurable (occupational injuries) employment, or

        (ii) any claimant or beneficiary,

        or

    (b) engages or has engaged a person under a contract for service to perform a service,

and the employees of, or any other person providing bookkeeping, clerical or other administrative services to, any such occupier or other person and any insured person, claimant or beneficiary or person in respect of whom such a benefit is claimed, shall furnish to a social welfare inspector all such information and produce for inspection all such registers, cards, wages sheets, records of wages and other documents as the social welfare inspector may reasonably require for the purposes of ascertaining whether contributions are or have been payable, or have been duly paid in respect of any person, or whether benefit is or was payable to or in respect of any person. [1994 Act, section 28].

(5) Any person who holds a certificate of authorisation under section 17 (as amended by section 28 of the Finance Act, 1992) of the Finance Act, 1970, shall, upon the request of a social welfare inspector, furnish such certificate for inspection by him.

(6) If any person—

    (a) wilfully delays or obstructs a social welfare inspector in the exercise of any duty or power under this section, or

    (b) refuses or neglects to answer any question or to furnish any information or to produce any document when required to do so under this section, or

    (c) conceals or prevents or attempts to conceal or prevent any person from appearing before or being examined by a social welfare inspector or any other person appointed under this section,

he shall be guilty of an offence.

(7) Notwithstanding the preceding provisions of this section, a person shall not be required under this section to give any evidence or answer any question tending to incriminate himself.

(8) Every social welfare inspector shall be furnished with a certificate of his appointment, and on entering any premises or place for the purposes of Parts II, III, IV, V, IX and this Part shall, if so requested, produce the said certificate.

(9) The premises or places liable to inspection under this section are any premises or places where a social welfare inspector has reasonable grounds for believing that—

(a) persons are, or have been, employed, or

(b) there are, or have been, self-employed persons.

and any premises or place where a social welfare inspector has reasonable grounds for believing that any documents relating to persons in employment or to self-employed persons are kept.

(10) Where any premises or place is liable to be inspected by an inspector or by an officer appointed, employed by, or under the control of, another Minister of the Government, the Minister may make arrangements with that other Minister for any of the powers or duties of a social welfare inspector appointed under this section to be vested in the inspector or officer employed by that other Minister and, where such an arrangement is made, such inspector or officer shall have all the powers of a social welfare inspector appointed under this section for the purposes of the inspection.

(10A) A social welfare inspector may exercise any of the powers or duties conferred on him by this section to investigate, at the request of the competent authority of another Member State or any other country with which the Minister has made a reciprocal arrangement under the provisions of section 238, any claim, by a person resident in the State, for or in respect of any social security payment under the legislation of another Member State, or under the legislation of any other country with which the Minister has made a reciprocal arrangement under the said provisions. [1994 Act, section 28].

(11) Where a person is required by subsection (4) to produce records required pursuant to regulations made under section 14(5), he shall, upon the request of a social welfare inspector, produce such records at his registered address or his principal place of business.

(12) A person who fails to comply with a request to produce records under subsection (11) within 21 days following the issue of such request in writing sent by registered post to him at his registered address or his principal place of business shall be guilty of an offence.

(13) Records of persons employed which an employer is obliged to maintain under regulations made under section 14(5) which are produced to a social welfare inspector shall be *prima facie* evidence that those persons were employed by that employer and of the earnings of such persons and of the periods during which such persons were employed by him.

(14) Where an employer issues to an employee a statement containing the particulars specified in section 9 of the Minimum Notice and Terms of Employment Act, 1973, he shall retain a copy of such statement for a period of 2 years from the date on which that statement was issued and shall furnish such copy on demand to a social welfare inspector for inspection under this section.

GENERAL NOTE

Subsection (1)

The Minister's power to appoint the Minister's officers to be social welfare inspectors is established by this subsection. Note that many of the issues raised by the *Bracken* case (see below) led to these powers being expanded by section 28 of the 1994 Act.

Subsection (2)

The inspector's jurisdiction in respect of the investigation and reporting of any claim for benefit is fixed by this subsection. S.I. No. 189 of 1993 allows the Minister's officers to require claimants to furnish such certificates, documents, information and evidence as may be required by that officer. This subsection directs that these powers may be invoked in respect of any claimant or beneficiary, the claimant or beneficiary spouse or employer, the person having custody of a child for whom child benefit is payable, a liable relative or that person's employer, or the personal representative of a deceased claimant. Article 10 of S.I. No. 189 of 1993 specifies that the duty to provide information extends to a change in circumstances: article 10(1)(b).

Subsection (3)
The broad powers given to inspectors under this subsection must be exercised with due regard to Constitutional law and the safeguards found in the subsection itself. For example, the power of entry can only be exercised "at all reasonable times", and the power to examine any person arises only where the Inspector may reasonably require information for the purposes of certain specified parts of the Act. Prior notification is not necessary. The subsection was broadened after *Minister for Social Welfare v. Bracken* H.C. Unrep. July 29, 1992.

Subsection (4)
This subsection specifies that the Inspector's powers in respect of the production of information and documents relevant to insurability and entitlement to benefit extend to the occupier of premises or places liable to inspection and any other person who has been employing someone in insurable employment or insurable (occupational injuries) employment or any claimant or beneficiary. This power extends to their servants or agents including, for example, service bureaus who prepare wages and PRSI accounts on behalf of other employers.

Subsection (5)
This subsection applies to subcontractors who hold a C2 certificate issued by the Revenue Commissioners under section 17 of the Finance Act 1990, as amended. This certificate must be produced for inspection on request by an inspector.

Subsections (6) and (7)
Subsection (6) sets out a number of offences in relation to conduct which impedes social welfare inspectors in discharging their duties under the Act. Subsection (7) provides that the rule against self-incrimination is to operate in the context of providing information to an inspector and the subsection (6) offences. Subsection (3) was broadened, following *Minister for Social Welfare v. Bracken* H.C. Unrep. July 29, 1992, to make it clear that consent, permission to enter, or prior notification is not a necessary precondition to the extent of this right of entry.

Subsection (9)
The power to enter premises or places was broadened under section 7 of the Social Welfare (No. 2) Act 1987 to cover cases where the inspector reasonably believes a person has been self-employed as well as employed under a contract of service. Some industries have recently changed the basis upon which persons are employed, particularly in the service sectors. Milk roundsmen and home heating fuel delivery men in particular have become self employed in an attempt to reduce overheads, particularly employer's PRSI. There is concern that this trend may be exploited by some employers who may falsely claim that persons are employed under a contract for services when in reality the person is employed under a contract of service and the power to inspect is broadened in this new subsection to meet this situation.

Clearly the phrase "premises or place" covers not only the place of employment but also the office premises and home of the employer: it also covers the office and home of the person employed. Some misgivings about the invasion of the citizens home were expressed in Dáil Eireann *vis-à-vis* the Inspector who, by this subsection, is given a power of entry without warrant: 376 *Dáil Debates* Cols. 2574 to 2577. Subsection (8) requires the Inspector to furnish the person in charge of the premises or place with a certificate of appointment but this is the only requirement of notice the Act provides for. One Deputy was of the belief that the power of entry must be exercised reasonably: the legislation does not so provide but the Constitution would require this.

Subsection (10)
This subsection allows the minister by arrangement to delegate to another Minister these powers of inspection which may then be exercised by that other Minister's appointee. The subsection applies when the premises in question are liable to be inspected by that other Minister's officers (*e.g.* Department of Enterprise and Employment officials).

Subsections (11) and (12)
Section 14(5) makes provision for the keeping of records relating to employment periods and the earnings of employees during these employment periods. This subsection dates back to the 1987 (No. 2) Act. Prior to implementation of this subsection, the Department of Social

Welfare found it difficult to operate their powers of inspection because many employers refused to make records available on the ground that records, or part of them, were located elsewhere *e.g.* in the hands of an accountant or solicitor. On contacting the holder the Department often found that only a portion of the records were held by that person. That "evasive action" as the Minister called it, is countered by requiring that the records prescribed are to be produced by employers at their registered address or place of business.

Subsection (13)

This prima facie rule of evidence is constitutionally necessary as a result of several decisions in which absolute rules of evidence have been declared unconstitutional.

Subsection (14)

The Minimum Notice and Terms of Employment Act 1973, sets out a statutory requirement that an employer must issue to an employee a statement which sets out the terms of the employee's contract of employment. The notice must be given within one month of employment commencing. The notice will contain information about the date employment commenced, details of payments by way of wages or salary including bonus payments, conditions of work, holiday entitlement, sick pay and pension entitlement, and periods of notice, *etc*. The notice can either be by written statement or in a readily accessible form such as an employment agreement registered under the Industrial Relations Acts.

Under this subsection the employer is bound to keep a copy of the statement for two years from the date it was issued, and furnish a copy to an inspector upon demand.

CHAPTER 4

OFFENCES, MISCELLANEOUS CONTROL PROVISIONS AND PROCEEDINGS

Offences

False statements and offences, including offences relating to bodies corporate

213.—(1) If, for the purpose of—

(a) obtaining or establishing entitlement to payment of any benefit for himself or for any other person, or

(b) obtaining or establishing entitlement to payment of any benefit for himself or for any other person which is in excess of that which he was entitled to, or

(c) avoiding the making by himself or any other person of any repayment under this Act,

or for any other purpose connected with this Act, any person—

(i) knowingly makes any statement or representation (whether written or verbal) which is to his knowledge false or misleading in any material respect, or knowingly conceals any material fact, or

(ii) produces or furnishes, or causes or knowingly allows to be produced or furnished, any document or information which he knows to be false in a material particular,

he shall be guilty of an offence.

(2) An employer or any servant or agent of an employer who aids, abets, counsels or procures an employee in the employment of that employer to commit any offence under subsection (1) shall be guilty of an offence.

(3) A person convicted of an offence under this section in relation to child benefit shall be disqualified for the receipt of child benefit for the period of 3 months immediately following the date of the conviction.

(4) Where a person is convicted of an offence under subsection (1) or (2) and by reason of that offence any benefit (other than child benefit) was

received by an employee of his which he was not entitled to receive, such person shall be liable to pay to the Minister on demand a sum not exceeding the amount of such benefit which by reason of the said offence was paid to that employee while in his employment and that sum, if not so repaid, may be recovered by the Minister as a debt under statute in any court of competent jurisdiction.

(5) Notwithstanding the provisions of subsection (5) [sic] or any other provisions of this Act under which amounts of benefit (other than child benefit) may be recovered, the amount recovered by the Minister, in any case may not exceed the amount of benefit received by the employee which he was not entitled to receive.

(6) Regulations under this Act may provide for offences consisting of contraventions of or failures to comply with such regulations and, where such offences are provided for, a person guilty of any such offence shall be liable on summary conviction to the penalties provided for in section 218(1)(a).

(7) Where an offence under this Act is committed by a body corporate and, in the case of an offence under subsection (1), where the offence is committed by an employee or officer of the body corporate, and is proved to have been so committed with the consent, connivance or approval of or to have been attributable to any wilful neglect on the part of any person, being a director, manager, secretary or any other officer of the body corporate or a person who was purporting to act in any such capacity, that person, as well as the body corporate, shall be guilty of an offence and shall be liable to be proceeded against and punished as if he were guilty of the first-mentioned offence.

(8) It shall be a defence to a prosecution for an offence under subsection (7) for a person to show that the offence was committed without his knowledge and that he exercised all such diligence to prevent the commission of the offence as he ought to have exercised, having regard to the nature of his position as director, manager, secretary or other officer and to all the circumstances.

(9) Any summons or other document required to be served for the purpose of proceedings under this Act on a body corporate may be served—

(a) by leaving it at or sending it by post to the registered office of the body corporate,

(b) by leaving it at or sending it by post to any place in the State at which the body corporate conducts business, or

(c) by sending it by post to any person who is a director, manager, secretary or other officer of the body corporate or is purporting to act in any such capacity at the place where that person resides.

(10) Where a person is in receipt of assistance or has made a claim for assistance which has not been finally determined, and his means have increased since the date of latest investigation thereof, or, if no such investigation has taken place, since the date of making the claim, the person shall, within such period as may be prescribed, give or cause to be given to the Minister notification in writing of the increase.

(11) A person who fails or neglects to comply with the provisions of subsection (10) shall be guilty of an offence.

GENERAL NOTE

Subsection (1)

This subsection makes it an offence for any person to: (i) knowingly make any statement or representation which is to that person's knowledge false or misleading in any material respect, or (ii) knowingly conceal any material fact, or (iii) produce or furnish, or allow to be produced or furnished, any document or information which is known to be false in some material particular. Such acts or omissions, however, must be for one of the three purposes, namely, establishing entitlement for any person, or obtaining excessive amounts of benefit for any person, or avoiding the duty to make a repayment. False statements relating to levels of PRSI contribution, for example, are not within this subsection.

The constituent elements in this offence were clarified by Carroll J. in *State (Wilson) v. Justice Neilan* H.C. Unrep. April 18, 1985.

It should be noted that in *Wosser v. Dublin Corporation*, an FAT decision (*U.D. 42/89*), it was decided that the dismissal of an employee for claiming disability benefit while simultaneously working was not an employment-related fraud which gave an employer the right to dismiss the employee, the Tribunal remarking that it is not for an employer to substitute inquiries and a penalty for those that may be exercised by the Department under this section.

Subsection (2)

This subsection provides a separate offence in relation to an employer, the employer's servant or agent, who aids, abets, counsels or procures some employee of that employer to commit a subsection (1) offence. It is clearly intended to create liability for the employer, whether an individual or a body corporate, should that employer facilitate or encourage employees to claim unemployment benefit while working, for example.

Subsection (3)

The three-month disqualification provided for in this subsection will not operate if the person convicted of the offence is not the beneficiary.

Subsections (4) and (5)

These provisions were inserted into Irish social welfare law by section 22 of the 1989 Act. The provisions in subsection (4) are directed at employers who collude with their employees in benefit fraud cases prosecuted under subsection (1) above.

If an employer is convicted of a statutory offence in connection with the fraudulent obtaining of any benefit, assistance or family income supplement by an employee of his, in circumstances where the employee was not so entitled—typically where the employer gives false information which leads the Department to believe the employee was in fact unemployed or paid at a certain level—the Department may seek restitution from the employer. The amount is due, on demand, and is to be such amount as does not exceed the amount irregularly obtained by the employee while in the employ of the offender.

Subsection (6)

This power to provide criminal offences by way of delegated legislation is used occasionally, particularly in relation to procedural failings such as the failure of an employer to report an industrial accident under S.I. No. 67 of 1967.

Subsections (7) and (8)

If the prosecution of a body corporate under subsection (1) reveals that the offence was committed by an employee or officer of that body corporate with the consent, connivance or approval of, or due to the wilful default of, an actual or apparent company officer, that company officer, if he or she is within the subsection, may be proceeded against separately as if guilty of the subsection (1) offence. The defence provided for in subsection (8) makes it clear that the offence is one of omission insofar as the company officer cannot avoid a conviction by showing lack of knowledge that a subsection (1) offence has been committed if diligence would have prevented the commission of the offence.

Subsections (10) and (11)

These subsections oblige a claimant for social assistance to notify the Minister of any increase in means that have taken place following upon the granting of the claim or before final determination or investigation of the claim.

The periods prescribed by S.I. No. 417 of 1994 are three months for old-age (non-contributory) and blind pensions: in all other cases the period is seven days.

Offences in relation to employment contributions

214.—(1) If an employer—

(a) fails to pay at or within a prescribed time any employment contribution which he is liable under Part II to pay,

(b) deducts or attempts to deduct the whole or any part of any employer's contribution in respect of a person from that person's remuneration,

(c) makes a deduction from the remuneration of a person in respect of any employment contribution which the employer is liable under

Part II to pay and fails to pay at or within a prescribed time the employment contribution in respect of which the deduction was made [1994 Act, Schedule C]

(d) adjusts the methods of payment of reckonable earnings to an employed contributor who was employed in consecutive weeks in order to ensure that the employed contributor is exempted in any week from the employment contribution payable under section 10(1)(b) by virtue of section 10(7)(a) and regulations made thereunder, or [1994 Act, Schedule C]

(e) adjusts the amount of payment of reckonable earnings to an employed contributor in order to avoid payment of contributions at the rate specified in section 10(1)(d)(ii) [1994 Act, Schedule C].

the employer shall be guilty of an offence.

(2) An employer, or a servant or agent acting on behalf of such employer, who, for the purpose of evading or reducing the amount of his liability in respect of employment contributions which he is liable to pay under Part II and which he has not paid—

(a) knowingly makes any statement or representation (whether written or verbal) which is to his knowledge false or misleading in any material respect, or knowingly conceals any material fact, or

(b) produces or furnishes, or causes or knowingly allows to be produced or furnished, any document or information which he knows to be false in a material particular,

shall be guilty of an offence.

(3) Where records are required to be kept by employers under regulations made under section 14(5) in so far as they relate to the recording of payment of earnings and the periods to which such earnings refer such records shall be recorded at or before the time of payment of such earnings.

(4) A person who fails to comply with subsection (3) shall be guilty of an offence.

(5) A person who is guilty of an offence under this section (other than an offence under subsection (1)(d)) shall be liable—

(a) on summary conviction, to the penalties provided in section 218(1)(a), or

(b) on conviction on indictment, to a fine not exceeding £10,000 or such amount as is equivalent to twice the amount so unpaid or deducted, whichever is the greater, or to imprisonment for a term not exceeding 3 years, or to both.

(6) A person who is guilty of an offence under subsection (1)(d) shall be liable on summary conviction to a fine not exceeding £1,000 or on conviction on indictment to a fine not exceeding £10,000.

(7) (a) Where an employer has been convicted under this section of the offence of failing to pay any employment contributions which he is liable under Part II to pay, he shall be liable to pay to the Social Insurance Fund a sum equal to the amount which he has failed to pay and, on such conviction, if notice of the intention to do so has been served with the summons or warrant, evidence may be given of the failure on the part of the employer to pay other employment contributions in respect of the same person during the 3 years preceding the date when the notice was so served, and on proof of such failure the court may order the employer to pay to the Social Insurance Fund a sum equal to the total of all the employment contributions which he is so proved to have failed to pay, and the employer's right of appeal against the conviction under the section shall include a right to appeal against such an order.

(b) Any sum paid by an employer under this subsection shall be treated as a payment in satisfaction of the unpaid employment contributions, and the insured person's portion of those employment contributions shall not be recoverable by the employer from the insured person.

(8) Nothing in this section or in regulations under this section shall be construed as preventing the Minister from recovering by means of civil proceedings any sums due to the Social Insurance Fund.

GENERAL NOTE

Subsection (1)

Failure to pay over employment contributions under section 10, the deduction or attempts to deduct the employer's portion of such contributions from the employee's remuneration, or the failure to pay over the sum deducted, are each criminal offences, as is any false adjustment of the method of weekly payment of reckonable earnings in order to obtain exemption from liability to pay employment contributions. The offence is committed by the employer and not the employee. The period prescribed is nine days from the end of the relevant period: see article 22 of S.I. No. 298 of 1989 (employment contributions).

Subsection (2)

Separate criminal offences are provided in respect of an employer, or an employer's servant or agent who acts on behalf of the employer, if such a person, for the purpose of evading or reducing liability to pay employment contributions:

    (i) knowingly makes a statement or representation which that person knows to be false or misleading in any material respect, or,

    (ii) knowingly conceals any material fact, or,

    (iii) produces or furnishes or allows to be produced or furnished, any document or information known to be false in any material particular.

Subsections (3) and (4)

This subsection requires employers to maintain records of remuneration paid and the periods within which the remuneration was earned so as to facilitate the investigation of claims to benefit. These records must be maintained at or before the time of payment. These regulations are found in S.I. No. 298 of 1989.

Subsections (5) and (6)

An employer convicted of falsely adjusting an employee's earnings in order to evade liability to pay an employment contribution under subsection (1)(d) is liable, following summary conviction, to a fine of up to £1,000: if convicted on indictment the maximum fine is £10,000. A person convicted of any of the other offences set out in this section is liable, on summary conviction to a maximum fine of £1,000 or imprisonment for up to 12 months. If convicted on indictment, to a fine not exceeding £10,000 or double the amount unpaid or undeducted, whichever is the greater, or imprisonment for up to three years, or indeed both penalties.

Subsections (7) and (8)

Notwithstanding the right of the Minister to obtain sums due to the Fund by civil proceedings, subsection (7)(a) makes an employer convicted of the offence of failing to pay due employment contributions liable to pay the amount that the employer is convicted of failing to pay to the Fund. The summons or warrant may specify that evidence may be given of other such failures during the preceding three-year period, and upon conviction these other specified amounts may also be payable by order of the Court. An appeal lies against conviction and this three-year arrears provision is also capable of being appealed against. Upon conviction, the employer who makes the payment is not able to deduct the employee's contribution from employee remuneration partially to offset the payment so made.

Notification by employer, etc. of commencement of employment

215.—(1) The Minister may require—

    (a) an employer or any other person to notify him of the date of the commencement of the employment of—

        (i) any person in his employment,

        (ii) any person engaged by him under a contract for service to perform a service, or

    (b) a person engaged under a contract for service to perform a service to notify him of the date on which any person was engaged to perform that service either with him or on his behalf whether under a contract for service or under any other arrangements made or to be made by him.

(2) The circumstances in which notification may be required under subsection (1) and the manner of that notification shall be prescribed in regulations.

(3) A person who fails to comply with this section or regulations made hereunder shall be guilty of an offence.

GENERAL NOTE

Section 2 of the No. 2 Act of 1989 marked the beginning of concerted action within the Department of Social Welfare in relation to benefit frauds by employees and independent contractors. Prior to 1987 many prosecutions took on a limited character because it was difficult to show precisely when a claimant had commenced work while still drawing benefit and in the absence of detailed information the Department was not able to prove that concurrent working and benefit claims had lasted for considerable periods of time. The fact that some employers may have colluded made it essential for the 1987 reforms to oblige employers to notify the Department about the commencement of employment of whatever nature.

This section is an enabling provision and the duty to notify has been imposed in certain employment sectors where abuses have been consistently detected or suspected.

Records to be maintained

215A.—(1) For the purpose of this Act the Minister may by regulations require—

(a) an employer or any other person to maintain such records as may be prescribed of any person in his employment and of any person engaged by him under a contract for service to perform a service, or

(b) a person engaged under a contract for service to perform a service to maintain such records as may be prescribed of any person engaged to perform that service either with him or on his behalf whether under a contract for service or under any other arrangements made or to be made by him.

(2) Records required to be maintained under subsection (1) shall be held at such place and for such period as may be prescribed.

(3) A person who fails to comply with this section shall be guilty of an offence.". [1993 (No. 2) Act, section 14].

GENERAL NOTE

This section was inserted by section 14 of the No. 2 Act of 1993. The regulation in question is S.I. No. 24 of 1994. For these purposes a specified industry is defined as the construction industry, including the building, alteration, decoration, repair or demolition of any building or structure. The employer is required to maintain a record of employees or sub-contractors so engaged by him with particulars of name, address, RSI number and date of commencement of the employment. The record must be readily accessible at the premises or place of employment.

Subsection (2)

The industries which are required to notify are found in the Social Welfare (Notification by Employers of Commencement of Employment) Regulations 1988 (S.I. No. 296 of 1988, as amended by S.I. No. 196 of 1994). Employers in the construction, contract cleaning, forestry, security, road haulage, private road transport, catering and licensed bar trade industries are required to notify the Department when engaging new employees. The same obligation is imposed in relation to the engagement of sub-contractors, save in the contract cleaning, security and licensed bar trade industries. The regulations also set out the information which is to be notified to the Minister.

For the penalties following upon conviction see section 218.

Information to be furnished by employers to Minister

216.—(1) An employer shall furnish to the Minister in writing in respect of any person who is or was in his employment such particulars, including particulars as to periods of employment, as are required by the Minister to enable determination or review of a claim to any benefit by or in respect of that person.

(2) Regulations may specify the particulars which an employer shall furnish under subsection (1) and prescribe the manner in which such particulars shall be so furnished.

(3) A person who fails to comply with this section or regulations made under subsection (2) shall be guilty of an offence.

GENERAL NOTE

This section requires employers to furnish in writing details concerning employees, current or past, so as to allow the Minister to determine or review a claim to any benefit by that employee.

For the penalties following a conviction see section 218.

Application of Probation of Offenders Act, 1907

217.—Where—

    (a) (i) the employer of an employed contributor is charged with an offence in relation to payment of employment contributions in respect of that contributor, or

        (ii) a person is charged under this Act with an offence in relation to the receipt of any benefit,

    and

    (b) the court proposes to make an order under section 1(1) of the Probation of Offenders Act, 1907,

the court shall not make such order until it is satisfied that all arrears in respect of such contributions have been paid by such employer or any amounts due to be repaid in respect of such benefit have been repaid.

GENERAL NOTE

This section provides employers and other accused persons with an incentive for making payment or restitution of contributions not paid or benefits overpaid by preventing a court from making a probation order if the accused has actually made payment or restitution at the time of sentencing.

Penalties

218.—(1) Except where otherwise provided for, a person guilty of an offence under this Act shall be liable—

    (a) on summary conviction, to a fine not exceeding £1,000 or imprisonment for a term not exceeding 12 months, or to both, or

    (b) on conviction on indictment, to a fine not exceeding £10,000 or imprisonment for a term not exceeding 3 years, or to both.

(2) Where a person, after conviction of an offence under this Act continues to contravene the provision concerned, he shall be guilty of an offence on every day on which the contravention continues and for each such offence he shall be liable to a fine, on summary conviction, not exceeding £200 or, on conviction on indictment, not exceeding £2,000.

GENERAL NOTE

Except where the Act otherwise provides, the penalty to be imposed following summary conviction for an offence under the Act is to be a fine of up to £1,000 or imprisonment for up to 12 months, or both; if the conviction is upon indictment, the fine may be up to £10,000 or imprisonment for up to three years, or both. Examples where the Act otherwise provides can be found in sections 213(3) and 214(6).

If the offence is continuing even after a conviction, the offender is guilty of an offence for each day on which contravention occurs and the penalty for each offence is to be up to £200 on summary conviction, £2,000 if the offence is successfully prosecuted on indictment.

Miscellaneous Control Provisions

Failure to keep records

219.—(1) Where—
(a) an employer has failed to keep records under regulations made under section 14(5) or 215A or has failed to make a notification under regulations made under section 215, or
(b) any other person who engages a person (referred to in this section as a 'contracted person') under a contract for service to perform a service, has failed to keep records under regulations made under section 215A or has failed to make a notification under regulations made under section 215,

and an employee or a contracted person (as the case may be) receives payment, due wholly or partly by reason of that failure, of benefit which he was not entitled to receive in respect of any day on which he was in the employment of the said employer or engaged under a contract for service by the other person, such employer or other person (as the case may be) shall be liable to pay to the Minister on demand a sum not exceeding the amount of benefit which was paid to the said employee or contracted person (as the case may be) and that sum, if not repaid by the employee or contracted person (as the case may be), may be recovered by the Minister as a simple contract debt in any court of competent jurisdiction.

(2) It shall be presumed until the contrary is shown that any payment aforesaid was made wholly or partly by reason of the failure of the employer or other person who engages a person under a contract for service to keep the said records or to make the said notification referred to in subsection (1).

(3) Where there is a material difference between any document issued by or on behalf of an employer or other person who engages a person under a contract for service, to an employee or contracted person (as the case may be) and any other document furnished to the Minister or to the Collector-General and the employee or contracted person (as the case may be) wholly or partly as a result of that difference, receives benefit to which he was not entitled, such employer or other person (as the case may be) shall be liable to pay to the Minister on demand a sum not exceeding the amount of benefit which was paid to the said employee or contracted person (as the case may be) and such sum, if not repaid by the employee or contracted person (as the case may be), may be recovered by the Minister as a simple contract debt in any court of competent jurisdiction.

(4) For the purposes of subsection (3) an employee or contracted person (as the case may be) shall include the employee's or contracted person's spouse and any other member of the employee's or contracted person's household (as the case may be) whose entitlement to benefit is regulated or adjusted by the income of the employee or contracted person (as the case may be).

(5) Notwithstanding the provisions of subsection (1) or (3) or any other provisions of this Act under which amounts of benefit may be recovered, the amount recovered by the Minister in any case may not exceed the amount of benefit received by the employee or contracted person (as the case may be) which he was not entitled to receive.". [1994 Act, section 29].

General Note

The statutory instruments that set out the details of an employer's obligation to maintain contribution records under section 15(5) of the Principal Act are the Social Welfare (Contributions) Regulations 1953 (S.I. No. 5 of 1953) as amended, and the Social Welfare (Collection of Employment Contributions by the Collector General) Regulations 1979 (S.I. No. 77 of 1979), as amended.

The statutory instruments made under section 15A of the Principal Act are the Social Welfare (Notification of Employers of Commencement of Employment) Regulations 1988 (S.I. No. 296 of 1988), and the Social Welfare (Commencement of Employment) Regulations 1989 (S.I. No. 339 of 1989).

The regulations of 1988 and 1989 apply to the construction, contract cleaning, forestry and security industries in respect of recruitment of employees or self-employed persons. The notification requirements are demanding because of a perceived lack of stringency on the part of some employers in these industries.

This section provides that where employers in these industries, or in the general sector covered by the 1953 Regulations, fail to notify or keep records respectively, and the default leads to an employee being wrongly in receipt of a benefit, allowance, pension, as stated, then the employer shall be obliged to pay the Minister, on demand, a sum not exceeding the amount so wrongly paid to the employee.

The payment should have been made wholly or partly by reason of the employer's default.

Subsection (3) makes similar provision when the employer issues documents to an employee which are materially different to other documents the employer has provided to the Minister or to the Revenue Commissioners.

These provisions were enhanced by the 1994 Act, section 29.

Loss of benefit because of employer's default

220.—(1) Where an employer has failed or neglected—

(a) to pay any employment contribution which under Part II he is liable to pay in respect of an employed contributor in his employment, or

(b) to comply, in relation to any such employed contributor, with any requirement of Part II or regulations which relates to the payment or collection of employment contributions,

and by reason thereof the employed contributor or any other person has lost, in whole or in part, any benefit to which he would have been entitled, such contributor or other person shall be entitled to recover from the employer as a simple contract debt in any court of competent jurisdiction a sum equal to the amount of the benefit so lost.

(2) Where an employed contributor or other person has lost benefit in a case referred to in subsection (1) and has not taken proceedings under that subsection, the Minister may, in the name of and on behalf of such contributor or other person, recover from the employer as a simple contract debt in any court of competent jurisdiction a sum equal to the amount of the benefit lost.

(3) Where, by virtue of regulations made under section 14—

(a) employment contributions which have not been paid have been treated as paid, or

(b) employment contributions which have been paid late have been treated as paid on the due dates,

and by reason thereof benefit which would otherwise have been lost was paid, there shall be due to the Social Insurance Fund by the employer the amount of the benefit which would have been so lost.

(4) Proceedings may be taken under this section notwithstanding that proceedings have been taken under any other provision of Part II or this Part in respect of the same failure or neglect.

(5) In ascertaining, for the purposes of this section, the amount of benefit lost by an employed contributor or other person by reason of a failure or neglect referred to in subsection (1), account shall not be taken of any assistance paid to such contributor or other person during a period when he was losing benefit by reason of such failure or neglect.

(6) The amount of assistance paid to an employed contributor or other person during a period when he was losing benefit by reason of a failure or neglect referred to in subsection (1) may be recovered by the Minister—

   (a) in case the full amount of the benefit which was lost has been recovered by such contributor or other person, from such contributor or other person—

      (i) by deduction from any benefit or assistance to which such contributor or other person may be or become entitled, or

      (ii) as a simple contract debt in any court of competent jurisdiction, or

   (b) in any other case, from the employer guilty of the failure or neglect as a simple contract debt in any court of competent jurisdiction,

and, if the amount of the assistance is recovered by the Minister from the employer, the sum recoverable by such contributor or other person from the employer under this section shall be reduced by the amount of such assistance.

(7) Any sums recovered by the Minister under subsection (6) shall be paid into the Exchequer.

(8) In this section "benefit" means benefit under Part II.

GENERAL NOTE

Should an employer's non-compliance with obligations to pay employment contributions or any of the detailed requirements relating to payment or collection of contributions, result in loss of benefit, in whole or in part, an employed contributor is entitled to seek the award of a sum corresponding to the loss as a simple contract debt in any court of competent jurisdiction. This will normally be the District Court where jurisdiction is fixed at a ceiling of £5,000.

It should be noted that under section 14(2)(e) it is possible for the Minister to deem contributions to be paid if the non-payment has occurred without the consent or connivance, or negligence of, the insured person. In such a case benefit will be payable. For this reason subsection (3) provides that where the insured person does not seek to exercise the subsection (1) right, the Minister may exercise this right on behalf of the insured person. Presumably the Minister's power to proceed under subsection (2) on behalf of the insured person arises only when the insured person has not been awarded benefit but lacks the means or is reluctant to proceed against the defaulting employer; damages recovered under subsection (2) are, presumably, ultimately paid to the insured person while damages under subsection (3) go to the Fund.

The force of these recovery powers are highlighted by subsection (5) which provides that in calculating the benefit lost, account is not to be taken of any assistance payment (e.g. unemployment assistance or supplementary welfare allowance) which is paid by virtue of non-qualification for benefit because of the employer's default. If assistance was capable of being referred to, lost benefit may be small or indeed nil in some cases. Subsection (6) provides that any assistance paid as a result of the insured person failing to establish entitlement to an insurance payment can be recovered by the Minister if (a) the insured person has recovered the full amount of lost benefit by way of deduction from an assistance or insurance payment to which they have become entitled or if the amount of lost benefit has been recovered by the insured person in court proceedings, or (b) in any other case, from the employer in court proceedings.

Information required by Minister

221.—For the purposes of controlling and investigating entitlement to any benefit, under this Act or under schemes administered by or on behalf of the Minister, the Minister may require such persons as may be prescribed to provide him with such information in relation to such persons or classes of persons as the Minister may determine and any person so prescribed shall be required to provide such information as may be required.

GENERAL NOTE

This section overlaps with the control provisions found in sections 215 and 216 of this Act. However, those sections required employers to notify the Minister of commencement of employment and the employment records of employees respectively. This section has a broader ambit by allowing the Minister, by regulation, to prescribe classes of person who must provide information about claimants. This anti-abuse provision has been used to require all institutions of higher education to provide the Minister with details concerning all students who are registered at the commencement of each academic year: see S.I. No. 196 of 1991, as amended by S.I. No. 311 of 1992.

Exchange of information

222.—(1) Information held by the Minister for the purposes of this Act (including the purpose of collection by the Revenue Commissioners of employment and self-employment contributions) may be transferred by the Minister to the Revenue Commissioners, and information held by the Revenue Commissioners for the purposes of this Act or the Income Tax Acts, relating to employers, the reckonable earnings of employed contributors or reckonable income or reckonable emoluments of self-employed contributors or of any payments made under this Act, may be transferred by the Revenue Commissioners to the Minister.

(2) Information held by the Minister for the purposes of this Act or the control of schemes administered by or on behalf of the Minister or the Department of Social Welfare may be transferred by the Minister to another Minister of the Government or a specified body, and information held by another Minister of the Government or a specified body which is required for the said purposes or the control of any such scheme administered by another Minister of the Government or a specified body may be transferred by that Minister of the Government or the specified body to the Minister.

(3) In subsection (2) "a specified body" means a local authority (for the purposes of the Local Government Act, 1941), a health board, the Garda Síochána or any other body established—

(a) by or under any enactment (other than the Companies Acts, 1963 to 1990), or

(b) under the Companies Acts, 1963 to 1990, in pursuance of powers conferred by or under any other enactment,

and financed wholly or partly by means of moneys provided or loans made or guaranteed, by a Minister of the Government or the issue of shares held by or on behalf of a Minister of the Government and a subsidiary of any such body.

GENERAL NOTE

This section seems to be directed at establishing that such transfers are not to be seen as incompatible with the provisions of the Data Protection Act, 1988. The transfer of information held by social security agencies has been a matter of great concern to the Council of Europe and it has great implications for privacy law and the Council of Europe Convention of Data Processing and in particular the Recommendations of the Council of Europe 1986, discussed by Clark, *Data Protection—National Needs and International Obligations* (1987) 5 ILT (N.S.) 173. There are privacy implications under the Constitution that this section seems to ignore, particularly in relation to authorisation to transfer "information"—the term is not defined or qualified—to the gardai: see *Murphy v. P.M.P.A. Ins* H.C. Unrep. February 21, 1978. See generally, Clark, *Privacy, Data Protection and Social Welfare* (1988) 6 ILT (N.S.) 207–211.

COMMENCEMENT

March 30, 1988.

Personal social services number

223.—(1) The Minister may allocate and issue a personal social services number to a person in such manner as he deems fit.

(2) A claimant or beneficiary under this Act shall be required to furnish to an officer of the Minister such information, as may be prescribed, which

is necessary for the allocation and issue of a personal social services number under subsection (1).

(3) For the purposes of this Act, including the making of a claim for benefit or the payment of any such benefit, a person shall furnish to an officer of the Minister, his personal social services number and that of his spouse, if any, and any child dependant.

(4) In this section a reference to a personal social services number shall be construed as including a reference to a number known as a revenue and social insurance number.

GENERAL NOTE

The legislative history behind this section is somewhat short, appearing in Irish social welfare law in the Social Welfare Act, 1993, but when introduced at that time, this seemingly innocuous provision was the cause of a protracted and interesting debate at Committee Stage in Dáil Eireann. The section seeks to give a legislative basis for the Departmental practice of allocating and issuing personal social services numbers to individuals, these numbers being a unique means of identification for persons who seek to use the social welfare and taxation agencies. This section also requires persons to provide "such information, as may be prescribed", before the number may be issued, and the section also requires claimants to furnish their number, or the number of a spouse and child dependant, if any, at the time of making a claim for benefit, or when benefit is paid. In fact the revenue and social insurance number, already used by the Revenue Commissioners and the Department of Social Welfare, already serves this purpose and the number, by subsection (4), is now to be called a "personal social services number". This measure is in essence an anti-fraud measure, to be used to cross-check claims by reference to social welfare and taxation data, and the number is issued by the Department of Social Welfare. The number will be recorded on a plastic card and claimants must use this number if a claim is to be processed.

The section, as presented, must be seen in the context of Irish data protection law and the provisions of section 31 of the Social Welfare Act, 1988. The Data Protection Act, 1988 requires the Department of Social Welfare to observe certain provisions, principally the data protection principles in section 2 of the Act, if personal privacy and confidentiality of information are to be respected. While the Social Welfare Act, 1988 does not directly contradict or compromise the data protection principles, the Department of Social Welfare is permitted to exchange personal data with other Government agencies and prescribed bodies, including the Gardai. It must be doubted whether the broad terms of section 31 represent a reasonable or balanced use of the power to modify the absolute terms of the data protection principles on the ground of fiscal efficiency. Administrative convenience is probably given greater emphasis than claimant privacy, at least in this writer's view; see (1988) 6 I.L.T. 207.

This section, however, represents a compromise between providing no legislative basis for the use of such numbers and a broader proposal to allow these numbers to be used for purposes other than social welfare or taxation purposes. In 1991 it was proposed that PRSI numbers would be issued to school children and that these numbers would be required if correspondence between parents and the Department of Education took place. The Data Protection Commissioner, in his 1991 Annual Report, was critical of such a proposal and he called for the proposal to be shelved pending a debate on the use of these numbers and legislative proposals to delimit a proper use of such identifiers. The Government have acceded to this prudent counsel offered by the Commissioner. Nevertheless, the section was criticised in Dáil Eireann. Some Deputies saw this as the thin end of a large anti-civil liberties wedge. Others were critical of the failure to specify in the section what information has to be provided, and others complained that social welfare claimants were being further stigmatised: see 428 Dáil Debates Cols. 923–934.

Proceedings

Provisions relating to prosecutions

224.—(1) Proceedings for an offence under this Act shall not be instituted except by or with the consent of the Minister or by an officer authorised in that behalf by special or general directions of the Minister.

(2) A prosecution for a summary offence under this Act may be brought at the suit of the Minister.

(3) Notwithstanding the provisions of subsection (1) or any provision in any enactment specifying the period within which proceedings may be commenced, a prosecution for a summary offence under this Act may be brought at any time within whichever of the following periods later expires—

(a) the period of 6 months commencing on the date on which evidence sufficient to justify the institution of that prosecution came into the possession of the Minister, or

(b) the period of two years commencing on the date on which the offence was committed.

(4) For the purposes of subsection (3), a certificate, sealed with the official seal of the Minister, as to the date on which such evidence as aforesaid came into his possession shall be sufficient evidence thereof until the contrary is shown.

(5) Where in a prosecution for an offence under this Act it is shown to the satisfaction of the court—

(a) that an application has been made by a person (in this section referred to as "the defendant") for any benefit, and

(b) that as a result of that application any such benefit has been paid to any person (whether or not such benefit was that applied for and whether or not it was paid to the defendant),

the defendant shall be presumed to have given any information contained in the application (or to have caused it to be given on his behalf) and, where such information is false, with full knowledge of such falsity and with intent that it should deceive; but this presumption may be rebutted.

(6) For the purpose of the institution of proceedings under this Act a certificate, purporting to be given by an officer of the Minister authorised in that behalf by the Minister and to be signed by that officer, certifying the following facts, namely, that a person is an officer of the Minister and that he has been authorised under a special or general direction of the Minister to institute such proceedings, or that the Minister has consented to the institution of such proceedings, shall be sufficient evidence in any legal proceedings of the matters certified in the certificate, until the contrary is shown.

(7) (a) In proceedings instituted by virtue of section 14, a certificate purporting to be signed by the Collector-General which certifies that a stated amount is due and payable by the defendant shall be evidence until the contrary is proved that that amount is due and payable, and when tendered in evidence shall be deemed until the contrary is proved to have been signed by him.

(b) For the purposes of this subsection, the rules of the court concerned for the time being applicable to civil proceedings shall apply to proceedings by virtue of section 14.

GENERAL NOTE

The Minister, or a duly authorised officer of the Minister, must consent to the commencement of proceedings against any person for an offence under the Act. Prosecution for a summary offence can be brought at the suit of the Minister. Despite the general statutory requirement that summary proceedings against an accused should commence within six months of the date of the offence, summary proceedings for an offence may be brought within six months from the date on which sufficient evidence justifying the prosecution came into the possession of the Minister, or two years from the date on which the offence was committed, whichever is the later. For the purpose of establishing when sufficient evidence was in the possession of the Minister, an official certificate is to be adequate evidence thereof unless the contrary is shown.

The accused is faced with a sweeping rebuttable presumption in proceedings under the Act. If the Court is satisfied that the defendant has made a claim for benefit and that, as a result of that application, benefit has been paid to any person (the defendant or the defendant's spouse, for example) it is presumed that any information which was given was given by the defendant and where the information was false that the defendant had full knowledge of the falsity and that the information was given with the intent to deceive. Subsections (6) and (7) allow certificates to be adduced as evidence of the competence of the Minister's officials to institute proceedings and as proof that contributions are due, unless the contrary is shown.

Evidence of records, computer readouts, photocopies, microfilms and copies of original documents in proceedings

225.—(1) In this section—

"copy record" means any copy of an original record being a record made for the purposes of or in connection with this Act or schemes administered by the Department of Social Welfare or a copy of that copy made in accordance with either of the methods referred to in subsection (2) and accompanied by the certificate referred to in subsection (3);

"original record" means any document, record, or record of an entry in a document or record or information stored by means of any mechanical or electronic device, whether or not in a legible form, which was made or stored by the Minister or a specified agency for the purposes of or in connection with this Act or schemes administered by the Department of Social Welfare at the time of or shortly after the event recorded and which is in the possession of the Minister or a specified agency;

"provable record" means an original record or a copy record;

"specified agency" means An Post or a person authorised to carry on banking business under section 9 of the Central Bank Act, 1971.

(2) The Minister or a specified agency may, where by reason of the deterioration of, or inconvenience in storing, or technical obsolescence in the manner of keeping any original record or any copy record, make a legible copy of the record or store information concerning that record otherwise than in a legible form so that the information is capable of being used to make a legible copy of the record, and the Minister or the specified agency may thereupon destroy the original record or the copy record:

Provided that any authorisation required by the National Archives Act, 1986, for such destruction has been granted.

(3) In any proceedings a certificate signed by an officer of the Minister or a specified agency, as the case may be, stating that a copy record has been made in accordance with the provisions of subsection (2) shall be evidence of the fact of the making of such copy record and that it is a true copy, until the contrary is shown.

(4) A document purporting to be a certificate under subsection (3) shall be deemed to be such a certificate without proof of the signature of the person purporting to sign the certificate or that such person was a proper person to so sign, until the contrary is shown.

(5) In any proceedings any provable record may be given in evidence and shall be *prima facie* evidence of any fact therein stated or event thereby recorded:

Provided that the court is satisfied of the reliability of the system used to make or compile, in the case of an original record, that record, and in the case of a copy record, the original on which it was based.

(6) Where information contained in a provable record is in a form which would normally not be comprehensible to a person who has no knowledge of that type of information, an explanation of its meaning by a suitably qualified person shall be admissible.

(7) In any proceedings a certificate signed by an officer of the Minister or a specified agency, as the case may be, stating that a full and detailed search

has been made for a provable record of an event in every place where such records are kept by the Minister or the agency, as the case may be, and that no such record has been found shall be *prima facie* evidence that the event did not happen.

Provided that the court is satisfied—

(a) of the reliability of the system used to compile or make and keep such records,

(b) that, if the event had happened, a record would have been made of it, and

(c) that the system is such that the only reasonable explanation for the absence of a record is that the event did not happen.

(8) This section shall apply to any original record or to any copy record made before the 26th day of March, 1989, in accordance with either of the methods referred to in subsection (2) but the proviso to that subsection shall not have effect in relation to anything deemed to have been done under that subsection before the commencement of section 7 of the National Archives Act, 1986.

GENERAL NOTE

This section provides that in any proceedings for an offence committed under the Social Welfare Acts, a certificate, signed by an officer and certifying facts recorded on a computer or microfilm will, absent the original document, be prima facie evidence of the facts so certified. The provision also extends to An Post and the Associated Banks for payment of money orders is often made by way of these agencies. If this is done, the original document can be destroyed if any prior authorisation which may be required under the National Archives Act, 1986 has been obtained. Before the record is to be prima facie evidence the court must be satisfied that the information system used to compile the record was reliable. Records which are not intelligible to a non-expert can be explained by a specialist and such an explanation may be admissible.

CHAPTER 5

ALIENATION OF BOOKS AND DOCUMENTS

Application

226.—In this Chapter "a document to which this Chapter applies" means every book, card, order, voucher or other document issued to any person and upon the delivery or production or in respect of the possession of which by such person on or after a date indicated expressly or by implication in such document and subsequent to the issue of such document any benefit is payable to him.

GENERAL NOTE

This is a definition section which defines the range of documents to which Chapter 5 applies. In brief, documents which have been issued to a beneficiary so as to enable the beneficiary to obtain a social welfare payment are covered in this definition. The most relevant document is a Child Benefit order book which allows the beneficiary to cash monthly vouchers at a designated bank or post office branch.

Prohibition of alienation of documents

227.—Every person who buys, takes in exchange or takes in pawn any document to which this Chapter applies shall be guilty of an offence.

GENERAL NOTE

This section is used to counteract moneylending activities which are facilitated by the lender taking a benefit book, often in exchange for an illegal loan. The loan being either secured via the book or repaid by allowing the beneficiary to cash the voucher and pay over the proceeds to the lender. Until recently this section was not widely used.

Avoidance of alienation of documents

228.—Every alienation or purported alienation of a document to which this Chapter applies, whether made by way of sale, exchange or hypothecation shall be and be deemed always to have been void and of no effect.

GENERAL NOTE

This section invalidates any alienation of a document as defined in section 226. It is wider in scope than the preceding section for this provision also applies to a temporary pledge of the document as well as a sale exchange or pawn of the document.

It should be noted that the Consumer Credit Bill, 1994 seeks to make it a criminal offence to obtain possession of documents of this kind.

Return of documents on demand

229.—(1) Every person who, by virtue of an alienation or purported alienation declared by this Chapter to be void, has in his possession a document to which this Chapter applies shall, in the case of any such document issued in respect of any benefit, on demand by a social welfare inspector forthwith deliver such document to such inspector or, where no such demand is made by a social welfare inspector, on demand by the owner of such document or his duly authorised agent, forthwith deliver such document to such owner or agent.

(2) Every person who, on a demand being made on him under this section, fails to deliver in accordance with this section a document which he is required by this section so to deliver shall be guilty of an offence.

(3) Where a person is convicted of an offence under this section the court by which he is so convicted may, where the circumstances so require, make such order as the court shall think proper for securing the delivery of the document in respect of which the offence was committed to the owner thereof or, where appropriate, to a social welfare inspector.

GENERAL NOTE

Where a document has been alienated within the terms of this section, the person who has possession of the document is obliged to deliver that document to a social welfare inspector upon demand or, where no such demand has been made, to the owner of the document, or the owner's agent, upon the demand of that person. Failure to comply is an offence. The penalty is stipulated in section 218.

CHAPTER 6

MISCELLANEOUS PROVISIONS

Provisions as to maintenance

230.—Regulations may provide for determining the circumstances in which a person is or is not to be deemed for the purposes of Part II to be wholly or mainly maintaining another person.

GENERAL NOTE

The regulations in question are not to be confused with regulations defining adult or child dependants, i.e. S.I. No. 417 of 1994.

Free certificates

231.—(1) The Minister may arrange for the issue for the purposes of Part II of medical certificates or certificates of expected or actual confinement free of charge.

(2) The expenses incurred in giving effect to this section shall not exceed such sums as may from time to time be agreed upon between the Minister and the Minister for Finance.

GENERAL NOTE

Part II relates to social insurance claimants. For the purpose of disability benefit, maternity benefit, occupational injury benefits or invalidity pension, the Minister may, under this section, arrange for the issue of medical certificates free of charge to the claimant, the Minister, by arrangement with the Minister for Finance, meeting the costs of such an arrangement.

Stamp duty

232.—Stamp duty shall not be chargeable upon any document by which any payment, refund, repayment or return pursuant to this Act is made.

GENERAL NOTE

For stamp duty generally, see *Doing Business in Ireland* (eds., Ussher and O'Connor) section 5.10.

Birth, marriage and death certificates

233.—(1) Where, for the purposes of this Act (other than Chapter 11 of Part III), the age, marriage or death of any person is required to be proved by the production of a certificate of birth, marriage or death any person shall, on presenting a written requisition in such form and containing such particulars as may be directed by the Minister for Health, be entitled to obtain, on payment of the fee set out therefor—
  (a) a copy of an entry in a register of birth— 70p,
  (b) a copy of an entry in a register of deaths— 70p,
  (c) a copy of an entry in a register of marriages—70p,
certified under the hand of the register or superintendent registrar or other person having the custody thereof.

(2) Where, for the purposes of Chapter 11 of Part III or regulations made under that Chapter, the age, marriage or death of any person is required to be proved by the production of a certificate of birth, marriage or death, any person shall, on presenting a written request in such form and containing such particulars as may be directed by the Minister for Health, be entitled to obtain free of charge a certified copy of the entry of the birth, marriage or death (as the case may be) of that person in the register of births, marriages or deaths (as the case may be) under the hand of the registrar or superintendent registrar or other person having the custody thereof.

(3) Forms for the purposes of subsections (1) and (2) shall be supplied on request without any charge by every registrar of births and deaths and by every superintendent registrar or other person having the custody of the register.

(4) The Minister for Health may, with the consent of the Minister and the Minister for Finance, by regulations alter the fees set out in subsection (1).

GENERAL NOTE

By the use of a form which satisfies the Minister for Health, claimants are able to obtain copies of birth, death or marriage certificates, when needed for the purposes of the Act (*e.g.*

establishing entitlement for a widow's pension) at a reduced rate of 70 pence for each such certificate. Supplementary welfare allowance claimants however may obtain such certificates free of charge under subsection (2).

Inalienability

234.—Subject to this Act, every assignment of or charge on, and every agreement to assign or charge, any benefit shall be void and on the bankruptcy of any person entitled to benefit, shall not pass to any trustee or other person acting on behalf of the creditors.

GENERAL NOTE

This section makes it clear that benefit is a personal right and the assignment of, or charge on, any such benefit is void. Upon the bankruptcy of a beneficiary there shall be no right in the trustee in bankruptcy to have access to this benefit for the advantage of the bankrupt's creditors. Note also the provisions in sections 226–229 which invalidate dealings in certain documents and indeed makes certain dealings criminal acts.

Means for purpose of Debtors Act (Ireland), 1872

235.—Any sum received by any person by way of benefit shall not be included in calculating that person's means for the purposes of section 6 of the Debtors Act (Ireland), 1872.

GENERAL NOTE

Sums payable as benefit are not to be regarded as part of that person's means when that person's assets are calculated under section 6 of the Debtors Act (Ireland) 1872. On personal insolvency see the Bankruptcy Act, 1988.

Exclusion in assessment of damages

236.—(1) In assessing damages in any action under the Fatal Injuries Act, 1956, or Part IV of the Civil Liability Act, 1961, whether commenced before or after the 24th day of February, 1981, there shall not be taken into account any child benefit, survivor's pension, orphan's (contributory) allowance, lone parent's allowance in the case of a person who qualifies for such allowance by virtue of being a widow or widower or widow's or orphan's (non-contributory) pension [1995 Act, Schedule D].

(2) Subject to sections 75 and 237, in assessing damages in any action in respect of injury or disease or in computing the amount of compensation under paragraph (1)(a)(ii) of the First Schedule to the Workmen's Compensation Act, 1906, or under Rule 2 or 4 of the Second Schedule to the Workmen's Compensation Act, 1934, there shall not be taken into account any benefit under Part II, widow's or orphan's (non-contributory) pension or child benefit.

GENERAL NOTE

This section directs a number of ways in which certain benefits and pensions are to be treated when a claim for certain kinds of compensation are made and the claimant has received a benefit or pension previously.

The disregarding of these benefits and allowances in claims brought under these statutory causes of action, viz. Fatal Injuries, Civil Liability, and Workmen's Compensation is due to the "family" nature of the welfare payment: on the policy issues see Clark, *Damages and the Social Welfare Overlap* (1984) 19 Ir.Jur. (N.S.) 40.

Taking of disability benefit and invalidity pension into account in assessing certain damages

237.—(1) Notwithstanding section 2 of the Civil Liability Act, 1964, and section 236, in assessing damages in any action in respect of liability for personal injuries not causing death relating to the use of a mechanically propelled vehicle (within the meaning of section 3 of the Road Traffic Act, 1961), there shall be taken into account the value of any rights arising from such injuries which have accrued, or are likely to accrue, to the injured person in respect of disability benefit (including any amount payable therewith by way of pay-related benefit) or invalidity pension under Part II for the period of five years beginning with the time when the cause of action accrued.

(2) The reference in subsection (1) to damages shall, in a case where the damages are subject to reduction under the law of contributory negligence or are limited by or under any Act, be construed as a reference to the total damages which would have been recoverable apart from the reduction or limitation.

(3) This section shall apply—

(a) in assessing damages in any action in respect of liability for personal injuries not causing death relating to the use of a mechanically propelled vehicle, which is required to be covered by an approved policy of insurance, where such action is instituted on or after the 30th day of March, 1984, and

(b) in assessing damages in any other action in respect of liability for personal injuries not causing death relating to the use of a mechanically propelled vehicle, where such action is instituted on or after the 4th day of April, 1990.

(4) In subsection (3)—

"approved policy of insurance" means a policy of insurance which, by virtue of section 62 of the Road Traffic Act, 1961 (as amended by the European Communities (Road Traffic) (Compulsory Insurance) Regulations, 1975 (S.I. No. 178 of 1975)) is an approved policy of insurance for the purposes of that Act;

"mechanically propelled vehicle" has the meaning assigned by section 3 of the Road Traffic Act, 1961.

GENERAL NOTE

The legislative history of this section goes back to s.12 of the 1984 Act.

This section implements one of the recommendations of the Prices Advisory Committee (Motor Insurance), *Report of Enquiry into the Cost and Methods of providing Motor Insurance, (1982)* (Pl. 1323). The Committee suggested that motor insurance premiums may be reduced in a variety of ways, one of which would be to allow a person who injures another in a motor accident to offset damages payable by reference to social welfare payments received by the injured party. Prior to section 12 of the 1984 Act the position was governed by section 2 of the Civil Liability (Amendment) Act, 1964 (No. 17) which directed that such benefits should not be taken into account in assessing damages. Section 68 of the 1981 Act however directed that where a person recovers damages for personal injury the court shall take into account all occupational injuries benefits received or likely to be received in the five-year period following accrual of the cause of action. Section 68 is here extended into motor accident cases when the accident victim receives disability benefit or invalidity pension. Indeed, this section goes further than section 68 of the 1981 Act by expressing providing that pay-related benefits are also to be taken into account.

Section 46 of the 1990 Act made the disregard established by the 1984 Act applicable to public sector drivers and vehicles. These disregards however involve issues of fact, and where the defendant seeks to offset disability benefit payments in the future, the court may decline to make such a deduction if the evidence indicates that the plaintiff's entitlements may operate for a limited time: *O'Loughlin v. Teeling* [1988] I.L.R.M. 617.

Reciprocal arrangements

238.—(1) The Minister may make such orders as may be necessary to carry out any reciprocal or other arrangements made with any international organisation, any other State or Government or the proper authority under any other Government, in respect of matters relating to insurance and benefits under Part II, old age (non-contributory) and blind pensions, widow's or orphan's (non-contributory) pensions, unemployment assistance and child benefit, and may by any such order make such adaptations of and modifications in respect of these matters as he considers necessary.

(2) The Minister may by order amend or revoke an order under this section.

GENERAL NOTE

The power to make reciprocal arrangements with other states or Governments has been exercised frequently in relation to social security arrangements. In the E.U., the issue of reciprocal recognition is addressed by Council Reg. 1408 of 1971. The most important recent reciprocal arrangements are as follows:

Social Welfare (Agreement with the Republic of Austria on Social Security) Order 1989 (S.I. No. 307 of 1989).

Social Welfare (Agreement with Canada on Social Security) Order 1991 (S.I. No. 317 of 1991).

Social Welfare (Agreement with Australia on Social Security) Order 1992 (S.I. No. 84 of 1992).

Social Welfare (Agreement with the United States of America on Social Security) Order 1993 (S.I. No. 243 of 1993).

Social Welfare (Agreement with New Zealand on Social Security) Order 1994 (S.I. No. 76 of 1994).

Provision of consultancy, training and contract services, etc.

238A.—(1) The minister may, with the consent of the Minister for Finance, for gain or otherwise, promote and enter into, with a specified body—

(a) a contract or an agreement for the provision by him to, or

(b) a contrct, agreement or a joint venture for the provision by him with, that body of consultancy, advisory, training, technical assistance or contract services or the sale or provision of computer products, inside and outside the State.

(2) In this section 'a specified body' means—

(a) a body established by or under any enactment (other than the Companies Acts, 1963 to 1990),

(b) a body established under the Companies Acts, 1963 to 1990.

(c) a body formed or established under the laws of a state other than the State and corresponding to a body referred to in paragraphs (a) and (b),

(d) an institution of the European Communities,

(e) a competent authority of a state other than the State, or

(f) the United Nations, the World Bank or any other international institution recognised by the State. [1994 Act, section 33].

GENERAL NOTE

This section was introduced into the Social Welfare Bill, 1994 at Committee Stage in Dáil Eireann by the Minister. Dr Woods explained this section at 139 Seanad Debates Cols. 1468–1469 in the following terms:

"The various skills which have been developed within my Department have resulted in numerous approaches from public and private organisations overseas seeking support on a consultancy basis. Over the past number of years, many groups from all over the world have visited Ireland to study how my Department operates. In the past month alone delegations from Poland, Russia and Slovakia have been here and a group from the Republic of Albania is scheduled to visit within the next few weeks.

In what I hope will set a new trend for Government Departments, my Department is to use our social welfare business expertise on a commercial basis. This is a new and exciting venture in public administration. With the opening up of eastern European countries many opportunities are presenting themselves. My Department is well positioned to maximise these opportunities in the development of new markets, which is an essential component of the *Programme for Competitiveness and Work*. This new role reflects the Government's determination to develop joint ventures between public and private sectors and to create commercial units within Departments which will develop and market the considerable expertise within the Civil Service, thereby bringing returns to the taxpayer in terms of business opportunities and jobs for young people.

For example, my Department is currently working with the Digital Equipment Corporation, our main computer supplier, to identify opportunities for marketing specialist products and services from Ireland to social welfare authorities in other countries. A number of approaches have been made from interested parties and these are being pursued. In addition, my Department is in discussion with E.U. officials with a view to providing social welfare expertise for the emerging states.

It is widely recognised within the EU and the developing states that we have a considerable expertise in the social security area. The challenge is to translate that high level of expertise into the creation of skilled jobs for Irish people while at the same time assisting these developing countries to make the successful transition to a modern European state".

Administration of social welfare schemes

239.—(1) The Minister may delegate to such persons as may be prescribed, any function in relation to the administration of any benefit as may be prescribed and any such delegation shall be subject to such conditions and in such circumstances as may be prescribed.

(2) Regulations made under this section may apply to the whole State or to a specified part or parts of the State.

GENERAL NOTE

This section empowers the Minister to make regulations delegating certain administrative functions of the Department of Social Welfare to other organisations. Under existing law certain functions are carried out by other organisations such as An Post in relation to the encashment of pension orders at post offices. The Minister explained that " . . . relationships between my Department and An Post is being placed on a more formal footing in the context of current plans for the development of Post Office services. While there are no immediate plans to devolve further functions, developments in technology and otherwise will open up considerable possibilities in this area in the future and the provision in section 41 is designed to enable me to take advantage of any such possibilities for the benefit of social welfare clients."

STATUTORY INSTRUMENT

Social Welfare (Household Budgeting) Regulations, 1993 (S.I. No. 196 of 1993).

Budgeting in relation to social welfare payments

240.—(1) The Minister may make regulations to provide that where a beneficiary consents, an amount of his benefit, which is determined by consultation and agreement between the Minister and the said beneficiary, may be withheld and paid separately by the Minister to such specified body as may be designated by the beneficiary.

(2) Regulations made under subsection (1) may, in particular and without prejudice to the generality of that subsection—

(a) provide for the withdrawal of consent by a beneficiary,

(b) provide for the time and manner in which such withdrawal shall take place, and

(c) provide for the adjustment of any amount of benefit as a result of such withdrawal.

(3) In this section "a specified body" means a local authority (for the purposes of the Local Government Act, 1941), or any other body established—

(a) by or under any enactment (other than the Companies Acts, 1963 to 1990), or

(b) under the Companies Acts, 1963 to 1990, in pursuance of powers conferred by or under other enactments, and financed wholly or partly by means of moneys provided or loans made or guaranteed by a Minister of the Government or the issue of shares held by or on behalf of a Minister of the Government and a subsidiary of any such body.

GENERAL NOTE

This enabling provision introduced in the 1991 Act, takes existing regulations on diverted payments into new territory. Existing diverted payments procedure tend to favour diversion to relatives, guardians or institutions providing care to the claimant. The regulations will allow diversion of payments to specified bodies. The Minister explained that the section "provides that, with the consent of the recipient, the Minister may withhold from any social welfare payment an amount to be agreed and the amount may then be paid to a body or organisation as designated by the recipient. This provision can be used, for example, to have a person's ESB bill or local authority rent paid directly by the Department to the relevant body".

STATUTORY INSTRUMENT

Social Welfare (Household Budgeting) Regulations, 1993 (S.I. No. 196 of 1993).

Regulations varying rates of benefit or assistance

241.—(1) Notwithstanding anything in this Act the Minister may by regulations increase temporarily or vary all or any of the rates of benefit (other than child benefit or family income supplement).

(2) Regulations under subsection (1) shall not so vary the rate of any benefit as to reduce the amount of the rate payable at the commencement of the regulations.

GENERAL NOTE

This power to increase temporarily or vary rates of benefit is used annually so as to make a double rate of payment at Christmas time: this is known as the Christmas bonus payment: see for example S.I. No. 437 of 1994.

Effect of means on certain rates of assistance

242.—Notwithstanding the provisions of this Act, in the case of a person who is in receipt of any assistance under Part III and whose means exceed a prescribed amount, the Minister may by regulations, where the amount payable is not a multiple of £2, increase such amount to the next multiple of £2 in respect of such class of person or classes of persons as may be prescribed.

GENERAL NOTE

This is a technical means-testing provision which enables the Minister, by regulation, to round up the rate of a social assistance payment to an appropriate minimum amount of £2 where the means test results in a payment of less than £2 being payable.

243.—The Minister may make regulations in relation to any benefit, and the regulations may apply (with or without modification) or make provisions corresponding (with or without modification) to any provisions of this Act.

Application of provisions of this Act, etc. by regulations

244.—(1) In the case of any section of this Act which confers powers on the Minister to apply by regulations any provisions of this Act to matters referred to in that section, such powers shall be deemed to include powers to apply any provisions of any enactment, whether passed before or after the 26th day of March, 1989, which amends or extends this Act.

(2) The powers conferred on the Minister under subsection (3) of section 23 of the Housing (Private Rented Dwellings) Act, 1982, in relation to regulations under subsection (1) of that section (which relates to payments under the rent allowance scheme) to apply (with or without modification), or make provision corresponding (with or without modification) to, any provisions of this Act shall be deemed to include powers to apply any provisions of, or provisions made under, any enactment, whether passed before or after the 26th day of March, 1989, which amends or extends this Act.

GENERAL NOTE

This section appeared in section 26 of the Social Welfare Act 1989.

The intention behind subsection (1) is to ensure that where under the Principal Act the Minister is given the power to apply, by regulations, any provisions of that Act to matters referred to in that section, the power is deemed to include powers to apply any amending legislation.

Subsection (2) relates to the powers conferred on the Minister by the Housing (Private Rented Dwellings) Act, 1982. Section 23(3) of that Act confers power on the Minister in respect of the payment of the social welfare rent allowance. Under the 1989 Act the Minister's powers under section 23(3) of the 1982 Act are deemed to extend to powers in the Principal Act or any amending legislation.

Payment of increases in respect of qualified children

245.—The Minister may provide by regulations for the payment of increases in respect of qualified children at the full rate to either parent of the children concerned notwithstanding that each parent is entitled to an increase in benefit in respect of qualified children.

GENERAL NOTE

This provision remains in force despite the fact that it was intended as a transitional provision following upon implementation of the Third Equality Directive in the (No. 2) Act of 1985.

Notwithstanding the general tenor of that Act, which provided that where both parents were in receipt of short-term insurance benefits, any child addition would be payable at 50 per cent of the scale rate, this section enables the Minister to pay the full rate of a child dependant addition in respect of each child.

Adult dependant (payment of allowances in certain circumstances).

245A.—(1) Subject to subsection (2), regulations may provide for entitling to an increase of benefit or assistance (other than suplementary welfare allowance), as the case may be, payable in respect of an adult dependant, a claimant or beneficiary who would be entitled thereto but for the fact that his spouse has income in excess of a prescribed amount.

(2) Regulations for the purposes of subsection (1) shall provide that the increase payable by virtue thereof shall be payable at a rate less than the appropriate rate specified in the Second or Fourth Schedule, as the case may be, and the rate specified by the regulations may vary by reference to the amount by which the income of the spouse exceeds the amount prescribed for the purposes of subsection (1).

(3) Notwithstanding the provisions of this Act, in the case of a person who qualifies for an increase in respect of an adult dependant by virtue of regulations made under this section, any increase in benefit or assistance, as the case may be, in respect of a qualified child who normally resides with

the beneficiary and with the spouse of the beneficiary shall be payable at the rate of one-half of the appropriate amount.

(4) In this section 'benefit' means benefit under Part II [1995 Act, section 15(1).

GENERAL NOTE

In introducing this provision to Dáil Eireann, Mr De Rossa said (450 *Dáil Debates* Cols. 1932–1933):

"Deputies will be aware of the rules governing the payment of the adult dependant allowance where the adult dependant has earnings in excess of £60 a week. These rules have been criticised in recent years because the full allowance is lost as soon as weekly earnings exceed the £60 limit. This has given rise to distortions in certain industries where extra working or overtime is not availed of—and in some cases, pay increases are foregone— because of the impact on the spouse's adult dependant allowance. With a view to resolving these difficulties, I propose to bring in new arrangements early next year in which I will provide a rate of adult dependant allowance related to earnings. It may be necessary for administrative reasons to introduce the new arrangements on a phased basis for different schemes.

Section 15 provides for giving regulatory powers to the Minister to enable an adult dependant allowance to be paid in respect of a spouse or partner who has weekly income in excess of a prescribed amount. It is my intention that the adult dependant allowance payable in these circumstances will be tapered by reference to the level of the spouse's or partner's income. In addition, child dependant allowances in respect of qualified children will continue to be payable at half rate.

The details of the new arrangements are being worked out and I propose to make the necessary regulations later this year with a view to implementing them from early next year. My objective is to ensure a higher level of earnings before the full adult dependant allowance is withdrawn from the spouse—a significant contribution to removing one of the poverty traps which currently keep people out of employment or on very low pay".

PART VII

DECISIONS, APPEALS AND SOCIAL WELFARE TRIBUNAL

CHAPTER 1

DECIDING OFFICERS AND DECISIONS BY DECIDING OFFICERS

Appointment and Functions of Deciding Officers

Appointment of deciding officers

246.—The Minister may appoint such and so many of his officers as he thinks proper to be deciding officers for the purposes of this Act, and every person so appointed shall hold office as a deciding officer during the pleasure of the Minister.

GENERAL NOTE

This section empowers the Minister to appoint a number of officials to serve as deciding officers. They continue to be officials within the Department, hold office in accordance with the section (*i.e.* at the Minister's pleasure) but are required to act quasi-judicially.

Decisions by deciding officers

247.—(1) Subject to this Act, and in accordance with any relevant regulations, every question to which this section applies shall be decided by a deciding officer.

(2) This section applies to every question arising under—
(a) Part II (social insurance) being a question—
    (i) in relation to a claim for benefit,
    (ii) as to whether a person is or was disqualified for benefit,
    (iii) as to the period of any disqualification for benefit,
    (iv) as to whether an employment is or was insurable employment or insurable (occupational injuries) employment,
    (v) as to whether a person is or was employed in an insurable employment or insurable (occupational injuries) employment,
    (vi) as to what rate of employment contribution is or was payable by an employer in respect of an employed contributor,
    (vii) as to who is or was the employer of an employed contributor,
    (viii) as to whether a person is or was entitled to become a voluntary contributor,
    (ix) on any such other matter relating to Part II as may be prescribed,
    (x) as to whether an employment is or was an insurable self-employment,
    (xi) as to whether a person is or was in insurable self-employment, or
    (xii) as to what rate of self-employment contribution is or was payable by a self-employed contributor,
(b) Part III (social assistance) other than Chapter 11 (supplementary welfare allowance),
(c) Part IV (child benefit),
(d) Part V (family income supplement), and
(e) Part VI (general provisions relating to social insurance, social assistance and insurability).
(3) A reference in subsection (2)(a) to a question arising in relation to a claim for benefit includes a reference to a question whether benefit is or is not or was or was not payable.

GENERAL NOTE

Subsection (1)
This subsection makes it clear that the jurisdiction of a deciding officer is fixed by this Act.

Subsection (2)
This subsection establishes the areas of jurisdiction open to a deciding officer. Note that deciding officers, under subsection (2)(b), have no jurisdiction in relation to supplementary welfare allowance.

Following upon the making of a valid claim by a claimant in accordance with the Claims and Payments Regulations, the merits of the claim will initially be judged by a deciding officer. Deciding officers are Department officials who are distributed throughout the State in order to give an application a, hopefully, more speedy response than if each claim were processed centrally, *e.g.* in Dublin. Deciding officers are required to act in accordance with the principles of Natural and Constitutional Justice and the decision-making powers of the deciding officer were examined by Murphy J. in *Corcoran v. The Minister for Social Welfare and Others* H.C. June 7, 1991. In that case a deciding officer, examining a motor vehicle owned by a claimant, concluded that the claimant had under-represented his resources and thus withdrew the claimant's qualification certificate, terminating his entitlement to unemployment assistance. On the propriety of such a decision, Murphy J. said:

"It seems to me that the Deciding Officer was entitled to have regard to the personal circumstances of the Applicant; the obvious demands on his very limited resources; the value of the vehicle which he owned; the cost of maintaining it and the purposes for which it might be used. If he drew, as it seems to me he did draw, the inference that the Applicant had a more substantial income or alternatively an undisclosed source of income which would result in the Applicant exceeding the maximum permitted statutory figure, that such a decision could not be described as unreasonable less still as "plainly and unambiguously flying in the face of fundamental reason and commonsense" which is the criterion laid down by the Supreme Court in *The State (Keegan) v. Stardust Compensation Tribunal* 1986 I.R. 642 as the test by which decisions of Administrative Tribunals will be judged".

Revised Decisions by Deciding Officers

Revision of decisions by deciding officers

248.—(1) A deciding officer may, at any time—

(a) revise any decision of a deciding officer, if it appears to him that the decision was erroneous in the light of new evidence or of new facts which have been brought to his notice since the date on which it was given or by reason of some mistake having been made in relation to the law or the facts, or if it appears to him that there has been any relevant change of circumstances since the decision was given, or

(b) revise any decision of an appeals officer if it appears to him that there has been any relevant change of circumstances which has come to notice since the decision was given,

and the provisions of this Part as to appeals shall apply to the revised decision in the same manner as they apply to an original decision of a deciding officer.

(2) Subsection (1)(a) shall not apply to a decision relating to a matter which is on appeal or reference under sections 250 and 257 unless the revised decision would be in favour of a claimant.

GENERAL NOTE

Subsection (1)(a) gives a deciding officer the jurisdiction to revise any decision of any deciding officer (including presumably a deciding officer's own decisions) in the light of new facts rendering the initial decision erroneous, a previous mistake having been made rendering the decision wrong in law or fact, or because of an intervening change in circumstances. As such, this provision is unexceptional and gives the adjudication system a necessary measure of flexibility and responsiveness.

Subsection (1)(b) is relatively new, dating from section 31 of the 1993 Act. As it stands it is a remarkable provision. It gives a deciding officer the power to revise any decision of an appeals officer if it appears to the deciding officer that there has been any relevant change in circumstances which has come to notice since the decision was given. The appeals officer is supposed to be an independent quasi-judicial figure, but, under this provision, a decision can be revised by the initial decision maker in circumstances which are loosely defined by the section, insofar as a revised decision can include a reversal of the appeals officer's decision. There can, however, be an appeal against any decision revised by the deciding officer. This provision nevertheless further undermines the independence of the appeals officer and the reforms undertaken by Part V of the Social Welfare Act, 1990. It reverses the decisions in *Lundy v. Minister for Social Welfare* and *O'Connor v. Minister for Social Welfare*, both decisions of Keane J. of April 30, 1993.

Subsection (3) prevents a deciding officer from exercising review powers under subsection (1)(a) if a section 250 (referral to an appeals officer) or section 257 (appeal to an appeals officer) referral or appeal has been made unless such a review benefits the claimant.

Effect of revised decisions by deciding officers

249.—A revised decision given by a deciding officer shall take effect as follows—

(a) where any benefit, assistance, child benefit or family income supplement will, by virtue of the revised decision be disallowed or reduced and the revised decision is given owing to the original decision having been given, or having continued in effect, by reason of any statement or representation (whether written or verbal) which was to the knowledge of the person making it false or misleading in a material respect or by reason of the wilful concealment of any material fact, it shall take effect as from the date on which the original decision took effect, but the original decision may, in the discretion of the deciding officer, continue to apply to any period covered by the original decision to which such false or misleading statement or representation or such wilful concealment of any material fact does not relate;

(b) where any benefit, assistance, child benefit or family income supplement will, by virtue of the revised decision be disallowed or reduced and the revised decision is given in the light of new evidence or new facts (relating to periods prior to and subsequent to the commencement of this Act) which have been brought to the notice of the deciding officer since the original decision was given, it shall take effect from such date as the deciding officer shall determine having regard to the new facts or new evidence;

(c) in any other case, it shall take effect as from the date considered appropriate by the deciding officer having regard to the circumstances of the case.

GENERAL NOTE

This section provides the various effects that a revised decision by a deciding officer will have in individual cases.

Subsection (a) provides that where a decision is revised and the revision results in benefit being disallowed or reduced, and the initial decision was due to some misrepresentation or concealment of a material fact when the person so misrepresenting or concealing acted knowingly or wilfully, as the case may be, the revised decision will take effect from the date of the original decision. This will mean that an overpayment will have been made. However, the deciding officer has a discretion whereby the original decision may operate until such time as the deciding officer may determine.

Subsection (b) provides that where a revised decision results in benefit being disallowed or reduced, and the revision is the result of new evidence or new facts made known to the officer after the original decision was made, the revised decision is to take effect from such date as the deciding officer determines to be appropriate. This may result in an overpayment liability being reduced or eliminated.

Subsection (c) provides that in all other cases, *e.g.* the claimant has not made any false statement and the original decision was incorrect by virtue of an administrative error, the revised decision takes effect from the date the deciding officer considers appropriate.

Reference by deciding officer to appeals officer

250.—A deciding officer may, if he so thinks proper, instead of deciding it himself, refer in the prescribed manner any question which falls to be decided by him to an appeals officer.

GENERAL NOTE

It is understood that this referral power is used sparingly. However, it is often used where a class of person comes forward (*e.g.* strikers) and issues of eligibility have to be resolved uniformly for several claimants. It resembles an "Administrative Case Stated" procedure.

CHAPTER 2

APPEALS OFFICERS, CHIEF APPEALS OFFICER AND DECISIONS BY APPEALS OFFICERS

Appointment of appeals officers

251.—The Minister may appoint such and so many of his officers as he thinks proper to be appeals officers for the purposes of this Act, except the provisions relating to supplementary welfare allowance, and every person so appointed shall hold office as an appeals officer during the pleasure of the Minister.

Chief Appeals Officer

GENERAL NOTE

Appeals officers remain officers of the Minister during their tenure as appeals officers and they hold office at the pleasure of the Minister. This has been criticised as undermining the independence of the appeals officer. As civil servants, appeals officers are also felt to be steeped in the culture and traditions of the Department of Social Welfare and, therefore, less likely to take an independent line on matters of policy or adjudication than an objectively independent tribunal would be: See Clark (1978) 13 Ir.Jur. 365.

Nevertheless, the appeals officer must observe principles of Natural and Constitutional Justice. It is also well settled that the appeals officer as a quasi-judicial figure must discharge his functions accordingly. For instance, Ministerial directives and medical reports irregularly submitted by a medical assessor are inadmissible. In the leading case of *McLoughlin v. Minister of Social Welfare* [1958] I.R. 1, the appeals officer relied on a memorandum submitted by the Minister for Finance in rejecting the claim of the appellant that he was not employed in the Civil Service and therefore was not insurable. O'Dálaigh J. indicated that when the appeals officer believed himself bound by such a direction this was "an abdication by him from his duty as an appeals officer". See also *Kiely v. Minister for Social Welfare* [1977] I.R. 267.

Chief Appeals Officer

252.—One of the appeals officers shall be designated by the Minister to be the Chief Appeals Officer and another of them shall be designated by the Minister to act as the deputy for the Chief Appeals Officer when that Officer is not available.

GENERAL NOTE

The Chief Appeals Officer and Deputy Appeals officer have, under the regulations, certain administrative functions and powers such as to allocation of appeals, the appointment of assessors and the revision of erroneous decisions by appeals officers. These are set out by later sections in this Part.

Reference of appeal to High Court by Chief Appeals Officer

253.—The Chief Appeals Officer may, where he considers it appropriate, refer any question which has been referred to an appeals officer, other than a question to which section 265 applies, for the decision of the High Court.

GENERAL NOTE

This provision was added to the appeals system as part of the extensive reforms effected in the 1990 Act in order to bring about greater independence. This section empowers the Chief Appeals Officer to refer issues arising under the Act, in respect of entitlement, to the High Court. The previous provision empowered the Chief Appeals Officer to request the Minister so to refer the matter but the Minister retained the right to make the ultimate decision.

Annual reports by Chief Appeals Officer

254.—(1) As soon as may be after the end of each year, but not later than six months thereafter, the Chief Appeals Officer shall make a report to the Minister of his activities and the activities of the appeals officers under this Part during that year and the Minister shall cause copies of the report to be laid before each House of the Oireachtas.

(2) A report under subsection (1) shall be in such form and shall include information in regard to such matters (if any) other than those referred to in that subsection as the Minister may direct.

(3) The Chief Appeals Officer shall, whenever so requested by the Minister, furnish to him information in relation to such matters as he may specify concerning his activities or the activities of appeals officers under this Part.

GENERAL NOTE

These provisions were included in the 1990 reforms in order to bring greater transparency into the Appeals system. When introducing this to the Dáil the Minister indicated that the Annual Report would be compiled by the Chief Appeals Officer under the direction of the Minister. The Minister indicated that the *Commission on Social Welfare* had recommended the publication of such an annual report. The report will give details of the number and types of appeals but also contain commentary on trends, incidence of types of appeals and analysis of need for legislative change, particular reference being made to the implication of decisions for Departmental policy-making. The Minister fully endorsed the Commission on Social Welfare:

"Publication of an annual report will make an important contribution to the task of developing public confidence in the social welfare appeals office as well as emphasising its independent status" (397 *Dáil Debates* Col. 1883).

For consequential amendments to the Rules of the Superior Courts, see S.I. No. 67 of 1991.

Appointment of assessors by Chief Appeals Officer

255.—(a) The Chief Appeals Officer may appoint any person whom he considers suitable to sit as an assessor with an appeals officer when any question which appears to the Chief Appeals Officer to require the assistance of assessors is heard.

(b) The Chief Appeals Officer may constitute, on the basis of districts or otherwise as he considers appropriate, panels of persons to sit as assessors with appeals officers and members may be selected in such manner as he may determine from such panels to so sit when any question which, in the opinion of the Chief Appeals Officer, is appropriate for the assistance of assessors is heard.

GENERAL NOTE

Assessors have been a feature of the appeals system since 1952. Assessors are appointed under subsection (a) in order to provide assistance to the appeals officer on matters which require either local or specialist knowledge, such as job availability or medical matters. For this reason, assessors are likely to be appointed to sit on unemployment or sickness-related appeals. Assessors are appointed on a panel basis, the assessor being nominated by trades union or employers' organisations. Since 1990, the rôle of assessors is fixed by reference to the Chief Appeals officer who appoints the assessors and, since 1992, draws up the panels of assessors. Previously these powers were exercised by the Minister. Assessors are not paid but expenses can be paid under section 261(2). In fact, the appointment of panels is administratively difficult, and in practice appeals are heard without an assessor if the appellant waives the need for the assessor at the oral appeal. Assessors do not have any clearly defined role. They do not constitute part of the adjudicative process and decisions are made on the merits of the appeal by the appeals officer alone. The leading case on the role of the assessor is *Kiely v. Minister for Social Welfare* [1977] I.R. 267.

The Supreme Court, in ruling on the role of the medical assessor under the Social Welfare (Occupational Injuries) Act, 1966, emphatically stated that medical assessors are not to take any active part in the proceedings themselves. Medical assessors are not to cross-examine witnesses: they are not to prompt the appeals officer into asking questions viewed by the assessor as pertinent to the appeal. Nor, it seems, are they to submit opinions on the medical condition of the appellant or the merits of the appeal. Their function is to give information on medical matters when so requested by the appeals officer. In Henchy J.'s words, the medical assessor's function is, "to act as a medical dictionary (and not as a medical report) available for consultation by the appeals officer".

There are compelling reasons for these limitations. The assessor and appeals officer should not compromise themselves by appearing to present or conduct the case, either for the claimant or the deciding officer. Nevertheless it can be argued that, should the assessors take an active role in unemployment benefit appeals and actually assist in weighing the merits of the appellant's submissions, quite considerable advantages may result. It is arguable that given the fact that the appeals officer is not truly independent—he remains, after all, an officer of the Department of Social Welfare—the interests of justice require that a counter-balance to any possible bias towards the Department be introduced into the appeals system. The participating assessor could provide a more effective means of ensuring that the appeals system is independent and not merely another level of internal administrative review. This will only be achieved if the assessors appreciate this fundamental principle. Recent studies in Britain suggest that claimants perceive the three-member tribunal model to be more effective where lay members take an active role in deliberations and proceedings. Lay-member participation offsets the tendency of the chairman to overawe claimant and lay-member alike. In *Judging Social Security* (1992) (Clarendon) the authors of the study, Baldwin, Wikeley and Young complain about the tendency towards legalism and the fact that if a tribunal chairman is allowed to dominate lay members, this undermines the self confidence of lay members and results in claimant satisfaction in the entire process.

Other functions of Chief Appeals Officer

256.—(1) The Chief Appeals Officer shall have such other functions in relation to appeals under this Part as may be prescribed.

(2) In this section "functions" includes powers, duties and obligations.

Procedures for Appeals

GENERAL NOTE

See Part II of the Social Welfare (Appeals) Regulations 1990 (S.I. No. 344 of 1990) for other functions not found in this Act.

Appeals and references to appeals officers

257.—(1) If any person is dissatisfied with the decision given by a deciding officer, the question shall, on notice of appeal being given to the Chief Appeals Officer within the prescribed time, be referred to an appeals officer.

(2) Regulations may provide for the procedure to be followed on appeals and references under this Part.

(3) An appeals officer, when deciding a question referred under subsection (1), shall not be confined to the grounds on which the decision of the deciding officer was based, but may decide the question as if it were being decided for the first time.

GENERAL NOTE

The prescribed time as laid down in S.I. No. 344 of 1990 is 21 days. This can be extended at the discretion of the Chief Appeals Officer. The procedures to be followed are laid down in S.I. No. 344 of 1990. it is very important to note that appeals may be heard summarily or orally. There is no guidance in the Act or the Regulations on just when an oral hearing is appropriate but *Kiely* does provide a clear statement of policy.

While the decision of the appeals officer appears at first sight to be an unfettered discretionary power the Supreme Court, in *Kiely v. Minister for Social Welfare* [1977] IR. 267, indicated that, essentially, the basic rule is that there is a right to an oral hearing. Henchy J. said:

"an oral hearing is mandatory unless the case is of such a nature that it can be determined without an oral hearing, that is, summarily. An appeal is of such a nature that it can be determined summarily if a determination of the claim can fairly be made on a consideration of the documentary evidence. If, however, there are unresolved conflicts in the documentary evidence, as to any matter essential to a ruling of the claim, the intention of the Regulations is that those conflicts shall be resolved by an oral hearing".

Notwithstanding this direction, the Minister has indicated that about one-half of appellants are given an oral hearing; 397 *Dáil Debates* Col. 397.

In the 1990 Act provision was made requiring the Chief Appeals Officer, upon the Minister's direction, to order an oral appeal in a particular case. This was criticised as being incompatible with the trend towards an independent appeals system but the 1993 Consolidation Act carries this over in section 270 above.

Under the regulations, claimants have a right to be represented by a member of their family or, with the consent of the appeals officer, any other person. In *Corcoran v. Minister for Social Welfare* H.C. Unrep. June 7, 1991, Murphy J. ruled that a social welfare claimant is not entitled to legal representation before it, at least in cases where there is no suspicion of the claimant having committed a criminal or civil wrong. As long as the Tribunal observes principles of Constitutional justice and does not mislead the claimant there is no right, in such a context, to be legally represented.

Subsection (3) makes it clear that the appeals officer does not just hear an appeal; a decision *de novo* can be made by the appeals officer.

Power to take evidence on oath

258.—An appeals officer shall, on the hearing of any matter referred to him under this Part have power to take evidence on oath and for that purpose may administer oaths to persons attending as witnesses at such hearing.

GENERAL NOTE

These powers are frequently exercised: see *Corcoran v. Minister for Social Welfare* H.C. Unrep. June 7, 1991.

Notification to persons to attend and give evidence or produce documents at appeal hearing

259.—(1) An appeals officer may, by giving notice in that behalf in writing to any person, require the person to attend at such time and place as is specified in the notice to give evidence in relation to any matter referred to such appeals officer under this Part or to produce any documents in his possession, custody or control which relate to any such matter.

(2) A notice under subsection (1) may be given either by delivering it to the person to whom it relates or by sending it by post in a prepaid registered letter addressed to that person at the address at which he ordinarily resides or at his place of business.

(3) A person to whom a notice under subsection (1) has been given and who refuses or wilfully neglects to attend in accordance with the notice or who, having so attended, refuses to give evidence or refuses or wilfully fails to produce any document to which the notice relates shall be guilty of an offence and shall be liable on summary conviction to a fine not exceeding £1,000.

(4) Where a person required to attend to give evidence or to produce documents under subsection (1) fails to attend or to produce such documents, an appeals officer may, on serving notice on that person, apply to the District Court for an order directing that person to attend or to produce such documents as required.

GENERAL NOTE

This power to summon witnesses and documents is exercised against a wide range of persons such as former employers of the claimant, for example. Appeals are heard at employment exchanges or at the Executive Office in D'Olier Street, Dublin. In 1990 the power to serve an effective notice was broadened so as to include that person's place of business as well as ordinary residence.

Procedure where assessor appointed

260.—Any matter referred to an appeals officer under this Part and to be heard by the appeals officer sitting with an assessor appointed under section 255 may, with the consent of the parties appearing at the hearing, but not otherwise, be proceeded with in the absence of the assessor.

GENERAL NOTE

Where an appeal is to be heard before an appeals officer sitting with an assessor, and no assessor is available, the appeal can only proceed if the claimant consents. In practice, the only other option is to adjourn the appeal but claimants are told that such an adjournment may be for several weeks and consent is normally forthcoming.

Award of expenses

261.—(1) An appeals officer may, in relation to any matter referred to him under this Part, award to any person any costs or expenses (including expenses representing loss of remunerative time) which he considers reasonable, and the award shall be payable by the Minister.

(2) The Minister may pay to assessors referred to in section 255 such amounts in respect of expenses (including expenses representing loss of remunerative time) as the Minister, with the sanction of the Minister for Finance, determines.

GENERAL NOTE

The power to award expenses covers claimants, witnesses and some others. At one time representatives could also be awarded expenses in the form of a flat fee (*e.g.* solicitors) but this practice has apparently ended.

Revised Decisions by Chief Appeals Officer and by Appeals Officers

Revision by appeals officer of decisions of appeals officers

262.—An appeals officer may, at any time revise any decision of an appeals officer, if it appears to him that the decision was erroneous in the light of new evidence or of new facts brought to his notice since the date on which it was given, or if it appears to him that there has been any relevant change of circumstances since the decision was given.

GENERAL NOTE

Apart from this power, it should be noted that under section 248(1)(b) similar powers of revision are now given to deciding officers. This is an absurd situation which undermines the independence of the Appeals Office.

Revision by Chief Appeals Officer of decisions of appeals officers

263.—The Chief Appeals Officer may, at any time, revise any decision of an appeals officer, if it appears to him that the decision was erroneous by reason of some mistake having been made in relation to the law or the facts.

GENERAL NOTE

This power of revision can be defended as being a useful means of ensuring uniformity of approach in decision-making.

Effect of revised decisions by appeals officers

264.—A revised decision given by an appeals officer shall take effect as follows—

(a) where any benefit, assistance, child benefit or family income supplement will, by virtue of the revised decision be disallowed or reduced and the revised decision is given owing to the original decision having been given, or having continued in effect, by reason of any statement or representation (whether written or verbal) which was to the knowledge of the person making it false or misleading in a material respect or by reason of the wilful concealment of any material fact, it shall take effect as from the date on which the original decision took effect, but the original decision may, in the discretion of the appeals officer, continue to apply to any period covered by the original decision to which such false or misleading statement or representation or such wilful concealment of any material fact does not relate;

(b) where any benefit, assistance, child benefit or family income supplement will, by virtue of the revised decision, be disallowed or reduced and the revised decision is given in the light of new evidence or new facts (relating to periods prior to and subsequent to the commencement of this Act) which have been brought to the notice of the appeals officer since the original decision was given, it shall take effect from such date as the appeals officer shall determine having regard to the new facts or new evidence;

(c) in any other case, it shall take effect as from the date considered appropriate by the appeals officer having regard to the circumstances of the case.

GENERAL NOTE

This section corresponds with the revision provisions in relation to revised decisions by deciding officers. Thus, decisions revised as a result of claimant fraud or concealment of material facts which result in loss or reduction of benefits dates back to the original date of the decision, rendering the claimant liable to repay excess benefits already paid. In other cases the revising appeals officer can fix the effective date as is thought appropriate.

Decision of appeals officer to be final and conclusive

265.—The decision of an appeals officer on any question—

(a) specified in section 247(2)(a)(i), (ii) or (iii), other than a question arising under Chapter 10 of Part II as to whether an accident arose out of and in the course of employment, and

(b) arising under Part III, IV, V, VI, VIII or this Part,

shall, subject to sections 248(1)(b), 262, 263 and 271, be final and conclusive.

GENERAL NOTE

This section basically directs that decisions of an appeals officer, on issues of fact, are final and conclusive. Appeals officers' decisions which are capable of being revised are not so immune; nor are decisions on the insurability of workers or issues concerning whether an accident was an industrial accident under Chapter 10 of Part II. Notwithstanding this section, section 271 sets out a broad right of appeal on questions of law. Where a claimant is unhappy with the way in which issues of fact and evidence were resolved, he may, notwithstanding this section, bring an appeal by way of judicial review: see *Thompson v. Minister for Social Welfare* H.C. Unrep. March 16, 1989 for an example of this. The reluctance of a court to allow section 265 to oust the jurisdiction of the courts is illustrated by *Kingham v. Minister for Social Welfare* H.C. Unrep. November 25, 1985. Jurisdictional issues are not as relevant as section 265 would appear to suggest.

CHAPTER 3

SUPPLEMENTARY WELFARE ALLOWANCE— DETERMINATIONS AND APPEALS

Determination of entitlement to supplementary welfare allowance

266.—Any function in relation to the determination of the entitlement of any person to supplementary welfare allowance and the amount of any such allowance shall, subject to section 267, be a function of the chief executive officer (within the meaning of section 13 of the Health Act, 1970) of the health board.

GENERAL NOTE

This section provides that issues of entitlement are to be a function of the chief executive officer of each of the eight health boards created under the Health Act 1970. In practice, issues of entitlement are resolved at local health centre level by community welfare officers who report to their immediate superiors, the superintendent community welfare officers. Within the health boards supplementary welfare allowance is regarded as a part of the community care programme.

Appeals

267.—(1) Where a person is dissatisfied with the determination by an officer of a health board of a claim by him for supplementary welfare allowance, an appeal shall lie against such determination to a person (being either another officer of the health board or a person not such an officer) appointed or designated by the Minister.

(2) The Minister may by regulations made under section 188 provide for the making and determination of appeals under this section.

GENERAL NOTE

A dissatisfied applicant has under this section a right of appeal against the way in which a claim for supplementary welfare has been processed. However, the person appointed or designated to hear this appeal is generally the programme manager for the community care programme, so doubts about the formal independence of the appeals system have been strongly felt for many years.

Despite the permissive nature of this section, there are no statutory rules governing the way in which appeals are heard or resolved. The Commission on Social Welfare recommended that supplementary welfare appeals should be integrated into an amended independent appeals mechanism. In late 1994 the then Minister, Dr Woods, promised legislation to improve the appeals system in supplementary welfare cases, although it does not appear to be policy to effect a total integration into the structures found in Chapter 2 of this Part.

Case law involving the health boards stresses the duty to act judicially and in accordance with Natural and Constitutional justice: *McConnell v. E.H.B.* H.C. Unrep. June 1, 1983; case law also reveals an alarming tendency to regard Ministerial Directives as having the force of law, even when *ultra vires*: *Kershaw v. E.H.B.* H.C. Unrep. November 12, 1984.

Revision of determinations of entitlement to supplementary welfare allowance

268.—An officer of a health board who is duly authorised to determine entitlement to a supplementary welfare allowance may, at any time revise any determination of entitlement to such allowance if it appears to him that the determination was erroneous in the light of new evidence or of new facts which have been brought to his notice since the date on which the determination was given or if it appears to him in a case where an allowance has been payable that there has been any relevant change of circumstances since the determination was given.

GENERAL NOTE
This section sets out the powers of a community welfare officer or superintendent welfare officer to revise earlier decisions made in relation to supplementary welfare allowances.

Effect of revised determinations by officers of health board

269.—A revised determination of entitlement to a supplementary welfare allowance given by an officer of a health board shall take effect as follows—
  (a) where any supplementary welfare allowance will, by virtue of the revised determination be disallowed or reduced and the revised determination is given owing to the original determination having been given, or having continued in effect, by reason of any statement or representation (whether written or verbal) which was to the knowledge of the person making it false or misleading in a material respect or by reason of the wilful concealment of any material fact, it shall take effect as from the date on which the original determination took effect, but the original determination may, in the discretion of the officer of the health board, continue to apply to any period covered by the original determination to which such false or misleading statement or representation or such wilful concealment of any material fact does not relate;
  (b) where any supplementary welfare allowance will, by virtue of the revised determination, be disallowed or reduced and the revised determination is given in the light of new evidence or new facts (relating to periods prior to and subsequent to the commencement of this Act) which have been brought to the notice of the officer of the health board since the original determination was given, it shall take effect from such date as the officer of the health board shall determine having regard to the new facts or new evidence;
  (c) in any other case, it shall take effect as from the date considered appropriate by the officer of the health board having regard to the circumstances of the case.

GENERAL NOTE
These provisions effect the same rules that apply to revised decisions of social welfare deciding officers and appeals officers: see sections 249 and 264 respectively.

CHAPTER 4

GENERAL PROVISIONS RELATING TO DECISIONS AND APPEALS

Appeals—oral hearings

270.—Notwithstanding section 257(2), where the Minister or a person designated by him considers that the circumstances of a particular case warrant an oral hearing of the appeal, the Minister or any person so designated by him may direct the Chief Appeals Officer that the appeal be determined by way of an oral hearing.

GENERAL NOTE
See the General Note to section 257 above.

Appeals to High Court

271.—Any person who is dissatisfied with—

   (a) the decision of an appeals officer, or
   (b) the revised decision of the Chief Appeals Officer,
on any question, other than a question to which section 265 applies, may appeal that decision or revised decision, as the case may be, to the High Court on any question of law.

GENERAL NOTE

See the General Note to section 265 above.

Certificate by deciding officer, appeals officer or officer of health board

272.—A document purporting to be a certificate of a decision made pursuant to this Act by a deciding officer or an appeals officer and to be signed by him shall be *prima facie* evidence of the making of the said decision and of the terms thereof, without proof of the signature of such officer or of his official capacity.

GENERAL NOTE

Prior to the 1990 reforms, there was no constitutional or statutory requirement that a decision on entitlement be given in writing or that reasons for a decision be given to a claimant/appellant. A certificate of the decision basically states if the appeal has been allowed or disallowed.

This section makes such certificates prima facie evidence of the decision.

Under article 18 of S.I. No. 344 of 1990, the appeals officer is required to append to a decision a note of the reasons if the decision is against the appellant. These are to be forwarded to the appellant by the Chief Appeals Officer.

Revision to include revision consisting of reversal

273.—A reference in this Part to a revised decision given by a deciding officer or an appeals officer or a revised determination given by an officer of a health board includes a reference to a revised decision or determination which reverses the original decision or determination.

CHAPTER 5

SOCIAL WELFARE TRIBUNAL

Application for adjudication by Social Welfare Tribunal

274.—Where, in relation to a stoppage of work or a trade dispute, a deciding officer and appeals officer have decided that a person is disqualified under section 47(1) for receiving unemployment benefit or under section 125(3) for receiving unemployment assistance, that person may, notwithstanding any other provision of this Act, apply to the Social Welfare Tribunal (in this Chapter referred to as "the Tribunal") for an adjudication under this Chapter.

GENERAL NOTE

This short chapter creates a separate adjudicative body, the Social Welfare Tribunal, which is required to consider whether social welfare payments should be available to persons engaged in an industrial dispute, notwithstanding the trade dispute disqualification in sections 47 (unemployment benefit) and 125 (unemployment assistance). The background to, and effects of, these provisions are worthy of extensive treatment.

The Clover Meats case and the 1982 legislation

Social welfare claimants have their application for unemployment benefit or unemployment assistance determined, in the first instance, by a deciding officer. If the decision goes against the claimant, a right of appeal lies to an appeals officer who, sitting with assessors, can consider the application *de novo*. A further appeal lies to the High Court on any question of law. The remedies of certiorari, prohibition and mandamus are also available and it is against this background that the *Clover Meats* dispute and the resulting litigation should be seen.

The *Clover Meat Company* plant in Waterford had two separate factories. One factory processed beef into beef products, the other processed pig meat. Due to difficulties in obtaining a reliable supply of cattle, *Clover Meats* decided to close down the beef factory. The company proposed to lay off only those workers who were employed in the beef factory; the union, the I.T.G.W.U., insisted that selection for lay off should depend on seniority, regardless of whether the worker was employed in the bacon or beef factory. *Clover Meats* refused to accede to this because, they argued, the bacon factory would be less efficient if workers were laid off and other persons, formerly employed in the beef factory, had to be retrained. Agreement could not be reached and the Company dismissed 356 workers who had been employed in both the beef and bacon factories. These workers were refused unemployment benefit or assistance because, in the view of the deciding officer, there was a "trade dispute" that had led to "a stoppage of work", even though no industrial action was taken or contemplated by the dismissed workers. An appeal to an appeals officer was dismissed, despite the fact that the employer testified before both the deciding officer and the appeals officer that no trade dispute existed. In the High Court, McMahon J. refused to grant an order of mandamus directing the Minister to pay unemployment benefit to one of the workers. In McMahon J.'s view the dismissal of the 356 beef and bacon factory workers was the result of a failure by the union to agree on a formula to decide who would be retained to work in the bacon factory. This failure to agree produced a stoppage of work due to a trade dispute within the meaning of "trade dispute", as defined in section 35(6) of the Social Welfare (Consolidation) Act, 1981: see *Irish Times* February 11, 1982 for a report on this litigation.

This controversial dispute, in a marginal Dáil constituency at a time of great political uncertainty, led the then Fianna Fáil Government to agree to pay all the Clover Meats workforce their respective social welfare "entitlements" from the date of dismissal until the resumption of work 10 weeks later. More importantly, the Administration agreed to amend the law on social welfare payments to strikers.

Although the simple way of proceeding would involve a change in the law, there is no attempt to amend the definition of "trade dispute", the basis of McMahon J.'s decision in the High Court: rather, the legislation broadens the focus of the trade dispute disqualification to make it material to consider whether a claimant has been "unreasonably deprived of his employment". This is a radical and imaginative approach to this problem.

The Social Welfare (No. 2) Act, 1982 interposed a new Tribunal, the Social Welfare Tribunal, between two of the existing appellate tiers, namely the appeals officer and the High Court. The Tribunal is *not* directed to review the decision of the appeals officer, whether on matters of fact or matters of law. There have been several cases in which the Tribunal has been asked to review the decision of the appeals officer, particularly on the question of whether there is a trade dispute or on the question of whether the applicants come within the proviso, but the Tribunal has indicated on each occasion that it has no jurisdiction to do this. The Tribunal is to decide the issue of wrongful deprivation of employment by reference to statutory criteria that have nothing to do with the trade dispute disqualification. It follows that the correctness or otherwise of the appeals officer's decision on the meaning of "trade dispute", "stoppage of work", the proviso or any other technical aspect of the trade dispute disqualification is not in issue. An appeals officer may decide that a claimant is "participating" or is "directly interested" but this does not prevent the Tribunal from holding the claimant entitled to social welfare payments if the facts disclose unreasonable behaviour by the employer.

Adjudications by Social Welfare Tribunal

275.—The following provisions shall apply in relation to an adjudication under this Chapter—

    (a) the Tribunal shall, before making the adjudication, take into account all the circumstances of the stoppage of work concerned and the trade dispute which caused the stoppage of work, including (without prejudice to the generality of the foregoing)—

(i) the question whether the applicant is or was available for work and willing to work, but is or was deprived of his employment through some act or omission on the part of the employer concerned which amounted to unfair or unjust treatment of the applicant,

(ii) the question whether the applicant is or was prevented by the employer from attending for work at his place of employment or was temporarily laid off by the employer, without (in either such case) any reasonable or adequate consultation by the employer with the applicant or with a trade union acting on his behalf, or without (in either case) the use by the employer or by any body acting on his behalf of the services normally availed of by employers in the interests of good industrial relations,

(iii) the question whether any action or decision by the employer, amounting to a worsening of the terms or conditions of employ-ment of the applicant and taken without any or any adequate consultation with, or any or any adequate notice to, the appli-cant, was a cause of the stoppage or work or of the trade dispute which caused the stoppage of work and was material grounds for such stoppage or such trade dispute,

(iv) the question whether the conduct of the applicant or of a trade union acting on his behalf was reasonable;

(b) the Tribunal shall, having heard such evidence as has been adduced before it, and such representations as have been made to it, by the applicant and the employer and having considered whether the conduct of the applicant or of a trade union acting on his behalf was reasonable and whether the employer or a body acting on his behalf was willing to avail of the services normally availed of in the interests of good industrial relations, decide whether the applicant is or was unreasonably deprived of his employment and whether (if it decides that he is or was so deprived) he shall, notwithstanding the decision under section 47(1) or under section 125(3) of the deciding officer or appeals officer, be qualified to receive unemployment benefit or unemployment assistance and (where appropriate) for what period he shall be so qualified:
Provided that the other conditions for the receipt of such benefit or such assistance are satisfied;

(c) a decision of the Tribunal on an application for an adjudication shall be final and conclusive, but an appeal shall lie to the High Court on a question of law:
Provided that a person interested (including the Minister) may apply to the Tribunal for a review of its decision and, if the Tribunal is satisfied that a material change has occurred in the circumstances of the stoppage of work or of the trade dispute which caused the stoppage of work, or that there is new evidence or new facts which in the opinion of the Tribunal could have affected its decision, it may review its decision and such a review shall be treated as an adjudication under this section.

GENERAL NOTE

The Tribunal is directed to "take into account all the circumstances of the stoppage of work concerned and of the trade dispute which caused the stoppage of work". Suppose an employer locks out his workforce because of a union prohibition against overtime working, this action by the union being a direct response to a management decision to force a number of compulsory redundancies. This "stoppage of work" would be caused, not by the ban but by the action of the employer. Whether this would constitute "unreasonable deprivation" of employment would, at first sight, require the Tribunal to rule on the merits of the trade dispute, a sometimes difficult and politically unpalatable task. The Tribunal has so far avoided being dragged into this vortex by concentrating upon the less controversial aspect of section 275(a)(i), that is, who is responsible for causing the "stoppage of work". This is hardly surprising, given that the legislation was drawn against the backcloth of the *Clover Meats* dispute, but this switch in emphasis—away from "trade dispute" to the "stoppage of work"— is facilitated by the guidelines contained in the legislation which state that it is material to consider the factors set out in section 275(a)(i) to (iv).

While these factors are not intended to limit the generality of the early part of the section, which requires the Tribunal to look at all the circumstances of the stoppage of work . . . *and the trade dispute* [my italics], it is evident that this will be the effect. Ministerial pronouncements while the Bill was going through Dáil Eireann indicate that this was intentional. What may not be intentional, however, is this: can the claimant, under the "all the circumstances of the stoppage of work . . . and the trade dispute" provision argue that he was wrongly deprived of his employment when the primary culprit in this respect is not the claimant's employer but, rather, a trade union which may indeed represent the claimant at the claimant's workplace. There have been two Tribunal decisions in which the Tribunal considered that trade union officials acting for the claimants may not have functioned effectively or conscientiously *vis-à-vis* industrial relations difficulties involving the claimants and on both occasions the Tribunal felt that the facts disclosed fell short of enabling the Tribunal to conclude that the claimants were unreasonably deprived of the employment by virtue of intransigence or unreasonable behaviour on the part of trade union officials. The legislation does not require that the Tribunal must find that the claimant was unreasonably deprived of his employment *by his employer* but this was presumably the intention behind the Act. Nevertheless in these two adjudications, *Morrissey v. Ronayne Shipping Ltd* (1986) and *Reynolds v. Veha Ltd* (1986) the Tribunal did *not* take the central issue, that is, who is responsible for precipitating the stoppage of work and/or trade dispute, as a fundamental element in its jurisdiction to authorise the payment of unemployment benefit. Indeed in *Reynolds v. Veha Ltd* the claimants alleged directly that the stoppage of work was the result of "the unreasonable and undemocratic action of" their own union in not calling a secret ballot. The Tribunal found, on the facts, that no such allegation could be sustained against the union but it seems reasonably clear that if this had been upheld, on the facts, benefit would have been paid. This would appear to be a ludicrous situation. It cannot be defended on the ground that the Act specifically authorises the Tribunal to look at the conduct of the applicant or a trade union acting for the applicant. Surely the Act intends this factor to be a counterweight to any unfair conduct by the employer, at least when the union or union officials act irresponsibly. The entire trade dispute disqualification has traditionally depended on some notion of unity of interest between workers and it would seem strange to allow union officials to be "disowned" by those who are represented by that official when the official fails to act in accordance with the wishes of that claimant. This development was not anticipated when the Bill was before Dáil Eireann although it was then attacked on other grounds. It was said to be yet another example of *ad hoc* social legislation. Several of the clauses were attacked as being "woolly and not fully and properly drafted" and several of the key concepts were said to be too subjective or ill defined, particularly "unfair and unjust treatment" and "adequate consultation". The most trenchant observations on the philosophy that forms the basis of the legislation were directed at the consequences for industrial relations practices. The main spokesman for the Opposition felt there was a real danger that the legislation would encourage and prolong strikes because of the payment of unemployment benefits to those on strike. The view was expressed that there was a danger that the focus of attention in industrial disputes would shift from the Labour Court and other conciliation procedures to this Tribunal:

"I see a danger that the initial reaction of anyone involved in a strike or trade dispute situation will be to get this tribunal to adjudicate as soon as possible on the rights and wrongs and ensure that, if possible, a finding is obtained against the employer so that social welfare benefits will be obtained".

Subsequent experience suggests that the Tribunal has not prolonged trade disputes by giving "speedy" decisions that lead to the State subsidising industrial action. Of the first 25 decisions handed down by the Tribunal six of those disputes were unresolved on the day the decision was delivered. In the other 19 cases, the decision was handed down after the dispute had been resolved; indeed, these 19 cases were resolved before the date of the hearing. If this pattern continues then it seems unlikely that any attempt to obtain a "quick" decision will be frustrated by the delays that inevitably follow from the relatively complex procedures that the Tribunal must observe.

The fear that the Tribunal would be drawn into making value judgements on who is at fault *vis-à-vis* the *trade dispute* reveals a misunderstanding of this legislation. The Tribunal is directed to concentrate on procedural issues rather than issues of a substantive nature. This point was in fact made by the Minister for Social Welfare, albeit obliquely, at Second Reading but the decisions of the Tribunal provide the most compelling evidence of this.

Emerging Guidelines

It would be difficult for any Tribunal to maintain an absolutely clear distinction between substantive and procedural justice, given the way in which the 1982 legislation was drafted. The Tribunal have nevertheless managed to avoid being drawn into making value judgements on the "trade dispute" itself. It is however inevitable that future disputes will require the tribunal to consider whether a failure by an employer to observe procedural niceties can be outweighed by the merits of the employer's claim.

This problem is likely to emerge when an employer demonstrates that the business is in financial difficulties and, unless immediate steps are taken to improve cost effectiveness through redundancies or changes in work practices, closure is inevitable. However the decision of the Tribunal in *Brennan v. Comer International Ltd* (1982) suggests that the merits of the employer's argument will not excuse a failure to exhaust existing dispute machinery. Further, *Jones v. Quigley Co. of Europe* (1989) indicates that management actions cannot be justified by difficulties of interpreting a Labour Court recommendation.

In *Comer International* management allegations of impropriety by a shop steward led to an unofficial strike. At a mass meeting of strikers, a motion to return to work was carried but the employers locked out the workers until the workers agreed to a variety of changes in their terms and conditions of employment, none of which were in any way connected with the original stoppage of work. The most important changes involved a reduction in bonus payments and union acceptance of a pay increase offer which was less than the Joint Industrial Council rate for the industry and smaller than the increase offered to similar workers in an associated company. The Tribunal held that making the reopening of the factory conditional on acceptance of a package that had nothing to do with the original dispute constituted "unfair treatment" of the workers concerned. No judgement on the merits of the package appears in the Tribunal decision. It is also evident that these proposals represented "a worsening of the terms and conditions of the applicant".

An employer who tries to broaden the argument, by suggesting for example that redundancies would be agreed at generous compensation levels, would be unlikely to find this factor of any real assistance; the statutory criteria, as interpreted by the Tribunal, indicate that the Tribunal will not "second guess" or pass judgement on management decisions which relate to trading or commercial strategy: "the Company's right to seek changes in conditions of employment in the interests of efficiency and viability must be recognised and respected". It is the reasonableness of the methods used to introduce such changes that fall under the scrutiny of the Tribunal. Several recent decisions illustrate this point. In *Sallinger v. Radionics Ltd* (1985) the Tribunal held that although the employer had a legitimate and well-founded interest to protect, the pilfering of electrical equipment by employees was costing him over £80,000 annually, the introduction of compulsory stop and search procedures for employees, a measure which precipitated a stoppage of work, was held to be inappropriate. Other procedures which would not have led to the stoppage of work were available to the employer and his failure to pursue these meant that the workers had been unreasonably deprived of their employment. Similarly, if an employer summarily dismisses members of his workforce in a manner that infringes principles of Natural justice and possibly the Constitutional rights of those employees, any subsequent protest by way of a stoppage of work will probably be held to be the direct result of the unreasonable behaviour of the employer. Failure to observe good industrial relations practice and the employer's refusal to discuss the dismissals were held, in *O'Brien v. Dawn Meats (Grannagh) Ltd* (1986) to amount to unreasonable behaviour that could legitimise industrial action. Further, in *King v. Cerdac Ltd* (1985) the Tribunal clearly indicated that strike action called by a union could, in appropriate circumstances, be "justified by unreasonableness on the part of the employer". The failure to adopt conciliation and arbitration procedures will normally result in the employer being held to bear the primary responsibility for any stoppage of work that results unless these procedures can be shown to be ineffective: *Kelly v. Irish Meat Producers* (1985); *Cox v. Irish Country Bacon* (1990).

Failure to adopt dispute procedures cannot be excused by the employer explaining that he did not regard the workforce as being involved in a dispute, if the facts objectively demonstrate differences exist. The employer must also adopt consultative procedures which are effective. If an employer seeks to change work practices in the name of rationalisation and in order to increase productivity, there should, if at all possible, be adequate notice given to employees and their representatives. In *Cox v. Hanley Meats Group* (1985) merger talks involving three companies produced a package of proposals which were presented to the workforce. The workforce agreed that drastic changes were necessary but they rejected the Group's view that these terms were non-negotiable and had to be immediately implemented. There was evidence of delay in consulting the unions. The Tribunal held that the Group was responsible for creating an "atmosphere of crisis" and the stoppage which ensued was primarily due to failure to process the changes by way of normal procedures. However, cases like *Power v. Dunnes Stores* (1988) represent a compromise solution insofar as an initial walk-out by employees, followed by foot-dragging by the employer, led to an appeal being allowed in part, benefit being payable in respect of the latter portion of the stoppage.

Where the focus falls upon the conduct of the claimant, the claimant's colleagues, and the trade unions involved in the dispute and stoppage of work, a similar emphasis on observing dispute procedures, to the exclusion of industrial action, is also evident in Tribunal decisions. The Tribunal has recognised that resort to any kind of industrial action, except where the employer acts in a high-handed and severely prejudicial manner, *e.g.* by summarily dismissing workers without hearing their side of the story, will result in benefit being denied on the ground that "if workers decide to embark on such action instead of going through normal procedures they must, of course, be prepared to accept the consequences that may stem from such action", *e.g.* loss of benefit, suspension and lay off: *Goulding v. Irish Metal Industries* (1986); *Murphy-Walsh v. Cow & Gate* (1991).

The Tribunal has held that a trade union which calls for official industrial action will, in most cases, be held to be acting precipitously. Union members affected are unlikely to be entitled to benefits. The case of *Sheridan v. Shamrock Forge & Tool Co.* (1984) involved a recognition dispute between the employer and a group of six clerical workers who had decided to join A.S.T.M.S. The employer recognised the I.T.G.W.U. for the entire workforce but indicated that, if the I.T.G.W.U. agreed, there would be no difficulty in recognising A.S.T.M.S. as representative of clerical workers. A.S.T.M.S. called for industrial action. The six workers began a sit-in which led to their suspension and claims for unemployment benefit. The Tribunal decided that action taken in furtherance of a recognition claim was the reason for the suspension. The applicant, by his own decision, was not available for work until recognition was granted: "a resumption of normal working insofar as the company was concerned was conditional only on a cessation of the sit-in". The union's impatience at not being granted recognition immediately was compounded by the fact that the claim was to be considered by the Federated Union of Employers and the Irish Congress of Trade Unions and A.S.T.M.S. had failed to wait for existing disputes procedures to run their course.

Unofficial action will also be regarded as an inappropriate response by trade union members to industrial relations difficulties, when other means of resolving these problems exist. Nor can the workforce refuse to undertake work unless extra payment is obtained for this work if other methods of securing the disputed payments existed. The Tribunal's decision in *Gleeson v. Plessey Office Systems Ltd* (1986) indicates just how determined the Tribunal seems to be to provide counterweights to industrial action. Failure to reach agreement on a pay increase resulted in a stoppage of work. The workers returned to their place of employment, indicating that while they were prepared to resume work, they reserved the right to pursue the claim by resorting to future, unspecified, industrial action. The employer refused to allow the workers back unless they promised not to undertake further industrial action. The Tribunal held that at no time had the employer unreasonably refused to allow a resumption of work. The Tribunal remarked that, apart from conceding the claim, there was nothing else the employer could do to protect the business and provide for future employment.

Even where the dispute involves one worker only, resort to industrial action may not be a legitimate response to a dispute. The adjudicator of the Tribunal in *Jordan v. Standard Printed Products Ltd* (1987) is remarkable in several respects. Jordan was employed as a bookbinder. A pay award to this category of worker was negotiated nationally: the agreement involved payment of back pay. Jordan's employer refused to pay this to Jordan. He commenced a work-to-rule which severely affected part of the employer's business and the employer dismissed him. The E.A.T. found that Jordan had been unfairly dismissed and recommended reinstatement. Jordan claimed unemployment benefit for the period between dismissal and reinstatement. The Tribunal held that Jordan had not been unreasonably deprived of his employment, notwithstanding the E.A.T.'s conclusion that he had been unfairly dismissed. Given the small amount of money involved, £167, Jordan's resort to a work-to-rule was the primary reason for his dismissal. His inexperience in industrial relations matters did not excuse such behaviour. Perhaps the most curious point about this case arises, not from the Tribunal's decision, but from the initial decision made under section 47: how can there be a trade dispute within the statutory definition when only one workman is engaged in a dispute with an employer? The statutory definition requires workers, in the plural, to be involved in a dispute with other workers or an employer or employers. Where a group of workers strike, the refusal of the employer to negotiate with one employee only is not going to constitute unreasonable deprivation: see *Healy v. Waterford Crystal Ltd* (1991).

One important procedural principle has emerged from the cases: "employees are entitled to know what precisely is involved before being expected to agree to new terms and conditions to be introduced by the employer". This statement was made by the Tribunal in *D'Alton and Others v. Longford Printing and Publishing Co.* (1984). This decision indicates that an employer may impose redundancies upon his workforce but he is obliged to negotiate before resorting to compulsory lay-offs in order to force an agreement. If, however, the employer fails to implement a Labour Court recommendation on redundancy levels, this would not breach any of the statutory guidelines because the only obligation under section 301A(2)(a)(ii) is to avail of the services of a body such as the Irish Labour Court. The Tribunal would, one suspects, be reluctant to hold that an employer has acted unreasonably in failing to *implement* a Labour Court recommendation because the employer must be presumed to be competent and the best judge of what is economically necessary to make the business efficient. The Tribunal sometimes permits the employer a degree of latitude in cases where the claimant asserts that the employer has acted arbitrarily. A finding that the employer has not acted in accordance with good industrial relations practice will not be fatal to the employer's position; benefits or assistance may still be denied. In *Comer v. Clery & Co. (1941) Ltd* (1983) the union claimed that the lay-off of I.U.D.W. & C. members at two days' notice without short-term pay was both unfair and the result of management failure to afford greater consultation with that union's representatives. If greater consultation had taken place the union felt some agreement could have been reached. Somewhat surprisingly perhaps the Tribunal declared "this, however, is strictly an industrial relations matter which has little relevance to the application before the Tribunal". Similarly, in *Purcell v. P. J. Crotty & Son* (1986) the Tribunal remarked that the employer could have laid off certain members of the workforce but later events made this failure irrelevant.

While the company in the *Clery & Co. (1941)* case was able to show that, in the circumstances, it had no alternative but to lay-off the workforce, the employer in *Donohoe v. Whessoe (Ireland) Ltd* (1984) was held to have resorted to the lay-off procedure without due consideration of any other course of action. In that case, the employer sought to introduce new work practices into their engineering firm, in particular, welders would lift their own plate rather than having cranemen and labourers do it for them. The company had already agreed redundancies with M.P. and G.W.U. but the agreement did not automatically include payments for new work practices. N.E.E.T.U. officials agreed to co-operate in principle but wanted agreement on payments before practices could be introduced. These negotiations began in September 1982 but no agreement was reached. In October 1982, following a refusal to commence new work practices, the 22 N.E.E.T.U. members were laid off, even though there was work available. Overtime worked by welders who were not N.E.E.T.U. members kept work proceeding as normal. The notice of lay-off given to the 22 N.E.E.T.U. welders stated that they were laid off because these men were not prepared to do their own labouring. While the Tribunal accepted that the company needed to introduce these new work practices because existing costs were too high the Tribunal, for the purpose of this adjudication, had to allocate "responsibility"; in this limited sense the Tribunal was obliged to make a judgement on the merits of the dispute. The Tribunal noted that the dispute was not about whether these practices would be introduced—N.E.E.T.U. accepted them—the dispute arose because agreement had not been reached on when, and on what terms, these changes would be introduced. The Tribunal found it significant that neither the union nor the employer had suggested referral to an outside agency for arbitration. The fact that it was the employer who was seeking a change in the *status quo* was, in the Tribunal's view, crucial. The onus rested on the employer to ensure that all normal negotiating procedures were exhausted before laying off these workers. The Tribunal found that while N.E.E.T.U. officials were not above criticism—they had not fully co-operated in attempts to resolve the company's difficulties—the union "could not be held to have been culpably responsible for the situation of lay-offs that arose. It is normal custom and practice for trade unions, in cases where new work practices involving increased productivity are being introduced by an employer, to seek to negotiate an increased payment before the proposed changes are brought into effect. If, however, new work practices are proposed, a union will "not be acting responsibly if it failed to cooperate in having the issue resolved through the accepted procedure". Proof of co-operation by the union, however, will be sought by the Tribunal if benefit is to be paid. Even if the union has been tardy in seeking third-party intervention, the employer will bear primary responsibility if third party intervention is not sought before new work practices are introduced: *Sallinger v. Radionics Ltd* (1985). However, *Scanlon v. Bus Eireann* (1988) points up the fact that a Labour Court adjudication is an important consideration and that the employer does not act unreasonably in requiring workers to observe the recommendation three months after it was made, the employer in the meantime seeking to negotiate implementation by agreement.

The lesson that can be gathered from these cases is that industrial action will be fatal to any claim for unemployment benefit, unless the employer provides a *nova causa interveniens*. In *Loughman v. Roscrea Meat Products* (1983) butchers made a claim for compensation due to the introduction of Moslem ritual killing for export markets. The Labour Court recommended that negotiations take place because some degree of additional work was involved. Negotiations were inconclusive; a go-slow began on May 13, 1982 which led to immediate lay-offs. During the lay-off, new terms of employment were proposed by the employer, some of which were not pertinent to the dispute. The workers, at a meeting of May 29, resolved to return to work if the issue of remuneration was referred to the Labour Court for a binding arbitration and other proposed changes were the subject of further negotiation. The employer refused to agree. The Tribunal held the butchers entitled to unemployment benefit from May 29 onwards. While the butchers were initially responsible for the stoppage of work on May 13, the employer's "unreasonable" response to the proposals was not compatible with good industrial relations practices; the employer's action at that time was, in effect, a lock-out without good cause. Similarly in *O'Connor v. Patrick McCormack (Joinery) Ltd* (1986) a recognition claim was met by closure of the factory for no other apparent reason and entitlement was established.

To like effect is *Burns v. Hanson Industries Ltd* (1985). Seven workers were suspended by their employer when they refused to carry out lawful instructions. The employer demanded the resignation of four of these workers as a precondition to reopening the factory, which had closed down because the seven workers were key employees and the remaining workers could not undertake any work. The Tribunal held that while the suspension was initially justified, the employer was responsible for prolonging the strike by demanding the resignation of some of the suspended workers. Benefit was payable to the seven suspended employees as from the date when the demand for resignation was made. A suspension that implements an E.A.T. recommendation however will be viewed in a different light: *Heavey v. Dunnes Stores* (1991).

Social Welfare Tribunal

276.—(1) There shall be a Tribunal, which shall be known as the Social Welfare Tribunal, to hear and decide applications for adjudications under this Chapter.

(2) The Tribunal shall consist of a chairman and four ordinary members.

(3) The members of the Tribunal shall be appointed by the Minister and shall be eligible for re-appointment.

    (4) (a) Two ordinary members of the Tribunal shall be persons representative of workers and nominated for appointment as such members by the body known as the Irish Congress of Trade Unions.

        (b) The two other ordinary members of the Tribunal shall be persons representative of employers and nominated for appointment as such members by an organisation representative of employers.

(5) The term of office of a member of the Tribunal shall be such period as is specified by the Minister when appointing such member.

    (6) (a) A member of the Tribunal may, by letter addressed to the Minister, resign his membership.

        (b) A member of the tribunal may be removed from office by the Minister.

    (7) (a) Whenever a vacancy occurs in the membership of the Tribunal and is caused by the resignation, removal from office or death of an ordinary member mentioned in subsection (4)(a), the vacancy shall be filled by the Minister by appointment in the manner specified in that subsection.

        (b) Whenever a vacancy occurs in the membership of the Tribunal and is caused by the resignation, removal from office or death of an ordinary member mentioned in subsection (4)(b), the vacancy shall be filled by the Minister by appointment in the manner specified in that subsection.

(8) In the case of a member of the Tribunal filling a vacancy caused by the resignation, removal from office or death of a member before the completion of the term of office of the last-mentioned member, the member filling that vacancy shall hold office for the remainder of the term of office of the person who so resigned, died or was so removed from office.

(9) A member of the Tribunal shall be paid such remuneration (if any) and allowances as may be determined by the Minister with the consent of the Minister for Finance.

(10) The Minister may, with the consent of the Minister for Finance, appoint such employees of the Tribunal as he considers necessary to assist the Tribunal in the performance of its functions, and such employees shall hold office on such terms and receive such remunerations as the Minister for Finance determines.

(11) (a) The Tribunal, on the hearing of an application under this Chapter, shall have power to take evidence on oath and for that purpose may cause to be administered oaths to persons attending as witnesses at such hearing.

(b) If a person gives false evidence before the Tribunal in such circumstances that, if he had given the evidence before a court, he would be guilty of perjury, he shall be guilty of that offence.

(c) The Tribunal may, by giving notice in that behalf in writing to any person, require such person to attend at such time and place as is specified in the notice to give evidence in relation to any matter referred to the Tribunal under this Chapter or to produce any documents in his possession, custody or control which relate to any such matter.

(d) A notice under paragraph (c) may be given either by delivering it to the person to whom it relates or by sending it by post in a prepaid registered letter addressed to such person at the address at which he ordinarily resides.

(e) A person to whom a notice under paragraph (c) has been given and who refuses or wilfully neglects to attend in accordance with the notice or who, having so attended, refuses to give evidence or refuses or wilfully fails to produce any document to which the notice relates shall be guilty of an offence and shall be liable on summary conviction thereof to a fine not exceeding £100.

(12) The Minister may make regulations giving effect to this section and such regulations may, in particular but without prejudice to the generality of the foregoing, provide for all or any of the following matters—

(a) the procedure to be followed regarding the making of applications to the Tribunal,

(b) the times and places of hearings by the Tribunal,

(c) the representation of parties attending hearings by the Tribunal,

(d) the procedure regarding the hearing of applications by the Tribunal,

(e) the publication and notification of decisions of the Tribunal,

(f) notices relating to applications or hearings by the Tribunal,

(g) the award by the Tribunal of costs and expenses and the payment of such awards,

(h) an official seal of the Tribunal.

GENERAL NOTE

The Tribunal

There are five members of the Social Welfare Tribunal, including the Chairman. All are appointed by the Minister although the members of the Tribunal are likely to be nominees of I.C.T.U. and two others nominated by I.B.E.C. In the main the procedures to be followed and the powers of the Tribunal are to be found in the Social Welfare (Social Welfare Tribunal) Regulations 1982 (S.I. No. 309 of 1982). An application for an adjudication may be made on a form approved by the Tribunal, within 21 days after receipt of the appeals officer's decision disqualifying the applicant from unemployment benefit or assistance respectively. The Tribunal may however accept an application at any time. A copy of the application, containing a statement of facts, must then be forwarded to the employer who must, within 14 days of receipt, enter an appearance by sending to the secretary of the Tribunal a statement indicating the extent to which the facts and contentions are admitted or disputed. An extension of time may be granted to the employer, the Chairman deciding what period of time should be granted. A copy of the employer's notice of appearance is forwarded to the applicant. The date, time and place for hearing the application is fixed by the Chairman, notice being given to all persons appearing to be interested. A right to representation is given to all persons summoned to the hearing, either through counsel, solicitor, trade union or employers' association representative, or, with the leave of the Tribunal, by any other person.

Unlike other social welfare appeals, where procedure during the course of the hearing is at the discretion of the appeals officer, a party to the application may make an opening statement, call witnesses, cross examine, give evidence on his own behalf and make a final address to the Tribunal. The decision of the Tribunal may be taken by a majority of the members. The decision is recorded and a copy is sent to the applicant, the employer and any other interested person. This is a great improvement on all other social welfare appeals where the decision is not recorded in detail, the applicant being entitled to notice of the decision and not a copy of the decision itself. The extensive powers for reviewing the Tribunal decisions, by the Tribunal itself, suggest that the right of appeal to the High Court on questions of law is unlikely to be exercised with any degree of frequency. There was, however, one respect in which the original powers of the Tribunal to review earlier decisions were quite deficient. The power to review earlier decisions could only be exercised by the Tribunal if there had been a change in circumstances between the hearing and the application to review. The Tribunal could not review its earlier decision if the facts disclosed at the hearing were inaccurate or if new facts which existed at the time of the hearing came to light after the date of the hearing. This anomaly came to light when the claimants in the *Clery's* case (above) sought to have the Tribunal review its decision in the light of facts not known at the time of the original hearing. After consultations with the Attorney General, the Tribunal indicated that it did not have the jurisdiction to review its decision unless a change in circumstances had occurred. The power to review was accordingly broadened in the 1987 (No. 2) Act. Although the regulations are silent on this point, decisions are reached after submissions have ended by attempts to negotiate unanimity of view amongst tribunal members. Although the decisions are not always unanimous, the written adjudication does not include statements of dissent.

The jurisdiction of the Tribunal is fixed by the Act. It is not the correctness of the appeal officer's decision that is under review. The Tribunal are directed to consider entirely new issues; who is responsible for causing the stoppage of work? Have the usual procedures been exhausted? Have the employer or the unions involved acted reasonably? These are factors immaterial to the appeals officer's decision under sections 47 and 125.

This jurisdictional dichotomy is graphically illustrated in *Comer v. Clery & Co. (1941) Ltd* (1983). The I.T.G.W.U. issued a call for strike action to all members employed in Clery & Co., a large Dublin department store. The management responded by closing the store on the morning of the day strike action was to commence. Comer, a member of I.U.D.W. & C. could not gain access to his place of employment. Comer sought unemployment benefit, claiming before the deciding officer and the appeals officer, that I.U.D.W. & C. workers were not involved in the dispute. The I.T.G.W.U. were pressing for an increase in pay for its members; all I.U.D.W. & C. members on the other hand were bound by a pay agreement that could not be renegotiated until May 1984. Both the deciding officer and the appeals officer refused benefits to Comer and all other I.U.D.W. & C. members. Before the Social Welfare Tribunal the union sought to argue that Comer and others were not "directly interested" in the outcome of the I.T.G.W.U. dispute with Clery & Co. because of the binding nature of the collective agreement, operative until May 1984. The Tribunal pointed out that it was only concerned to ensure that the refusal to pay unemployment benefit or assistance resulted from the trade dispute disqualification. Comer's sole recourse was to exercise his right of appeal to the High Court and not "appeal" to the Tribunal.

PART VIII

OVERPAYMENTS, REPAYMENTS, SUSPENSION OF PAYMENT, ETC.

Interim payments and suspension of payment

277.—(1) Regulations may make provision in relation to matters arising—

(a) pending the decision or determination under Part II, III, IV, V, VI, VII, or this Part (whether in the first instance or on an appeal or reference, and whether originally or on revision) of any claim for benefit, assistance, child benefit or family income supplement or of any question affecting any person's right to any such benefit, assistance, child benefit or family income supplement or to receipt thereof or any person's liability for contributions, or

(b) out of the effect of any appeal or revision of any decision or determination under Part II, III, IV, V, VI, VII, or this Part on any such claim or question.

(2) Where it appears to the Minister that a question has arisen or may arise as to whether—

(a) the conditions for the receipt of benefit, assistance (other than supplementary welfare allowance), child benefit or family income supplement payable under a decision are or were fulfilled, or

(b) a decision that any such benefit, assistance, child benefit or family income supplement is payable ought to be revised under this section, he may direct that payment of the said benefit, assistance, child benefit or family income supplement shall be suspended in whole or in part until the question has been decided.

(3) Where it appears to an officer of a health board who is duly authorised to determine entitlement to supplementary welfare allowance that a question has arisen or may arise as to whether—

(a) the conditions for the receipt of an allowance payable under a determination are or were fulfilled, or

(b) a determination of entitlement ought to be revised under this section, payment of the supplementary welfare allowance may be suspended in whole or in part until that question has been determined.

GENERAL NOTE

Subsection (1)

This subsection is an enabling section which allows the Minister, by regulation, to determine how a pending claim, appeal or reference may be treated in the period between the making of the claim and the ultimate decision thereon. No regulations have been made under this subsection but the intention behind it is to allow the Minister to direct that interim payments will be made to persons in this situation.

Subsection (2)

This subsection empowers the Minister to direct that insurance and assistance payments to a particular claimant or beneficiary, including child benefit and F.I.S. beneficiaries, may be suspended in whole or in part when issues of entitlement, whether on an original application or by reason of revision, arise from time to time. Note that the Minister's powers will be exercised by the Minister's officers, and that principles of Natural and Constitutional justice will regulate the exercise of this power, in both a procedural sense (*e.g. McDonnell v. E.H.B.* H.C. Unrep.; *Thompson v. Minister for Social Welfare* H.C. Unrep. March 16, 1989) and in substantive terms (*e.g. Healy & Healy v. E.H.B.* H.C. Unrep. March 11, 1988). In *Thompson v. Minister for Social Welfare (supra)* O'Hanlon J. said:

"before a deciding officer proceeds to a decision that an applicant who has been in receipt of unemployment assistance for some time, should have continuing payment disallowed, he should inform the person concerned that the position is being reviewed by him; the grounds upon which he is considering disallowing further payment; and the person concerned should be given an opportunity to answer the case made against him".

Subsection (2) , therefore, does not authorise interruption of a payment already being made without these requirements being met.

Subsection (3)

This subsection authorises interruption of supplementary welfare allowance, or deferral of a decision on a new claim, if issues of eligibility arise. Again, the decision to interrupt a payment already being made is subject to Constitutional principles which are capable of being judicially reviewed: see above note to subsection (2) and the cases referred to.

Overpayments

278.—Where, in accordance with the provisions of sections 249, 264 or 269, a decision or determination is varied or reversed by a deciding officer, an appeals officer or an officer of the health board (as the case may be) so as to disallow or reduce any benefit, assistance, child benefit or family income supplement paid or payable to a person—

(a) any benefit paid in pursuance of the original decision shall be repayable to the Social Insurance Fund to the extent to which it would not have been payable if the decision on the appeal or revision had been given in the first instance and such person and any other person to whom the benefit was paid on behalf of such person, or the personal representative of such person, shall be liable to pay to the said Fund, on demand made in that behalf by an officer of the Minister, the sum so repayable,

(b) any assistance (other than supplementary welfare allowance under Part III), child benefit or family income supplement paid in pursuance of the original decision shall be repayable to the Minister to the extent to which it would not have been payable if the decision on the appeal or revision had been given in the first instance and such person and any other person to whom the said assistance, child benefit or family income supplement (as the case may be) was paid on behalf of such person, or the personal representative of such person, shall be liable to pay to the Minister, on demand made in that behalf by an officer of the Minister, the sum so repayable,

(c) any supplementary welfare allowance paid in pursuance of the original determination shall be repayable to the health board to the extent to which it would not have been payable if the revised determination had been given in the first instance and such person and any other person to whom the supplementary welfare allowance was paid on behalf of such person, or the personal representative of such person, shall be liable to pay on demand by the health board the sum so repayable.

GENERAL NOTE

Following the making of a revised decision by a deciding officer (section 249), an appeals officer (section 264) or a health board official *vis-á-vis* supplementary welfare allowance (section 269), the revised decision where it results:

(a) in an overpayment of an insurance payment, will create an obligation to repay to the Social Insurance Fund any overpayment, upon demand being made by an officer of the Minister,

(b) in any overpayment of an assistance payment, will create an obligation to repay the overpayment to the Minister upon demand being made by one of the Minister's officers,

(c) in any overpayment of supplementary welfare allowance, will create an obligation to repay the overpayment to the health board in question, on demand.

Note that personal representatives of such a person may be addressees of such demands.

Section 278 is extremely sweeping in its terms. It is not uncommon for the demand to be made even if the claimant has made no misrepresentation, as for example, in a case where one deciding officer reviews a claimant's eligibility and decides that the original claim was invalid. In such a case the Department may seek the return of all sums paid, notwithstanding the claimant's blamelessness. A claimant in such a situation may possibly invoke a defence of estoppel or legitimate expectation, although this is a somewhat speculative issue in Irish law.

Repayment of benefit, assistance, etc. overpaid

279.—Where, in any case, other than a case involving a revised decision or determination in accordance with sections 249, 264 or 269, a person has been—

   (a) in receipt of any benefit, assistance, child benefit or family income supplement for any period during which that person was not entitled thereto, or

   (b) in receipt of such benefit, assistance, child benefit or supplement at a rate higher than that to which he was entitled,

then that person and any other person to whom such benefit, assistance, child benefit or supplement was paid on behalf of such person, or the personal representative of such person, shall be liable to pay—

     (i) to the Social Insurance Fund, in the case of benefit,

     (ii) to the Minister, in the case of assistance (other than supplementary welfare allowance), child benefit or family income supplement, and

     (iii) to the health board, in the case of supplementary welfare allowance,

on demand any sums paid to that person in respect of the said benefit, assistance, child benefit or supplement during such period or, as the case may be, a sum representing the difference between such benefit, assistance, child benefit or supplement at the rate actually paid and benefit, assistance, child benefit or supplement at the rate to which he was entitled.

GENERAL NOTE

   The power to seek the return of payments made as a matter of administrative error (*e.g.* the wrong insurance records have been assessed by the Department in processing an insurance benefit or pension claim) is established via this section.

Distribution of assets

280.—(1) The personal representative of a person who was at any time in receipt of assistance shall, not less than three months before commencing to distribute the assets of that person—

   (a) inform the Minister, by notice in writing delivered to the Minister, of his intention to distribute the assets, and provide the Minister with a schedule of the assets of the estate, and

   (b) if requested in writing by the Minister within three months of the furnishing of the notice and schedule of assets referred to in paragraph (a), ensure that sufficient assets are retained, to the extent (if any) appropriate, to repay any sum which may be determined to be due to the Minister or the State (as the case may be) in respect of—

     (i) payment of assistance to the person at a time when the person was not entitled to receive such assistance, or

     (ii) payment of assistance to the person of an amount in excess of the amount which the person was entitled to receive.

   (2) Notwithstanding any other provision of this Act, for the purposes of determining the sum which is due to the Minister under subsection (1), the means of the deceased person for the period in respect of which assistance was paid to him shall, in the absence of evidence to the contrary, be calculated on the basis that his assets at the time of his death belonged to him for that entire period.

   (3) A personal representative who contravenes subsection (1) and who distributes the assets of the person whose estate he represents without payment of any sum which is due to the Minister in respect of—

   (a) payments of assistance to the person at a time when the person was not entitled to receive such assistance, or

   (b) payments of assistance to the person of amounts in excess of the amounts which the person was entitled to receive,

shall be personally liable to repay to the Minister an amount equal to the amount (if any) which the Minister would have received if, in the administration of the estate of the person, the sum aforesaid had been duly taken into account and repaid to the Minister to the extent (if any) appropriate, having regard to the assets of the person, and such amount shall be a debt due by the personal representative to the Minister.

(4) Any proceedings to recover assistance due to the Minister as a debt due to the State under subsection (3) of section 281 shall be maintainable against the estate of a deceased person if brought at any time within the period of two years commencing on the date on which the notice and the schedule of assets under paragraph (a) of subsection (1) is received by the Minister or within any other period fixed in any other enactment, whichever is the longer.

GENERAL NOTE

This section provides extensive procedural means whereby a deceased person's estate could be made liable to repay any monies paid by way of social assistance when, following the beneficiary's death, it appears that the deceased held assessable means which were not disclosed at the making of a claim for assistance, thereby resulting in an overpayment being made. This is not a new problem, *e.g. Sligo Board v. Lee* [1935] I.R. 673 but the method of counteracting the problem as found in this section evolved from the area of old-age (non-contributory) pensions in the entire field of social assistance through section 35 of the Social Welfare Act, 1993, as from June 25, 1993.

Under this section, where a recipient of any assistance payment or pension dies, the personal representative of that person must deliver to the Minister a notice in writing of intention to distribute assets of the deceased and provide a schedule of the assets of the estate. This notice must be given at least three months prior to the intended distribution, and because the Act does not contain any limitation period (*i.e.* the obligation arises whenever a person was "at any time" in receipt of assistance) the obligation to give this notice would appear to arise if assets have not been distributed prior to commencement of the section on June 25, 1993: prior to that date the only obligation to give notice arose if the deceased had obtained old-age (non-contributory) pension: see section 33 of the Act of 1991.

Following upon this notice the Minister has a further three months within which the Minister may serve upon the personal representative of the deceased a "request" to hold sufficient assets necessary to repay any monies paid to the deceased as assistance which were overpaid, or which were not payable at all. Presumably the notice will specify the amount so necessary. Non-observance will result in personal liability for the personal representative of the deceased (subsection (3)).

Unless there is evidence to the contrary, the assets of the deceased are deemed to be those in the deceased's possession at the time of death, and it is further presumed that they belonged to the deceased for the period of the claim.

These powers are used frequently: *e.g. Lundy v. Minister for Social Welfare* and *O'Connor v. Minister for Social Welfare*, [1993] 3 I.R. 406.

A claim may be brought against the estate of the deceased within two years of the date of delivery of the schedule of assets, or any period fixed by any other Act, whichever is the larger.

Recovery of sums due by civil proceedings or by deduction from other payments

281.—(1) All sums due to the Social Insurance Fund, other than in accordance with section 279, shall be recoverable as debts due to the State and, without prejudice to any other remedy (notwithstanding the assignment by any regulations under section 14(2) to the Collector-General or any other person of any function referred to in that section in relation to employment contributions or the assignment by any regulations under section 20(2) to the Collector-General of any function referred to in that section in relation to self-employment contributions) may be recovered by the Minister as a debt under statute or simple contract debt in any court of competent jurisdiction.

(2) Notwithstanding section 224, or any provision in any other enactment specifying the period within which proceedings may be commenced to recover a debt under statute or simple contract debt, any proceedings for

the recovery of any sums due to the Social Insurance Fund by way of employment contributions under section 10(1) or self-employment contributions under section 18(1) may be brought and shall be maintainable at any time.

(3) All sums due to the Minister, other than in accordance with section 279, under this Act shall be recoverable as debts due to the State and may, without prejudice to any other remedy, be recovered by the Minister as a debt under statute or simple contract debt in any court of competent jurisdiction.

(4) Every sum repaid to or recovered by the Minister under this Act shall be paid into or disposed of for the benefit of the Exchequer or the Social Insurance Fund, as appropriate, in such manner as the Minister for Finance shall direct.

(5) All sums due to a health board under this Act shall be recoverable as debts due to the State and may, without prejudice to any other remedy, be recovered by the health board as a debt under statute or simple contract debt in any court of competent jurisdiction.

(6) Any benefit or assistance repayable in accordance with section 278 or section 279 may, without prejudice to any other method of recovery, be recovered by deduction from any benefit or assistance (except supplementary welfare allowance) to which such person then is or becomes entitled.

(7) (a) Any child benefit repayable in accordance with section 278 or section 279 may, without prejudice to any other method of recovery, be recovered by deduction from any payment or payments on account of child benefit to which such person then is or becomes entitled.

(b) Any family income supplement repayable in accordance with section 278 or section 279 may, without prejudice to any other method of recovery, be recovered by deduction from any payment or payments on account of family income supplement to which such person then is or becomes entitled.

(8) The power conferred on the Minister by this section to deduct from any payments on account of benefit, assistance, child benefit or family income supplement to which a person becomes entitled any sums payable by the person to the Minister or the health board under this section, may be exercised, notwithstanding that proceedings have been instituted in a court for the recovery of the sums which the person is liable to repay to the Minister or the health board as aforesaid or that an order has been made by a court requiring the payment by the person of the sums which he is liable to pay to the Minister or the health board under this section, and any costs required by such order to be paid to the Minister or the health board shall be deemed, for the purposes of this section, to be sums payable by the person to the Minister or the health board (as the case may be) under this section.

GENERAL NOTE

This section sets out the general principles which govern the recovery of overpayments by way of civil action, or by other means of recapment, including deductibility from future entitlements.

Subsection (1)

Save for payments actually made following upon a lawful demand under section 279, all sums due to the Social Insurance Fund are to be recoverable as debts, either as a debt under statute or as a simple contract debt in a court of competent jurisdiction (*i.e.* District Court up to £5,000; Circuit Court up to £30,000).

Subsection (2)

In relation to the recoverability of unpaid employment or self-employment contributions, these debts are recoverable and the normal limitation periods (six years since breach of contract) do not apply thereto.

Subsection (3)

This section empowers the Minister to recover as a debt, any monies due to the State in the form of overpayments of social assistance, by analogy with subsection (1).

Subsection (4)

Sums recovered under this Act are to be held, or disposed of, for either the Fund or the Exchequer, as the Minister for Finance shall direct.

Subsection (6)

Save in cases of overpayments of child benefit or family income supplement, and without prejudice to other means of recoupment, overpayments under sections 278 and 279 may be recovered by deducting sums due from any benefit or assistance other than supplementary welfare allowance.

Subsection (7)

Overpayments of child benefit can only be recovered by deduction from child benefit and the same is true of family income supplement. A civil action in debt is of course also open to the Department, notwithstanding this subsection.

Subsection (8)

Even if a court order directing repayment has been made, or proceedings are pending, the power to deduct overpayments from existing entitlements is unaffected.

Repayment of amounts due to be deferred, suspended, reduced or cancelled

282.—Notwithstanding anything to the contrary, where a person is required to repay an amount of any benefit, assistance (other supplementary welfare allowance), child benefit or family income supplement in accordance with the provisions of this Act, an officer of the Minister authorised by him for this purpose or in the case of supplementary welfare allowance an officer of a health board may, in accordance with such code of practice as shall be prescribed, defer, suspend, reduce or cancel repayment of any such amount.

GENERAL NOTE

No such code of practice has been made publicly available.

Effect of decision for purposes of proceedings

283.—In any proceedings for an offence under this Act, or in any proceedings involving any issue related to the payment of contributions, or for the recovery of any sums due to the Minister or the Social Insurance Fund, a decision on any question relevant to the proceedings given in accordance with this Act shall, unless an appeal or reference in respect of the decision is pending or the prescribed time for appealing against the decision has not expired, be conclusive for the purpose of those proceedings and—

(a) if any such decision which might be so given has not been obtained and the decision is necessary for the determination of the proceedings, the question shall be submitted for decision in accordance with this Act, and

(b) where any such appeal or reference is pending or the time for so appealing has not expired or any question has been submitted under paragraph (a), the court dealing with the case shall adjourn the proceedings until such time as a final decision on the question has been obtained.

PART IX

LIABILITY TO MAINTAIN FAMILY

Interpretation

284.—(1) In this Part—

"allowance" means deserted wife's allowance, lone parent's allowance or supplementary welfare allowance;

"antecedent order" means—

   (a) an order under section 286(4),

   (b) an order under section 286(5) (insofar as it is deemed to be an order under section 17 of the Enforcement of Court Orders Act, 1926), or

   (c) an order under section 286(5) (insofar as it is deemed to be an order under section 5 of the Enforcement of Court Orders Act, 1940);

"attachment of earnings order" means an order under section 287;

"benefit" means deserted wife's benefit;

"competent authority" in relation to deserted wife's benefit, deserted wife's allowance and lone parent's allowance means the Minister, and in relation to supplementary welfare allowance means the health board which granted that allowance to a recipient;

"earnings" means any sums payable to a person—

   (a) by way of wages or salary (including any fees, bonus, commission, overtime pay or other emoluments payable in addition to wages or salary or payable under a contract of service),

   (b) by way of pension or other like benefit in respect of employment (including an annuity in respect of past services, whether or not rendered to the person paying the annuity, and including periodical payments by way of compensation for the loss, abolition or relinquishment, or diminution in the emoluments, of any office or employment);

"order of the Court" means a maintenance order, a lump sum order, a variation order or an interim order under the Family Law (Maintenance of Spouses and Children) Act, 1976, an order under section 10 of that Act or an order of the Court made on foot of a separation agreement.

(2) Every reference in this Part to a person who is liable to maintain another person shall be construed as meaning a person who by virtue of section 285 is liable to maintain such other person.

GENERAL NOTE

This section is the definition section for Part IX of the 1993 Consolidation Act.

This Part, in historical terms, dates back to the Social Welfare Act, 1989 and it represents an attempt by the State to transfer all or some of the cost of child maintenance to liable members of the family.

In introducing this reform to Dáil Éireann in 1989 the Minister for Social Welfare, Dr Woods, had this to say about the problem of marital breakdown as a result of desertion by one spouse (387 *Dáil Debates* Col. 2488):

"The break-up of marriage through desertion is an increasing problem in our society today. In 1978 there were 5,237 women in receipt of deserted wife's benefit or allowance. This grew to 13,617 for 1988. This represents an increase of 8,380 or 160 per cent in a ten year period. Expenditure has shown a corresponding increase rising from £5.6 million in 1978 to £52 million in 1988. The State has always shown concern for deserted wives and will continue to do so. They are paid at the same rate as widows".

Apart from the liable relative provisions found in sections 214 and 215 of the Social Welfare (Consolidation) Act, 1981, which are only applicable to supplementary welfare allowances and which have never been operated by the health boards, there were no formal legislative provisions which allowed the State to transfer the cost of providing income maintenance from the State to the deserting spouse. The State did attempt to deflect the cost of income maintenance by requiring a deserted wife to show that she had made reasonable efforts to obtain support from her spouse as a condition precedent to eligibility for deserted wife's benefit or allowances. This, however, was not generally productive, particularly in low income family units. In terms of the effect this had on relations between spouses the requirement often did more harm than good and it has not been possible for commentators to support this kind of approach (see, for example, the *Finer Report on One Parent Families* (Cmnd. 5629)) because the emphasis placed on legal proceedings as the primary method of obtaining income support was unrealistic, particularly when the deserting spouse had formed another relationship and was therefore unlikely or unwilling to put the needs of the former relationship before those of his or her current one. *Finer* also found that in this context the husband simply did not have the resources to discharge all these commitments so State support was essentially the only effective method of income support. Notwithstanding this reality, and the fact that the evidence in the United Kingdom is that liable relative proceedings net only a fraction of the amount of money disbursed through the social security system, Dr Woods said the new measures provide a new mechanism which will "impose a liability on a husband to maintain his wife and family and, likewise to impose the same liability on a wife to maintain her husband and family": see 122 *Seanad Debates* Col. 683. This measure was first announced on August 29, 1988: see *Irish Times* August 30, 1988.

In Ireland the only comprehensive study of the private law and State systems of income maintenance following family breakdown is that of Peter Ward. This study, completed in the late 1980s, reviewed the files held by the District Court and the Department of Social Welfare. In the case of maintenance applications under the Family Law (Maintenance of Spouses and Children) Act 1976, the majority of maintenance awards were set by the courts at levels which were below the scale rate for supplementary welfare allowance. Even then, default rates were high: some 87 per cent of the orders paid through the District Court Clerk were not paid regularly; 28 per cent had apparently never been paid and 49 per cent had been in arrears for six months or more. In such a context the majority of families affected by family breakdown are largely dependant on social welfare payments. Peter Ward's study *Financial Consequences of Marital Breakdown* was published by the Combat Poverty Agency in 1990.

These provisions came into force on November 29, 1990, as a result of S.I. No. 273 of 1990.

Liability to maintain family

285.—For the purposes of sections 110, 152, 158 and 171 and without prejudice to any obligations imposed by law or otherwise, the following provisions shall have effect, that is to say—
  (a) a man shall be liable to maintain—
    (i) his wife, and
    (ii) any child of his, being a child who is under the age of 18 years or (save for the purposes of section 171) who is of or over that age and under the age of 21 years, and is receiving full-time education or instruction by day at any university, college, school or other educational establishment,
  and
  (b) a woman shall be liable to maintain—
    (i) her husband, and
    (ii) any child of hers, being a child who is under the age of 18 years or (save for the purposes of section 171) who is of or over that age and under the age of 21 years, and is receiving full-time education or instruction by day at any university, college, school or other educational establishment.

DEFINITIONS

"receiving full-time education": article 8 of S.I. No. 417 of 1994.

GENERAL NOTE

These provisions operate in substitution for the pre-existing liable relative provisions found in the Principal Act of 1981 in respect of supplementary welfare allowance (*i.e.* sections 214 and 215).

Section 285 imposes upon a person the duty to support a spouse or a child when the child is under 18 years of age or, when older than 18 but below 21 years of age, undergoing full-time education or instruction, by day, at any university, college, school or other educational establishment. The form of words is slightly different to that found in the former sections 214 and 215. However, a man does not, it seems, have any legal duty to support children born to his wife if that child is not the child of that man: on the evidentiary issues see *S. v. S.* [1983] I.R. 68.

Contribution towards benefit or allowance

286.—(1) Where a benefit or allowance is paid to any recipient, every person who is liable to maintain that recipient or to maintain any child in respect of whom an increase in such benefit or allowance is granted, shall be liable to contribute to the competent authority such amount as that authority may determine to be appropriate towards such benefit or allowance.

(2) Where a person who is liable to contribute under subsection (1) (subsequently referred to in this Part as "the liable relative") fails or neglects to contribute, the competent authority may apply to the District Court for an order directing the liable relative to make such contribution towards the benefit or allowance.

(3) The competent authority, before making an application to the District Court under subsection (2), shall serve notice of the application on the liable relative.

(4) Where the District Court is satisfied that, at the time of the hearing of an application by the competent authority under subsection (2), the liable relative had failed or neglected to make the contribution required under subsection (1) and was able to contribute to the benefit or allowance granted, the District Court shall fix the amount of the contribution to be made by the liable relative and shall order the payment thereof to the competent authority by way of such payments as the Court shall think proper.

(5) An order made by the District Court under subsection (4) shall, for the purposes of its variation or enforcement, be deemed to be an order for payment by instalments made under section 17 of the Enforcement of Court Orders Act, 1926, and the said section 17 shall be construed accordingly.

(6) The District Court may, on the application of either the liable relative or the competent authority, vary in accordance with the provisions of section 5 of the Enforcement of Court Orders Act, 1940, an order made by it under subsection (4) and the said section 5 shall, with any necessary modifications, be construed accordingly:

Provided that any such application made by either party be notified to the other party in advance.

(7) The District Court may, on application by the competent authority in whose favour an order was made under subsection (4) for an order for the arrest and imprisonment of the debtor under section 6 of the Enforcement of Court Orders Act, 1940, proceed in accordance with the provisions of the said section 6.

(8) The provisions of—

(a) section 4(1) (inserted by section 3(3) of the Courts (No. 2) Act, 1986) of the Enforcement of Court Orders Act, 1940 (which relates to the duration of instalment orders), and

(b) section 5(4) (inserted by section 3 of the Courts (No. 2) Act, 1986) of the Enforcement of Court Orders Act, 1940 (which relates to the duration of variation orders),

shall not apply to orders made under subsection (4) of this section.

DEFINITIONS

See section 284.

GENERAL NOTE

Subsections (1) to (4)

These provisions, with minor drafting amendments, were introduced in the 1989 Act so as to provide a legal mechanism whereby the duty to support can be made effective.

When any benefit or allowance is paid to any recipient, subsection (1) directs that any person obliged to maintain that recipient, or any child in respect of which a child dependant addition is added to the benefit or allowance, shall be liable to contribute an appropriate amount towards such benefit or allowance. "Benefit or allowance" is limited to deserted wives' allowance (lone parents' allowance), supplementary welfare allowance, or deserted wives' benefit. Failure to make the appropriate contribution following a "voluntary" agreement can lead to proceedings before the District Court. The appropriate authority, normally the Department of Social Welfare save in cases of supplementary welfare allowance when the appropriate authority will be the health board making the payment, makes an application to the District Court. The District Court, if satisfied that at the time of application the person liable to contribute has failed or neglected to make the contribution required—an appropriate amount—and was able to contribute to the benefit or allowance granted, shall fix the amount of the contribution to be made by the person so liable. There is some flexibility here. Note that all the District Court has to determine is that the liable relative has failed or neglected to make the contribution fixed by the competent authority and that he was able to contribute. The District Court could find, for example, that the competent authority had placed an unreasonable obligation on the liable relative, but, as long as the liable relative was able to contribute something towards the benefit or allowance granted, the District Court could nevertheless fix the amount of the contribution. The appropriate amount of the contribution is nowhere defined. This raises questions about the factors the District Court shall have regard to. If the liable relative has attached himself or herself to another family unit or is supporting aged parents for example, do these voluntary obligations take precedence over the liable relative obligations? In fixing the appropriate amount what financial considerations are relevant? Is income relevant or can cash or non-cash assets be taken into account? Is the District Court to take account of marital misconduct when fixing the appropriate amount in cases of supplementary welfare allowance being paid to the spouse of the liable relative? Can the District Court direct that a liable relative be obliged to transfer part of the liable relative's own social welfare entitlements to the competent authority?

Subsections (5) to (7)
These provisions were absent from the 1989 measures introduced in order to implement the policy of making liable relatives contribute towards the cost of benefits or allowances. As initially introduced, the 1989 Act was not a great success, as the Minister for Social Welfare, Mr McCreevy, stated when introducing these provisions, in the 1992 Bill, to Dáil Eireann:

"Since the provisions of the 1989 Act came into force on 29 November 1900, 5,796 cases in payment have been examined to determine liability on the part of a spouse to make contributions to the Department.

The circumstances of the liable relatives in these cases examined to date can be classified as follows: (1) employed/self-employed, 16 per cent.; (2) social welfare recipient, 47 per cent.; (3) whereabouts cannot be traced at present, 37 per cent.

Maintenance recovery action is at present pursued by the Department only in the case of persons within category (1) at present, that is, those in employment with the means to make some contribution towards the relevant payment of benefit or allowance. There are at present 1,018 cases in this category, including 83 cases where the liable relative is resident in the U.K. To date, 32 determination orders have been issued to liable relatives directing that weekly payments be made to the Department. The total weekly value of these orders if £1,707. The recovery of payments on these orders has, however, not been very successful. To date, total receipts amount to £1,056. Payments have so far been received from six cases only. Nine cases have so far been prepared for civil debt proceedings for non-compliance with the determination orders.

Deputies would realise from the figures I have given that even since 1989 we have not been very successful in receiving payments from liable relatives". (417 *Dáil Debates* Col. 2039).

These provisions enhance the status and effectiveness of orders made by the District Court. When such orders are made they are deemed to be Instalment Orders under the Enforcement of Court Orders Act, 1926. The Minister or the health board are able to enforce the order without having to return to court following a default by the liable relative. The procedure to be followed and the forms to be used in relation to applications are to be found in the District Court (Social Welfare—Contribution Towards Benefit or Allowance) Rules 1992 (S.I. No. 47 of 1992).

Attachment of earnings order

287.—(1) (a) On application to the District Court by a competent authority on whose application the District Court has made an antecedent order, the Court may, to secure payments under the antecedent order, if it is satisfied that the liable relative is a person to whom earnings fall to be paid, make an attachment of earnings order.

(b) References in paragraph (a) to an antecedent order made by the District Court shall include references to such an order made, varied or affirmed on appeal from that Court.

(2) An attachment of earnings order shall be an order directed to a person who (at the time of the making of the order or at any time thereafter) has the liable relative in his employment and shall operate as a direction to that person to make, at such times as may be specified in the order, periodical deductions of such amounts (specified in the order) as may be appropriate, having regard to the normal deduction rate (within the meaning of subsection (4)(a)) and the protected earnings rate (within the meaning of subsection (4)(b)), from the liable relative's earnings and to pay the amounts deducted at such times as the Court may order to the District Court clerk specified by the attachment of earnings order for transmission to the person or competent authority entitled to receive payments made under the relevant antecedent order.

(3) An attachment of earnings order shall not be made without the consent of the liable relative, unless the District Court is satisfied that the liable relative has, without reasonable excuse, defaulted in the making of any payment under the relevant antecedent order.

(4) An attachment of earnings order shall—

(a) specify the normal deduction rate, that is to say, the rate at which the District Court considers it reasonable that the earnings to which the order relates should be applied in satisfying the relevant antecedent order, not exceeding the rate appearing to the District Court to be necessary for the purpose of—

　(i) securing payment of the sums falling due from time to time under the relevant antecedent order, and

　(ii) securing payment within a reasonable period of any sums already due and unpaid under the relevant antecedent order,

(b) specify the protected earnings rate, that is to say, the rate below which, having regard to the resources and the needs of the liable relative, the District Court considers it proper that the relevant earnings should not be reduced by a payment made in pursuance of the attachment of earnings order, and

(c) contain, so far as they are known to the District Court, such particulars as it considers appropriate for the purpose of enabling the liable relative to be identified by the person to whom the order is directed.

(5) Payments under an attachment of earnings order shall be in lieu of payments of the like total amount under the relevant antecedent order that have not been made and that, but for the attachment of earnings order, would fall to be made under the relevant antecedent order.

GENERAL NOTE

This section seeks to enhance the enforcement mechanism in relation to section 286 orders by allowing the competent authority (but not the person liable to be maintained) to seek an attachment-of-earnings order from the District Court. The order is only applicable in respect of wages or salary payable under a contract or service, or a pension, payable by an employer. This section is modelled on Part III of the Family Law (Maintenance of Spouses and Children) Act, 1976.

Obligations on employer in relation to attachment of earnings order

288.—(1) Where an attachment of earnings order or an order varying it is made, the employer for the time being affected by it shall, if it has been served upon him, comply with it; but he shall be under no liability for non-compliance therewith before 10 days have elapsed since the service.

(2) Where an attachment of earnings order is served on any person and the liable relative is not in his employment or the liable relative subsequently ceases to be in his employment, that person shall (in either case) within 10 days from the date of service or, as the case may be, the cesser, give notice of that fact to the District Court.

(3) On any occasion when a person makes, in compliance with an attachment of earnings order, a deduction from a liable relative's earnings, he shall give to the liable relative a statement in writing of the total amount of the deduction.

(4) Such court registrar or court clerk as may be specified by an attachment of earnings order shall cause the order to be served on the employer to whom it is directed and on any subsequent employer of the liable relative concerned of whom the registrar or clerk so specified becomes aware and such service may be effected by leaving the order or a copy of the order at, or sending the order or a copy of the order by registered prepaid post to, the residence or place of business in the State of the person to be served.

GENERAL NOTE

This section sets out the obligations which an employer must meet once an attachment of earnings order is served upon the employer. If the order is valid, *i.e.* the liable relative is in that person's employment, compliance is legally necessary once 10 days have elapsed since service of the order.

For the forms used in this procedure see S.I. No. 47 of 1992.

Payments under attachment of earnings order

289.—Any payments made to a District Court clerk under an attachment of earnings order shall, when transmitted by him to the competent authority entitled to receive those payments, be deemed to be payments made by the liable relative so as to discharge any sums payable under the relevant antecedent order.

DEFINITIONS

See section 284.

GENERAL NOTE

For the forms used under this procedure see S.I. No. 47 of 1992.

Powers of District Court

290.—(1) In relation to an attachment of earnings order or an application for such an order, the District Court that made the order or to which the application is made may, before or at the hearing or while the order is in force—

(a) order the liable relative to give to the District Court, within a specified period, a statement in writing signed by him containing—
   (i) the name and address of any person by whom earnings are paid to him,
   (ii) specified particulars as to his earnings and expected earnings and as to his resources and needs, and
   (iii) specified particulars for enabling the liable relative to be identified by any employer of his, and
(b) order that any person appearing to the District Court to have the liable relative in his employment to give to the Court, within a

specified period, a statement signed by that person, or on his behalf, containing specified particulars of the liable relative's earnings and expected earnings.

(2) Notice of an application for an attachment of earnings order served on a liable relative may include a requirement that he shall give to the District Court, within the period and in the manner specified in the notice, a statement in writing of the matters referred to in paragraph (a) of subsection (1) and of any other matters which are or may be relevant to the determination of the normal deduction rate and the protected earnings rate to be specified in the order.

(3) In any proceedings in relation to an attachment of earnings order, a statement given to the District Court in compliance with an order under paragraph (a) or (b) of subsection (1) or with a requirement under subsection (2) shall be admissible as evidence of the facts stated therein, and a document purporting to be such a statement shall be deemed, unless the contrary is shown, to be a statement so given.

DEFINITIONS
See section 284.

GENERAL NOTE
For forms used in this procedure see S.I. No. 47 of 1992.

Changes in employment

291.—Where an attachment of earnings order is in force—
(a) the liable relative shall notify in writing the District Court that made the order of every occasion on which he leaves any employment, or becomes employed or re-employed, not later (in each case) than 10 days from the date on which he does so,
(b) the liable relative shall, on any occasion on which he becomes employed or re-employed, include in his notification under paragraph (a) particulars of his earnings and expected earnings from the relevant employment,
(c) any person who becomes an employer of the liable relative and knows that the order is in force and by what Court it was made shall, within 10 days of his becoming the liable relative's employer or of acquiring that knowledge (whichever is the later), notify the District Court in writing that he is the liable relative's employer, and include in his notification a statement of the liable relative's earnings and expected earnings, and
(d) any person who is an employer of the liable relative and knows that the order is in force and by what Court it was made shall, within 10 days of such occurrence notify the competent authority and the District Court in writing of any increase in earnings paid to the liable relative.

DEFINITIONS
See section 284.

GENERAL NOTE
This section places absolute obligations upon the liable relative to notify the District Court of any changes in employment, as well as to provide information about earnings and expected earnings in relation to such employment. The employer who is aware of the existence of an order under section 287 is also under similar obligations as a result of this section.

Determinations by District Court

292.—(1) Where an attachment of earnings order is in force, the District Court that made the order shall, on the application of the employer concerned or the liable relative or competent authority to whom payments are being made under the order, determine whether payments (or any portions thereof) to the liable relative of a particular class or description specified by the application are earnings for the purpose of the order, and the employer shall give effect to any determination for the time being in force under this section.

(2) Where an application under this section is made by the employer, he shall not incur any liability for non-compliance with the order as respects any payments (or any portions thereof) of the class or description specified by the application which are made by him to the liable relative while the application or any appeal in consequence thereof or any decision in relation to the application or appeal is pending, but the foregoing provisions of this subsection shall not, unless the District Court otherwise orders, apply as respects such payments (or any portions thereof) if the employer subsequently withdraws the application or, as the case may be, abandons the appeal.

GENERAL NOTE

This section provides that an employer, a liable relative, or a competent authority may apply to the District Court so as to resolve issues relating to the applicability of the attachment of earnings order to certain payments (*e.g.* bonus payments, redundancy payments for example). Ward (*op cit.*) outlines the difficulties that have arisen under the 1976 Act in relation to disputed payments.

Subsection (2) is intended to ensure that employer references should be *bona fide.*

Liable relative in service of State

293.—(1) Where a liable relative is in the service of the State, a local authority for the purposes of the Local Government Act, 1941, a harbour authority within the meaning of the Harbours Act, 1946, a health board, a vocational education committee established by the Vocational Education Act, 1930, or a committee of agriculture established by the Agriculture Act, 1931, or is a member of either House of the Oireachtas—

  (a) in a case where a liable relative in the service of the State is employed in a department, office, organisation, service, undertaking or other body, its chief officer (or such other officer as the Minister of the Government by whom the department, office, organisation, service, undertaking or other body is administered by may from time to time designate) shall, for the purposes of this Act, be regarded as having the liable relative in his employment,

  (b) in a case where a liable relative is in the service of such an authority, board or committee, its chief officer shall, for the purposes of this Act, be regarded as having the liable relative in his employment,

  (c) in any other case, where a liable relative is paid out of the Central Fund or out of moneys provided by the Oireachtas, the Secretary of the Department of Finance (or such other officer of the Minister for Finance as that Minister may from time to time designate) shall, for the purposes of this Act, be regarded as having the liable relative in his employment, and

  (d) any earnings of a liable relative paid out of the Central Fund or out of moneys provided by the Oireachtas shall be regarded as paid by the chief officer referred to in paragraph (a) or (b), as the case may be, the Secretary of the Department of Finance or such other officer as may be designated under paragraph (a) or (c), as the case may be, as may be appropriate.

(2) If any question arises in proceedings for or arising out of an attachment of earnings order as to what department, office, organisation,

service, undertaking or other body a liable relative in the service of the State is employed in for the purposes of this section, the question may be referred to and determined by the Minister for Finance.

(3) A document purporting to contain a determination of the Minister for Finance under subsection (2) and to be signed by an officer of the Minister for Finance shall, in any such proceedings as are mentioned in that subsection, be admissible in evidence and be deemed, unless the contrary is shown, to contain an accurate statement of that determination.

(4) In this section references to a liable relative in the service of the State shall include references to a liable relative to whom earnings are paid directly out of moneys provided by the Oireachtas.

GENERAL NOTE

This section resolves issues of interpretation for employees in the Public Service *vis-à-vis* questions of service of notices (*e.g.* under section 288) and factual issues about the identity of a specific employer.

Discharge, variation or lapse of attachment of earnings order

294.—(1) The District Court that made an attachment of earnings order may, if it thinks fit, on the application of the competent attachment of authority, the liable relative, or the District Court clerk on whose application the order was made, make an order discharging or varying that order.

(2) Where an order varying an attachment of earnings order is made under this section, the employer shall, if it has been served upon him, comply with it, but he shall be under no liability for non-compliance before 10 days have elapsed since the service.

(3) Where an employer affected by an attachment of earnings order ceases to have the liable relative in his employment, the order shall, in so far as that employer is concerned, lapse (except as respects deductions from earnings paid after the cesser by that employer and payment to the person in whose favour the order was made of deductions from earnings made at any time by that employer).

(4) The lapse of an order under subsection (3) shall not prevent its remaining in force for other purposes.

GENERAL NOTE

For the forms used under this procedure see S.I. No. 47 of 1992.

Cesser

295.—(1) An attachment of earnings order shall cease to have effect upon the discharge of the relevant antecedent order, except as regards payments under the attachment of earnings order in respect of any time before the date of the discharge.

(2) Where an attachment of earnings order ceases to have effect, the clerk or registrar of the Court that made the order shall give notice of the cesser to the employer.

GENERAL NOTE

For forms used under this procedure see S.I. No. 295 of 1992.

Offences

296.—(1) When, without reasonable excuse, a person—

(a) fails to comply with subsection (1) or (2) of section 288 or section 291 or an order under section 290 or section 294(2), or

(b) gives to a court a statement pursuant to section 290(1), or a notification under section 291, that is false or misleading, or fails to give any statement,

and the competent authority as a result fails to obtain a sum of money due under an attachment of earnings order, that sum may be sued for as a simple contract debt in any court of competent jurisdiction by the competent authority or the District Court clerk to whom such sum falls to be paid, and that court may order the person to pay to the competent authority or the District Court clerk, as appropriate, such amount (not exceeding the sum aforesaid) as in all the circumstances the court considers proper for distribution in such manner and in such amounts as the court may specify to the competent authority for whose benefit the attachment of earnings order was made.

(2) Where a person gives a District Court—

(a) a statement pursuant to section 290, or

(b) a notification under section 291,

that is to his knowledge false or misleading, he shall be guilty of an offence and shall be liable on summary conviction to a fine not exceeding £1,000 or to imprisonment for a term not exceeding 6 months or to both.

(3) A person who contravenes section 288(3) shall be guilty of an offence and shall be liable on summary conviction to a fine not exceeding £1,000.

GENERAL NOTE

These offences may be committed by the liable relative or an employer of the liable relative. The civil liability provisions in subsection (1) parallel those found in sections 219 and 220.

Payments under order of court to offset contributions

297.—Where an order of the Court has been granted to a person who is in receipt of a benefit or allowance, the payments made under that order shall offset either in whole or part, as the competent authority may determine, contributions due by the person liable to contribute pursuant to section 286(1) to such benefit or allowance.

GENERAL NOTE

The health board or Department of Social Welfare is given a discretion to treat payments made under an attachment of earnings order as offsetting, in whole or in part, the section 286(1) liability which is itself defined as the antecedent order. This section is explicable on the ground that payments made may not meet the sum fixed by the court under section 286(4).

Recipient of benefit or allowance to transfer to competent authority payments under order of court

298.—(1) A person who is in receipt of a benefit or allowance shall be liable to transfer to the competent authority payments made to that person in compliance with an order of the Court.

(2) A person who claims a benefit or allowance may be required by the competent authority to consent to the transfer to the competent authority of payments made to that person in compliance with an order of the court, such transfer to be conditional on the award of benefit or allowance to that person.

(3) Where a person who is in receipt of benefit or allowance fails to comply with the provisions of subsection (1) the benefit or allowance being paid to that person shall be reduced by the amount which that person is liable under subsection (1) to transfer to the Minister.

The payment of monies on the foot of a court order to the dependant spouse will result in the transfer of those monies to the competent authority. The penalty for non-transfer by the dependant spouse is a reduction in benefit or allowance: the word "shall" rather than "may" is used.

COMMENCEMENT
November 29, 1990 (S.I. No. 273 of 1990).

Investigations by health boards

299.—(1) A health board may investigate into any question arising on or in relation to supplementary welfare allowance granted by the board and may, for the purpose of such investigation, require a liable relative or any employer of any such person to furnish the health board with such information and to produce to the health board for inspection such documents relating to that person as the health board may reasonably require.

(2) Where a liable relative or the employer of any such person fails to comply with the provisions of subsection (1) he shall be guilty of an offence and shall be liable on summary conviction to a fine not exceeding £1,000 or on conviction on indictment to a fine not exceeding £10,000.

GENERAL NOTE
For powers of the Department of Social Welfare see section 221.

PART X

COMMENCEMENT, REPEALS AND CONTINUANCE

Repeals

300.—The enactments specified in column (2) of the Fifth Schedule (referred to in this Part as "the repealed enactments") are hereby repealed to the extent specified in column (3) of that Schedule:

Provided that without prejudice to the Interpretation Act, 1937, the provisions of the repealed enactments shall continue to apply to benefit, assistance, child benefit or family income supplement prior to the commencement of this Act to the same extent as if this Act had not been passed.

Continuity of repealed enactments

301.—The continuity of the operation of the law relating to the matters provided for in the repealed enactments shall not be affected by the substitution of this Act for those enactments, and—

(a) so much of any enactment or document (including enactments contained in this Act) as refers, whether expressly or by implication, to, or to things done or falling to be done under or for the purposes of, any provision of this Act, shall, if and so far as the nature of the subject matter of the enactment or document permits, be construed as including, in relation to the times, years or periods, circumstances or purposes in relation to which the corresponding provision in the repealed enactments has or had effect, a reference to, or, as the case may be, to things done or falling to be done under or for the purposes of, that corresponding provision;

(b) so much of any enactment or document (including repealed enactments and enactments and documents passed or made after the commencement of this Act) as refers, whether expressly or by implication, to, or to things done or falling to be done under or for the purposes of, any provision of the repealed enactments shall, if and so far as the nature of the subject matter of the enactment or document permits, be construed as including, in relation to the times, years or periods, circumstances or purposes in relation to which the corresponding provision of this Act has effect, a reference to, or, as the case may be, to things done or deemed to be done or falling to be done under or for the purposes of, that corresponding provision.

Continuance of instruments, officers and documents

302.—(1) All officers appointed under the repealed enactments or any enactments repealed by the Social Welfare (Consolidation) Act, 1981, and holding office immediately before the commencement of this Act shall continue in office as if appointed under this Act.

(2) All instruments made and documents issued under the repealed enactments or any enactments repealed by the Social Welfare (Consolidation) Act, 1981, and in force immediately before the commencement of this Act (other than the provisions of any instruments which are incorporated in this Act) shall continue in force as if made or issued under this Act.

Continuity of insurance under old codes

303.—(1) Regulations may be made, subject to such modifications, additions and exceptions as may be specified, for the purpose of ensuring that persons insured or deemed to be or treated as insured within the prescribed period before the 5th day of January, 1953, under the National Insurance Act, 1911, the Unemployment Insurance Act, 1920, (or any scheme under that Act) or the Widows' and Orphans' Pensions Act, 1935, may continue to be insured under the provisions of Part II or otherwise to preserve the rights conferred on them by virtue of those enactments.

(2) Regulations under subsection (1) shall, in such manner and subject to such conditions as may be specified, in particular, provide in relation to persons so insured, for modifying the contribution conditions for receipt of benefit under Part II to take account of contributions paid or deemed to be paid or treated as paid under the said enactments and periods of insurance thereunder.

(3) Without prejudice to any specific power conferred by subsections (1) and (2), regulations may be made for facilitating their operation or the introduction of the system of insurance established by the Social Welfare Act, 1952, including, in particular, regulations providing—

(a) for modifying, as respects the period before the 5th day of January, 1953, any provisions of or made under any enactment repealed or amended by Part V of that Act, or

(b) for making any savings or additional savings from the effect of any repeal or amendment effected by that Act.

Commencement

304.—(1) Subject to this Part, this Act shall come into operation on such day as the Minister may appoint by order.

(2) The provisions of the Sixth Schedule shall come into operation—

(a) in respect of paragraph 1, on such day or days as the Minister may appoint by order or orders and different days may be so appointed for different provisions of that paragraph,

(b) in respect of paragraph 2, on such day as the Minister may appoint by order,

(c) in respect of paragraph 3, on such day as the Minister may appoint by order, and

(d) in respect of paragraph 4, on such day as the Minister may appoint by order.

GENERAL NOTE

Under the Social Welfare (Consolidation) Act, 1993 Commencement Order, 1993 (S.I. No. 335 of 1993) the Act came into force on November 16, 1993.

Section 9 FIRST SCHEDULE

EMPLOYMENTS, EXCEPTED EMPLOYMENTS AND EXCEPTED SELF-EMPLOYED CONTRIBUTORS

PART I

EMPLOYMENTS

1. Employment in the State under any contract of service or apprenticeship, written or oral, whether expressed or implied, and whether the employed person is paid by the employer or some other person, and whether under one or more employers, and whether paid by time or by the piece or partly by time and partly by the piece, or otherwise, or without any money payment.

2. Employment under such a contract as aforesaid—

(a) as master or a member of the crew of—
(i) any ship registered in the State, or
(ii) any other ship or vessel of which the owner, or, if there is more than one owner, the managing owner or manager, resides or has his principal place of business in the State, or

(b) as captain or a member of the crew of—
(i) any aircraft registered in the State, or
(ii) any other aircraft of which the owner, or, if there is more than one owner, the managing owner or manager, resides or has his principal place of business in the State.

3. Employment in the civil service of the Government or the civil service of the State and employment such that the service therein of the employed person is, or is capable of being, deemed under section 24 of the Superannuation Act, 1936, to be service in the civil service of the Government or the civil service of the State.

4. Employment as a member of the Defence Forces.

5. Employment under any local or other public authority.

6. Employment as a court messenger under section 4 of the Enforcement of Court Orders Act, 1926.

7. Employment as a trainee midwife, student midwife, pupil midwife, probationary midwife, trainee nurse, student nurse, pupil nurse or probationary nurse. In this paragraph "nurse" includes a nursery or children's nurse.

8. Employment by the Minister as manager of an employment office.

9. Employment as a member of the Garda Síochána.

10. Employment where the employed person is a person in Holy Orders or other minister of religion or a person living in a religious community as a member thereof.

11. Employment by An Post as a sub-postmaster remunerated by scale payment.

Section 9 PART II

EXCEPTED EMPLOYMENTS

1. Employment in the service of the husband or wife of the employed person.

2. Employment of a casual nature otherwise than for the purposes of the employer's trade or business, and otherwise than for the purposes of any game or recreation where the persons employed are engaged or paid through a club.

3. Employment by a prescribed relative of the employed person, being either employment in the common home of the employer and the employed person or employment specified by regulations as corresponding to employment in the common home of the employer and the employed person.

4. Employment specified in regulations as being of such a nature that it is ordinarily adopted as subsidiary employment only and not as the principal means of livelihood.

5. Employment specified in regulations as being of inconsiderable extent.

6. Employment under a scheme administered by An Foras Áiseanna Saothair and known as the Social Employment Scheme.

Section 17   Part III

EXCEPTED SELF-EMPLOYED CONTRIBUTORS

1. A prescribed relative of a self-employed contributor not being a partner, where he participates in the business of the self-employed contributor and performs the same tasks or ancillary tasks.

2. A self-employed contributor who—
   - (a) by virtue of the provisions of Chapter 2 of Part III is in receipt of unemployment assistance, or
   - (b) by virtue of the provisions of Chapter 3 of Part III is in receipt of pre-retirement allowance.

3. A person, the aggregate of whose total reckonable income, reckonable emoluments or reckonable earnings (if any) before deducting so much of any deduction—
   - (a) allowed by virtue of the provisions referred to in section 33 of the Finance Act, 1975, to be deducted or set off against income in charging it to income tax, or
   - (b) allowed in accordance with Regulations 59 and 60 of the Income Tax (Employments) Regulations, 1960 (S.I. No. 28 of 1960) (inserted by the Income Tax (Employments) Regulations, 1972 (S.I. No. 260 of 1972)) to be deducted on payment of emoluments or earnings,

is below a prescribed amount.

4. An employed contributor or a person who is in receipt of a pension arising from a previous employment of his or of his spouse, in the case of either of whom the income for the contribution year does not include reckonable emoluments or in the case of reckonable income, income to which Chapter II or III of Part IV of the Income Tax Act, 1967, applies.

5. A person employed in any one or more of the employments specified in regulations under section 11, being employments in respect of which the contribution payable under the said regulations are reckoned only in relation to the grant of survivor's pension [1995 Act, Schedule D] deserted wife's benefit or orphan's (contributory) allowance and are not reckoned in relation to the grant of any other benefit.

6. A person who is regarded as not resident or not ordinarily resident in the State in accordance with the provisions of the Income Tax Acts and whose reckonable income for that year does not include income to which Chapter II or III of Part IV of the Income Tax Act, 1967, applies.

SECOND SCHEDULE

RATES OF BENEFITS

PART I

RATES OF PERIODICAL BENEFITS AND INCREASES THEREOF

Description of benefit	Weekly rate	Increase for adult dependant (where payable)	Increase for each qualified child in excess of two (where payable)	Increase for prescribed relative (where payable)	Increase where the person has attained pension-able age and is living alone (where payable)	Increase where the person has attained the age of 80 years (where payable)
(1)	(2)	(3)	(4)	(5)	(6)	(7)
	£	£	£	£	£	£
1. Disability Benefit, Unemployment Benefit and Injury Benefit and Health and Safety Benefit	62.50	37.50	13.20	—	—	—
2. Death Benefit						
(a) pension payable to a widow (section 60(2)) or widower (section 60(6))	83.90	—	17.00	34.70	4.90	—
(b) pension payable to a parent						
(i) reduced rate	37.70	—	—	34.70	4.90	—
(ii) maximum rate	83.90	—	—	34.70	4.90	—
(c) pension payable to an orphan	43.60	—	—	—	—	—
3. Old Age (Contributory) Pension and Retirement Pension:	72.80	48.10	15.20	33.70	4.90	4.80
additional increase for an adult dependant who has attained pensionable age	—	4.20	—	—	—	—
4. Invalidity Pension	64.20	42.30	15.20	34.70	4.90	4.80
additional increase for a beneficiary who has attained the age of 65 years	8.60	—	—	—	—	—
5. Survivor's Pension and Deserted Wife's Benefit [1995 Act, Schedule D]	66.10	—	17.00	34.70	4.90	4.80
6. Orphan's (Contributory) Allowance	41.40	—	—	—	—	—

GENERAL NOTE

For reduced rates of disability benefit, unemployment benefit, Health and Safety benefit, old age (contributory) pension, retirement pension, survivor's pension and deserted wife's benefit, see S.I. No. 146 of 1995.

PART II

OCCUPATIONAL INJURIES BENEFITS— GRATUITIES AND GRANT

Description of Grant (1)	Amount (2)
	£
1. Disablement Benefit: Maximum gratuity	5,980

2. Death Benefit:
  (a) Widower's gratuity ....
  (b) Grant in respect of funeral expenses ....
	4,360
	300

Section 54

PART III

DISABLEMENT PENSION

Degree of disablement (1)	Weekly rate (2)
	£
100 per cent	85.60
90 ,, ,, ...	77.00
80 ,, ,, ...	68.50
70 ,, ,, ...	59.90
60 ,, ,, ...	51.40
50 ,, ,, ...	42.80
40 ,, ,, ...	34.20
30 ,, ,, ...	25.70
20 ,, ,, ...	17.10

Sections 56 and 57

PART IV

INCREASES OF DISABLEMENT PENSION

Description of Increase (1)	Weekly Rate (2)
	£
1. Increase where the person is permanently incapable of work	62.50

2. Increase where the beneficiary requires constant attendance:
  (a) limit of increase except in cases of exceptionally severe disablement
  (b) limit in any other case ....
	
	34.70
	69.50

[inserted by 1995 Act, section 3(1)].

GENERAL NOTE

For certain reduced rates of occupational injuries payments, see S.I. No. 137 of 1995.

1993 No. 27

THIRD SCHEDULE

RULES AS TO CALCULATION OF MEANS

Sections 119 and 127   PART I

UNEMPLOYMENT ASSISTANCE AND PRE-RETIREMENT ALLOWANCE

1. In the calculation of the means of a person for the purposes of Chapters 2 and 3 of Part III, the following things and no other things shall be deemed to constitute the means of a person—

(1) other than in circumstances and subject to such conditions and for such periods as may be prescribed the yearly value ascertained in the prescribed manner of all property belonging to him or to his spouse (not being property personally used or enjoyed by him or by his spouse or a farm of land leased either by him or by his spouse under a lease which was certified by the Irish Land Commission to be *bona fide* and in accordance with sound land use practice) which is invested or otherwise put to profitable use or is capable of being, but is not, invested or put to profitable use; [1995 Act Schedule C]

(2) all income which he or his spouse may reasonably expect to receive during the succeeding year in cash, whether as contributions to the expenses of the household or otherwise, but excluding—

(a) all moneys earned by his spouse from insurable employment and insurable self-employment,

(b) any moneys received by way of benefit, pension, assistance, allowance or supplement under Part II, III, IV or V, "or by way of a payment corresponding to child benefit under Part IV, from another Member State.", [1994 Act, section 18].

(c) any income arising from a bonus under a scheme administered by the Minister for the Gaeltacht for the making of special grants to parents or guardians resident in the Gaeltacht or Breac-Ghaeltacht (as defined in such scheme) of children attending primary schools,

(d) in the case of a qualified applicant under a scheme administered by the Minister for the Gaeltacht and known as Scéim na bhFoghlaimeoirí Gaeilge, any income received under that scheme in respect of a person who is temporarily resident with the qualified applicant, together with any other income received in respect of such temporary resident,

(e) an amount of an allowance, dependant's allowance, disability pension or wound pension under the Army Pensions Acts, 1923 to 1980, or a combination of such allowances and such pensions so far as such amount does not exceed £80 per year.

(f) any moneys received from a charitable organisation, being a body whose activities are carried on otherwise than for profit (but excluding any public or local authority) and one of whose functions is to assist persons in need by making grants of money to them,

(g) such amount, as may be prescribed, of income from employment by a health board or by a person approved by a health board, as a home help", and [1994 Act, section 18].

(h) any moneys received by way of training allowance from an organisation while undergoing a course of rehabilitation training provided by the organisation (being an organisation approved of by the Minister for Health for the purposes of the provision of such training),

(i) any moneys, except so far as they exceed £104 per year, received by such person or by the spouse of such person in respect of work as an outworker under a scheme that is, in the opinion of the Minister, charitable in character and purpose,

(j) where he or his spouse is engaged on a seasonal basis in the occupation of fishing, one-half of so much of the income derived therefrom as does not exceed £120 per year and one-third of so much of such income as exceeds £120 per year but does not exceed £300 per year,

(k) payments by a health board in respect of a child who is boarded out,

(l) [repealed 1995 Act, Schedule C].

(m) such amount as may be prescribed of all moneys earned by him in respect of current personal employment under a contract of service;

(n) in such cases as may be prescribed, any moneys received by way of a maintenance grant under a scheme administered by the Minister for Education under the Local Authorities (Higher Education Grants) Acts, 1968 to 1992,

(o) any moneys received by way of a mobility allowance payable under section 61 of the Health Act, 1970.

(p) such income, as may be prescribed, arising from such activities as may be prescribed; [1994 Act, section 18].

(q) subject to paragraph (6), any moneys derived from insurable employment of a seasonal nature; [1995 No. 2 Act, section 11]

(3) the yearly value ascertained in the prescribed manner of any advantage accuring to him or to his spouse from—

(a) the use of property (other than a domestic dwelling or farm building owned and occupied, furniture and personal effects) which is personally used or enjoyed by him or by his spouse, and

(b) the leasing by him or by his spouse of a farm of land under a lease which was certified by the Irish Land Commission to be *bona fide* and in accordance with sound land use practice;

(4) all income and the yearly value ascertained in the prescribed manner of all property of which he or his spouse have directly or indirectly deprived themselves in order to qualify for the receipt of unemployment assistance or pre-retirement allowance, but where such income or the yearly value of the property so ascertained has reduced since the date of calculation, the calculation may be revised, subject to such conditions and in such circumstances as may be prescribed:

Provided that any such regulations shall not cause the income or yearly value of the property taken to be part of the means to be increased;

(5) the yearly value of any benefit or privilege enjoyed by him or by his spouse, including the estimated value to the household in the succeeding year deriving from all income earned by his spouse from insurable employment and insurable self-employment.

(6) In the case of a person who makes a claim for unemployment assistance in respect of a day of unemployment which occurs during a period in which he is engaged in insurable employment of a seasonal nature, the value, ascertained in the prescribed manner, of any moneys derived from the said employment and the value so calculated shall be deemed to constitute the weekly means of that person from such employment for the purposes of Chapter 2 of Part III; [1995 No. 2 Act, section 11]

2. For the purposes of Rules 1(2) and 1(5), the income of a person shall, in the absence of other means of ascertaining it, be taken to be the income actually received during the year immediately preceding the date of calculation.

"3. For the purposes of Rules 1 and 2 'spouse' means—

(a) each person of a married couple who are living together, or

(b) a man and woman who are not married to each other but are cohabiting together as husband and wife." [1995 Act, section 16]

Sections 134, 142, 152, 155, 157 and 163   Part II

Old Age (Non-Contributory), Blind, Widow's and Orphan's (Non-Contributory) Pensions, Deserted Wife's, Prisoner's Wife's, Lone Parent's and Carer's Allowances

1. Subject to paragraphs (2) and (3), in calculating the means of a person, account shall be taken of the following—

(1) other than in such circumstances and subject to such conditions and for such periods as may be prescribed the yearly value of any property belonging to the person (not being property personally used or enjoyed by the person or a farm of land leased by him under a lease which was certified by the Irish Land Commission to be *bona fide* and in accordance with sound land use practice) which is invested or is otherwise put to profitable use by the person or which, though capable of investment or profitable use is not invested or put to profitable use by the person, the yearly value of the property being calculated as follows: [1995 Act, Schedule C]

(a) the first £200 of the capital value of the property shall be excluded, and

(b) the yearly value of the next £375 of the capital value of the property shall be taken to be one-twentieth part of the capital value, and

(c) the yearly value of so much of the capital value of the property as exceeds £575 shall be taken to be one-tenth part of the capital value,

but no account shall be taken under any other provision of these Rules of any appropriation of the property for the purpose of current expenditure;

(2) in the application of paragraph (1) for the purposes of widow's (non-contributory) pension, orphan's (non-contributory) pension, deserted wife's allowance, prisoner's wife's

allowance or lone parent's allowance, the following subparagraphs shall be substituted for subparagraphs (a), (b) and (c) of that paragraph:

"(a) the first £200 of the capital value of the property shall be excluded, and

(b) in the case of a lone parent, an additional £100 of the capital value of the property shall be excluded in respect of each qualified child normally residing with the lone parent in respect of whom an increase of allowance is claimable, and

(c) the yearly value of any remainder of the capital value of the property shall be taken to be one-twentieth part of such remainder.";

(3) where, for the purposes of old age (non-contributory) pension, blind pension, widow's (non-contributory) pension, deserted wife's allowance, prisoner's wife's allowance, lone parent's allowance or carer's allowance, the means are or include means assessed in accordance with paragraph (1) or paragraphs (1) and (2), as the case may be, and the means as so assessed are not less than £52, the means shall be taken to be increased by £52;

(4) all income in cash (including, in the case of widow's (non-contributory) pension, orphan's (non-contributory) pension, deserted wife's allowance, prisoner's wife's allowance or lone parent's allowance, the net cash value of such non-cash benefits as may be prescribed, and such income received by a qualified child or qualified children as may be prescribed), which the person may reasonably expect to receive during the year succeeding the date of calculation, but excluding—

(a) any sums arising from the investment or profitable use of property (not being property personally used or enjoyed by the person or a farm of land leased by him under a lease which was certified by the Irish Land Commission to be *bona fide* and in accordance with sound land use practice),

(b) any sums received by way of benefit, pension, assistance, allowance or supplement under Part II, III, IV or V, "or by way of a payment, corresponding to child benefit under Part IV, from another Member State,", [1994 Act, section 18].

(c) any income arising from a bonus under a scheme administered by the Minister for Education for the making of special grants to parents or guardians resident in the Gaeltacht or Breac-Ghaeltacht (as defined in such scheme) of children attending primary schools,

(d) in the case of a qualified applicant under a scheme administered by the Minister for the Gaeltacht and known as Scéim na bhFoghlaimeoirí Gaeilge, any income received under that scheme in respect of a person who is temporarily resident with the qualified applicant, together with any other income received in respect of such temporary resident,

(e) (i) any moneys from a charitable organisation, being a body whose activities are carried on otherwise than for profit (but excluding any public or local authority) and one of whose functions is to assist persons in need by making grants of money to them, and

(ii) any income, other than income of the kind specified in clause (i), from voluntary or gratuitous payments in so far as it does not exceed £52.25 per year,

(f) any income arising by way of—

(i) infectious diseases maintenance allowance to or in respect of the person or the person's dependants,

(ii) payments by a health board in respect of a child who is boarded out,

(iii) disabled person's maintenance allowance to the person, or,

(iv) a mobility allowance payable under section 61 of the Health Act, 1970, to the person,

(g) subject to Rule 5, an amount of an allowance, dependent's allowance, disability pension or wound pension under the Army Pensions Acts, 1923 to 1980, (including, for the purposes of this subparagraph, a British war pension) or of a combination of such allowances and such pensions except so far as such amount exceeds £80 per year,

(h) in the case of a blind person, his earnings (including wages and profit from any form of self-employment) as a blind person except and in so far as the annual amount of such earnings is calculated to exceed an amount made up as follows— £312, plus £208 if his spouse is living with or is wholly or mainly maintained by him or, being a single person, widow or widower, is maintaining wholly or mainly a person over the age of 16 years having the care of one or more than one qualified child who normally resides or reside with him, plus £104 for each qualified child normally residing with him of whom account has not already been taken in accordance with this paragraph in calculating the means of another person,

    (i) any income arising from a grant or allowance in pursuance of a scheme for promoting the welfare of the blind prepared under section 2 of the Blind Persons Act, 1920,

    (j) in the case of a person who is not a blind person or a lone parent, and who has a qualified child who normally resides with him, his earnings (including wages and profit from any form of self-employment), except and insofar as the annual amount of such earnings is calculated to exceed £104 for each such child of whom account has not already been taken in accordance with this paragraph in calculating the means of another person,

    (jj) in the case of a lone parent, such amount, as may be prescribed, of his earnings (including wages and profit from any form of self-employment), together with one-half of the amount of his earnings, if any, in excess of the amount so prescribed," [1994 Act, section 15].

    (k) in the case of a person who is not a blind person, any moneys, except so far as they exceed £52 per year, received by the person in respect of employment as an outworker under a scheme that is, in the opinion of the Minister, charitable in character and purpose,

    (l) such amount, as may be prescribed, of income from employment by a health board or by a person approved by a health board, as a home help," [1994 Act, section 18].

    (m) [repealed, 1995 Act, Schedule C].

and such income shall, in the absence of other means for ascertaining it, be taken to be that actually received during the year immediately preceding the date of calculation:

Provided that, where such income is attributable to a period prior to the year immediately preceding the date of calculation but is received in a subsequent year, it shall be regarded for the purposes of this paragraph as having been received in the year to which it is attributable;

    (n) any moneys received by way of training allowance from an organisation while undergoing a course of rehabilitation training provided by the organisation (being an organisation approved of by the Minister for Health for the purposes of the provision of such training),

    (o) in the case of lone parent's allowance, any moneys received by way of a maintenance grant under a scheme administered by the Minister for Education under the Local Authorities (Higher Education Grants) Acts, 1968 to 1992,

    (p) such income, as may be prescribed, arising from such activities as may be prescribed;" [1994 Act, section 18].

    (5) the yearly value of any advantage accruing to the person from—

    (a) the use or enjoyment of property (other than a domestic dwelling or a farm building owned and occupied, furniture and personal effects) which is personally used or enjoyed by the person, and

    (b) a farm of land leased by the person under a lease which was certified by the Irish Land Commission to be *bona fide* and in accordance with sound land use practice, but for the purposes of this Rule a cottage provided under the Labourers Acts, 1883 to 1965, and vested in the person or the spouse of that person pursuant to those Acts or pursuant to the Housing Acts, 1966 to 1984, shall not be treated as property which is personally used or enjoyed by that person or the spouse of that person so long as payment of the purchase annuity has not been completed;

    (6) in the case of carer's allowance, such amount as the Minister determines that the relevant pensioner (as defined in section 163) could reasonably be expected to contribute to the support of the carer but in determining such amount, no account shall be taken of any sums received by the relevant pensioner under Part II, III or IV.

2. (1) Notwithstanding the provisions of this Schedule, for the purposes of old age (non-contributory) pension, the gross proceeds derived from the sale of the principal residence of the claimant or beneficiary or, in the case of a married couple who are living together, the spouse of the claimant or beneficiary where such spouse has attained pensionable age, shall not, subject—

    (a) to such limit,

    (b) to such conditions,

    (c) in such circumstances, and

    (d) for such periods,

as shall be prescribed, be taken into account in calculating the means of the claimant or pensioner.

    (2) Notwithstanding the provisions of this Schedule, for the purposes of—

    (a) widow's (non-contributory) pension,

    (b) deserted wife's allowance,

    (c) prisoner's wife's allowance, or

    (d) lone parent's allowance,

where the claimant or beneficiary has attained pensionable age, the gross proceeds derived from the sale of the principal residence of the claimant or beneficiary shall not, subject—

        (i) to such limit,

       (ii) to such conditions,

     (iii) in such circumstances, and

     (iv) for such periods,

as may be prescribed, be taken into account in calculating the means of the claimant or beneficiary.

(3) In this Rule "gross proceeds derived from the sale of the principal residence" means—

    (a) the agreed sale price of the residence, or

    (b) where the claimant or beneficiary purchases alternative accommodation, the difference between the agreed sale price of the former residence and the agreed purchase price of the replacement residence.

(4) Paragraphs (1) and (2) shall not apply to any sums arising from the investment or profitable use of the gross proceeds derived from the sale of the principal residence.

3. (1) Subject to paragraph (2), if it appears that any person has, whether before or after the commencement of this Act, directly or indirectly deprived himself of any income or property in order to qualify himself for the receipt of the pension or allowance in question, or for the receipt thereof at a higher rate than that to which he would otherwise be entitled, that income or the yearly value of that property shall for the purposes of these Rules be taken to be part of the means of that person.

    (2) (a) Subject to subparagraph (b), paragraph (1) shall not apply to any assignment—

        (i) which is an assignment to a child or children of the assignor, and

       (ii) which is an assignment of property consisting of a farm of land (together with or without the stock and chattels thereon) the rateable value of which (including the buildings thereon) does not exceed £30 and of which the assignor is the owner and the occupier or the occupier only.

      (b) Subparagraph (a) shall not apply to an assignment by a person who, at any time within the 3 years ending when the relevant claim for a pension or allowance or application for an increase of a pension or allowance is made, was as respects any agricultural lands exceeding £30 in rateable value or aggregate rateable value, the owner and occupier thereof, the occupier only thereof or the owner and occupier of part thereof and the occupier only of the remainder.

      (c) In this paragraph "assignment" includes any form of conveyance, transfer or other transaction by which a person parts with the ownership or possession of property.

(3) In the case of a person to whom paragraph (1) applies, where the income or the yearly value of the property taken to be part of his means for the purposes of that paragraph has reduced since the date of calculation, the calculation may be revised, subject to such conditions and in such circumstances as may be prescribed, but regulations made under this paragraph shall not cause the income or the yearly value of the property taken to be part of his means to be increased.

4. (1) In the case of an old age (non-contributory) pension, blind pension or a carer's allowance, the following provisions shall have effect when calculating the means of a person who is one of a couple living together—

    (a) the means of the person shall be taken to be one-half of the total means of the couple;

    (b) the person shall be deemed to be entitled to one-half of all property to which the person or the other member of the couple is entitled or to which the person and the other member of the couple are jointly entitled;

    (c) for the purposes of this Rule, the means of each member of the couple shall first be determined in accordance with these Rules (each being regarded as an applicant for a pension or a pension at a higher rate or carer's allowance, as the case may be) and the total means shall be the sum of the means of each member as so determined;

    (d) where one member of the couple dies, nothing which was reckoned for the purposes of pension, or would (if such deceased member had been entitled to receive any pension) have been so reckoned, as means of the deceased member shall be so reckoned as means of the surviving member for the purpose of reducing the pension of the surviving member if any payment in respect of that pension was made before the death of the deceased member or becomes payable in respect of a period previous or part of which was previous to that death.

"(1A) In the case of carer's allowance, in calculating the means of the other member of the couple for the purposes of paragraph (1), such amount as may be prescribed shall be disregarded.". [1995 Act, section 12].

(2) In paragraph (1) "couple" means a married couple who are living together or a man and woman who are not married to each other but are cohabiting as husband and wife.

(3) In calculating the means of a person who is one of a married couple living apart from his spouse, any sum paid by him to his spouse under a separation order shall be deducted in calculating his means.

5. Notwithstanding these Rules, where—

    (a) an old age (non-contributory) pension, blind pension, widow's (non-contributory) pension, orphan's (non-contributory) pension, deserted wife's allowance, prisoner's wife's allowance or lone parent's allowance or carer's allowance [1995 Act, Schedule C] is in course of payment to or in respect of a person or the spouse of the person or both of them, and

    (b) a pension or pensions (in this Rule referred to as "the other pension"), not being a pension or pensions mentioned in paragraph (a), is in course of payment to or in respect of the person or the spouse of the person or both of them,

in calculating the means of the person or of the spouse or of both of them for the purposes of old age (non-contributory) pension, blind pension, widow's (non-contributory) pension, orphan's (non-contributory) pension, deserted wife's allowance, prisoner's wife's allowance or lone parent's allowance or carer's allowance [1995 Act, Schedule C] (as the case may require) any portion of the amount of an increase in the other pension or the aggregate increase, where more than one increase in the other pension has occurred, which, if it were reckoned as means, would result in a reduction in the amount of the pension or combined pensions (as the case may be) which would be greater than the amount by which the other pension has been increased, shall not be reckoned as means.

6. Notwithstanding this Schedule, the amount of any allowance, special allowance, dependent's allowance, disability pension or wound pension under the Army Pensions Acts, 1923 to 1980, or pension under the Military Service (Pensions) Acts, 1924 to 1964, arising out of service in the period commencing on the 23rd day of April, 1916, and ending on the 30th day of September, 1923, or pension under the Connaught Rangers (Pensions) Acts, 1936 to 1964, shall be disregarded in the calculation of means for the purposes of Chapters 4, 5, 6, 7, 8, 9 and 10 of Part III.

Section 177   PART III

SUPPLEMENTARY WELFARE ALLOWANCE

1. In calculating the weekly means of a person for supplementary welfare allowance account shall be taken of the following—

(1) all income in cash, including the net cash value of any non-cash earnings derived from personal exertions and the actual or estimated amount of any household income, whether as contributions to the expenses of the household or otherwise, but excluding—

    (a) any sums received by way of child benefit under Part IV, "or a payment corresponding to the said benefit from another Member State," [1994 Act, section 18].

    (b) payments by a health board in respect of a child who is boarded out,

    (c) in the case of a qualified applicant under a scheme administered by the Minister for the Gaeltacht and known as Scéim na bhFoghlaimeoirí Gaeilge, any income received under that scheme in respect of a person who is temporarily resident with the qualified applicant, together with any other income received in respect of such temporary resident,

    (d) any sums received by way of allowance for domiciliary care of handicapped children under section 61 of the Health Act, 1970,

    (e) any sums arising from the investment or profitable use of property (not being property personally used or enjoyed by such person or a farm of land leased by him under a lease which was certified by the Irish Land Commission to be *bona fide* and in accordance with sound land use practice),

    (f) any moneys received from a charitable organisation, being a body whose activities are carried on otherwise than for profit (but excluding any public or local authority) and one of whose functions is to assist persons in need by making grants of money to them, and

(g) such amount, as may be prescribed, of income from employment by a health board or by a person approved by a health board, as a home help,

(h) any moneys received by way of training allowance from an organisation while undergoing a course of rehabilitation training provided by the organisation (being an organisation approved of by the Minister for Health for the purposes of the provision of such training),

(i) any moneys received by way of a mobility allowance payable under section 61 of the Health Act, 1970,

(j) such income, as may be prescribed, arising from such activities as may be prescribed;" [1994 Act, section 18].

(2) the value of any property belonging to such person (not being property personally used or enjoyed by him or a farm of land leased by him under a lease which was certified by the Irish Land Commission to be *bona fide* and in accordance with sound land use practice) which is invested or is otherwise put to profitable use or which, though capable of investment or profitable use, is not invested or put to profitable use, the yearly value of the first £400 of the property being taken to be one-twentieth part of the capital value and the yearly value of so much of the capital value of the property as exceeds the sum of £400 being taken to be one-tenth part of the capital value; and the weekly value of the property being calculated as one fifty-second part of the yearly value so calculated;

(3) the value of advantage accruing to such person from—

(a) the use or enjoyment of property (other than a domestic dwelling or a farm building owned and occupied, or furniture and personal effects) which is personally used or enjoyed by him, and

(b) the leasing by him of a farm of land under a lease which was certified by the Irish Land Commission to be *bona fide* and in accordance with sound land use practice;

(4) the value of any benefit or privilege enjoyed by such person;

(5) all income and the value of all property of which such person has directly or indirectly deprived himself in order to qualify himself for the receipt of supplementary welfare allowance.

2. The Minister may by regulations vary the provisions of Rule 1.

FOURTH SCHEDULE

RATES OF ASSISTANCE

PART I

RATES OF PERIODICAL SOCIAL ASSISTANCE AND INCREASES THEREOF

Description of assistance, (1)	Weekly rate (2)	Increase for adult dependant (where payable) (3)	Increase for each qualified child (where payable) (4)	Increase for each prescribed relative under section 167 where payable) (5)	Increase for where the person has attained pensionable age and is living alone (where payable) (6)	Increase where the person has attained the age of 80 years (where payable) (7)
	£	£	£	£	£	£
1. Unemployment Assistance:						
(a) in the case of a person to whom section 121(1)(a) applies	62.50	37.50	13.20	—	—	—
(b) in the case of a person to whom section 121(1)(b) applies	60.40	37.50	13.20	—	—	—
2. Pre-Retirement Allowance	62.50	37.50	13.20	—	—	—
3. Old Age (non-contributory) Pension and Blind Pension	62.50	—	13.20	34.70	4.90	4.80
4. Widow's (Non-Contributory) Pension, Deserted Wife's Allowance and Prisoner's Wife's Allowance	62.50	—	—	34.70	4.90	4.80
5. Lone Parent's Allowance	62.50	—	15.20	—	4.90	4.80
6. Carer's Allowance	62.50	—	13.20	—	—	—
7. Orphan's (Non-Contributory) Pension	41.40	—	—	—	—	—
8. Supplementary Welfare Allowance	60.40	37.50	13.20	—	—	—

Section 137   PART II

INCREASE OF OLD AGE (NON-CONTRIBUTORY) PENSION AND BLIND PENSION FOR ONE OF A COUPLE

Means of claimant or pensioner	Weekly rate of increase
	£
Where the weekly means of the claimant or pensioner do not exceed £6	37.50
exceed £6 but do not exceed £8	36.50
exceed £8 but do not exceed £10	35.50
exceed £10 but do not exceed £12	34.50
exceed £12 but do not exceed £14	33.50
exceed £14 but do not exceed £16	32.50
exceed £16 but do not exceed £18	31.50
exceed £18 but do not exceed £20	30.50
exceed £20 but do not exceed £22	29.50
exceed £22 but do not exceed £24	28.50
exceed £24 but do not exceed £26	27.50
exceed £26 but do not exceed £28	26.50
exceed £28 but do not exceed £30	25.50
exceed £30 but do not exceed £32	24.50
exceed £32 but do not exceed £34	23.50
exceed £34 but do not exceed £36	22.50
exceed £36 but do not exceed £38	21.50
exceed £38 but do not exceed £40	20.50
exceed £40 but do not exceed £42	19.50
exceed £42 but do not exceed £44	18.50
exceed £44 but do not exceed £46	17.50
exceed £46 but do not exceed £48	16.50
exceed £48 but do not exceed £50	15.50
exceed £50 but do not exceed £52	14.50
exceed £52 but do not exceed £54	13.50
exceed £54 but do not exceed £56	12.50
exceed £56 but do not exceed £58	11.50
exceed £58 but do not exceed £60	10.50
exceed £60 but do not exceed £62	9.50
exceed £62 but do not exceed £64	8.50
exceed £64 but do not exceed £66	7.50
exceed £66	nil

[Parts I and II inserted by 1995 Act, section 4(1)].

Section 194   PART III

AMOUNTS OF CHILD BENEFIT

Amount for each of first two children (1)	Amount for each child in excess of two (2)
£27.00	£32.00

[Part III inserted by 1995 Act, section 5(1)].

FIFTH SCHEDULE

ENACTMENTS REPEALED

Number and Year (1)	Short Title (2)	Extent of Repeal (3)
No. 1 of 1981	Social Welfare (Consolidation) Act, 1981	The whole Act (other than Part VI).
No. 3 of 1981	Social Welfare (Amendment) Act, 1981	The whole Act.
No. 29 of 1981	Social Welfare (Temporary Provisions) Act, 1981	The whole Act.
No. 2 of 1982	Social Welfare Act, 1982	The whole Act.
No. 23 of 1982	Social Welfare (No. 2) Act, 1982	The whole Act.
No. 6 of 1983	Social Welfare Act, 1983	The whole Act.
No. 5 of 1984	Social Welfare Act, 1984	The whole Act.
No. 27 of 1984	Social Welfare (Amendment) Act, 1984	The whole Act.
No. 5 of 1985	Social Welfare Act, 1985	The whole Act.
No. 14 of 1985	Social Welfare (No. 2) Act, 1985	The whole Act.
No. 8 of 1986	Social Welfare Act, 1986	The whole Act.
No. 2 of 1987	Social Welfare Act, 1987	The whole Act.
No. 29 of 1987	Social Welfare (No. 2) Act, 1987	The whole Act.
No. 7 of 1988	Social Welfare Act, 1988	The whole Act (other than subsection .8(1) and (4) of section 1, and section 27).
No. 4 of 1989	Social Welfare Act, 1989	The whole Act (other than section 13).
No. 12 of 1989	Social Welfare (No. 2) Act, 1989	The whole Act.
No. 5 of 1990	Social Welfare Act, 1990	The whole Act (other than subsections (1), (3), (4) and (5) of section 1, and sections 15 and 25 to 30).
No. 7 of 1991	Social Welfare Act, 1991	The whole Act (other than section 1(1) and (3), section 2(1) in so far as it relates to the definition of "the Pensions Act", sections 37, 39 and 46, Part VIII and Schedule C).
No. 5 of 1992	Social Welfare Act, 1992	The whole Act (other than section 1(1), section 2 in so far as it relates to the definition of "the Pensions Act" and Part X).
No. 5 of 1993	Social Welfare Act, 1993	The whole Act (other than section 1(1), section 2(1) in so far as it relates to the definition of "the Pensions Act" and Part VII).

Section 304   SIXTH SCHEDULE

COMMENCEMENT OF CERTAIN PROVISIONS

Amendment of section 96

1.—Section 96 of this Act is hereby amended by—
    (a) the substitution for subsection (1) of the following subsection:
      "(1) The contribution conditions for invalidity pension are—
          (a) that before the relevant date the claimant has qualifying contributions in respect of not less than 260 contribution weeks since his entry into insurance, and
          (b) that before the relevant date the claimant has qualifying contributions or credited contributions in respect of not less than 48 contribution weeks in the last complete contribution year before that date, and
          (c) that the claimant has prescribed reckonable weekly earnings in excess of a prescribed amount in a prescribed period.", and
    (b) the insertion after subsection (6) of the following subsections:
      "(7) Subject to subsection (8), regulations may provide for entitling to invalidity pension persons who would be entitled thereto but for the fact that the condition set out in subsection (1)(c) is not satisfied.
      (8) Regulations for the purposes of subsection (7) shall provide that pension payable by virtue thereof shall be payable at a rate less than that specified in the Second Schedule, and the rate specified by the regulations may vary with the extent to which the condition set out in subsection (1)(c) is satisfied.".

Disqualifications—fraudulent claims

2.—(1) This Act is hereby amended by the insertion after section 174 of the following section:

"Disqualifications

    174A.—In any case where a person is disqualified for receiving any benefit, assistance or family income supplement in accordance with section 249A or section 213(2A), his needs for the period of disqualification shall be disregarded for the purpose of ascertaining his entitlement to supplementary welfare allowance except in so far as such needs include the need to provide for his adult or child dependants.".

(2) This Act is hereby amended by the insertion after section 249 of the following section:

    "249A.—In the case of a person whose claim for benefit, assistance or family income supplement is disallowed or reduced in accordance with section 249(a), a deciding officer may, having regard to the circumstances of the case, disqualify that person for receiving any benefit, assistance or family income supplement, as the case may be, for a period of up to 9 weeks and the period of disqualification shall commence—
          (a) where any such benefit, assistance or family income supplement is so reduced, on the day on which the revised decision is given, or
          (b) in any other case, on the day on which that person subsequently becomes entitled to any benefit, assistance or family income supplement, as the case may be,
and any such period of disqualification shall be treated as though it were a period in respect of which such benefit, assistance or family income supplement, as the case may be, was paid.".

Amendment of section 179

3.—This Act is hereby amended by the substitution for section 179 of the following section:

"Weekly or monthly supplements

    179.—(1) Subject to this Chapter, in the case of a person whose means are insufficient to meet his needs, regulations may provide for a weekly or monthly payment to supplement that person's income.

    (2) Regulations under subsection (1) may prescribe the class or classes of persons to whom and the conditions and circumstances under which a payment under subsection (1) may be made and the amount of such a payment (either generally or in relation to a particular class or classes of persons).".

Amendment of section 213

4.—Section 213 of this Act is hereby amended by the insertion after subsection (2) of the following subsection:

"(2A) In the case of a person convicted of an offence under this section the period of disqualification applied in accordance with the provisions of section 249A shall be extended to 3 months and the provisions of that section shall be construed and have effect accordingly.".

INDEX

References are to Sections or Schedules to the 1993 Act (as amended)

Index